"Lott turns conventional wisdom concerning violent crime and handguns on its head."
—*Chicago Tribune Books*

"An intriguing and shocking look at crime, guns, and gun-control policy."
—*Kirkus Reviews*

"This book is a refreshing, well-documented case for responsible gun ownership."
—*Bookviews*

"For anyone with an open mind on either side of this subject this book will provide a thorough grounding. It is also likely to be the standard reference on the subject for years to come."
—Stan Liebowitz, *Dallas Morning News*

"John Lott's work to uncover the truth about the costs and benefits of guns in America is as valuable as it is provocative. Too much of today's public debate over gun ownership and laws ignores the empirical evidence. Based on carefully proven facts, Professor Lott shatters the orthodox thinking about guns and debunks the most prominent myths about gun use that dominate the policy debate. For those who are convinced that the truth matters in formulating public policy and for anyone interested in the role of guns in our society, *More Guns, Less Crime* is must reading."
—Edwin Meese III, U.S. Attorney General, 1985–88

"*More Guns, Less Crime* is one of the most important books of our time. It provides thoroughly researched facts on a life-and-death subject that is too often discussed on the basis of unsubstantiated beliefs and hysterical emotions."
—Thomas Sowell

"Armed with reams of statistics, John Lott has documented many surprising linkages between guns and crime. *More Guns, Less Crime* demonstrates that what is at stake is not just the right to carry arms but rather our performance in controlling a diverse array of criminal behaviors. Perhaps most disturbing is Lott's documentation of the role of the media and academic commentators in distorting research findings that they regard as politically incorrect."
—W. Kip Viscusi, Cogan Professor of Law and Director of the Program on Empirical Legal Studies, Harvard Law School

"John Lott has done the most extensive, thorough, and sophisticated study we have on the effects of loosening gun control laws. Regardless of whether one agrees with his conclusions, his work is mandatory reading for anyone who is open-minded and serious about the gun control issue. Especially fascinating is his account of the often unscrupulous reactions to his research by gun control advocates, academic critics, and the news media."
—Gary Kleck, Professor of Criminology and Criminal Justice, Florida State University

"Until John Lott came along, the standard research paper on firearms and violence consisted of a longitudinal or cross-sectional study on a small and artfully selected data set with few meaningful statistical controls. Lott's work, embracing all of the data that are relevant to his analysis, has created a new standard, which future scholarship in this area, in order to be credible, will have to live up to."
—Dan Polsby, Kirkland & Ellis Professor of Law, Northwestern University

"His empirical analysis sets a standard that will be difficult to match. . . . This has got to be the most extensive empirical study of crime deterrence that has been done to date."
—*Public Choice*

"The most important book ever published about firearms policy. . . . [I]t should be read by everyone who cares about firearms policy, which is literally a matter of life or death. . . . [T]he more people who read *More Guns, Less Crime*, the sooner streets in every state will become safe zones for good citizens, rather than for predators."
—David B. Kopel, *Chronicles*

"Lott impressively marshals the evidence in support of his position in his best-selling (for an academic book) *More Guns, Less Crime*. As a result, Lott has become one of the few members of the legal academy whose name is now bandied about on talk shows, in legislative sessions, and in the print media. . . . [F]or those who argue that the serious evaluation of data is an important and underutilized guide to good public policy, this book poses a real challenge. For make no mistake, Lott has painstakingly constructed a massive data set, analyzed it exhaustively, and commendably shared it with scholars across the country. In these respects, he deserves high praise for following the scientific protocol so faithfully."
—Ian Ayres and John J. Donohue III, *American Law and Economics Review*

More Guns, Less Crime

MORE GUNS, LESS CRIME

UNDERSTANDING CRIME AND GUN-CONTROL LAWS

THIRD EDITION

JOHN R. LOTT, JR.

THE UNIVERSITY OF CHICAGO PRESS

CHICAGO AND LONDON

John R. Lott, Jr., is the author of five books, including
Freedomnomics and *Are Predatory Commitments Credible? Who
Should the Courts Believe?*

The University of Chicago Press, Chicago 60637
The University of Chicago Press, Ltd., London
© 1998, 2000, 2010 by The University of Chicago
All rights reserved. Published 2010
Printed in the United States of America
19 18 17 16 15 14 13 12 11 10   1 2 3 4 5

ISBN-13: 978-0-226- 49366-4 (paper)
ISBN-10: 0-226-49366-0 (paper)

Library of Congress Cataloging-in-Publication Data

Lott, John R.
  More guns, less crime : understanding crime and gun-control
laws / John R. Lott, Jr.—3rd ed.
     p. cm.
  Includes bibliographical references and index.
  ISBN-13: 978-0-226-49366-4 (pbk. : alk. paper)
  ISBN-10: 0-226-49366-0 (pbk. : alk. paper)
  1. Firearms—Law and legislation—United States. 2. Firearms
and crime—United States. I. Title.
  KF3941.L68 2010
  344.7305'33—dc22
                    2009036622

⊗ The paper used in this publication meets the minimum re-
quirements of the American National Standard for Information
Sciences—Permanence of Paper for Printed Library Materials,
ANSI Z39.48-1992.

CONTENTS

Ten years have passed since the last edition of this book. Much has happened in those years. Now thirty-nine states have right-to-carry laws, a huge increase from the eighteen states with them when David Mustard and I first examined the relationship between such laws and crime. That original research in this book covered the sixteen years from 1977 through 1992. The second edition extended it by four years and covered twenty-eight states. Now, this new edition covers thirty-nine states and twenty-nine years from 1977 through 2005. That is a lot of crime data to study, especially with so many more states having adopted the law during the time.

By now, dozens of academics have published studies on right-to-carry laws using national data. These studies have either confirmed the beneficial link between gun ownership and crime or at least not found any indication that ownership *increases* crime. Not too surprisingly, depending on the precise methods used and the exact data set, the results have varied. Some claim no effect from these laws, but not a single refereed study finds the opposite result, that right-to-carry laws have a bad effect on crime.

Unfortunately, even normally level-headed scholars can get very emotional debating guns. Perhaps I am naive, but I have continued to be amazed by the great lengths people can go to attack others and to distort research. I had no idea of the political intensity of the gun issue when I entered into this hornet's nest.

Right-to-carry laws are still the focus of this new edition, but I will address questions about some new laws as well. One of them is the Castle Doctrine, which states that it is not necessary for a would-be victim to retreat as far as possible before using a gun defensively. The federal assault weapons ban will also be studied. The federal assault weapons ban started in 1994 but ended in 2004. Rarely do we get a chance to look at the impact of gun laws when they are first passed and then when they are eliminated.

Not only have laws changed, but also the Supreme Court has ruled on important gun rights cases. A case of possible historic significance was the Supreme Court striking down the DC handgun ban in June 2008. The handgun ban in Chicago is currently being challenged in the courts, and it is possible that the Supreme Court will review that case also. Since the DC ruling, there has been a lot of renewed interest in the impact of gun bans on crime and suicide rates, and those same questions will be brought up again when deciding whether the Second Amendment applies to states as well as to areas controlled by the federal government, such DC.

The legal questions will also now focus on how much the government can regulate gun ownership and on the ability to carry guns. The courts will turn from the simple legal question of whether governments at any level can ban guns to more complicated questions of what specific regulations are to be allowed.

Since the second edition came out in 2000, I have continued working on gun-control issues. The research that John Whitley and I did on gun storage laws was published in the *Journal of Law and Economics* and is extended and updated in the new chapter. I have also updated previous research on multiple victim public shootings, work originally done together with Bill Landes. My previous work on gun show regulations and assault weapons has also been extended.

I have had a lot of help on these different projects. Research assistants have been extremely helpful with the very large data sets used in these studies. I need to thank Brian Blasé, James Knowles, and Maxim Lott for putting the new data together.

Finally, I would like to thank academics at George Mason University Law School, Chapman University Law School, the University of Florida, and the University of Miami for their helpful comments on the entirely new chapter added at the end of this book. I would also like to thank six anonymous referees for their comments.

PREFACE TO THE SECOND EDITION

The debate set off by this book was quite astonishing to me. Despite attacks early on when my paper was published in the *Journal of Legal Studies,* I was still rather unprepared for the publicity generated by the book in 1998. This expanded edition not only discusses the ensuing political debate and responds to the various criticisms, but also extends the data set to cover additional years. Replicating the results over additional years is important, so as to verify the original research. The new extended and broadened data set has also allowed me to study new gun laws, ranging from safe-storage provisions to one-gun-a-month purchase rules. It has also allowed me to extend my study of the Brady law and its impact to its first three years. Other extensions of the data set include entirely new city-level statistics, which made it possible to account more fully for policing policies.

Since I finished writing the first edition of this book in 1997, I have continued working on many related gun and crime issues. A new section of the book draws on continued research that I am conducting with numerous talented coauthors: William Landes on multiple-victim public shootings, John Whitley on safe-storage gun laws, and Kevin Cremin on police policies. Other work was published in the May 1998 *American Economic Review* under the title "Criminal Deterrence, Geographic Spillovers, and the Right to Carry

Concealed Handguns," coauthored with Stephen Bronars. Also, an article of mine, "The Concealed Handgun Debate," was published in the January 1998 issue of the *Journal of Legal Studies*.

I am grateful for the many opportunities to present my new research in a variety of academic forums and for the many useful comments that I have received. The research on guns and crime has been presented at (a partial listing) Arizona State University, Auburn University, the University of Chicago, Claremont Graduate School, the University of Houston, the University of Illinois, the University of Kansas, the University of Miami, New York University, the University of Oklahoma, the University of Southern California, Rice University, the University of Texas at Austin, the University of Texas at Dallas, the University of Virginia, the College of William and Mary, and Yeshiva University School of Law, as well as at the "Economics of Law Enforcement" Conference at Harvard Law School, the Association of American Law Schools meetings, the American Economic Association meetings, the American Society of Criminology meetings, the Midwestern Economic Association meetings, the National Lawyers Conference, the Southern Economic Association meetings, and the Western Economic Association meetings. Other presentations have been made at such places as the Chicago Crime Commission, the Kansas Koch Crime Commission, the American Enterprise Institute, and the Heritage Foundation.

Finally, I must thank the Yale Law School, where I am a senior research scholar, for providing me with the opportunity to write the new material that has been added to the book. I must also especially thank George Priest, who made this opportunity possible. The input of my wife and sons has been extremely important, and its importance has only been exceeded by their tolerance in putting up with the long working hours required to finish this revision.

PREFACE TO THE FIRST EDITION

Does allowing people to own or carry guns deter violent crime? Or does it simply cause more citizens to harm each other? Using the most comprehensive data set on crime yet assembled, this book examines the relationship between gun laws, arrest and conviction rates, the socioeconomic and demographic compositions of counties and states, and different rates of violent crime and property crime. The efficacy of the Brady Law, concealed-handgun laws, waiting periods, and background checks is evaluated for the first time using nationwide, county-level data.

The book begins with a description of the arguments for and against gun control and of how the claims should be tested. A large portion of the existing research is critically reviewed. Several chapters then empirically examine what facts influence the crime rate and answer the questions posed above. Finally, I respond to the political and academic attacks leveled against the original version of my work, which was published in the January 1997 issue of the *Journal of Legal Studies*.

I would like to thank my wife, Gertrud Fremling, for patiently reading and commenting on many early drafts of this book, and my four children for sitting through more dinnertime conversations on the topics covered here than anyone should be forced to endure. David Mustard also assisted me in collecting the data for the original article, which serves as the basis for some of the discussions in chapters 4 and 5. Ongoing research with Steve Bronars and William Landes has contributed to this book. Maxim Lott provided valuable research assistance with the polling data.

For their comments on different portions of the work included in this book, I would like to thank Gary Becker, Steve Bronars, Clayton Cramer, Ed Glaeser, Hide Ichimura, Jon Karpoff, C. B. Kates, Gary Kleck, David Kopel, William Landes, Wally Mullin, Derek Neal, Dan Polsby, Robert Reed, Tom Smith, seminar participants at the University of Chicago (the Economics and Legal Organization, the Rational Choice, and Divinity School workshops), Harvard University, Yale University, Stanford University, Northwestern University, Emory University, Fordham University, Valparaiso University, the American Law and Economics Association Meetings, the American Society of Criminology, the Western Economic Association Meetings, and the Cato Institute. I also benefited from presentations at the annual conventions of the Illinois Police Association and the National Association of Treasury Agents. Further, I would like to express my appreciation to the John M. Olin Law and Economics Program at the University of Chicago Law School for its generous funding (a topic dealt with at length in chapter 7).

1 | Introduction

American culture is a gun culture—not merely in the sense that in 2009 about 124 million people lived in households that owned a total of about 270 million guns,[1] but in the broader sense that guns pervade our debates on crime and are constantly present in movies and the news. How many times have we read about shootings, or how many times have we heard about tragic accidental gun deaths—bad guys shooting innocent victims, bad guys shooting each other in drug wars, shots fired in self-defense, police shootings of criminals, let alone shooting in wars? We are inundated by images through the television and the press. Our kids are fascinated by computer war games and toy guns.

So we're obsessed with guns. But the big question is: What do we really know? How many times have most of us actually used a gun or seen a gun being used? How many of us have ever seen somebody in real life threatening somebody else with a gun, witnessed a shooting, or seen people defend themselves by displaying or firing guns?

The truth is that most of us have very little firsthand experience with using guns as weapons. Even the vast majority of police officers have never exchanged shots with a suspect.[2] Most of us receive our images of guns and their use through television, film, and newspapers.

Unfortunately, the images from the screen and the newspapers are often unrepresentative or biased because of the sensationalism and exaggeration typically employed to sell news and entertainment. A couple of instances of news reporting are especially instructive in illustrating this bias. In a highly publicized incident, a Dallas man became the first Texas resident charged with using a permitted concealed weapon in a fatal shooting.[3] Only long after the initial wave of publicity did the press report that the person had been savagely beaten and in fear for his life before firing the gun. In another case a Japanese student was shot on his way to a Halloween party in Louisiana in 1992. It made international headlines and showed how defensive gun use can go tragically wrong.[4] However, this incident was a rare event: in the entire United States during a year, only about 30 people are accidentally killed by private citizens who mistakenly believe the victim to be an intruder.[5] By comparison, police accidentally kill as many as 330 innocent individuals annually.[6] In neither the Louisiana case nor the Texas case did the courts find the shooting to be criminal.

While news stories sometimes chronicle the defensive uses of guns, such discussions are rare compared to those depicting violent crime committed with guns. Since in many defensive cases a handgun is simply brandished, and no one is harmed, many defensive uses are never even reported to the police. I believe that this underreporting of defensive gun use is large, and this belief has been confirmed by the many stories I received from people across the country after the publicity broke on my original study. On the roughly one hundred radio talk shows on which I discussed that study, many people called in to say that they believed having a gun to defend themselves with had saved their lives. For instance, on a Philadelphia radio station, a New Jersey woman told how two men simultaneously had tried to open both front doors of the car she was in. When she brandished her gun and yelled, the men backed away and fled. Given the stringent gun-control laws in New Jersey, the woman said she never thought seriously of reporting the attempted attack to the police.

Similarly, while I was on a trip to testify before the Nebraska Senate, John Haxby—a television newsman for the CBS affiliate in Omaha—privately revealed to me a frightening experience that he had faced in the summer of 1995 while visiting in Arizona. At about 10 A.M., while riding in a car with his brother at the wheel, they stopped for a red light. A man appeared wielding a "butcher's knife" and opened the passenger door, but just as he was lunging towards John, the attacker suddenly turned and ran away. As John turned to his brother, he saw that his brother was holding a handgun. His brother was one of many who had acquired permits under the concealed-handgun law passed in Arizona the previous year.

Philip Van Cleave, a former reserve deputy sheriff in Texas, wrote me, "Are criminals afraid of a law-abiding citizen with a gun? You bet. Most cases of a criminal being scared off by an armed citizen are probably not reported. But I have seen a criminal who was so frightened of an armed, seventy-year-old woman that in his panic to get away, he turned and ran right into a wall! (He was busy trying to kick down her door, when she opened a curtain and pointed a gun at him.)"

Such stories are not limited to the United States. On February 3, 1996, outside a bar in Texcoco, Mexico (a city thirty miles east of Mexico City), a woman used a gun to stop a man from raping her. When the man lunged at the woman, "ripping her clothes and trying to rape her," she pulled a .22-caliber pistol from her purse and shot her attacker once in the chest, killing him.[7] The case generated much attention in Mexico when a judge initially refused to dismiss murder charges against the woman because she was viewed as being responsible for the attempted rape, having "enticed" the attacker "by having a drink with him at the bar."[8]

A national survey that I conducted during 2002 indicates that about 95 percent of the time that people use guns defensively, they merely have to brandish a weapon to break off an attack. Such stories are not hard to find: pizza deliverymen defend themselves against robbers, carjackings are thwarted, robberies at automatic teller machines are prevented, and numerous armed robberies on the streets and in stores are foiled,[9] though these do not receive the national coverage of other gun crimes.[10] Yet the cases covered by the news media are hardly typical; most encounters reported involve a shooting that ends in a fatality.[11]

A typical dramatic news story involved an Atlanta woman who prevented a carjacking and the kidnapping of her child; she was forced to shoot her assailant:

A College Park woman shot and killed an armed man she says was trying to carjack her van with her and her 1-year-old daughter inside, police said Monday. . . .

Jackson told police that the gunman accosted her as she drove into the parking lot of an apartment complex on Camp Creek Parkway. She had planned to watch a broadcast of the Evander Holyfield–Mike Tyson fight with friends at the complex.

She fired after the man pointed a revolver at her and ordered her to "move over," she told police. She offered to take her daughter and give up the van, but the man refused, police said.

"She was pleading with the guy to let her take the baby and leave the van, but he blocked the door," said College Park Detective Reed Pollard. "She was protecting herself and the baby."

Jackson, who told police she bought the .44-caliber handgun in September after her home was burglarized, said she fired several shots from the gun, which she kept concealed in a canvas bag beside her car seat. "She didn't try to remove it," Pollard said. "She just fired."[12]

Although the mother saved herself and her baby by her quick actions, it was a risky situation that might have ended differently. Even though there was no police officer to help protect her or her child, defending herself was not necessarily the only alternative. She could have behaved passively, and the criminal might have changed his mind and simply taken the van, letting the mother and child go. Even if he had taken the child, he might later have let the baby go unharmed. Indeed, some conventional wisdom claims that the best approach is not to resist an attack. According to a recent *Los Angeles Times* article, "'active compliance' is the surest way to survive a robbery. Victims who engage in active resistance . . . have the best odds of hanging on to their property. Unfortunately, they also have much better odds of winding up dead."[13]

Yet the evidence suggests that the College Park woman probably engaged in the correct action. While resistance is generally associated with higher probabilities of serious injury to the victim, not all types of resistance are equally risky. By examining the data provided from 1979 to 1987 by the Department of Justice's National Crime Victimization Survey,[14] Lawrence Southwick, confirming earlier estimates by Gary Kleck, found that the probability of serious injury from an attack is 2.5 times greater for women offering no resistance than for women resisting with a gun. In contrast, the probability of women being seriously injured was almost 4 times greater when resisting without a gun than when resisting with a gun. In other words, the best advice is to resist with a gun, but if no gun is available, it is better to offer no resistance than to fight.[15]

Men also fare better with guns, but the benefits are substantially smaller. Behaving passively is 1.4 times more likely to result in serious injury than resisting with a gun. Male victims, like females, also run the greatest risk when they resist without a gun, yet the difference is again much smaller:

resistance without a gun is only 1.5 times as likely to result in serious injury than resistance with a gun. The much smaller difference for men reflects the fact that a gun produces a smaller change in a man's ability to defend himself than it does for a woman.

Although usually skewed toward the dramatic, news stories do shed light on how criminals think. Anecdotes about criminals who choose victims whom they perceive as weak are the most typical. While "weak" victims are frequently women and the elderly, this is not always the case. For example, in a taped conversation with police investigators reported in the *Cincinnati Enquirer* (October 9, 1996, p. B2), Darnell "Bubba" Lowery described how he and Walter "Fatman" Raglin robbed and murdered musician Michael Bany on December 29, 1995:

> Mr. Lowery said on the tape that he and Walter "Fatman" Raglin, who is also charged with aggravated robbery and aggravated murder and is on trial in another courtroom, had planned to rob a cab driver or a "dope boy."
>
> He said he gave his gun and bullets to Mr. Raglin. They decided against robbing a cab driver or drug dealer because both sometimes carried guns, he said.
>
> Instead, they saw a man walking across the parking lot with some kind of musical instrument. He said as he looked out for police, Mr. Raglin approached the man and asked for money.
>
> After getting the money, Mr. Raglin asked if the man's car was a stick or an automatic shift. Then Mr. Raglin shot the man.

Criminals are motivated by self-preservation, and handguns can therefore be a deterrent. The potential defensive nature of guns is further evidenced by the different rates of so-called "hot burglaries," where a resident is at home when a criminal strikes.[16] In Canada and Britain, both with tough gun-control laws, almost half of all burglaries are "hot burglaries." In contrast, the United States, with fewer restrictions, has a "hot burglary" rate of only 13 percent. Criminals are not just behaving differently by accident. Convicted American felons reveal in surveys that they are much more worried about armed victims than about running into the police.[17] The fear of potentially armed victims causes American burglars to spend more time than their foreign counterparts "casing" a house to ensure that nobody is home. Felons frequently comment in these interviews that they avoid late-night burglaries because "that's the way to get shot."[18]

To an economist such as myself, the notion of deterrence—which causes criminals to avoid cab drivers, "dope boys," or homes where the residents are in—is not too surprising. We see the same basic relationships in all other areas of life: when the price of apples rises relative to that of oranges, people buy fewer apples and more oranges. To the non-economist, it may appear cold to make this comparison, but just as grocery shoppers switch to cheaper types of produce, criminals switch to attacking more vulnerable prey. Economists call this, appropriately enough, "the substitution effect."

Deterrence matters not only to those who actively take defensive actions. People who defend themselves may indirectly benefit other citizens. In the Cincinnati murder case just described, cab drivers and drug dealers who carry guns produce a benefit for cab drivers and drug dealers without guns. In the example involving "hot burglaries," homeowners who defend themselves make burglars generally wary of breaking into homes. These spillover effects are frequently referred to as "third-party effects" or "external benefits." In both cases criminals cannot know in advance who is armed.

The case for allowing concealed handguns—as opposed to openly carried handguns—relies on this argument. When guns are concealed, criminals are unable to tell whether the victim is armed before striking, which raises the risk to criminals of committing many types of crimes. On the other hand, with "open-carry" handgun laws, a potential victim's defensive ability is readily identified, which makes it easier for criminals to choose the more vulnerable prey. In interviews with felony prisoners in ten state correctional systems, 56 percent claimed that they would not attack a potential victim who was known to be armed. Indeed, the criminals in states with high civilian gun ownership were the most worried about encountering armed victims.[19]

Other examples suggest that more than just common crimes may be prevented by law-abiding citizens carrying concealed handguns. Referring to the July, 1984, massacre at a San Ysidro, California, McDonald's restaurant, Israeli criminologist Abraham Tennenbaum described

> what occurred at a [crowded venue in] Jerusalem some weeks before the California McDonald's massacre: three terrorists who attempted to machine-gun the throng managed to kill only one victim before being shot down by handgun-carrying Israelis. Presented to the press the next day, the surviving terrorist complained that his group had not realized that Israeli civilians were armed. The terrorists had planned to machine-gun a succession of crowd spots, thinking that they would be able to escape before the police or army could arrive to deal with them.[20]

On March 13, 1997, seven young seventh- and eighth-grade Israeli girls were shot to death by a Jordanian soldier while visiting Jordan's so-called Island of Peace. Reportedly, the Israelis had "complied with Jordanian requests to leave their weapons behind when they entered the border enclave. Otherwise, they might have been able to stop the shooting, several parents said."[21]

Obviously, arming citizens has not stopped terrorism in Israel; however, terrorists have responded to the relatively greater cost of shooting in public places by resorting to more bombings. This is exactly what the substitution effect discussed above would predict. Is Israel better off with bombings instead of mass public shootings? That is not completely clear, although one might point out that if the terrorists previously chose shooting attacks rather than bombings but now can only be effective by using bombs, their actions are limited in a way that should make terrorist attacks less effective (even if only slightly).[22]

Substitutability means that the most obvious explanations may not always be correct. For example, when the February 23, 1997, shooting at the Empire State Building left one person dead and six injured, it was not New York's gun laws but Florida's—where the gun was sold—that came under attack. New York City Mayor Rudolph W. Giuliani immediately called for national gun-licensing laws.[23] While it is possible that even stricter gun-sale regulations in Florida might have prevented this and other shootings, we might ask, Why did the gunman travel to New York rather than remain in Florida to do the shooting? And could someone intent on committing the crime and willing to travel to Florida still have gotten a gun illegally some other way? It is important to study whether states that adopt concealed-handgun laws similar to those in Israel experience the same virtual elimination of mass public shootings. Such states may also run the risk that would-be attackers will substitute bombings for shootings, though there is the same potential downside to successfully banning guns. The question still boils down to an empirical one: Which policy will save the largest number of lives?

The Numbers Debate and Crime

Unfortunately, the debate over crime involves many commonly accepted "facts" that simply are not true. For example, take the claim that individuals are frequently killed by people they know.[24] As shown in table 1.1, according to the FBI's *Uniform Crime Reports*, 58 percent of the country's murders

Table 1.1 Murderers and victims: relationship and characteristics

	Percent of cases involving the relationship	Percent of victims	Percent of offenders
Relationship		—	—
Family	18%		
Acquaintance (non-friend and friend)	40		
Stranger	13		
Unknown	30		
Total	101		
Race			
Black		38%	33%
White		54	42
Hispanic		2	2
Other		5	4
Unknown		1	19
Total		100	100
Sex			
Female		29	9
Male		71	72
Unknown		0	19
Total		100	100

Source: U.S. Dept. of Justice, FBI staff, *Uniform Crime Reports,* (Washington, DC: U.S. Govt. Printing Office, 1992
Note: Nonfriend acquaintances include drug pushers and buyers, gang members, prostitutes and their clients, bar customers, gamblers, cab drivers killed by their customers, neighbors, other nonfriend acquaintances, and friends. The total equals more than 100 percent because of rounding. The average age of victims was 33; that of offenders was 30.

were committed either by family members (18 percent) or by those who "knew" the victims (40 percent). Although the victims' relationship to their attackers could not be determined in 30 percent of the cases, 13 percent of all murders were committed by complete strangers.[25]

Surely the impression created by these numbers has been that most victims are murdered by close acquaintances. Yet this is far from the truth. In interpreting the numbers, one must understand how these classifications are made. In this case, "murderers who know their victims" is a very broad category. A huge but not clearly determined portion of this category includes rival gang members who know each other.[26] In larger urban areas, where most murders occur, the majority of murders are due to gang-related turf wars over drugs.

The Chicago Police Department, which keeps unusually detailed numbers on these crimes, finds that just 5 percent of all murders in the city from 1990 to 1995 were committed by nonfamily friends, neighbors, or roommates.[27] This is clearly important in understanding crime. The list of nonfriend acquaintance murderers is filled with cases in which the relationships would not be regarded by most people as particularly close: for example, relationships between drug pushers and buyers, gang members, prostitutes and their clients, bar customers, gamblers, and cabdrivers killed by their customers.

While I do not wish to downplay domestic violence, most people do not envision gang members or drug buyers and pushers killing each other when they hear that 58 percent of murder victims were either relatives or acquaintances of their murderers.[28] If family members are included, no more than 17 percent of all murders in Chicago for 1990–95 involved family members, friends, neighbors, or roommates.[29] While the total number of murders in Chicago grew from 395 in 1965 to 814 in 1995, the number involving family members, friends, neighbors, or roommates remained virtually unchanged. What has grown is the number of murders by nonfriend acquaintances, strangers, identified gangs, and persons unknown.[30]

Few murderers could be classified as previously law-abiding citizens. In the largest seventy-five counties in the United States in 1988, over 89 percent of adult murderers had criminal records as adults.[31] Evidence for Boston, the one city where reliable data have been collected, shows that, from 1990 to 1994, 76 percent of juvenile murder victims and 77 percent of juveniles who murdered other juveniles had prior criminal arraignments.[32]

Claims of the large number of murders committed against acquaintances also create a misleading fear of those we know. To put it bluntly, criminals are not typical citizens. As is well known, young males from their mid-teens to mid-thirties commit a disproportionate share of crime,[33] but even this categorization can be substantially narrowed. We know that criminals tend to have low IQs as well as atypical personalities.

For example, delinquents generally tend to be more "assertive, unafraid, aggressive, unconventional, extroverted, and poorly socialized," while nondeliquents are "self-controlled, concerned about their relations with others, willing to be guided by social standards, and rich in internal feelings like insecurity, helplessness, love (or lack of love), and anxiety."[34] Other evidence indicates that criminals tend to be more impulsive and put relatively little weight on future events.[35] Finally, we cannot ignore the unfortunate fact that crime (particularly violent crime, and especially murder) is disproportionately committed against blacks by blacks.[36]

The news media also play an important role in shaping what we perceive as the greatest threats to our safety. Because we live in such a national news market, we learn very quickly about tragedies in other parts of the country.[37] As a result, some events appear to be much more common than they actually are. For instance, children are much less likely to be accidentally killed by guns (particularly handguns) than most people think. Consider the following numbers: In 2006 there were a total of 642 accidental firearm deaths in the entire country. A relatively small portion of these involved children under age ten: 13 deaths involved children up to four years of age and 18 more deaths involved five- to nine-year-olds.[38] In comparison, 1,305 children died in motor-vehicle crashes and another 392 died when they were struck by motor vehicles, 651 died from drowning, and 348 were killed by fire and burns. Almost three times as many children drown in bathtubs each year than die from all types of firearm accidents.

Of course, any child's death is tragic, and it offers little consolation to point out that common fixtures in life from pools to heaters result in even more deaths. Yet the very rules that seek to save lives can result in more deaths. For example, banning swimming pools would help prevent drowning, and banning bicycles would eliminate bicycling accidents, but if fewer people exercise, life spans will be shortened. Heaters may start fires, but they also keep people from getting sick and from freezing to death. So whether we want to allow pools or space heaters depends not only on whether some people may end up being harmed, but also on whether more people are helped than hurt.

Similar trade-offs exist for gun-control issues, such as gun locks. As former president Clinton argued many times, "We protect aspirin bottles in this country better than we protect guns from accidents by children."[39] Yet gun locks require that guns be unloaded, and a locked, unloaded gun does not offer ready protection from intruders.[40] The debate is not simply over whether one wants to save lives or not. Rather, it involves the question of how many of these two hundred accidental gun deaths would have been avoided under different rules versus the extent to which such rules would have reduced the ability to defend against criminals. Without looking at data, one can only guess the net effects.[41] Unfortunately, despite the best intentions, evidence indicates that child-resistant bottle caps actually have resulted in "3,500 additional poisonings of children under age 5 annually from [aspirin-related drugs] . . . [as] consumers have been lulled into a less-safety-conscious mode of behavior by the existence of safety caps."[42] If President Clinton had been aware of such research, he surely wouldn't have referred to aspirin bottles when telling us how to deal with guns.[43]

Another common argument made in favor of banning guns involves the number of people who die from guns each year: there were 17,034 homicides and 18,169 suicides in 1992 alone.[44] Yet, just because a law is passed to ban guns, it does not automatically follow that the total number of deaths will decline. Given the large stock of guns in the country and given the difficulties the government faces in preventing other illegal items, such as drugs, from entering the country, it is quite doubtful that the government would be able to eliminate most guns. This raises the important question: Would the law primarily reduce the number of guns held by law-abiding citizens? How would such a law alter the relative balance of power between criminals and law-abiding citizens?

Suppose it were indeed possible to remove all guns. Other problems are still likely to arise. Perhaps successfully removing guns would discourage murders and other crimes because criminals would find knives and clubs poor alternatives. But on the other hand it would be easier for criminals to prey on the weakest citizens, who would find it more difficult to defend themselves. Suicide raises other questions. It is simply not sufficient to point to the number of people who kill themselves with guns. The debate must be over what substitute methods are available and whether they appear sufficiently less attractive. Even evidence about the "success rate" of different methods of suicide is not enough, because we need to ask why people choose the method that they do. If people who were more intent than others on successfully killing themselves previously chose guns, forcing them to use other methods might raise the reported "success rate" for these other methods. Broader concerns for the general public also arise. For example, even if we banned many of the obvious ways of committing suicide, many methods exist that we could never really control. And these substitute methods might endanger others in ways that shootings do not. For example, deliberately crashing one's car, throwing oneself in front of a train, or jumping off a building.

This book attempts to measure this trade-off for guns. Our primary questions are the following: Will allowing citizens to carry concealed handguns mean that otherwise law-abiding people will harm each other? Will the threat of self-defense by citizens armed with guns primarily deter criminals? Without a doubt, both "bad" and "good" uses of guns occur. The question isn't really whether both occur; it is, rather: Which is more important? In general, do concealed handguns save or cost lives? Even a devoted believer in deterrence cannot answer this question without examining the data, because these two different effects clearly exist, and they work in opposite directions.

To some, however, the logic is fairly straightforward. Philip Cook argues that "if you introduce a gun into a violent encounter, it increases the chance that someone will die."[45] A large number of murders may arise from unintentional fits of rage that are quickly regretted, and simply keeping guns out of people's reach would prevent deaths.[46] Others point to the horrible public shootings that occur not just in the United States but in recent years around the world, from the two worst high school shootings in Germany to Mumbai, India, where 163 people were killed.

The survey evidence of defensive gun use weighs importantly in this debate. At the lowest end of these estimates, the U.S. Department of Justice's National Crime Victimization Survey reports that each year there are "only" 110,000 defensive uses of guns during assaults, robberies, and household burglaries.[47] Other national polls weight regions by population and thus have the advantage, unlike the National Crime Victimization Survey, of not relying too heavily on data from urban areas.[48] These national polls should also produce more honest answers, since a law-enforcement agency is not asking the questions.[49] They imply much higher defensive use rates. Fifteen national polls, including those by organizations such as the *Los Angeles Times*, Gallup, and Peter Hart Research Associates, imply that there are 760,000 defensive handgun uses to 3.6 million defensive uses of any type of gun per year.[50] Yet even if these estimates are wrong by a very large factor, they still suggest that defensive gun use is extremely common.

Some evidence on whether concealed-handgun laws will lead to increased crimes is readily available. Between October 1, 1987, when Florida's "concealed-carry" law took effect, and the end of 1996, over 380,000 licenses had been issued, and only 72 had been revoked because of crimes committed by license holders (most of which did not involve the permitted gun).[51] A statewide breakdown on the nature of those crimes is not available, but Dade County records indicate that four crimes involving a permitted handgun took place there between September 1987 and August 1992, and none of those cases resulted in injury.[52] Similarly, Multnomah County, Oregon, issued 11,140 permits over the period from January 1990 to October 1994; only five permit holders were involved in shootings, three of which were considered justified by grand juries. Of the other two cases, one involved a shooting in a domestic dispute, and the other involved an accident that occurred while a gun was being unloaded; neither resulted in a fatality.[53]

In Virginia, "Not a single Virginia permit-holder has been involved in violent crime."[54] In the first year following the enactment of concealed-carry legislation in Texas, more than 114,000 licenses were issued, and only 17 have so far been revoked by the Department of Public Safety (reasons not specified).[55] After Nevada's first year, "Law enforcement officials throughout the state could not document one case of a fatality that resulted from irresponsible gun use by someone who obtained a permit under the new law."[56] Speaking for the Kentucky Chiefs of Police Association, Lt. Col. Bill Dorsey, Covington assistant police chief, concluded that after the law had been in effect for nine months, "We haven't seen any cases where a [concealed-carry] permit holder has committed an offense with a firearm,"[57] In North Carolina, "Permit-holding gun owners have not had a single permit revoked as a result of use of a gun in a crime."[58] Similarly, for South Carolina, "Only one person who has received a pistol permit since 1989 has been indicted on a felony charge, a comparison of permit and circuit court records shows. That charge, . . . for allegedly transferring stolen property last year, was dropped by prosecutors after evidence failed to support the charge."[59]

During state legislative hearings on concealed-handgun laws, the most commonly raised concerns involved fears that armed citizens would attack each other in the heat of the moment following car accidents or accidentally shoot a police officer. The evidence shows that such fears are unfounded: although thirty-one states had so-called nondiscretionary concealed-handgun laws when this book was first written, some of them decades old, there existed only one recorded incident of a permitted, concealed handgun being used in a shooting following a traffic accident, and that involved self-defense.[60] No permit holder has ever shot a police officer, and there have been cases where permit holders have used their guns to save officers' lives.

Let us return to the fundamental issue of self-protection. For many people, the ultimate concern boils down to protection from violence. Unfortunately, our legal system cannot provide people with all the protection that they desire, and yet individuals are often prevented from defending themselves. A particularly tragic event occurred in 1996 in Baltimore:

Less than a year ago, James Edward Scott shot and wounded an intruder in the back yard of his West Baltimore home, and according to neighbors, authorities took away his gun.

Tuesday night, someone apparently broke into his three-story row house again. But this time the 83-year-old Scott didn't have his .22-caliber rifle, and police said he was strangled when he confronted the burglar.

"If he would have had the gun, he would be OK," said one neighbor who declined to give his name, fearing retribution from the attacker, who had not been arrested as of yesterday. . . .

Neighbors said burglars repeatedly broke into Scott's home. Ruses [a neighbor] said Scott often talked about "the people who would harass him because he worked out back by himself."[61]

Others find themselves in a position in which either they no longer report attacks to the police when they have used a gun to defend themselves, or they no longer carry guns for self-defense. Josie Cash learned this lesson the hard way, though charges against her were ultimately dropped. "The Rockford [Illinois] woman used her gun to scare off muggers who tried to take her pizza delivery money. But when she reported the incident to police, they filed felony charges against her for carrying a concealed weapon."[62]

A well-known story involved Alan Berg, a liberal Denver talk-show host who took great delight in provoking and insulting those he disagreed with. Berg attempted to obtain a permit after receiving death threats from white supremacists, but the police first attempted to talk him out of applying and then ultimately rejected his request. Shortly after his request was denied, Berg was murdered by members of the Aryan Nations.[63]

As a Chicago cabdriver told me, "What good is a police officer going to do me if you pulled a knife or a gun on me right now?"[64] Nor are rural, low-crime areas immune from these concerns. Illinois State Representative Terry Deering (Democrat) noted that "we live in areas where if we have a state trooper on duty at any given time in a whole county, we feel very fortunate. Some counties in downstate rural Illinois don't even have 24-hour police protection."[65] The police cannot feasibly protect everybody all the time, and perhaps because of this, police officers are typically sympathetic to law-abiding citizens who own guns.[66]

Mail-in surveys are seldom accurate, because only those who feel intensely about an issue are likely to respond, but they provide the best information that we have on police officers' views. A 2005 mail survey of twenty-two thousand chiefs of police and sheriffs conducted by the National Association of Chiefs of Police found that 92 percent believed that law-abiding citizens should continue to be able to purchase guns for self-defense.[67] Sixty percent thought that a national concealed-handgun permit law will "reduce rates of violent crime." The Southern States Police Benevolent Association surveyed its eleven thousand members during June of 1993 (36 percent responded) and reported similar findings: 96 percent of those who responded agreed with the statement, "People should have the right to own a gun for self-protection," and 71 percent did not believe that stricter handgun laws would reduce the number of violent crimes.[68] A national reader survey conducted in 1991 by *Law Enforcement Technology* magazine found that 76 percent of street officers and 59 percent of managerial officers agreed that all trained, responsible adults should be able to obtain handgun-carry permits.[69] By similarly overwhelming percentages, these officers and police chiefs rejected claims that the Brady law would lower the crime rate.

The passage of concealed-handgun laws has also caused former opponents in law enforcement to change their positions. Recently in Texas, "vocal opponent" Harris County District Attorney John Holmes admitted, "I'm eating a lot of crow on this issue. It's not something I necessarily like to do, but I'm doing it on this."[70] Soon after the implementation of the Florida law, the president and the executive director of the Florida Chiefs of Police and the head of the Florida Sheriff's Association all admitted that they had changed their views on the subject. They also admitted that despite their best efforts to document problems arising from the law, they have been unable to do so.[71] The experience in Kentucky has been similar; as Campbell County Sheriff John Dunn says, "I have changed my opinion of this [program]. Frankly, I anticipated a certain type of people applying to carry firearms, people I would be uncomfortable with being able to carry a concealed weapon. That has not been the case. These are all just everyday citizens who feel they need some protection."[72]

Support among rank-and-file police officers and the general population for the right of individuals to carry guns for self-protection is even higher than it is among police chiefs. A national poll by the Lawrence Research group (September 21—28, 1996) found that by a margin of 69 to 28 percent, registered voters favor "a law allowing law-abiding citizens to be issued a permit to carry a firearm for personal protection outside their home."[73] A recent national polling by the Zogby International (July 2009) appears even more supportive of at least allowing some law-abiding citizens to carry concealed handguns. They found that 83 percent supported "laws that allow residents to carry firearms to protect themselves," while only 11 opposed them.[74] Perhaps just as telling, a 2008 Gallup poll found that the percent of people who favor a ban on handguns had fallen to a fifty-year low.[75]

A National Opinion Research Center poll also provides some insights into who supports tighter restrictions on gun ownership; it claims that "the less educated and those who haven't been threatened with a gun are most supportive of gun control."[76] If this is true, it appears that those most supportive of restrictions also tend to be those least directly threatened by crime.[77]

State legislators also acknowledge the inability of the police to be always available, even in the most public places, by voting to allow themselves unusually broad rights to carry concealed handguns. During the 1996 legislative session, for example, Georgia "state legislators quietly gave themselves and a few top officials the right to carry concealed guns to places most residents can't: schools, churches, political rallies, and even the Capitol."[78] Even local prosecutors in California strenuously objected to restrictions on their rights to carry concealed handguns.[79]

Although people with concealed handgun permits must generally view the police as offering insufficient protection, it is difficult to discern any pattern of political orientation among celebrities who have concealed-handgun permits: Bill Cosby, Cybill Shepherd, Howard Stern, Donald Trump, Arthur O. Sulzberger (chairman of the *New York Times*), union bosses, Laurence Rockefeller, Tom Selleck, and Robert De Niro. The reasons these people gave on their applications for permits were similar. Laurence Rockefeller's reason was that he carries "large sums of money"; Arthur Sulzberger wrote that he carries "large sums of money, securities, etc."; and William Buckley listed "protection of personal property when traveling in and about the city" as his reason.[80] Some made their decision to carry a gun after being victims of crime.[81]

And when the *Denver Post* asked Sen. Ben Nighthorse Campbell (R-Colo.) "how it looks for a senator to be packing heat," he responded, "You'd be surprised how many senators have guns." Campbell said that "he needed the gun back in the days when he exhibited his Native American jewelry and traveled long distances between craft shows."[82]

Emotion, Rationality, and Deterrence

In 1995 two children, ten and eleven years old, dropped a five-year-old boy from the fourteenth floor of a vacant Chicago Housing Authority apartment.[83] The reason? The five-year-old refused to steal candy for them. Or consider the case of Vincent Drost, a promising musician in the process of composing a symphony, who was stabbed to death immediately after making a call from a pay telephone to his girlfriend. The reason? According to the newspapers, "His five teenage attackers told police they wanted to have some fun and simply wanted 'to do' somebody."[84] It is not difficult to find crimes such as "the fatal beating of a school teacher" described as "extremely wicked, shockingly evil." The defense attorney in this crime described the act as one of "insane jealousy."[85]

The notion of "irrational" crime is enshrined by forty-seven states that recognize insanity defenses.[86] Criminal law recognizes that emotions can overwhelm our normal judgments in other ways.[87] For example, under the Model Penal Code, intentional homicide results in the penalty for manslaughter when it "is committed under the influence of extreme mental or emotional disturbance for which there is reasonable explanation or excuse."[88] These mitigating factors are often discussed in terms of the "heat of passion" or "cooling time," the latter phrase referring to "the interval in which 'blood' can be expected 'to cool'" or the time required for "reason to reassert itself."[89] Another related distinction is drawn between first- and second-degree murder: "The deliberate killer is guilty of first-degree murder; the impulsive killer is not."[90] In practice, the distinction between these two grades appears to rely less on premeditation than on whether the act was done without emotion or "in cold blood," "as is the case [when] someone who kills for money . . . displays calculation and greed."[91]

Some academics go beyond these cases or laws to make more general claims about the motives behind crime. Thomas Carroll, an associate professor of sociology at the University of Missouri at Kansas City, states that "murder is an irrational act, [and] we don't have explanations for irrational behavior."[92] From this he draws the conclusion that "there's really no statistical explanation" for what causes murder rates to fluctuate. Do criminals respond to disincentives? Or are emotions and attitudes the determining factors in crime? If violent acts occur merely because of random emotions, stronger penalties would only reduce crime to the extent that the people least able to control such violent feelings can be imprisoned.

There are obvious difficulties with taking this argument against deterrence to its extreme. For example, as long as "even a handful" of criminals respond to deterrence, increasing penalties will reduce crime. Higher probabilities of arrest or conviction as well as longer prison terms might then possibly "pay" for themselves. As the cases in the previous section have illustrated, criminal decisions—from when to break into a residence, whom to attack, or whether to attack people by using guns or bombs—appear difficult to explain without reference to deterrence. Some researchers try to draw a distinction between crimes that they view as "more rational," like robbery and burglary, and others, such as murder. If such a distinction is valid, one might argue that deterrence would then at least be effective for the more "rational" crimes.

Yet even if we assume that most criminals are largely irrational, deterrence issues raise some tough questions about human nature, questions that are at the heart of very different views of crime and how to combat it. Still it is important to draw a distinction between "irrational" behavior and the notion that deterrence doesn't matter. One doesn't necessarily imply the other. For instance, some people may hold strange, unfathomable objectives, but this does not mean that they cannot be discouraged from doing things that bring increasingly undesirable consequences. While we may not solve the deeper mysteries of how the human mind works, I hope that the following uncontroversial example can help show how deterrence works.

Suppose that a hypothetical Mr. Smith is passed over for promotion. He kept a stiff upper lip at work, but after he gets home, he kicks his dog. Now this might appear entirely irrational: the dog did not misbehave. Obviously, Mr. Smith got angry at his boss, but he took it out on his poor dog instead. Could we conclude that he is an emotional, irrational individual not responding to incentives? Hardly. The reason that he did not respond forcefully to his boss is probably that he feared the consequences. Expressing his anger at the boss might have resulted in being fired or passed up for future promotions. An alternative way to vent his frustration would have been to kick his co-workers or throw things around the office. But again, Mr. Smith chose not to engage in such behavior because of the likely consequences for his job and possible assault charges. In economic terms, the costs are too high. He managed to bottle up his anger until he gets home and kicks his dog. The dog is a "low-cost" victim.

Here lies the perplexity: the whole act may be viewed as highly irrational—after all, Mr. Smith doesn't truly accomplish anything. But still he tries to minimize the bad consequences of venting his anger. Perhaps we could label Mr. Smith's behavior as "semirational," a mixture of seemingly senseless emotion and rational behavior at the same time.

What about changing the set of punishments in the example above? What if Mr. Smith had a "killer dog," that bit anyone who abused it (equivalent to arming potential victims)? Or what if Mr. Smith were likely to be arrested and convicted for animal abuse? Several scenarios are plausible. First, he might have found another victim, perhaps a family member, to hit or kick. Or he might have modified his outwardly aggressive acts by merely yelling at family and neighbors or demolishing something. Or he might have repressed his anger—either by bottling up his frustration or finding some nonviolent substitute, such as watching a video, to help him forget the day's events.

Responding to disincentives is by no means limited to "rational" humans. Economists have produced a large number of studies that investigate whether animals take the costs of doing things into account.[93] Animal subjects have included both rats and pigeons, and the typical experiment measures the amount of some desired treat or standard laboratory food or fluid that is consumed in relation to the number of times the animal must push a lever to get the item. Other experiments alter the amount of the item received for a given number of lever pushes. These experiments have been tried in many different contexts. For example, does an animal's willingness to work for special treats, such as root beer or cherry cola, depend upon the existence of unlimited supplies of water or standard laboratory food? These experiments consistently show that as the "cost" of obtaining the food increases, the animal obtains less food. In economic terms, "Demand curves are downward sloping."

As for human beings, a large economics literature exists that overwhelmingly demonstrates that people commit fewer crimes if criminal penalties are more severe or more certain. Whether we consider the number of airliners hijacked in the 1970s,[94] evasion of the military draft,[95] or international data on violent and property crimes,[96] stiffer penalties or higher probabilities of conviction result in fewer violations of the law. Sociologists are more cautious, but the National Research Council of the U.S. National Academy of Sciences established the Panel on Research on Deterrent and Incapacitative Effects in 1978 to evaluate the many academic studies of deterrence. The panel concluded as follows: "Taken as a whole, the evidence consistently finds a negative association between crime rates and the risks of apprehension, conviction or imprisonment. . . . the evidence certainly favors a proposition supporting deterrence more than it favors one asserting that deterrence is absent."[97]

This debate on incentives and how people respond to them arises repeatedly in many different contexts. Take gun-buyback programs. Surely the intention of such programs is good, but why should we believe that they will greatly influence the number of guns on the street? True, the guns purchased are removed from circulation, and these programs may help to stigmatize gun ownership. Yet if they continue, one effect of such programs will be to increase the return to buying a gun. The price that a person is willing to pay for a gun today increases as the price for which it can be sold rises. In the extreme case, if the price offered in these gun-buyback programs ever became sufficiently high, people would simply buy guns in order to sell them through these programs. This would hardly distress gun manufacturers. Empirical work on this question reveals no impact on crime from these programs.[98]

Introspection can go only so far. Ultimately, the issue of whether sanctions or other costs deter criminals can be decided only empirically. To what extent will concealed-handgun laws or gun-control laws raise these costs? To what extent will criminals be deterred by these costs? In chapter 2 we will consider how to test these questions.

An Overview

This book offers a critical review of the existing evidence on gun control and crime. The primary focus will be on whether gun laws save or cost lives.

To answer these questions I use a wide array of data. For instance, I have employed polls that allow us to track how gun ownership has changed over time in different states, as well as the massive FBI yearly crime rate data for all 3,054 U.S. counties from 1977 to 1992. I use additional, more recently available data for 1993 and 1994 later to check my results. Over the last decade, gun ownership has been growing for virtually all demographic groups, though the fastest growing group of gun owners is Republican women, thirty to forty-four years of age, who live in rural areas. National crime rates have been falling at the same time as gun ownership has been rising. Likewise, states experiencing the greatest reductions in crime are also the ones with the fastest growing percentages of gun ownership.

Overall, my conclusion is that criminals as a group tend to behave rationally—when crime becomes more difficult, less crime is committed. Higher arrest and conviction rates dramatically reduce crime. Criminals also move out of jurisdictions in which criminal deterrence increases. Yet criminals respond to more than just the actions taken by the police and the courts. Citizens can take private actions that also deter crime. Allowing citizens to carry concealed handguns reduces violent crimes, and the reductions coincide very closely with the number of concealed-handgun permits issued. Mass shootings in public places are reduced when law-abiding citizens are allowed to carry concealed handguns.

Not all crime categories showed reductions, however. Allowing concealed handguns might cause small increases in larceny and auto theft. When potential victims are able to arm themselves, some criminals turn away from crimes like robbery that require direct attacks and turn instead to such crimes as auto theft, where the probability of direct contact with victims is small.

There were other surprises as well. While the support for the strictest gun-control laws is usually strongest in large cities, the largest drops in violent crime from legalized concealed handguns occurred in the most urban counties with the greatest populations and the highest crime rates. Given the limited resources available to law enforcement and our desire to spend those resources wisely to reduce crime, the results of my studies have implications for where police should concentrate their efforts. For example, I found that increasing arrest rates in the most crime-prone areas led to the greatest reductions in crime. Comparisons can also be made across different methods of fighting crime. Of all the methods studied so far by economists, the carrying of concealed handguns appears to be the most cost-effective method for reducing crime. Accident and suicide rates were unaltered by the presence of concealed handguns.

Guns also appear to be the great equalizer among the sexes. Murder rates decline when either more women or more men carry concealed handguns, but the effect is especially pronounced for women. One additional woman carrying a concealed handgun reduces the murder rate for women by about 3–4 times more than one additional man carrying a concealed handgun reduces the murder rate for men. This occurs because allowing a woman to defend herself changes her ability to defend herself much more than it would for a man. After all, men are usually bigger and stronger.

While some evidence indicates that increased penalties for using a gun in the commission of a crime reduce crime, the effect is small. Furthermore, I find no crime-reduction benefits from state-mandated waiting periods and background checks before allowing people to purchase guns. At the federal level, the Brady law has proven to be no more effective. Surprisingly, there is also little benefit from training requirements or age restrictions for concealed-handgun permits.

2 | How to Test the Effects of Gun Control

The Existing Literature

Despite intense feelings on both sides of the gun debate, I believe everyone is at heart motivated by the same concerns: Will gun control increase or decrease the number of lives lost? Will these laws improve or degrade the quality of life when it comes to violent crime? The common fears we all share with regard to murders, rapes, robberies, and aggravated assaults motivate this discussion. Even those who debate the meaning of the Constitution's Second Amendment cannot help but be influenced by the answers to these questions.[1]

Anecdotal evidence is undoubtedly useful in understanding the issues at hand, but it has definite limits in developing public policy. Good arguments exist on both sides, and neither side has a monopoly on stories of tragedies that might have been avoided if the law had only been different. One side presents the details of a loved one senselessly murdered in a massacre like the April 2007 Virginia Tech shooting, where thirty-two people were killed. The other side points to an attack during a service at the New Life Church in Colorado with seven thousand people attending—an attack that was stopped by a concealed-carry permit holder.

Surveys have filled many important gaps in our knowledge; nevertheless, they suffer from many inherent problems. For example, how accurately can a person judge whether the presence of a gun actually saved her life or whether it really prevented a criminal from attacking? Might people's policy preferences influence how they answer the pollster's questions? Other serious concerns arise with survey data. Does a criminal who is thwarted from committing one particular crime merely substitute another victim or another type of crime? Or might this general deterrence raise the costs of these undesirable activities enough so that some criminals stop committing crimes? Survey data just has not been able to answer such questions.

To study these issues more effectively, academics have turned to statistics on crime. Depending on what one counts as academic research, there are at least two hundred studies on gun control. The existing work falls into two categories, using either "time-series" or "cross-sectional" data. Time-series data deal with one particular area (a city, county, or state) over many years; cross-sectional data look across many different geographic areas within the same year. The vast majority of gun-control studies that examine time-series data present a comparison of the average murder rates before and after the change in laws; those that examine cross-sectional data compare murder rates across places with and without certain laws. Unfortunately, these studies make no attempt to relate fluctuations in crime rates to changing law-enforcement factors like arrest or conviction rates, prison-sentence lengths, or other obvious variables.

Both time-series and cross-sectional analyses have their limitations. Let us first examine the cross-sectional studies. Suppose, as happens to be true, that areas with the highest crime rates are the ones that most frequently adopt the most stringent gun-control laws. Even if restrictions on guns were to lower the crime rates, it might appear otherwise. Suppose crime rates were lowered, but not by enough to reach the level of rates in low-crime areas that did not adopt the laws. In that case, looking across areas would make it appear that stricter gun control produced higher crime. Would this be proof that stricter gun control caused higher crime? Hardly. Ideally, one should examine how the high-crime areas that adopted the controls changed over time—not only relative to their past levels but also relative to areas without the controls. Economists refer to this as an "endogeneity" problem. The adoption of the policy is a reaction (that is, "endogenous") to other events, in this case crime.[2] To correctly estimate the impact of a law on crime, one must be able to distinguish and isolate the influence of crime on the adoption of the law.

For time-series data, other problems arise. For example, while the ideal study accounts for other factors that may help explain changing crime rates, a pure time-series study complicates such a task. Many potential causes of crime might fluctuate in any one jurisdiction over time, and it is very difficult to know which one of those changes might be responsible for the shifting crime rate. If two or more events occur at the same time in a particular jurisdiction, examining only that jurisdiction will not help us distinguish which event was responsible for the change in crime. Evidence is usually much stronger if a law changes in many different places at different times, and one can see whether similar crime patterns exist before and after such changes.

The solution to these problems is to combine both time-series and cross-sectional evidence and then allow separate variables, so that each year the national or regional changes in crime rates can be separated out and distinguished from any local deviations.[3] For example, crime may have fallen nationally between 1991 and 1992, but this study is able to identify whether there exists an additional decline over and above that national drop for states that have adopted concealed-handgun laws. I also use a set of measures that control for the average differences in crime rates across places even after demographic, income, and other factors have been accounted for. No previous gun-control studies had taken this approach when the first edition of this book was written.

The largest cross-sectional gun-control study examined 170 cities in 1980.[4] While this study controlled for many differences across cities, no variables were used to deal with issues of deterrence (such as arrest or conviction rates or prison-sentence lengths). It also suffered from the bias discussed above that these cross-sectional studies face in showing a positive relationship between gun control and crime.

The time-series work on gun control that has been most heavily cited by the media was done by three criminologists at the University of Maryland who looked at five different counties (one at a time) from three different states (three counties from Florida, one county from Mississippi, and one from Oregon) from 1973 to 1992 (though a different time period was used for Miami).[5] While this study has received a great deal of media attention, it suffers from serious problems. Even though these concealed-handgun laws were state laws, the authors say that they were primarily interested in studying the effect in urban areas. Yet they do not explain how they chose the particular counties used in their study. For example, why examine Tampa but not Fort Lauderdale, or Jacksonville but not Orlando? Like most previous studies, their research does not account for any other variables that might also help explain the crime rates.

Some cross-sectional studies have taken a different approach and used the types of statistical techniques found in medical case studies. Possibly the best known paper was done by Arthur Kellermann and his many coauthors,[6] who purport to show that "keeping a gun in the home was strongly and independently associated with an increased risk of homicide."[7] The claim is that the gun will be more likely to kill someone the gun owner knows than the criminal. The data for this test consists of a "case sample" (444 homicides that occurred in the victim's homes in three counties) and a "control" group (388 "matched" individuals who lived near the deceased and were the same sex and race as well as the same age range). After information was obtained from relatives of the homicide victim or the control subjects regarding such things as whether they owned a gun or had a drug or alcohol problem, these authors attempted to see if the probability of a homicide was correlated with the ownership of a gun.

There are many problems with Kellermann et al.'s paper that undercut the misleading impression that victims were killed by the gun in the home. For example, they fail to report that in only 8 of these 444 homicide cases could it be established that the "gun involved had been kept in the home."[8] Counting only the deaths from defensive gun use also ignores the much larger number of effective defensive gun uses that don't require that the gun be fired. Indeed, in less than one out of every thousand defensive gun uses is the attacker killed. More important, the question posed by the authors cannot be tested properly using their chosen methodology because of the endogeneity problem discussed earlier with respect to cross-sectional data.

To demonstrate this, suppose that the same statistical method—with a matching control group—was used to do an analogous study on the efficacy of hospital care. Assume that we collected data just as these authors did; that is, we got a list of all the people who died in a particular county over the period of a year, and we asked their relatives whether they had been admitted to a hospital during the previous year. We would also put together a control sample with people of similar ages, sex, race, and neighborhoods, and ask these men and women whether they had been in a hospital during the past year. My bet is that we would find a very strong positive relationship between those who spent time in hospitals and those who died, quite probably a stronger relationship than in Kellermann's study on homicides and gun ownership. If so, would we take that as evidence that hospitals kill people? I would hope not. We would understand that, although our methods controlled for age, sex, race, and neighborhood, the people who had visited a hospital during the past year and the people in the "control" sample who did not visit a hospital were really not the same types of people. The difference is pretty obvious: those hospitalized were undoubtedly sick, and thus it should come as no surprise that they would face a higher probability of dying.

The relationship between homicides and gun ownership is no different. The finding that those who are more likely to own guns suffer a higher homicide rate makes us ask, Why were they more likely to own guns? Could it be that they were at greater risk of being attacked? Is it possible that this difference arose because of a higher rate of illegal activities among those in the case study group than among those in the control group? Owning a gun could lower the probability of attack but still leave it higher than the probability faced by those who never felt the need to buy a gun to begin with. The fact that all or virtually all the homicide victims were killed by weapons brought into their homes by intruders makes this all the more plausible.

Unfortunately, the case study method was not designed for studying these types of social issues. Compare these endogeneity concerns with a laboratory experiment to test the effectiveness of a new drug. Some patients with the disease are provided with the drug, while others are given a placebo. The random assignment of who gets the drug and who receives the placebo is extremely important. A comparable approach to the link between homicide and guns would have researchers randomly place guns inside certain households and also randomly determine in which households guns would be forbidden. Who receives a gun would not be determined by other factors that might themselves be related to whether a person faces a high probability of being killed.

So how does one solve this causation problem? Think for a moment about the preceding hospital example. One approach would be to examine a change in something like the cost of going to hospitals. For example, if the cost of going to hospitals fell, one could see whether some people who would otherwise not have gone to the hospital would now seek help there. As we observed an increase in the number of people going to hospitals, we could then check to see whether this was associated with an increase or decrease in the number of deaths. By examining changes in hospital care prices, we could see what happens to people who now choose to go to the hospital and who were otherwise similar in terms of characteristics that would determine their probability of living.

Obviously, despite these concerns over previous work, only statistical evidence can reveal the net effect of gun laws on crimes and accidental deaths. The laws being studied here range from those that allow concealed-handgun permits to those demanding waiting periods or setting mandatory minimum sentences for using a gun in the commission of a crime. Instead of just examining how crime changes in a particular city or state, I analyze the first systematic national evidence for all 3,054 counties in the United States over the sixteen years from 1977 to 1992 and ask whether these rules saved or cost lives. I attempt to control for a change in the price people face in defending themselves by looking at the change in the laws regarding the carrying of concealed handguns. I will also use the data to examine why certain states have adopted concealed-handgun laws while others have not.

This book is the first to study the questions of deterrence using these data. While many recent studies employ proxies for deterrence—such as police expenditures or general levels of imprisonment—I am able to use arrest rates by type of crime and also, for a subset of the data, conviction rates and sentence lengths by type of crime.[9] I also attempt to analyze a question noted but not empirically addressed in this literature: the concern over causality related to increases in both handgun use and crime rates. Do higher crime rates lead to increased handgun ownership or the reverse? The issue is more complicated than simply whether carrying concealed firearms reduces murders, because questions arise about whether criminals might substitute one type of crime for another as well as the extent to which accidental handgun deaths might increase.

The Impact of Concealed Handguns on Crime

Many economic studies have found evidence broadly consistent with the deterrent effect of punishment.[10] The notion is that the expected penalty affects the prospective criminal's desire to commit a crime. Expectations about the penalty include the probabilities of arrest and conviction, and the length of the prison sentence. It is reasonable to disentangle the probability of arrest from the probability of conviction, since accused individuals appear to suffer large reputational penalties simply from being arrested.[11] Likewise, conviction also imposes many different penalties (for example, lost licenses, lost voting rights, further reductions in earnings, and so on) even if the criminal is never sentenced to prison.[12]

While these points are well understood, the net effect of concealed-handgun laws is ambiguous and awaits testing that controls for other factors influencing the returns to crime. The first difficulty involves the availability of detailed county-level data on a variety of crimes in 3,054 counties during the period from 1977 to 1992. Unfortunately, for the time period we are studying, the FBI's *Uniform Crime Reports* include arrest-rate data but not conviction rates or prison sentences. While I make use of the arrest-rate information, I include a separate variable for each county to account for the different average crime rates each county faces,[13] which admittedly constitutes a rather imperfect way to control for cross-county differences such as expected penalties.

Fortunately, however, alternative variables are available to help us measure changes in legal regimes that affect the crime rate. One such method is to use another crime category to explain the changes in the crime rate being studied. Ideally, one would pick a crime rate that moves with the crime rate being studied (presumably because of changes in the legal system or other social conditions that affect crime), but is unrelated to changes in laws regulating the right to carry firearms. Additional motivations for controlling other crime rates include James Q. Wilson's and George Kelling's "broken window" effect, where less serious crimes left undeterred will lead to more serious ones.[14] Finally, after telephoning law-enforcement officials in all fifty states, I was able to collect time-series, county-level conviction rates and mean prison-sentence lengths for three states (Arizona, Oregon, and Washington).

The FBI crime reports include seven categories of crime: murder and non-negligent manslaughter, rape, aggravated assault, robbery, auto theft, burglary, and larceny.[15] Two additional summary categories were included: violent crimes (including murder, rape, aggravated assault, and robbery) and property crimes (including auto theft, burglary, and larceny). Although they are widely reported measures in the press, these broader categories are somewhat problematic in that all crimes are given the same weight (for example, one murder equals one aggravated assault).

The most serious crimes also make up only a very small portion of this index and account for very little of the variation in the total number of violent crimes across counties (see table 2.1). For example, the average county has about eight murders, and counties differ from this number by an average of twelve murders. Obviously, the number of murders cannot be less than zero; the average difference is greater than the average simply because while 46 percent of the counties had no murders in 1992, some counties had a very large number of murders (forty-one counties had more than a hundred murders, and two counties had over one thousand murders). In comparison, the average county experienced 619 violent crimes, and counties differ from this amount by an average of 935. Not only does the murder rate contribute just a little more than 1 percent to the total number of violent crimes, but the average difference in murders across counties also explains just a little more than 1 percent of the differences in violent crimes across counties.

Table 2.1 The most common crimes and the variation in their prevalence across counties (1992)

	Average number of crimes	Percent of crime category	Dispersion	Percent of variation in general category due to each crime	Number of counties
Violent crime	619.1		934.50		2,853
Murder	7.8	1.3%	11.60	1.2%	2,954
Rape	35.4	5.7%	48.96	5.2%	2,853
Robbery	224.8	36.3%	380.70	40.7%	2,954
Aggravated assault	367.5	59.4%	534.80	57.2%	2,954
Property crime	4,078.2		5,672		2,954
Auto theft	533.9	13.1%	868	15.3%	2,954
Burglary	969.1	23.8%	1,331	23.4%	2,954
Larceny	2,575.2	63.1%	3.516	62.0%	2,954

Note: Dispersion provides a measure of variation for each crime category; it is a measure of the average difference between the overall average and each county's number of crimes. The total of the percents for specific crimes in the violent-crime category does not equal 100 percent because not all counties report consistent measures of rape. Other differences are due to rounding errors.

Even the narrower categories are somewhat broad for our purposes. For example, robbery includes not only street robberies, which seem the most likely to be affected by concealed-handgun laws, but also bank robberies, too. And for the bank robberies the additional return to permitting citizens to be armed would appear to be small because of the presence of armed guards.[16] Likewise, larceny involves crimes of "stealth," which includes those committed by pickpockets, purse snatchers, shoplifters, and bike thieves, and such crimes as theft from buildings, coin machines, and motor vehicles. However, while most of these fit the categories in which concealed-handgun laws are likely to do little to discourage criminals, pickpockets do come into direct contact with their victims.

This aggregation of crime categories makes it difficult to isolate crimes that might be deterred by increased handgun ownership and crimes that might be increasing as a result of a substitution effect. Generally, the crimes most likely to be deterred by concealed-handgun laws are those involving direct contact between the victim and the criminal, especially when they occur in places where victims otherwise would not be allowed to carry firearms. Aggravated assault, murder, robbery, and rape are both confrontational and likely to occur where guns were not previously allowed.

In contrast, crimes like auto theft of unattended cars seem unlikely to be deterred by gun ownership. While larceny is more debatable, in general—to the extent that these crimes actually involve "stealth"—the probability that victims will notice the crime being committed seems low, and thus the opportunities to use a gun are relatively rare. The effect on burglary is am-

biguous from a theoretical standpoint. It is true that if nondiscretionary laws
cause more people to own a guns, burglars will face greater risks when breaking into houses, and this should reduce the number of burglaries. However,
if some of those who already own guns now obtain right-to-carry permits,
the relative cost of crimes like armed street robbery and certain other types
of robberies (where an armed patron may be present) should rise relative to
that for burglary or residential robbery. This may cause some criminals to engage in burglaries instead of armed street robbery. Indeed, a recent Texas poll
suggests that such substitution may be substantial: 97 percent of first-time
applicants for concealed-handgun permits already owned a handgun.[17]

Previous concealed-handgun studies that rely on state-level data suffer from an important potential problem: they ignore the heterogeneity within states.[18] From my telephone conversations with many law-
enforcement officials, it has become very clear that there was a large
variation across counties within a state in terms of how freely gun permits
were granted to residents prior to the adoption of nondiscretionary right-
to-carry laws.[19] All those I talked to strongly indicated that the most populous counties had previously adopted by far the most restrictive practices
in issuing permits. The implication for existing studies is that simply using
state-level data rather than county data will bias the results against finding any impact from passing right-to-carry provisions. Those counties that
were unaffected by the law must be separated from those counties where
the change could be quite dramatic. Even cross-sectional city data will not
solve this problem, because without time-series data it is impossible to determine the impact of a change in the law for a particular city.[20]

There are two ways of handling this problem. First, for the national
sample, one can see whether the passage of nondiscretionary right-to-carry
laws produces systematically different effects in the high- and low-
population counties. Second, for three states—Arizona, Oregon, and
Pennsylvania—I acquired time-series data on the number of right-to-carry
permits for each county. The normal difficulty with using data on the
number of permits involves the question of causality: Do more permits
make crimes more costly, or do higher crime rates lead to more permits?
The change in the number of permits before and after the change in the
state laws allows us to rank the counties on the basis of how restrictive
they had actually been in issuing permits prior to the change in the law. Of
course there is still the question of why the state concealed-handgun law
changed, but since we are dealing with county-level rather than state-level
data, we benefit from the fact that those counties with the most restrictive

policies regarding permits were also the most likely to have the new laws imposed upon them by the state.

Using county-level data also has another important advantage in that both crime and arrest rates vary widely within states. In fact, as indicated in table 2.2, the variation in both crime rates and arrest rates across states is almost always smaller than the average within-state variation across counties. With the exception of the rates for robbery, the variation in crime rates

Table 2.2 Comparing the variation in crime rates across states and across counties within states from 1977 to 1992

	Percent of variation across states relative to the average variation within states
Crime rates per 100,000 population	
Violent-crime rate	111%
Murder rate	75
Murder rate with guns (from 1982 to 1991)	61
Rape rate	69
Aggravated-assault rate	83
Robbery rate	166
Property-crime rate	66
Auto theft rate	74
Burglary rate	69
Larceny rate	61
Arrest rates (number of arrests divided by number of offenses)*	
Violent crimes	21
Murder	21
Rape	17
Robbery	21
Aggravated assault	32
Property crime	18
Burglary	23
Larceny	15
Auto theft	15
Truncating arrest rates to be no greater than one	
Violent crime	44
Murder	30
Rape	34
Robbery	25
Aggravated assault	41
Property crimes	43
Burglary	33
Larceny	46
Auto theft	31

Note: The percents are computed as the standard deviation of state means divided by the average within-state standard deviations across counties.
*Because of multiple arrests for a crime and because of the lags between the time when a crime occurs and the time an arrest takes place, the arrest rate for counties and states can be greater than one. This is much more likely to occur for counties than for states.

across states is from 61 to 83 percent of their average variation within states. (The difference in violent-crime rates arises because robberies make up such a large fraction of the total crimes in this category.) For arrest rates, the numbers are much more dramatic; the variation across states is as small as 15 percent of the average of the variation within states.

These results imply that it is no more accurate to view all the counties in the typical state as a homogenous unit than it is to view all the states in the United States as a homogenous unit. For example, when a state's arrest rate rises, it may make a big difference whether that increase is taking place in the most or least crime-prone counties. Widely differing estimates of the deterrent effect of increasing a state's average arrest rate may be made, depending on which types of counties are experiencing the changes in arrest rates and depending on how sensitive the crime rates are to arrest-rate changes in those particular counties. Aggregating these data may thus make it more difficult to discern the true relationship between deterrence and crime.

Another way of illustrating the differences between state and county data is simply to compare the counties with the highest and lowest crime rates to the states with the highest and lowest rates. Tables 2.3 and 2.4 list

Table 2.3 Murder rates: state and county variation in the states with the ten highest and ten lowest murder rates (1992)

States ranked by level of murder rate (10 highest; 10 lowest)	Murder rate per 100,000	County with highest murder rate	Highest county murder rate per 100,000	Number of counties with zero murder rate
Louisiana (1)	15.3	Orleans	57	5
New York (2)	13.2	Kings	28	13
Texas (3)	12.7	Delta	64	116
California (4)	12.66	Los Angeles	21	8
Maryland (5)	12.1	Baltimore	46	4
Illinois (6)	11.21	St. Clair	31	67
Arkansas (7)	10.8	Chicot	53	19
Georgia (8)	10.7	Taliaferro	224	62
North Carolina (9)	10.4	Graham	56	16
South Carolina (10)	10.35	Jasper	32	4
Nebraska (41)	3.2	Pierce	13	72
Utah (42)	2.99	Kane	20	15
Massachusetts (43)	2.97	Suffolk	12	2
Montana (44)	2.22	Meager	55	32
North Dakota (45)	1.9	Golden Valley	53	44
Maine (46)	1.7	Washington	5.5	7
New Hampshire (47)	1.5	Carroll	5.5	5
Iowa (48)	1.1	Wayne	14	71
Vermont (49)	0.7	Chittenden	2.2	9
South Dakota (50)	0.6	Bon Homme	14	49

Table 2.4 Rape rates: state and county variation in the states with the ten highest and ten lowest rape rates (1992)

States ranked by level of rape rate (10 highest; 10 lowest)	Rape rate per 100,000	County with highest rape rate	Highest county rape rate per 100,000	County with lowest rape rate	Lowest county rape rate per 100,000
Alaska (1)	98	North Slope	473	Matanuska-Susitna	14
Delaware (2)	86	Sussex	118	New Castle	74
Michigan (3)	79	Branch	198	Keweenaw	0
Washington (4)	71	Ferry	237	Garfield	0
South Carolina (5)	59	Dillon	97	2 counties	0
Nevada (6)	55	Washoe	82	5 counties	0
Florida (7)	53.7	Putnam	178	3 counties	0
Texas (8)	53.5	Rains	130	70 counties	0
Oregon (9)	53	Multnomah	95	3 counties	0
South Dakota (10)	50	Pennington	136	24 counties	0
Mississippi (41)	29	Harrison	108	11 counties	0
Pennsylvania (42)	27.4	Fulton	85	2 counties	0
Connecticut (43)	26.8	New Haven	38	Windham	1
Wisconsin (44)	26.4	Menominee	98	10 counties	0
North Dakota (45)	25	Morton	81	33 counties	0
Maine (46)	23	Franklin	41	Sagadahoc	0
West Virginia (47)	22	Cabell	99	8 counties	0
Montana (48)	21	Mineral	179	24 counties	0
Iowa (49)	13	Buchanan	62	40 counties	0
Vermont (50)	12	Chittenden	47	Orange	0

the ten safest and ten most dangerous states by murder and rape rates, along with those same crime rates for the safest and most dangerous counties in each state. (When rates were zero in more than one county, the number of counties is given.) Two conclusions are clear from these tables. First, even the states with the highest murder and rape rates have counties with no murders or rapes, and these counties in the most dangerous states are much safer than the safest states, according to the average state crime rates for the safest states. Second, while the counties with the highest murder rates tend to be well-known places like Orleans (New Orleans, Louisiana), Kings (Brooklyn, N.Y.), Los Angeles, and Baltimore, there are a few relatively small, rural counties that, for very short periods of time, garner the top spots in a state. The reverse is not true, however: counties with the lowest murder rates are always small, rural ones.

The two exceptions to this general situation are the two states with the highest rape rates: Alaska and Delaware. Alaska, possibly because of the imbalance of men and women in the population, has high rape rates over the entire state.[21] Even Matanuska-Susitna, which is the Alaskan borough with the lowest rape rate, has a higher rape rate than either Iowa or Vermont. Delaware, which has a very narrow range between the highest and lowest county rape rates, is another exception. However, at least part of the reason for a nonzero rape rate in New Castle county (although this doesn't explain the overall high rape rate in the state) is that Delaware has only three counties, each with a relatively large population, and these large numbers virtually guarantee that some rapes take place.

Perhaps the relatively small across-state variation, as compared to within-state variations, is not so surprising, as states tend to average out differences when they include both rural and urban areas. Yet when coupled with the preceding discussion on the differing effects of concealed-handgun provisions on different counties in the same state, these numbers strongly imply that it is risky to assume that states are homogenous units with respect either to how crimes are punished or how the laws that affect gun usage are changed. Unfortunately, this emphasis on state-level data pervades the entire crime literature, which focuses on state- or city-level data and fails to recognize the differences between rural and urban counties.

However, using county-level data has some drawbacks. Because of the low crime rates in many low-population counties, it is quite common to find huge variations in the arrest and conviction rates from year to year. These variations arise both because the year in which the offense occurs frequently differs from the year in which the arrests and/or convictions occur, and because an offense may involve more than one offender. Unfortunately, the FBI data set allows us neither to link the years in which offenses and arrests occurred nor to link offenders with a particular crime. In counties where only a couple of murders occur annually, arrests or convictions can be many times higher than the number of offenses in a year. This data problem appears especially noticeable for counties with few people and for crimes that are relatively infrequent, like murder and rape.

One partial solution is to limit the sample to counties with large populations. Counties with a large number of crimes have a significantly smoother flow of arrests and convictions relative to offenses. An alternative solution is to take a moving average of the arrest or conviction rates over several years, though this reduces the length of the usable sample period, depending on how many years are used to compute this average. Furthermore, the moving-average solution does nothing to alleviate the effect of multiple suspects being arrested for a single crime.

Another concern is that otherwise law-abiding citizens may have carried concealed handguns even before it was legal to do so.[22] If nondiscretionary laws do not alter the total number of concealed handguns carried by otherwise law-abiding citizens, but merely legalize their previous actions, passing these laws seems unlikely to affect crime rates. The only real effect from making concealed handguns legal could arise from people being more willing to use them to defend themselves, though this might also imply that they would be more likely to make mistakes in using them.

It is also possible that concealed-firearm laws both make individuals safer and increase crime rates at the same time. As Sam Peltzman has pointed out in the context of automobile safety regulations, increasing safety may lead drivers to offset these gains by taking more risks as they drive.[23] Indeed, recent studies indicate that drivers in cars equipped with air bags drive more recklessly and get into accidents at sufficiently higher rates to offset the life-saving effect of air bags for the driver and actually increase the total risk of death for others.[24] The same thing is possible with regard to crime. For example, allowing citizens to carry concealed firearms may encourage them to risk entering more dangerous neighborhoods or to begin traveling during times they previously avoided:

> Martha Hayden, a Dallas saleswoman, said the right-to-carry law introduced in Texas this year has turned her life around.
>
> She was pistol-whipped by a thief outside her home in 1993, suffering 300 stitches to the head, and said she was "terrified" of even taking out the garbage after the attack.
>
> But now she packs a .357 Smith and Wesson. "It gives me a sense of security; it allows you to get on with your life," she said.[25]

Staying inside her house may have reduced Ms. Hayden's probability of being assaulted again, but since her decision to engage in these riskier activities is a voluntary one, she at least believes that this is an acceptable risk. Likewise, society as a whole might be better off even if crime rates were to rise as a result of concealed-handgun laws.

Finally, we must also address the issues of why certain states adopted concealed-handgun laws and whether higher offense rates result in lower arrest rates. To the extent that states adopted the laws because crime was rising, econometric estimates that fail to account for this relationship will underpredict the drop in crime and perhaps improperly blame some of the higher crime rates on the measures taken to help solve the problem, such as increasing the police force. To explain this problem differently, crime rates may have risen even though concealed-handgun laws were passed, but the rates might have risen even higher if the laws had not been passed.

Likewise, if the laws were adopted when crime rates were falling, the bias would be in the opposite direction. None of the previous gun-control studies deal with this type of potential bias.[26]

The basic problem is one of causation. Does the change in the laws alter the crime rate, or does the change in the crime rate alter the law? Do higher crime rates lower the arrest rate or the reverse? Does the arrest rate really drive the changes in crime rates? And are any errors in measuring crime driving the relationship between crime and arrest rates? Fortunately, we can deal with these potential biases by using well-known techniques that let us see what relationships, if any still exist after we try to explain the arrest rates and the adoption of these laws. For example, we can see how arrest rates change in response to changes in crime rates and then examine to what extent the unexplained portion of the arrest rates helps explain the crime rate. We will find that accounting for these concerns actually strengthens the general initial findings. My general approach, however, is to examine first how concealed-handgun laws and crime rates, as well as arrest rates and crime rates, tend to move in comparison to one another before we try to deal with more complicated relationships.

3 | Gun Ownership, Gun Laws, and the Data on Crime

Who Owns Guns?

Before studying what determines the crime rate, let's look at what types of people own guns and how this has been changing over time.

Information on gun ownership rates is difficult to obtain, and the only way to overcome this problem is to rely on surveys. The largest, most extensive polls are the exit polls conducted during the general elections every two years. Only these surveys interview enough people to get a useful estimate of gun ownership in individual states. Presidential election polls for 1988 and 1996 included a question on whether a person owned a gun, as well as information on the person's age, sex, race, income, place of residence, and political views. In 2004, a question on whether a person's family owned a gun was included. The available 1992, 2000, and 2008 survey data did not include a question on gun ownership.

Using the individual respondent data in the 1988 CBS News General Election Exit Poll and the 1996 Voter News Service National General Election Exit Poll, we can construct a very detailed description of the people who own guns. The Voter News Service poll collected data for a consortium of national news bureaus (CNN, CBS, ABC, NBC, Fox, and AP). I will soon discuss an exit poll survey from the 2004 presidential elec-

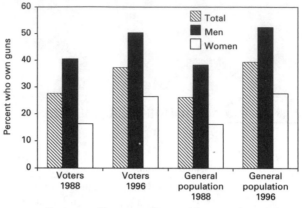

Gun ownership among voters and the general population

Figure 3.1. Percent of women and men who owned guns in 1988 and 1996: examining both voters and the general population

tion, but the gun ownership question is sufficiently different that I want to treat the 2004 survey separately.

What stands out immediately is the large increase in the number of people identifying themselves as gun owners (see figure 3.1). In 1988, 27.4 percent of voters owned guns.[1] By 1996, the number of voters owning guns had risen to 37 percent. In general, the percentages of voters and the general population who appear to own guns are extremely similar; among the general population, gun ownership rose from 26 to 39 percent,[2] which represented 76 million adults in 1996. Perhaps in retrospect, given all the news media discussions about high crime rates in the last couple of decades, this increase is not very surprising. Just as spending on private security has grown dramatically—reaching $82 billion in 1996, more than twice the amount spent in 1980 (even after taking into account inflation)—more people have been obtaining guns.[3] The large rise in gun sales that took place immediately before the Brady law went into effect in 1994 accounts for some of the increase.[4]

Three points must be made about these numbers. First, the form of the question changed somewhat between these two years. In 1988 people were asked, "Are you any of the following? (Check as many as apply)," and the list included "Gun Owner." In 1996 respondents were asked to record "yes" or "no" to the question, "Are you a gun owner?" This difference may have accounted for part, though not all, of the change.[5] Second, Tom Smith, director of the General Social Survey, told me he guessed that voters might own guns "by up to 5 percent more" than nonvoters, though this was difficult to know for sure because in polls of the general population, over 60 percent of respondents claim to have voted, but we know that only around 50 percent did vote.[6] Given the size of the error in the General Social Survey regarding the percentage of those surveyed who were actual voters, it is nevertheless possible that nonvoters own guns by a few percentage points more than voters.[7]

Finally, there is strong reason to believe that women greatly underreport gun ownership. The most dramatic evidence of this arises from a comparison of the ownership rates for married men and married women. If the issue is whether women have immediate access to a gun in their house when they are threatened with a crime, it is the presence of a gun that is relevant, not ownership. For example, the 1988 poll data show that 20 percent of married women acknowledged owning a gun, which doesn't come close to the 47 percent figure reported for married men. Obviously, some women interpret this poll question literally regarding personal ownership as opposed to family ownership. If married women were assumed to own guns at the same rate as married men, the gun ownership rate in 1988 would increase from 27 to 36 percent.[8] Unfortunately, the 1996 data do not allow such a comparison, though presumably a similar effect is also occurring. The estimates reported in the figures do not attempt to adjust for these three considerations.

The other finding that stands out is that while some types of people are more likely than others to own guns, large numbers of people in all groups own guns. Almost one in four voters who identify themselves as liberals and almost one in three Democrats own a gun (see figure 3.2). The most typical gun owner may be a rural, white male, middle-aged or older, who is a conservative Republican earning between $30,000 and $75,000. Women, however, experienced the greatest growth in gun ownership during this eight-year period, with an increase of over 70 percent: between the years 1988 and 1996, women went from owning guns at 41 percent of the rate of men to over 53 percent.

High-income people are also more likely to own guns. In 1996, people earning over $100,000 per year were 7 percentage points more likely to own guns than those making less than $15,000. The gap between those earning $30,000 to $75,000 and those making less than $15,000 was over 10 percentage points. These differences in gun ownership between high- and low-income people changed little between the two polls.

When comparing these poll results with the information shown in table 1.1 on murder victims' and offenders' race, the poll results imply that, at least for blacks and whites, gun ownership does not explain why blacks have higher murder rates. For example, while white gun ownership exceeds that

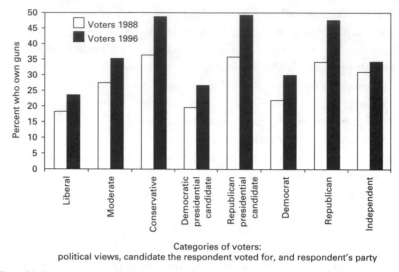

Categories of voters:
political views, candidate the respondent voted for, and respondent's party

Figure 3.2. Percent of different groups of voters who owned guns in 1988 and 1996

for blacks by about 40 percent in 1996 (see figure 3.3), and the vast majority of violent crimes are committed against members of the offender's own racial group, blacks are 4.6 times more likely to be murdered and 5.1 times more likely to be offenders than are whites. Even if blacks underreported their gun ownership rate, it still couldn't explain the gap in crime rates. Even a 100 percent gun ownership rate among blacks would still leave a gap in gun ownership that is smaller than the gap in crime rates.

The polls also indicate that families that included union members tended to own guns at relatively high and more quickly growing rates (see figure 3.3). While the income categories in these polls varied across the two years, it is clear that gun ownership increased across all ranges of income. In fact, of the categories examined, only one experienced declines in gun ownership—people living in urban areas with a population of over 500,000 (see figure 3.4). Not too surprisingly, while rural areas have the highest gun ownership rates and the lowest crime rates, cities with more than 500,000 people have the lowest gun ownership rates and the highest crime rates (for example, in 1993 cities with over 500,000 people had murder rates that were over 60 percent higher than the rates in cities with populations between 50,000 and 500,000).

For a subset of the relatively large states, the polls include enough respondents to provide a fairly accurate description of gun ownership even at the state level, as shown in table 3.1. The 1988 survey was extensive enough to provide us with over 1,000 respondents for twenty-one states, and over 770 respondents for three other states. The 1996 survey was less extensive, with only fourteen of the states surveyed having at least 100 respondents. Since these fourteen states were relatively more urban, they tended to have lower gun ownership rates than the nation as a whole.

The polls show that the increase in gun ownership was nationwide and not limited to any particular group. Of the fourteen states with enough respondents to make state-level comparisons, thirteen states had more people owning guns in 1996 than 1988. Six states each had over a million

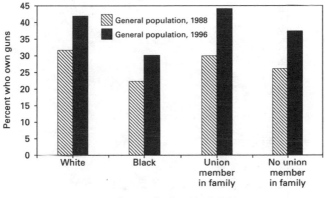

Figure 3.3. Percent of people by race and by union membership who own guns

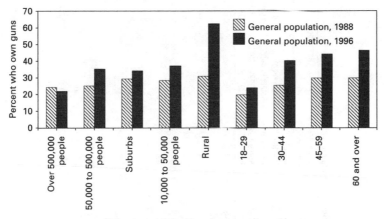

Figure 3.4. Percent of people living in different-size communities and in different age groups who owned guns in 1988 and 1996

Table 3.1 Gun-ownership rates by state

State	CBS General Election Exit Poll (November 8, 1988) surveyed 34,245 people			Voter News Service General Election Exit Poll (November 5, 1996) surveyed 3,818 people			Estimated change in states over time	
	Percent of voting population owning a gun[1] (1)	Percent of state's adults owning a gun[1] (2)	Estimated number of adults owning a gun, using column 2 (3)	Percent of voting population owning a gun[2] (4)	Percent of state's adults owning a gun[2] (5)	Estimated number of adults owning a gun, using column 5 (6)	Change in percent of adults owning a gun (7)	Change in the number of adults owning a gun (8)
United States	27.4%	26%	47.3 million	37%	38.9%	76.7 million	12.9%	29.4 million
California	23%	21%	6 million	33%	32%	10 million	11%	4 million
Connecticut	14%	10%	337,000	10%	12%	377,000	2%	40,000
Florida	28%	29%	3.6 million	35%	31%	4.4 million	2%	800,000
Illinois	19%	17%	1.9 million	34%	36%	4.3 million	19%	2.4 million
Indiana	29%	32%	1.74 million	32%	31%	1.8 million	-1%	60,000
Iowa	29%	31%	847,000	—	—	—	—	—
Maryland	23%	22%	1 million	—	—	—	—	—
Massachusetts	15%	16%	951,000	12%	11%	638,000	-5%	-313,000
Michigan	27%	28%	2.5 million	38%	37%	3.5 million	9%	1 million
Minnesota	33%	28%	1.2 million	—	—	—	—	—
Mississippi	40%	40%	1 million	—	—	—	—	—
Missouri	37%	31%	1.6 million	—	—	—	—	—

Nevada	30%	38%	404,000	—	—	—	—	—
New Jersey	12%	11%	810,000	14%	13%	1.04 million	2%	230,000
New Mexico	38%	41%	608,000	—	—	—	—	—
New York	13%	11%	2 million	20%	18%	3.3 million	7%	1.3 million
North Carolina	35%	32%	2.1 million	45%	43%	4.8 million	11%	2.7 million
Ohio	25%	28%	2.97 million	32%	32%	3.57 million	4%	600,000
Oregon	40%	36%	996,000	—	—	—	—	—
Pennsylvania	24%	19%	2.2 million	30%	29%	3.5 million	10%	1.3 million
Texas	38%	37%	6.1 million	34%	34%	6.4 million	-3%	300,000
Vermont	34%	35%	193,000	—	—	—	—	—
Washington	33%	31%	1.5 million	—	—	—	—	—
Wisconsin	29%	29%	1.4 million	43%	45%	2.3 million	16%	900,000

Source: The polls used are the General Election Exit Polls from CBS (1988) and Voter News Service (1996). The estimated percent of the voting population owning a gun is obtained by using the weighting of responses supplied by the polling organizations. The estimated percent of the general population owning a gun uses a weight that I constructed from the census to account for the difference between the percentage of males and females: whites, blacks, Hispanics and others; and these groups by age categories that are in the voting population relative to the actual state-level populations recorded by the census.

[1] State poll numbers based upon at least 770 respondents per state.

[2] State poll numbers based upon at least one hundred respondents per state. Other states were surveyed, but the number of respondents in each state was too small to provide an accurate measure of gun ownership p. These responses were still useful in determining the national ownership rate, even if they were not sufficient to help determine the rate in an individual state.

more people owning guns. Only Massachusetts saw a decline in gun ownership.

States differ significantly in the percentage of people who own guns. On the lower end in 1988, in states like New York, New Jersey, and Connecticut, only 10 or 11 percent of the population owned guns. Despite its reputation, Texas no longer ranks first in gun ownership; California currently takes that title—approximately 10 million of its citizens own guns. In fact, the percentage of people who own guns in Texas is now below the national average.

National Election Pool survey data are available for the 2004 presidential election,[9] but there are two problems. First, the gun ownership survey question changes significantly. Instead of asking whether an individual personally owns a gun, the question is now "Do you or does someone else in your household own a gun?" As noted previously, many respondents in the earlier surveys may have indicated that they owned a gun simply because there was a gun in the home even if the gun was technically owned by another person in the household. Presumably asking if a gun is owned in the household will cause more people to answer "yes" than they had to the question of whether they personally own a gun, but how large the effect is remains an empirical question.

Just as important, there is strong evidence that Republicans and conservatives "refused to be interviewed [by the exit pollsters] in disproportionately higher numbers, thus skewing the results."[10] A similar problem appears to have occurred with the 2000 general voter exit poll, but a study by those who conducted the exit poll concluded: "[This systematic refusal] was higher in 2004 than in previous years for which we have data."[11] This skewness in the survey data generated quite a controversy after the 2004 presidential election, as John Kerry supporters argued that the difference between the actual vote totals for their candidate and what had been predicted by the exit poll survey implied some type of fraud had occurred. Since Republicans and conservatives are much more likely to own guns than the general population, this last bias works to understate the percent of the overall population that owns guns.[12]

There is some evidence that changing questions on gun ownership significantly affected the rate that people say that they own a gun. If the difference between married men and married women had remained unchanged, it would suggest that the results are not greatly affected. While there is still a ten-percentage-point gap between the rates that married men and women report that there are guns in their household (53 to 43 percent), it is quite a bit smaller than the twenty-seven-percentage point gap (a difference of more than 2 to 1) shown for 1988. I would have greatly preferred making this comparison to 1996, where the overall poll results are more comparable, but it still seems likely that changing the question did cause more people (primarily women) to answer "yes" to the survey question in 2004.

In any case, both the change in questions and the higher rate at which Republicans and conservatives refused to answer survey questions make it difficult to directly compare the 2004 exit polls with those from 1988 and 1996. However, since one error works to overstate gun ownership while another works to understate it, without additional information it is not clear whether these errors work to overstate or understate the true gun ownership rate. With that in mind, it makes more sense to limit the 2004 survey results to making comparisons between different groups in the 2004 sample than to compare the changes between 1996 and 2004.

Given these caveats, the poll results shown in figures 3.5a and 3.5b indicate that 41 percent of Americans live in households with guns (this is slightly higher than the 37 percent who reported owning a gun in 1996). The demographic patterns are very similar to patterns shown for 1988 and 1996. For all the categories, the relative gun ownership rankings of the different groups in 2004 are exactly the same as they were in 1996. Men are more likely than women to say that they live in a household with guns. Conservatives are more likely than moderates to own guns and moderates more likely than liberals, and the same pattern occurs whether they voted for the Democratic or Republican presidential candidate and regardless of political affiliation.

The male/female ratio of gun ownership in 2004 remains virtually the same as in 1996. The percent of married women with guns rose at the same time that it fell for single women. Gun ownership in the most urbanized areas has increased relative to ownership in rural areas (urban areas increased from being 32 percent of the level of rural areas to 41 percent), and white gun ownership has increased slightly relative to black ownership (from 40 percent more to 49 percent more).

The one category of comparisons used earlier that cannot be made here involves gun ownership in union households. Not all respondents were asked whether their household owned guns or whether someone in their household belonged to a union, and there was no overlap between the two samples.

Table 3.2 shows the breakdown in gun ownership rates by state for the thirty-eight states where at least 100 people were asked whether their

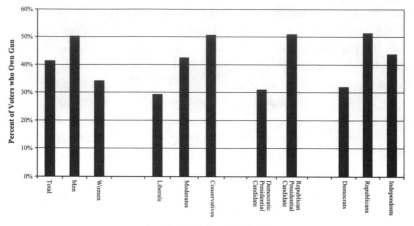

Figure 3.5a. Percent of voters who own guns by gender and political views

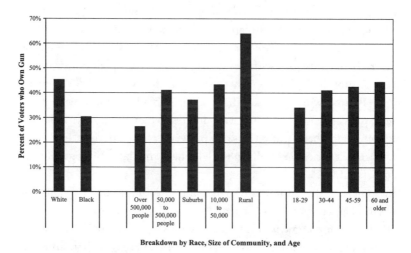

Figure 3.5b. Percent of voters who own guns by race, size of community, and age

household owns a gun. The results show a much wider range of gun ownership than was observed in either of the two previous surveys—ranging from 87 percent in Nebraska to 13 percent in Rhode Island. The seven states with the highest gun ownership rates and the two states with the lowest rates in 2004 had samples that were too small to be included in either of the two previous years. With the exception of slight drops in gun ownership rates in California, Illinois, and New York, all the other states showed an increase from 1996 to 2004.

Table 3.2 Gun ownership rate by state in 2004, using the question in the 2004 presidential exit poll survey "Do you or does someone else in your household own a gun?"

State	Gun ownership rate
Alabama	58%
Arizona	40%
California	31%
Colorado	33%
Connecticut	27%
Delaware	16%
Florida	39%
Georgia	50%
Idaho	47%
Illinois	30%
Indiana	60%
Iowa	59%
Kansas	62%
Louisana	65%
Maine	32%
Maryland	34%
Massachusetts	22%
Michigan	56%
Minnesota	44%
Missouri	45%
Montana	84%
Nebraska	87%
New Hampshire	37%
New Jersey	30%
New York	18%
North Carolina	56%
Ohio	35%
Oklahoma	71%
Oregon	44%
Pennsylvania	33%
Rhode Island	13%
South Carolina	34%
Tennessee	49%
Texas	48%
Utah	69%
Virginia	32%
Washington	56%
Wisconsin	44%
All States	41%

Understanding Different Gun Laws and Crime Rate Data

While murder rates have exhibited no clear trend over the last twenty years, they are currently 60 percent higher than in 1965.[13] Driven by substantial increases in rapes, robberies, and aggravated assaults, violent crime was 46 percent higher in 1995 than in 1976 and 240 percent higher than in 1965. As shown in figure 3.6, violent-crime rates peaked in 1991, but, with the exception of murder, they are still substantially above the rates in previous decades.

Such high violent-crime rates make people quite concerned about crime, and even the recent declines have not allayed their fears. By 2007, stories of people who had used guns to defend themselves had helped motivate thirty-nine states to adopt nondiscretionary (also referred to as "shall-issue," "right-to-carry," or "do-issue") concealed-handgun laws, which require law-enforcement officials or a licensing agency to issue, without subjective discretion, concealed-weapons permits to all qualified applicants (see figures 3.7a and 3.7b for the state laws in 1996 and 2007). This constitutes a dramatic increase from the eight states that had enacted nondiscretionary concealed-weapons laws prior to 1985. The requirements that must be met vary by state, and generally include the following: lack of a significant criminal record, an age restriction of either 18 or 21, various fees, training, and a lack of significant mental illness. The first three requirements, regarding criminal record, age, and payment of a fee, are the most common. Two states, Vermont and Idaho (with the exception of Boise), do not require permits, though the laws against convicted felons carrying guns still apply. In contrast, discretionary laws allow local law-enforcement officials or judges to make case-by-case decisions about whether to grant permits, based on the applicant's ability to prove a "compelling need."

When the data set used in this book was originally put together, county-level crime data was available for the period between 1977 and 1992. During that time, ten states—Florida (1987), Georgia (1989), Idaho (1990), Maine (1985),[14] Mississippi (1990), Montana (1991), Oregon (1990), Pennsylvania (1989), Virginia (1988),[15] and West Virginia (1989)—adopted nondiscretionary right-to-carry firearm laws. Pennsylvania is a special case because Philadelphia was exempted from the state law during the sample period, though people with permits from the surrounding Pennsylvania counties were allowed to carry concealed handguns into the city. Eight other states (Alabama, Connecticut, Indiana, New Hampshire, North Dakota, South Dakota, Vermont, and Washington) have had right-to-carry laws on the books for decades.[16] Between 1993 and 2007, twenty-one additional states adopted shall-issue laws. The last two chapters of this book will analyze later changes.

Keeping in mind all the serious causation problems discussed earlier for cross-sectional data, table 3.3 provides a first and very superficial look at the data for the last year originally examined in this book (1992) as well as the last year that FBI crime rate data are available. The table shows how crime rates varied with the type of concealed-handgun law. Despite the problem with cross-sectional data, according to the data presented in the table for 1992, the difference is quite suggestive: violent crimes are 81 percent higher in states without nondiscretionary laws. For murder, states that ban the concealed carrying of guns have murder rates 127 percent higher than states with the most liberal concealed-carry laws. After almost all the states have adopted these laws in 2007, the difference is much smaller: just 25 percent for violent crime and 28 percent for murder. States with non-discretionary laws have less violent crime, but the differences for property crimes are smaller and less consistent.

Since the primary data that we will focus on are at the county level, we are asking whether crime rates change in counties whose states adopt nondiscretionary concealed-handgun laws. We are also asking whether the crime rates change relative to other changes in counties located in states without such laws. Using a reference library (Lexis/Nexis) that contains an extensive collection of news stories and state laws, I conducted a search to determine the exact dates on which these laws took effect. Because of delays in implementing the laws even after they went into effect, I defined counties in states with nondiscretionary laws as being subject to these laws beginning with the first full year for which the law was in effect. While all the tables shown in this book use the second measure, both measures produced similar results.

The number of arrests and offenses for each type of crime in every county from 1977 to 1992 was provided by the FBI's *Uniform Crime Reports;* in addition, however, I contacted the state department of corrections, attorney general, secretary of state, and state police offices in every state in an effort to compile data on conviction rates, sentence lengths, and concealed-weapons permits by county. The Bureau of Justice Statistics also released a list of contacts in every state that might provide state-level criminal justice data. Unfortunately, county data on the total number of outstanding concealed-carry pistol permits were available only for Arizona, California,

A. Violent crime

B. Murder

C. Rape

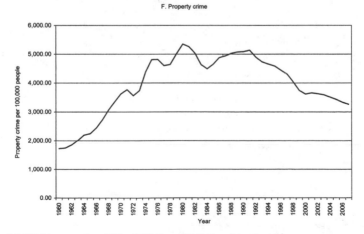

Figure 3.6. U.S. Crime rates from 1960 to 2006 (from FBI's *Uniform Crime Reports*)

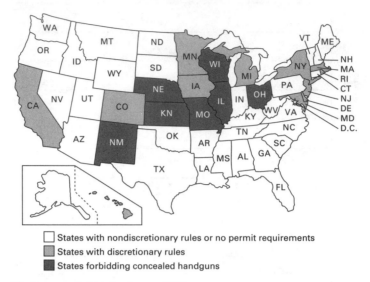

States with nondiscretionary rules or no permit requirements
States with discretionary rules
States forbidding concealed handguns

Figure 3.7a. State concealed-handgun laws as of 1996

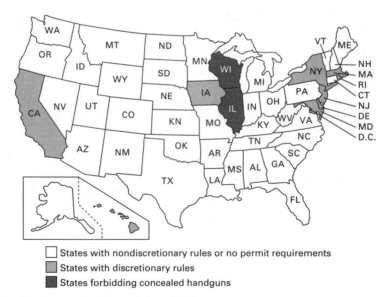

States with nondiscretionary rules or no permit requirements
States with discretionary rules
States forbidding concealed handguns

Figure 3.7b. State concealed-handgun laws as of 2007

Table 3.3 Crime rates in states and the District of Columbia that are shall-issue and are more restrictive in letting citizens carry concealed handguns

	1992 Crime rate per 100,000 people			2007 Crime rate per 100,000 people		
Type of crime	States with nondiscretionary concealed handgun laws	All other states	Percentage higher crime rate in states without nondiscretionary laws	States with nondiscretionary concealed handgun laws	All other states	Percentage higher crime rate in states without nondiscretionary laws
Violent crime	378.8	684.5	81	403.2	505.2	25
Murder	5.1	9.5	86	5	6.4	28
Rape	35	43.6	25	34.7	25.3	−27
Aggravated assault	339.9	417.4	23	262	286.6	9
Robbery	108.8	222.6	105	101.5	186.9	84
Property crime	3,786.3	4,696.8	24	3244	3,047.4	−6
Auto theft	334.2	533.4	60	314.1	399.2	27
Burglary	840.3	1,074.7	28	714.4	573.8	−20
Larceny	2,611.8	3,088.7	18	2,215.4	2,074.4	−6

Florida, Oregon, Pennsylvania, and Washington, and time-series county data before and after a change in the law were only available for Arizona (1994–96), Oregon (1990–92), and Pennsylvania (1986–92). Since the Oregon nondiscretionary law was passed in 1990, I sought data on the number of permits in 1989 by calling up every county sheriff in Oregon, and 25 of the 36 counties provided that information. (The remaining counties stated that records had not been kept.)[17] For Oregon, data on county-level conviction rates and sentence lengths were also available from 1977 to 1992.

One difficulty with the sentence-length data is that Oregon passed a sentencing-reform act that took effect in November 1989 and required criminals to serve at least 85 percent of their sentences; thus, judges may have correspondingly altered their sentencing practices. This change was phased in over time because the law only applied to crimes committed after it went into effect in 1989. In addition, the Oregon system did not keep complete records prior to 1987, and the percentage recorded decreased as one looked further into the past. One solution to both of these problems is to allow the sentence-length variable to have different effects in each year.[18] A similar problem exists for Arizona, which adopted a truth-in-sentencing reform in the fall of 1994. We must note, finally, that Arizona differs from Oregon and Pennsylvania in that it already allowed handguns to be carried openly before passing its concealed-handgun law; thus, one might expect to find a somewhat smaller response to adopting a concealed-handgun law.

In addition to using separate variables to measure the average crime rate in each county,[19] I collected data from the Bureau of the Census to try to control for other demographic characteristics that might influence the crime rate. These data included information on the population density per square mile, total county population, and detailed information on the racial and age breakdown of the county (percent of population by each racial group and by sex between 10 and 19 years of age, between 20 and 29, between 30 and 39, between 40 and 49, between 50 and 64, and 65 and over).[20] While a large literature discusses the likelihood that younger males will engage in crime,[21] controlling for these other categories allows us to account for the groups considered most vulnerable (for example, females in the case of rape).[22] Evidence reported by Glaeser and Sacerdote confirms the higher crime rates experienced in cities and examines the effects on these rates of social and family influences as well as the changing pecuniary benefits from crime;[23] the present study, however, is the first to explicitly control for population density (see appendix 3 for a more complete discussion of the data).

An additional set of income data was also used. These included real per-capita personal income, real per-capita unemployment insurance payments, real per-capita income-maintenance payments, and real per-capita retirement payments per person over 65 years of age.[24] Unemployment insurance and income-maintenance payments from the Commerce Department's Regional Economic Information System (REIS) data set were included in an attempt to provide annual, county-level measures of unemployment and the distribution of income.

Finally, I recognize that other legal changes regarding how guns are used and when they can be obtained can alter the levels of crime. For example, penalties involving improper gun use might also have been changing simultaneously with changes in the requirements for obtaining permits to carry concealed handguns. In order to see whether such changes might confound my ability to infer the causes of any observed changes in crime rates, I read through various editions of *State Laws and Published Ordinances—Firearms* (published by the Bureau of Alcohol, Tobacco, and Firearms: 1976, 1986, 1989, and 1994). Except for the laws regarding machine guns and sawed-off shotguns, the laws involving the use of guns did not change significantly when the rules regarding concealed-handgun permits were changed.[25] A survey by Marvell and Moody that addresses the somewhat broader question of sentencing-enhancement laws for felonies committed with deadly weapons (firearms, explosives, and knives) from 1970 to 1992 also confirms this general finding.[26] Yet Marvell and Moody's dates still allow us to examine the deterrent effect of criminal penalties specifically targeted at the use of deadly weapons during this earlier period.[27]

States also differ in terms of their required waiting periods for handgun purchases. Again using the Bureau of Alcohol, Tobacco, and Firearms' *State Laws and Published Ordinances—Firearms,* I identified states with waiting periods and conducted a Lexis search on the ordinances to determine exactly when those laws went into effect. Thirteen of the nineteen states with waiting periods instituted them prior to the beginning of the sample period.[28]

4 | Concealed-Handgun Laws and Crime Rates: The Empirical Evidence

While our initial comparison of crime rates in states with and without concealed-handgun laws was suggestive, obviously many other factors must be accounted for. The next three chapters use common statistical techniques known as regression analysis to control for these factors. (For those who are interested, a more complete discussion of regressions and statistical significance is provided in appendix 1.) The following discussion provides information on a wide range of law-enforcement activities, but the primary focus is on the link between the private ownership of guns and crime. What gun laws affect crime? Does increased gun ownership increase or decrease murders? How do more lenient gun ownership laws affect accidental deaths and suicide?

The analysis begins by examining both county- and state-level crime data. We then examine how gun ownership benefits different groups, such as women and minorities. To test whether crime-rate changes are a result of concealed-handgun laws, it is not enough simply to see whether these laws lower crime rates; any changes in crime rates must also be linked to the changes in the number of concealed-handgun permits. We must also remember that the laws are not all the same: different states adopt different training and age requirements for obtaining a permit. These differences allow us to investigate whether the form of the concealed-handgun law matters as well as to test the importance of other gun-control laws. Finally, evidence is provided on whether criminals move to other places when concealed-handgun laws are passed.

The book is organized to examine the simplest evidence first and then gradually considers more complicated issues. The first estimates measure whether the average crime rate falls in counties when they adopt concealed-handgun laws. By looking across counties or states at the same time that we examine them over time, we can test not only whether places with the most permits have the greatest reductions in crime, but also whether those with the greatest *increases* in permits have the greatest reductions in crime. Similarly, we can investigate how total gun ownership is related to the level of crime. Tracking gun ownership in individual states over time allows us to investigate how a crime in a state changes as its gun ownership rates change.

Using County and State Data for the United States

The first group of estimates reported in table 4.1 attempts to explain crime rates. There are nine different categories of crime. Each column in the table presents the changes in the crime rate for the crime in the column heading. The numbers in each row represent the impact that a particular explanatory variable has on each crime rate. There are three pieces of information for most of the explanatory variables: (1) the percent change in the crime rate attributed to a particular change in the explanatory variable; (2) the percentage of the variation in the crime rate that can be explained by the variation in the explanatory variable;[1] and (3) one, two, or three asterisks denote whether a particular effect is statistically significant at least at the 1, 5, or 10 percent level, where the 1 percent level represents the most reliable result.[2]

While I am primarily interested in nondiscretionary laws, the estimates also account for many other variables: the arrest rate for each type of crime; population density and the number of people living in a county; measures of income, unemployment, and poverty; the percentage of the population that is a certain sex and race by ten-year age groupings (10 to 19 years of age, 20 to 29 years of age); and the set of variables described in the previous section to control for other county and year differences. The results clearly imply that nondiscretionary laws coincide with fewer murders, aggravated assaults, and rapes.[3] On the other hand, auto-theft and larceny rates rise.

Table 4.1 The effect of nondiscretionary concealed-handgun laws on crime rates: National, County-Level, Cross-Sectional, Time-Series Evidence

Change in explanatory variable	Percent change in various crime rates for changes in explanatory variables								
	Violent crime	Murder	Rape	Aggravated assault	Robbery	Property crime	Burglary	Larceny	Auto theft
Nondiscretionary law adopted	-4.9%* (1%)	-7.7%* (2%)	-5.3%* (1%)	-7.01%* (1%)	-2.2%*** (3%)	2.7%* (1%)	.05% (.02%)	3.3%* (1%)	7.1%* (1%)
Arrest rate for the crime category (e.g., violent crime murder, etc.) increased by 100 percentage points	-0.48% (9%)	-1.39%* (7%)	-0.81%* (4%)	-0.896%* (9%)	-0.57%* (4%)	-0.76%* (10%)	-2.4%* (11%)	-0.18%* (4%)	-0.18%* (3%)
Population per square mile increased by 1,000	6%* (5%)	-2%* (1%)	-2% (1%)	0.58% (4%)	31.6%* (17%)	0.48%* (1%)	-7%* (9%)	3.7%* (4%)	48%* (36%)
Real per-capita personal income increased by $1,000	0.79%* (1%)	1.63%* (2%)	-0.59%*** (1%)	0.47% (1%)	0.47% (1%)	-1.02%* (3%)	-1.84%* (4%)	-1.23%* (2%)	1.5%* (2%)
Real per-capita unemployment Ins. increased by $100	-2.2%* (.07%)	-4.6%* (1%)	-4.7%* (1%)	-1.9%* (.05%)	0.7% (.01%)	3.8%* (2%)	6.0%* (3%)	1.9%* (.08%)	2.1%* (.06%)
Real per-capita income maintenance increased by $100	-0.7% (.3%)	2.5%** (1%)	-1.7% (.7%)	1.39% (.7%)	-3.2%* (1%)	1.9%* (2%)	3.9%* (4%)	0.2% (.1%)	3.3%* (2%)
Real per-capita retirement payments per person over 65 increased by $1,000	-0.197% (.5%)	-1.3% (3%)	-0.24% (4%)	-0.68% (2%)	-0.55% (1%)	-0.87% (4%)	-1.06% (7%)	-0.63% (2%)	-0.93% (2%)
Population increased by 100,000	0.86% (1%)	-0.34%* (.4%)	-2.94% (3%)	0.45%* (.06%)	-0.61%*** (.06%)	-2.18%* (6%)	-2.14%* (5%)	-3.10%* (6%)	-0.04%* (.05%)

Note: The percentage reported in parentheses is the percent of a standard deviation change in the endogenous variable that can be explained by one-standard-deviation change in the exogenous variable. Year and county dummies are not shown, and the results for demographic variables are shown in appendix. All regressions use weighted least squares, where the weighting is each county's population. Entire sample used for all counties over the 1977–1992 period.

*The result is statistically significant at the 1 percent level for a two-tailed *t*-test.

**The result is statistically significant at the 5 percent level for a two-tailed *t*-test.

***The result is statistically significant at the 10 percent level for a two-tailed *t*-test.

Both changes are consistent with my discussion of the direct and substitution effects produced by concealed weapons.[4]

The results are also large, indicating how important the laws can be. When state concealed-handgun laws went into effect in a county, murders fell by about 8 percent, rapes fell by 5 percent, and aggravated assaults fell by 7 percent.[5] In 1992 the following numbers were reported: 18,469 murders; 79,272 rapes; 538,368 robberies; and 861,103 aggravated assaults in counties without nondiscretionary laws. The estimated coefficients suggest that if these counties had been subject to state concealed-handgun laws and had thus been forced to issue handgun permits, murders in the United States would have declined by about 1,400.

What about increased accidental deaths from concealed weapons? The entire number of accidental handgun deaths in the United States in 1988 was only 200 (the last year for which these data are available for the entire United States).[6] Of this total, 22 accidental deaths were in states with concealed-handgun laws, while 178 occurred in states without these laws. The reduction in murders is as much as eight times greater than the total number of accidental deaths in concealed-handgun states. We will revisit the impact of concealed-handgun laws on accidental deaths in chapter 5, but if these initial results are accurate, the net effect of allowing concealed handguns is clearly to save lives, even if concealed handguns were somehow responsible for all accidental handgun deaths.[7]

As with murders, the results indicate that the number of rapes in states without nondiscretionary laws would have declined by 4,200. Aggravated assaults would have declined by 60,000, and robberies by 12,000.[8]

On the other hand, property-crime rates increased after nondiscretionary laws were implemented. If states without concealed-handgun laws had passed such laws, there would have been 247,000 more property crimes in 1992 (a 2.7 percent increase). The increase is small compared to the changes that we observed for murder, rape, and aggravated assault, though it is about the same size as the change for robbery. Criminals respond to the threat of being shot while committing such crimes as robbery by choosing to commit less risky crimes that involve minimal contact with the victim.[9]

It is possible to put a rough dollar value on the losses from crime in the United States and thus on the potential gains from nondiscretionary laws. A recent National Institute of Justice study estimates the costs to victims of different types of crime by measuring lost productivity; out-of-pocket expenses, such as those for medical bills and property losses; and losses from fear, pain, suffering, and lost quality of life.[10] While the use of jury awards to measure losses such as fear, pain, suffering, and lost quality of life may be questioned, such estimates allow us to compare the reduction in violent crimes with the increase in property crimes.

By combining the estimated reduction in crime from table 4.1 with the National Institute of Justice's estimates of what these crimes would have cost victims had they occurred, table 4.2 reports the gain from allowing concealed handguns to be $5.7 billion in 1992 dollars. The reduction in violent crimes represents a gain of $6.2 billion ($4.2 billion from murder, $1.4 billion from aggravated assault, $374 million from rape, and $98 million from robbery), while the increase in property crimes represents a loss of $417 million ($343 million from auto theft, $73 million from larceny, and $1.5 million from burglary). However, while $5.7 billion is substantial, to put it into perspective, it still equals only about 1.23 percent of the total losses to victims from these crime categories. These estimates are probably most sensitive to the value of life used (in the National Institute of Justice Study this was set at $1.84 million in 1992 dollars). Higher estimated values of life would obviously increase the net gains from the passage of concealed-handgun laws, while lower values would reduce the gains. To the extent that people are taking greater risks regarding crime because of any increased sense of safety produced by concealed-handgun laws,[11] the preceding numbers underestimate the total savings from allowing concealed handguns.

The arrest rate produces the most consistent effect on crime. Higher arrest rates are associated with lower crime rates for all categories of crime. Variation in the probability of arrest accounts for 3 to 11 percent of the variation in the various crime rates.[12] Again, the way to think about this is that the typical observed change in the arrest rate explains up to about 11 percent of the typical change in the crime rate. The crime most responsive to the arrest rate is burglary (11 percent), followed by property crimes (10 percent); aggravated assault and violent crimes more generally (9 percent); murder (7 percent); rape, robbery, and larceny (4 percent); and auto theft (3 percent).

For property crimes, the variation in the percentage of the population that is black, male, and between 10 and 19 years of age explains 22 percent of the ups and downs in the property-crime rate.[13] For violent crimes, the same number is 5 percent (see appendix 5). Other patterns also show up in the data. Not surprisingly, a higher percentage of young females is positively and significantly associated with the occurrence of a greater number of rapes.[14] Population density appears to be most important in explaining

Table 4.2 The effect of nondiscretionary concealed-handgun laws on victims' costs: What if all states had adopted nondiscretionary laws?

Crime category	Change in number of crimes if states without nondiscretionary laws in 1992 had adopted them			Change in victims' costs if states without nondiscretionary laws in 1992 had adopted them		
	Estimates using county-level data	Estimates using county-level data and state time trends	Estimates using state-level data	Estimates using county-level data	Estimates using county-level data and state time trends	Estimates using state-level data
Murder	-1,410	-1,840	-1,590	-$4.2 billion	-5.57 billion	-$4.8 billion
Rape	-4,200	-3,700	-4,800	-$374 million	-$334 million	-$431 million
Aggravated assault	-60,400	-61,100	-93,900	-$1.4 billion	-$1.4 billion	-$2.2 billion
Robbery	-11,900	-10,990	-62,900	-$98 million	-$90 million	-$518 million
Burglary	1,100	-112,700	-180,800	$1.5 million	-$162 million	-$261 million
Larceny	191,700	-93,300	-180,300	$73 million	-$35 million	-$69 million
Auto theft	89,900	-41,500	-11,100	$343 million	-$2 million	-$42 million
Total change in victims' costs				-$5.7 billion	-$7.6 billion	-$8.3 billion

Note: Estimates of the costs of crime are in 1992 dollars, from the National Institute of Justice's study.

robbery, burglary, and auto-theft rates, with the typical variation in population density explaining 36 percent of the typical change across observations in auto theft.

Perhaps most surprising is the relatively small, even if frequently significant, effect of a county's per-capita income on crime rates. Changes in real per-capita income account for no more than 4 percent of the changes in crime, and in seven of the specifications it explains at most 2 percent of the change. It is *not* safer to live in a high-income neighborhood if other characteristics (for example, demographics) are the same. Generally, high-income areas experience more violent crimes but fewer property crimes. The two notable exceptions to this rule are rape and auto theft: high-income areas experience fewer rapes and more auto theft. If the race, sex, and age variables are replaced with separate variables showing the percentage of the population that is black and white, 50 percent of the variation in the murder rate is explained by variations in the percentage of the population that is black. Yet because of the high rates at which blacks are arrested and incarcerated or are victims of crimes (for example, 38 percent of all murder victims in 1992 were black; see table 1.1), this is not unexpected.

One general caveat should be made in evaluating the coefficients involving the demographic variables. Given the very small portions of the total populations that fall into some of these narrow categories (this is particularly true for minority populations), the effect on the crime rate from a one-percentage-point increase in the percentage of the population in that category greatly overstates the true importance of that age, sex, or race grouping. The assumption of a one-percentage-point change is arbitrary and is only provided to give the reader a rough idea of what these coefficients mean. For a better understanding of these variables' impact, relatively more weight should be placed on the second number, which shows how much of the variation in the various crime rates can be explained by the normal changes in each explanatory variable.[15]

We can take another look at how sensitive the results from table 4.1 are and examine how they vary with different subsets of the following variables: the nondiscretionary law, the nondiscretionary law and the arrest rates, and the nondiscretionary law and the variables that account for the national changes in crime rates across years. Each specification yields results that show even more significant effects from the nondiscretionary law, though when results exclude variables that measure how crime rates differ across counties, they are likely to tell us more about which states adopt these laws than about the impact of these laws on crime.[16] The low-crime states are the most likely to pass these laws, and their crime rates become even lower after their passage. I will attempt to account for this fact later in chapter 6.

To further test the sensitivity of the results to the various control variables used, I reestimated the specifications in table 4.1 without using either the percentages of the populations that fall into the different sex, race, and age categories or the measures of income; this tended to produce similar though somewhat more significant results with respect to concealed-handgun laws. And the estimated gains from passing concealed-handgun laws were also larger.

While these regressions account for nationwide changes in crime rates on average over time, one concern is that individual states are likely to have their own unique time trends. The question here is whether the states adopting nondiscretionary concealed-handgun laws experienced falling crime rates over the entire time period. This cannot be true for all states as a whole, because as figure 3.5 shows, violent crimes have definitely not been diminishing during the entire period. However, if this downward trend existed for the states that adopted nondiscretionary laws, the variables shown in table 4.1 could indicate that the average crime rate was lower after the laws were passed, even though the drop in the average level was due merely to a continuation of a downward trend that began before the law took effect. To address this issue, I reestimated the specifications shown in table 4.1 by including state dummy variables that were each interacted with a time-trend variable.[17] This makes it possible to account not only for the national changes in crime rates with the individual year variables but also for any differences in state-specific trends.

When these individual state time trends were included, all results indicated that the concealed-handgun laws lowered crime, though the coefficients were not statistically significant for aggravated assault and larceny. Under this specification, the passage of nondiscretionary concealed-handgun laws in states that did not have them in 1992 would have reduced murders in that year by 1,839; rapes by 3,727; aggravated assaults by 10,990; robberies by 61,064; burglaries by 112,665; larcenies by 93,274; and auto thefts by 41,512. The total value of this reduction in crime in 1992 dollars would have been $7.6 billion. With the exceptions of aggravated assault and burglary, violent-crime rates still experienced larger drops from the adoption of concealed-handgun laws than did property crimes.

Despite the concerns over the aggregation issues discussed earlier, economists have relied on state-level data in analyzing crime primarily because of the difficulty and extra time required to assemble county-level data. As shown in tables 2.2–2.4, the large within-state heterogeneity raises significant concerns about relying too heavily on state-level data.

To provide a comparison with other crime studies relying on state-level data, table 4.3 reestimates the specifications reported in table 4.1 using state-level rather than county-level data. While the results in these two tables are generally similar, two differences immediately manifest themselves: (1) the specifications now imply that nondiscretionary concealed-handgun laws lower all types of crime, and (2) concealed-handgun laws explain much more of the variation in crime rates, while arrest rates (with the exception of robbery) explain much less of the variation.[18] Concealed-handgun laws lower both violent- and property-crime rates, but violent crimes are more affected by concealed handguns, falling two-and-one-half times more than those for property crimes.

Suppose we rely on the state-level results rather than the county-level estimates. We would then conclude that if all states had adopted nondiscretionary concealed-handgun laws in 1992, about 1,600 fewer murders and 4,800 fewer rapes would have been committed.[19] Overall, table 4.3 allows us to calculate that the estimated monetary gain from reductions in crime produced by nondiscretionary concealed-handgun laws was $8.3 billion in 1992 dollars (again, see table 4.2 for the precise breakdown). Yet, at least in the case of property crimes, the concealed-handgun law coefficients are sensitive to whether the regressions are run at the state or county level. This suggests that aggregating observations into units as large as states is a bad idea.[20]

Differential Effects across Counties, between Men and Women, and by Race and Income

Let us now return to other issues concerning the county-level data. Criminal deterrence is unlikely to have the same impact across all counties. For instance, increasing the number of arrests can have different effects on crime in different areas, depending on the stigma attached to arrest. In areas where crime is rampant, the stigma of being arrested may be small, and that means that an increase in arrest rates has a correspondingly small effect.[21] To test this, the specifications shown in table 4.1 were reestimated by breaking down the sample into two groups: (1) counties with above-median crime rates and (2) counties with below-median crime rates. Each set of data was reexamined separately.

Table 4.3 Aggregating the data: state-level, cross-sectional, time-series evidence

Change in explanatory variable	Percent change in various crime rates for changes in explanatory variables								
	Violent crime	Murder	Rape	Aggravated assault	Robbery	Property crime	Burglary	Larceny	Auto theft
Nondiscretionary law adopted	-10.1% (5.8%)	-8.62%** (5%)	-6.07%** (4.7%)	-10.9%* (6.5%)	-14.21%* (5.7%)	-4.19%** (4.8%)	-0.88% (.43%)	-8.25%* (7.6%)	-3.14% (3.8%)
Arrest rate for the crime category increased by 100 percentage points	-8.02%* (1.5%)	-7.3%* (5.3%)	-2.05%*** (.69%)	-15.3%* (3.9%)	-10.5%* (14.4%)	-59.9% (8.1%)	-14.5%* (6.5%)	-71.5%* (7.6%)	-65.7%* (10.4%)

Note: Except for the use of state dummies in place of county dummies, the control variables are the same as those used in table 4.1 including year dummies, though they are not all reported. The percent reported in parentheses is the percent of a standard deviation change in the endogenous variable that can be explained by a one-standard-deviation change in the exogenous variable. All regressions use weighted least squares, where the weighting is according to each state's population. Entire sample used over the 1977 to 1992 period.

*The result is statistically significant at the 1 percent level for a two-tailed t-test.

**The result is statistically significant at the 5 percent level for a two-tailed t-test.

***The result is statistically significant at the 10 percent level for a two-tailed t-test.

As table 4.4 shows, concealed-handgun laws do indeed affect high- and low-crime counties similarly. The coefficient signs are consistently the same for both low- and high-crime counties, though for two of the crime categories—rape and aggravated assault—concealed-handgun laws have statistically significant effects only in the relatively high-crime counties. For most violent crimes—such as murder, rape, and aggravated assault—concealed-weapons laws have much greater deterrent effects in high-crime counties. In contrast, for robbery, property crimes, auto theft, burglary, and larceny, the effect appears to be greatest in low-crime counties.

Table 4.4 also shows that the deterrent effect of arrests is significantly different, at least at the 5 percent level, between high- and low-crime counties for eight of the nine crime categories (the one exception being violent crimes). The results further reject the hypothesis that arrests would be associated with greater stigma in low-crime areas. Additional arrests in low- and high-crime counties generate extremely similar changes in the aggregate category of violent crime, but the arrest-rate coefficient for murder is almost three times greater in high-crime counties than in low-crime counties. If these results suggest any conclusion, it is that for most crimes, tougher measures have more of an impact in high-crime areas.

The effect of gun ownership by women deserves a special comment. Despite the relatively small number of women who obtain concealed-handgun permits, the concealed-handgun coefficient for explaining rapes in the first three sets of results is consistently similar in size to the effect that this variable has on other violent crime. January 1996 data for Washington and Oregon reveal that women constituted 18.6 and 22.9 percent, respectively, of those with concealed-handgun permits.[22] The set of women who were the most likely targets of rape probably chose to carry concealed handguns at much higher rates than women in general. The preceding results show that rapists are particularly deterred by handguns. As mentioned earlier, the National Crime Victimization Survey data show that providing a woman with a gun has a much greater effect on her ability to defend herself against a crime than providing a gun to a man. Thus even if few women carry handguns, the change in the "cost" of attacking women could still be as great as the change in the "cost" of attacking men, despite the much higher number of men who are becoming armed. To phrase this differently, if one more woman carries a handgun, the extra protection for women in general is greater than the extra protection for men if one more man carries a handgun.[23]

These results raise a possible concern as to whether women have the

Table 4.4 Aggregating the data: Do law-enforcement and nondiscretionary laws have the same effects in high- and low-crime areas?

Change in explanatory variable	Percent change in various crime rates for changes in explanatory variables								
	Violent crime	Murder	Rape	Aggravated assault	Robbery	Property crime	Burglary	Larceny	Auto theft
Sample where county crime rates are above the median									
Nondiscretionary law adopted	−6.0%*	−9.9%*	−7.2%*	−4.5%*	−3.4%*	1.6%*	0.4%	3.0%*	5.2%*
Arrest rate for the crime category increased by 100 percentage points	−5.2%*	−12.3%*	−3.3%*	−6.3%*	−29.4%*	−53.5%*	−56.5%*	−59.6%*	−13.3%*
Sample where county crime rates are below the median									
Nondiscretionary law adopted	−3.7%**	−4.4%**	−3.0%	−0.3%	−7.9%*	8.8%*	3%**	8.7%*	7.2%*
Arrest rate for the crime category increased by 100 percentage points	−5.2%*	−4.9%*	−6.6%*	−6.8%*	−3.7%*	−13.5%*	−27.1%*	−10%*	−1.4%*

Note: The control variables are the same as those used in table 4.1, including year and county dummies, though they are not reported. All regressions use weighted least squares, where the weighting is each county's population. Entire sample used over the 1977 to 1992 period.

*The result is statistically significant at the 1 percent level for a two-tailed *t*-test.

**The result is statistically significant at the 5 percent level for a two-tailed *t*-test.

right incentive to carry concealed handguns. Despite the fact that women who carry concealed handguns make other women so much safer, it is possible that women might decide not to carry them because they see their own personal gain as much smaller than the total benefit to all women. While the problem is particularly pronounced for women, people in general often take into account only the benefits that they individually receive from carrying a gun and not the crime-reduction benefits that they are generating for others.[24]

As mentioned in chapter 2, an important concern is that passing a nondiscretionary concealed-handgun law should not affect all counties equally. In particular, when states had discretionary laws, counties with the highest populations were also those that most severely restricted people's ability to carry concealed weapons. Adopting nondiscretionary laws therefore produced the greatest change in the number of permits in the more populous counties. Thus, a significant advantage of using this county data is that it allows us to take advantage of county-level variation in the impact of nondiscretionary concealed-handgun laws. To test this variation across counties, figures 4.1 and 4.2 repeat all the specifications in table 4.1 but examine instead whether the effect of the nondiscretionary law varies with county population or population density. (The simplest way to do this is to multiply the nondiscretionary-law variable by either the county population or population density.) While all the other coefficients remain virtually unchanged, this new interaction implies the same crime-reducing effects from the nondiscretionary law as reported earlier. In all but one case the coefficients are more significant and larger.

The coefficients are consistent with the hypothesis that the new laws induce the greatest changes in the largest counties, which have a much greater response in both directions to changes in the laws. Violent crimes fall more and property crimes rise more in the largest counties. The figures indicate how effects vary for counties of different sizes. For example, when counties with almost 600,000 people (two standard deviations above the mean population) pass a concealed-handgun law, the murder rate falls by 12 percent. That is reduced 7.4 times more than for the average county (75,773 people).

Although the law-enforcement officials that I talked to continually mentioned population as being the key variable, I also reexamined whether the laws had different effects in more densely populated counties. Given the close relationship between county population and population density, it is not too surprising to find that the impact of concealed handguns in

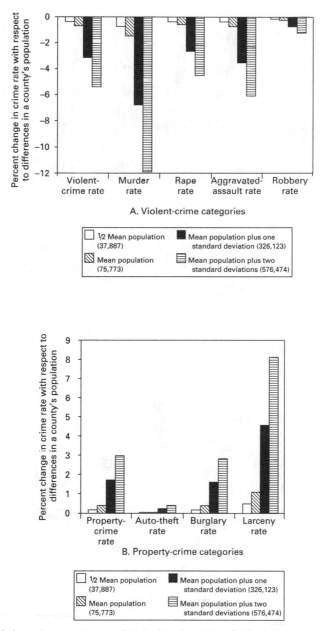

Figure 4.1. Do larger changes in crime rates from nondiscretionary concealed-handgun laws occur in more populous counties?

A. Violent-crime categories

□ ½ Mean population (107.2)

■ Mean population plus one standard deviation (1,635.6)

▨ Mean population (214.3)

▤ Mean population plus two standard deviations (3,056.8)

B. Property-crime categories

□ ½ Mean population (107.2)

■ Mean population plus one standard deviation (1,635.6)

▨ Mean population (214.3)

▤ Mean population plus two standard deviations (3,056.8)

Figure 4.2. Do larger changes in crime rates from nondiscretionary concealed-handgun laws occur in more densely populated counties?

more densely populated areas is greater than in sparsely populated counties. Passing a concealed-handgun law lowers the murder rate in counties with about 3,000 people per square mile (the levels found in Fairfax, Virginia; Orleans, Louisiana, which contains New Orleans; and Ramsey, Minnesota, which contains St. Paul) by 8.5 percent, 12 times more than it lowers murders in the average county. The only real difference between the results for population and population density occur for the burglary rate, where concealed-handgun laws are associated with a small reduction in burglaries for the most densely populated areas.

Figures 4.3 and 4.4 provide a similar breakdown by income and by the percentage of the population that is black. Higher-income areas and counties with relatively more blacks both have particularly large drops in crime associated with concealed-handgun laws. Counties with a 37 percent black population experienced 11 percent declines in both murder and aggravated assaults. The differences with respect to income were not as large.[25]

With the extremely high rates of murder and other crimes committed against blacks, it is understandable why so many blacks are concerned about gun control. University of Florida criminologist Gary Kleck says, "Blacks are more likely to have been victims of crime or to live in neighborhoods where there's a lot of crime involving guns. So, generally, blacks are more pro-control than whites are." Nationally, polls indicate that 83 percent of blacks support police permits for all gun purchases.[26] While many blacks want to make guns harder to get, the irony is that blacks actually benefit more than other groups from concealed-handgun laws. Allowing potential victims a means for self-defense is more important in crime-prone neighborhoods. Even more strikingly, the history of gun control in the United States has often been a series of attempts to disarm blacks.[27] In explaining the urgency of adopting the U.S. Constitution's Fourteenth Amendment, Duke University Law Professor William Van Alstyne writes,

> It was, after all, the defenselessness of the Negroes (denied legal rights to keep and bear arms by state law) from attack by night riders—even to protect their own lives, their own families, and their own homes—that made it imperative that they, as citizens, could no longer be kept defenseless by a regime of state law denying them the common right to keep and bear arms.[28]

Indeed, even in the 1960s, much of the increased regulation of firearms stemmed from the fear generated by Black Panthers who openly carried guns.

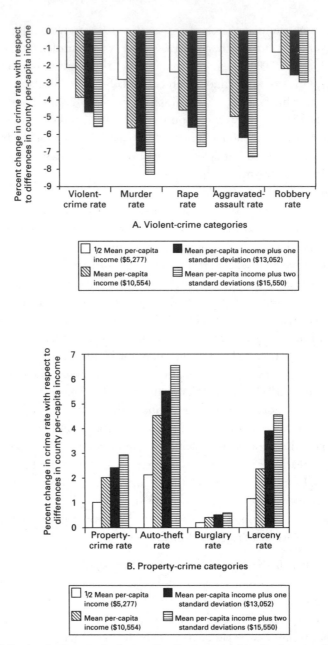

A. Violent-crime categories

☐ 1/2 Mean per-capita income ($5,277)	■ Mean per-capita income plus one standard deviation ($13,052)
▨ Mean per-capita income ($10,554)	▤ Mean per-capita income plus two standard deviations ($15,550)

B. Property-crime categories

☐ 1/2 Mean per-capita income ($5,277)	■ Mean per-capita income plus one standard deviation ($13,052)
▨ Mean per-capita income ($10,554)	▤ Mean per-capita income plus two standard deviations ($15,550)

Figure 4.3. How does the change in crime from nondiscretionary concealed-handgun laws vary with county per-capita income?

Figure 4.4. How does the change in crime from nondiscretionary concealed-handgun laws vary with the percent of a county's population that is black?

Alexis Herman, the current Secretary of Labor, experienced firsthand the physical risks of growing up black in Alabama. Describing her difficult confirmation hearings, an Associated Press story included the following story:

> Anyone who thought the frustrations of waiting for confirmation would discourage her knew nothing about the lessons Herman learned from her father. They forgot that he sued to integrate the Democratic Party in Alabama, and later became the state's first black ward leader. They never heard about the night he put a pistol in his young daughter's hands and stepped out of the car to confront the Ku Klux Klan.
>
> "He taught me that you have to face adversity. He taught me to stand by my principles," Herman said in the interview. "He also taught me how to work within the system for change."
>
> Herman said her father never raised his voice, but he always kept a small silver pistol under the driver's seat of his DeSoto as he drove from community meeting to community meeting around Mobile. She always sat close by his side, unless the pistol was out. "The only way that I ever knew trouble was around was that the gun would come out from under the driver's seat and he'd put it by his side," she said.
>
> As they left the home of a minister one Christmas Eve, the pistol was on the car seat. She was 5. "It was a dark road, a dirt road to get back to the main highway," she recalled. "We were driven off the road by another car, and they were Klansmen."
>
> She hid on the floor and her father pressed the pistol's white handle into her palm. "He told me, 'If anybody opens this door, I want you to pull this trigger.'" He locked the door behind him and walked ahead to keep them away from the car. She crouched in the dark, listening until the shouts and scuffling died down.
>
> Eventually, the minister came to the car to drive Herman home. Her father, who had been beaten, rode in another car.[29]

Recently, after testifying before the Illinois state House of Representatives on whether to pass a concealed-handgun bill, I was approached by a black representative from Chicago who supported the bill.[30] He told me that, at least for Illinois, he was not surprised by my finding that areas with large minority populations gained the most from these laws. Noting the high rate at which young, black males are stopped by police and the fact that it is currently a felony to possess a concealed handgun, he said that an honest, law-abiding, young, black male would be "nuts" to carry a concealed handgun in Illinois. He mentioned a case that had occurred just a week earlier: Alonzo Spellman—a black professional football player for the Chicago Bears—had been arrested in Chicago after a routine traffic violation revealed that he had a handgun in his car.[31] Noting the inability of the police to protect people in heavily black areas when "bad guys" already had illegal guns, the representative said he believed that the current power imbalance between law-abiding people and criminals was greatest in black areas.

Perhaps it is not too surprising that blacks and those living in urban areas gain the most from being able to defend themselves with concealed handguns, since the absence of police appears most acute in black, central-city neighborhoods. Until 1983, the American Housing Survey annually asked sixty thousand households whether their neighborhoods had adequate police protection. Black, central-city residents were about twice as likely as whites generally to report that they did not have adequate protection, and six times more likely to say that they had considered moving because of an insufficient police presence in their neighborhoods.[32]

These results should at least give pause to the frequent attempts to pass city ordinances and state laws banning low-cost, "Saturday night specials." Indeed, the results have implications for many gun-control rules that raise gun prices. Law-abiding minorities in the most crime-prone areas produced the greatest crime reductions from being able to defend themselves. Unfortunately, however unintentionally, these new laws risk disarming precisely these poor minorities.

Using Other Crime Rates to Explain the Changes in the Crime Rates Being Studied

Other concerns still exist regarding the specifications employed here. Admittedly, although arrest rates and average differences in individual counties are controlled for, more can be done to account for the changing environments that determine the level of crime. One method is to use changes in other crime rates to help us understand why the crime rates that we are studying are changing over time. Table 4.5 reruns the specifications used to generate figure 4.1A but includes either the burglary or robbery rates as proxies for other changes in the criminal justice system. Robbery and burglary are the violent- and property-crime categories that are the least related to changes in concealed-handgun laws, but

Table 4.5 Using crime rates that are relatively unrelated to changes in nondiscretionary laws as a method of controlling for other changes in the legal environment: controlling for robbery and burglary rates

Change in the explanatory variable	Percent change in various crime rates for changes in explanatory variables								
	Violent crime	Murder	Rape	Aggravated assault	Robbery	Property crime	Burglary	Larceny	Auto theft
Controlling for robbery rates									
Nondiscretionary law adopted multiplied by county population (evaluated at mean county population)	−2.6%*	−4.3%*	−1.9%*	−2.6%*	—	1.4%*	0.08%	1.3%*	3.7%*
	1%	1.1%	0.4%	0.4%	—	0.5%	0.04%	0.4%	0.5%
Arrest rate for the crime category increased by 100 percentage points	−0.038*	−0.13*	−0.07*	−0.08*	—	−0.06*	−0.20*	−0.015*	−0.014*
	7%	7%	4%	8%	—	8%	9%	3%	2%
Controlling for burglary rates									
Nondiscretionary law adopted multiplied by *county population (evaluated at mean county population)	−2.4%*	−4.3%*	−2.0%*	−2.6%*	0.4%	1.8%*	—	1.4%*	3.6%*
	1%	1.1%	0.4%	0.4%	0.04%	0.7%	—	0.4%	0.5%
Arrest rate for the crime category increased by 100 percentage points	−0.026*	−0.13*	−0.05*	−0.05*	−0.043*	−0.05*	—	−0.01*	−0.01*
	5%	6%	3%	5%	3%	6%	—	2%	2%

Note: While not all the coefficient estimates are reported, all the control variables are the same as those used in table 4.1, including year and county dummies. All regressions use weighted least squares, where the weighting is each county's population. Net violent and property-crime rates are respectively net of robbery and burglary rates to avoid producing any artificial collinearity. Likewise, the arrest rates for those values omit the portion of the corresponding arrest rates due to arrests for robbery and burglary. While not reported, the coefficients for the robbery and burglary rates were extremely statistically significant and positive. Entire sample used over the 1977 to 1992 period.

*The result is statistically significant at the 1 percent level for a two-tailed t-test.

they still tend to move up and down together with all the other types of crimes.[33]

There is some evidence that changes in burglary or robbery rates reflect other changes in the criminal justice system that are omitted by the other factors already accounted for. This is suggested by their very high correlations with other crime categories.[34] The two sets of specifications reported in table 4.5 closely bound the earlier estimates, and the estimates continue to imply that the introduction of concealed-handgun laws coincided with similarly large drops in violent crimes and increases in property crimes. These results differ from the preceding results in that the nondiscretionary laws are not significant related to robberies. The estimates on the other control variables also remain essentially unchanged.[35]

Crime: Changes in Levels Versus Changes in Trends

The preceding results in this chapter examined whether the average crime rate fell after the nondiscretionary laws went into effect. If changes in the law affect behavior with a lag, changes in the trend are probably more relevant. Therefore, a more important question is: How has the crime trend changed with the change in laws? Examining whether there is a change in levels or a change in whether the crime rate is rising or falling could yield very different results. For example, if the crime rate was rising right up until the law was adopted but falling thereafter, some values that appeared while crime rate was rising could equal some that appeared as it was falling. In other words, deceptively similar levels can represent dramatically different trends over time.

I used several methods to examine changes in the trends exhibited over time in crime rates. First, I reestimated the regressions in table 4.1, using year-to-year changes on all explanatory variables (see table 4.6). These regressions were run using both a variable that equals 1 when a nondiscretionary law is in effect as well as the change in that variable (called "differencing" the variable) to see if the initial passage of the law had an impact. The results consistently indicate that the law lowered the rates of violent crime, rape, and aggravated assault. Nondiscretionary laws discourage murder in both specifications, but the effect is only statistically significant when the nondiscretionary variable is also differenced. The property-crime results are in line with those of earlier tables, showing that nondiscretionary laws produce increases in property crime. Violent crimes decreased by an average of about 2 percent annually, whereas property crimes increased by an average of about 5 percent.

Table 4.6 Results of rerunning the regressions on differences

	Endogenous variables in terms of first differences of the natural logarithm of the crime rate								
Exogenous variables	Δln(Violent-crime rate)	Δln(Murder rate)	Δln(Rape rate)	Δln(Aggravated-assault rate)	Δln(Robbery rate)	Δln(Property-crime rate)	Δln(Burglary rate)	Δln(Larceny rate)	Δln(Auto-theft rate)
All variables except for the nondiscretionary dummy differenced									
Nondiscretionary law adopted	−2.2%***	−2.6%	−5.2%*	−4.6%*	−3.3%****	5.2%*	3.5%*	5.2%*	12.8%*
First differences in the arrest rate for the crime category	−0.05%*	−0.15%*	−0.09%*	−0.09%*	−0.06%*	−0.08%*	−0.24%*	−0.02%*	−0.02%*
All variables differenced									
First differences in the dummy for nondiscretionary law adopted	−2.7%*	−3.6%***	−3.9%*	−5.4%*	−0.7%	4.8%*	0.7%	6.2%*	24.2%*
First differences in the arrest rate for the crime category	−0.05%*	−0.15%*	−0.09%*	−0.09%*	−0.06%*	−0.08%*	−.24%*	−0.02%*	−0.02%*

Note: The variables for income; population; race, sex, and age of the population; and density are all in terms of first differences. While not all the coefficient estimates are reported, all the control variables used in Table 4.1 are used here, including year and county dummies. All regressions use weighted least squares, where the weighting is each county's population. Entire sample used over the 1977 to 1992 period.

*The result is statistically significant at the 1 percent level for a two-tailed t-test.

***The result is statistically significant at the 10 percent level for a two-tailed t-test.

****The result is statistically significant at the 11 percent level for a two-tailed t-test.

Table 4.7 Permits granted by state: Florida, Oregon, and Pennsylvania

Year	Florida	Oregon	Pennsylvania
1987	17,000[a]	N.A.	N.A.
1988	33,451	N.A.	267,335[c]
1989	51,335	N.A.	314,925
1990	65,636	N.A.	360,649
1991	67,043	N.A.	399,428
1992	75,578	22,197[b]	360,919
1993	95,187	32,049	426,011
1994	134,008	43,216	492,421
1995	163,757	65,394	571,208
1996	192,016	78,258	N.A.

[a]Estimate of the number of concealed-handgun permits issued immediately before Florida's law went into effect from David McDowall, Colin Loftin, and Brian Wiersema, "Easing Concealed Firearms Laws: Effects on Homicide in Three States," *Journal of Criminal Law and Criminology*, 86 (Fall 1995): 194.
[b]December 31, 1991.
[c]Number of permits issued under discretionary law.

As one might expect, the nondiscretionary laws affected crime immediately, with an additional change spread out over time. Why would the entire effect not be immediate? An obvious explanation is that not everyone who would eventually obtain a permit to carry a concealed handgun did so right away. For instance, as shown by the data in table 4.7, the number of permits granted in Florida, Oregon, and Pennsylvania was still increasing substantially long after the nondiscretionary law was put into effect. Florida's law was passed in 1987, Oregon's in 1990, and Pennsylvania's in 1989.

Reestimating the regression results from table 4.1 to account for different time trends in the crime rates before and after the passage of the law provides consistent strong evidence that the deterrent impact of concealed handguns increases with time. For most violent crimes, the time trend prior to the passage of the law indicates that crime was rising. The results using the simple time trends for these violent-crime categories are reported in table 4.8. Figures 4.5 through 4.9 illustrate how the violent-crime rate varies before and after the implementation of nondiscretionary concealed-handgun laws when both the linear and squared time trends are employed. Comparing the slopes of the crime trends before and after the enactment of the laws shows that the trends become more negative to a degree that is statistically significant after the laws were passed.[36]

These results answer another possible objection: whether the findings are simply a result of so-called crime cycles. Crime rates rise or fall over time. If concealed-handgun laws were adopted at the peaks of these cycles (say, because concern over crime is great), the ensuing decline in crime might have occurred anyway without any help from the new laws. To deal

Table 4.8 Change in time trends for crime rates before and after the adoption of nondiscretionary laws

	Percent change in various crime rates for change in explanatory variable							
	Violent crime	Murder	Rape	Aggravated assault	Robbery	Property crime	Auto theft	Burglary	Larceny
Change in the crime rate from the difference in the annual change in crime rates in the years before and after the change in the law (annual rate after the law − annual rate before the law)	−0.9%*	−3%*	−1.4%*	−0.5%*	−2.7%*	−0.6%*	−0.3%**	−1.5%*	−0.1%

Note: The control variables are the same as those used in table 4.1, including year and county dummies, though they are not reported, because the coefficient estimates are very similar to those reported earlier. All regressions use weighted least squares, where the weighting is each county's population. Entire sample used over the 1977 to 1992 period.
*The result is statistically significant at the 1 percent level for a two-tailed t-test.
**The result is statistically significant at the 5 percent level for a two-tailed t-test.

with this, I controlled not only for national crime patterns but also for individual county patterns by using burglary or robbery rates to explain the movement in the other crime rates. I even tried to control for individual state trends. Yet the simplest way of concisely illustrating that my results are not merely a product of the "normal" ups and downs in crime rates is to look again at the graphs in figures 4.5–4.9. With the exception of aggravated assault, the drops not only begin right when the laws pass but also take the crime rates well below what they had been before the passage of the laws. It is difficult to believe that, on the average, state legislatures could have timed the passage of these laws so accurately as to coincide with the peaks of crime waves; nor can the resulting declines be explained simply as reversions to normal levels.

Was the Impact of Nondiscretionary Concealed-Handgun Laws the Same Everywhere?

Just as we found that the impact of nondiscretionary laws changed over time, we expect to find differences across states. The reason is the same in both cases: deterrence increases with the number of permits. While the information obtained from state government officials only pertained to why permits were issued at different rates across counties within a given state, the rate at which new permits are issued at the state level may also vary based upon population and population density. If this is true, then it should be possible to explain the differential effect that non-discretionary laws have on crime in each of the states that passed such laws in the same way that we examined differences across counties.

Table 4.9 reexamines my earlier regressions, where I took into account that concealed-handgun laws have different effects across counties, depending upon how lenient officials had been in issuing permits under a previously discretionary system. The one change from earlier tables is that a different coefficient is used for the counties in each of the ten states that changed their laws during the 1977 to 1992 period. At least for violent crimes, the results indicate a very consistent effect of nondiscretionary concealed-handgun laws across states. Nine of the ten states experienced declines in violent-crime rates as a result of these laws, and eight of the ten states experienced declines in murder rates; in the states where violent crimes, murders, or robberies rose, the increases were very small. In fact, the largest increases were smaller than the smallest declines in the states where those crime rates fell.

Generally, the states with the largest decreases in any one category

Figure 4.5. The effect of concealed-handgun laws on violent crimes

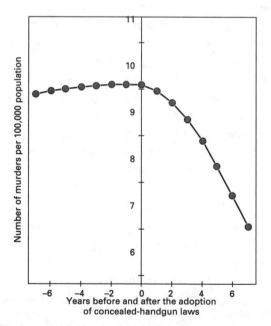

Figure 4.6. The effect of concealed-handgun laws on murders

Figure 4.7. The effect of concealed-handgun laws on rapes

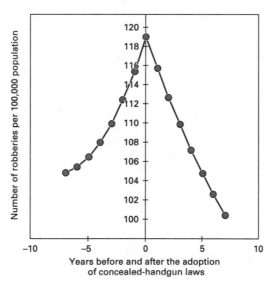

Figure 4.8. The effect of concealed-handgun laws on robberies

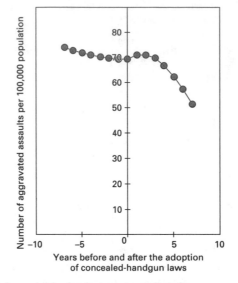

Figure 4.9. The effect of concealed-handgun laws on aggravated assaults

tended to have relatively large decreases across all the violent-crime categories, although the "leader" in each category varied across all the violent-crime categories.[37] Likewise, the states with relatively small crime decreases (for example, Georgia, Oregon, Pennsylvania, and Virginia) tended to exhibit little change across all the categories.

Property crimes, on the other hand, exhibited no clear pattern. Property crimes fell in five states and increased in five states, and the size of any decrease or increase was quite small and unsystematic.

Ideally, any comparison across states would be based on changes in the number of permits issued rather than simply the enactment of the non-discretionary law. States with the largest increases in permits should show the largest decreases in crime rates. Unfortunately, only a few states have recorded time-series data on the number of permits issued. I will use such data in chapter 5. For the moment, it is still useful to see whether the patterns in crime-rate changes found earlier across counties are also found across states. In particular, we would like to know whether the largest declines occurred in states with the largest or most dense populations, which we believed had the greatest increase in permits. The justification for the county-level differences was very strong because it was based on conversations with individual state officials, but those officials were not asked to

Table 4.9 State-specific impact of nondiscretionary concealed-handgun laws

	Violent crime	Murder	Rape	Aggravated assault	Robbery	Property crime	Auto theft	Burglary	Larceny
Florida	-4%	-10%	-8%	-4%	0.3%	1%	2%	0.3%	2%
Georgia	0.2	-2	0.5	-0.2	0	1	1	1	1
Idaho	-3	-1	0.1	-3	-7	-1	-3	-3	-1
Maine	-17	-5	1	-24	-8	1	-4	-2	2
Mississippi	-3	0.6	3	-8	0	-0.2	3	2	-1
Montana	-10	-5	-10	-12	-6	-4	-5	5	-4
Oregon	-3	-1	-1	-3	-4	-2	3	-4	-2
Pennsylvania	-1	-3	-1	1	-2	1	3	-1	3
Virginia	-2	1	-1	-2	-2	-1	-2	-2	-1
West Virginia	-1	-11	-5	-1	1	3	0	4	2
Summary of the coefficients' signs									
Negative	9	8	6	9	6	5	4	5	5
Positive	1	2	4	1	4	5	6	5	5

Note: The table uses arrest rates adjusted for counties wherein the adoption of nondiscretionary concealed-handgun laws was most likely to represent a real change from past practice by multiplying the nondiscretionary-law variables by the population in each county. The percents are evaluated at the mean county population.

make judgments across states (nor was it likely that they could do so). Further, there is much more heterogeneity across counties, and a greater number of observations. The relationship posited earlier for county populations also seems particularly tenuous when dealing with state-level data because a state with a large population could be made up of a large number of counties with small populations.

With this list of reservations in mind, let us look at the results we get by using state-level density data. Table 4.10 provides the results with respect to population density, and we find that, just as in the case of counties, larger declines in crime were recorded in the most densely populated states. The differences are quite large: the most densely populated states experienced decreases in violent crimes that were about three times greater than the decreases in states with the average density. The results were similar when state populations were taken into account.

Other Gun-Control Laws and Different Types of Concealed-Handgun Laws

Two common restrictions on handguns arise from (1) increased sentencing penalties for crimes involving the use of a gun and (2) waiting periods required before a citizen can obtain a permit for a gun. How did these two types of laws affect crime rates? Could it be that these laws—rather than concealed-handgun laws—explain the deterrent effects? To answer this question, I reestimated the regressions in tables 4.1 and 4.3 by (1) adding a variable to control for state laws that increase sentencing penalties when crimes involve guns and (2) adding variables to measure the impact of waiting periods.[38] It is not clear whether adding an extra day to a waiting period had much of an effect; therefore, I included a variable for when the waiting period went into effect along with variables for the length of the waiting period in days and the length in days squared to pick up any differential impact from longer lengths. In both sets of regressions, the variable for nondiscretionary concealed-handgun laws remains generally consistent with the earlier results.[39] While the coefficients for arrest rates are not reported here, they also remain very similar to those shown previously.

So what about these other gun laws? The pattern that emerges from table 4.11 is much more ambiguous. The results for county-level data suggest that harsher sentences for the use of deadly weapons reduce violent crimes, especially crimes of aggravated assault and robbery. While the same county-level data frequently imply an impact on murder, rape, aggravated

Table 4.10 Effects of concealed-handgun laws across states related to differences in state population density

State population density	Violent crimes	Murder	Rape	Aggravated assault	Robbery	Property crimes	Auto theft	Burglary	Larceny
1/2 Mean 179 per square mile	–2.7%	–3.2%	–5%	–1%	–7%	–1%	3%	–5%	1%
Mean 358 per square mile	–5.4	–6.3	–10	–2	–14	–1	6	–10	2
Plus 1 standard deviation 778 per square mile	–11.8	–13.7	–21	–4	–29	–3	12	–22	4
Plus 2 standard deviations 1,197 per square mile	–18.2	–21.1	–32	–6	–45	–5	19	–33	7

Note: The regressions used for this table multiplied the variable for whether the law was enacted by that state's population density. The control variables used to generate these estimates are the same as those used in table 4.1, including year and county dummies, though they are not reported, because the coefficient estimates are very similar to those reported earlier. All regressions use weighted least squares, where the weighting is each state's population.

Table 4.11 Controlling for other gun laws

Exogenous variables	Violent crime	Murder	Rape	Aggravated assault	Robbery	Property crime	Burglary	Larceny	Auto theft
County-level regressions									
Nondiscretionary law adopted	−4.2%*	−8.7%*	−6%*	−5.5%*	−2%	3.6%*	1%	4.5%*	8.2%*
Enhanced sentencing law adopted	−4%	−0.3%	1.1%	−1.5%***	−2.9%***	−0.001%	−2%	1.2%***	−1.8%***
Waiting law adopted	2.3%	23%*	25%*	−9.4%**	−9%***	2%	2%	−0.3%	−8%***
Percent change in crime by increasing the waiting period by one day: linear effect	−0.08%	−9.4%*	−13.6%*	6.5%*	−11%*	−1.5%***	−4.5%*	1.2%	−1%
Percent change in crime by increasing the waiting period by one day: squared effect	−0.08%	0.55%*	0.8%*	−0.5%*	0.73%*	0.019%	0.23%*	−0.17%*	0.099%
State-level regressions									
Nondiscretionary law adopted	−10.1%*	−8.1%**	−5.7%***	−10.2%*	−13.3%*	−3.4%	−7.6%*	−2.2%	−1%
Enhanced sentencing law adopted	3.5%	3%	3%	−2.8%	1%	3%***	0.5%	3.7%*	2%
Waiting law adopted	10%	6.8%	22%*	2.6%	15%	3.3%	6.5%	2.3%	−3.1%
Percent change in crime by increasing the waiting period by one day: linear effect	−3%	−3%	−10%*	−0.65%	−10%**	−0.95%	−2.2%	−0.53%	−2.4%
Percent change in crime by increasing the waiting period by one day: squared effect	0.12%	−0.13%	0.59%*	−0.041%	0.59%**	−0.021%	0.05%	−0.06%	−0.25%

Note: The control variables are the same as those used in table 4.1, including year and county dummies, though they are not reported, because the coefficient estimates are very similar to those reported earlier. All regressions use weighted least squares, where the weighting is each county's population.

*The result is statistically significant at the 1 percent level for a two-tailed t-test.

**The result is statistically significant at the 5 percent level for a two-tailed t-test.

***The result is statistically significant at the 10 percent level for a two-tailed .

assault, and robbery, the effects are quite inconsistent. For example, simply requiring the waiting period appears to raise murder and rape rates but lower the rates for aggravated assault and robbery. The lengths of waiting periods also result in inconsistent patterns: longer periods at first lower and then raise the murder and rape rates, with the reverse occurring for aggravated assault. Using state level data fails to confirm any statistically significant effects for the violent-crime categories. First, it reveals no statistically significant or economically consistent relationship between either the presence of waiting periods or their length and violent-crime rates. The directions of the effects also differ from those found using county data. Taken together, the results make it very difficult to argue that waiting periods (particularly long ones) have an overall beneficial effect on crime rates. In addition, one other finding is clear: laws involving sentence length and waiting periods do not alter my earlier findings with respect to nondiscretionary laws; that is, the earlier results for nondiscretionary laws cannot merely be reflecting the impact of other gun laws.

The Importance of the Types of Concealed-Handgun Laws Adopted: Training and Age Requirements

Finally, we need to consider how concealed-handgun laws vary across states and whether the exact rules matter much. Several obvious differences exist: whether a training period is required, and if so, how long that period is; whether any minimum age limits are imposed; the number of years for which the permit is valid; where people are allowed to carry the gun (for example, whether schools, bars, and government buildings are excluded); residency requirements; and how much the permit costs. Six of these characteristics are reported in table 4.12 for the thirty-seven states with nondiscretionary laws in 2005.

A major issue in legislative debates on concealed-handgun laws is whether citizens will receive sufficient training to cope with situations that can require difficult, split-second decisions. Steve Grabowski, president of the Nebraska state chapter of the Fraternal Order of Police, notes that "police training is much more extensive than that required for concealed-handgun permits. The few hours of firearms instruction won't prepare a citizen to use the gun efficiently in a stress situation, which is a challenge even for professionals."[40] Others respond that significantly more training is required to use a gun offensively, as a police officer may be called on to do, than defensively. Law-abiding citizens appear reticent to use their guns

Table 4.12 Characteristics of different nondiscretionary concealed-handgun laws as of 2005

State	Last major change	Permit duration (years)	Training hours (length)	Age requirement	Initial permit fee	Renewal fee	Issuing agency
Alabama	1936	1	0	18	0	15	Sheriff
Alaska	2003	None	None	None	None	None	None
Arizona	2004	5	8	21	60	60	Dept. of Public Safety
Arkansas	1995	4	5	21	144.25	50	State Police
Colorado	2003	5	8	21	52.5	25	Sheriff
Connecticut	1986	5	5	21	35	35	State Police
Florida	1995	5	2	21	117	65	Dept. of State
Georgia	1996	5	0	21	50	50	Judge of probate court
Idaho	1996	4	7	21	56	48	Sheriff
Indiana	1980	4	0	18	10	10	Chief of police or sheriff
Kentucky	1996	5	8	21	60	60	Sheriff
Louisiana	1996	4	9	21	100	100	Dept. of Public Safety
Maine	1985	4	5	18	35	20	Chief of police or sheriff
Michigan	2000	5	8	21	105	105	State Police
Minnesota	2003	5	6	21	100	75	Sheriff
Mississippi	1990	4	0	21	124	74	Dept. of Public Safety
Missouri	2003	3	8	23	100	50	Sheriff
Montana[a]	1991	4	4	18	55	25	Sheriff
Nevada	1995	5	8	21	50	25	Sheriff

New Hampshire	1923	4	0	21	10	10	Chief of police
New Mexico	2004	0	15	18	100	100	Dept. of Public Safety
North Carolina	2002	5	8	21	90	75	Sheriff
North Dakota	1985	3	0	18	25	25	Bureau of Criminal Investigation
Ohio	2004	5	12	21	69	55	Sheriff
Oklahoma	1995	5	8	23	125	85	State Bureau of Criminal Investigation
Oregon	1993	4	5	21	65	50	Sheriff
Pennsylvania	1995	5	0	21	19	19	Chief of police or sheriff
South Carolina	1996	4	6	21	55	55	State Law Enforcement Division
South Dakota	1986	4	0	18	10	10	Chief of police or sheriff
Tennessee	1996	4	9	21	115	50	Dept. of Public Safety
Texas	1995	4	10	21	140	140	Dept. of Public Safety
Utah	1995	5	4	21	64	10	Dept. of Public Safety
Vermont	None	None	None	None	None	None	None
Virginia	1995	5	5	21	50	50	Clerk of circuit court
Washington	1995	5	0	21	60	32	Judge, chief of police, or sheriff
West Virginia	1996	5	5	18	90	90	Sheriff
Wyoming	1994	5	5	18	50	50	Attorney general

*Montana does not require a permit outside the city limits for the largest six cities.

and, as noted earlier, in the majority of cases simply brandishing the gun is sufficient to deter an attack.

Reestimating the earlier regressions, I included measures for whether a training period was required, for the length of the training period, and for the age limit.[41] The presence or length of the training periods typically show no effect on crime, and although the effects are significant for robbery, the size of the effect is very small. On the other hand, age limits display quite different and statistically significant coefficients for different crimes. The 21-year-old age limit appears to lower murder rates, but it tends to reduce the decline in rape and overall violent-crime rates that is normally associated with nondiscretionary concealed-handgun laws. Because of these different effects, it is difficult to draw firm conclusions regarding the effect of age limits.

Additional Data on Crime Rates

After I originally put the data together for this study, and indeed after I had written virtually all the first edition of this book, additional county-level data became available for 1993 and 1994 from the FBI's *Uniform Crime Reports*. These data allow us to evaluate the impact of the Brady law, which went into effect in 1994. Four additional states (Alaska, Arizona, Tennessee, and Wyoming) also had right-to-carry laws in effect for at least part of the year. The new information allows us to double-check whether the results shown earlier were mere aberrations.

Table 4.13 reexamines the results from tables 4.1, 4.8, and 4.11 with these new data, and the findings are generally very similar to those already reported. The results in section A that correspond to table 4.1 imply an even larger drop in murder rates related to the passage of concealed-handgun laws (10 percent versus 7.7 percent previously), though the declines in the rates for overall violent crime as well as rape and aggravated assault are smaller. Robbery is also no longer statistically significant, and the point estimate is even positive. As noted earlier, given the inverted V shape of crime-rate trends over time, comparing the average crime rates before and after the passage of these laws is not enough, since crime rates that are rising before the law and falling afterward can produce similar average crime rates in the two periods. To deal with this, section B of table 4.13 corresponds to the results reported earlier in table 4.8. The estimates are again quite similar to those reported earlier. The effect on rape is larger than those previously

Table 4.13 Earlier results reexamined using additional data for 1993 and 1994

Change in explanatory variable	Percent change in various crime rates for changes in explanatory variables				
	Violent crime	Murder	Rape	Aggravated assault	Robbery
Section A: Nondiscretionary law adopted	−4.4%*	−10.0%*	−3.0%*	−5.7%*	0.6%
Section B: The difference in the annual change in crime rates in the years before and after the change in the law (annual rate after the law minus annual rate before the law)	−0.5%*	−2.9%*	−1.7%*	−0.3%*	−2.2%*
Section C: Brady law adopted	3%	−2.3%	3.9%***	3.7%***	−3.9%

Note: This table uses county-level, violent-crime data from the *Uniform Crime Report* that were not available until the rest of the book was written. Here I was not able to control for all the variables used in table 4.1. All regressions use weighted least squares, where the weighting is each county's population. Section C also controls for the other variables that were included in Table 4.11 to account for changes in other gun laws. Section A corresponds to the regressions in table 4.1, section B to those in table 4.8, and section C to those in table 4.11, except that a dummy variable for the Brady law was added for those states that did not previously have at least a five-day waiting period.
*The result is statistically significant at the 1 percent level for a two-tailed *t*-test.
***The result is statistically significant at the 10 percent level for a two-tailed *t*-test.

reported, while the effects for aggravated assault and robbery are somewhat smaller. All the results indicate that concealed-handgun laws reduce crime, and all the findings are statistically significant.

Finally, section C of table 4.13 provides some very interesting estimates of the Brady law's impact by using a variable that equals 1 only for those states that did not previously have at least a five-day waiting period. The claims about the criminals who have been denied access to guns as a result of this law are not necessarily evidence that the Brady law lowers crime rates. Unfortunately, these claims tell us nothing about whether criminals are ultimately able to obtain guns illegally. In addition, to the extent that law-abiding citizens find it more difficult to obtain guns, they may be less able to defend themselves. For example, a woman who is being stalked may no longer be able to obtain a gun quickly to scare off an attacker. Numerous newspaper accounts tell of women who were attempting to buy guns because of threats by former lovers and were murdered or raped during the required waiting period.[42]

The evidence from 1994 indicates that the Brady law has been associated with significant increases in rapes and aggravated assaults, and the declines in murder and robbery have been statistically insignificant. All the other gun-control laws examined in table 4.11 were also controlled for here, but because their estimated impacts were essentially unchanged, they are not reported.

What Happens to Neighboring Counties in Adjacent States When Nondiscretionary Handgun Laws are Adopted?

If you put more resources in one place, it will displace some of the crime.

—Al L'Ecuyer, West Boylston

(Massachusetts) Police Chief[43]

Up to this point we have asked what happens to crime rates in places that have adopted nondiscretionary laws. If these laws do discourage criminals, however, they may react in several ways. We already have discussed two: criminals could stop committing crimes, or they could commit other, less dangerous crimes, such as those involving property, where the probability of contact with armed victims is low. Yet, as the epigraph for this section notes, a third possibility is that criminals may commit crimes in other areas where potential victims are not armed. A fourth outcome is also possible: eliminating crime in one area can help eliminate crime in other areas as well. This last outcome may occur if criminals had been using the county that adopted the law as a staging area. Crime-prone, poverty-stricken areas of cities may find that some of their crime spills over to adjacent areas.

This section seeks to test what effect concealed-handgun laws and higher arrest rates have on crime rates in adjacent counties in neighboring states. Since concealed-handgun laws are almost always passed at the state level, comparing adjacent counties in neighboring states allows us to examine the differential effect of concealed-handgun laws. Evidence that changes in a state's laws coincide with changes in crime rates in neighboring states will support the claim that the laws affect criminals. If these laws do not affect criminals, neighboring states should experience no changes in their crime rates.

Although any findings that nondiscretionary concealed-handgun laws cause criminals to leave the jurisdictions that adopt these laws would provide additional evidence of deterrence, such findings would also imply that simply looking at the direct effect of concealed-handgun laws on crime overestimates the total gain to society from these laws. In the extreme, if the entire reduction in crime from concealed-handgun laws was simply transferred to other areas, society as a whole would be no better off with these laws, even though individual jurisdictions benefited. While the evidence would confirm the importance of deterrence, adopting such a law in a single state might have a greater deterrent impact than if the entire nation adopted the law. The deterrent effect of adopting nondiscretionary

Table 4.14 Estimates of the impact of nondiscretionary concealed-handgun laws on neighboring counties

| Type of crime | Percent change in own crime rate | | |
	Own county has nondiscretionary law	Average neighbor has nondiscretionary law	Average neighbor and own county have nondiscretionary law
Violent crime	−5.5%	0	−5.7%
Murder	−7.6%	3.5%	−4.1%
Rape	−6.2%	6%	0
Robbery	−4%	2.8%	−1.1%
Aggravated assault	−7.4%	−3.3%	−10.7%
Property crime	1%	1%	2%
Auto theft	−1.3%	2%	3.4%
Burglary	1%	4.7%	−1%
Larceny	9%	−2%	10.8%

concealed-handgun laws in additional states could also decline as more states adopted the laws.

To investigate these issues, I reran the regressions reported in table 4.1, using only those counties that were within fifty miles of counties in neighboring states. In addition to the variable that examines whether your own state has a nondiscretionary concealed-handgun law, I added three new variables. One variable averages the dummy variables for whether adjacent counties in neighboring counties have such laws. A second variable examines what happens when your county and your neighboring county adopt these laws. Finally, the neighboring counties' arrest rates are added, though I do not bother reporting them, because the evidence indicates that only the arrest rates in your own county, not your neighboring counties, matter in determining your crime rate.

The results reported in table 4.14 confirm that deterrent effects do spill over into neighboring areas. For all the violent-crime categories, adopting a concealed-handgun law reduces the number of violent crimes in your county, but these results also show that criminals who commit murder, rape, and robbery apparently move to adjacent states without the laws. The one violent-crime category that does not fit this pattern is aggravated assault: adopting a nondiscretionary concealed-handgun law lowers the number of aggravated assaults in neighboring counties. With respect to the benefits of all counties adopting the laws, the last column shows that all categories of violent crime are reduced the most when all counties adopt such laws. The results imply that murder rates decline by over 8 percent and aggravated assaults by around 21 percent when a county and its neighbors adopt concealed-handgun laws.

As a final test, I generated the figures showing crime trends before and after a neighbor's adoption of the law by the method previously used, in addition to the time trends for before and after one's own adoption of the concealed-handgun laws. The use of an additional squared term allows us to see if the effect on crime is not linear. Figures 4.10–4.13 provide a graphic display of the findings for the different violent-crime categories, though the results for the individual violent-crime categories are equally dramatic. In all violent-crime categories, the adoption of concealed-handgun laws produces an immediate and large increase in violent-crime rates in neighboring counties. And in all the categories except aggravated assaults the spillover increases over time just as the counties with the nondiscretionary law see their own crime rates continue to to fall. The symmetry and timing between the reduction in counties with non-discretionary laws and increases in neighboring counties without the laws is striking.

Overall, these results provide strong additional evidence for the deter-

Figure 4.10. Impact on murder rate from a neighbor's adoption of nondiscretionary concealed-handgun law

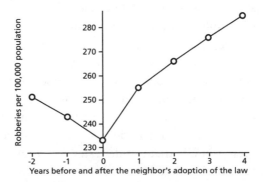

Figure 4.11. Impact on robbery rate from a neighbor's adoption of nondiscretionary concealed-handgun law

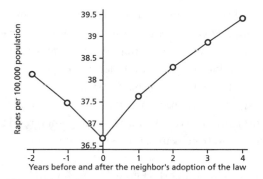

Figure 4.12. Impact on rape rate from a neighbor's adoption of nondiscretionary concealed-handgun law

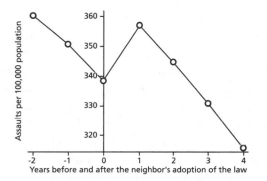

Figure 4.13. Impact on aggravated-assault rate from a neighbor's adoption of nondiscretionary concealed-handgun law

rent effect of nondiscretionary concealed-handgun laws. They imply that the earlier estimate of the total social benefit from these laws may have overestimated the initial benefits, but underestimated the long-term benefits as more states adopt these laws. In the long run, the negative spillover effect subsides, and the adoption of these laws in all neighboring states has the greatest deterrent effect on crime.

Conclusions

The empirical work provides strong evidence that concealed-handgun laws reduce violent crime and that higher arrest rates deter all types of crime. The results confirm what law-enforcement officials have said—that nondiscretionary laws cause a greatest change in the number of permits issued for concealed handguns in the most populous, urbanized counties.

This provides additional support for the claim that the greatest declines in crime rates are related to the greatest increases in concealed-handgun permits. The impact of concealed-handgun laws varies with a county's level of crime, its population and population density, its per-capita income, and the percentage of the population that is black. Despite the opposition to these laws in large, urban, densely populated areas, those are the areas that benefit the most from the laws. Minorities and women tend to be the ones with the most to gain from being allowed to protect themselves.

Some of the broader issues concerning criminal deterrence discussed in chapter 1 were evaluated, and the hypotheses used produced information about the locations where increased police efforts had the most significant deterrent effects on crime. Splitting the data set into high-and low-crime counties shows that arrest rates do not affect crime rates equally in all counties: the greatest return to increasing arrest rates is in the most crime-prone areas.

The results also confirm some of the potential aggregation problems with state-level data. The county-level data explain about six times more variation in violent-crime rates and eight times more variation in property-crime rates than do state-level data. Generally, the effect of concealed-handgun laws on crime appeared much greater when state-level regressions were estimated. However, one conclusion is clear: the very different results for state- and county-level data should make us very cautious in aggregating crime data. The differences in county characteristics show that dramatically greater differences exist among counties within any state than among different states. Whether increased arrest rates are concentrated in the highest-crime counties in a state or spread out equally across all counties makes a big difference in their impact on crime. Likewise, it is a mistake to think that concealed-handgun laws change crime rates in all counties in a state equally. The data should definitely remain as disaggregated as possible.

The three sets of estimates that rely on county-level data, state-level data, or county-level data that accounts for how the law affected different counties have their own strengths and weaknesses. While using county-level data avoids the aggregation problems present with state-level data, the initial county-level regressions rely heavily on variation in state laws and thus are limited to comparing the variation in these fifty jurisdictions. If weight is thus given to any of the results, it would appear that the greatest weight should be given to the county-level regressions that interact the nondiscretionary-law variable with measures of how liberally different counties issued permits under the preexisting discretionary systems. These regressions not only avoid the aggregation problems but also take fullest advantage of the relationship between county-level variations in crime rates and the impact of nondiscretionary laws. They provide the strongest evidence that concealed-handgun laws reduce all types of crime. Despite these different approaches, one point is clear: the results are remarkably consistent with respect to the deterrent effect of nondiscretionary concealed-handgun laws on violent crime. Two of these three sets of estimates imply that concealed-handgun laws also result in lower property-crime rates, although these rates decline less than the rates for violent crimes.

This study represents a significant change in the general approach to crime studies. This is the first study to use cross-sectional time-series evidence at both the county and state levels. Instead of simply using either cross-sectional state- or city-level data, this study has made use of the much larger variations in arrest rates and crime rates between rural and urban areas, and it has been possible to control for whether the lower crime rates resulted from the gun laws themselves or from other differences in these areas (for example, low crime rates) that lead to the adoption of these laws.

5 | The Victims and the Benefits from Protection

Concealed-Handgun Laws, the Method of Murder, and the Choice of Murder Victims

Do laws allowing individuals to carry concealed handguns cause criminals to change the methods they use to commit murders? For example, the number of murders perpetrated with guns may rise after such laws are passed, even though the total number of murders falls. While concealed-handgun laws raise the risk of committing murders with guns, murderers may also find it relatively more dangerous to kill using other methods once people start carrying concealed handguns, and they may therefore choose to use guns to put themselves on a more even basis with their potential prey. Using data on the methods of murder from the Mortality Detail Records provided by the U.S. Department of Health and Human Services, I reran the murder-rate regression from table 4.1 on counties with populations over 100,000 during the period from 1982 to 1991. I then separated murders committed with guns from all other murders. Table 5.1 shows that carrying concealed handguns appears to have been associated with approximately equal drops in both categories of murders. Carrying concealed handguns appears to make all types of murders relatively less attractive.

We may also wonder whether concealed-handgun laws have any effect on the types of

Table 5.1 Do concealed-handgun laws influence whether murders are committed with or without guns? Murder methods for counties with more than 100,000 people from 1982 to 1991

Exogenous variables	ln(Total murders)	ln(Murder with guns)	ln(Murders by nongun methods)
Nondiscretionary law adopted	−9.7%*	−9.0%***	−8.9%***
Arrest rate for murder increased by 100 percentage points	−0.15%*	−0.10%*	−0.14%*

Note: While not all the coefficient estimates are reported, all the control variables are the same as those used in table 4.1, including the year and county dummies. All regressions use weighted least squares, where the weighting is each county's population. The first column uses the UCR numbers for counties with more than 100,000 people. The second column uses the numbers on total gun deaths available from the Mortality Detail Records, and the third column takes the difference between the UCR numbers for total murders and Mortality Detail Records of gun deaths. Endogenous variables are in murders per 100,000 population.

*The result is statistically significant at the 1 percent level for a two-tailed *t*-test.

***The result is statistically significant at the 10 percent level for a two-tailed *t*-test.

people who are likely to be murdered. The *Supplementary Homicide Reports* of the FBI's *Uniform Crime Reports* contain annual, state-level data from 1977 to 1992 on the percent of victims by sex, race, and age, as well as information on the whether the victims and the offenders knew each other (whether they were members of the same family, knew each other but were not members of the same family, were strangers, or no relationship was known).[1] Table 5.2, which uses the same setup as in table 4.1, is intended to explain these characteristics of the victims. The regressions indicate no statistically significant relationship between the concealed-handgun law and a victim's sex, race, relationships with offenders, or age (the last is not shown). However, while they are not quite statistically significant, two of the estimates appear important and imply that in states with concealed-handgun laws victims know their nonfamily offenders 2.6 percentage points more frequently than not, and that the number of victims for whom it was not possible to determine whether a relationship existed declined by 2.9 percentage points.

This raises the question of whether the possible presence of concealed handguns causes criminals to prefer committing crimes against people they know, since presumably they would be more likely to know if an acquaintance carried a concealed handgun. The principal relationship between age and concealed handguns is that the concealed weapon deters crime against adults more than against young people—because only adults can legally carry concealed handguns—but the effect is statistically insignificant.[2] Some of the benefits from allowing adults to carry concealed handguns may be conferred on younger people whom these adults protect. In addition, when criminals who attack adults leave states that pass concealed-handgun laws, there might also be fewer criminals left

Table 5.2 Changes in characteristics of murder victims: annual, state-level data from the *Uniform Crime Reports, Supplementary Homicide Reports,* from 1977 to 1992

| | Percent change in various endogenous variables for changes in explanatory variables | | | | | | | | | |
| | By victim's sex | | | By victim's race | | | By victim's relationship to offender | | | |
Change in explanatory variable	Percent of male victims	Percent of female victims	Percent of victims, sex unknown	Percent of victims that are white	Percent of victims that are black	Percent of victims that are Hispanic	Percent of victims where the offender is known to victim but is not in family	Percent of victims where the offender is in the family	Percent of victims where the offender is a stranger	Percent victims where the relationship is unknown
Nondiscretionary law adopted	0.39	−0.44	0.05	0.01	0.70	−0.87	2.58	−0.25	0.54	−2.88
Arrest rate for murder increased by 100 percentage points	0.068	−0.14	0.07	−2.02**	1.32**	0.33	1.74**	−1.45*	0.79	−1.08

To interpret this table, the first coefficient (0.39) implies that the percent of male victims increases by 0.39 percentage points if a state adopts a nondiscretionary concealed-handgun law. While not all the coefficient estimates are reported, all the control variables are the same as those used in table 2.3, including the year and state dummies. All regressions use weighted least squares, where the weighting is each state's population.

*The result is statistically significant at the 1 percent level for a two-tailed *t*-test.

**The result is statistically significant at the 5 percent level for a two-tailed *t*-test.

to attack the children. The earlier evidence from figures 4.10–4.13 indicates that concealed-handgun laws actually drive criminals away, leaving fewer criminals to attack either adults or those under eighteen. Younger people may also benefit from concealed-carry laws simply because criminals cannot always easily determine who is eligible to carry a concealed handgun. Attackers may find seventeen-year-olds difficult to distinguish from eighteen-year-olds.

The arrest rates for murder produce more interesting results. The percent of white victims and the percent of victims killed by family members both declined when arrest rates were increased, while the percent of black victims and the percent killed by non–family members whom they knew both increased. The results imply that higher arrest rates have a much greater deterrent effect on murders involving whites and family members. One explanation is that whites with higher incomes face a greater increase in expected penalties for any given increase in the probability of arrest.

Mass Public Shootings

Chapter 1 noted the understandable fear that people have of mass public shootings like the one at Virginia Tech University. To record the number of mass public shootings by state from 1977 to 1992, a search was done of news-article databases (Nexis) for the same period examined in the rest of this study. A mass public shooting is defined as one that occurred in a public place and involved two or more people either killed or injured by the shooting. The crimes excluded involved gang activity; drug dealing; a holdup or a robbery; drive-by shootings that explicitly or implicitly involved gang activity, organized crime, or professional hits; and serial killings, or killings that took place over the span of more than one day. The places where public shootings occurred included such sites as schools, churches, businesses, bars, streets, government buildings, public transit facilities, places of employment, parks, health care facilities, malls, and restaurants.

Unlike the crime data we have been using, these data are available only at the state level. Table 5.3 shows the mean rate at which such killings occurred both before and after the adoption of the nondiscretionary concealed-handgun laws in the ten states that changed their laws during the 1977 to 1992 period and, more broadly, for all states that either did or did not have such laws during the period. In each case the before-and-after means are quite statistically significantly different at least at the 1 percent

Table 5.3 Mass shooting deaths and injuries

	Mean death and injury rate per year for years in which the states do not have nondiscretionary concealed-handgun laws (1)	Mean death and injury rate per year for years in which the states do have nondiscretionary concealed-handgun laws (2)
	A. Comparing the before-and-after mean mass shooting deaths and injuries for states that changed their concealed-handgun laws during the 1977–1992 period[1]	
Number of mass shooting deaths and injuries for the ten states that changed their laws during the 1977–1992 period	1.63	1.19
Mass shooting deaths and injuries per 100,000 population for the ten states that changed their laws during the 1977–1992 period	0.039	0.012
	B. Comparing the mean mass shooting deaths and injuries for all states with nondiscretionary concealed-handgun laws and those without such laws[2]	
Number of mass shooting deaths and injuries	2.09	0.89
Mass shooting deaths and injuries per 100,000 population	0.041	0.037

[1]Column 1 for section A has 128 observations; column 2 has 32 observations.
[2]Column 1 for section B has 656 observations; column 2 has 160 observations.

level,[3] with the rates being dramatically lower when nondiscretionary concealed-handgun laws were in effect. For those states from which data are available before and after the passage of such laws, the mean per-capita death rate from mass shootings in those states plummets by 69 percent.[4]

To make sure that these differences were not due to some other factor, I reestimated the specifications used earlier to explain murder rates for the state-level regressions with time trends before and after the adoption of the nondiscretionary concealed-handgun laws. The variable being explained is now the total number of deaths or injuries due to mass public shootings in a state.[5]

Figure 5.1 shows that although the total number of deaths and injuries from mass public shootings actually rises slightly immediately after a nondiscretionary concealed-handgun law is implemented, it quickly falls after that, with the rate reaching zero five years after the law is enacted.[6] Why there is an initial increase is not immediately obvious, though during this early period relatively few people have concealed-handgun permits. Perhaps those planning such shootings do them sooner than they otherwise would have, before too many citizens acquire concealed-handgun

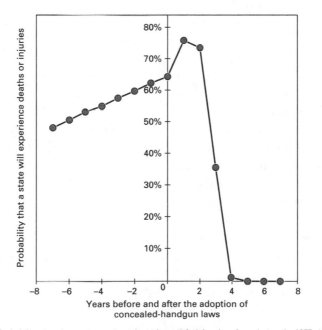

Figure 5.1. Probability that the ten states that adopted concealed-handgun laws during the 1977–1992 period experienced deaths or injuries from a shooting spree in a public place

permits. One additional qualification should also be made. While nondis-cretionary concealed-handgun laws reduced deaths and injuries from mass public shootings to zero after five years in the ten states that changed their laws during the 1977 to 1992 period, a look at the mean death and injury rates from mass public shootings in the eight states that passed such laws before 1977 shows that these rates were quite low but definitely not zero. This tempers the conclusion here and implies that while deaths and inju-ries from mass public shootings fall dramatically after nondiscretionary concealed-handgun laws are passed, it is unlikely that the true rate will drop to zero for the average state that adopts these laws.

County Data for Arizona, Pennsylvania, and Oregon, and State Data for Florida

One problem with the preceding results was the use of county population as a proxy for how restrictive counties were in allowing concealed-handgun permits before the passage of nondiscretionary laws. Since I am still go-ing to control for county-specific levels of crime with county dummies, a better measure would have been to use the actual change in the num-ber of gun permits before and after the adoption of a concealed-handgun law. The per-capita number of permits provides a more direct measure of the expected costs that criminals face in attacking people. Knowing the number of permits also allows us to calculate the benefit from issuing an additional permit.

Fortunately, the information on the number of permits issued by county is available for three states: Arizona, Oregon, and Pennsylvania. Florida also provides yearly permit data at the state level. Arizona and Or-egon also provided additional information on the conviction rate and the mean prison-sentence length. However, for Oregon, because the sentence-length variable is not directly comparable over time, it is interacted with all the individual year variables, so that we can still retain any cross-sectional information in the data. One difficulty with the Arizona sentence-length and conviction data is that they are available only from 1990 to 1995, and since the nondiscretionary concealed-handgun law did not take effect until July 1994, we cannot control for all the other variables that we control for in the other regressions.

Unlike Oregon and Pennsylvania, Arizona did not allow private citizens to carry concealed handguns prior to July 1994 (and permits were not actu-ally issued until the end of the year), so the value of concealed-handgun permits equals zero for this earlier period. Unfortunately, however, because Arizona changed its law so near the end of this period, I cannot control for all the variables that I controlled for in the other regressions. Florida's data are even more limited, but they allow the study of the simple relationship between crime and permits at the state level for a relatively long period of time.

The results in table 5.4 for Pennsylvania and table 5.5 for Oregon provide a couple of consistent patterns.[7] The most economically and statistically important relationship involves the arrest rate: higher arrest rates consistently imply lower crime rates, and in twelve of the sixteen regressions the effect is statistically significant. Five cases for Pennsylvania (violent crime, murder, aggravated assault, robbery, and burglary) show that arrest rates explain more than 15 percent of the change in crime rates.[8] Automobile theft is the only crime for which the arrest rate is insignificant in both tables.

For Pennsylvania, murder and rape are the only crimes for which percapita concealed-handgun permits explain a greater percentage of the variation in crime rates than does the arrest rate. However, increased concealed-handgun licensing explains more than 10 percent of the variation in murder, rape, aggravated assault, and burglary rates. Violent crimes, with the exception of robbery, show that greater numbers of concealed-handgun permits lower violent crime rates, while property crimes exhibit very little relationship. The portion of the variation for property crimes that is explained by concealed-handgun licensing is only about one-tenth as large as the variation for violent crimes that is explained by such licensing, which is not too surprising, given the much more direct impact that concealed handguns have on violent crime.[9] The regressions for Oregon weakly imply a similar relationship between concealed-handgun use and crime, but the effect is only strongly statistically significant for larceny; it is weakly significant for murder.

The Oregon data also show that higher conviction rates consistently result in significantly lower crime rates. The change in conviction rates explains 4 to 20 percent of the change in the corresponding crime rates;[10] however, for five of the seven crime categories, increases in conviction rates appear to produce a smaller deterrent effect than increases in arrest rates.[11] The greatest differences between the deterrent effects of arrest and conviction rates produce an interesting pattern. For rape, increasing the arrest rate by 1 percent produces more than ten times the deterrent effect of increasing the conviction rate for those who have been arrested by 1 percent.

Table 5.4 Crime and county data on concealed-handgun permits: Pennsylvania counties with populations greater than 200,000

Percent change in the crime rate	Crimes per 100,000 population								
	Violent crime	Murder	Rape	Aggravated assault	Robbery	Property crime	Auto theft	Burglary	Larceny
Due to a 1 percent change in the number of right-to-carry pistol permits/population over 21 between 1988 and each year since the law was implemented	−5.3%***	−26.7%*	−5.7%***	−4.8%***	1.2%	−0.12%	1.5%	−1.4%	0.7%
Due to a 1 percent change in the arrest rate for the crime category	−0.79%*	−0.37%*	−0.08%	−0.76%*	−0.84%*	−0.41%***	−0.065%	−1.1%*	0.13%

Note: While not all the coefficient estimates are reported, all the control variables are the same as those used in table 4.1, including year and county dummies. All regressions use weighted least squares, where the weighting is each county's population. The nondiscretionary-law-times-county-population variable that was used in the earlier regressions instead of the variable for change in right-to-carry permits was tried here and produced very similar results. I also tried controlling for either the robbery or burglary rates, but I obtained very similar results.

*The result is statistically significant at the 1 percent level for a two-tailed *t*-test.

***The result is statistically significant at the 10 percent level for a two-tailed *t*-test.

Table 5.5 Crime and county data on concealed-handgun permits: Oregon data

Percent change in the crime rate	Crimes per 100,000 population							
	Murder	Rape	Aggravated assault	Robbery	Auto theft	Burglary	Larceny
Due to a 1 percent change in the number of right-to-carry pistol permits/population over 21 between 1988 and each year since the law was implemented	−37%****	−6.7%	−4.8%	−4.7%	12%	2.7%	−9%**
Due to a 1 percent change in the arrest rate for the crime category	−0.34%*	−1%*	−0.4%*	−0.4%*	−.04%*	−0.7%*	−0.9%*
Due to a 1 percent change in the conviction rate for the crime category	−0.2%*	−0.09%*	−1.5%***	−0.19%*	−0.37%*	−0.27%*	−0.86%*

Note: While not all the coefficient estimates are reported, all the control variables are the same as those used in table 4.1, including year and county dummies. I also controlled for sentence length, but the different reporting practices used by Oregon over this period make its use somewhat problematic. To deal with this problem, the sentence-length variable was interacted with year-dummy variables. Thus, while the variable is not consistent over time, it is still valuable in distinguishing penalties across counties at a particular point in time. The categories for violent and property crimes are eliminated because the mean sentence-length data supplied by Oregon did not allow us to use these two categories. All regressions use weighted least squares, where the weighting is each county's population.

*The result is statistically significant at the 1 percent level for a two-tailed *t*-test.

**The result is statistically significant at the 5 percent level for a two-tailed *t*-test.

***The result is statistically significant at the 10 percent level for a two-tailed *t*-test.

****The result is statistically significant at the 11 percent level for a two-tailed *t*-test.

For auto theft, arrest seems more important than conviction: a 1 percent increase in the arrest rate reduces crime by about ten times more than the same increase in convictions. These results are consistent with the assumption that arrests produce large penalties in terms of shame or negative reputation.[12] In fact, the existing evidence shows that the reputational penalties from arrest and conviction can dwarf the legally imposed penalties.[13] This is some of the first evidence that the reputational penalties from arrests alone provide significant deterrence for some crimes.

One possible explanation for these results is that Oregon simultaneously passed both the nondiscretionary concealed-handgun law and a waiting period. The statistics in table 4.11 suggest that the long waiting period imposed by the Oregon law (fifteen days) increased murder by 5 percent, rape by 2 percent, and robbery by 6 percent. At least in the case of murder, which is weakly statistically significant in any case, the estimates from tables 4.11 and 5.5 together indicate that if Oregon had not adopted its waiting period, the drop in murder resulting from the concealed-handgun law would have been statistically significant at the 5 percent level.

The results for sentence length are not shown, but the t-statistics are frequently near zero, and the coefficients indicate no clear pattern. One possible explanation for this result is that all the changes in sentencing rules produced a great deal of noise in this variable, not only over time but also across counties. For example, after 1989, whether a crime was prosecuted under the pre- or post-1989 rules depended on when the crime took place. If the average time between when the offense occurred and when the prosecution took place differed across counties, the recorded sentence length could vary even if the actual time served was the same.

Florida's state-level data showing the changes in crime rates and changes in the number of concealed-handgun permits are quite suggestive (see figure 5.2). Cuba's Mariel Boat Lift created a sudden upsurge in Florida's murder rate from 1980 through 1982. By 1983 the murder rate had return to its pre-Mariel level, and it remained relatively constant or exhibited a slight upward trend until the state adopted its nondiscretionary concealed-handgun law in 1987. Murder-rate data are not available for 1988 because of changes in the reporting process, but the available evidence indicates that the murder rate began to drop when the law was adopted, and the size of the drop corresponded with the number of concealed-handgun permits outstanding. Ironically, the first post-1987 upward movement in murder rates occurred in 1992, when Florida began to require a waiting period and background check before issuing permits.

Figure 5.2A. Cumulative percent change in Florida's murder rate

Figure 5.2B. Concealed-handgun permits after implementation of the law in Florida

Finally, a very limited data set for Arizona produces no significant relationship between the change in concealed-handgun permits and the various measures of crime rates. In fact, the coefficient signs themselves indicate no consistent pattern; the fourteen coefficients are equally divided between negative and positive signs, though six of the specifications imply that the variation in the number of concealed-handgun permits explains at least 8 percent of the variation in the corresponding crime rates.[14] This is likely to occur for several reasons. The sample is extremely small (only 64–89 observations, depending on which specification), and we have only a year and a half over which to observe the effect of the law. In addition, if Arizona holds true to the pattern observed in other states, the impact of these laws is smallest right after the law passes.

The results involving either the mean sentence length for those sentenced in a particular year or the actual time served for those ending their sentences also imply no consistent relationship between sentence length and crime rates. While the coefficients are negative in eleven of the fourteen specifications, they provide weak evidence of the deterrent effect of longer prison terms: only two coefficients are negative and statistically significant.

The Brady law also went into effect during this period.[15] Using the Arizona data to investigate the impact of the Brady law indicates that its only discernible effect was in the category of aggravated assault, where the statistics imply that it increased the number of aggravated assaults by 24 percent and the number of rapes by 3 percent. Yet it is important to remember that the data for Arizona covered only a very short period of time when this law was in effect, and other factors influencing crime could not be taken into account. While I do not believe that the Brady law was responsible for this large increase in assaults, I at least take this as evidence that the law did not reduce aggravated assaults and as confirmation of the belief that relying on this small sample for Arizona is problematic.

Overall, Pennsylvania's results provide more evidence that concealed-handgun ownership reduces violent crime, murder, rape, aggravated assault, and burglary. For Oregon, the evidence implies that murder and larceny decrease. While the Oregon data imply that the effect of handgun permits on murder is only marginally statistically significant, the point estimate is extremely large economically, implying that a doubling of permits reduces murder rates by 37 percent. The other coefficients for Pennsylvania and Oregon imply no significant relationship between the change in concealed-handgun ownership and crime rates. The evidence from the small sample for Arizona implies no relationship between crime and concealed-handgun ownership. All the results also support the claim that higher arrest and conviction rates deter crime, although—perhaps partly because of the relatively poor quality of the data—no systematic effect appears to arise from longer prison sentences.

Putting Dollar Values on the Crime-Reduction Benefits and Private Costs of Additional Concealed-Handgun Permits

By combining evidence that additional concealed handguns reduce crime with the monetary estimates of victim losses from crime produced by the National Institute of Justice, it is possible to attach a monetary value to the benefits of additional concealed-handgun permits. While the results for Arizona imply no real savings from reduced crime, the estimates for Pennsylvania indicate that potential costs to victims are reduced by $5,079 for each additional concealed-handgun permit, and for Oregon, the savings are $3,439 per permit. As noted in the discussion of table 4.2, the results are largely driven by the effect of concealed handguns in lowering murder rates (with savings of $4,986 for Pennsylvania and $3,202 for Oregon).[16]

These estimated gains appear to far exceed the private costs of owning a concealed handgun. The purchase price of handguns ranges from $100 or less for the least-expensive .25-caliber pistols to over $700 for the newest, ultracompact, 9-millimeter models.[17] The permit-filing fees can range from $19 every five years in Pennsylvania to a first-time, $65 fee with subsequent five-year renewals at $50 in Oregon, which also requires several hours of supervised safety training. Assuming a 5 percent real interest rate and the ability to amortize payments over ten years, purchasing a $300 handgun and paying the licensing fees every five years in Pennsylvania implies a yearly cost of only $43, excluding the time costs incurred. The estimated expenses are higher for Oregon, because of the higher fees and the costs in time and money of obtaining certified safety instruction. Even if these annual costs double, however, they are still quite small compared to the social benefits. While ammunition purchases and additional annual training would increase annualized costs, the long life span of guns and their resale value work to reduce the above estimates.

The results imply that handgun permits are being issued at much lower than optimal rates, perhaps because of the important externalities not directly captured by the handgun owners themselves. While the crime-reducing benefits of concealed handguns are shared by all those who are spared being attacked, the costs of providing this protection are borne exclusively by permit holders.

Accidental Deaths and Suicides

Even if nondiscretionary handgun permits reduce murder rates, we are still left with the question of what happens to the rates for accidental death.

As more people carry handguns, accidents may be more likely. Earlier, we saw that the number of murders prevented exceeded the entire number of accidental deaths. In the case of suicide, the nondiscretionary laws increase the probability that a gun will be available when an individual feels particularly depressed; thus, they could conceivably lead to an increase in the number of suicides. While only a small portion of accidental deaths are attributable to guns (see appendix 4), the question remains whether concealed-handgun laws affect the total number of deaths through their effect on accidental deaths.

To get a more precise answer to this question, I used county-level data from 1982 to 1991 in table 5.6 to test whether allowing concealed handguns increased accidental deaths. Data are available from the Mortality Detail Records (provided by the U.S. Department of Health and Human Services) for all counties from 1982 to 1988 and for counties with populations over 100,000 from 1989 to 1991. The specifications are identical to those shown in all the previous tables, with the exceptions that they no longer include variables related to arrest or conviction rates and that the variables to be explained are either measures of the number of accidental deaths from handguns or measures of accidental deaths from all other nonhandgun sources.

While there is some evidence that the racial composition of the population and the level of welfare payments affect accident rates, the impact of nondiscretionary concealed-handgun laws is consistently both quite small economically and insignificant statistically. The first estimate in column 1 implies that accidental deaths from handguns rose by about 0.5 percent when concealed-handgun laws were passed. With only 200 accidental handgun deaths nationwide during 1988 (22 accidental handgun deaths occurred in states with nondiscretionary laws), the implication is that enacting concealed-handgun laws in states that currently do not have them would increase the number of deaths by less than one (.851 deaths). Redoing these tests by adding together accidental handgun deaths and deaths from "unknown" types of guns produces similar results.

With 186 million people living in states without concealed-handgun laws in 1992,[18] the third specification implies that implementing such laws across those remaining states would have resulted in about nine more accidental handgun deaths.[19] Combining this finding with earlier estimates from table 4.1, we find that if the rest of the country had adopted concealed-handgun laws in 1992, the net reduction in total deaths would have been approximately 1,405 to 1,583.

Table 5.6 Did nondiscretionary concealed-handgun laws increase the number of accidental deaths? (1982–91 county-level data)

Change in explanatory variable	Deaths per 100,000 population Ordinary least squares, natural logarithm of endogenous variable		Tobit	
	Accidental deaths from handguns	Accidental deaths from nonhandgun sources	Accidental deaths from handguns	Accidental deaths from nonhandgun sources
Nondiscretionary law adopted	0.48%	9.9%***	0.574 more deaths	1.331 more deaths
Percent change in crime (for Tobit number of deaths per 100,000) for an increase in population of one person per square mile	−0.07%*	0.09%*	−0.004%	−0.016%
Percent change in crime (for Tobit number of deaths per 100,000) for an increase in $1,000 of real per-capita personal income	2.67%	−5.7%*	4.4%	−9%*

Note: While not all the coefficient estimates are reported, all the control variables are the same as those used in table 4.1, including year and county dummies. Absolute t-statistics are in parentheses. All regressions weight the data by each county's population.

*The result is statistically significant at the 1 percent level for a two-tailed t-test.

***The result is statistically significant at the 10 percent level for a two-tailed t-test.

One caveat should be added to these numbers, however: both columns 2 and 4 indicate that accidental deaths from nonhandgun sources increased by more than accidental deaths from handguns after the nondiscretionary concealed-handgun laws were implemented. To the extent that the former category increased because of uncontrolled factors that also increase accidental deaths from handguns, the results presented here are biased toward finding that concealed-handgun laws have increased accidental deaths from handguns.

Finally, I examined similar specifications using data on suicide rates. The possibility exists that if a person becomes depressed while away from home, the presence of a concealed handgun might encourage that person to act impulsively, whereas an enforced delay might ultimately prevent a suicide. If anything, the results implied a statistically insignificant and small increase in suicides (less than one-tenth of 1 percent). Hence it is reasonable to conclude that no relationship exists between concealed-handgun laws and suicide rates.

Total Gun Ownership and Crime

Traditionally, people have tried to use cross-country comparisons of gun ownership and crime rates to determine whether gun ownership enhances or detracts from safety.[20] Worldwide, there is no relationship between gun ownership and crime rates. Many countries, such as Switzerland, Finland, New Zealand, and Israel, have high gun ownership rates and low crime rates, while many other countries have both low gun ownership rates and either high or low crime rates. For example, in 1995 Switzerland's murder rate was 40 percent lower than Germany's despite having a three-times higher gun-ownership rate. Yet, making a reliable comparison across countries is an arduous task simply because it is difficult to obtain gun ownership data both over time and across countries, and to control for all the other differences across the legal systems and cultures across countries. International comparisons are also risky because polls underreport ownership in countries where gun ownership is illegal, and the polls are conducted by different polling organizations that ask questions in widely differing ways. How crime is measured also varies across countries.

Fortunately, more consistent data are available to investigate the relationship between total gun ownership in the United States and crime. In chapter 3, I presented poll data from general-election surveys that offer consistent polling across states, showing how gun ownership varied across states for 1988 and 1996. There is broad variation in gun ownership across states, and the crime rates also vary across states and over time. Even with rather few observations, however, these data suggest that we may be able to answer an obvious question: Is the crime rate higher in states with more guns?

To test the relationship between gun ownership and crime, I attempted to examine the relationship between the percentage of the adult population owning guns and the crime rate after accounting for the arrest rate, real personal income, population per square mile, state dummy variables, the percentage of blacks among each state's population, and a variable to pick up the average change in crime rates between 1988 and 1995. This last variable was also intended to help pick up any differences in the results that arise from the slightly different poll methods in the two years. Ideally, one would want to construct the same type of cross-sectional, time-series data set over many years and states that was used in the earlier discussions; unfortunately, however, such extensive poll data on gun ownership are not available. Because we lack the most recent data for the above-named variables, all the variables except for the percentage of the state's adult population that owns guns is for 1995.

As table 5.7 shows, a strong negative relationship exists between gun ownership and all of the crime rates except for rape, and the results are statistically significant for seven of the nine categories. Indeed, the effect of

Table 5.7 The relationship between state crime rates and the general election poll data on the percent of the state's adult population owning guns

Crime rates	Percent change in the crime rate from a 1 percentage point increase in a state's gun ownership rate	Estimated change in victim costs from a 1 percent increase in the number of guns nationwide
Violent crime	−4.1*	
Murder	−3.3*	$2.7 billion
Rape	0	
Aggravated assault	−4.3*	$44 million
Robbery	−4.3*	$200 million
Property crime	−1.5**	
Burglary	−1.6*	$54 million
Larceny	−1.3	$38 million
Auto theft	−3.2*	$17 million
Total savings		$3.1 billion

Note: While the other coefficient values are not reported here, these regression results control for the arrest rate, real personal income, population per square mile, state dummy variables, the percent of the state's population that is black, and a year-dummy variable for 1996 to pick up the average change in crime rate between the years. All regressions use weighted least squares, where the regressions are weighted by the state populations.
*The result is statistically significant at the 1 percent level for a two-tailed t-test.
**The result is statistically significant at the 5 percent level for a two-tailed t-test.

gun ownership on crime is quite large: a 1 percent increase in gun owner-ship reduces violent crime by 4.1 percent. The estimates from the National Institute of Justice of the costs to victims of crime imply that increasing gun ownership nationwide by 1 percent would reduce victim costs by $3.1 billion, though we must bear in mind that these conclusions are based on a relatively small sample. Similar estimates for accidental gun deaths or suicides reveal no significant relationships.

Conclusion

Nondiscretionary concealed-handgun laws have equal deterrent effects on murders committed both with and without guns. Despite differences in the rates at which women and men carry guns, no difference exists in the total benefit the two sexes derive in terms of reduced murder rates. The evidence strongly rejects claims that criminals will be more likely to use firearms when their potential victims are armed. Furthermore, the increased pres-ence of concealed handguns under nondiscretionary laws does not raise the number of accidental deaths or suicides from handguns.

As in other countries, people who engage in mass public shootings are deterred by the possibility that law-abiding citizens may be carrying guns. Such people may be deranged, but they still appear to care whether they will themselves be shot as they attempt to kill others. The results presented here are dramatic: states that adopted nondiscretionary laws during the 1977–1992 period virtually eliminated mass public shootings after four or five years. These results raise serious concerns over state and federal laws banning *all* guns from schools and the surrounding area. At least permit-ting school employees access to guns would seem to make schools less vulnerable to mass shootings.

One prominent concern about leniency in permitting people to carry concealed handguns is that the number of accidental deaths might rise, but I can find no statistically significant evidence that this occurs. Even the largest estimate of nine more accidental deaths per year is extremely small in comparison to the number of lives saved from fewer murders.

The evidence for Pennsylvania and Oregon also provides the first esti-mates of the annual social benefits that accrue from private expenditures on crime reduction. Each additional concealed-handgun permit reduces total losses to victims by between three and five thousand dollars. The results imply that handgun permits are being obtained at much lower than optimal rates in two of the three states for which I had the relevant data, perhaps because the individual owners bear all the costs of owning their handguns but receive only a small fraction of the total benefits. The evidence implies that concealed handguns are the most cost-effective method of reducing crime that has been analyzed by economists; they provide a higher return than increased law enforcement or incarceration, other private security devices, or social programs like early educational intervention.[21]

The general-election exit-poll data may also be used to calculate the change in total costs to crime victims when more people own guns. These preliminary estimates are quite dramatic, indicating that, nationwide, each 1 percent increase in the number of people owning guns reduces victim costs by over 3 billion dollars.

The data continue to supply strong evidence supporting the economic notion of deterrence. Higher arrest and conviction rates consistently and dramatically reduce the crime rate. Consistent with other recent work,[22] the results imply that increasing the arrest rate, independent of the probability of eventual conviction, imposes a significant penalty on criminals. Perhaps the most surprising result is that the deterrent effect of a 1 percent increase in arrest rates is much larger than the same increase in the probability of conviction. It was also surprising that while longer prison terms usually implied lower crime rates, the results were normally not statistically significant.

6 | What Determines Arrest Rates and the Passage of Concealed-Handgun Laws?

The regressions used in previous chapters took both the arrest rate and the passage of nondiscretionary concealed-handgun laws as given. This chapter deals with the unavoidably complicated issue of determining whether the variables I am using to explain the crime rate are in themselves determined by other variables. Essentially, the findings here confirm the deterrence effect of concealed-handgun laws and arrest rates.

Following the work of Isaac Ehrlich, I now let the arrest rate depend on crime rates as well as on population measures and the resources invested in police.[1] The following crime and police measures were used: the lagged crime rates; measures of police employment and payroll per capita, per violent crime, and per property crime at the state level (these three measures of employment are also broken down by whether police officers have the power to make arrests). The population measures were as follows: income; unemployment insurance payments; the percentages of county population by age, sex, and race (already used in table 4.1); and county and year dummy variables.[2] In an attempt to account for political influences, I further included the percentage of a state's population belonging to the National Rifle Association, along with the percentage voting for the Republican presidential candidate.[3]

Because presidential candidates and political

issues vary from election to election, the variables for the percentage voting Republican are not perfectly comparable across years. To account for these differences across elections, I used the variable for the percentage voting Republican in a presidential election for the years closest to that election. Thus, the percent of the vote obtained in 1980 was multiplied by the individual year variables for the years from 1979 to 1982, the percent of the vote obtained in 1984 was multiplied by the individual year variables for the years from 1983 to 1986, and so on through the 1992 election. A second set of regressions explaining the arrest rate also includes the change in the log of the crime rates as a proxy for the difficulties that police forces may face in adjusting to changing circumstances.[4] The time period studied in all these regressions, however, is more limited than in the previous tables because the state-level data on police employment and payroll available from the U.S. Department of Justices' Expenditure and Employment data set for the criminal justice system covered only the years from 1982 to 1992.

Aside from the concern over what determines the arrest rate, we want to answer another question: Why did some states adopt nondiscretionary concealed-handgun laws while others did not? As noted earlier, if states adopted such laws because crime rates were either rising or expected to rise, our preceding regression estimates (using ordinary least-squares) will underestimate the drop in crime. Similarly, if such laws were adopted because crime rates were falling, the bias is in the opposite direction—the regression will overestimate the drop in crime. Thus, in order to explain whether a county was likely to be in a state that had adopted concealed-handgun laws, I used the rates for both violent crime and property crime, along with the change in those crime rates.[5] To control for general political differences that might affect the chances for the passage of these laws, I also included the percentage of a state's population that belonged to the National Rifle Association; the Republican presidential candidate's percentage of the statewide vote; the percentage of blacks and whites in a state's population; the total population in the state; regional dummy variables for whether the state is in the South, Northeast, or Midwest; and year dummy variables.

The regressions reported here are different from those reported earlier because they allow us to let the crime rate depend on the variables for the concealed-handgun law and the arrest rate, as well as on other variables, but the variables for the concealed-handgun law and the arrest rate are in turn dependent on other variables.[6] While these estimates use the same set of control variables employed in the preceding tables, the results differ from all my previous estimates in one important respect: nondiscretionary concealed-handgun laws are associated with large, significant declines in all nine crime categories. I tried estimating a specification that mimicked the regressions in Ehrlich's study. Five of the nine crime categories implied that a change of one standard deviation in the predicted value of the nondiscretionary-law variable explains at least 10 percent of a change of one standard deviation in the corresponding crime rates. Nondiscretionary concealed-handgun laws explain 11 percent of the variation in violent crime, 7.5 percent of the variation in murder, 6 percent for rape, 10 percent for aggravated assault, and 5 percent for robbery. In fact, concealed-handgun laws explain a greater percentage of the change in murder rates than do arrest rates.

A second approach examined what happened to the results when the arrest rate was determined not only by past crime rates but also by the change in the crime rate in the previous year. The concern here is that rapid changes in crime rates make it more difficult for police agencies to maintain the arrest rates they had in the past. With the exception of robbery, the new set of estimates using the change in crime rates to explain arrest rates indicated that the effect of concealed-handgun laws was usually more statistically significant but economically smaller. For example, in the new set of estimates, concealed-handgun laws explained 3.9 percent of the variation in murder rates compared to 7.5 percent for the preceding estimates. While these results imply that even crimes involving relatively little contact between victims and criminals experienced declines, nondiscretionary concealed-handgun laws reduced violent crimes by more than they reduced property crimes.

Both sets of estimates provide strong evidence that higher arrest rates reduce crime rates. Among violent crimes, rape consistently appears to be the most sensitive to higher arrest rates. Among property crimes, larceny is the most sensitive to higher arrest rates.

The estimates explaining which states adopt concealed-handgun laws show that the states adopting these laws are relatively Republican with large National Rifle Association memberships and low but rising rates of violent crime and property crime. The set of regressions used to explain the arrest rate shows that arrest rates are lower in high-income, sparsely populated, Republican areas where crime rates are increasing. This evidence calls into question claims that police forces are not catching criminals in high-crime, densely populated areas.

I reestimated the state-level data using similar specifications. The coefficients on the variables for both arrest rates and concealed-handgun laws remained consistently negative and statistically significant. The state-level data again implied a much stronger effect from the passage of concealed-handgun laws and a much weaker effect from higher arrest rates. In order to use the longer data series available for the nonpolice employment and payroll variables, I even reestimated the regressions without those variables. This produced similar results.[7]

Finally, using the predicted values for the arrest rates allows us to investigate the significance of another weakness of the data. The arrest-rate data suffers not only from some missing observations but also from some instances where it is undefined when the crime rate in a county equals zero. This last issue is problematic only for murders and rapes in low-population counties. In these cases, both the numerator and denominator in the arrest rate equal zero, and it is not clear whether I should count this as an arrest rate equal to 100 or 0 percent, neither of which is correct, as it is truly undefined. The previously reported evidence arising from regressions that were run only on the larger counties (population over 10,000) sheds some light on this question, since these counties have fewer observations with undefined arrest rates. In addition, if the earlier reported evidence that adopting nondiscretionary concealed-handgun laws changed the number of permits the least in the lower-population counties, one would expect relatively little change in counties with missing observations.

The analysis presented in this section allowed us to try another, more appropriate approach to deal with this issue.[8] I created predicted arrest rates for these observations using the regressions that explain the arrest rate, and then I reestimated the regressions with the new, larger samples. While the coefficient for murder declined, implying a 5 percent drop when nondiscretionary laws are adopted, the coefficient for rape increased, implying a drop of more than 10 percent. Only very small changes appeared in the other estimates. All coefficients were statistically significant. The effect of arrest rates also remained negative and statistically significant. As one final test to deal with the problems that arise from using the arrest rates, I reestimated the regressions using only the predicted values for the nondiscretionary-law variable. In this case the coefficients were always negative and statistically significant, and they indicate that these laws produce an even larger negative effect on crime than the effect shown in the results already reported.

Conclusion

Explicitly accounting for the factors that influence a state's decision to adopt a nondiscretionary concealed-handgun law and that determine the arrest rate only serves to strengthen the earlier results: with this approach, both concealed-handgun laws and arrest rates explain much larger percentages of the changes in the crime rate than they did earlier. Several other facts are clear. Up through the early 1990s, nondiscretionary laws were adopted by relatively low-crime states in which the crime rate is rising. These states have also tended to vote Republican and to have high percentages of their populations enrolled in the National Rifle Association.

For studies that use the number of police officers as a proxy for the level of law enforcement, these results suggest some caution. Property-crime rates appear to have no systematic relationship to the number of police officers either with or without the power to make arrests. For violent crime, the presence of more police officers *with* arrest powers lowers the arrest rate, while a greater number of police officers *without* arrest powers raises the arrest rate.

Neither of these results alone is particularly troubling, because increasing the number of police officers could reduce the crime rate enough so that the arrest rate could fall even if the officers did not slack off. Theoretically, the relationship between the number of police officers and the arrest rate could go either way. Yet in the case of violent crimes, the drop in arrest rates associated with more police officers is too large to be explained by a drop in the crime rate. In fact, the direct relationship between the number of police officers and violent crime implies a positive relationship. There are many possible explanations for this. Quite plausibly, the presence of more police officers encourages people to come forward to report crime. Another possibility is that relatively large police forces tend to be unionized and have managed to require less work from their officers. The bottom line is that using the number of police officers directly as a proxy for the level of law enforcement is at best a risky proposition. We must control for many other factors before we know exactly what we are measuring.

7 | The Political and Academic Debate by 1998

The Political Process

When my original study was released in 1996, many commentators were ready to attack it. Anyone who had shown any interest in looking at the article was given a copy while I was in the process of revising it for the *Journal of Legal Studies,* although I quickly learned that it was not common practice to circulate studies to groups on both sides of the gun debate. Few comments were offered privately, but once the paper began to receive national press coverage, the attacks came very quickly.

Before the press coverage started, it was extremely difficult to get even a proponent of gun control to provide critical comments on the paper when I presented it at the Cato Institute in early August 1996. I approached twenty-two pro-control people before Jens Ludwig, a young assistant professor at Georgetown University, accepted my request to comment on the paper.

One of the more interesting experiences occurred when I asked Susan Glick, of the Violence Policy Center, to participate.[1] Glick, whom I called during June 1996, was one of the last people that I approached. She was unwilling to comment on my talk at Cato because she didn't want to "help give any publicity to the paper." Glick said that her appearance might help bring media attention to the paper that it wouldn't otherwise have gotten. When I pointed out that

C-SPAN was likely to cover the event, she said she didn't care because "we can get good media whenever we want." When I asked her if I could at least send her a copy of the paper because I would appreciate any comments that she might have, she said, "Forget it, there is no way that I am going to look at it. Don't send it."[2]

However, when the publicity broke on the story with an article in *USA Today* on August 2, she was among the many people who left telephone messages immediately asking for a copy of the paper. In her case, the media were calling, and she "need[ed] [my] paper to be able to criticize it." Because of all the commotion that day, I was unable to get back to her right away. ABC National Television News was doing a story on my study for that day, and when at around 3:00 P.M. the ABC reporter doing the story, Barry Serafin, called saying that certain objections had been raised about my paper, he mentioned that one of those who had criticized it was Ms. Glick. After talking to Mr. Serafin, I gave Glick a call to ask her if she still wanted a copy of my paper. She said that she wanted it sent to her right away and wondered if I could fax it to her. I then noted that her request seemed strange because I had just gotten off the telephone with Mr. Serafin at ABC News, who had told me that she had been very critical of the study, saying that it was "flawed." I asked how she could have said that there were flaws in the paper without even having looked at it yet. At that point Ms. Glick hung up the telephone.[3]

Many of the attacks from groups like Handgun Control, Inc. and the Violence Policy Center focused on claims that my study had been paid for by gun manufacturers or that the *Journal of Legal Studies* was not a peer-reviewed journal and that I had chosen to publish the study in a "student-edited journal" to avoid the close scrutiny that such a review would provide.[4] These attacks were completely false, and I believe that those making the charges knew them to be false. At least they had been told by all the relevant parties here at the University of Chicago and at the Olin Foundation that the funding issues were false, and the questions about publishing in a "student-edited journal" or one that was not peer-reviewed were well known to be false because of the prominence of the journal. Some statements involved claims that my work was inferior to an earlier study by three criminologists at the University of Maryland who had examined five counties.

Other statements, like those in the *Los Angeles Times,* tried to discredit the scholarliness of the study by claiming that "in academic circles, meanwhile, scholars found it curious that he would publicize his findings before they were subjected to peer review."[5] In fact, the paper was reviewed and accepted months before media stories started discussing it in August 1996.

The attacks claiming that this work had been paid for by gun manufacturers have been unrelenting. Congressman Charles Schumer (D-N.Y.) wrote as follows in the *Wall Street Journal*: "I'd like to point out one other 'association.' The Associated Press reports that Prof. Lott's fellowship at the University of Chicago is funded by the Olin Foundation, which is 'associated with the Olin Corporation,' one of the nation's largest gun manufacturers. Maybe that's a coincidence, too. But it's also a fact."[6] Others were even more direct. In a letter that the Violence Policy Center mass-mailed to newspapers around the country, M. Kristen Rand, the Center's federal policy director, wrote,

> Lott's work was, in essence, funded by the firearms industry—the primary beneficiary of increased handgun sales. Lott is the John M. Olin fellow at the University of Chicago law school, a position founded by the Olin Foundation. The foundation was established by John Olin of the Olin Corp., manufacturer of Winchester ammunition and maker of the infamous "Black Talon" bullet. Lott's study of concealed handgun laws is the product of gun-industry funding. . . . (See, as one of many examples, "Gun Industry Paid," *Omaha World Herald,* March 10, 1997, p. 8.)[7]

Dan Kotowski, executive director of the Illinois Council Against Handgun Violence, said that "the study was biased because it was funded by the parent company of Winchester, Inc., a firearms manufacturer."[8] Kotowski is also quoted as saying that the claimed link between Winchester and my study's conclusions was "enough to call into question the study's legitimacy. It's more than a coincidence."[9] Similar claims have been made by employees of Handgun Control, Inc. and other gun-control organizations.

Indeed, gun-control groups that were unwilling to comment publicly on my study at the Cato Institute forum had time to arrange press conferences that were held exactly at the time that I was presenting my paper in Washington. Their claims were widely reported by the press in the initial news reports on my findings. A typical story stated that "Lott's academic position is funded by a grant from the Olin Foundation, which is associated with the Olin Corp. Olin's Winchester division manufactures rifles and bullets,"[10] and it was covered in newspapers from the *Chicago Tribune* to the *Houston Chronicle* and the *Des Moines Register,* as well as in "highbrow" publications like *The National Journal.* The Associated Press released a partial correction stating that the Olin Foundation and Olin Corporation are separate organizations and that the Winchester subsidiary of the Olin Corporation makes ammunition, not guns, but a Nexis search of news stories revealed that only one newspaper in the entire country that had published the original report carried the Associated Press correction.[11]

Congressman Schumer's letter did produce a strong response from William Simon, the Olin Foundation's president and former U.S. Secretary of the Treasury, in the *Wall Street Journal* for September 6, 1996:

An Insult to Our Foundation

As president of the John M. Olin Foundation, I take great umbrage at Rep. Charles Schumer's scurrilous charge (Letters to the Editor, Sept. 4) that our foundation underwrites bogus research to advance the interests of companies that manufacture guns and ammunition. He asserts (falsely) that the John M. Olin Foundation is "associated" with the Olin Corp. and (falsely again) that the Olin Corp. is one of the nation's largest gun manufacturers. Mr. Schumer then suggests on the basis of these premises that Prof. John Lott's article on gun-control legislation (editorial page, Aug. 28) must have been fabricated because his research fellowship at the University of Chicago was funded by the John M. Olin Foundation.

This is an outrageous slander against our foundation, the Olin Corp., and the scholarly integrity of Prof. Lott. Mr. Schumer would have known that his charges were false if he had taken a little time to check his facts before rushing into print. Others have taken the trouble to do so. For example, Stephen Chapman of the *Chicago Tribune* looked into the charges surrounding Mr. Lott's study, and published an informative story in the Aug. 15 issue of that paper, which concluded that, in conducting his research, Prof. Lott was not influenced either by the John M. Olin Foundation or by the Olin Corp. Anyone wishing to comment on this controversy ought first to consult Mr. Chapman's article and, more importantly, should follow his example of sifting the facts before reaching a conclusion. For readers of the *Journal*, here are the key facts.

The John M. Olin Foundation, of which I have been president for nearly 20 years, is an independent foundation whose purpose is to support individuals and institutions working to strengthen the free enterprise system. We support academic programs at the finest institutions in the nation, including the University of Chicago, Harvard, Yale, Stanford, Columbia, the University of Virginia, and many others. We do not tell scholars what to write or what to say.

The foundation was created by the personal fortune of the late John M. Olin, and is not associated with the Olin Corp. The Olin Corp. has never sought to influence our deliberations. Our trustees have never taken into account the corporate interests of the Olin Corp. or any other company when reviewing grant proposals. We are as independent of the Olin Corp. as the Ford Foundation is of the Ford Motor Co.

The John M. Olin Foundation has supported for many years a program in law and economics at the University of Chicago Law School. This program is administered and directed by a committee of faculty members in the law school. This committee, after reviewing many applications in a very competitive process, awarded a research fellowship to Mr. Lott. We at the foundation had no knowledge of who applied for these fellowships, nor did we ever suggest that Mr. Lott should be awarded one of them. We did not commission his study, nor, indeed, did we even know of it until last month, when Mr. Lott presented his findings at a conference sponsored by a Washington think tank.

As a general rule, criticism of research studies should be based on factual grounds rather than on careless and irresponsible charges about the motives of the researcher. Mr. Lott's study should be evaluated on its own merits without imputing motives to him that do not exist. I urge Mr. Schumer to check his facts more carefully in the future.

Finally, it was incorrectly reported in the *Journal* (Sept. 5) that the John M. Olin Foundation is 'headed by members of the family that founded the Olin Corp.' This is untrue. The trustees and officers of the foundation have been selected by virtue of their devotion to John Olin's principles, not by virtue of family connections. Of our seven board members, only one is a member of the Olin family. None of our officers is a member of the Olin family—neither myself as president, nor our secretary-treasurer, nor our executive director.

This letter, I think, clarifies the funding issue, and I would only like to add that while the faculty at the Law School chose to award me this fellowship, even they did not inquire into the specific research I planned to undertake.[12] The judgment was made solely on the quality and quantity of my past research, and while much of my work has dealt with crime, this was my first project involving gun control. No one other than myself had any idea what research I was planning to do. However, even if one somehow believed that Olin were trying to buy research, it must be getting a very poor return on its money. Given the hundreds of people at the different universities who have received the same type of fellowship, I have been the only one to work on the issue of gun control.

Unfortunately, as the quote from Ms. Rand's letter and statements by many other gun-control advocates—made long after Simon's explanation—indicates, the facts about funding did little to curtail the comments of those spreading the false rumors.[13]

After these attacks on my funding, the gun-control organizations brought up new issues. For example, during the spring of 1997 the Violence Policy Center sent out a press release entitled "Who Is John Lott?" that claimed, among other things, "Lott believes that some crime is good for society, that wealthy criminals should not be punished as harshly as poor convicts." I had in fact been arguing that "individuals guilty of the same crime should face the same expected level of punishment" and that with limited resources to fight crime, it is not possible to eliminate all of it.[14] I would have thought that most people would recognize these silly assertions for what they were, but they were picked up and republished by publications such as the *New Republic*.[15]

The aversion to honest public debate has been demonstrated to me over and over again since my study first received attention. Recently, for example, Randy Roth, a visiting colleague at the University of Chicago Law School, asked me to appear on a radio program that he does from the University of Hawaii on a public radio station. I had almost completely stopped doing radio interviews a few months before because they were too much of an interruption to my work, but Randy, whom I have known only very briefly from lunch-table conversation, seemed like a very interesting person, and I thought that it would be fun to do the show with him. I can only trust that he doesn't normally have as much trouble as he had this time in getting an opposing viewpoint for his program. In a note that Randy shared with me, he described a conversation that he had with Brandon Stone, of the Honolulu Police Department, whom he had been trying for a while to get to participate. Randy wrote as follows on March 3, 1997:

> Brandon called to say he had not changed his mind—he will not participate in any gun-control radio show involving John Lott. Furthermore, he said he had discussed this with all the others who are active in this area (the Hawaii Firearms Coalition, I think he called it), and that they have "banded together"—none will participate in such a show.
>
> He said he didn't want to "impugn" John's character . . . [and] then he went on to talk about all the money involved in this issue, the fact that

[the] Olin Corp. is in the firearm business and financing John's chair, etc. He said John's study had been given to the media before experts first could discredit it, implying that this "tactic" was used because the study could not withstand the scrutiny of objective scholars.

He said the ideas promoted by John's study are "fringe ideas" and that they are "dangerous." When I pointed out that such ideas not only have been publicly debated in other states, but that some of those states actually have enacted legislation, he basically just said that Hawaii is a special place and other states have sometimes been adversely affected by unfair tactics by the pro-gun lobby.

I kept coming back to my belief that public debate is good and that my show would give him an opportunity to point out anything about John's study that he believes to be incorrect, irrelevant, distorted, or whatever. He kept saying that public debate does more harm than good when others misuse the forum. When he specifically mentions the firearm industry ("follow the money" was his suggestion, to understand what John's study is all about), I reminded him of John's association with the University of Chicago and his outstanding reputation, both for scholarship and integrity. He then said he realized John was "my friend," as though I couldn't be expected to be objective. He also said that John was "out of his field" in this area.

My hunch is that it's going to be extremely difficult finding a studio guest with the credentials and ability to do a good job on the pro-gun-control side.

After talking with Randy and in an attempt to create a balanced program, I also telephoned Mr. Stone. While we did not get into the detail that he went into with Randy, I did try to address his concerns over my funding and my own background in criminal justice as chief economist at the U.S. Sentencing Commission during the late 1980s. Stone also expressed his concerns to me that Hawaiians would not be best served by our debating the issue and that Hawaiians had already made up their minds on this topic. I said that he seemed like an articulate person and that it would be good to have a lively discussion on the subject, but he said that the program "could only do more harm than good" and that any pro-gun-control participation would only lend "credibility" to the discussion.[16]

Before I did my original study, I would never have expected it to receive the attention that it did. None of the refereed journal articles that I had produced had received so much attention. Many people have told me that this was politically naive. That may be, but this much is clear: I never would have guessed how much people fear discussion of these issues. I never would have known how much effort goes into deliberately ignoring certain findings in order to deny them news coverage. Nor would I have seen, after news coverage did occur, how much energy goes into attacking the integrity of those who present such findings, with such slight reference—or no reference at all—to the actual merits of the research. I was also surprised by the absolute confidence shown by gun-control advocates that they could garner extensive news coverage whenever they wanted.

Criticisms of the Original Study

A second line of attack came from academic, quasi-academic, and gun-control advocacy groups concerning the competence with which the study was conducted. Many of these objections were dealt with somewhere in the original study, which admittedly is very long. Yet it should have been easy enough for critics—especially academics—to check.

The attacks were fairly harsh, especially by the standards of academic discourse. For example,

> "They highlight things that support their hypothesis while they ignore things contrary to their hypothesis," said Daniel Webster, an assistant professor at Johns Hopkins University Center for Gun Policy and Research.
>
> "We think the study falls far short of any reasonable standard of good social science research in making [their] case," said economist Daniel Nagin of Carnegie-Mellon University, who has analyzed Lott's data with colleague Dan Black.[17]

I have made the data I used available to all academics who have requested them, and professors at twenty-four universities took advantage of that. Of those who have made the effort to use the extensive data set, Dan Black and Daniel Nagin have been the only ones to publicly criticize the study.

The response from some academics, particularly those at the Johns Hopkins Center for Gun Policy and Research, was highly unusual in many ways. For instance, who ever heard of academics mounting an attack on a scholarly study by engaging in a systematic letter-writing campaign to local newspapers around the country?[18] One letter from a citizen to the *Springfield (Illinois) State Journal-Register* noted, "Dear Editor: Golly, I'm impressed that the staff at Johns Hopkins University reads our local *State Journal-Register*. I wonder if they subscribe to it."[19]

The rest of this chapter briefly reviews the critiques and then provides my responses to their concerns. I discuss a number of issues below that represent criticisms raised in a variety of published or unpublished research papers as well as in the popular press:

1 Is the scale of the effect realistic?

Large reductions in violence are quite unlikely because they would be out of proportion to the small scale of the change in carrying firearms that the legislation produced. (Franklin Zimring and Gordon Hawkins, "Concealed-Handgun Permits: The Case of the Counterfeit Deterrent," *The Responsive Community* [Spring 1997]: 59, cited hereafter as Zimring and Hawkins, "Counterfeit Deterrent")

In some states, like Pennsylvania in 1996, almost 5 percent of the population has concealed-handgun permits. In others, like Florida, the portion is about 2 percent and growing quickly. The question here is whether these percentages of the population are sufficient to generate 8 percent reductions in murders or 5 percent reductions in rapes. One important point to take into account is that applicants for permits do not constitute a random sample of the population. Applicants are likely to be those most at risk. The relevant comparison is not between the percentage of the population being attacked and the percentage of the entire population holding permits, but between the percentage of the population most vulnerable to attack and the percentage of that population holding permits.

Let us consider some numbers from the sample to see how believable these results are. The yearly murder rate for the average county is 5.65 murders per 100,000 people, that is, .00565 percent of the people in the average county are murdered each year. An 8 percent change in this murder rate amounts to a reduction of 0.0005 percent. Obviously, even if only 2 percent of the population have handgun permits, that 2 percent is a huge number relative to the 0.0005 percent reduction in the murder rate. Even the largest category of violent crimes, aggravated assault, involves 180 cases per 100,000 people in the average county per year (that is, 0.18 percent of the people are victims of this crime in the typical year). A 7 percent change in this number implies that the assault rate declines from 0.18 percent of the population to 0.167 percent of the population. Again, this 0.013 percent change in the assault rate is quite small compared to the observed changes in the number of concealed-handgun permits.

Even if those who carry concealed handguns face exactly the same risk of being attacked as everyone else, a 2 percent increase in the portion of the population carrying concealed handguns seems comparable to the percentage-point reductions in crime. Bearing in mind that those carrying guns are most likely to be at risk, the drop in crime rates correlated with the presence of these guns even begins to seem relatively small. Assuming that just 2 percent of the population carries concealed handguns, the drop in the murder rate only requires that 0.025 percent of those with concealed-handgun permits successfully ward off a life-threatening attack to achieve the 0.0005 percent reduction in the murder rate. The analogous percentage for aggravated assaults is only 0.65 percent. In other words, if less than seven-tenths of one percent of those with concealed handguns successfully ward off an assault, that would account for the observed drop in the assault rate.

2 The importance of "crime cycles"

> Crime rates tend to be cyclical with somewhat predictable declines following several years of increases. . . . Shall-issue laws, as well as a number of other measures intended to reduce crime, tend to be enacted during periods of rising crime. Therefore, the reductions in violent crime . . . attribute[d] to the implementation of shall-issue laws may be due to the variety of other crime-fighting measures, or to a commonly observed downward drift in crime levels towards some long-term average. (Daniel W. Webster, "The Claims That Right-to-Carry Laws Reduce Violent Crime Are Unsubstantiated," The Johns Hopkins Center for Gun Policy and Research, copy obtained March 6, 1997, p. 1; cited hereafter as Webster, "Claims")

Despite claims to the contrary, the regressions do control for national and state crime trends in several different ways. At the national level, I use a separate variable for each year, a technique that allows me to account for the changes in average national crime rates from one year to another. Any national cycles in crime rates should be accounted for by this method. At the state level, some of the estimates use a separate time trend for each state, and the results with this method generally yielded even larger drops in violent-crime rates associated with nondiscretionary (shall-issue) laws.

To illustrate that the results are not merely due to the "normal" ups and downs for crime, we can look again at the diagrams in chapter 4 showing crime patterns before and after the adoption of the nondiscretionary laws. The declines not only begin right when the concealed-handgun laws pass, but the crime rates end up well below their levels prior to the law. Even if laws to combat crime are passed when crime is rising, why would one believe that they happened to be passed right at the peak of any crime cycle?

As to the concern that other changes in law enforcement may have been occurring at the same time, the estimates account for changes in other gun-control laws and changes in law enforcement as measured by arrest and conviction rates as well as by prison terms. No previous study of crime has attempted to control for as many different factors that might explain changes in the crime rate.

3 *Did I assume that there was an immediate and constant effect from these laws and that the effect should be the same everywhere?*

> The "statistical models assumed: (1) an immediate and constant effect of shall-issue laws, and (2) similar effects across different states and counties." (Webster, "Claims," p. 2; see also Dan Black and Daniel Nagin, "Do 'Right-to-Carry' Laws Deter Violent Crime?" *Journal of Legal Studies* 27 [January 1998], p. 213.)

One of the central arguments both in the original paper and in this book is that the size of the deterrent effect is related to the number of permits issued, and it takes many years before states reach their long-run level of permits. Again, the figures in chapter 4 illustrate this quite clearly.

I did not expect the number of permits to change equally across either counties or states. A major reason for the larger effect on crime in the more urban counties was that in rural areas, permit requests already were being approved; hence it was in urban areas that the number of permitted concealed handguns increased the most.

A week later, in response to a column that I published in the *Omaha World-Herald*,[20] Mr. Webster modified this claim somewhat:

> Lott claims that his analysis did not assume an immediate and constant effect, but that is contrary to his published article, in which the *vast majority* of the statistical models assume such an effect. (Daniel W. Webster, "Concealed-Gun Research Flawed," *Omaha World-Herald,* March 12, 1997; emphasis added.)

When one does research, it is most appropriate to take the simplest specifications first and then gradually make things more complicated. The simplest way of doing this is to examine the mean crime rates before and after the change in a law. Then one would examine the trends that existed before and after the law. This is the pattern that I followed in my earlier work, and I have followed the same pattern here. The bottom line should be, How did the different ways of examining the data affect the results? What occurs here is that (1) the average crime rate falls after the nondiscretionary concealed-handgun laws are adopted; (2) violent-crime rates were rising until these laws were adopted, and they fell dramatically after that; and (3) the magnitude of the drops, both across counties and states and over time, corresponds to the number of permits issued.

4 *When were these concealed-handgun laws adopted in different states?*

> Lott and Mustard also use incorrect dates of shall-issue law implementation in their analyses. For example, they claim that Virginia adopted its shall-issue law in 1988. . . . Some populous counties in Virginia continued to issue very few permits until 1995 (after the study period), when the state eliminated this discretion. Lott and Mustard identify 1985 as the year in which Maine liberalized its concealed-carry policy. It is unclear why they chose 1985 as the year of policy intervention, because the state changed its concealed-carry law in 1981, 1983, 1985, 1989, and 1991. (Webster, "Claims," p. 3; see also Daniel W. Webster, "Concealed-Gun Research Flawed," *Omaha World-Herald,* March 12, 1997; cited hereafter as Webster, "Flawed.")

I do think that Virginia's 1988 law clearly attempted to take away local discretion in issuing permits, and, indeed, all but three counties clearly complied with the intent of the law. However, to satisfy any skeptics, I examined whether reclassifying Virginia affected the results: it did not. The 1988 law read as follows:

> The court, after consulting the law-enforcement authorities of the county or city and receiving a report from the Central Criminal Records Exchange, *shall issue* such permit if the applicant is of good character, has demonstrated a need to carry such concealed weapon, which need may include but is not limited to lawful defense and security, is physically and mentally competent to carry such weapon, and is not prohibited by law from receiving, possessing, or transporting such weapon [emphasis added].[21]

As with Virginia, I relied on a study by Clayton Cramer and David Kopel to determine when Maine changed its law to a nondiscretionary law. Maine enacted a series of changes in its law in 1981, 1983, 1985, and 1991. The 1985 law did not completely eliminate discretion, but it provided the foundation for what they then considered to be a switch to a de facto shall-issue regime, which was upheld in a number of important state court decisions.[22] The bottom line, however (again, as with Virginia), is that reclassifying Maine (or even eliminating it from the data set) does not change the results much.

5 Should robbery be the crime most affected by the adoption of the nondiscretionary law?

Shall-issue laws were adopted principally to deter predatory street crime, the most common example of which is robbery by a stranger. But [the] results indicate that shall-issue laws had little or no effect on robbery rates. Instead the strongest deterrent effects estimated were for rape, aggravated assault, and murder. (Webster, "Claims," p. 3)

Is it credible that laws that allow citizens to carry guns in public appear to have almost no effect on robberies, most of which occur in public spaces, yet do reduce the number of rapes, most of which occur outside of public spaces within someone's home. (Jens Ludwig, speaking on *Morning Edition*, National Public Radio, 10:00 A.M. ET December 10, 1996.)

I have two responses. First, as anyone who has carefully read this book will know, it is simply not true that the results show "little or no effect on robbery rates." Whether the effect was greater for robbery or other violent crimes depends on whether one simply compares the mean crime rates before and after the laws (in which case the effect is relatively small for robbery) or compares the slopes before and after the law (in which case the effect for robbery is the largest).

Second, it is not clear that robbery should exhibit the largest impacts, primarily because the term *robbery* encompasses many crimes that are not street robberies. For instance, we do not expect bank or residential robberies to decrease; in fact, they could even rise. Allowing law-abiding citizens to carry concealed handguns makes street robberies more difficult, and thus may make other crimes like residential robbery *relatively* more attractive. Yet not only is it possible that these two different components of robbery could move in opposite directions, but to rank some of these different crimes, one requires information on how sensitive different types of criminals are to the increased threat.

Making claims about what will happen to different types of violent crimes is much more difficult than predicting the relative differences between, say, crimes that involve no contact with victims and crimes that do. Even here, however, some of these questions cannot be settled *a priori*. For example, when violent crimes decline, more people may feel free to walk around in neighborhoods, which implies that they are more likely to observe the illegal actions of strangers.[23] Criminals who commit violent crimes are also likely to commit some property crimes, and anything that can make an area unattractive to them will reduce both types of crime.

6 *Do concealed-handgun laws cause criminals to substitute property crimes for rape?*

> Lott and Mustard argue that criminals, in response to shall-issue laws, substitute property crimes unlikely to involve contact with victims. But their theory and findings do not comport with any credible criminological theory because theft is the motive for only a small fraction of the violent crimes for which Lott and Mustard find shall-issue effects. It is difficult to rationalize why a criminal would, for example, steal a car because he felt deterred from raping or assaulting someone. (Webster, "Claims," p. 4. See also Jens Ludwig, "Do Permissive Concealed-Carry Laws Reduce Violent Crime?" Georgetown University working paper, October 8, 1996, p. 19, hereafter cited as Ludwig, "Permissive Concealed-Carry Laws.")

No one believes that hard-core rapists who are committing their crimes only for sexual gratification will turn into auto thieves, though some thefts do also involve aggravated assault, rape, or murder.[24] Indeed, 16 percent of murders in Chicago from 1990 to 1995 occurred in the process of a robbery.[25] What is most likely to happen, however, is that robbers will try to obtain money by other means such as auto theft or larceny. Although it is not unusual for rape victims to be robbed, the decline in rape most likely reflects the would-be rapist's fear of being shot.

I am also not completely clear on what Webster means when he says that "theft is the motive for only a small fraction of violent crimes," since robbery accounted for as much as 34 percent of all violent crimes committed during the sample between 1977 and 1992 (and this excludes robberies that were committed when other more serious crimes like murder or rape occurred in connection with the robbery).

7 *Comparing crime rates for two to three years before nondiscretionary laws go into effect with crime rates for two to three years after the passage of such laws*

> If right-to-carry laws have an immediate, substantial impact on the crime rates, the coefficients on the right-to-carry laws immediately after the

enactment of the law should be substantially different from those immediately preceding the law's enactment. To test formally for the impact of right-to-carry laws, we see if the sum of the coefficients for two to three years prior to adoption is significantly different from the sum for two and three years following adoption. . . . Only in the murder equation do our findings agree with Lott and Mustard. In contrast to Lott and Mustard, we find evidence that robberies and larcenies are reduced when right-to-carry laws are passed and no evidence of an impact on rape and aggravated assaults. (Dan Black and Daniel Nagin, "Do 'Right-to-Carry' Laws Deter Violent Crime?" Carnegie-Mellon University working paper, October 16, 1996, p. 7)

Instead of the approach used earlier in this book (a simple time trend and time trend squared for the number of years before and after the concealed-handgun laws) Black and Nagin used ten different variables to examine these trends. Separate variables were used for the first year after the law, the second year after the law, the third year after the law, the fourth year after the law, and five or more years after the law. Similarly, five different variables were used to measure the effects for the five years leading up to the adoption of the law. They then compared the average coefficient values for the variables measuring the effects two to three years before the law with the average effect for the variables two to three years after the law.

A quick glance at figures 7.1–7.5, which plot their results, explains their findings. Generally, the pattern is very similar to what we reported earlier. In addition, as crime is rising right up until the law is adopted and falling thereafter, it is not surprising that some values when the crime rate is going down are equal to those when it was going up. It is the slopes of the lines and not simply their levels that matter. But more generally, why choose to compare only two to three years before and after to look for changes created by the law. Why not use all the data available?

Examining the entire period before the law versus the entire period after produces the significant results that I reported earlier in the book. Alternatively, one could have chosen to analyze the differences in crime rates between the year before the law went into effect and the year after, but one would hope that if deviations are made from any simple rule, some rationale for doing so would be given.

They claim that their results differ from ours because they find a statistically significant decline. This is puzzling; it is difficult to see why their results would be viewed as inconsistent with my argument. I had indeed also

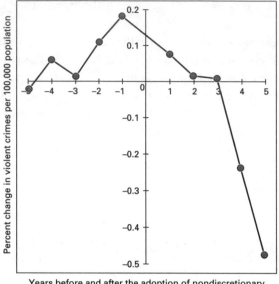

Figure 7.1. Average year-dummy effects for violent crimes, using Black's and Nagin's "full sample"

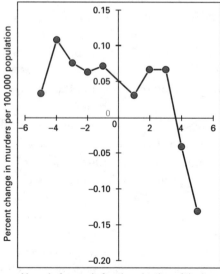

Figure 7.2. The effect of concealed-handgun laws on murder, using Black's and Nagin's "full sample"

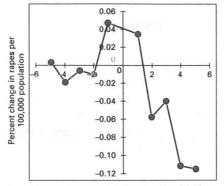

Figure 7.3. The effect of concealed-handgun laws on rapes, using Black's and Nagin's "full sample"

Figure 7.4. The effect of concealed-handgun laws on robbery, using Black's and Nagin's "full sample"

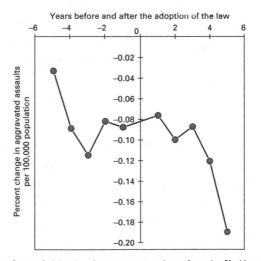

Figure 7.5. The effect of concealed-handgun laws on aggravated assaults, using Black's and Nagin's "full sample"

found some evidence that larcenies were reduced by nondiscretionary laws (for example, see the results using the state-level data or the results using two-stage least squares), but I chose to emphasize those results implying the smallest possible positive benefits from concealed-handgun laws.

The bottom line—even using their choice of the dates that they deem most appropriate—is that murder and robbery rates fall after the passage of the laws and that none of the other violent-crime categories experienced an increase. Looking further at whether violent-crime rates were rising or falling before and after these laws, one finds that violent-crime rates were almost always rising prior to the passage of the law and always falling after it.

8 *The impact of including Florida in the sample*

> Our concern is particularly severe for the state of Florida. With the Mariel boat lift of 1980 and the thriving drug trade, Florida's crime rates are quite volatile. Moreover, four years after the passage of the right-to-carry law in 1987, Florida passed several gun-related measures, including background checks of handgun buyers and a waiting period for handgun purchases. To test the sensitivity of the results to the inclusion of Florida, we reestimated the model . . . without Florida. Only in the robbery equation can we reject the hypothesis that the crime rate two and three years after adoptions is different than the crime rate two and three years prior to adoption. (Dan Black and Daniel Nagin, "Do 'Right-to-Carry' Laws Deter Violent Crime?" Carnegie-Mellon University working paper, October 16, 1996, p. 9)

> In fact, Nagin and Black said they found that virtually all of the claimed benefits of carry laws were attributable to changes in the crime rate in just one state: Florida. (Richard Morin, "Unconventional Wisdom: New facts and Hot Stats from the Social Sciences," *Washington Post,* March 23, 1997, p. C5)

This particular suggestion—that we should throw out the data for Florida because the drop in violent crimes is so large that it affects the results—is very ironic. Well after my work in 1996 got attention, Handgun Control, Inc., and other gun-control groups continued to cite the 1995 University of Maryland study, which claimed that if evidence existed of a detrimental impact of concealed handguns, it was for Florida.[26] If the Maryland study is to be believed, the inclusion of Florida must have biased my results in the opposite direction.[27]

Figure 7.6. Florida's murder rates

More important, as we shall see below, the reasons given by Black and Nagin for dropping Florida from the sample are simply not valid. Furthermore, the impact of excluding Florida is different from what they claim. Figure 7.6 shows the murder rate in Florida from the early 1980s until 1992. The Mariel boat lift did dramatically raise violent-crime rates like murder, but these rates had returned to their pre-Mariel levels by 1982. For murder, the rate was extremely stable until the nondiscretionary concealed-handgun law passed there in 1987, when it began to drop dramatically.

The claim that Florida should be removed from the data because a waiting period and a background check went into effect in 1992 is even weaker. If this were a valid reason for exclusion, why not exclude other states with these laws as well? Why only remove Florida? Seventeen other states had waiting periods in 1992. A more valid response would be to try to account for the impact of these other laws—as I did in chapter 4. Indeed, accounting for these other laws slightly strengthens the evidence that concealed handguns deter crime.

The graph for Florida in figure 7.6 produces other interesting results. The murder rate declined in each consecutive year following the implementation of the concealed-handgun law until 1992, the first year that these other, much touted, gun-control laws went into effect. I am not claiming that these laws caused murder rates to rise, but this graph surely

Figure 7.7. The effect of concealed-handgun laws on violent crimes, excluding Florida

makes it more difficult to argue that laws restricting the ability of law-abiding citizens to obtain guns would reduce crime.

While Black's and Nagin's explanations for dropping Florida from the data set are invalid, there is some justification for concern that results are being driven by a few unusual observations. Figure 7.7 shows the relationship between violent-crime rates and concealed-handgun laws when Florida is excluded. A careful comparison of this graph with that of figure 4.5, which includes Florida, reveals only a few very small differences.

As a more systematic response to this concern, I excluded Florida and reestimated all the regressions shown in this book. Indeed, there were eight regressions out of the more than one thousand discussed in which the exclusion of Florida did cause the coefficient for the nondiscretionary variable to lose its statistical significance, although it remained negative. The rest of the regression estimates either remained unchanged or (especially for aggravated assault and robbery) became larger and more statistically significant.

Black and Nagin seem to feel that their role in this debate is to see if they can find some specification using any combination of the data that weakens the results.[28] But traditional statistical tests of significance are based on the assumption that the researcher is not deliberately choosing which results to present. Even if a result is statistically significant at the 1 percent level, one would expect that one out of every one hundred regressions would not yield a statistically significant result; in other words, out of one thousand regressions, one would expect to find at least ten for which the impact of nondiscretionary concealed-handgun laws was not statistically significant.

> Lott's claims that Florida's concealed-carry law was responsible for lower murder rates in that state is questionable. Florida did not experience reductions in murders and rapes until four or five years after the law was liberalized. Lott attributes this "delayed effect" to the cumulative influence of increases in carrying permits. Other research attributes Florida's declines in murders in the 1990s to laws requiring background checks and waiting periods for handgun purchases that were implemented several years after gun-carrying laws were liberalized. (Webster, "Flawed")

Much of Webster's comment echoes the issues raised previously by Black and Nagin—indeed, I assume that he is referring to their piece when he mentions "other research." However, while I have tested whether other gun-control laws might explain these declines in crime (see table 4.11), Black and Nagin did not do so, but merely appealed to "other research" to support their affirmation. The preceding quotation seems to imply that my argument involved some sort of "tipping" point: as the number of permits rose, the murder rate eventually declined. As figure 7.6 illustrates, however, Florida's decline in murder rates corresponded closely with the rise in concealed-handgun permits: no lag appears in the decline; rather, the decline begins as soon as the law goes into effect.

9 *The impact of including Maine in the sample*

> One should also be wary of the impact that Maine has on Lott's graphs. . . . When Maine was removed from the analyses, the suggested delayed [effects of the law] on robberies and aggravated assaults vanished. (Webster, "Flawed")

This comment is curious not only because Mr. Webster does not cite a study to justify this claim but also because he has never asked for the data to examine these questions himself. Thus it is difficult to know how he arrived at this conclusion. A more direct response, however, is simply to show how the graphs change when Maine is excluded from the sample. As figures 7.8 and 7.9 show, the exclusion of Maine has very little effect.

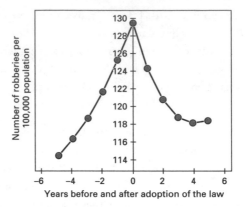

Figure 7.8. The effect of concealed-handgun laws on robberies, excluding Maine

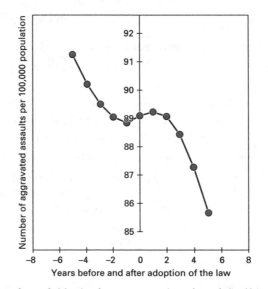

Figure 7.9. The effect of concealed-handgun laws on aggravated assaults, excluding Maine

10 *How much does the impact of these laws vary across states?*

[Dan Black and Dan Nagin] found the annual murder rate did go down in six of the ten states—but it went up in the other four, including a 100 per-cent increase in West Virginia. Rape dropped in five states—but increased in the other five. And the robbery rate went down in six states—but went up in four. "That's curious," Black said. If concealed weapons laws were really so beneficial, their impact should not be so "wildly" different from state to state. (Richard Morin, "Unconventional Wisdom: New Facts and Hot Stats from the Social Sciences," *Washington Post,* March 23, 1997, p. C5)

Unfortunately, Black's and Nagin's evidence was not based on statewide crime rates but on the crime rates for counties with over 100,000 people. This fact is important, for instance, in West Virginia, where it means that *only one single county*—Kanawha—was examined. The other fifty-four counties in West Virginia, which include 89 percent of the state's population, were excluded from their estimates. They used only one county for three of the ten states, and only three counties for another state. In fact, Black and Nagin managed to eliminate 85 percent of all counties in the nation in their analysis.

As shown in table 4.9 (see chapter 4), my estimates using all the counties certainly did not yield "wildly" different estimates across states. Violent-crime rates fell in nine of the ten states enacting new nondiscretionary concealed-handgun laws between 1977 and 1992. The differences that did exist across states can be explained by differences in the rates at which concealed-handgun permits were issued. Table 4.10 also provides evidence that the states that issued more permits experienced greater reductions in crime.

11 *Do the coefficient estimates for the demographic variables make sense?*

Perhaps even more surprising are the coefficient estimates for measures of a county's population that is black, female, and between the ages of 40 and 49 or over the age of 65. [Lott and Mustard find] evidence to suggest that these variables have a statistically significant, positive correlation with murder rates . . . and that black females ages 40 to 49 have a statistically significant positive correlation with the aggravated assault rate. . . . There remain two competing explanations for [these] findings. First, middle-aged and elderly African-American women could be actively [engaged] in the commission of car thefts, assaults, and murders across the United States. The more likely explanation is that [their results] are misspecified and, as a result, their coefficient estimates are biased. (Ludwig, "Permissive Concealed-Carry Laws," pp. 20–21. See also Albert W. Alschuler, "Two Guns, Four Guns, Six Guns, More: Does Arming the Pubic Reduce Crime?" *Valparaiso University Law Review* 31 (Spring 1997): 367.)

No, black females ages 40 to 49 are not responsible for a crime wave. Other results in the regressions that were not mentioned in this quotation indicate that the greater the percentage of women between the ages of 10 and 29, the greater the rape rate—but these estimates do not imply that young women are going out and committing rapes. To show that crime rates are higher where greater percentages of the population are of a certain demographic age group does not imply that the people in that group are committing the crimes. The positive relationship may exist because these people are relatively easy or attractive victims.

If such an objection were valid, it should also apply to my finding that in areas where personal incomes are high, auto-theft rates are also high. Should we infer from this that high-income individuals are more likely to steal cars? Presumably not. What is most likely is that wealthy individuals own cars that are attractive targets for auto thieves.

It is also important to note that the different demographic variables are very highly correlated with each other. The percentage of the population that is male and within a particular race and age grouping is very similar to the percentage that is female within that race and age group. Similar high correlations exist within racial groups across age groups. With thirty-six different demographic categories, determining whether an effect is specifically related to an individual category or simply arises because that category is correlated (whether negatively or positively) with another demographic group is difficult and not the object of this book. What I have tried to do is "overcontrol" for all possible demographic factors to make sure that any effects attributed to the right-to-carry law are not arising because I have accidentally left out some other factor.

12 *Can we compare counties with discretionary and nondiscretionary concealed-handgun laws?*

> Many counties with very permissive permit systems can be found in states with no shall-issue laws, such as Louisiana and California. For example, in El Dorado county in California, 1,289 concealed-carry permits were issued in 1995. With a population of 148,600, this implies that 0.87 percent of this county's population received concealed-carry permits in one year alone. In contrast, a total of 186,000 people in Florida had concealed-carry permits in 1996 out of a total state population of 13,958,000; that is, 1.33 percent of the population was licensed to carry concealed [guns]. Yet under [the] classification scheme used in most of their results, El Dorado county would not be classified as shall-issue, while every county in Florida would be so classified. (Jens Ludwig, "Permissive Concealed-Carry Laws," pp. 20–21.)

The simplest question that we are asking is, What happens to the crime rate when nondiscretionary laws are passed allowing law-abiding citizens to carry concealed handguns? The key here is the *change* in the leniency of the laws. The regressions have individual variables for each county that allow us to account for differences in the mean crime rate. The purpose of all the other variables is to explain why crime rates differ from this average. Under discretionary laws some counties are extremely liberal in granting permits—essentially behaving as if they had nondiscretionary laws. In the regressions, differences between counties with discretionary laws (including differences in how liberally they issued concealed-handgun permits) are already being partly "picked up" by these individual county variables. For my test to work, it is only necessary for nondiscretionary laws *on average* to increase the number of concealed-handgun permits.

True, the amount of change in the number of permits does vary across counties. As this book has documented, law officials in discretionary states across the country have said that the more rural counties with relatively low populations were much more liberal in granting permits under discretionary laws. Since no usable statistics are available regarding how easily permits are granted, I tested whether nondiscretionary laws changed the crime rates the most in counties with the largest or densest populations. The results confirmed that this was the case (see figure 4.1).

We also tried another approach to deal with this question. A few states did keep good records on the number of concealed-handgun permits issued at either the county or the state level. We reported earlier the results for Pennsylvania and Oregon (see tables 5.4 and 5.5 in chapter 5). Despite the small samples, we accounted for all the variables controlled for in the larger regressions, and the results confirmed that murder rates decline as the number of a permits issued in a county rises.

13 *Should changes in the arrest rate be accounted for when explaining changes in the crime rate?*

> The use of arrest rates as an explanatory variable is itself quite problematic. . . . Since the arrest rate is calculated as the number of arrests for a particular crime divided by the number of crimes committed, unobserved determinants of the crime rate will by construction also influence the arrest rate. When the arrest rate is included as an explanatory variable in a regression equation, this leads to the statistical problem known as "endogeneity," or "simultaneity bias." (Jens Ludwig, "Permissive Concealed-Carry Laws," pp. 7–8)

True, there is an endogeneity "problem." However, on theoretical grounds, the inclusion of the arrest rate is highly desirable. There is strong reason to believe that crime rates depend on the probability of punishment. In addition, to exclude variables that obviously should be included in the analysis would create even more important potential bias problems. Furthermore, the endogeneity problem was dealt with in the original paper: it was precisely our awareness of that problem that led us to use two-stage least squares to estimate the set of regressions, which is the recognized method of dealing with such a problem. As reported in chapter 6, the two-stage least-squares estimate provided even stronger evidence that concealed handguns deter crime.

The simplest point to make, however, is that excluding the arrest rate does not alter the findings regarding concealed handguns. Reestimating the regressions in tables 4.1 and 4.3 for the same samples and control variables produces virtually identical results. Ironically, two of my strongest critics, Dan Black and Dan Nagin, also tried excluding the arrest rates, and they admitted in early drafts of their paper that their results agreed with ours: "The inclusion of the arrest-rate variable has very little impact on the coefficient estimates of the right-to-carry laws."[29]

14 *Are the graphs in this book misleading?*

> Lott rebuts many of the criticisms of his study by pointing to his simple but misleading graphs. The graphs are visually compelling yet very deceptive. What is not obvious to the casual observer of the graphs is that each data point represents an aggregate average for states that liberalized their gun-carrying laws, but the states that make up the average are not the same each year. Lott examined 10 states he claims adopted "shall-issue" concealed-gun-carrying laws during his sample period. For many of the states studied, data were available for only one to three years after the laws were implemented. (Webster, "Flawed")

The graphs presented in the paper do indeed represent the average changes in crime rates before and after the implementation of these laws. The graphs consistently show that violent-crime rates are rising before these laws go into effect and falling afterward. Since some states only adopted nondiscretionary, "shall-issue" laws toward the end of the sample period, it was not possible to examine all the states for the same number of years after the laws were implemented. I disagree that this is "misleading" or "deceptive." The results were by no means generated by the aggregation itself, and anybody doubting the meaning of the graph can examine the regression results. Since the regressions already control for each county's average crime rate, any changes refer to deviations from that county's average crime rate.[30]

Ian Ayres and Steven Levitt use similar graphs and find similar results when they look at the deterrent effect of Lojack antitheft devices on cars (these are radio tracking devices that can be activated by police when a car is stolen).[31] In many ways, the theoretical deterrent effect of these devices is the same as that of concealed handguns: because the device is small and easy to hide, a criminal cannot easily know whether a car has the tracking device until the police arrive.

Future studies will be able to track these changes in crime over longer periods of time because more states will have had right-to-carry laws for longer periods of time. Such studies will ultimately help to test my findings. I have used all the data that was available at the time that David Mustard and I put this data set together. With 54,000 observations and hundreds of variables available over the 1977 to 1994 period, it is also by far the largest data set that has ever been put together for any study of crime, let alone for the study of gun control.[32] I find it ironic that my study is attacked for not having enough data when these same researchers have praised previous studies that relied on much shorter time periods for a single state or a few counties. For example, Mr. Webster expresses no such criticism when referring to a study conducted by the University of Maryland. Yet that study analyzed merely five counties and covered a shorter period of time after the law was enacted.[33]

15 *Should concealed-handgun laws have differential effects on the murder rates of youths and adults?*

Ludwig points out that in many states only adults may carry concealed weapons. So, according to Lott's deterrence theory, adults should be safer than young people. But this hasn't happened, Ludwig says. (Kathleen Schalch describing Jens Ludwig's arguments on *Morning Edition,* National Public Radio, 10:00 A.M. ET Tuesday, December 10, 1996.)

As noted in chapter 4, I tested the hypothesis that murder rates would be lower for adults than for adolescents under nondiscretionary concealed-handgun laws, and reported the results in the original paper. However, the results did not bear out this possibility. Concealed-handgun laws reduce murder rates for both adults and for adolescents. One explanation may simply be that young people also benefited from the carrying of concealed handguns by adults. Several plausible scenarios may explain this.

First, criminals may well tend to leave an area where law-abiding adults carry concealed handguns, and since all age groups live in the same neighborhood, this lowers crime rates for all population groups. Second, when gun-carrying adults are physically present, they may able to protect some youngsters in threatening situations.

Could some other factor be lowering the juvenile murder rate—something that is unrelated to concealed handguns? Perhaps, despite all the factors accounted for, the results of any research may be affected by unknown factors. But it is wrong to conclude, as Ludwig does, that "these findings are not consistent with the hypothesis that shall-issue laws decrease crime through a deterrence effect."[34]

16 *Are changes in the characteristics of victims consistent with the theory?*

> Lott and Mustard offer data on the character of victims in homicide cases. They report (astonishingly) that the proportion of stranger killings increases following the enactment of right-to-carry laws, while the proportion of intrafamily killings declines. That right-to-carry laws deter intrafamily homicides more than they deter stranger homicides is inconceivable. (Albert W. Alschuler, "Two Guns, Four Guns, Six Guns, More: Does Arming the Public Reduce Crime?" *Valparaiso University Law Review* 31 (1997): 369)

> Josh Sugarmann of the Violence Policy Center noted that most murders are committed by people who know each other. "Concealed-weapons laws are not passed to protect people from people they know," Sugarmann said. (Doug Finke, "Sides Stick to Their Guns, Concealed-Carry Bill Set for Showdown in General Assembly," *Springfield State Journal-Register,* March 31, 1997, p. 1)

As noted in the first chapter, the category of acquaintance murder is extremely broad (encompassing shootings of cab drivers, gang members, drug dealers or buyers, and prostitutes or their clients). For the Chicago data that we discussed, the number of acquaintance murders involving friends was actually only a small percentage of the total number of acquaintance murders. If the breakdown found for Chicago provides even the remotest proxy for the national data, it is not particularly surprising that the relative share of acquaintance murders involving friends should rise, because we expect that many of the murders in this category are unlikely to be affected by law-abiding citizens carrying concealed handguns. Family members may also find that concealed handguns protect them from other estranged family members. A wife seeking a divorce may find that a concealed handgun provides her protection against a husband who is unwilling to let go of the relationship, and attacks by such people do not always take place in a home. Surely there are many cases of spousal abuse where women fear for their lives and find that a handgun provides them with a significant degree of protection.

A recent case involving a woman who used a handgun to protect herself from an abusive husband created an important new legal precedent in California: for the first time, women are now allowed to use self-defense before they suffer serious blows. The *San Francisco Examiner* reported as follows:

> [Fay] Johnson, a 47-year-old mother of four, said that on July 2, 1995, she feared her 62-year-old husband, Clarence, would beat her as he always did after a weekend of drinking and hanging out with his motorcycle buddies.
>
> She had overspent her budget on supplies for a Fourth of July barbecue and didn't have dinner ready, and the house was not clean—so when she heard her husband's motorcycle pull into the driveway, she decided to take matters into her own hands.
>
> Johnson said she grabbed a loaded gun . . . [and fired,] hitting her husband five times. He survived and testified against her. She was arrested and spent 21 months in prison until her acquittal.
>
> "I regret being in jail, but I just wouldn't tolerate it anymore," said Johnson, a friendly, articulate woman who is celebrating her freedom with her children and six grandchildren. "It would have been suicide."
>
> Johnson said she had endured nearly 25 years of mental and physical abuse at the hands of her husband, whose usual form of punishment was slamming her head into a wall. The beatings got so bad, she said, that she had to be hospitalized twice and tried getting counseling until he found out and forced her to stop. She said the pressure of the abuse had culminated that fateful day.[35]

Pointing to women who use handguns to protect themselves from abusive husbands or boyfriends in no way proves that the primary effects of concealed-handgun laws will involve such uses of guns, but these cases should keep us from concluding that significant benefits for these women are "inconceivable."

With reference to Alschuler's discussion, however, two points must be made clear. First, the diverse breakdown of these groupings makes it difficult to predict on theoretical grounds how the number of murders among family members, acquaintances, strangers, or unknown cases should necessarily change relative to each other. Second, as Alschuler himself has noted, these estimates are suggestive; they are not statistically significant, in that we cannot say with much certainty how concealed-handgun laws have affected the proportions of victims across the categories mentioned above.

An additional response should be made to Sugarmann's claims. Even if one accepts the claim that nondiscretionary concealed-handgun laws do not reduce the number of murders against people who know each other (and I do not concede this), what about other types of murders, such as those arising from street robbery? For Chicago during the period from 1990 to 1995, 16 percent of all murders involved nonacquaintance robbery. Moreover, one must ask about nonfriend acquaintance murders (excluding prostitution, gang, and drug cases), murders by complete strangers, and at least some of those murders still classified as mysteries (an additional 22 to 46 percent of all murders). Since permitted handguns are virtually never used in crimes against others and they do not produce accidental deaths, should not the reduction of these other types of murders still be deemed important?[36]

17 *Do nondiscretionary concealed-handgun laws only affect crimes that occur in public places?*

> Handguns were freely available for home and business use in all the "shall-issue" jurisdictions prior to the new laws. The new carrying privilege would thus not affect home or business self-defense but should have most of its preventive impact on street crime and offenses occurring in other public places. But the study contains no qualitative analysis of different patterns within crime categories to corroborate the right-to-carry prevention hypothesis. (Zimring and Hawkins, "Counterfeit Deterrent," p. 54)

Contrary to the claim of Zimring and Hawkins, concealed handguns may very well affect crime in homes and businesses in several ways. First, being allowed to carry a concealed gun outside is likely to increase the number of guns owned by law-abiding citizens. Since these guns will be kept at least part of the time in the home, this should have a deterrent effect on crimes committed at home and also at one's business. Second, as some of the evidence suggests, nondiscretionary laws could even increase the number of crimes that occur in the home as criminals turn away from other crimes, like street robbery, for which the risks that criminals face have gone up.

These two effects would thus work in opposite directions. Finally, to the extent that nondiscretionary handgun laws drive criminals out of a certain geographical area, rates for all types of crimes could fall.

Aggregation of the crime categories makes it difficult to separate all the different substitution effects. Still, the results presented here are very consistent with the two primary dimensions that we focused on: whether there is contact between the criminal and the victim, and whether the crime occurs where law-abiding citizens could already legally carry a gun.

18 Is it reasonable to make comparisons across states?

> The sort of state that passes a "shall-issue" law in the 1980s is apt to be the same kind of place where ordinary citizens carrying concealed firearms might not be regarded as a major problem even before the law changed. . . . Idaho is not the same sort of place that New York is, and there seem to be systematic differences between states that change standards for concealed weapons and those that do not. (Zimring and Hawkins, "Counterfeit Deterrent," pp. 50–51)

The observed drop in crime rates in states that have enacted nondiscretionary concealed-handgun laws does not by itself imply that we will observe the same effect in other states that adopt such laws later. Several different issues arise here. First, the regressions used in this book have attempted to control for many differences that can explain the level of crime (for example, income, poverty, unemployment, population and population density, demographic characteristics, law enforcement, other gun laws). Admittedly, even my long list of variables does not pick up all the differences between states, which is the reason that a variable is added for each county or state to pick up the average differences in crime rates across places. Individual time trends are also allowed for each state.

Yet despite all these attempts to control for variables, some caution is still in order—especially when dealing with areas that are particularly extreme along dimensions that do not have obvious counterparts in areas with nondiscretionary laws. One obvious example would be New York City. While the regression results show that areas with the largest and most dense populations gain the most from nondiscretionary laws, there is always the possibility that the relationship changes for values of population and density that are different from those in places where we have been able to study the effects of these laws. To date, the fourth and fifth largest cities in the country have passed nondiscretionary laws (Houston and

Philadelphia), and additional experience with large cities may help determine whether these laws would be equally useful in a city like New York. If one were skeptical about the effects in large cities, the laws should first be changed in Los Angeles and Chicago.

A second issue is whether there is something unique about states that have adopted nondiscretionary laws, and whether that characteristic caused them not only to adopt the laws but also reduced the potential problems resulting from adoption. For example, if local legislators in a few states had special information confirming that the citizens in their state were uniquely trustworthy with regard to concealed handguns, that might have led these few states to pass the laws and have little difficulty with them. It could then "falsely" appear that nondiscretionary laws are generally successful. Such an argument may have been plausible at one time, but its force has declined as larger and more varied areas have been covered by these laws. Equally important is the fact that not all jurisdictions have willingly adopted these laws. Many urban areas, such as Atlanta and Philadelphia, fought strongly against them, but lost out to coalitions of rural and suburban representatives. Philadelphia's opposition was so strong that when Pennsylvania's nondiscretionary law was first passed, Philadelphia was partially exempted.

19 *Does my discussion provide a "theory" linking concealed-handgun ownership to reductions in crime? Do the data allow me to link the passage of these laws with the reduction in crime?*

> Two idiosyncratic aspects of the Lott and Mustard analysis deserve special mention. . . . In the first place, there is very little in the way of explicit theory advanced to explain where and when right-to-carry laws should operate as deterrents to the types of crime that can be frustrated by citizens carrying concealed handguns. . . . They have no data to measure the critical intermediate steps between passing the legislation and reductions in crime rates. This is the second important failing . . . that is not a recurrent feature in econometric studies. (Zimring and Hawkins, "Counterfeit Deterrent," pp. 52, 54)

This set of complaints is difficult to understand. The theory is obvious: A would-be criminal act is deterred by the risk of being shot. Many different tests described in this book support this theory. Not only does the drop in crime begin when nondiscretionary laws are adopted, but the extent of the decline is related to the number of permits issued in a state. Nondiscretionary laws reduce crime the most in areas with the greatest increases in the number of permits. As expected, crimes that involve criminals and victims in direct contact and crimes occurring in places where the victim was previously unable to carry a gun are the ones that consistently decrease the most.

20 *What can we infer about causality?*

Anyone who has taken a course in logical thinking has been exposed to the fallacy of arguing that because A happened (in this case, passage of a concealed-weapon law) and then B happened (the slowing of the rate of violent crime), A must surely have caused B. You can speculate that the passage of concealed-gun legislation caused a subsequent slowing of the rate of violent crime in various states, but you certainly can't prove it, despite the repeated claims that a University of Chicago law professor's "study" has offered "definitive scholarly proof." (Harold W. Andersen, "Gun Study Akin to Numbers Game," *Omaha World Herald,* April 3, 1997, p. 15)

An obvious danger arises in inferring causality because two events may coincide in time simply by chance, or some unknown factor may be the cause of both events. Random chance is a frequent concern with pure time-series data when there is just one change in a law. It is not hard to believe that when one is examining a single state, unrelated events A and B just happened to occur at the same time. Yet the data examined here involve many different states that changed their laws in many different years. The odds that one might falsely attribute the changes in the crime rate to changes in the concealed-handgun laws decline as one examines more experiences. The measures of statistical significance are in fact designed to tell us the likelihood that two events may have occurred randomly together.

The more serious possibility is that some other factor may have caused both the reduction in crime rates and the passage of the law to occur at the same time. For example, concern over crime might result in the passage of both concealed-handgun laws and tougher law-enforcement measures. Thus, if the arrest rate rose at the same time that the concealed-handgun law passed, not accounting for changes in the arrest rate might result in falsely attributing some of the reduction in crime rates to the concealed-handgun law. For a critic to attack the paper, the correct approach would have been to state what variables were not included in the analysis. Indeed, it is possible that the regressions do not control for some important factor. However, this study uses the most comprehensive set of control variables yet used in a study of crime, let alone any previous study on gun control. As noted in the introduction, the vast majority of gun-control studies do not take any other factors that may influence crime into account, and no previous study has included such variables as the arrest or conviction rate or sentence length.

Other pieces of evidence also help to tie together cause and effect. For example, the adoption of nondiscretionary concealed-handgun laws has not produced equal effects in all counties in a state. Since counties with easily identifiable characteristics (such as rural location and small population) tended to be much more liberal in granting permits prior to the change in the law, we would expect them to experience the smallest changes in crime rates, and this is in fact what we observe. States that were expected to issue the greatest number of new permits and did so after passing nondiscretionary laws observed the largest declines in crime. We know that the number of concealed-handgun permits in a state rises over time, so we expect to see a greater reduction in crime after a nondiscretionary law has been in effect for several years than right after it has passed. Again, this is what we observe. Finally, where data on the actual number of permits at the county level are available, we find that the number of murders declines as the number of permits increases.

The notion of statistical significance and the number of different specifications examined in this book are also important. Even if a relationship is false, it might be possible to find a few specifications out of a hundred that show a statistically significant relationship. Here we have presented over a thousand specifications that together provide an extremely consistent and statistically significant pattern about the relationship between nondiscretionary concealed-handgun laws and crime.

21 *Concerns about the arrest rates due to missing observations*

To control for variation in the probability of apprehension, the [Lott and Mustard] model specification includes the arrest ratio, which is the number of arrests per reported crime. Our replication analysis shows that the inclusion of this variable materially affects the size and composition of the estimation data set. Specifically, division by zero forces all counties with no reported crimes of a particular type in a given year to be dropped from the sample for that year. [Lott's and Mustard's] sample contains all counties, regardless of size, and this problem of dropping counties with no reported crimes is particularly severe in small counties with few crimes.

The frequencies of missing data are 46.6% for homicide, 30.5% for rape, 12.2% for aggravated assault, and 29.5% for robbery. Thus, the [Lott and Mustard] model excludes observations based on the realization of the dependent variable, potentially creating a substantial selection bias. Our strategy for finessing the missing data problem is to analyze only counties maintaining populations of at least 100,000 during the period 1977 to 1992. . . . Compared to the sample [comprising] all counties, the missing data rate in the large-county sample is low: 3.82% for homicide, 1.08% for rape, 1.18% for assault, and 1.09% for robberies. (Dan Black and Daniel Nagin, "Do 'Right-to-Carry' Laws Deter Violent Crime?" *Journal of Legal Studies* 27 [January 1998], forthcoming)

The arguments made by Black and Nagin have changed over time, and some of their statements are not consistent.[37] In part because of the public nature of their attacks, I have tried to deal with all of the different attacks, so that those who have heard them may hear my responses. The problem described immediately above by Black and Nagin is indeed something one should be concerned about, but I had already dealt with the problem of missing observations in the original paper, and I discuss it again here at the end of chapter 6. My original paper and chapter 4 also reported the results when the arrest rate was removed entirely from the regressions. The discussion by Black and Nagin exaggerates the extent of the problem and, depending on the crime category being examined, quite amazingly proposes to solve the missing data problem by throwing out data for between 77 and 87 percent of the counties.

Black and Nagin present a very misleading picture of the trade-offs involved with the solution that examined the more populous counties.[38] The relevant comparison is between weighted numbers of missing observations, not the total number of missing observations, since the regressions are weighted by county population and the missing observations tend to be from relatively small counties, which are given a smaller weight.[39] When this is done, the benefits obtained by excluding all counties with fewer than 100,000 people become much more questionable. The most extreme case is for aggravated assault, where Black and Nagin eliminate 86 percent of the sample (a 29 percent drop in the weighted frequency) in order to reduce weighted missing values from 2.8 to 1.5 percent. Even for murder, 77 percent of the sample is dropped, so that the weighted missing data declines from 11.7 to 1.9 percent. The rape and robbery categories lie between these two cases, both in terms of the number of counties with fewer than 100,000 people and in terms of the change in the amount of weighted missing data.[40]

Why they choose to emphasize the cut-off that they did is neither explained nor obvious. The current cost-benefit ratio is rather lopsided. For example, eliminating counties with fewer than 20,000 people would have removed 70 percent of the missing arrest ratios for murder and lost only 20 percent of the observations (the weighted frequencies are 23 and 6 percent respectively). There is nothing wrong with seeing whether the estimates provide the same results over counties of various sizes, but if that is their true motivation for excluding portions of the data, it should be clearly stated.

Despite ignoring all these observations, it is only when they *also* remove the data for Florida that they weaken my results for murder and rape (though the results for aggravated assault and robbery are even larger and more statistically significant). Only eighty-six counties with more than 100,000 people adopted nondiscretionary concealed-handgun laws between 1977 and 1992, and twenty of these counties are in Florida. Yet after all this exclusion of data, Black and Nagin still find no evidence that allowing law-abiding citizens to carry concealed handguns increases crime, and two violent-crime categories show a statistically significant drop in crime. The difference between their approach and mine is rather stark: I did not select which observations to include; I used all the data for all the counties over the entire period for which observations were available. When updated data have been available, they have all been used.

22 *What can we learn about the deterrent effect of concealed handguns from this study?*

> The regression study [that Lott and Mustard] report is an all-or-nothing proposition as far as knowledge of legal impact is concerned. If the model is wrong, if their bottom-line estimates of impact cannot withstand scrutiny, there is no intermediate knowledge of the law's effects on behavior that can help us sort out the manifold effects of such legislation. As soon as we find flaws in the major conclusions, the regression analyses tell us nothing. What we know from this study about the effects of "shall-carry" laws is, therefore, nothing at all. (Zimring and Hawkins, "Counterfeit Deterrent," p. 59)

Academics can reasonably differ about what factors account for changes in crime. Sociologists and criminologists, for example, have examined gun control without trying to control for changes in arrest or conviction rates. Others might be particularly concerned about the impact of drugs on crime. Economists such as myself try to include measures of deterrence, though I am also sympathetic to other concerns. In this book and my other research, my approach has not been to say that only one set of variables or even one specification can explain the crime rate. My attitude has been that if someone believes that a variable is important and has any plausible reason for including it, I have made an effort to include it. This book reports many different approaches and specifications—all of which support the conclusion that allowing law-abiding citizens to carry concealed handguns reduces crime. With each update of this research, I believe that no other study on crime has used as extensive a data set as used here.

23 Summarizing the concerns about the evidence that concealed-handgun laws deter crime

The gun lobby claims to have a new weapon in its arsenal this year—a study by economist John Lott. But the Lott study shoots blanks. In reviewing Lott's research and methodology, Carnegie-Mellon University Profs. Daniel Nagin and Dan Black, and Georgetown University's Prof. Jens Ludwig corrected for the many fatal flaws in Lott's original analysis and found no evidence of his claim that easing restrictions on carrying concealed handguns leads to a decrease in violent crime. Nagin, Black, and Ludwig recently concluded in a televised debate with Lott that "there is absolutely no credible evidence to support the idea that permissive concealed-carry laws reduce violent crime," and that "it would be a mistake to formulate policy based on the findings from Dr. Lott's study." (James Brady, "Concealed Handguns; Putting More Guns on Streets Won't Make America Safer," *Minneapolis Star Tribune,* March 21, 1997, p. 21A)

Unlike the authors of past papers on gun control such as Arthur Kellermann and the authors of the 1995 University of Maryland study, I immediately made my data available to all academics who requested it.[41] To date, my data have been supplied to academics at twenty-four universities, including Harvard, Stanford, the University of Pennsylvania, Emory, Vanderbilt, Louisiana State, Michigan State, Florida State, the University of Texas, the University of Houston, the University of Maryland, Georgetown, and the College of William and Mary.

James Brady's op-ed piece ignores the fact that some of these academics from Vanderbilt, Emory, and Texas paid their own way to attend the December 9, 1996, debate sponsored by his organization—Handgun Control. While Handgun Control insisted on rules that did not allow these academics to participate, I am sure that they would have spoken out to support the integrity of my original study.

Those who have attempted to replicate the findings in the original *Journal of Legal Studies* paper have been able to do so, and many have gone beyond this to provide additional support for the basic findings. For example, economists at Vanderbilt University have estimated over 10,000 regressions attempting to see whether the deterrent effects of nondiscretionary laws are at all sensitive to all possible combinations of the various data sets on demographics, income, population, arrest rates, and so on. Their results are quite consistent with those reported in this book.[42]

I have tried in this chapter to examine the critiques leveled against my work. In many cases, the concerns they describe were addressed in the original paper. In others, I believe that relatively simple responses exist to the complaints. However, even taking these critics at their worst, I still believe that a comment that I made at the December 9 discussion sponsored by Handgun Control still holds:

> Six months ago, who would have thought that Handgun Control would be rushing out studies to argue that allowing law-abiding citizens to carry concealed handguns would have no effect, or might have a delayed impact, in terms of dropping crimes? (*Morning Edition,* National Public Radio, 10:00 A.M. ET, December 10, 1996.

8 | Some Final Thoughts (1998)

As more than 30 diners sat in Sam's St. John's Seafood [in Jacksonville, Florida] about 7:20 P.M., a masked man entered the eatery and ordered everyone to the floor, said co-owner Sam Bajalia. The man grabbed waitress Amy Norton from where she and another waitress were huddled on the floor and tried to get her to open the cash register.

At that point, [Oscar] Moore stood up and shot him. Another diner . . . pulled out a .22-caliber derringer and fired at the man as he ran out of the restaurant. At least one shot hit the fleeing robber.

[The robber was later arrested when he sought medical care for his wound.] . . .

"I'm glad they were here because if that girl couldn't open the register, and he didn't get [any] money, he might have started shooting," Bajalia said.[1]

[It was] 1:30 A.M. when Angelic Nichole Hite, 26, the night manager, and Victoria Elizabeth Shaver, 20, the assistant manager at the Pizza Hut at 4450 Creedmoor Road, were leaving the restaurant with Marty Lee Hite, 39, the manager's husband. He had come to pick her up after work.

They saw a man wearing a ski mask, dark clothes, gloves, and holding a pistol walking toward them, and the Hites ran back inside the restaurant. Shaver apparently had reached her car already. . . . The couple couldn't close the door behind them because the robber ran up and wedged the barrel of his handgun in the opening. As they struggled to get the door closed, . . . the masked man twice said he would kill them if they didn't open it.

Marty Hite, who carried a .38-caliber handgun, pulled

out his weapon and fired three times through the opening, striking the robber in the abdomen and upper chest. The would-be bandit staggered away, and the Hites locked the door and called police.

The Wake County district attorney will review the shooting, but Raleigh police did not file charges against the manager's husband. Police said it appeared the couple retreated as far as they could and feared for their lives, which would make it a justified shooting.[2]

Many factors influence crime, with arrest and conviction rates being the most important. However, nondiscretionary concealed-handgun laws are also important, and they are the most cost-effective means of reducing crime. The cost of hiring more police in order to change arrest and conviction rates is much higher, and the net benefits per dollar spent are only at most a quarter as large as the benefits from concealed-handgun laws.[3] Even private, medium-security prisons cost state governments about $34 a day per prisoner ($12,267 per year).[4] For concealed handguns, the permit fees are usually the largest costs borne by private citizens. The durability of guns allows owners to recoup their investments over many years. Using my yearly cost estimate of $43 per concealed handgun for Pennsylvanians, concealed handguns pay for themselves if they have only 1/285 of the deterrent impact of an additional year in prison. This calculation even ignores the other costs of the legal system, such as prosecution and defense costs—criminals will expend greater effort to fight longer prison sentences in court. No other government policy appears to have anywhere near the same cost-benefit ratio as concealed-handgun laws.

Allowing citizens without criminal records or histories of significant mental illness to carry concealed handguns deters violent crimes and appears to produce an extremely small and statistically insignificant change in accidental deaths. If the rest of the country had adopted right-to-carry concealed-handgun provisions in 1992, about 1,500 murders and 4,000 rapes would have been avoided. On the other hand, consistent with the notion that criminals respond to incentives, county-level data provide some evidence that concealed-handgun laws are associated with increases in property crimes involving stealth and in crimes that involve minimal probability of contact between the criminal and the victim. Even though both the state-level data and the estimates that attempt to explain why the law and the arrest rates change indicate that crime in all the categories declines, the deterrent effect of nondiscretionary handgun laws is largest for violent crimes. Counties with the largest populations, where the deterrence of violent crimes is the greatest, are also the counties where the substitution of property crimes for violent crimes by criminals is the highest. The estimated annual gain in 1992 from allowing concealed handguns was over $5.74 billion.

Many commonly accepted notions are challenged by these findings. Urban areas tend to have the most restrictive gun-control rules and have fought the hardest against nondiscretionary concealed-handgun laws, yet they are the very places that benefit the most from nondiscretionary concealed-handgun laws. Not only do urban areas tend to gain in their fight against crime, but reductions in crime rates are greatest precisely in those urban areas that have the highest crime rates, largest and most dense populations, and greatest concentrations of minorities. To some this might not be too surprising. After all, law-abiding citizens in these areas must depend on themselves to a great extent for protection. Even if self-protection were accepted, concerns would still arise over whether these law-abiding citizens would use guns properly. This study provides a very strong answer: a few people do and will use permitted concealed handguns improperly, but the gains completely overwhelm these concerns.

Another surprise involves women and blacks. Both tend to be the strongest supporters of gun control, yet both obtain the largest benefits from nondiscretionary concealed-handgun laws in terms of reduced rates of murder and other crimes. Concealed handguns also appear to be the great equalizer among the sexes. Murder rates decline when either more women or more men carry concealed handguns, but the effect is especially pronounced for women. An additional woman carrying a concealed handgun reduces the murder rate for women by about three to four times more than an additional man carrying a concealed handgun reduces the murder rate for men. Providing a woman with a concealed handgun represents a much larger change in her ability to defend herself than it does for a man.

The benefits of concealed handguns are not limited to those who use them in self-defense. Because the guns may be concealed, criminals are unable to tell whether potential victims are carrying guns until they attack, thus making it less attractive for criminals to commit crimes that involve direct contact with victims. Citizens who have no intention of ever carrying concealed handguns in a sense get a "free ride" from the crime-fighting efforts of their fellow citizens. However, the "halo" effect created by these laws is apparently not limited to people who share the characteristics of those who carry the guns. The most obvious example is the drop in murders of children following the adoption of nondiscretionary laws. Arming older people not only may provide direct protection to these children, but also causes criminals to leave the area.

Nor is the "halo" effect limited to those who live in areas where people are allowed to carry guns. The violent-crime reduction from one's own state's adopting the law is in fact greatest when neighboring states also allow law-abiding citizens to carry concealed handguns. The evidence also indicates that the states with the most guns have the lowest crime rates. Urban areas may experience the most violent crime, but they also have the smallest number of guns. Blacks may be the racial group most vulnerable to violent crime, but they are also much less likely than whites to own guns.

These estimates make one wonder about all the attention given to other types of gun legislation. My estimates indicate that waiting periods and background checks appear to produce little if any crime deterrence. During the 1990s former president Clinton credited the Brady law with lowering crime because it had, according to him, been "taking guns out of the hands of criminals."[5] During the 1996 Democratic National Convention, Sarah Brady, after whose husband the bill was named, boasted that it "has helped keep more than 100,000 felons and other prohibited purchasers from buying handguns."[6] From 1994 until the Supreme Court's decision in 1997, backers of the Brady law focused almost exclusively on the value of background checks, the one part of the law that the Supreme Court specifically struck down.[7]

Actually, the downward crime trend started in 1991, well before the Brady law became effective in March 1994. With a national law that goes into effect only once, it is difficult to prove empirically that the law was what altered crime rates, because so many other events are likely to have occurred at that same time. One of the major advantages of the large data set examined in this book is that it includes data from many different states that have adopted nondiscretionary laws in many different years.

Others estimate a much smaller effect of the Brady law on gun sales. In 1996 the General Accounting Office reported that initial rejections based on background checks numbered about 60,000, of which over half were for purely technical reasons, mostly paperwork errors that were eventually corrected.[8] A much smaller number of rejections, 3,000, was due to convictions for violent crimes, and undoubtedly many of the people rejected proceeded to buy guns on the street. By the time the background-check provision was found unconstitutional, in June 1997, only four people had gone to jail for violations.

Presumably, no one would argue that rejected permits are meaningful by themselves. They merely proxy for what might happen to crime rates, provided that the law really stops criminals from getting guns. Do criminals simply get them from other sources? Or do the restrictions primarily inconvenience law-abiding citizens who want guns for self-defense? The results presented in this book are the first systematic national look at such gun laws, and if the national *Uniform Crime Report* data through 1994 or state waiting periods and background checks are any indication, the empirical evidence does not bode well for the Brady law. No statistically significant evidence has appeared that the Brady law has reduced crime, and there is some statistically significant evidence that rates for rape and aggravated assault have actually risen by about 4 percent relative to what they would have been without the law.

Yet research does not convince everybody. Perhaps the Supreme Court's June 1997 decision on the constitutionality of the Brady law's national background checks will shed light on how effective the Brady law was. The point of making the scope of the background check *national* was that without it, criminals would buy guns from jurisdictions without the checks and use them to commit crimes in the rest of the country. As these national standards are eliminated, and states and local jurisdictions discontinue their background checks,[9] will crime rates rise as quickly without this provision of the law as gun-control advocates claimed they fell because of it? My bet is no, they will not. If President Clinton and gun-control advocates are correct, a new crime wave should be evident by the time this book is published.

Since 1994, aside from required waiting periods, many new rules making gun ownership by law-abiding citizens more difficult have come into existence. There were 279,401 active, federal gun-dealer licenses in the nation when the new licensing regulations went fully into effect in April 1994. By 2000 there were 100,000, a decline of 64 percent, and by September 2009 it had fallen to 50,630.[10] This has undoubtedly made purchasing guns less convenient. Besides increasing licensing fees from $30 to $200 for first-time licenses and imposing renewal fees of $90, the 1994 Violent Crime Control and Law Enforcement Act imposed significant new regulatory requirements that were probably much more important in reducing the number of licensees.[11]

The Bureau of Alcohol, Tobacco, and Firearms (BATF) supports this decrease largely because it believes that it affects federal license holders who are illegally selling guns. The BATF's own (undoubtedly high) estimate is that about 1 percent of federal license holders illegally sell guns, and that this percentage has remained constant with the decline in licensed dealers.[12] If so, 155,115 licensees have lost their licenses in order to eliminate 1,551 illegal traffickers. Whether this lopsided trade-off justifies stiffer federal regulation is unclear, but other than simply pointing to the fact that crime continued on its downward course nationally during this period, no evidence has been offered. No attempt has been made to isolate this effect from many other changes that occurred over the same period of time.[13]

Changes in the law will also continue to have an impact. Proposals are being made by the U.S. Department of Justice to "require owners of firearms 'arsenals' to provide notice to law enforcement," where the definition of what constitutes an "arsenal" seems to be fairly subjective, and to "require gun owners to record the make, model, and serial number of their firearms as a condition of obtaining gun insurance." Other proposals would essentially make it impossible for private individuals to transfer firearms among themselves.

What implications does this study have for banning guns altogether? This book has not examined evidence on what the crime rate would be if all guns could be eliminated from society—no data were present in the data set for areas where guns were completely absent for any period of time, but the findings do suggest how costly the transition to that gun-free goal would be. If outlawing guns would primarily affect their ownership by law-abiding citizens, this research indicates that at least in the short run, we would expect crime rates to rise. The discussion is very similar to the debate over nuclear disarmament. A world without nuclear weapons might be better off, but unilateral disarmament may not be the best way to accomplish that goal. The large stock of guns in the United States, as well as the ease with which illegal items such as drugs find their way across borders implies that not only might the transition to a gun-free world be costly (if not impossible), but the transition might also take a long time.

Further, not everyone will benefit equally from the abolition of guns. For example, criminals will still maintain a large strength advantage over many of their victims (such as women and the elderly). To the extent that guns are an equalizer, their elimination will strengthen criminals relative to physically weak victims. As we have seen in discussing international crime data, eliminating guns alters criminals' behavior in other ways, such as reducing their fear of breaking into homes while the residents are there.

All these discussions, of course, ignore the issues that led the founding fathers to put the Second Amendment in the Constitution in the first place—important issues that are beyond the scope of this book.[14] They believed that an armed citizenry is the ultimate bulwark against tyrannical government. Possibly our trust in government has risen so much that we no longer fear what future governments might do. Having just fought a war for their independence against a government that had tried to confiscate their guns, the founding fathers felt very strongly about this issue.

What Can We Conclude?

How much confidence do I have in these results? The largest previous study on gun control produced findings similar to those reported here but examined only 170 cities within a single year. This book has examined over 54,000 observations (across 3,000 counties for eighteen years) and has controlled for a range of other factors never accounted for in previous crime studies. I have attempted to answer numerous questions. For example, do higher arrest or conviction rates reduce crime? What about changes in other handgun laws, such as penalizing the use of a gun in the commission of a crime, or the well-known waiting periods? Do income, poverty, unemployment, drug prices, or demographic changes matter? All these factors were found to influence crime rates, but no previous gun study had accounted for changing criminal penalties, and this study is the first to look at more than a few of any of these other considerations.

Preventing law-abiding citizens from carrying handguns does not end violence; it merely makes victims more vulnerable to attack. While people have strong views on either side of this debate, and one study is unlikely to end this discussion, the size and strength of my deterrence results and the lack of evidence that holders of permits for concealed handguns commit crimes should at least give pause to those who oppose concealed handguns. In the final analysis, one concern unites us all: Will allowing law-abiding citizens to carry concealed handguns save lives? The answer is yes, it will.

9 | Updating the Results in 2000

Updating the Basic Results

I started this research several years ago with data from 1977 to 1992, all the county data that were available at that time. When the book was first published, I had updated the data through 1994. It is now possible to expand the data even further, through 1996. This is quite important, since so many states very recently have passed right-to-carry laws. During 1994, Alaska, Arizona, Tennessee, and Wyoming enacted new right-to-carry laws, and during 1995, Arkansas, Nevada, North Carolina, Oklahoma, Texas, and Utah followed suit.[1] Between 1977 and 1996 a total of twenty states had changed their laws and had them in effect for at least one full year.[2]

Some commentators complained that even though my study was by far the largest statistical crime study ever, there were simply not enough data to properly evaluate the impact of the laws. Others suspected that the findings were simply a result of studying relatively unusual states.[3] Another criticism was that poverty was not properly accounted for.[4]

While the methods I used in the 1998 edition were by far the most comprehensive that I know of, I have continued to look into other methods. By putting together an entirely new data set—using city-level information—it is possible to go beyond my previous efforts and to also control for policing-policy variables such as arrest and conviction rates, number of police per-capita, expenditures on police per capita, and a proxy for the so-called broken-windows policing policy. The city-level data that I have now compiled include direct information on whether a city has adopted community policing, problem-oriented polic- ing, and/or the broken-windows approach.

One of the commentators on my book suggested that in addition to year-to-year changes in the national crime rate as well as state and county crime trends, another way to account for crime cycles is by measuring whether the crime rates are falling faster in right-to-carry states than in other states in their region rather than compared to just the nation as a whole. While it is impossible to use a separate variable for each year for each individual state, because that would falsely appear to explain all the year-to-year changes in average crime rates in a state, it is possible to group states together. This new set of estimates would account not only for whether the crime rates in concealed-handgun states are falling relative to the national crime rate but now also for whether they are falling relative to the crime rates in their region. To do this, the country is divided into five regions (Northeast, South, Midwest, Rocky Mountains, and Pacific) and variables are added to measure the year-to-year changes in crime by region.[5] All county- and city-level regressions will employ these additional control variables.

Some have criticized my earlier work for not doing enough to account for poverty rates. As a response, I have incorporated in this section of the book state-level measures of poverty and unemployment rates in addition to all the county-level variables that accounted for these factors earlier in this book. The execution rates for murders in each state are now included in estimates to explain the murder rate. Finally, new data on the number of permits granted in different states make it easier to link crime rates to the number of permits granted.

Reviewing the Basic Results

The central question is, How did crime rates change before and after the right-to-carry laws went into effect? The test used earlier in this book ex- amined the difference in the time trends before and after the laws were enacted.[6] With the extended data and the additional variables for the year- to-year changes in crime by region (so-called regional fixed year effects), state poverty, unemployment, and death-penalty execution rates, table 9.1 shows that this pattern closely resembles the pattern found earlier in the book: violent-crime rates were rising consistently before the right-to-carry laws and falling thereafter.[7] The change in these before-and-after trends was always extremely significant—at least at the 0.1 percent level. Compared to the results for tables 4.8 or 4.13, the effects were larger for overall violent crimes, rape, robbery, and aggravated assaults and smaller for murder. For each additional year that the laws were in effect, murders fell by an additional 1.5 percent, while rape, robbery, and aggravated assaults all fell by about by 3 percent each year. The other variables continued to produce results similar to those that were found earlier.[8]

While no previous crime study accounts for year-to-year changes in regional crime rates, it is possible to go even beyond that and combine different approaches. Including not only the factors accounted for in table 9.1 but also individual state time trends produces similar results. The annual declines in crime from right-to-carry laws are greater for murder (2.2 percent), rape (3.9 percent), and robbery rates (4.9 percent), while the impact on aggravated assaults (0.8 percent) and the property-crime rates (0.9 percent) is smaller.

Figures 9.1–9.5 illustrate how the violent-crime rates vary before and after the implementation of right-to-carry laws when both the linear and squared time trends are employed. Despite expanding the data through 1996 so that the legal changes in ten additional states could be examined, the results are similar to those previously shown in figures 4.5–4.9.[9] As in the earlier results, the longer the laws are in effect, the larger the decline in violent crime. The most dramatic results are again for rape and robbery rates, which were rising before the right-to-carry law was passed and falling thereafter. Robbery rates continued rising during the first full year that the law was in effect, but the rate of increase slowed and began to fall by the second year. It is this continued increase in robbery rates which kept the violent crimes as a whole from immediately declining. While aggravated assaults were falling on average before the right-to-carry law was adopted, figure 9.5 shows that the rate of decline accelerated after the law went into effect.

What Determines the Number of Permits Issued and What Is the Net Benefit from Issuing Another Permit?

The Number of Permits

The relationship between the percentage of the population with permits and the changes in crime rates is central to much of the debate over the right to carry. My previous work was based on the number of permits

Table 9.1 Reexamining the change in time trends before and after the adoption of nondiscretionary laws, using additional data for 1995 and 1996

	Percent change in various crime rates for changes in explanatory variables							
	Violent crime	Murder	Rape	Robbery	Aggravated assault	Property crime	Burglary	Larceny	Auto theft
Change in the crime rate from the difference in the annual change in crime rates in the years before and after the adoption of the right-to-carry law (annual rate of change after the law − annual rate of change before the law)	−2.3%*	−1.5%*	−3.2%*	−2.9%*	−3.0%*	−1.6%*	−2.5%*	−0.9%*	−2.1%*

Note: This table uses county-level violent and property-crime data from the *Uniform Crime Report* that were not available when I originally wrote the book. All regressions use weighted least squares, where the weighting is each county's population. The regressions correspond to those in tables 4.8 and 4.13. The one difference from the earlier estimates is that these regressions now also allow the regional fixed effects to vary by year.

*The result is significant at the 1 percent level for a two-tailed *t*-test.

Figure 9.1. The effect of concealed-handgun laws on violent crimes

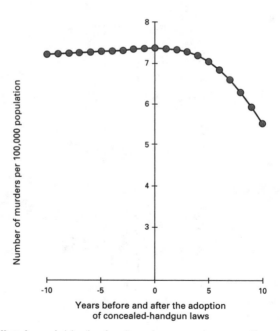

Figure 9.2. The effect of concealed-handgun laws on murders

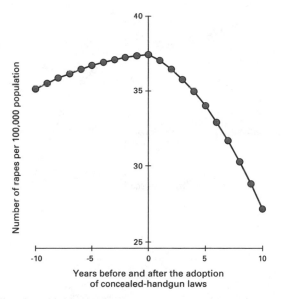

Figure 9.3. The effect of concealed-handgun laws on rapes

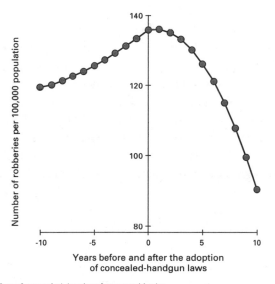

Figure 9.4. The effect of concealed-handgun laws on robberies

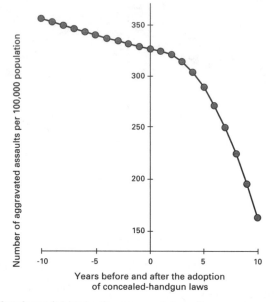

Figure 9.5. The effect of concealed-handgun laws on aggravated assaults

issued for counties in Oregon and Pennsylvania as well as on discussions with various government officials on what types of counties issued the most permits. The comparison across states assumed that what created the difference in permit rates across counties also applied across states. Some more state-level data have now become available on permit rates, but such data are still relatively scarce. In addition to Florida, Oregon, and Pennsylvania, I have also acquired some annual permit-rate data up to 1996 for Alaska, Arizona, Oklahoma, South Carolina, Texas, Utah, and Wyoming, though these states had these rules in effect for no more than a few years.

While these data are limited on the number of permit holders, they allow us to examine what factors determine permitting rates, which in turn lets us link the permitting rate to changes in crime. Permit prices, the amount of training required to get a permit, the length of time that permitting rules have been in effect, and the crime rate are all important factors in determining how many people will get permits. Permitting fees and prices charged for training courses are expected to reduce the number of permits issued, but another important cost of getting a permit is the time spent meeting the requirements. This is not to say that there are not also benefits from training (that is a separate issue), but in the narrow issue of how many permits will be issued, there is no doubt that longer training requirements discourage some people from getting permits.

What permitting rules are in place largely depends upon when the laws were first enacted. States that adopted right-to-carry laws more recently tend to have more restrictive licensing requirements. For example, the three states (Alaska, Arizona, and Texas) requiring at least ten hours of training adopted their rules during the last few years of the sample, and Arizona is the only right-to-carry state that requires additional training when permits are renewed. Six of the eight states with permitting fees of at least $100 have also enacted the law during the last few years. This raises the concern that the drops in crime from the passage of right-to-carry laws may be smaller in the states that have most recently adopted these laws simply because they have issued fewer permits.

Based on state-level data, table 9.2 shows the impact of permit fees, training requirements, and how long (in years) the law has been in effect. Because the evidence indicates that the number of new permits is likely to trail off over time, the estimates include both the number of years the law has been in effect and the number of years squared. Fees and training requirements were first investigated without square terms. Notice that only a small fraction of the population gets permits, ranging from less than 1 percent to 6 percent. With that in mind, the regression results show that for each $10 increase in fees, the population getting permits is reduced by about one half of a percentage point. And requiring five hours of training (rather than none) reduces the number of permits by about two-thirds of a percentage point. In a typical state without any fees or training requirements, the percentage of the population with permits would grow from about 3 percent to a little less than 6 percent after a decade.

I also ran more complicated specifications including squared terms for fees and training requirements. They gave similar results: fees discourage people from obtaining permits over almost the entire range (until fees go over $130, which is near the highest fee in the sample—$140 for Texas).

Table 9.2 What determines the rate at which people obtain permits?

	$10 increase in permit fee	5-hour increase in training requirement	5 years after the law has passed, assuming no fee or training requirement	10 years after the law has passed, assuming no fee or training requirement
Percentage of the state population with permits	−.5%*	−.6%*	4.8%*	6.1%*

*The result is significant at the 1 percent level for a two-tailed t-test.

Anecdotal evidence from newspapers indicates that yet another factor is important: the fear of an attack. Thus, crime and multiple-victim public shootings increase gun sales and concealed-handgun permits.[10] Other variables, such as violent-crime rates, murder rates, the number of multiple-victim public shootings, or the death rate from those attacks, are also important for determining how many people get permits, but they do not alter the impact of the previously mentioned variables. Each additional multiple-victim public shooting increases a state's number of permits by about two-tenths of a percentage point, and each additional person who is killed in such a shooting per 1 million people living in a state increases handgun permits by one-tenth of a percentage point.

The Crime Rate and the Estimated Number of Concealed Handguns

The above estimates allow us to revisit the impact of permits and crime rates. While the time-series data on permits issued in different states covers a relatively limited number of years, we do have detailed information on the factors that help determine the number of permits (the fees, training requirements, and how long the law has been in effect). The results from the specification shown in table 9.2 were used to construct "predicted values." Constructing a predicted percentage of a state's population with permits allows us to do more than relying on how crime rates change over time or on the anecdotal evidence I obtained from surveying different state permitting agencies.

These new results using state-level data, shown in table 9.3, indicate that violent-crime rates fell across the board as more permits were issued, with the largest drop occurring for robberies. These results correspond closely to the diagrams reported in figures 4.6–4.9 and 7.1–7.4, which indicate that robberies and rapes are most dramatically affected by the number of years that right-to-carry laws are in effect. The coefficients imply that for every 1,000 additional people with permits, there are 0.3 fewer murders, 2.4 fewer rapes, 21 fewer robberies, and 14.1 fewer aggravated assaults.[11] On the other hand, with the exception of burglary, property crime remained statistically unchanged as more people obtained permits.

Would society benefit from more people getting permits? As already noted, obtaining a permit costs money and takes time. Carrying around a gun is also inconvenient, and many states impose penalties if the gun does not remain concealed.[12] On the positive side, permit holders benefit from having the gun for protection and might also come to the rescue of others. But perhaps just as important are the benefits to general crime deterrence produced by concealed-carry laws, for they also help protect others indirectly, as criminals do not know which people can defend themselves until they attack. This raises the real risk that too few people will get permits, as permit holders personally bear all these costs but produce large benefits for others.

Whether too few permits are being issued depends on how the crime rate changes as more and more permits are issued and whether it is the permit holder or the general public who primarily reaps the benefit from more concealed carry.

The impact of increasing the number of permits on crime is shown in table 9.3, column 1. However, the impact does not need to be constant as more people get permits. Indeed, there may well exist what economists call "diminishing returns"—that is, the crime-reducing benefits from another person getting a permit falls as more people get permits. The reason behind this is twofold: first, those most at risk could be the first to get permits; second, once one adult in a public setting (e.g., a store) has a concealed handgun, the additional benefit from a second or third person being armed should be relatively smaller.

But it is also conceivable that the probability that a victim can defend herself must rise above a certain threshold before it does much to discourage criminals. For instance, if only a few women brandish guns, a would be rapist may believe that a defensive use is simply an exception and go after another woman. Perhaps if a large enough percentage of women defend themselves, the would-be rapist would decide that the risk to himself is too high.

One can test for diminishing returns from more permits by using a squared term for the percentage of the population with permits. The results (shown in column 2) indicate that right-to-carry states experience additional drops in all the violent-crime categories when more permits are issued. For murder, rape, and robbery, all states experience further reductions in crime from issuing more permits, though diminishing returns appear for murder and aggravated assault. (Only one state—Pennsylvania—approaches the number of permits beyond which there would be little further reduction in aggravated assaults from issuing more permits.) An important word of caution is in order here. These particular estimates of the percentage of the population that minimizes crime are rather speculative, because they represent predictions outside the range for which observed permit levels are available. (We thus cannot use these results to predict with confidence what would happen if a state got up to, say, 8 percent having permits.) Still, there is little doubt that issuing additional permits beyond what we have today lowers crime.

Table 9.3 Using the predicted percent of the population with permits to explain the changes in different crime rates for state data

	One-percentage-point change in the share of the state population with permits (1)	Pattern when a quadratic term is added for the percent of the population with permits (2)	Number by which total crimes are reduced when an additional 1 percent of the population obtains permits in 1996, using the estimates from column 1 for states that had a right-to-carry law in effect by that year (3)
Violent crime	−7%*	Drop reaches its maximum when 23% of the population has permits	
Murder	−4%****	Drop reaches its maximum when 8% of the population has permits	432 lives saved
Rape	−7%*	Drop is increasing at an increasing rate as more people get permits	3,862 fewer rapes
Robbery	−13.6%*	Drop tapers off, but so slowly that it is still falling when 100 percent of the population has permits	35,014 fewer robberies
Aggravated assault	−5%**	Drop reaches its maximum when 6 percent of the population has permits	28,562 fewer aggravated assaults
Property crime	−2.6%****	Drop continues at a constant rate	
Burglary	−10%*	Drop is increasing at an increasing rate as more people get permits	144,227 fewer burglaries
Larceny	−.6%	No significant pattern	27,922 fewer larcenies
Auto theft	−3%	Drop reaches its maximum when 3 percent of the population has permits	21,254 fewer auto thefts

Note: Using the National Institute of Justice estimates of what crime costs victims to estimate the net savings from 1 percent more of the population obtaining permits (or of each additional permit) in 1998 dollars, the cost is reduced by $3.45 billion ($2,516 per permit).

*The result is significant at the 1 percent level for a two-tailed t-test.

**The result is significant at the 5 percent level for a two-tailed t-test.

****The result is significant at the 15 percent level for a two-tailed t-test.

Chapter 5 employed county-level permit data from Oregon and Pennsylvania and used the estimated victimization costs from the National Institute of Justice to determine the net benefit to society from issuing an additional permit. Similar estimates can be made for the thirty-one states issuing permits in 1996: each one-percentage-point increase in the population obtaining permits is associated with a $3.45 billion annual net saving to crime victims (in 1998 dollars). Each additional permit produces a total societal benefit of $2,500 per year. While this estimate is smaller than my earlier figures for Oregon and Pennsylvania, the total benefits greatly exceed the total costs of getting a permit. In other words, the numbers suggest that not enough permits are being issued.

The results also indicate that permitting fees are highly detrimental. For each $10 increase in fees, the percentage of the population with permits falls by one half of one percentage point. For the thirty-one states with right-to-carry laws, this increases victimization costs by $1.7 billion. The large effect from higher permitting fees might be due to the poorest and most vulnerable being especially discouraged from obtaining a permit. Blacks living in higher-crime urban areas benefit disproportionately from concealed-handgun permits. High fees are more likely to deter individuals from carrying guns when those individuals are poor. When fees are high, there may be a smaller crime-reduction benefit from right-to-carry laws even if the same percentage of the population were to obtain permits.

To test this, I reestimated the relationship between predicted permits and crime by also including the direct impact of permit fees on the crime rate.[13] The regressions for violent crime, murder, robbery, and aggravated assault all indicate that, holding constant the percentage of the population with permits, higher fees greatly reduce the benefit from right-to-carry laws. For example, the drop in robberies from one percent of the population having permits is about two percentage points smaller when the fee is raised from $10 to $50.

Updating the Evidence on Who Benefits from Permits

While the preceding results relied on state-level data, we know from previous work (already presented in this book) that different parts of states obtained greatly varying benefits from issuing permits. This finding is confirmed with the new, updated data. But I will here discuss a somewhat different specification, linking the changes in crime more closely to the issuing of more permits. The percentage of the population with permits

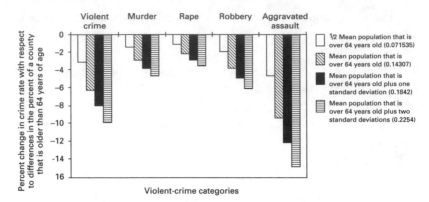

Figure 9.6. How does the change in crime from nondiscretionary concealed-handgun laws occur in counties with relatively more people over age sixty-four?

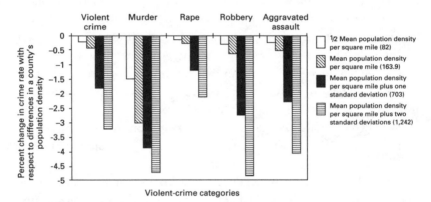

Figure 9.7. How does the change in crime from nondiscretionary concealed-handgun laws occur in the most densely populated counties?

is interacted with the percentage of the adult population in a county that is over sixty-four years of age, the population density per square mile, the percentage that is black, the percentage that is female, and per-capita personal income. The earlier interactions in chapter 4, reported with county population, are skipped over here because they again produce results that are extremely similar to the regressions with an interaction for population density.[14]

The results reported in figures 9.6–9.9 are all quite statistically significant and imply the same pattern reported earlier when using the data through 1992. The benefits of right-to-carry laws are not uniform across counties. Counties with a high portion of elderly people, blacks, and

Figure 9.8. How does the change in crime from nondiscretionary concealed-handgun laws vary with the percentage of a county's population that is black?

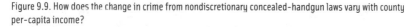

Figure 9.9. How does the change in crime from nondiscretionary concealed-handgun laws vary with county per-capita income?

females—the most vulnerable victims—all benefit disproportionately more from concealed-handgun laws. So do those living in counties that are densely populated.

Certain crime patterns do emerge. For example, in counties with many elderly people (23 percent of the population over age sixty-four) right-to-carry laws have a large deterrent effect against aggravated assaults and robberies but seem to have a relatively small effect on rapes. In contrast, counties with few elderly individuals (7 percent of their population over sixty-four years of age) have only about a third of the drop in violent crime that counties with many elderly people have. Heavily black areas benefit the most through reductions in robberies and rapes, while areas where women make up a larger share of the population and those living in the wealthiest areas obtain the largest benefits from drops in aggravated assaults and rapes. The benefit for blacks is very large. Increasing the percentage of the black population in a county from half the mean (4.4 percent) to two standard deviations above the mean (37 percent) increases the reduction in violent crime from right-to-carry laws from about one percentage point to over seven percentage points.

Unlike the earlier data presented in chapter 4, which represented crime through 1992, not all the states adopting right-to-carry laws during 1993–1996 moved from a discretionary to a nondiscretionary law. Some states had previously prohibited the carrying of concealed handguns. This is important because one of the reasons that I examined the interactions of population or population density with right-to-carry laws was that state government officials had told me that under a discretionary system lower-population counties had already tended to be more liberal in granting permits. Higher-population counties were thus expected to experience the largest increase in issuing permits and thus the largest drops in violent crime after a non-discretionary system was adopted. In fact, I find that the more populous counties in states changing from discretionary to nondiscretionary laws had a statistically bigger relative drop in violent-crime rates than states that changed from banning concealed handguns to nondiscretionary laws.

These updated results confirm my earlier findings that those who are relatively weaker physically (women and the elderly) and those who are most likely to be crime victims (blacks and those living in urban areas) tend to benefit the most from the passage of right-to-carry laws. Taken together, these results indicate that legislators should be sensitive not only to the costs of running the permitting program, but also to how the rules affect the number and types of people who get permits. Focusing only on setting fees to recoup the costs of the permitting system will end up being financially short sighted.

How Sensitive Are the Results to Different Specifications?

While I have tried to control for all sorts of factors that might explain changes in crime over time, it is indeed possible to get overzealous and account for *too many* variables. Including variables that do not really affect crime can actually create problems similar to excluding factors that should be included. Take a simple example of explaining how the stock market, say the Dow Jones industrials, changes over time. Obvious variables to include would be the interest rate and the expected growth in the economy, but many other variables—many of dubious importance—could possibly also be included. The problem arises when such variables are correlated to changes in stock prices merely by chance. An extreme case would be including the prices of various grocery store products. A store might sell thousands of items, and one—say, the price of peanut butter—might happen to be highly correlated with the stock prices over the particular period examined. We know that peanut butter has little to do with explaining overall stock prices, but if it just accidentally happens to move up and down with the movements in the stock market, other variables (like the interest rate) may no longer prove to be statistically significant.

There are ways to protect against this "dubious variable" problem. One is to expand the sample period. If no true causal relationship exists between the two variables, the probability that this coincidence will continue to occur during future years is low. And this is exactly what I have done as more data have become available: first by looking at data through 1992, then extending them to 1994, and in the second edition up until 1996. Another approach guarding against the "dubious variable" problem is to replicate the same test in many different places. Again, this is exactly what I have done here: I have studied the impact of right-to-carry laws in different states at different times. As charged by many a critic, it is still conceivable that some other factor just happened to occur also when an individual state passed the law, but the probability of mere coincidence falls as the experiences of more and more states are examined. It is also possible that adding variables that don't belong can cause you to get a more significant result for other factors than is warranted.

Generally, excluding variables that should be included is a more significant problem than including variables that should not be included, and in general I have tried to err on the side of including whatever possible factors can be included. Indeed, a strong case can be made that one must be careful not to include too many variables like state time trends, which can be endlessly added on and have little theoretical justification. Still, I do not consider any of these variables to be similar to the price of peanut butter at the local grocery store in the previous discussion, but obviously some researchers might believe that some variables should not be included. One way to investigate this issue is to include only those variables that different investigators view as relevant. In the early stages of my research, when I presented my original research as a working paper at seminars, I asked participants for other factors that should be included, and some of their comments were very helpful. I also tried in vain to ask pro-gun-control researchers what variables they wanted me to include in the regressions, but (as discussed in chapter 7) they did not make any suggestions when my initial research was circulated for comments. What comments they made after the publicity broke claimed that I had not controlled for factors that I had indeed accounted for.

Since the original research immediately received a lot of attention, I have let my critics decide for themselves what variables should be included by simply giving them complete access to the data. I know from personal communication that some critics (such as Black and Nagin) did indeed examine numerous different specifications.[15]

A more systematic, if time-consuming, approach is to try all possible combinations of these so-called control variables—factors which may be interesting but are included so that we can be sure of the importance of some other "focus" variables.[16] In my regressions to explain crime rates there are at least nine groups of control variables—population density, waiting periods and background checks, penalties for using guns in the commission of a crime, per-capita income, per-capita unemployment insurance payments, per-capita income maintenance payments, retirement payments per person for those over sixty-five, state poverty rate, and state unemployment rate.[17] To run all possible combinations of these nine groups of control variables requires 512 regressions. The regressions for murder rates also require a tenth control variable for the death-penalty execution rate and thus results in 1,024 combinations of control variables. Given the nine different crime categories, this amounts to 5,120 regressions.

This approach is decidedly biased toward not finding a consistent effect of the right-to-carry laws, because it includes many combinations of control variables that no researcher thinks are correct specifications. Indeed, even the strongest, best-accepted empirical relationships usually fail this test.[18] Since different people will have different preferences for what variables should be included, this massive set of results makes sense only if one knows what variables produce what results. If a range of conflicting estimates are then produced, people can judge for themselves what they think the "true" range of the estimates is.

Two sets of variables have been primarily used to test the impact of right-to-carry laws: crime trends before and after the adoption of right-to-carry laws and the percentage of people with permits. Yet another division is possible by focusing on counties with a large number of people to avoid the difficulty that low-population counties frequently have zero murder or rape rates and thus have "undefined" arrest rates.[19] Eliminating counties with fewer than 20,000 people removes about 70 percent of the missing arrest ratios for murder while sacrificing 20 percent of the observations (the population-weighted frequencies are 23 and 6 percent, respectively). Dropping out more populous counties reduces the sample size but has virtually no impact on further reducing the frequency of missing arrest rates. Even if I limit the estimates to the full sample and counties with more than 20,000 people, combining that with the two other types of specifications results in 20,480 regressions. Because of all the concerns over possible crime trends, all estimates include variables to account for the average differences across counties and years as well as by year within region as well as the thirty-six demographic variables.[20]

Figures 9.10–9.13 present the range of estimates associated with these different combinations of variables and specifications, both in terms of their extreme bounds and their median value. What immediately stands out when one examines all these estimates is how extremely consistent the violent-crime results are. For example, take figure 9.10. A one-percentage-point change in people with permits lowers violent-crime rates by 4.5–7.2 percent. Indeed, all the estimates (over two thousand of them) for overall violent crime, murder, rape, robbery, and aggravated assault indicate that increases in permits reduce crime. All the combinations of the other ten sets of control variables imply that a one-percentage-point increase in the population holding permits reduces murder rates by 2–3.9 percent annually. Compared to the state-level data, the benefits from right-to-carry laws are much smaller for robbery and much larger for aggravated assaults.

Figure 9.11 uses the simple before-and-after trends to examine the impact of the right-to-carry laws, and the results for the violent-crime rates are generally consistent with those shown in figure 9.10. Again, all the violent-crime-rate regressions show the same direction of impact from the concealed-handgun law. The median estimated declines in violent-crime rates are quite similar to those initially reported in table 9. 1. For each additional year that the right-to-carry laws are in effect, violent crimes decline by 2.4 percent, murders by 1.6 percent, rapes and aggravated assaults by over 3 percent, and robberies by 2.7 percent.

With the notable exception of burglaries, which consistently decline, figures 9.10 and 9.11 provide mixed evidence for whether right-to-carry laws increase or decrease other property crimes. Even when one focuses on estimates of one type, such as those using the percentage of the population with permits, the county- and state-level data yield inconsistent results. Yet,

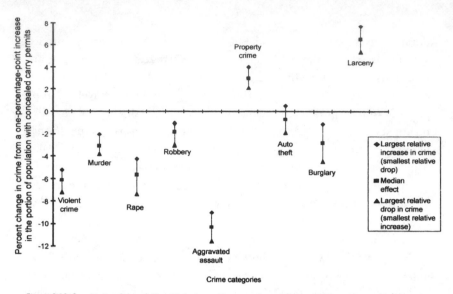

Figure 9.10. Sensitivity of the relationship between the percentage of the population with permits and annual changes in crime rates: data for all counties

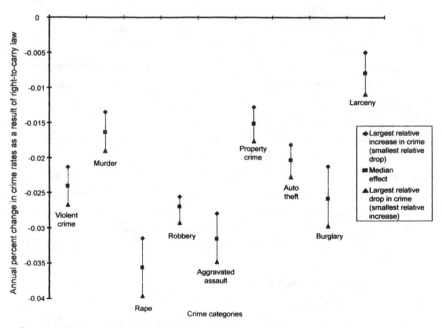

Figure 9.11. Sensitivity of the relationship between right-to-carry laws and annual changes in crime rates: data for all counties

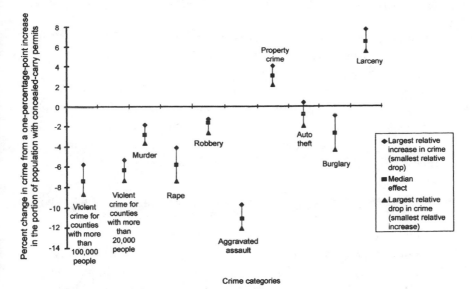

Figure 9.12. Sensitivity of the relationship between the percentage of the population with permits and annual changes in crime rates: data for counties with either more than 20,000 people or more than 100,000 people (all individual crime categories—that is, all categories except "violent crime"—are for counties with more than 20,000 people)

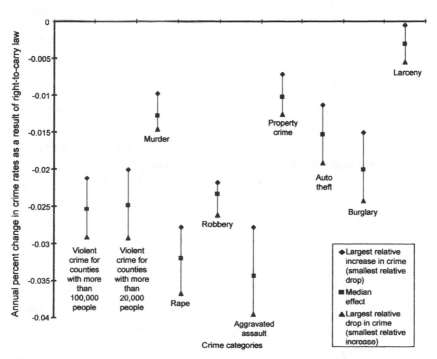

Figure 9.13. Sensitivity of the relationship between right-to-carry laws and annual changes in crime rates: data for counties with either more than 20,000 people or more than 100,000 people (all individual crime categories—that is, all categories except "violent crime"—are for counties with more than 20,000 people)

while the net effect of right-to-carry laws on larceny and auto theft is not clear, one conclusion can be drawn: the passage of right-to-carry laws has a consistently larger deterrent effect against violent crimes than property crimes and may even be associated with increases in property crimes.

Figures 9.12 and 9.13 limit the sample to the more populous counties and continue reaching very similar results. For counties with more than 20,000 people, the estimate ranges are always of the same sign and have magnitudes similar to those results which examined all the counties. Both figures also looked at the sensitivity of the overall violent-crime rate for counties over 100,000. The range of estimates was again very similar, though they implied a slightly larger benefit than for the more populous counties. For example, figure 9.12 shows that in counties with more than 20,000 people, violent crime declines by between 5.4 and 7.4 percentage points for each additional 1 percent of the population with permits, while the analogous drop for counties with more than 100,000 people is between 5.8 and 8.7 percentage points.

A total of 13,312 regressions for the various violent-crime categories are reported in this section. The evidence clearly indicates that right-to-carry laws are always associated with reductions in violent crime, and 89 percent of the results are statistically significant at least at the 1 percent level. The results are not sensitive to including particular control variables and always show that the benefits from these laws increase over time as more people obtain permits. The 8,192 regressions for property crime imply a less consistent relationship between right-to-carry laws and property crime, but even when drops in property crime are observed, the declines are smaller than the decrease in violent crime.

While limiting the sample size to only larger-population counties provides one possible method of dealing with "undefined" arrest rates, it has a serious drawback—information is lost by throwing out those counties with fewer than 20,000 people. Another approach is to control for either the violent- or property-crime arrest rate depending upon whether the crime rate being studied is that of violent or property crime. Even if a county has zero murders or rapes in a particular year, virtually all counties have at least some violent or property crime, thus eliminating the "undefined" arrest rate problem and still allowing us to account for county-level changes over time in the effectiveness of law enforcement. This approach also helps mitigate any spurious relationship between crime and arrest rates that might arise because the arrest rate is a function of the crime rate. Reestimating the 4,096 regressions in figure 9.10 for murder, rape, robbery, aggravated assault, auto theft, burglary, and larceny with this new measure of arrest rates again produces very similar results.

City Crime Data

County data, rather than city data, allow the entire country to be examined. This is important, since, obviously, not everyone lives in cities. Such data further allow us to deal with differences in how permits are issued, such as the discretion states grant to local law enforcement. Relying on county data allows a detailed analysis of many important factors, such as arrest and conviction rates, the number of police, expenditures on police, (sometimes) prison sentences, and proxies for policing policies like the so-called broken-windows strategy (according to which police focus on less serious property crimes as a means of reducing overall violent crime). Yet a drawback with county data is that policing policies cannot be dealt with well, for such policy decisions are made at the level of individual police departments—not at the county level.[21] With a few exceptions such as San Francisco, Philadelphia, and New York, where county and city boundaries coincide, only city-level data can be used to study these issues.

The focus of my research is guns and crime, but I had to make sure that I accounted for whatever policing policies are being employed.[22] Three policing strategies dominate the discussion: community-oriented policing, problem-oriented policing, and the broken-windows approach. While community-oriented policing is said to involve local community organizations directly in the policing effort, problem-oriented policing is sometimes viewed as a less intrusive version of the broken-windows policy. Problem-oriented policing began as directing patrols on the basis of identified crime patterns but nowadays involves the police in everything from cleaning housing projects and surveying their tenants to helping citizens design parking garages to reduce auto theft.[23] An extensive Westlaw database search was conducted to categorize which cities adopted which policing strategies as well as their adoption and rescission dates.[24]

Other recent research of mine demonstrates the importance of racial and gender hiring decrees on the effectiveness of police departments.[25] When hiring rules are changed so as to create equal pass rates on hiring exams across different racial groups—typically by replacing intelligence tests with what some claim are arbitrary psychological tests—the evidence indicates that the quality of new hires falls across the board. And the longer these new hiring policies are in place, the more detrimental the effect on police departments. As with the right-to-carry laws, simple before-and-after trends were included to measure the changing impact of these rules over time.

Let us return to the main focus, guns and crime. To examine the impact of right-to-carry laws, the following list of variables has been accounted for: city population, arrest rate by type of crime, unemployment rate, percentage of families headed by females, family poverty rate, median family income, per-capita income, percentage of the population living below poverty, percentage of the population that is white, percentage that is black, percentage that is Hispanic, percentage that is female, percentage that is less than five years of age, percentage that is between five and seventeen, percentage that is between eighteen and twenty-five, percentage that is between twenty-six and sixty-four, percentage that is sixty-five and older, median population age, percentage of the population over age twenty-five with a high school diploma, percentage of the population over age twenty-five with a college degree, and other types of gun-control laws (waiting periods, background checks, and additional penalties for using guns in the commission of a crime). As with the earlier county- and state-level data, variables are included to measure the length of state waiting periods, as well as the change in average crime rates from state waiting periods, background checks, penalties for using a gun in the commission of crime, and whether the federal Brady law altered existing state rules. Again, all estimates include variables to account for the average differences across counties and years as well as by year within region.

Table 9.4 provides strong evidence that even when detailed information on policing policies is taken into account, passing concealed-handgun laws deters violent crime. The benefit in terms of reduced murder rates is particularly large, with a drop of 2.7 percent each additional year that the right-to-carry law is in effect. The drop experienced for rapes is 1.5 percent per year. The one violent crime for which the decline is not statistically significant is aggravated assault. On the other hand, property crimes increase after the adoption of right-to-carry laws, confirming some of the earlier findings.

Consent decrees—which mandate police hiring rules that ensure equal pass rates by race and sex—significantly and adversely affect all crime categories but rape. For each additional year that the consent decree is in effect, overall violent crimes rise by 2.4 percent and property crimes rise by 1.9 percent.

The evidence for the before-and-after average crime rates for the different types of policing policies is more mixed, and my research does not

Table 9.4 Accounting for policing policies using city-level data

	Percent change in various crime rates for changes in explanatory variables								
	Violent crime	Murder	Rape	Robbery	Aggravated assault	Property crime	Burglary	Larceny	Auto theft
Change in the crime rate from the difference in the annual change in crime rates in the years before and after the adoption of a right-to-carry law (annual rate of change after the law − annual rate of change before the law)	−1.2%**	−2.7%*	−1.5%**	−1.0%*	−0.6%	0.92%**	1.0%*	0.7%**	1.2%**
Change in the crime rate after imposition of a consent decree regarding the hiring of police officers	2.4%*	0.4%***	−0.27%	3.5%*	1.4%*	1.9%*	2.4%*	2.0%*	0.5%**
Change in the average crime rate after implementation of community policing	−3.3%[a]	2.2%	−4.9%[a]	−1.7%[b]	−2.5%[b]	1.6%[a]	−1.2%[c]	2.5%[a]	7.7%[a]
Change in the average crime rate after implementation of problem-oriented policing	2.4%	−4.1%	−4.5%	3.6%	2.6%	1.8%	−1.8%	−2.7%	24.9%[a]
Change in the average crime rate after implementation of broken-window policing	−0.8%	6.7%[c]	−10.1%[a]	−3.8%[a]	2.3%	−6.4%[a]	−5.6%[a]	−12.3%[a]	18.2%[a]
Average crime rate after adoption of one-gun-a-month purchase rule	9.3%	14.7%[d]	6.8%	7.9%[d]	15.8%[c]	−0.6%	2.7%	−4.9%	.1%
Change in the average crime rate in a state after a neighboring state adopts a one-gun-a-month rule	9.6%[a]	18.4%[a]	11.5%	4.1%	17.2%[a]	13%[a]	10.6%[b]	14.3%[c]	11%[c]

[a]The result is significant at the 1 percent level for a two-tailed t-test.
[b]The result is significant at the 5 percent level for a two-tailed t-test.
[c]The result is significant at the 10 percent level for a two-tailed t-test.
[d]The result is significant at the 12 percent level for a two-tailed t-test.
*The F-test is significant at the 1 percent level.
**The F-test is significant at the 5 percent level.
***The F-test is significant at the 10 percent level.

attempt to deal with issues of why the different rules were adopted to begin with.[26] In ten cases, the policing policies produce significant reductions in crime, but in six cases there are significant increases in crime. Including cases that are not statistically significant still produces no consistent pattern: the policing policies are associated with declines in crime in fifteen cases and increases in twelve cases. A possible explanation for such results might be that adopting new policing policies reallocates resources within the police department, causing some crime rates to go down while others go up. Indeed, each of the three policing policies is associated with increases in some categories of crime and decreases in others. It is difficult to pick out many patterns, but community policing reduces violent crimes at the expense of increased property crimes.

Revisiting Multiple-Victim Public Shootings

Student eyewitnesses and shooting victims of the Pearl High School (Mississippi) rampage used phrases like "unreal" and "like a horror movie" as they testified Wednesday about seeing Luke Woodham methodically point his deer rifle at them and pull the trigger at least six times. . . . The day's most vivid testimony came from a gutsy hero of the day. Assistant principal Joel Myrick heard the initial shot and watched Woodham choosing his victims. When Woodham appeared headed for a science wing where early classes were already under way, Myrick ran for his pickup and grabbed his .45-caliber pistol. He rounded the school building in time to see Woodham leaving the school and getting into his mother's white Chevy Corsica. He watched its back tires smoke from Woodham's failure to remove the parking brake. Then he ordered him to stop. "I had my pistol's sights on him. I could see the whites of his knuckles" on the steering wheel, Myrick said. He reached into the car and opened the driver-side door, then ordered Woodham to lie on the ground. "I put my foot on his back area and pointed my pistol at him," Myrick testified.[27]

Multiple-victim public shootings were not a central issue in the gun debate when I originally finished writing this book in the spring of 1997. My results on multiple-victim public shootings, presented in chapter 5, were obtained long before the first public school attacks occurred in October 1997. Since that time, two of the eight public school shootings (Pearl, Mississippi, and Edinboro, Pennsylvania) were stopped only when citizens with guns interceded.[28] In the Pearl, Mississippi, case, Myrick stopped the killer from proceeding to the nearby junior high school and continuing his attack there. These two cases also involved the fewest people harmed in any of the attacks. The armed citizens managed to stop the attackers well before the police even had arrived at the scene—4½ minutes before in the Pearl, Mississippi, case and 11 minutes before in Edinboro.

In a third instance, at Columbine High School in Littleton, Colorado, an armed guard was able to delay the attackers and allow many students to escape the building, even though he was assigned to the school because he had failed to pass his shooting proficiency test. The use of homemade grenades, however, prevented the guard from fighting longer. There is some irony in Dylan Klebold, one of the two killers, strongly opposing the proposed right-to-carry law that was being considered in Colorado at the time of the massacre.[29] In the attack on the Jewish community center in Los Angeles in which five people were wounded, the attacker had apparently "scouted three of the West Coast's most prominent Jewish institutions— the Museum of Tolerance, the Skirball Cultural Center and the University of Judaism—but found security too tight."[30]

It is remarkable how little public discussion there has been on the topic of allowing people to defend themselves. It has only been since 1995 that we have had a federal law banning guns by people other than police within one thousand feet of a school.[31]

Together with my colleague William Landes, I compiled data on all the multiple-victim public shootings occurring in the United States from 1977 to 1999, during which time twenty-three states adopted right-to-carry laws. As with earlier numbers reported in this book, the incidents we considered were cases with at least two people killed or injured in a public place. We excluded gang wars or shootings that were by-products of another crime, such as robbery. The United States averaged twenty-nine such shootings annually, with an average of 1.5 people killed and 2.5 wounded in each incident.

What can stop these attacks? We examined a range of different gun laws, including waiting periods, as well the frequency and level of punishment. However, while arrest and conviction rates, prison sentences, and the death penalty reduce murders generally, they have no significant effect on public shootings. There is a simple reason for this: Those who commit these crimes usually die in the attack. They are killed in the attack or, as in the Colorado shooting, they commit suicide. The normal penalties simply do not apply.

In the deranged minds of the attackers, their goal is to kill and injure as many people as possible. Some appear to do it for the publicity, which is related to the harm inflicted. Some may do it only because they value harming others. The best way to prevent these attacks might therefore be to limit the carnage they can cause if they do attack. We find only one policy that effectively accomplishes this: the passage of right-to-carry laws.

Even after accounting for the factors that we have used in the other estimates, when different states passed right-to-carry laws during the twenty-three years we studied, the number of multiple-victim public shootings declined by a whopping 67 percent. Deaths from all these shootings plummeted by 75 percent, and injuries by 81 percent. Figure 9.14 demonstrates how the raw number of attacks changes before and after the passage of right-to-carry laws. The extensive research that we have done indicates that these results hold up very well when the long list of factors discussed in this book is taken into account. The very few attacks that still occur in states after enactment of right-to-carry laws tend to occur in particular places where concealed handguns are forbidden, such as schools.

Concealed-handgun laws significantly reduce multiple-victim public shootings in public places (but have no systematic effects on bombings). The estimates imply that the average state passing these laws reduces the total number of murders and injuries per year from 1.91 to .42 and the number of shootings from .42 to .14. Despite expecting a deterrent effect from these laws because of the high probability that one or more potential victims or bystanders will be armed, the drop in murders and injuries is still surprisingly large. And as we shall see, alternative measures of shootings

Figure 9.14. Murders from multiple-victim public shootings per 100,000 people: data from 1977 to 1995 and adding other factors that might explain the drop do not seem to reduce the magnitude of the law's effect.[32]

The reason why the deterrent effect on multiple-victim public attacks is greater than on attacks on individual victims is fairly straightforward. Say the probability that a victim has a permitted concealed handgun is 5 percent. That will raise the expected costs to the criminal and produce some deterrence. Yet if one hundred adults are present on a train or in a restaurant, even if the probability that any one of them will be able to offer a defense is only 5 percent, the probability that at least someone there has a permitted concealed handgun is near 100 percent.[33] The results for multiple-victim public shootings are consistent with the central findings of this book: as the probability that victims are going to be able to defend themselves increases, the level of deterrence increases.

Concealed-handgun laws also have an important advantage over uniformed police, for would-be attackers can aim their initial assault at a single officer, or alternatively wait until he leaves the area. With concealed carrying by ordinary citizens, it is not known who is armed until the criminal actually attacks. Concealed-handgun laws might therefore also require fewer people carrying weapons. Some school systems (such as Baltimore) have recognized this problem and made nonuniformed police officers "part of the faculty at each school."[34]

Despite all the debate about criminals behaving irrationally, reducing their ability to accomplish their warped goals reduces their willingness to attack. Yet even if mass murder is the only goal, the possibility of a law-abiding citizen carrying a concealed handgun in a restaurant or on a train is apparently enough to convince many would-be killers that they will not be successful. Unfortunately, without concealed carry, ordinary citizens are sitting ducks, waiting to be victimized.

Other Gun-Control Laws

"Gun control? It's the best thing you can do for crooks and gangsters," Gravano said. "I want you to have nothing. If I'm a bad guy, I'm always gonna have a gun. Safety locks? You will pull the trigger with a lock on, and I'll pull the trigger. We'll see who wins."[35]
—Sammy "the Bull" Gravano, the Mafia turncoat, when asked about gun control

Every couple of years we see a big push for new gun-control laws. Unfortunately, the discussion focuses on only the possible benefits and ignores any costs. Waiting periods may allow for a "cooling-off period," but they may also make it difficult for people to obtain a gun quickly for self-defense. Gun locks may prevent accidental gun deaths involving young children, but they may also make it difficult for people to use a gun quickly for self-defense.[36] The exaggerated stories about accidental gun deaths, particularly those involving young children, might scare people into not owning guns for protection, even though guns offer by far the most effective means of defending oneself and one's family.

Some laws, such as the Brady law, may prevent some criminals from buying guns through legal channels, such as regular gun stores. Nevertheless, such laws are not going to prevent criminals from obtaining guns through other means, including theft. Just as the government has had difficulty in stopping gangs from getting drugs to sell, it is dubious that the government would succeed in stopping criminals from acquiring guns to defend their drug turf.

Similar points can be made about one-gun-a-month rules. The cost that they impose upon the law abiding may be small. Yet there is still a security issue here: someone being threatened might immediately want to store guns at several places so that one is always easily within reach. The one-gun-a-month rule makes that impossible. Besides this issue, the rule is primarily an inconvenience for those who buy guns as gifts or who want to take their families hunting.

The enactment dates for the safe-storage laws and one-gun-a-month rules are shown in table 9.5.[37] For the implementation dates of safe-storage laws, I relied primarily on an article published in the *Journal of the American Medical Association,* though this contained only laws passed up through the end of 1993.[38] Handgun Control's Web site provided information on the three states that passed laws after this date. The laws share certain common features, such as making it a crime to store firearms in a way that a reasonable person would know allows a child to gain use of a weapon. The primary differences involve exactly what penalties are imposed and the age at which a child's access becomes allowed. While Connecticut, California, and Florida classify such violations as felonies, other states classify them as misdemeanors. The age at which children's access is permitted also varies across states, ranging from twelve in Virginia to eighteen in North Carolina and Delaware. Most state rules protect owners from liability if firearms are stored in a locked box, secured with a trigger lock, or obtained through unlawful entry.

The state-level estimates are shown in table 9.6. Only the right-to-carry

Table 9.5 Enactment dates of other gun control laws

State	Date law went into effect
Safe-storage laws:[a]	
Florida	10/1/89
Iowa	4/5/90
Connecticut	10/1/90
Nevada	10/1/91
California	1/1/92
New Jersey	1/17/92
Wisconsin	4/16/92
Hawaii	6/29/92
Virginia	7/1/92
Maryland	10/1/92
Minnesota	8/1/93
North Carolina	12/1/93
Delaware	10/1/94
Rhode Island	9/15/95
Texas	1/1/96
One-gun-a-month laws:[b]	
South Carolina	1976
Virginia	7/93
Maryland	10/1/96

[a]Source for the dates of enactment of safe-storage laws through the end of 1993 is Peter Cummings, David C. Grossman, Frederick P. Rivara, and Thomas D. Koepsell, "State Gun Safe Storage Laws and Child Mortality Due to Firearms," *Journal of the American Medical Association,* 278 (October 1, 1997): 1084–86. The other dates were obtained from the Handgun Control Web site at http://www.handguncontrol.org/caplaws.htm.
[b]Data were obtained through a Nexis/Lexis search. Lynn Waltz, "Virginia Law Cuts Gun Pipeline to Capital's Criminals," *Norfolk Virginian-Pilot,* September 8, 1996, p. A7.

laws are associated with significant reductions in crime rates. Among the violent-crime categories, the Brady law is only significantly related to rape, which increased by 3.6 percent after the law passed. (While the coefficients indicate that the law resulted in more murders and robberies but fewer aggravated assaults and as a consequence fewer overall violent crimes, none of those effects are even close to being statistically significant.) Only the impact of the Brady law on rape rates is consistent with the earlier results that we found for the data up through 1994.

Safe-storage rules also seem to cause some real problems. Passage of these laws is significantly related to almost 9 percent more rapes and robberies and 5.6 percent more burglaries. In terms of total crime in 1996, the presence of the law in just these fifteen states was associated with 3,600 more rapes, 22,500 more robberies, and 64,000 more burglaries. These increases might reflect the increased difficulty victims have in reaching a

Table 9.6 Evaluating other gun-control laws using state-level data

	Percent change in various crime rates for changes in explanatory variables							
	Violent crime	Murder	Rape	Robbery	Aggravated assault	Property crime	Burglary	Larceny	Auto theft
Change in the crime rate from the difference in the annual change in crime rates in the years before and after the adoption of the right-to-carry law (annual rate of change after the law – annual rate of change before the law)	−2.0%*	−3.2%*	−1.4%*	−3.8%*	−2.3%*	−1.3%*	−2.9%*	−0.8%***	0.06%
Change in the average crime rate after the adoption of Brady law	−2.4%	3.6%	3.6%[a]	0.02%	−4.2%	−0.6%	0.7%	−0.6%	2.5%
Change in the average crime rate after the adoption of safe-storage rules	0.04%	1.3%	8.9%[a]	8.9%[a]	−4.4%	2.5%	5.6%[b]	2.0%	−0.6%

[a]The result is significant at the 1 percent level for a two-tailed *t*-test.
[b]The result is significant at the 5 percent level for a two-tailed *t*-test.
*The F-test is significant at the 1 percent level.
***The F-test is significant at the 10 percent level.

gun to protect themselves. However, a contributing factor might be the horror stories that often accompany the passage of these laws, reducing people's desire to own a gun in the first place. The increase in burglaries is particularly notable. Burglars appeared to be less afraid of entering homes after these laws were passed. Additional state data would be required to answer the question of whether "hot burglaries"—burglaries occurring while the residents are in the dwelling—increased and whether burglars spent less time casing dwellings after these laws were passed. Evidence of these other changes would help confirm that these laws have emboldened criminals.

On the other side of this question is the number of accidental gun deaths that will be prevented. The General Accounting Office reported in 1991 that mechanical safety locks are unreliable in preventing children over six years of age from using a gun,[39] but there is still the question of how many of these children's lives might have been saved, and even if locks are unreliable for older children, some deaths may be prevented. Even if one believes that the high-end estimated benefits are correct, that as many as 31 of the 136 children under age fifteen who had died from accidental gunshots in 1996 would have been saved by nationwide safe-storage laws, table 9.6 implies some caution.[40] The effect for murders was not statistically significant, but it still provides the best estimate that we have and the size of the effect is still instructive. It indicates that in just these fifteen states, 109 lives would be lost from this law. If the entire country had these safe-storage laws, the total lost lives would have risen to 255.

Yet other research that I have done with John Whitley indicates that this is the most optimistic possible outcome from safe-storage laws. We find no support for the theory that safe-storage laws reduce either juvenile accidental gun deaths or suicides. Instead, these storage requirements appear to impair people's ability to use guns defensively. Because accidental shooters also tend to be the ones most likely to violate the new law, safe-storage laws increase violent and property crimes against low-risk citizens with no observable offsetting benefit in terms of reduced accidents or suicides. Just as important, we found that examining the simple before-and-after average effects of the law underestimates the increases in crime that result from safe-storage laws. When the before-and-after trends are accounted for, the group of fifteen states that adopted these laws faced an annual average increase of over 300 more murders, 3,860 more rapes, 24,650 more robberies, and over 25,000 more aggravated assaults during the first five full years after the passage of the safe-storage laws. Using the National Institute of Justice estimates of victim costs from crime indicates that the average annual costs borne by victims averaged over $2.6 billion.

The one-gun-a-month rule seems to have negative consequences, too. But only three states passed these laws during the twenty years studied, so there is always the issue of whether enough data exist and whether other factors might have played a role. Nevertheless, the passage of these laws was associated with more murders, more robberies, and more aggravated assaults, and the effects appear to be quite large.

One possible suspicion, however, is that the large effect of one-gun-a-month rules merely reflects some regional crime increases, increases that just happen to coincide with the adoption of these laws. To counter this potential problem, I again allowed year-to-year average differences to vary by region, as I had done for the county- and city-level data. The results for right-to-carry laws were essentially unchanged, and the pattern for other gun-control laws remained very similar, though some of the statistical significance declined. The Brady law was still associated with a statistically significant increase in rapes. Using the simple before-and-after averages, safe-storage laws were still associated with statistically significant increases in rape, robbery, and burglary. Indeed, not only did the coefficients remain significant at the 1 percent level, but the results actually implied slightly larger increases in these crime categories, with the effect from state storage laws on rape now increasing to 9 percent, on robbery to 9.9 percent, and on burglary to 6.8 percent.

The Political and Academic Debate Continued
Attacking the Messenger

David Yassky [member of the board of directors of Handgun Control, Inc.]: The people who fund your studies are gun manufacturers.

Lott: That is a lie.

Yassky: That is not a lie. That is not a lie.

Lott: That is a lie.

Yassky: It is paid for by gun manufacturers who manufacture firearms.

—From *Debates/Debates,* a nationally syndicated program on public television that was broadcast during the week of April 22, 1999

Michael Beard [president of the Coalition to Stop Gun Violence]: Yes, and you're unbiased. You work for, what, the Olin Foundation, which manufactures firearms . . .

Lott: No I don't. I work for the University of Chicago.

Beard: Who pays your salary?

Lott: The University of Chicago pays my salary.

Beard: Through the Olin Foundation.

Lott: No, that's not true.

—From *CNN Today,* June 18, 1999; 1:29 P.M. Eastern Time

Gun-control advocates all too frequently use these types of arguments in debates. Often callers on radio shows make similar claims. Even if the claim merely diverts the discussion away from whether guns save more lives than they cost, my guess is that the gun-control organizations view the personal attack as a success.[41] Unfortunately, no matter how many times I deny the charge or explain that no, I did not apply for money from the Olin Foundation; no, I was paid by the University of Chicago; no, the Olin Foundation and the Olin Corporation are separate entities; and no, it was the faculty at the University of Chicago who decided on my appointment and they asked no questions about my future research topics, many people still tune out after these charges are raised.

During 1999, numerous newspaper columns also made similar claims, for instance: "John R. Lott Jr., the latest darling of gun advocates everywhere. He's the Olin Fellow of Law and Economics at the University of Chicago School of Law. (That's 'Olin' as in Olin-Winchester, one of the world's leading manufacturers of ammunition)."[42] Or "They fail to mention that Lott is a John M. Olin fellow. This Olin Foundation is funded through the Olin Corp., the parent company of Winchester Ammunition. Winchester makes more money as the sale of handguns goes up."[43] Letter writers to newspapers have also chimed in: "It was particularly helpful that he exposed Professor John R. Lott Jr. as an intellectually dishonest toady of the bullet manufacturing industry."[44] Even after being given facts to the contrary, some state legislators have continued making claims like "The Lott study's been thrown out. . . . It's a joke. . . . Professor Lott is funded by the Olin Corporation which is funded by Winchester."[45] And, of course, Internet news-group discussions are filled with such assertions.[46] Others bring up the topic only to point out that while others believe it to be important, they do not personally believe that it is relevant.[47]

Gun-control groups have repeatedly attacked me rather than my findings and distorted the research I have done in other areas. State legislators in Michigan, Missouri, Nebraska, and Maryland have begun calling me up to ask whether it is true that I don't think that police departments should hire black or female police officers. Handgun Control and the Violence Policy Center spread claims such as "Lott has argued that the hiring of more women and minorities in law enforcement has actually increased crime rates."[48] They have made this claim on their Web sites, in debates, and on radio programs.[49] In fact, I had stated that this would be the wrong conclusion to reach. The paper argued: "But it would be a serious mistake not to realize that this simple relationship is masking that the new rules reduce the quality of new hires from other groups."[50] The affirmative action rules which changed the testing standards lowered the quality of new police hires across the board, and that was showing itself in the simple relationship between minority hires and crime.[51]

On the upside, many have come to my defense. One academic review of my book noted, "The personal (and, to those who know him, completely unfounded) attacks on John Lott's integrity were made with such ferocity and in so many media outlets nationwide that one can only conclude that Lott was, with apologies to our gracious First Lady [Hillary Clinton], the target of a vast left-wing conspiracy to discredit his politically incorrect findings."[52] Another academic review wrote: "the ease with which gun-control advocates could get misleading and even false claims published by the press raises important public choice questions. Many of these claims were highly personal and vicious, including outright lies about alleged funding of Lott's research by the firearms industry . . . , about the outlet for his then forthcoming work . . . , about Lott's fringe ideas . . . , and about his lack of qualifications. . . . Most academics probably would have withdrawn back into the sheltered halls of their universities rather than expose themselves to the vicious public attacks that John Lott faced."[53] Other academics have written that "gun control groups attempted to discredit his work by smearing him with accusations that they had to know were patently false"[54] and about the "vicious campaign of lies and distortions."[55] Publications for police officer associations have also been very supportive.[56]

Once in a while, I have come to feel that there is a well-organized campaign to impugn my findings, especially on days when I have done radio talk shows for stations based in different parts of the country and callers state word for word the exact same charge that I have been paid to do my research by gun makers. Originally, I had thought that these personal attacks would fade away after a year or so, but they have now continued for three years, so unfortunately they will probably continue. The most disconcerting aspect of this, especially for my family, has been the numerous physical threats, including an instance of a note on our apartment door.[57]

Yet the gun-control organizations still realized that they had to do more to counter my work. In December 1996, Handgun Control had organized a debate that was broadcast on C-SPAN between myself and three critics: Dan Black, Dan Nagin, and Jens Ludwig. However, none of the researchers that they invited were able to claim that concealed-handgun laws increased crime. I can only imagine that this put Handgun Control in a bind. It is hard to oppose legislation or a referendum by arguing that concealed-handgun laws do no harm. Not being able to find support from the researchers that they work closely with, Handgun Control finally came out with its own numbers in a press release on January 18, 1999, arguing that between 1992 and 1997 violent-crime rates were falling more quickly in the states that most restricted concealed handguns than in the states with more liberal rules.

Their claim was widely and uncritically reported in publications from *Newsweek* to *USA Today,* as well as during the spring 1999 campaign to pass a concealed-handgun law in Missouri.[58] Press coverage and Handgun Control itself usually referred to this contention as coming from the FBI.[59]

Handgun Control examined the change in violent crime between only two years, 1992 and 1997, and strangely enough they chose to classify states according to what their laws were in 1997, at the end of the period. This odd classification makes a considerable difference, for some states' right-to-carry laws did not even go into effect until late 1996, with few permits issued until 1997. It makes no sense to attribute the increase in crime to a law for the five years before the law goes into effect. A third of the states with right-to-carry laws did not enact them until after late 1995. Of course, the way any trained researcher would approach the question is to separate the change in crime rates before and after the different states changed their laws. That is only common sense. Only changes in crime after the law goes into effect can be attributed to the passage of the law.

Given the evidence in this book, I would also argue that since one is examining the change in crime rates, it is important to separate out those states that have had changes in permits and those that have not. If a state has had its right-to-carry law in place for decades, it is extremely unlikely that it will be experiencing any additional growth in permits and thus it should not be expecting any additional changes in its crime rates from this law. Handgun Control also did not account for any other factors that could have influenced crime. Nor did they even classify states consistently across their own press releases issued within months of each other.[60]

During the Missouri campaign, many reporters called me up to comment about the "FBI numbers" on crime rates.[61] When I would point out that the claim was actually based on a report produced by Handgun Control, they said that they didn't know what to do with the conflicting claims. Editorials and news stories in the *St. Louis Post-Dispatch* and the *Kansas City Star* normally just accepted the Handgun Control assertion as established truth.

After repeatedly encountering this response from reporters, I started suggesting to reporters that they ask some local academic (a statistician, criminologist, or economist) to evaluate the two conflicting claims. One reporter with the *St. Louis Post-Dispatch,* Kim Bell, expressed the concern that they might run into a professor with a preconceived bias and that would make the test unfair. I told her that I was willing to take that risk, but that if she were concerned about that problem, she could always approach a few different academics. Others who refused to take me up on this challenge included Bill Freivogel, deputy editor at the *Post-Dispatch,* and Rich Hood, an editor at the *Kansas City Star.* Rather, their newspapers simply presented Handgun Control's claims as fact.

Criticisms of the Book

Some reviewers clearly have not even bothered to read my book, or at least it didn't matter to them whether they read it. A review in the *British Journal of Criminology* claimed that "there is nothing in Lott's study to connect this more general information to the specific county-based data on the issuing of concealed-carry permits," "Lott is dealing with a time frame entirely prior to the introduction of the non-discretionary concealed-carry laws in most of the states which now have them," and "he has pre-occupied himself exclusively with 'good guns' owned by 'good people.'"[62] Another book review, in the *New England Journal of Medicine,* starts off by falsely claiming that I "approvingly" quote Archie Bunker's suggestion to stop airplane hijacking by arming "all the passengers."[63]

As of this writing (September 1999), Handgun Control's Web site still continues to assert the same "major criticisms" of my research—"where are the robbery effects?" "auto theft as a substitute for rape," "Lott fails to account for other initiatives—including other gun control laws," "Lott fails to account for cyclical changes in crime rates"—and the same claims about misclassifying state laws.[64] Ironically, they also continue citing the McDowall et. al. (1995) study that we discussed in chapter 2, which examined a total of only five counties picked from three states, attempted to account for no other factors that might be changing over the same period of time, and examined only murders with guns.[65]

Time magazine reported that "Other critics raise questions about whether Lott massaged the numbers. One arcane quarrel: for statistical purposes, Lott dropped from his study sample any counties that had no reported murders or assaults for a given year."[66] It also said that "the book does not account for fluctuating factors like poverty levels and policing techniques." After the story on my book ran, I called up the reporter, Romesh Ratnesar, and said that I knew that he had read the book carefully, so I was surprised that he would write these claims as if they were true. I, as well as critics like Black and Nagin, had looked at the evidence once arrest rates were excluded so as to include those counties with zero arrest rates. What was particularly disappointing was that I had spent the time to obtain all the data that were available. The county-level data were used for all the years and for all the counties for which they were available, both when I did the original paper and when I wrote the book. As to the other claim, I had measures of poverty and policing techniques like the broken-window strategy included.

While I appreciated that the *Time* magazine piece was published, claims that "the book does not account" for these factors are clearly wrong. Ratnesar agreed that these issues were dealt with in the book, but that his role was not to serve as a "referee" between the two sides. His job was to report what the claims were.[67]

I keep on being amazed at the absolute faith that so many news media people place in the gun-control organizations and the "facts" issued by them. Take another example: Molly Ivins, a syndicated columnist, asserted that "[Lott] himself admits, he didn't look at any other causative factors— no other variables, as they say."[68] She also argued that "Lott's study supposedly showed that when 10 Western states passed 'right-to-carry' laws between 1985 and 1992, they had less violent crime" and that "according to the author's research, getting rid of black women older than 40 would do more to stop murder than anything else we could try." Syndicated columnist Tom Teepen wrote a very similar column a year earlier in which he also claimed that this book "failed to consider other anti-crime variables in making its cause-and-effect claims, a fundamental gaffe."[69]

I did get a chance to talk with Mr. Teepen, and he told me that he wrote his review without even reading the book. He apparently relied on conversations that he had with people at Handgun Control and the Violence Policy Center. When I talked to Cynthia Tucker, an editor at the *Atlanta Journal-Constitution*, where Mr. Teepen is based, about having a letter responding to the charges Mr. Teepen made, she found it "unbelievable" that he would have written the review without first looking at the book. She grudgingly said that if it were true, they would publish as a response a short letter, but that she would have to check into it first. Needless to say, the newspaper published my letter the following Sunday.[70] In contrast, unfortunately, Ms. Ivins never returned my telephone calls or responded to my e-mail messages and never corrected her claims.[71]

Undoubtedly, some of the claims constitute simple mistakes, but more than a few reflect columnists and others being too quick to accept whatever gun-control groups tell them. I will spare the reader the long list of other false claims reported in the press.[72] Yet, obviously, many people, particularly those with gun-control organizations, continually make statements that they know are false—safe in the knowledge that only a tiny fraction of readers or listeners ever check the assertions. Unfortunately, the gun-control organizations risk losing significant credibility only with the few who read the book.[73]

Other critiques by academics and the media—some old, some new—require more in-depth discussions. The rest of this section reviews the critiques and then provides my responses.

1 *How do we know that these findings are not a result of the normal ups and downs in crime rates?*

The central problem is that crime moves in waves, yet Lott's analysis does not include variables that can explain these cycles. (David Hemenway, "Book Review of *More Guns, Less Crime*," *New England Journal of Medicine,* December 31, 1998)

Jens Ludwig, assistant professor of public policy at Georgetown University, argued that Lott's data don't prove "anything about what laws do to crime." He noted that crime rates, including homicide, are cyclical: They rise and fall every five to 10 years or so in response to forces that are not well understood. Ludwig suggested that this pattern explains the apparent effectiveness of concealed weapons laws. Imagine, he said, a state where the murder cycle is on the upswing and approaching its peak and public concern is correspondingly high. Then a particularly ghastly mass shooting occurs. Panicked legislators respond by passing a law that allows equally panicked citizens to carry concealed weapons. A year or two later, the murder rate goes down, as Lott's study found. (Richard Morin, "Guns and Gun Massacres: A Contrary View," *Washington Post,* May 30, 1999, p. B5)

Lott's variables are not good predictors of crime waves. Nor does he provide
for any effect of history in the way he models crime. For example, the year
1982 could as well follow 1991 as 1981 in his analyses. (David Hemenway,
"More Guns, Less Crime," *New England Journal of Medicine*, May 20, 1999)

Even my most determined critics concede one point: violent-crime rates
fell at the point in time that the right-to-carry laws went into effect. The
real question is: Why did the crime rates fall? Do these laws simply happen
to get passed right when crime rates hit their peaks? Why don't we observe
this coincidence of timing for other gun-control laws?

It is logically possible that such coincidental timing could take place.
But there is more evidence besides decreases in crime after right-to-carry
laws are adopted. First, the size of the drop is closely related to the number
of permits issued (as indicated in the first edition and confirmed by the
additional data shown here). Second, the additional evidence presented
here goes even further: it is not just the number of permits, but also the
type of people who obtain permits that is important. For example, high
fees discourage the poor, the very people who are most vulnerable to
crime, from getting permits. Third, if it is merely coincidental timing, why
do violent-crime rates start rising in adjacent counties in states without
right-to-carry laws exactly when states that have adopted right-to-carry
laws are experiencing a drop in violent crime?

Finally, as the period of time studied gets progressively longer, the
results are less likely to be due to crime cycles, since any possible crime
"cycles" involve crime not only going down but also "up." If crime happened to hit a peak, say, every ten years, and right-to-carry laws tended
to be passed right at the peak, then the reported effect of the law would
spuriously show a negative impact right after the enactment. However,
five years after that an equally large positive spurious effect on crime would
have to show up. Instead, my results reveal permanent reductions in crime
that only become larger with time, as more people acquire concealed-
carry permits.

Furthermore, my study accounted for possible crime cycles in many
ways: individual year variables accounted for average national changes in
crime rates, and different approaches in chapter 4 controlled for individual
state and county time trends and did not take away the effects of concealed
carry. To the contrary, they resulted in similar or even stronger estimates
for the deterrence effect. Other estimates used robbery or burglary rates to
help account for any left-out factors in explaining other crime rates. Since

crime rates generally tend to move together, this method also allows one to detect individual county trends. In updating the book, I have included estimates that account for the separate average year-to-year changes in five different regions in the country. Despite all these additional controls the deterrence effect continues to show up strongly.

It is simply false to claim, "nor does he provide for any effect of history," as I have variables that account for "changes" in crime rates from previous years. I have variables that measure explicitly the number of years that the law has been in effect as well as the number of years until it goes into effect. In addition, I have used individual state linear time trends that explicitly allow crime rates to change systematically over time.

Earlier discussions in chapter 7 on crime cycles (pp. 134–35) and causality (pp. 157–58) also explain why these concerns are misplaced.

2 Does it make sense to control for nonlinear time trends for each state?

The results suggest that the Lott and Mustard model, which includes only a single national trend, does not adequately capture local time trends in crime rates. To test for this possibility, we generalized the Lott and Mustard model to include state-specific trends in an effort to control for these unobserved factors. . . . we report the results for models with a quadratic time trend. The only significant impact estimate is for assaults, and its sign is positive, not negative. (Dan Black and Dan Nagin, "Do Right-to-Carry Laws Deter Violent Crime?" *Journal of Legal Studies,* January 1998, p. 218)

Much more was controlled for than "a single national trend" in my study (e.g., as just mentioned above, state and county trends as well as other crime rates). While it is reasonable to include individual linear state trends or nonlinear trends for regions, including nonlinear trends for individual states makes no sense. The approach by Black and Nagin is particularly noteworthy because it is the one case in which an academic study has claimed that a statistically significant, even if small, increase in any type of violent crime (aggravated assault) occurs after the law.

Consider a hypothetical case in which the crime rate for each and every state follows the pattern that Black and Nagin found in their earlier paper and that I showed in this book (discussed in chapter 7, pp. 134–38): crime rates were rising up until the law went into effect and falling thereafter. Allowing a separate quadratic time trend for each state results in the time trend picking up both the upward path before the law and the downward path thereafter. If the different state crime patterns all peaked in the year in which their state law went into effect, the state-specific quadratic trends would account for all the impact of the law. A variable measuring the average crime rates before and after the law would then no longer reflect whether the law raised or lowered the crime rate.[74] This is analogous to the "dubious variable" problem discussed earlier. If enough state-specific trends are included, there will be nothing left for the other variables to explain.

If shall-issue laws deter crime, we would expect crime rates to rise until the law was passed and then to rise more slowly or to fall. The effect should increase over time as more permits are issued and more criminals adjust to the increased risks that they face. But the quadratic specification used by Black and Nagin replicates that pattern, state by state. Their results show not that the effect from the quadratic curve is insignificant, but that the deviation of the law's effect from a quadratic curve over time is generally insignificant.

To see this more clearly, take the hypothetical case illustrated in figure 9.15, in which a state faced rising crime rates.[75] The figure shows imaginary data for crime in a state that passed its shall-issue law in 1991. (The dots in the figure display what the crime rate was in different years.) The pattern would clearly support the hypothesis that concealed-handgun laws deter violent crime, but the pattern can easily be fitted with a quadratic curve, as demonstrated with the curved line. There is no systematic drop left over for any measure of the right-to-carry law to detect—in terms of the figure, the difference between the dots and the curved line shows no particular pattern.

Phrased differently, the deterrence hypothesis implies a state-specific time pattern in crime rates (because different states did or did not pass shall-issue laws, or passed them at different dates). All Black and Nagin have shown is that they can fit such a state-specific pattern with a state-specific

Figure 9.15. Fitting a nonlinear trend to individual states

quadratic time trend, and do this well enough that the residuals no longer show a pattern.

3 *Should one expect an immediate and constant effect from right-to-carry laws with the same effect everywhere?*

> While he includes a chapter that contains replies to his critics, unfortunately he doesn't directly respond to the key Black and Nagin finding that formal statistical tests reject his methods. The closest he gets to addressing this point is to acknowledge "the more serious possibility is that some other factor may have caused both the reduction in crime rates and the passage of the law to occur at the same time," but then goes on to say that he has "presented over a thousand [statistical model] specifications" that reveal "an extremely consistent pattern" that right-to-carry laws reduce crime. Another view would be that a thousand versions of a demonstrably invalid analytical approach produce boxes full of invalid results. (Jens Ludwig, "Guns and Numbers," *Washington Monthly,* June 1998, p. 51)[76]

> We applied a number of specification tests suggested by James J. Heckman and V. Joseph Hotz. The results are available from us on request. The specifics of the findings, however, are less important than the overall conclusion that is implied. The results show that commonly the model either overestimates or underestimates the crime rate of adopting states in the years prior to adoption. (Dan Black and Dan Nagin, "Do Right-to-Carry Laws Deter Violent Crime?" *Journal of Legal Studies,* January 1998, p. 218)

Black and Nagin actually spent only a few brief sentences on this issue at the very end of their paper. Nevertheless, I did respond to this general point in the original book. Their test is based upon the claim that I believe "that [right-to-carry] laws have an impact on crime rates that is constant over time."[77] True, when one looks at the simple before-and-after average crime rates, as in the first test presented in table 4.1 and a corresponding table in my original work with Mustard, this was the assumption that was being made.[78] Figure 9.16 illustrates the crime pattern assumed by that test. But I emphasized that looking at the before-and-after averages was not a very good way to test the impact of the right-to-carry laws (e.g., see p. 92), and I presented better, more complicated specifications, and these showed even larger benefits from these laws. Black and Nagin's test confirms the very criticisms that I was making of these initial simplifying assumptions.

Figure 9.16. What was the crime pattern being assumed in the simple test provided in table 4.1?

Looking at the before-and-after averages merely provides a simplified starting point. If criminals respond to the risk of meeting a potential victim who is carrying a concealed handgun, the deterrent effect of a concealed-handgun law should be related to the number of concealed handguns being carried and that should rise gradually over time. It was precisely because of these concerns that I included a variable for the number of years since the law had been in effect. As consistently demonstrated in figure 1 in my original paper as well as the figures in this book (e.g., pp. 82–83), these estimated time trends confirm that crime rates were rising before the law went into effect and falling afterward, with the effect increasing as more years went by.

As already discussed in the book, I did not expect the impact to be the same across all states, for obviously all states cannot be expected to issue permits at the same rate (see the response to point 3 on pp. 135–36). Indeed, this is one of the reasons why I examined whether the drops in crime rates were greatest in urban, high-population areas.

On this issue David Friedman, a professor at the University of Santa Clara Law School, wrote that "The simplifying assumptions used in one of the regressions reported in the Lott and Mustard paper (Table 3) are not true—something that should be obvious to anyone who has read Lott and Mustard's original article, which included a variety of other regressions designed to deal with the complications assumed away in that one. Black and Nagin simply applied tests of the specification to demonstrate that they were not true."[79] Similar points have also been raised in academic reviews of the book: "Another tactic was to criticize one part of the research by raising issues that Lott actually raised and addressed in another part of the study. Those criticisms that were not uninformed or misleading were generally irrelevant since taking them into account did not change his empirical results. Nonetheless, they were widely cited by an unquestioning press."[80]

4 *Do right-to-carry laws significantly reduce the robbery rate?*

Q. What's your take on John Lott's study and subsequent book that concludes concealed weapon laws lower the crime rate? (Lott's book is titled "More Guns, Less Crime," University of Chicago Press, 1998.)

A. His basic premise in his study is that these laws encourage private citizens to carry guns and therefore discourage criminal attacks, like homicides and rapes. Think for a second. Most murders and rapes occur in homes. So where would you see the greatest impact if his premise were true? You would see it in armed robbery. But there's no effect on armed robbery. His study is flawed, but it's costing us enormous problems. People are citing it everywhere. (Quote in the St. Paul, Minnesota, newspaper the *Pioneer Planet,* August 3, 1998, from an interview with Bob Walker, president of Handgun Control, Inc.)

Both the preceding quotes and many other criticisms are based on not recognizing that a law can be associated with reduced crime even when the average crime rate in the period after the law is the same as or higher than the average crime rate before the law.[81] For example, look at the four diagrams in figure 9.17. The first two diagrams show dramatic changes in crime rates from the law, but very different before-and-after average crime rates. In the first diagram (17*a*), the average crime rate after the law is lower than the average crime rate before it, while the reverse is true in the second diagram. The second diagram (17*b*) corresponds to an example in which the simple variable measuring the average effect from the law would have falsely indicated that the law actually "increased" the average crime rate, while in actual fact the crime rate was rising right up until the law passed and falling thereafter. If I had another figure where the inverted V shape was perfectly symmetrical, the before-and-after averages would have been the same. (With this in mind, it would be useful to reexamine the earlier estimates for robbery shown in figures 4.8 and 7.4.)

The third diagram (17*c*) illustrates the importance of looking at more than simple before-and-after averages in another way. A simple variable measuring the before-and-after averages would indicate that the average crime rate "fell" after the law was adopted, yet once one graphs out the before-and-after trends it is clear that this average effect is quite misleading—the crime rate was falling until the law went into effect and rising

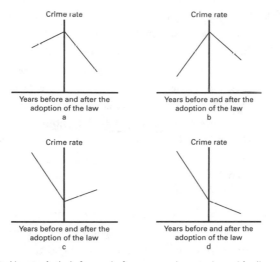

Figure 9.17. Why looking at only the before-and-after average crime rates is so misleading

thereafter. Finally, the fourth diagram (17*d*) shows a case in which the average crime rate is obviously lower after the law than beforehand but the drop is merely a continuation of an existing trend. Indeed, if anything, the rate of decline in crime rates appears to have slowed down after the law. Looking at the simple before-and-after averages provides a very misleading picture of the changing trends in crime rates.

5 *Is the way criminals learn about victims' ability to defend themselves inconsistent with the results?*

Zimring and Hawkins observe that there are two potential transmission mechanisms by which potential criminals respond to the passage of a shall issue law. The first, which they term the announcement effect, changes the conduct of potential criminals because the publicity attendant to the enactment of the law makes them fear the prospect of encountering an armed victim. The second, which they call the crime hazard model, implies that potential criminals will respond to the actual increased risk they face from the increased arming of the citizenry. Lott adheres to the standard economist's view that the latter mechanism is the more important of the two—but he doesn't fully probe its implications. Recidivists and individuals closely tied to criminal enterprises are likely to learn more quickly than non-repeat criminals about the actual probability of encountering a concealed weapon in a particular situation. Therefore, we suspect that shall issue laws are more likely to deter recidivists. . . . Thus, if Lott's theory were true, we would also suspect that the proportion of crime committed by recidivists should be decreasing and that crime categories with higher proportions of recidivism—and robbery is likely in this category—should exhibit the highest reductions. Once again, though, the lack of a strong observed effect for robbery raises tensions between the theoretical predictions and Lott's evidence. (Ian Ayres and John J. Donohue III, "Nondiscretionary Concealed Weapons Laws: A Case Study of Statistics, Standards of Proof, and Public Policy," *American Law and Economics Review* 1, nos. 1–2 [Fall 1999]: 458–59)

I have always viewed both the mentioned mechanisms as plausible. Yet the question of emphasis is an empirical issue. Was there a once-and-for-all drop in violent crimes when the law passed? Did the drop in violent crimes increase over time as more people obtained permits? Or was there some combination of these two influences? The data strongly suggest that criminals respond more to the actual increased risk, rather than the announcement per se. Indeed, all the data support this conclusion: table 4.6, the before- and after-law time trends, the county-level permit data for Oregon and Pennsylvania, and the new results focusing on the predicted percentage of the population with permits. The deterrence effect is closely related to the percentage of the population with permits.

I have no problem with Ayres and Donohue's hypothesis that criminals who keep on committing a particular crime will learn the new risks faster than will criminals who only commit crimes occasionally.[82] However, that hypothesis will be difficult to evaluate, for data on the number and types of crimes committed by criminals are known to be notoriously suspect, as they come from surveys of criminals themselves. Some of the criminals appear to be bragging to surveyors and claim many thousands of crimes each year. But one thing is clear from these surveys: criminals often commit many different types of crimes, and hence it is generally incorrect to say that criminals only learn from one type of crime. In any case, even if Ayres and Donohue believe that robbers are more likely to learn from their crimes, the estimated deterrent effect on robbery turns out to be very large when the before-and-after trends are compared.[83]

It is interesting that one set of critiques attacks me for allegedly assuming a once-and-for-all drop in crime from right-to-carry laws (see point 3 above), while at the same time I am attacked for assuming that the drop can be related only to the number of permits issued.

6 *Have prominent "pro-gun" researchers questioned the findings in my book?*

> To dispel the notion that Lott is simply being victimized by the "PC crowd," it may be helpful to mention the reaction of Gary Kleck, a Florida State criminologist known for his generally "pro-gun" views. . . . Kleck argues in his recent book that it is "more likely [that] the declines in crime coinciding with relaxation of carry laws were largely attributable to other factors not controlled in the Lott and Mustard analysis." (Jens Ludwig, "Guns and Numbers," *Washington Monthly,* June 1998, p. 51)

> Even Gary Kleck, a researcher long praised by the NRA and identified as an authority on gun-violence prevention by Lott himself, has dismissed the findings. (Sarah Brady, "Q: Would New Requirements for Gun Buyers Save Lives? Yes: Stop Deadly, Unregulated Sales to Minors, at Gun Shows and on the Internet," *Insight,* June 21, 1999, p. 24)

The quote by Kleck has frequently been mentioned by Jim and Sarah Brady and other members of Handgun Control and the Violence Policy Center.[84] However, it is a rather selective reading of what he wrote. Their claim that Kleck "dismissed the findings" is hard to reconcile with Kleck's comment in the very same piece that my research "represents the most authoritative study" on these issues.[85]

Let me try to explain the meaning of Kleck's quote. I have talked to Gary on several occasions about what additional variables I should control for, but he has been unable to concretely suggest anything; it rather seemed to be more a "feeling" of his that there might be other factors out there. But the issue is more complicated than simply stating that something else should be accounted for: there must exist some left-out factor that just happened to be changing in all the twenty states that had enacted right-to-carry laws for at least a year between 1977 and 1996. Perhaps one can find some left-out national change in some specific year, yet this would not have much of an effect on the regression results.

Gary Kleck has long felt strongly that guns have no net effect on the crime rate. Why he has felt that way has never been clear to me (though I have asked), especially considering his own survey results, which indicate that citizens use guns to stop violent crime about 2.5 million times each year—a large order of magnitude bigger than the reported number of crimes committed with guns.[86] Thus, the couple of sentences that gun-control advocates refer to from what Gary has written about my research did not totally surprise me. Gary told me that he thought it was "quite

amusing" that people from Handgun Control and other gun-control organizations were now starting to cite him as an expert. He also said that
he thought that the quotes were being misused, and that he still stood by
the blurb for my book—the blurb stating that my research represented
"the most extensive, thorough, and sophisticated study we have on the
effects of loosening gun control laws."

7 *Are the CBS and Voter News Service polls accurately reflecting how gun ownership rates vary
across states?*

> Douglas Weil: But the most important information is that the Voter News
> Service, which conducted the 1996 poll has said the poll cannot be used in
> the manner Dr. Lott used it. It cannot be used to say anything about gun
> ownership in any state, and it cannot be used to compare gun ownership
> to the earlier 1988 voter poll. ("More Guns, Less Crime? A Debate between
> John Lott, Author of *More Guns, Less Crime,* and Douglas Weil, Research Di-
> rector of Handgun Control, Inc.," an on-line debate sponsored by *Time*
> magazine, transcript from July 1, 1998)

Statistics from the CBS and Voter News Service exit polls (discussed in chapters 3 and 5) were originally "weighted" by these organizations to reflect
the share of different racial, sex, and age groups in the national population.
For example, white females between thirty and thirty-nine make up 6 percent of the population but may end up accounting for a larger percentage
of those surveyed in a poll. If white females in that age group are overrepresented in the calculations made to determine what voters support,
the poll will not accurately reflect how voters as a whole will vote in an
election. To correct this, polls were adjusted so that different groups are
weighted according to their actual shares of either the voting or the general population. It is therefore necessary for the researcher to use a state's
demographics to adjust that state's poll results himself, because the shares
that different groups make of state populations differ from their shares of
the national population. That is precisely what I did.

There were also differences in how the 1988 and 1996 surveys were
phrased, and I already discussed those biases right at the beginning of chapter 3. In the notes accompanying that discussion, I mentioned that these
biases do not appreciably affect changes in survey results between these
two years. The important point is that the changes in how the questions
were worded should not alter the relative ranking of states or what types of

people are more likely to own guns. Regressions using data from the two years used variables that account for the average difference across years as well as the average differences across states to account for any biases.

8 *Have I ignored the costs of gun violence?*

> He ignores the huge cost on medical systems that gun violence causes. (Steve Young of the Bell Campaign, an anti-gun group, as quoted in Frank Main, "Economist Says Guns Fight Crime," *Chicago Sun-Times,* July 8, 1999, p. 6)

The costs of crime include medical or other costs of crime, such as lost time from a job or replacement costs for damage and replacement costs for items taken or destroyed. I do not ignore such costs. But unlike my critics, neither do I ignore the crimes that are stopped because people are able to defend themselves. The net effect is what is relevant, and that is directly measured by what happens to the number of crimes. To the extent that people commit crimes with permitted concealed handguns, the number of crimes will rise. To the extent that such handguns deter criminals, the number of crimes will decline. When criminals substitute different types of crimes, the issue then is how the medical and other costs of those different crimes compare. As to the costs of different crimes, I relied on a study produced the National Institute of Justice, rather than produce my own independent numbers.

An interesting contrast to my work is a recent paper published in the *Journal of the American Medical Association* which claimed to show that there were "$2.3 billion in lifetime medical costs for people shot in 1994." Jens Ludwig, one of the authors of the study, argues that "cities such as Chicago could use the study in their lawsuits against the gun industry."[87] But the correct question is not whether guns involve medical costs but whether total medical costs are greater with or without guns. The logic is akin to determining whether police should be allowed to carry guns only by looking at the number of wrongful shootings, and not the times that guns are used to protect officers or deter criminals. Eliminating guns will not eliminate violence and the costs associated with those attacks. Indeed, from a historical perspective, murder rates were higher in England before guns were invented. Medical costs also include costs from suicides and attempted suicides, and the evidence discussed in chapter 5 indicates that suicides will still occur at pretty much the same rate even if guns are not present. For example, crashing one's car in an attempt to kill oneself can produce substantial medical costs, but even methods like overdosing on sleeping pills or slitting one's wrists with a knife involve medical costs.

9 *What happens to the evidence when Florida and counties with fewer than 100,000 people are removed from the sample?*

> Lott does not respond to Black and Nagin's finding that excluding Florida and small counties (with population less than 100,000) from his samples destroys the statistical significance of all of the violent-crime categories except assault. This suggests that Lott's results are not as robust as he claims. True, Lott's thesis is not embarrassed by varying degrees of deterrence across states (especially since he shows that this variance may be related to the number of permits issued). However, his thesis is shaken by the considerable number of state specific crime categories where concealed-handgun laws are associated with an increase in crime and where the overall significance of his results is undermined by the exclusion of Florida and small counties. (Ian Ayres and John J. Donohue III, "Nondiscretionary Concealed Weapons Laws: A Case Study of Statistics, Standards of Proof, and Public Policy," *American Law and Economics Review* 1, nos. 1–2 [Fall 1999]: 463)

I had clearly dealt with this issue in the first edition of the book. Dropping all counties with fewer than 100,000 people plus Florida reduces the significance in regressions that examine only the average crime rates before and after the law is adopted. Making these changes increases the impact of the law when one examines the before-and-after trends. As the careful reader might guess, the reason that the before-and-after average is not significant for some crimes is that dropping all these observations actually causes the changes to look more like the inverted V that we have so frequently discussed. Picking and choosing which observations to include, which single specification to report, and even which crime categories to report (Black and Nagin do not report the overall violent-crime rates) allows them to knock down the significance of two of the crime categories. (By any standards that I know, a t-statistic of 1.9 for robberies is still statistically significant at better than the 5 percent level, and their coefficient still implies a drop in before-and-after averages of 4.6 percent.) Dropping 87 percent of the sample and reporting only the specifications examining the before-and-after averages may be Black and Nagin's preferred sample and specification, but even these results imply significant benefits and no cost from passing right-to-carry laws. If they had reported the overall violent-crime rate, they would have shown that overall violent crime fell after the right-to-carry laws were passed.

Table 9.7 uses the updated data to examine the importance of dropping out counties with fewer than 100,000 people as well as Florida. The impact of the law is greater for overall violent-crime rates and aggravated assaults and smaller for the other three violent-crime categories. Each additional year after the law goes into effect produces an additional 3 percent drop in violent-crime rates.

When Black and Nagin break down the differences by individual states, they claim to find three crime categories in which one of the ten states had a statistically significant increase in crime rates (West Virginia for murder, Mississippi for rape, and Pennsylvania for robbery). But their results do not show the variation across states, for they are derived from only a small subset of observations from those states. The West Virginia sample included only one of its fifty-five counties, as it was the only one with more than 100,000 people. The Mississippi data included just three of its eighty-two counties. The results reported earlier in table 4.9 provide the information on how the right-to-carry laws affected the crime rates across states.

10 *Are the results valid only when Maine and Florida are included?*

I will try to summarize the argument here. Ian Ayres and John Donohue are concerned about the inclusion of Maine and Florida for several reasons: (1) the results discussed by Black and Nagin, (2) the issue of whether the crack epidemic might have just happened to cause the relative crime rates to rise in non-right-to-carry states in the late 1980s, and (3) objections to whether Cramer and Kopel were correct in classifying Maine as a right-to-carry state. To satisfy their concerns, Ayres and Donohue use several different approaches, such as dropping both Maine and Florida out of the sample. They also divide the shall-issue dummy variable into two separate variables: a variable to measure the average before-and-after crime rates for those states that adopted their right-to carry laws before December 1987 (Maine and Florida) and a similar variable to measure the average before-and-after crime rates for those states that adopted their crime rates after December 1987.

Ayres and Donohue find that violent-crime rates consistently fall in states adopting right-to-carry laws after 1987, but the effect is often statistically

Table 9.7 What is the impact of removing both counties with fewer than 100,000 people and Florida from the sample?

	Percent change in various crime rates for changes in explanatory variables							
	Violent crime	Murder	Rape	Robbery	Aggravated assault	Property crime	Burglary	Larceny	Auto theft
Change in the crime rate from the difference in the annual change in crime rates in the years before and after the adoption of the right-to-carry law (annual rate of change after the law − annual rate of change before the law)	−3.3%*	−0.45%****	−2.6%**	−3.0%*	−4.7%*	−0.8%	−2.1%**	−0.24%	−1.8%**

*The F-test is significant at the 1 percent level.
**The F-test is significant at the 5 percent level.
****The F-test is significant at the 15 percent level.

insignificant. The drops in violent crime appear much larger and more significant for the earlier states. Indeed, as reported earlier in this book, Maine and Florida experience two of the three largest overall drops in violent crime (see table 4.9). Yet the focus on the before-and-after averages again obscures the benefits from right-to-carry laws.

The results presented in table 9.8 take the two approaches that I have been using: the estimated number of permits issued in a state and the differences between the trends in crime rates before and after the adoption of the right-to-carry laws. With the exception of rape, Maine and Florida experience greater drops in all violent-crime categories, but all the violent-crime rates decline for states adopting right-to-carry laws during the post-1987 period and all but two of these declines are statistically significant at least at the 10 percent level. The estimates using the percentage of the population with permits imply that there were no statistically different effects for the two sets of states for murder and rape.

11 *Was it proper to assume that more permits were issued in the more populous counties after right-to-carry laws were adopted?*

> Since the links between the issuance of permits and the crime reduction that Lott attributes to the shall issue laws is so crucial to establishing causality, more research on this issue is needed. Lott's county population proxies rely on his assumption that population density is a good predictor of the difficulty in obtaining permits under discretionary laws. However, if many states went directly from prohibiting concealed weapons to a non-discretionary law (like Arizona), Lott's assumed relationship between permits and density would break down. (Ian Ayres and John J. Donohue III, "Nondiscretionary Concealed Weapons Laws: A Case Study of Statistics, Standards of Proof, and Public Policy," *American Law and Economics* Review 1, nos. 1–2 [Fall 1999]: 446)

The original tests shown in figures 4.1 and 4.2 were based upon conversations that I had had with state officials in nondiscretionary states. If the state officials' claims were correct that high-population counties had been much more restrictive in issuing permits than low-population counties, adoption of right-to-carry laws would have seen the biggest issuance of permits in these counties and thus the biggest drops in crime. The results confirmed this prediction. Obviously, this claim depends upon all the states switching from discretionary to nondiscretionary laws, and indeed all the states examined for the tests shown in these earlier figures did make that change.

Table 9.8 Reexamining the claim that states adopting the law before and after December 1987 were differently affected by right-to-carry laws

	Percent change in various crime rates for changes in explanatory variables								
	Violent crime	Murder	Rape	Robbery	Aggravated assault	Property crime	Burglary	Larceny	Auto theft
States adopting law prior to December 1987: one-percentage-point change in the share of the state population with permits to carry concealed handguns	-15.8%[a]	-5.4%[b]	-3.9%[d]	-9.7%[a]	-19.1%[a]	-15.5%[a]	-6.1%[a]	-22.6%[a]	-8.9%[a]
States adopting law after December 1987: one-percentage-point change in the share of the state population with permits to carry concealed handguns	-4.1%[a]	-2.7%[a]	-5.0%[a]	-1.0%	-7.8%[a]	4.8%[a]	-2.0%[a]	8.7%[a]	0.34%
States adopting law prior to December 1987: change in the crime rate from the difference in the annual change in crime rates in the years before and after the adoption of the right-to-carry law (annual rate of change after the law − annual rate of change before the law)	-7.2%*	-9.2%*	-0.9%	-7.1%*	-5.7%*	-2.4%*	-1.1%	-4.1%*	-4.1%*
States adopting law after December 1987: change in the crime rate from the difference in the annual change in crime rates in the years before and after the adoption of the right-to-carry law (annual rate of change after the law − annual rate of change before the law)	-1.7%*	-0.7%***	-3.3%*	-2.9%*	-2.4%*	-0.7%*	-2.4%*	0.5%*	-1.4%*

[a]The result is significant at the 1 percent level for a two-tailed t-test.
[b]The result is significant at the 5 percent level for a two-tailed t-test.
[d]The result is significant at the 12 percent level for a two-tailed t-test.
*The F-test is significant at the 1 percent level.
*The result is significant at the 1 percent level.
***The F-test is significant at the 10 percent level.

None of the states during 1977–1992 switched from not issuing any permits to nondiscretionary rules. Arizona made its change in late 1994.

The updated results in this chapter have continued to remain conscious of this issue, and I found that the more populous counties in states that changed from discretionary to nondiscretionary laws had bigger relative drops in violent-crime rates than states that changed from banning concealed handguns to nondiscretionary laws.

12 *Did the passage of right-to-carry laws result in more guns being carried in public places?*

> Perhaps by "more guns," Lott means more guns carried in public places. However, surveys indicate that 5–11% of US adults admit to carrying guns, dwarfing the 1% or so of the population that obtained concealed-weapon permits. . . . And if those who got permits were merely legitimating what they were already doing before the new laws, it would mean there was no increase at all in carrying or in actual risks to criminals. One can always speculate that criminals' perceptions of risk outran reality, but that is all this is—a speculation. More likely, the declines in crime coinciding with relaxation of carry laws were largely attributable to other factors not controlled in the Lott and Mustard analysis. (Tim Lambert, "Do More Guns Cause Less Crime?" from his posting on his Web site at the School of Computer Science and Engineering, University of New South Wales [http://www.cse.unsw.EDU.AU/~lambert/guns/lott/])

The survey results mentioned by Lambert refer to all transportation or carrying of guns by Americans. They include not only carrying concealed handguns (whether legally or illegally) but also people who have guns with them to go hunting or who may simply be transporting guns between residences.[88] On the other hand, any survey that focused solely on the illegal carrying of concealed handguns prior to the adoption of the law would find it difficult to get people to admit that they had been violating the law.

The 1 percent figure Lambert picks for carrying concealed handguns is also very misleadingly low. As I have shown in this book, permitting rates depend upon many factors (such as the level of fees and the amount of training required), but they also depend crucially on the number of years that the permitting rules have been in effect. The longer the amount of time that the rules are in effect, the more people who obtain permits. Not everyone who will eventually obtain a permit will apply for it immediately. With the large number of states that have only recently granted permits to people it is misleading to think that the current permit rate tells us the rate at which people in those states will be carrying concealed handguns even a few years from now.

Given how extremely law abiding these permit holders tend to be, it seems doubtful that most people carrying concealed handguns with permits were illegally carrying concealed handguns before the passage of the right-to-carry law. In many states, illegally carrying a concealed weapon would be the type of violation that would prevent people from ever even getting a permit. There is no evidence that these permit holders have violated this particular law. Yet even if as many as 10 percent of permit holders had previously been illegally carrying a concealed handgun, the coefficients from table 9.3 would still imply that for every 900 additional people with permits there are 0.3 fewer murders and 2.4 fewer rapes.

Finally, while the evidence linking the rate at which permits are issued and the drops in crime rates is important, it is only one portion of the evidence. For example, if there was no change in the number of people carrying concealed handguns, why did violent-crime rates in neighboring counties without the law increase at the same time that they were falling in neighboring counties with the right-to-carry law?

13 *Shouldn't permit holders be required to have the same type of training as police officers?*

Proponents of [right-to-carry] legislation contend that citizens will be adequately trained to handle firearms responsibly, but this is rarely true. Police departments require officers to go through a great deal of safety and proficiency training before issued a gun—followed by regular refresher courses and qualifications throughout the officer's career. Citizens armed under the provisions of non-discretionary carry laws are not so highly trained, and frequently not trained at all, thereby further increasing the risk of injury and death with a firearm. (From the Web page of Handgun Control, Inc., entitled "Will the Real John Lott Please Stand Up?")

Police officers face a much more difficult job than citizens with concealed handguns. An officer cannot be satisfied if the criminal runs away after he brandishes a gun. Instead, police must act offensively, which is much more dangerous. Citizens are rarely put in situations that require the skill of pursuing an attacker.

There are both costs and benefits to training. Yet the question is ultimately an empirical one. Training requirements improve the deterrence effect for concealed-handgun laws, but the effects are small. What I do find is that longer training periods reduce the number of people obtaining permits, and the net effect of increased training is clearly to reduce the deterrent effect of adopting right-to-carry laws.

Conclusion

The noise came suddenly from behind early Tuesday—feet rapidly pounding the pavement, voices cursing. Before Jim Shaver could turn around, he was knocked to the ground at East 13th Avenue and Mill Street, fighting off punches from two young men. Police said the assailants figured they'd found a drug dealer to rob, someone who'd have both drugs and money. They couldn't have been more wrong. Their victim was a 49-year-old nurse on his way to work—a nurse with a concealed weapons permit. The fists kept flying, even as Shaver told them—twice, he said—that he had a gun. Fearing for his life, Shaver pulled a .22-caliber revolver out of his coat pocket and fired several shots. One of them hit 19-year-old Damien Alexander Long in the right hip. Long's alleged accomplice, Brandon Heath Durrett, 20, wasn't injured. The pair ran off.[89]

A man who police said kidnapped a 2-year-old child and robbed a disabled elderly woman of a medical monitor was in jail Friday after he was captured and held at gun point by a man with a license to carry a concealed handgun. . . . "I have never pulled a gun on anyone before, and I wouldn't have pulled a gun on this man if he had not run off with that little girl," [the man who stopped the crime] said. "That mother was screaming for her child. She was quite upset."[90]

Awe-struck Phoenix police declared Mr. Vertigan a hero and gave him $500 and a new pistol for catching a cop killer after running out of ammunition in a gunfight with three heavily armed men. Mr. Vertigan . . . came upon three armed Mexican drug-traffickers fatally ambushing a uniformed Phoenix policeman who was patrolling alone in Phoenix's tough Maryvale precinct. Firing 14 shots with his left hand during a slam-and-bump car chase that left the killers' license number imprinted on the front of his own car, Mr. Vertigan emptied his Glock 31 .357 Sig. He wounded the shooter, who was firing at him, and forced the getaway car to crash, slowing the shooter's partners long enough for pursuing police to seize them, as well as a pound of cocaine "eight balls" they were dealing from their white Lincoln. "I always felt that if my life was in danger or anyone around me was in immediate danger I never would hesitate to use that gun. Unfortunately, that day came," Mr. Vertigan said.[91]

A man who tried to commit an armed robbery at a Bensalem convenience store Friday morning was thwarted by a customer who pulled out his own gun and fired five shots at the crook. . . . Fearing he would be killed, police said, the customer began shooting at the suspect. . . . Police said the clerks were "a little shaken up" after the attempted robbery—but they guessed that the would-be robber was probably just as shocked. "I'll bet he never expected that to happen," said Fred Harran, Bensalem's deputy director of public safety.[92]

All these recent cases involved individuals with permitted concealed hand-guns. During 1999 concealed permit holders have prevented bank robber-ies, stopped what could have been a bloody attack by gang members at a teenage girl's high school graduation party, and stopped carjackings.[93] In the couple of months during which I was updating this book, armed citizens have helped capture murderers who had escaped prison; stopped hostage taking at a business, a situation that otherwise surely would have resulted in multiple deaths; and prevented robberies and rapes.[94] Residen-tial attacks that were stopped by citizens with guns during 1999 were ex-tremely common.[95]

One of the bigger puzzles to me has been the news coverage on guns. Admittedly, some of it is easy to explain. Suppose a media outlet has two stories to choose from: one in which there is a dead body on the ground and it is a sympathetic person like a victim, another in which a woman brandishes a gun and the attacker runs away, no shots are fired, no dead bodies are on the ground, and no crime is actually consummated. It seems pretty obvious which story is going to get the news coverage. Yet if we re-ally want to answer the question of which policies will save lives, we must take into consideration not only the newsworthy bad events but also the bad events that never happen because people are able to defend themselves. Unfortunately, the newsworthy bad events give people a warped impres-sion of the costs and benefits from having guns around.

Even when defensive gun uses are mentioned in the press, those men-tions do not focus on typical defensive gun uses. The news stories focus primarily on the extremely rare cases in which the attacker is killed, though a few times press stories do mention cases of a gun being used to seri-ously wound an attacker. News coverage of defensive gun uses in which a would-be victim simply brandished a gun are essentially unheard-of. I don't think one has to rely on a conspiracy explanation to understand why this type of news coverage occurs, for it is not that surprising that dead attackers are considered more newsworthy than prevented attacks in which nobody was harmed. Even so, it is still important to recognize how this coverage can color people's perspective on how guns are used defensively. Since most people probably are very reticent to take a life, if they believe that defensive gun use almost always results in the death of an attacker, they will become more uncomfortable with guns.

While these examples are easily understood, some other news coverage is not as obvious. Take the case of accidental gun deaths involving young children, which we discussed in chapter 1. My guess is that people believe these events to be much more frequent than they actually are. When I have given talks, I have sometimes asked the audience how many children under age five or ten die from accidental gun shots each year; the answers are frequently in the thousand-plus range. A few answers might mention only hundreds of deaths per year. No one comes close to the Centers for Disease Control numbers: seventeen accidental gun deaths for children under age five and forty-two for children under ten in 1996. The information that forty children under age five drown each year in five-gallon water buckets or that eighty drown in bathtubs always astounds the audience. People remember national news reports of young children dying from accidental handgun shots in the home. In contrast, when was the last time that you heard on the national news of a child drowning in a five-gallon water bucket?[96]

As a father of four boys and one daughter, I can't imagine what life would be like if one of my children died for any reason, including guns. But why so much more attention is given to guns when so many other risks pose a greater threat to our children is not immediately obvious to me. Indeed, it is difficult to think of anything other than guns that is as prevalent around American homes, and that is anywhere near as potentially dangerous, yet is responsible for as low an accidental death rate. With around 80 million people owning a total of 200–240 million guns, the vast majority of gun owners must be extremely careful or such gun accidents would be much more frequent.

I have asked some reporters why they think accidental gun deaths receive so much coverage, and the only answer seems to be that these events get coverage because they are so rare. Dog bites man is simply not newsworthy because it is so common, but man bites dog, well, that is news. Yet this explanation still troubles me, for there are other equally rare deaths involving children that get very little news coverage.

Another puzzle is the lack of coverage given to cases in which citizens with guns have prevented multiple-victim public shootings from occurring. Given the intense concern generated by these attacks, one would think that people would be interested in knowing how these attacks were stopped.

For a simple comparison, take the justified news coverage accorded the heroic actions of Dave Sanders, the Columbine High School teacher who helped protect some of the students and was killed in the process. By the Sunday morning five days after the incident, a Lexis-Nexis search (a type of on-line computer search that includes news media databases) indicates that over 250 of the slightly over 1,000 news stories around the country on this tragedy had mentioned this hero.

Contrast this with other school attacks in which the crimes were stopped well before the police were able to arrive. Take, for example, the October 1997 shooting spree at a high school in Pearl, Mississippi, described at the beginning of this section, which left two students dead. It was stopped by Joel Myrick, an assistant principal. He retrieved his permitted concealed handgun from his car and physically immobilized the shooter for about five minutes before police arrived.

A Lexis-Nexis search indicates that 687 articles appeared in the first month after the attack. Only 19 stories mentioned Myrick in any way. Only a little more than half of these mentioned he used a gun to stop the attack. Some stories simply stated Myrick was "credited by police with helping capture the boy" or that "Myrick disarmed the shooter." A later story reported by Dan Rather on CBS noted that "Myrick eventually subdued the young gunman." Such stories provide no explanation of how Myrick accomplished this feat.

The school-related shooting in Edinboro, Pennsylvania, which left one teacher dead, was stopped only after James Strand, the owner of a nearby restaurant, pointed a shotgun at the shooter when he was finishing reloading his gun. The police did not arrive until eleven minutes later. At least 596 news stories discussed this crime during the next month, yet only 35 mentioned Strand. Once again, the media ignored that a gun was used to stop the crime. The *New York Daily News* explained that Strand "persuaded [the killer] to surrender," while the *Atlanta Journal* wrote how he "chased [the killer] down and held him until police came." Saying that Strand "persuaded" the attacker makes it sound as if Strand were simply an effective speaker.

Neither Myrick nor Strand was killed during their heroics. That might explain why they were ignored to a greater degree than Dave Sanders in the Columbine attack. Yet one suspects a more politically correct explanation—especially when the media generally ignore defensive gun use. With five public-school-related shootings occurring during the 1997–1998 school year, one might have thought that the fact that two of them were stopped by guns would register in the public debate over such shootings.

The media bias can be amply illustrated by other examples as well. Take the example of the July attack in Atlanta, which left nine people dead. Mark Barton killed people working at two stock brokerages.[97] It did deserve the extensive news coverage that it received. Yet, within the next week and a half, there were three cases around Atlanta in which citizens with guns stopped similar attacks from occurring, and these incidents were given virtually no news coverage. They were an attack at a Lavonia, Georgia, store by a fired worker; an attack by a mental patient at an Atlanta hospital; and an Atlanta truckjacking.[98] The last two incidents were stopped by citizens with permitted concealed handguns. The first was stopped by someone who had only been allowed to buy a gun hours before the attack because of Georgia's instant background check system. Meanwhile, a week after the Atlanta massacre, another attack, which left three people dead at a business in Birmingham, Alabama, again generated national television news coverage on all the networks and was the lead story on the CBS and NBC evening news.[99]

Again, I can see that bad events that never occur are not nearly as newsworthy as actual bad events. Yet multiple-victim attacks using methods other than guns are frequently ignored. On May 3, 1999, Steve Abrams drove his Cadillac into a crowded preschool playground because he "wanted to execute innocent children."[100] Two children died horrible deaths as one was mangled under the wheels and the other pinned to a tree by the car, and another five were badly injured. One woman's son was so badly mauled that "teachers and other parents stepped between [her] and the Cadillac to prevent her from seeing her son's battered body" even though he was still alive. Yet only one television network provided even a passing reference to this attack.[101] One very obvious news angle, it seems to me, would be to link this attack to the various public school attacks. Compare this news coverage with the attention generated by Buford Furrow's August 10, 1999, assault on a Jewish community center, which left five people wounded, three of them young boys.[102] Multiple-victim knife attacks have been ignored by the national media, and few people would realize that there were 1,884 bombing incidents in the United States in 1996, which left a total of 34 people dead and 365 people injured.[103]

The news coverage is also constantly framed as, "Is more gun control the answer?"[104] The question is never asked, "Have increased regulations encouraged these attacks by making potential victims more vulnerable? Do these attacks demonstrate the importance of letting people be able to defend themselves?"

We are constantly bombarded with pro-gun-control claims. While my research, when it is referred to in the press, is labeled as "controversial" or worse, the claims from the Clinton administration and Handgun Control, Inc., are reported without reference to any academics who might object to them. For years the Clinton administration has been placing public service ads claiming that "thirteen children die every day from guns," linking this claim with elementary school children's voices or pictures. But few of these thirteen deaths fit the image of innocent young children. Nine of these deaths per day involve "children" between seventeen and nineteen years old, primarily homicides involving gang members. Eleven of the deaths per day involved fifteen- to nineteen-year olds. This does not alleviate the sorrow created by these deaths or the 1.9 children under age fifteen that die from guns every day, but it strains credulity to have this number mentioned as evidence justifying the importance of trigger locks.

Much of the debate today is framed so as to blame the greater accessibility of guns in America for the recent school violence. Gun-control groups claim that today "guns are less regulated than toasters or teddy bears."[105] The solutions range from banning gun possession for those under twenty-one to imprisoning adults whose guns are misused by minors under eighteen.

Yet, to the contrary, gun availability has never before been as restricted as it is now. As late as 1967, it was possible for a thirteen-year-old virtually anywhere in the United States to walk into a hardware store and buy a rifle. Relatively few states even had age restrictions for buying handguns from a store. Buying a rifle through the mail was easy. Private transfers of guns to juveniles were also unrestricted.

It was common for schools to have shooting clubs. Even in New York City, virtually every public high school had a shooting club up until 1969. It was common for high school students to take their guns with them to school on the subways in the morning and turn them over to their homeroom teacher or the gym coach so the heavy guns would simply be out of the way. After school, students would pick up their guns when it was time for practice. The federal government would even give students rifles and pay for their ammunition. Students regularly competed in citywide shooting contests, with the winners being awarded university scholarships.

Contrast those days with regulations today. College or elementary students are now expelled from school for even accidentally bringing a water pistol. Schools prohibit images of guns, knives, or other weapons on shirts, on hats, or in pictures. Elementary school students have been suspended for carrying around a mere picture of a gun. High schools have refused to publish yearbook pictures of students sitting on howitzers, even when the picture shows graduating students who are joining the military. School superintendents have lost their jobs for even raising the question of whether someone at a school should have a gun for protection.[106]

Since the 1960s, the growth of federal gun control has been dramatic. Before the Brady law in 1994, background checks and waiting periods were not required in most states. It was not a federal crime for those under eighteen to possess a handgun until 1994. The 1990s saw dramatically higher fees for registered dealers as well as many added paperwork requirements. Federal gun laws in 1930 amounted to only 3,571 words. They expanded to 19,907 words in 1960 and then more than quadrupled to 88,413 words in 1999.[107]

The growth in state laws has kept pace. By 1997, California's gun-control statutes contained an incredible 158,643 words, nearly the length of the King James Version of the New Testament. And in 1999, at least four new gun laws have already been signed into law by the governor. Even a "gun-friendly" state government such as Texas has gun-control provisions containing over 41,000 words. None of this even begins to include the burgeoning local regulations on everything from licensing to mandatory gun locks.

Yet without academic evidence that existing regulations such as gun-free zones, the Brady law, and gun locks produce desirable results, it is surprising that in 2000 we are now debating what new gun-control laws to pass. With that in mind, 294 academics from institutions as diverse as Harvard, Stanford, Northwestern, the University of Pennsylvania, and UCLA released an open letter to Congress during 1999 stating that the proposed new gun laws are "ill advised." They wrote that "With the 20,000 gun laws already on the books, we advise Congress, before enacting yet more new laws, to investigate whether many of the existing laws may have contributed to the problems we currently face."[108]

An effective as well as moving piece I recently read was written by Dale Anema, a father whose son was trapped for hours inside the Columbine High School building during the April 1999 attack. His agony while waiting to hear what happened to his son touches any parent's worst fears. Because he had witnessed this tragedy, he described his disbelief over the policy debate:

> Two pending gun bills are immediately dropped by the Colorado legislature. One is a proposal to make it easier for law-abiding citizens to carry concealed weapons; the other is a measure to prohibit municipalities from suing gun manufacturers. I wonder: If two crazy hoodlums can walk into a "gun-free" zone full of our kids, and police are totally incapable of defending the children, why would anyone want to make it harder for law-abiding adults to defend themselves and others? . . . Of course, nobody on TV mentions that perhaps gun-free zones are potential magnets to crazed killers.[109]

10 | A Decade Later: Nine More Years of Data and Nine More States

Introduction

Ten years have passed since the second edition of this book. During that time, both the argument and the data have been hotly debated. This debate has often been unpleasant, vociferous, and even disingenuous. To say that my career has suffered as a result is something of an understatement and, alas, an unpleasant warning to other scholars who dare to go against the academic grain. And yet, as this chapter will document, within the scholarly community the research has withstood criticism and remains sound. Further, the additional ten years of data provide continued strong support for the arguments I initially put forward on right-to-carry and other gun-control laws.

I would never have predicted that I would still be working on gun control a decade and a half after I started thinking about the issue. Back in 1993, I had done extensive research on crime, having served as chief economist at the United States Sentencing Commission, but the issues I was interested in were corporate and white-collar crime. I had little interest in the gun-control issue, and I rarely read academic papers on the topic. It is strange how seemingly small decisions can cascade into results that one would never guess. In my case, the impetus came when I was teaching at the Wharton Business School from a couple students asking if I could spend a little bit of one class talking about gun control and crime. That simple request made me sit down and read many of the existing academic papers. It made me realize how incredibly poorly done the research had been.

Generally, one tries to do work that matters to society, but one is rarely successful. Still, I frequently doubt that the research was personally worth it. The personal attacks and misstatements about my work and other aspects of my life have come fast and furious for years. As Matt Bai, then of *Newsweek*, wrote in 2001, "Lott may be brilliant, but his theories are so controversial that some academics won't so much as look at him when he's standing in a room."[1] One academic paper in 2003 by law professor John Donohue suggested that there could be "blood on Lott and Mustard's hands" because our research may have caused states to adopt right-to-carry laws. Donohue used terms such as "now discredited work," "fraud," and "blight on democracy," and warned I was causing "harm to the democratic process" by "encouraging the adoption of laws on false pretenses."[2] He was still making similar claims in academic seminars five years later.[3]

Others impugned my methodology, insisting that researchers could not replicate my results showing that right-to-carry laws reduce crime. One even alleged that I paid off editors at the University of Chicago Press to publish other research that supported my findings.[4]

Obviously, though, there is much more to this debate than the personal attacks, and we will turn to those empirical issues first. The following sections will revisit the risks and benefits of letting law-abiding people carry concealed handguns. Do bans on concealed handguns make people safer? Do those who carry concealed handguns represent a threat to others? Do they use their guns to commit crime? To look at the impact of right-to-carry laws on crime rates, I will update the data previously examined in this book by nine years—through 2005—to see if it alters the relationship between right-to-carry laws and crime rates.

The more-guns-less-crime thesis will be examined by looking at what happens to crime rates when cities or countries ban guns. The evidence should make gun-control advocates pause, as all the gun bans that I have studied show that murder rates increase after the ban is enacted.

The chapter will then summarize the conclusions that other published studies have reached, and I will discuss the objections raised against my research, including which type of data is best, county- or state-level data. Finally, the impact of other gun-control laws, such as assault weapons bans, gun show regulations, safe-storage rules, and the Castle Doctrine, will be examined. This is the first study to look at the Castle Doctrine, which eliminates the requirement that people in their own home have to retreat as far as possible before defending themselves.

The Continuing Debate

Del. Eleanor Holmes Norton (D-D.C.) and gun control groups are concerned that some visitors attending President-elect Obama's inauguration may try to pack heat because of a rule allowing concealed weapons in national parks.

   The Bush administration recently altered federal regulations to allow people with permits to carry concealed firearms while in national parks if the park falls within a state or district that allows concealed weapons.

   Washington D.C. does not allow concealed weapons, but Norton and others think confusion over the rule could lead visitors to bring guns to Obama's Jan. 20 inauguration, which will be held on two miles of National Park land.
—*The Hill*, December 27, 2008[5]

On January 9, 2009, the National Park Service was tasked to live by the same rules that the Bureau of Land Management and the U.S. Forest Service and the rest of the nation use [and apply each state's right-to-carry laws to the national parks in that state]. On January 10, 2009, the earth rotated. The sun rose. The Constitution still worked. Law-abiding citizens were still, well, law-abiding. Apparently, we all survived.
—Representative Rob Bishop (R-UT), January 15, 2009[6]

Despite all our experience with permitted concealed handguns, the debate continues. There are always fears about what might happen. Whether it is concealed-handgun laws, assault weapons bans, gun shows, one-gun-a-month rules, banning inexpensive guns, or safe-storage laws, the same issues always reappear. Do guns on balance save lives or cost lives? Will gun-control laws primarily disarm law-abiding citizens or criminals?

   In the United States, we have a lot of experience with concealed-handgun permit holders. In 2007, there were about 5 million Americans permitted to carry concealed handguns (see table 10.1). Thirty-nine states have right-to-carry laws and nine have may-issue laws. Only two states, Illinois and Wisconsin, still completely ban people from carrying concealed handguns.[7] That is a big change from just the eight states that had right-to-carry laws in the early 1980s.

   The precise number of people legally carrying concealed guns isn't known, because three of the right-to-carry states (Alaska, Montana, and Vermont) do not require permits to carry a concealed handgun in all or

Table 10.1 Permits and percent of adult population with permits by state in 2007

State	Number of permits	Percent of adults with permits
Alabama (estimate)[a]	>281,000	>8%
Alaska (no permit required—permits acquired to carry gun in other states)	9,547	1.91%
Arizona	99,370	2.12%
Arkansas	54,919	2.58%
California	?	
Colorado	28,454	0.78%
Connecticut	133,252	4.94%
Delaware	?	
Florida	445,038	3.13%
Georgia	>300,000	>4.31%
Hawaii	0	0%
Idaho	48,364	4.42%
Illinois	Banned	0%
Indiana	295,643	6.21%
Iowa	28,383	1.25%
Kansas	8,958	0.43%
Kentucky	95,638	2.97%
Louisiana	14,084	0.44%
Maine	?	
Maryland (Feb. 2006)	36,755	0.86%
Massachusetts (fall 2006)[b]	<203,302	<4.04%
Michigan	155,000	2.02%
Minnesota	50,777	1.29%
Mississippi	47,500	2.20%
Missouri	36,105	0.81%
Montana (Dec. 2008); no permit required in 98% of state	17,974	2.44%
Nebraska	2,109	0.16%
Nevada	?	
New Hampshire (nonresidents only; state does not collect county info for residents)	29,609	2.92%
New Jersey (Jan. 13, 2009)[c]	10,821	0.17%
New Mexico	10,566	0.72%
New York City only	2,555	0.02%
North Carolina	95,502	1.39%
North Dakota	8,364	1.68%
Ohio	97,912	1.12%
Oklahoma	57,540	2.12%
Oregon	96,005	3.33%
Pennsylvania	668,372	6.89%
Rhode Island	?	

Table 10.1 (*continued*)

State	Number of permits	Percent of adults with permits
South Carolina	56,715	1.69
South Dakota	41,000	6.87
Tennessee	179,356	3.83
Texas	288,909	1.68
Utah	108,100	5.92
Vermont	No permit required	
Virginia	146,874	2.51
Washington	236,975	4.82
West Virginia	82,000	5.73
Wisconsin	Concealed carry banned	
Wyoming	12,278	3.09
Total	>4,621,625	>2.03

Note: Many of these data were collected by Chris Bird, and I appreciate his sharing this with me. Sources for active concealed-carry permits as of the following dates: Alaska Department of Public Safety as of Aug. 17, 2007; Donna J. Street, administrative supervisor, Arizona Department of Public Safety, Dec. 2007; Arkansas State Police, Aug. 20, 2007; Colorado Sheriffs Association, Dec. 31, 2006; Connecticut State Police, Sept. 6, 2007; Florida Department of Agriculture and Consumer Services, July 31, 2007; Hawaii state senator Sam Slom, Jan. 18, 2009; Sam Knowles, Program Services Bureau, Iowa Department of Public Safety, Dec. 2007; Idaho State Police, Aug. 22, 2007; Kansas Attorney General's Office, Aug. 1, 2007; Kentucky State Police, Aug. 1, 2007; Louisiana State Police, Aug. 28, 2007; for Maryland, http://www.marylandshallissue.org/ccwdata.html; Mississippi Department of Public Safety, Aug. 29, 2007; Missouri Highway Patrol, Aug. 3, 2007; Nebraska State Patrol, Aug. 30, 2007; New Jersey state assemblyman Michael Carroll; New Mexico Department of Public Safety, Aug. 14, 2007; North Carolina Department of Justice, Sept. 12, 2007; Office of North Dakota Attorney General, Bureau of Criminal Investigation, Aug. 30, 2007; Ohio Attorney General's Office, June 30, 2007; Oklahoma State Bureau of Investigation, July 17, 2007; Oregon State Police, Sept. 4, 2007; Pennsylvania State Police, Apr. 27, 2007; South Carolina Law Enforcement Division, Sept. 5, 2007; Tennessee Department of Safety, May 8, 2007; Virginia State Police, Aug. 5, 2007; State of Washington, Department of Licensing, Sept. 5, 2007. Other information: Alabama (Stan Diel, "Metro Zarea Loaded with Concealed Guns Records Show More than 1 in 10 Adults May Have Carry Permits; For Many, 'It's an Insurance Policy,'" *Birmingham News*, Feb. 18, 2007, p. A1; and Christopher Pelton, "Packing Heat, Discretely," *Florence Times Daily*, Aug. 6, 2008), Georgia ("Gun Permit Holders Praise New Georgia Law," WALB News, May 15, 2008 [http://www.walb.com/Global/story.asp?S=8331521&nav=5kZQ]; this information was also confirmed by Ed Stone with GeorgiaCarry.org), Indiana (Lt. Jerry Berkey, Indiana State Police, 317–232–8263), Massachusetts (Bob Hohler, "Many Players Regard Firearm as a Necessity," *Boston Globe*, Nov. 10, 2006 [unable to verify independently]), Michigan (Dawson Bell, "Michigan Sees Fewer Gun Deaths—with More Permits," *Detroit Free Press*, Jan. 6, 2008), Minnesota (http://www.madfi.org/permitcount.asp), Montana (Ted Richardson, customer support technician, Montana Department of Justice; permits as of Dec. 12, 2008), New Hampshire (Rosemary Ruby, counter clerk 4, New Hampshire State Police, Permits and Licenses Unit), New York City (Chris Faherty, "Concealed Pistols Permits Drop in City," *New York Sun*, Aug. 29, 2007), South Dakota (Ben Shouse, "South Dakotans No. 1 in Permits to Conceal Guns," *Argus Leader*, Dec. 17, 2006), Texas (Texas Department of Public Safety, Dec. 31, 2007 [http://www.txdps.state.tx.us/administration/crime_records/chl/PDF/ActLicAndInstr/ActiveLicandInstr2007.pdf]), Utah (Utah Department of Public Safety [http://www.des.utah.gov/bci/brady_statistics.html#]), and West Virginia ("West Virginia Reciprocity Started," *Centre Daily Times* [State College, PA], Aug. 30, 2007).

[a]The estimate for Alabama was obtained from the six counties for which permit information was available. Data were available for six counties. The state rate was obtained assuming that the entire state averaged the lowest rate shown for these counties. One of these counties is Jefferson County, the most densely populated county in the state, where Birmingham is located. Even though urban counties generally tend to have lower rates of permit holding in Jefferson County, 11 percent of adults have permits. If that rate holds for the rest of the state, about 387,000 Alabamans would have permits.

[b]While a class A license to carry firearms is required in order to carry, some licenses are restricted by the issuing police department to prohibit carrying.

[c]9,798 of these were for retired police officers; 1,023 were for private citizens.

virtually all areas in those states. Alaska and Montana grant permits so that their residents can carry concealed handguns in other states, and Montana residents need permits to carry guns only within the city limits of Montana's six largest cities. Vermont doesn't require or grant any permits. In addition, the figures are difficult to determine precisely in states like Alabama, where the permits are issued by the sixty-four local sheriffs' offices and can only be obtained by contacting each office.[8]

Interestingly, no state that has adopted a right-to-carry law has ever rescinded it or even held a state legislative hearing to consider rescinding it.[9] In some states the adoption of right-to-carry laws was controversial, but there seems to be no buyer's remorse. In fact, the only changes that have been made to right-to-carry laws have been to loosen the requirements for getting a permit.

One particularly surprising fact is the high rate at which state legislators seem to have concealed-handgun permits.[10] In South Carolina, 20 percent of the state legislature had permits in early 2008. In Tennessee, 25 percent have permits.[11] Exactly a third of the twenty-four Virginia state legislators from the area around Norfolk, Virginia, have permits.[12]

The debate over concealed-handgun laws has implications for gun-control regulations generally. If permit holders can actually be trusted to carry their guns in public—in restaurants or bars, on buses, at sports stadiums—it is hard to imagine where law-abiding citizens cannot be trusted with guns. The evidence on concealed-handgun laws is also relevant for debates over banning handguns in general—concealed-handgun laws may provide us with the best direct evidence of the costs and benefits of owning handguns.

Even with this level of satisfaction among voters and state legislators, gun-control groups and some liberal academics still strongly advocate more restrictions. The following sections will first examine whether law-abiding concealed-handgun permit holders follow the law and do not pose a threat to others. Then I will present the latest data on how gun-control laws affect crime. I will discuss recent major court cases, including the U.S. Supreme Court 2008 decision to overturn the District of Columbia's handgun ban as well as ongoing legal attempts to overturn the Chicago handgun ban and bans in public housing. As the court cases often turn on the question of whether handgun bans reduce crime, I will discuss this issue at length. I will then turn to answering objections that have been raised against my work and critically discuss some of the recent literature on gun control.

Concealed-Carry Permit Holders: Villains or Saints?

[Obama] differs with McCain and Clinton about whether people should be allowed to carry concealed guns. Clinton and McCain oppose outlawing it.

"I am not in favor of concealed weapons," Obama said. "I think that creates a potential atmosphere where more innocent people could (get shot during) altercations."

—Mike Wereschagin and David M. Brown, "Candidates' Gun Control Positions May Figure in Pa. Vote," *Pittsburgh Tribune-Review*, Apr. 2, 2008

[State Representative Michael] DeBose [a Southside Cleveland Democrat] twice voted against a measure to allow Ohioans to carry concealed weapons. It became law in 2004.

DeBose voted his conscience. He feared that [concealed-handgun] permits would lead to a massive influx of new guns in the streets and a jump in gun violence. He feared that Cleveland would become the O.K. Corral, patrolled by legions of freshly minted permit holders.

"I was wrong," he said Friday.

"I'm going to get a permit and so is my wife.

"I've changed my mind. You need a way to protect yourself and your family."

—Cleveland Plain Dealer, May 15, 2007[13]

The gun-control debate largely focuses on what *might* go wrong, rather than evidence on what actually happens. For example, after 9/11, many were fearful that letting pilots carry guns on planes would endanger passengers' safety. Some worried that a gun being accidentally discharged would lead to an explosive depressurization, causing a plane to crash.[14] Yet Boeing and other airplane manufacturers testified that bullet holes in the airplane's skin would have little effect on cabin pressure and would not cause a crash.[15] Still, the Bush Administration strongly fought against allowing pilots to carry guns.[16]

The debate implies that arming pilots is either something that has not been tried before or that it has been tried and failed. But arming pilots is actually nothing new. Until 1963, American commercial passenger pilots on any flight carrying U.S. mail were *required* to carry handguns.[17] The practice was mandated during the 1920s because the federal government wanted to insure that the U.S. mail would be protected if a plane were forced to land away from an airport. Pilots were still allowed to carry guns as recently as 1987, and the pilots' union for American Airlines and the Airline Pilots Security Alliance claim that up to 10 percent of pilots regularly continued to do so up to that time.[18] Most significantly, there are no recorded instances of any significant gun-related problem arising from a legally armed pilot.[19]

Since 2003, pilots have again been allowed to carry guns on planes, providing they now go through an extensive training and psychological evaluation program.[20] In March 2008, there was one case where a pilot accidentally discharged his gun on a U.S. Airways flight from Denver to Charlotte.[21] The plane experienced no problems and landed safely. Ironically, the accident was caused by federal regulations that require a pilot to put a trigger lock on a loaded gun as the plane was landing.[22] But some academics have used this incident to argue that armed pilots should no longer be countenanced.[23]

Similar fears are expressed over what might happen with guns in school. But many are unaware of the long history of schools permitting concealed handguns. Prior to 1995, when the Federal Safe School Zone Act was passed, many states had allowed concealed-handgun permit holders to carry guns on school property.[24] And even since 1995, Oregon, New Hampshire, and Utah have continued to let permit holders carry guns at school. Many other states adopted limited restrictions, such as allowing a gun only in the school parking lot or when someone is picking up a student.

Yet, over all this time, there has not been a single example of an improper use of a permitted concealed handgun at a school, not even the improper exposure of the gun or an accidental gunshot.[25]

Ignoring this evidence, however, critics continue to argue that permitted concealed handguns make people less safe. Take, for example, the following argument from Brady Campaign president Paul Helmke:

> But the *Sun-Sentinel* found 216 [concealed permit holders] with active warrants, 128 with domestic violence restraining orders, nine people charged with felonies or reckless—or violent reckless demeanors, six red—registered sex offenders, at least one prison inmate, and another 1400 people who had pled guilty or no-contest to felony charges, all had concealed-carry permits in the state of Florida.[26]

Also consider this rather simplified account from John Donohue of our positions on the issue:

> Now, John [Lott] and I have debated on the issue of right to carry laws, laws that say citizens who have not yet been convicted of a felony, or not yet been involuntarily committed to a mental hospital should be allowed to carry a gun wherever they want. John thinks this is a great idea, offers statistics to prove it. Let me just mention that in Texas, even if you have been committed to a mental hospital, if you can get a note from your doctor, they'll give you that concealed handgun permit. North Dakota really

set a new low. They actually gave one of these permits to a blind permit holder. This is, to be frank, insanity.[27]

These arguments both ignore a crucial question: Did these permit holders actually harm others? I asked Megan O'Matz and John Maines, the reporters who wrote the *South Florida Sun-Sentinel* piece that Helmke refers to, if they had any evidence that any of the individuals they had flagged had committed any crimes while they had a concealed-handgun permit.[28] The newspaper would not allow the reporters to respond directly, but Sally Kestin, their editor, confirmed that there were no examples of these permit holders committing crimes or using their guns improperly while they had permits.[29]

The numbers the *Sun-Sentinel* presented are also somewhat misleading. The 1,400 people referred to who had pleaded guilty or no contest to felony charges had their criminal records expunged by a judge. Presumably, judges only expunge criminal records when they are convinced that there were special circumstances in their cases and that the individuals did not represent a threat to others. Thus, it is not too surprising that these individuals have not committed any crimes. Gun-control groups and these reporters instead claim that a "loophole" allowed those permits to be granted. But the Florida legislature apparently doesn't agree—since the *Sun-Sentinel* article was run in January 28, 2007, no changes have been made to the law. Indeed, no serious discussion even took place in the legislature.

True, some of Florida's then 410,000 permit holders may indeed have been granted permits improperly. But if O'Matz and Maines are correct, those 344 errors amount to merely 0.08 percent of the permits issued. Again, none of those improperly granted permits led to any problems.

As for Donohue's statement, it inaccurately describes the Texas concealed-handgun law.[30] It is simply not true that people are forbidden to obtain a concealed-handgun permit only if they have a felony. It is stricter than that, as one misdemeanor is sufficient for denial. To be eligible for a permit in Texas, a person must not (1) have been convicted of a felony, (2) have been charged with a class A or class B misdemeanor or convicted of such a crime during the previous five years, (3) have been disqualified under federal or state law from purchasing a handgun, (4) have been delinquent in making child support payments or taxes, (5) have been in default on student loans, (6) be chemically dependent, or (7) be under a court protective order or subject to a restraining order. The applicant must also have lived in Texas for at least six months and be at least 21 years old.

The prohibitions on individuals with a history of mental illness are also much more restrictive than Donohue implies. The prohibition applies not only to those involuntarily committed, but also to those who have voluntarily sought psychiatric hospitalization in the preceding two years and to those who have ever been diagnosed "by a licensed physician that the person suffers or has suffered from a psychiatric disorder" related to schizophrenia or delusional disorder, bipolar disorder, chronic dementia, dissociative identity disorder, intermittent explosive disorder, or antisocial personality disorder.

Furthermore, somebody can't simply "get a note from your doctor" to get a permit. The doctor must have his primary practice in psychiatry and must state that the specific "condition is in remission and not reasonably likely to develop at a future time."

Donohue's discussion of the "new low" in North Dakota is also misleading. It is surely easy to ridicule the notion of a legally blind person using a gun for self-defense. Carey McWilliams, the blind permit holder, noted, "A lot of people thought a blind guy with a gun was a funny story. They didn't know the facts or that I've had legitimate training."[31] McWilliams is legally blind, but he has some minimal sight and can differentiate light from darkness. Even with his longtime poor vision, he was able to take target-shooting courses in college. Yet McWilliams only planned for a very limited role in using the gun—"The person would have to actually be attacking me. Then I would put the gun right up against the attacker's body and fire the gun so I wouldn't hit anyone else."

So if McWilliams is denied a gun, how should he defend himself if he's attacked? As McWilliams notes, "It's much easier to attack a blind person than other people."

More important, there have been no problems with McWilliams or with any other legally blind persons with permits, be it in North Dakota or any other state. And there has been no move in the North Dakota legislature to change the law.

We have gone through the numbers before on how law-abiding permit holders are, but given the continued concerns, here are some updated numbers:

ARIZONA. There were 99,370 active permits as of December 1, 2007. During 2007, 33 permits were revoked for any reason—a 0.03 percent rate.[32] There was one case where a permit holder committed murder with a gun in 2002.[33]

FLORIDA. Between, October 1, 1987, and November 30, 2008, Florida issued permits to 1,439,446 people, many of whom have had their permits renewed multiple times. Only 166 had their permits revoked for any type of firearms related violation—about 0.01 percent.[34] These revocations overwhelmingly involved individuals accidentally carrying concealed handguns into restricted areas.

INDIANA. In 2007, there were approximately 300,000 active permits, and 744 were revoked—just under 0.25 percent. According to Indiana State Police Lt. Jerry Berkey, who oversees permit revocations, revocations "rarely" involve the use of a gun. "I have heard of a couple being revoked over the years for improperly discharging their weapons, one involved a player on the Pacers, but I can't think of one involving murder or other violent crime."[35]

KENTUCKY. During 2000, 74 of the 66,000 permits were revoked for any reason—about 0.1 percent. No permit holder was convicted of a violent crime.[36] The most common charge against permit holders, accounting for 20 of the 74 revocations, was a lack of vehicle insurance.

MICHIGAN. During 2007, there were over 155,000 licensed permit holders and 163 revocations—about 0.1 percent.[37] Over the period from July 1, 2001, to June 30, 2007, there was one permit holder convicted of manslaughter, though it did not involve the use of a gun.[38] Three other people were also convicted of "intentionally discharging a firearm at a dwelling." No one was convicted of "intentionally discharging a firearm at or towards another person."

MISSOURI. Ninety-six of the 50,507 permit holders had their permits revoked in 2008—a 0.19 percent rate.[39]

MONTANA. As of December 12, 2008, Montana had 17,974 active permits, and during 2008 there were 20 revocations—0.1 percent. Ted Richardson, who handles the revocation records, commented, "Revocations almost never involve the use of a gun."[40] When asked if any violent crimes were committed by permit holders, Richardson replied, "Not that I have seen."

NEW HAMPSHIRE. Local sheriffs handle permits for New Hampshire residents, so systematic statewide information is only available for nonresident permits. As of December 31, 2007, there were 29,609 active permits held by nonresidents. Rosemary Ruby with the New Hampshire State Police Permits and Licenses Unit said, "The number of revocations is in the range of

2 to 5 per year, never more than five permits." That is a revocation rate of between 0.007 and 0.017 percent per year. She stated that she had "no recollection of revocation for murder or other serious crimes. Simple assault is the worst, nothing even major sticks out."[41]

NORTH CAROLINA. With 246,243 permits issued and 789 revocations, about 0.3 percent of North Carolina permit holders have had their permits revoked over the twelve years from when permits started being issued in December 1, 1995, and December 31, 2008.[42] Local sheriffs revoke the permits and the state only collects the total number of revocations reported to them by the sheriffs. To check the reasons for revocations, I called the sheriff's office for several counties. Tamara Road, an administration support supervisor in Mecklenburg County, the county for Charlotte, reported there were 8,200 permit holders as of December 2008. She said that "no one has had their permit revoked for violent crime. . . . I don't know of any cases where someone has had their permit revoked for improperly using their gun."[43]

Sergeant Bum Gardiner, with the Wake County Sheriff's Office (the county for the state capitol of Raleigh and home of North Carolina State University), has overseen the permit division for seven years and said, "I don't know of one revocation involving the use of a gun. . . . One frequent reason [for revocation] is when the police pull someone over for a traffic violation, [permit holders] fail to tell them that they are a CCW holder." When he was asked why he thought permit holders would forget this, Gardiner said that he couldn't really think of a reason other than they simply forgot they were required to do so. Sheriffs in smaller counties, such as Johnson County, gave similar answers.[44]

OHIO. From April 2004 to the beginning of August 2006, 73,530 permits were issued in Ohio. There were 217 revocations, but 69 of these came from the Cuyahoga County Sheriff's Office after a weapons instructor was accused of not providing the training required by state law.[45] Excluding revocations due to improper training, about 0.2 percent of permit holders had their permits revoked. There were no reported incidents of any permit holder having his permit revoked for committing a violent crime. In 2007, there were 108,386 permits and 171 were revoked—a rate of 0.16 percent. A major reason for revocations was that a licensee moves out of state or dies.[46] The *Cincinnati Post* wrote about the behavior of permit holders, "Toby Hoover of Toledo, director of the Ohio Coalition Against Guns . . . whose group opposes the law, conceded, 'There's been no increase in violence.'"[47]

PENNSYLVANIA. Pennsylvania has more active permits issued than any other state. In April 2007, there were 668,372 permits. The state also had by far the most permit revocations that year: 2,318, translating into a rate of 0.345 percent.[48] However, this was an unusually high year, with the revocation rates during 2003 to 2005 running from 0.23 percent to 0.26 percent.[49]

Interestingly, while Philadelphia accounted for only about 4 percent of the permits issued in the state during 2007, it accounted for 32 percent (744) of all revocations. Philadelphia is the only county in the state that regularly revokes permits for such trivial reasons as parking tickets, notifications to the sheriff's office by the permit holder that he is moving to another address in the city, failure to pay child support, and a host of other, similar reasons.[50] Going to court can usually overturn these revocations, but the process is costly and time-consuming. The easier alternative is to wait one year and then reapply for a new permit.

Still Philadelphia's share of revocations in the state has gone down somewhat over time. In 2000, 40 percent of all revocations in Pennsylvania had taken place in Philadelphia.[51] As noted, by 2007 that share had dropped to 32 percent.

Excluding Philadelphia from the calculation, the revocation rate in 2007 for any reason was 0.25 percent (for the years 2003–2005 the number ranges from 0.15 percent to 0.17 percent). Over half these revocations result from "Protection from Abuse" orders, the vast majority apparently filed in divorce proceedings.[52] Kim Stolfer, chairman of the Pennsylvania-based Firearm Owners Against Crime, states that "a large number of these filings are to obtain concessions in divorce proceedings."[53]

TEXAS. In 2006, there were 258,162 active permit holders. Out of these, 140 were convicted of either a misdemeanor or a felony, a rate of 0.05 percent. That is about one-seventh the conviction rate in the general adult population, and the convictions among permit holders tend to be for much less serious offenses.[54] The most frequent type of revocation, with 33 cases, involved carrying a weapon without their license with them. The next largest category involved domestic violence, with 23 cases.

Similar numbers have been reported in Texas every year. Over the preceding four years, from 2002 to 2005, the average rate at which permit holders were convicted of a misdemeanor or a felony was 0.04 percent.[55]

UTAH. With 134,398 active concealed-handgun permits as of December 1, 2008, there were 12 revocations for any type of violent crime over the preceding twelve months—a 0.009 percent rate. None of those involved any use of a gun. Thirteen revocations involved any type of firearms-related offense, a revocation rate of less than 0.01 percent. Clark Aposhian, chairman of the State of Utah Concealed Weapon Hearing/Licensing Board, said, "Typically if they just list it as a firearms offense, it is just a more minor offense like carrying a gun into a secure area. The Salt Lake police at the airport handled some of those. If it was intentional, it would have been handled by Homeland Security." In total, 0.22 percent of permit holders had their permits revoked for any reason, and by far the most common reason for revocations involved "alcohol violations."[56]

Since 1994, two permit holders have been convicted of murder, including a police officer who shot his wife.[57] The other murder was not committed with a gun.

WYOMING. Over the four years from 2005 to 2008, 31 permits were revoked. The average yearly revocation rate was 0.06 percent. When asked about the reasons for the revocations, Chris Lynch, a records analyst with the Wyoming Division of Criminal Investigations, noted, "The biggest one that I remember is an individual whose permit was revoked for tax evasion."[58] None of the cases involved a violent crime or the improper use of a gun.

The information that I have collected for other states is more anecdotal and frequently required contacting individual county sheriffs' offices,[59] but the general impression is that their permit holders behave similarly to the permit holders in the states listed above.

With about 5 million people with concealed-handgun permits in the United States in 2007, it is hard to look at these revocation rates and not realize how incredibly law abiding permit holders really are. While all states don't provide detailed records of the reasons that permit are revoked, when a licensee kills someone, it gets extensive news coverage. From 1990 through July 2008, I found twenty-three cases where a permit holder committed murder with a gun (twenty of those cases resulted in convictions, and in the other three murderers died at the scene). Seven permit holders committed murder in Texas; three in Ohio; two in Florida, Pennsylvania, and Utah; and one permit holder committed a murder with a gun in each of the following states: Arizona, Alabama, Indiana, Maine, North Carolina, Tennessee, and Virginia.[60]

Beyond these twenty-three murder cases, one permit holder was convicted of negligent homicide (a misdemeanor), and two cases resulted in convictions but no prison time served. These three cases are interesting, showing how even obviously defensive gun uses can result in criminal charges:

Clay Wallace (February 1999)—Wallace, 75 years old, and his friend, Robert Qualls, 65, got into a fight in Black Oak, Arkansas.[61] Qualls knocked Wallace down twice,[62] punching and kicking him.[63] When Wallace was on the ground the second time he pulled out his revolver and shot Qualls once in the chest.[64] Jurors were initially deadlocked on the case, but the judge ordered them back to deliberations, and they came back with a guilty verdict on the misdemeanor charge of negligent homicide.[65] Wallace was sentenced to one year in county jail.

Kenneth Ray Gumm (September 2007)—Gumm, a 67-year-old retired certified security guard with law enforcement education and training, was attacked by Dale Turney, 47, who had a blood alcohol level of .08 and had taken methamphetamines.[66] Turney was angry because he felt that Gumm had cut in front of him in traffic. Turney followed Gumm into a parking lot, where Turney's car blocked Gumm's, preventing him from driving. Turney screamed at Gumm, saying, "You're history," and he chased Gumm around his car. Gumm has "health problems [and] couldn't run away or fight him" and "'backed away from Turney approximately two times around his (Gumm's) car before Turney pushed his shoulder." Claiming, "I thought my life was going to end," Gumm then shot Turney once in his chest. The prosecutor argued that Gumm "was not justified, in the circumstances that existed, to use deadly force in defense of a misdemeanor assault and battery."[67] Convicted of manslaughter, Gumm received a suspended sentence and was placed on probation. No prison time was served and no fine imposed.

Esteban Garza (April 2006)—While eating breakfast at a cafe with his brother-in-law, Garza, 50, argued with others at another table.[68] Fernando Gutierrez, 43, attacked Garza, pushing him to the ground and then shoving him through the glass in the front door.[69] Garza then fatally shot Gutierrez and wounded two bystanders (though no additional charges were ever prosecuted). The prosecutor argued that the response against Gutierrez was excessive. Garza was convicted of second-degree murder and received ten years probation. No prison time was served.[70]

The courts' convictions of Gumm and Garza but refusal to sentence them to jail perhaps indicates the courts' desire not to punish either man seriously, while also discouraging such ready use of a weapon.

The Brady Campaign and other gun-control organizations cherry-pick a few cases, while omitting important facts, such as whether the permit holder was found to have used justifiable force. For instance, in its account of a Texas case from 1997, the Brady Campaign makes it appear as if the permit holder, Pete Kanakidis, shot an innocent bystander named Arroyo: "Arroyo was not involved in the argument and was sitting alone in the driver's seat of a truck."[71]

The Associated Press provided some important details that the jury apparently thought were important about Arroyo's not being a passive bystander:[72]

> Mr. Arroyo drove two other men to Mr. Kanakidis' repair shop in River Oaks on May 30. Mr. Kanakidis had fired one of the men and reportedly planned to fire the other man that day.
>
> Police said the two men beat up Mr. Kanakidis and ran from the shop. Mr. Kanakidis then got his gun from his truck and shot Mr. Arroyo, who was backing up his vehicle. Mr. Kanakidis told police he thought Mr. Arroyo was going to run over him.

The *San Antonio Express-News* described how "[Kanakidis] said his nose was broken, he was knocked to the ground and was choked as the men repeatedly attacked him."[73]

Or take the case of Harold Glover in Tulsa, Oklahoma, in 1997. While the Brady Campaign notes that the person who was shot, Cecil Herndon, had a pocketknife, he is described as just "standing outside the vehicle" and "not acting in a 'life-threatening' manner," and Glover is said to have "acted without cause."[74] Left out of the discussion is that Glover was acquitted, that Herndon had "verbally threatened to cut him with a knife," and that Glover was cleared of acting improperly.[75]

In yet another example, in Austin, Texas, a taxi driver named Wayne Lambert shot two men. The Brady Campaign version of the story fails to note that Lambert suffered a gash over his left eye that required eighteen stitches and that he claimed he fired in self-defense.[76] There was no jury verdict, because Lambert died before trial.

Possibly most telling is that the Brady Campaign and the Violence Policy Center keep track of arrests of permit holders, not convictions—ignoring that defensive gun uses frequently result in arrests simply because a police officer can't be sure what happened.[77] But accurate accounts of these cases are important, because they really demonstrate the exact opposite point that the Brady Campaign is making—that permitted concealed handguns, in fact, help to protect people from getting killed when attacked.

Overall, from 1990 through July 2008, the twenty cases where someone has been convicted of murder with a gun and the three other cases where the killers died at the scene amount to slightly more than one murder per year. Permit holders committed murder at 1/182nd the rate of the general public.[78] This is an amazing difference.

Comparing the states provides some interesting lessons. The variation in state revocation rates is primarily related to the possible reasons that one can have his permit revoked, rather than differences in the rates at which permit holders commit violent crime. Murder and violent crime rates by permit holders are essentially zero whether there are many or a few reasons for screening if someone can get a permit. For example, no permit holder has killed a spouse during divorce proceedings, thus indicating that even if the rules in Pennsylvania could be extended to other states, it clearly wouldn't reduce the number of spousal murders—the number is already zero.

Since permit holders are so very law-abiding and so rarely use their guns to cause harm, it doesn't take many examples of defensive gun use by permit holders to imply there are net benefits. A quick review of news stories over just the month from December 14, 2008, to January 11, 2009, yields articles on ten cases where permitted concealed-handgun holders stopped violent crimes. Here are some of the cases:[79]

> Hammond, Indiana (January 11, 2009)—"An attempted robbery early Sunday morning turned fatal for one of the suspects, police said. A 38-year-old man and his girlfriend were exiting their sport-utility vehicle in the parking lot of McTavern's bar in the 7400 block of Indianapolis Boulevard when two people attempted to rob the couple, according to a Hammond police news release."[80] "Hammond police believe a man who shot and killed a would-be robber outside of a bar there early Sunday legitimately acted in self defense. . . . 'We do believe that his version of the story is true and credible,' Miller said, adding that the man had a valid license to carry the weapon and purchased it legally."[81]

> Orlando, Florida (January 9, 2009)—"Orange County sheriff's deputies said two men with a sawed-off shotgun tried to rob a man at a car wash on Orange Blossom Trail Friday night."[82] "'During this attempted robbery, the victim, who holds a concealed weapons permit, pulled out his weapon and fired shots into the bad guy,' said Orange County Sheriff's Office Commander Paul Hopkins. . . . For the bad guys out there, you never know who you're dealing with,' Hopkins said. 'When you go out to commit this crime, you might be the one who's lying dead in the parking lot.'"[83]

Ocoee, Florida (January 5, 2009)—"A convenience store customer in Ocoee turned the tables on suspected robbers Monday night, and authorities continued to search for two people Tuesday evening. . . . The customer . . . grabbed his gun and went back inside and saw the suspected robber beating a female clerk with a beer bottle. The customer said he told the assailant he had a gun, but the man turned toward him and the customer fired two shots, killing the suspect. . . . The customer was asked whether he had a permit to carry a concealed weapon, and he responded that he did."[84]

West Park, Florida (December 26, 2008)—"An armed robber who held a West Park man at gunpoint outside his home early this morning was killed when his victim pulled out a gun and fired first, the Broward County Sheriff's Office said. Brian Kelley, 22, was returning to his apartment in the 4100 block of Southwest 19th Street about 4:39 a.m. when he said Kenneth Nelson, 42, came up from behind him and put a gun to his head, according to sheriff's office spokesman Mike Jachles. Kelley pulled out his own handgun and fired, striking and killing Nelson, of Hollywood. Homicides detectives questioned Kelley after the shooting but did not take him into custody. Kelley acted in self-defense, investigators believe."[85]

Terrel, Texas (December 17, 2008)—"A man walking his dog in Terrell on Wednesday fatally shot an armed 17-year-old robber, police said. The incident happened at about 10:20 p.m. . . . Police said, a group of teen robbers surrounded the man. According to investigators, Markee Lamar Johnson pulled out a gun and the 47-year-old man, a licensed concealed handgun owner, fired shots. . . . 'It would be a clear example of someone exercising their rights to protect themselves under the law,' Capt. A. D. Sanson said."[86]

Fort Smith, Arkansas (December 14, 2008)—"She's a woman who knows how to protect herself as two men who tried to rob her found out. What they didn't know was the woman is licensed to carry a concealed weapon . . . and yes, she was packing heat. . . . [Police said] 'When she pulled over to check her tires one of those persons in that other car got out and attempted to rob her at knife point. She pointed that [handgun] at her attacker and he backed away, got in the car and they fled.'"[87]

Obviously, on top of this should be included the crimes that never occured because would-be attackers decided it was too risky to attack in the first place.

So What Has Happened over the Last Decade?

Six years after new rules made it much easier to get a license to carry concealed weapons, the number of Michiganders legally packing heat has increased more than six-fold.

But dire predictions about increased violence and bloodshed have largely gone unfulfilled, according to law enforcement officials and, to the extent they can be measured, crime statistics.

The incidence of violent crime in Michigan in the six years since the law went into effect has been, on average, below the rate of the previous six years. The overall incidence of death from firearms, including suicide and accidents, also has declined.

More than 155,000 Michiganders—about one in every 65—are now authorized to carry loaded guns as they go about their everyday affairs, according to Michigan State Police records.

About 25,000 people had CCW permits in Michigan before the law changed in 2001.

—"Michigan Sees Fewer Gun Deaths—with More Permits," *Detroit Free Press*, January 6, 2008

The first edition of this book studied data up to 1994. The second edition expanded the data up to 1996. Since then a lot has changed. Kentucky, Louisiana, and South Carolina's right-to-carry laws were in effect for their first full year in 1997. There was a four-year hiatus before Michigan adopted its right-to-carry law in 2001, followed by Colorado, Minnesota, and Missouri in 2003 and New Mexico and Ohio in 2004. I have now extended the county- and state-level data up through 2005.[88] Kansas and Nebraska adopted right-to-carry laws the next year. Twenty-nine states that have now adopted right-to-carry laws did so at some point during the twenty-nine-year period I have data for, from 1977 to 2005. On average, states had their laws in effect for just over ten years, with 86 percent of the states having had the laws in effect for at least nine years.

This update will focus heavily on state-level data where the change in crime rates is broken down in yearly intervals. There are several reasons for this. Regardless of which data set is used, the results are similar for both county- and state-level data. Results from the state-level data show smaller estimated benefits from right-to-carry laws. They should not be seen as "the" estimate but rather as a lower bound on the benefits. Nevertheless, as we will see, these estimated benefits are still very large. Some of my critics (e.g., criminologists Michael D. Maltz and Joseph Targonski as well as economists Ian Ayres and John Donohue) insist that they are much more likely to accept state-level than county-level results. Although I disagree with their claims, I will present the data that they believe are best.

It's necessary to look at the year-by-year changes in the crime rates before and after the adoption of right-to-carry laws, especially due to the way some summary statistics have been misused by critics. The bottom line is this: if you see a pattern using trends that you don't observe with the year-by-year breakdowns, it means that there is something wrong with your use of trends. Trends are supposed to help summarize the changes in crime, but if they don't do a good job summarizing more complex relationships, there is a problem. Just as I explained earlier how simple before-and-after averages can hide what is going on with changes in crime rates, some set-ups with a before-and-after average and even a before-and-after trend can also be misleading. We will get deeper into this statistical issue later, but I want to provide some explanation up front, because presenting these more disaggregated changes before and after the right-to-carry laws will take up a lot more space.

One other note should be made before proceeding. Just as was done in the previous chapters, the estimates are going to account for not only all the law enforcement variables (arrest, execution, and imprisonment rates), income and poverty measures (poverty and unemployment rates, per capita real income, as well as income maintenance, retirement, and un-employment payments), the thirty-six measures of demographic changes, and the national average changes in crime rates from year to year and average differences across states (the fixed year and state effects).[89] In addition, the estimates account for the differences in various concealed-handgun laws and other types of gun-control laws. The law enforcement, income and poverty measures, and demographics are exactly the same as described in previous chapters.

Other gun laws besides right-to-carry laws might also affect crime, and the estimates therefore take into account one-gun-a-month regulations, assault weapons bans (whether there are state bans when the federal ban is not enforced), background checks on the private transfer of guns (essentially "closing" the so-called gun show loophole), the Castle Doctrine (which absolves people of having to retreat when they are being threatened with deadly force), one-gun-a-month rules, and bans on relatively inexpensive guns (so-called Saturday night specials).

These gun laws may be important for explaining changes in crime rates. But, perhaps more important, these other gun-control laws appear likely to be hot topics in the near future. Shortly after the November 2008 election, Barack Obama's transition Web site noted that Obama and Joe Biden "support closing the gun show loophole and making guns in this country childproof. They also support making the federal Assault Weapons Ban that expired in 2004 permanent."[90]

Due to the big differences between concealed-carry laws in different states, as well as differences in the percentages actually getting permits, I also account for the different permit requirements in the estimates. They include the state's permit fee, the number of hours of training required to get the permit, how long the permit lasts, and the minimum age requirement.

Some examples of differences across states help illustrate the need to control for these variables. For example, today in Alaska there are no longer any fees or training requirements (see table 10.2). Yet, in the beginning of this decade Alaska charged fees of over $100 and training took sixteen hours. In 2005, Texas had fees well over $140 with a ten-hour training requirement, but Pennsylvania had a $19 fee and no training requirement. Given those differences, it is not too surprising that Pennsylvania had issued more than twice as many permits as Texas despite a population half the size. And Indiana, with about a quarter of Texas's adult population, has virtually the same rules as Pennsylvania and also has more permit holders than Texas.

As we demonstrated in chapter 9, the rules to get permits do matter. One important pattern stands out. As table 10.3 shows, the states that have passed concealed-handgun permits most recently have made it much more difficult to obtain a permit, and therefore should issue fewer permits overall than states that passed the laws earlier. Later-adopting states had, on average, higher fees for getting a permit (even adjusted for inflation), longer training hours, and older minimum required ages. From the 1980s on, the late-adopting states also have permits with shorter durations.

Further, the most recent right-to-carry states have tended to impose more restrictions on where concealed handguns can be carried. For example, later states more frequently prohibit concealed handguns in restaurants or schools or at amusement parks. Some states allow businesses to prohibit customers from carrying guns on their premises. Such prohibitions make carrying a gun very inconvenient and should further reduce the rate at which people get permits.[91] In sum, the more "reluctant" states have not only waited longer to allow concealed carry, but have also, when finally passing the law, imposed more restrictions.

Permit holders are often still prohibited from carrying a gun in many public places. In Kansas, for example, prosecutors are forbidden to carry their concealed handguns in court. This has further repercussions. If they

Table 10.2 Criteria for concealed-handgun permits in right-to-carry states in 2005

State	Last major change	Permit duration (years)	Training length (hours)	Age requirement	Initial permit fee	Renewal fee	Issuing agency
Alabama	1936	1	0	18	15	15	Sheriff
Alaska	2003	None	None	None	None	None	None
Arizona	2004	5	8	21	60	60	Dept. of Public Safety
Arkansas	1995	4	5	21	144.25	50	State Police
Colorado	2003	5	8	21	52.5	25	Sheriff
Connecticut	1986	5	5	21	35	35	State Police
Florida	1995	5	2	21	117	65	Dept. of State
Georgia	1996	5	0	21	50	50	Judge of probate court
Idaho	1996	4	7	21	56	48	Sheriff
Indiana	1980	4	0	18	10	10	Chief of police or sheriff
Kentucky	1996	5	8	21	60	60	Sheriff
Louisiana	1996	4	9	21	100	100	Dept. of Public Safety
Maine	1985	4	5	18	35	20	Chief of police or sheriff
Michigan	2000	5	8	21	105	105	State police
Minnesota	2003	5	6	21	100	75	Sheriff
Mississippi	1990	4	0	21	124	74	Dept. of Public Safety
Missouri	2003	3	8	23	100	50	Sheriff

State	Year						Position
Montana	1991	4	4	18	55	25	Sheriff
Nevada	1995	5	8	21	50	25	Sheriff
New Hampshire	1923	4	0	21	10	10	Chief of police
New Mexico	2004	0	15	18	100	100	Dept. of Public Safety
North Carolina	2002	5	8	21	90	75	Sheriff
North Dakota	1985	3	0	18	25	25	Bureau of Criminal Investigation
Ohio	2004	5	12	21	69	55	Sheriff
Oklahoma	1995	5	8	23	125	85	State Bureau of Criminal Investigation
Oregon	1993	4	5	21	65	50	Sheriff
Pennsylvania	1995	5	0	21	19	19	Chief of police or sheriff
South Carolina	1996	4	6	21	55	55	State Law Enforcement Division
South Dakota	1986	4	0	18	10	10	Chief of police or sheriff
Tennessee	1996	4	9	21	115	50	Dept. of Public Safety
Texas	1995	4	10	21	140	140	Dept. of Public Safety
Utah	1995	5	4	21	64	10	Dept. of Public Safety
Vermont	None	None	None	None	None	None	None
Virginia	1995	5	5	21	50	50	Clerk of circuit court
Washington	1995	5	0	21	60	32	Judge, chief of police, or sheriff
West Virginia	1996	5	5	18	90	90	Sheriff
Wyoming	1994	5	5	18	50	50	Attorney general

Table 10.3 Criteria for permits based on when the right-to-carry laws went into effect

First full year that the state's right-to-carry law went into effect	Average permit fee (real 2007 dollars)	Permit duration (years)[a]	Average training time to qualify for a permit (hours)	Average age at which one can get a permit[b]
Prior to 1977	$21.90	3.71	0.7	19.3
1980s	$71.49	4.67	4.0	20.0
1990s	$80.27	4.3	5.45	20.5
2000s	$93.16	4.17	9.5	20.8

Note: Values are for 2005.
[a]Excluding Vermont, which had no permits.
[b]Excluding Vermont, which had no age requirements.

can't take a gun into court, it prevents them from carrying a gun when they enter or leave the building. One prosecutor explained the problem this way:[92]

> [Wyandotte County District Attorney Jerome] Gorman, who has received several written death threats over the years, said he works in two courthouse buildings and he and his staff often walk between them.
>
> "We're out in exposed areas, not behind a locked door," he said.
>
> He recalled that several years ago, he was standing in line at a mall with his wife and daughter waiting to see Santa Claus when he spotted the family of a man he convicted of involuntary manslaughter. When Gorman saw them talking among themselves, he left with his family.
>
> "It was time to get away, but I could have been in a position where they saw me before I saw them," he said.

These restrictions appear to have a large effect on permit-issuing rates. In 2008, applications for permits in Georgia soared by 79 percent, a much larger increase than seen in other states after Obama's election.[93] One of the most prominent reasons given for the increase was "a law change last year that opened up the places where a concealed weapon is allowed."

The fees, training requirements, permit duration, and number of prohibited places all have important implications for studying right-to-carry laws. If criminals are indeed discouraged by a higher probability of a potential victim being able to defend herself, then states that only recently adopted right-to-carry laws should have fewer permit holders and a smaller reduction in crime rates.

A problem of growing inconvenience for future research involves the increasing issuance of nonresidential permits. Two states in particular (Florida and Utah) are giving out a large number of permits to out-of-state residents.

Utah's permits for out-of-state residents are honored in twenty-eight states, while Florida's are honored in twenty-seven states. The changes have been particularly significant during the last few years, and over 100,000 permits in these two states are now held by out-of-state residents.[94] Over time, permits issued by Florida and Utah will have a great impact on researchers knowing how may people in other states possess concealed-handgun permits.

The Results

My primary approach here is to let the estimated changes in crime rates "take their own shape" rather than assume that they fit a straight line or some other particular shape.

As a first pass, the regressions account for all the possible influences and consider the year-by-year effects by two-year intervals, from nine years before the right-to-carry law is passed until fourteen years after the law.[95] Two other variables measure the crime rates ten or more years before the law goes into effect and fifteen or more years afterward. Thus, rather than a before-and-after trend and possibly also a variable to measure any changes in the before-and-after averages, this approach has fourteen variables to measure more precisely how crime rates are changing before and after right-to-carry laws are adopted. Only for 2.6 percent of the sample do states that have adopted a right-to-carry law have their laws in effect for at least fifteen or more complete years. Any changes in crime rates for these right-to-carry states are relative to the changes in crime rates for the states without these laws.

Figures 10.1a–10.1i show some dramatic results. There are large drops in overall violent crime, murder, rape, and aggravated assault that begin right after the right-to-carry laws have gone into effect. In all those crime categories, the crime rates consistently stay much lower than they were before the law.

The murder rate for these right-to-carry states fell consistently every year relative to non-right-to-carry states. When the laws were passed, the average murder rate in right-to-carry states was 6.3 per 100,000 people. By the first and second full years of the law it had fallen to 5.9. And by nine to ten years after the law, it had declined to 5.2. That averages to about a 1.7 percent drop in murder rates per year for ten years. The drops were statistically significant by years 5 and 6.[96] The detailed estimates are shown in appendix 6.

Overall violent crime rates also dropped. On average, states with right-to-carry laws start out at 475 crimes per 100,000 people, then fall to to 436

Figure 10.1a. Violent-crime rates before and after adoption of right-to-carry laws

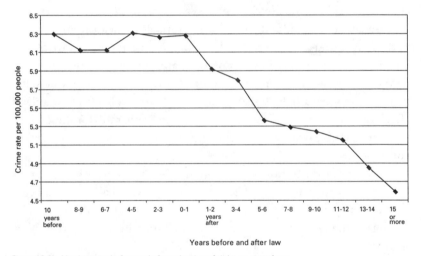

Figure 10.1b. Murder rates before and after adoption of right-to-carry laws

by the first and second full years of the law, and stay down in the 415–40 range after that.[97] A similar pattern holds for rape and aggravated assault. Rape was on average at 40.2 per 100,000 people when the law was passed and ended up at 35.7 (a 12 percent drop) by nine to ten years later.[98]

The story is somewhat more complicated for aggravated assault. While there are large, statistically significant drops in crime as soon as one to two years after the law, assault rates were already declining in the years before the law. If that trend were to have continued in the absence of a

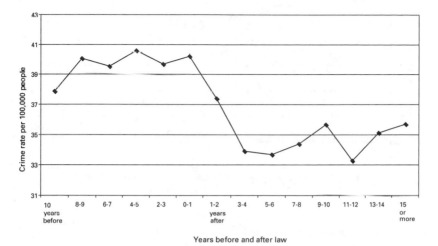

Figure 10.1c. Rape rates before and after adoption of right-to-carry laws

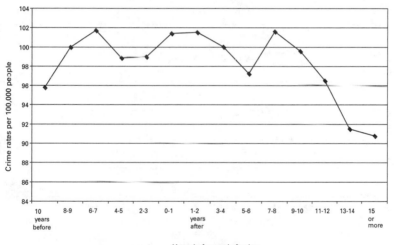

Figure 10.1d. Robbery rates before and after adoption of right-to-carry laws

right-to-carry law, the drop would have finally caught up with the crime rates that we observe by years 11 to 12 after the law. Still, even under that assumption, a right-to-carry law appears to have lowered the number of assaults for ten years.

For robbery, the drop isn't as obvious or as immediate. There are two sets of years in the figure after the law is passed where the robbery rate was slightly higher than it was immediately before the law (years 1 and 2, and

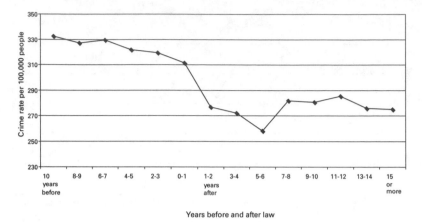

Figure 10.1e. Aggravated-assault rates before and after adoption of right-to-carry laws

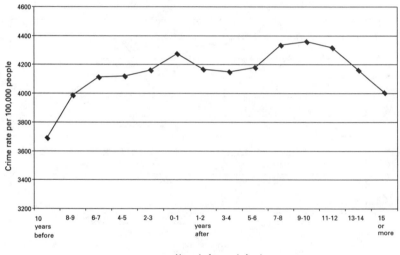

Figure 10.1f. Property-crime rates before and after adoption of right-to-carry laws

years 7 and 8), and there are six observations where it was lower. Robbery is one case where simple before-and-after trends would indicate a much more statistically significant drop in crime rates than is observed for the method being used here. But this disaggregated way provides a more accurate picture, and we have to accept that the results for robbery are not extremely strong.

Consistent with the previously reported research in this book, violent

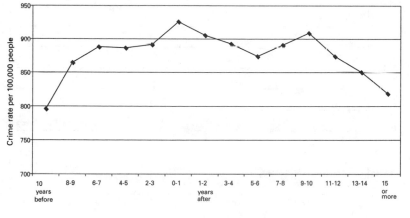

Figure 10.1g. Burglary rates before and after adoption of right-to-carry laws

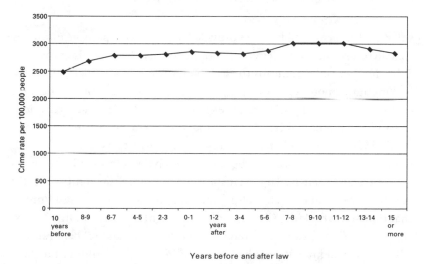

Figure 10.1h. Larceny rates before and after adoption of right-to-carry laws

crime rates are improving relative to property-crime rates, at least larceny and auto theft. If anything, larceny and auto theft keep rising after right-to-carry laws are passed. However, burglary rates go from increasing before the law to generally falling afterward. And indeed, right-to-carry laws should have a bigger impact on violent crimes where victims and criminals come into direct contact.

While we will continue to focus on the year-by-year estimates, the mea-

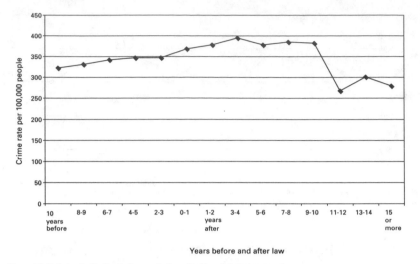

Figure 10.1i. Auto-theft rates before and after adoption of right-to-carry laws

sures used earlier in this book are provided here. For comparison, estimates that do not account for differences in right-to-carry laws are also provided. Table 10.4 generally confirms these previous results for earlier periods by looking at the more restrictive, simple before-and-after average crime rates (with their obvious limitations), the change in the before-and-after crime rate trends, and the combined before-and-after averages and trends. All the results indicate that violent crime falls after right-to-carry laws are passed, but the results vary based on whether one analyzes before-and-after averages or trends. There is a large, statistically significant drop in murder rates across all specifications. The before-and-after average comparison implies that right-to-carry laws reduce murder by roughly 20 percent. In all cases, right-to-carry laws cause the trends in murder, rape, and robbery rates to fall. For each additional year that the law is in effect, the murder rate falls by about 2 percent and the rape and robbery rates fall by about 1 percent relative to states without the law.

An alternative way of asking whether concealed-carry laws reduce crime is to see how crime rate changes vary across different states. (We provided a much simpler version of this previously in table 4.9 on page 80.) These estimates let us check how many states benefit from letting individuals defend themselves.

Tables 10.5a–10.5d show this breakdown using all the control variables for the four violent crime categories for all twenty-nine states that enacted right-to-carry laws between 1977 and 2005. The year-by-year breakdowns for

Table 10.4 The impact of right-to-carry laws on violent crime rates, 1977–2005

	Murder	Rape	Robbery	Aggravated assault
Estimates accounting for everything but differences in right-to-carry laws:				
Simple before-and-after averages	−4.5%[b]	−5.7%[a]	−1%	−5.9%[a]
Change in before-and-after crime trends:				
Change in crime rate trend (annual rate of change after the law minus annual rate of change before the law)	−1.54%*	−1.2%*	−0.6%	−0.7%
Combination of before-and-after averages and trends:				
Shift in crime rates after the law	−0.4%	−8.3%	−0.6%	−3.3%
Change in crime rate trend (annual rate of change after the law minus annual rate of change before the law)	−1.52%*	−0.7%**	−0.7%	0.15%
Estimates accounting for everything including differences in right-to-carry laws:				
Simple before-and-after averages	−20.3%[c]	−14%	−5.7%	−12.9%
Change in before-and-after crime trends:				
Change in crime rate trend (annual rate of change after the law minus annual rate of change before the law)	−2%*	−1%*	−0.8%***	0.5%
Combination of before-and-after averages and trends:				
Shift in crime rates after the law	12.4%	−12.2%	−2.1%	−13.6%
Change in crime rate trend (annual rate of change after the law minus annual rate of change before the law)	−2%*	−1%*	−1%***	0.55%

* Statistically significant at the 1 percent level for an *F*-test.
** Statistically significant at the 5 percent level for an *F*-test.
*** Statistically significant at the 10 percent level for an *F*-test.
[a] Statistically significant at the 1 percent level for a two-tailed *t*-test.
[b] Statistically significant at the 5 percent level for a two-tailed *t*-test.
[c] Statistically significant at the 10 percent level for a two-tailed *t*-test.

crime rates do not show the results for as many years as in the figures because the tables would prove too large. Instead, I simply put together the year-by-year changes after year 10 after the law into one 10+ year category.

Two important questions can be answered from using this state-by-state breakdown. The first is: following concealed-carry laws being passed, how many states experience a drop versus an increase in crime? Because of random events, one doesn't expect crime in every state to fall. This is likely true even after an extremely effective law is adopted. But what we can do is see if the percentage of states where crime rates fell after the law is large compared to the percentage in states where crime remained the same or increased so that we can rule out randomness as a cause. Secondly, we can study how large the increases or decreases are.

The odds that a typical state experiences a drop in murder or rape after

Table 10.5a Changes in murder rates by state over time

	Years before law in effect						Years after law in effect						Change in murder rates		
	10 or more	9–8	7–6	5–4	3–2	1–0	1–2	3–4	5–6	7–8	9–10	11 or more	Average yearly change before and after law	Net impact by year 6	Net impact by year 10
Alaska	11.7	9.9	9.5	10.7	7.0	9.3	9.1	8.3	7.5	7.4	6.6		−1.91	−9.0	−23.1
Arizona	9.8	11.0	10.6	10.0	7.8	9.0	10.4	8.9	7.6	7.5	8.9		−1.03	−0.4	−5.1
Arkansas	12.7		15.2	16.3	14.8	16.4	8.7	7.6	7.8	8.0	9.6		−6.73	−74.8	−120.3
Colorado	4.7	4.1	4.7	5.5	3.4	4.3									
Florida	19.8	22.4	27.6	27.4	29.2	27.0		10.5	10.7	11.1	11.4	14.2	−14.01	−98.8	−193.5
Georgia	13.9		12.1	13.6	14.3	15.8	11.6	10.3	9.6	9.2	10.6	12.3	−3.36	−47.7	−83.4
Idaho	3.0	1.9	2.3	1.8	2.5	1.8	1.7	1.8	2.6		1.6	1.6	−0.37	2.1	1.5
Kentucky	11.4		8.8	7.7	6.1	6.7	5.8	6.4	6.4	7.3	6.9		−1.56	−4.2	−1.8
Louisiana	15.2	12.6	14.0	14.1	18.5	18.7	15.7	14.5	15.2	16.5			−0.03	−32.4	−95.1
Maine		2.5	2.7		2.5	2.5	2.0	2.5	1.4	1.3	1.7	1.6	−0.79	−4.8	−10.8
Michigan	8.5	7.1	7.0	7.1	7.7	7.4		5.8					−1.66	−4.9	−4.8
Minnesota	3.3		4.5	4.3	3.6	2.8	2.2						−1.51	−1.9	−1.8
Mississippi	17.4		18.7	17.9	15.8	15.9	8.5	14.6	15.3	19.3	16.1	19.4	−1.63	−28.3	−17.7
Missouri	5.5	6.2	6.5	6.5	6.2	6.2									
Montana	4.4	3.4	4.2	3.0	3.1	2.8	2.2			3.2	2.5	2.5	−0.88	−1.9	−1.8
Nevada	14.3	10.6	10.0	10.4	10.8	12.7	13.7	11.9	7.0		7.1		−1.57	−16.8	−33.6
New Mexico	7.2	8.9	9.8	7.5	5.9	6.4	7.4						−0.24	2.9	3

North Carolina	6.3	5.8	6.0	7.6	8.2	9.8	8.5	8.6	9.4	10.6		1.99	-7.6	-6.3
Ohio	3.7	3.2		3.4	4.1	4.5	5.1		5.0	5.1		1.31	1.8	1.8
Oklahoma	11.1	11.4	10.5	10.0	9.0	12.3	6.8					-5.2	-37.8	-81.3
Oregon	5.8	6.9	8.1	7.2	5.4	4.5	4.3	4.1	4.2	2.9	3.5	-2.76	-9.8	-21
Pennsylvania	7.1	7.4	7.5	7.7	8.0	8.5	6.8	6.5	8.3	7.4	8.1	-0.32	-11.5	-15.9
South Carolina	9.8	9.5	10.1	9.1	8.9	8.5	8.4	8.4	11.8			0.4	4.9	15
Tennessee	14.9	16.5	15.5	16	14.8	12.4	10.6	10.7	12.1	11.9	12.8	-3.47	-17.7	-20.1
Texas	16.1	15.7	15.2		12.6	11.1	10.7	10	5.9	6.1		-8.56	-33.1	-62.7
Utah	3.6	4.4	3.9	4.0	3.8	3.6	3.2	3.3	3.0			-0.7	-3.3	-5.4
Virginia		9.5	9.4	9.7	9	9.1	7.9	6.6	7.1	7.4	6.0	-2.19	-14.6	-25.5
West Virginia	5.4	5.8	5.8	5.6	6.5	6.8	5.7	6.4	3.9	2.8	4.1	-1.11	-11.9	-20.7
Wyoming	4.1	4.0	2.1	4.0	2.9	2.5	2.1	3.7	2.4	2.8		-0.64	1.1	1.8
Percentage of states where crime fell												89%	82%	82%
Drop in murders per 100,000 people for states where murder rates fell												-62.25	-473.1	-794.4
Increase in murders per 100,000 people for states where murder rates rose												3.71	12.9	21.6

Note: Blanks indicate that not enough information was available to calculate an estimate for those years.

Table 10.5b Changes in rape rates by state over time

	Years before law in effect						Years after law in effect						Change in rape rates		
	10 or more	9–8	7–6	5–4	3–2	1–0	1–2	3–4	5–6	7–8	9–10	11 or more	Average yearly change before and after law	Net impact by year 6	Net impact by year 10
Alaska	153.8	221.7	190.2	159.9	217.8	218.0	80.3	69.8	77.1	44.9	43.3		−130.5	−426.8	−774.6
Arizona	64.0	61.2	54.2	46.9	35.5	35.6	33.6		29.5	28.3	34.3	34.7	−17.5	−8.1	−16.7
Arkansas	100.8	105.6		127.2	110.0	105.3	41.7	33.8	41.8	39.5	59.2		−66.6	−198.5	−310.4
Colorado	26.7	25.1	38.0	39.5	32.6	41.3									
Florida		217.3	228.3	224.9	215.4	213.1	50.3	58.5	69.3	86.9		93.4	−148.1	−461.1	−587.2
Georgia	41.3	45.8	43.6	47.2	51.5	61.9		43.6	43.4	41.4	44.6	44.5	−5.0	−36.9	−74.7
Idaho	18.3	16.4	17.7	20.3	36.0	29.1	29.1	27.0	24.7	26.3	27.2	27.9	6.7	−6.6	−11.4
Kentucky	44.2	43.5	35.1	41.1	36.0	33.8	33.4	31.5	33.4	33.5			−6.0	−3.1	−3.4
Louisiana	70.0	64.6	55.5	49.3	60.0	61.9	41.3	38.1	37.1	45.2			−19.8	−69.1	−85.7
Maine		12.1	8.5		9.9	8.4	14.9	18.9	18.3	18.6	17.5	15.3	7.5	26.8	46.0
Michigan	103.0	101.2	100.0	94.1	96.4	104.4									
Minnesota	42.5		64.3	61.8	61.3	55.6	41.6						−15.5	−14.0	−14.0
Mississippi	57.3	67.4	72.8	63.5	74.1	88.2		51.2	55.1	61.1	74.5	69.8	−8.2	−70.1	−110.8
Missouri	29.3	30.8	31.3	33.9	24.4	28.4									
Montana	30.1	22.9	25.9	18.2	19.0	17.6	21.4			15.7	16.9	18.9	−4.1	3.8	1.2
Nevada	47.0	44.6	44.6	40.0	41.1	57.2	53.4	44.1	26.8	24.1	22.4		−11.8	−47.2	−115.1
New Mexico	141.7	184.1	142.9	78.3	66.9	59.3	54.1						−58.1	−5.2	−5.2

North Carolina	18.3	22.5	23.5	26.1	31.7	39.6	31.3	28.6	27.0	28.5	31.2	—	2.4	-31.9	-51.3
Ohio	39.0	37.4	—	42.6	45.0	42.6	39.8	—	35.0	33.9	34.7	—	-1.5	-2.8	-2.8
Oklahoma	101.3	101.6	97.8	108.5	99.2	103.1	46.8	43.9	37.5	41.2	37.2	—	-64.3	-124.5	-262.1
Oregon	73.2	63.4	63.3	50.4	51.1	53.2	—	—	—	—	—	45.1	-17.3	-18.7	-42.4
Pennsylvania	29.7	—	28.9	29.3	28.2	26.0	26.4	24.5	24.3	27.7	25.9	—	-2.7	-2.7	-1.0
South Carolina	50.7	56.4	—	68.2	60.8	54.5	48.9	42.4	42.1	42.0	35.1	—	-16.0	-30.1	-61.9
Tennessee	83.4	91.5	90.5	89.5	75.6	80.3	47.1	47.6	44.7	47.9	46.9	—	-38.3	-101.5	-167.3
Texas	163.8	181.5	—	159.7	145.7	140.0	47.1	45.3	44.7	47.9	46.9	—	-113.6	-190.9	-190.9
Utah	39.7	36.0	—	52.4	47.6	42.0	41.8	40.8	52.1	55.3	65.5	—	7.6	8.8	45.6
Virginia	23.4	23.3	23.9	22.8	22.7	22.8	27.0	26.6	32.0	28.3	—	22.3	4.1	17.4	22.9
West Virginia	39.0	37.6	37.2	36.5	36.9	29.2	23.4	20.7	20.4	20.5	21.5	18.3	-15.4	-23.1	-40.6
Wyoming	58.3	41.8	46.1	40.3	32.9	38.9	34.4	32.1	28.8	27.2	21.5	19.6	-15.8	-21.5	-50.7
Percentage of states where crime fell													81%	85%	85%
Drop in rapes per 100,000 people for states where rape rates fell													-776.0	-1,894	-2,980
Increase in rapes per 100,000 people for states where rape rates rose													28.2	52.9	115.6

Note: Blanks indicate that not enough information was available to calculate an estimate for those years

Table 10.5c Changes in robbery rates by state over time

	Years before law in effect						Years after law in effect						Change in robbery rates		
	10 or more	9–8	7–6	5–4	3–2	1–0	1–2	3–4	5–6	7–8	9–10	11 or more	Average yearly change before and after law	Net impact by year 6	Net impact by year 10
Alaska	130.4	160.3	162.1	134	160.8	194.7	155.1	141.1	112.9	83.5	50.4		−48.4	−525	−1,292
Arizona	189.7	201.0	185.9	176.8	124.4	139.1	173.8	188.9	178.1	194.4	189.2		15.4	371	687
Arkansas	167.9		244.3	253.9	224.6	233.5	114.1	119.6	116.3	148.2	166.5		−91.9	−1,051	−1,508
Colorado	80.7	59.4	72.0	69.3	53.2	70.6									
Florida		617.8	892.8	701.2	810.4	970.5	357.3	398.7	375.2	389.9		425.6	−409.2	−5,341	−7,083
Georgia	197.9		146.7	169.8	225.7	289.3	257.2	225.6	209.6	224.7	248.8	218.6	24.9	−526	−841
Idaho	40.9	27.6	24.7	21.8		13.8	20.5	14.9	22.0	24.0	23.1	18.4	−5.3	48	106
Kentucky	91.9	117.8	72.9	76.3	70.4	84.3	90.7	103.7	100.9	107.8			15.2	127	198
Louisiana	233.6	235	229.1	223.8	260.2	299.2	239.1	244	238.1	201			−16.2	−529	−824
Maine		65.2	46.5		35.9	36.3	28.0	26.1	23.3	22.6	27.0	28.9	−20	−94	−163
Michigan	234.7	194.5	191.5	158.1		191.5	117.9	113.9					−78.2	−454	−454
Minnesota	102.3	118.5	127.2	115.3	84.7	82.6									
Mississippi	159.3	142.4	135.6	125	140.6	159.2		158.3	185	224.9	186.3	226.2	52.5	74	353
Missouri	121.8	136.8	124.5		129.1	114.0	114.0						−11.2		
Montana	34.7	26.5		19.3	22.2	22.2	25.3		22.2	19.5	20.9	27.1	−2	10	−2
Nevada	365.1	337.7	312.9	284.7	325.1	316.2	307.6	269.2	191.8		151.2		−93.7	−541	−1,036
New Mexico	123.6	123.6	149.1	104.5	95.4	80.7									

State															
North Carolina	51.1	65.2	87.7	111.9	131.6	150.9	163.9	191.5	200.7	217.7			93.7	161	511
Ohio	103.4	104.8	105.1	120.7	133.5	139.2			85.1	97.7			-98.9	-544	-1,095
Oklahoma	160.1	206.8	221.1	196.3	177.3	183.1	106.6	119.6	78.2	124.1	104.7	136.9	-83.9	-287	-604
Oregon	161.5	193.3	227.8	246.6	242	169.7	174.3	158.9	171.7	225.6	201.4	184.0	4.8	-38	207
Pennsylvania	165.2		196.4	193	178.9	172.6	176.2	179.5	186.8	204.4	192.4		59	172	300
South Carolina	89.4	104.5	133.1	155.8	161.7								-41.6	-314	-258
Tennessee	264.9	320.2	318.4	286.5	251.9	223.2	210.8	217.1	256.3	266.1		307.1	-195.9	-1,547	-2,180
Texas	344.7		474.1	460.8	390.1	354.2	171.5	174.8	200.6	250.7	246.9				
Utah	65.1	63.4		54.2	46.5	55.5	68.9	69.2	76.1	69.6	55.0		10.8	143	185
Virginia	101.2	109.7	106.3	97.1	94.9	103.6	107.2	111.8			134.9	98.1	13.1	97	191
West Virginia	41.5	48.5	51.3	48.9	44.0	45.5	37.7	40.3	36.1	40.6	50.0		-5.7	-68	-83
Wyoming	33.8	27.2	24.4	20.1	16.8	16.4	17.9	18.8	12.1	16.1	15.6		-7	-1	-4
Percentage of states where crime fell													64%	64%	64%
Drop in robberies per 100,000 people for states where robbery rates fell													-1,209.2	-11,861	-1,7426
Increase in robberies per 100,000 people for states where robbery rates rose													289.3	1,203	2,738

Note: Blanks indicate that not enough information was available to calculate an estimate for those years.

Table 10.5d Changes in aggravated assault rates by state over time

	Years before law in effect						Years after law in effect						Change in aggravated assault rates		
	10 or more	9–8	7–6	5–4	3–2	1–0	1–2	3–4	5–6	7–8	9–10	11 or more	Average yearly change before and after law	Net impact by year 6	Net impact by year 10
Alaska	333.9	449.8	423.9	351.5	348.1	457.7	526.3	484.2	574.5	414.8	272.7		60.3	635	-48
Arizona	684.5	719.4	680.2	619.6	523.1	538.4	495.7		381.7	417.1	463.2	509.6	-174	-599	-1,188
Arkansas	332.6		368.6	390.9	394.6	354.7	359.8	344.0	362.9	375.7	449.0		10	8	354
Colorado	285.7	221.2	187.5	184.1	184.8	197.4									
Florida	711.0	665.0	686.9	676.8	675.1	613.3		602.4	626.4	635.4		689.7	-32.9	7	73
Georgia	353	378.4	344.4	354.3	317.7	390.6	227.5	413.6	373.8	376.4	337.2	295.9	3	19	-184
Idaho	303	323.9	289.9	220.5	211.9	221.5		207.2	238.9		244.9	209.4	-36.2	27	97
Kentucky	321.9	339.1	363.3	506.3	415.2	216.7	187	221.5	230.6	214.4			-147	-33	-41
Louisiana	471.3		347.7	381.0	507.8	517.9	559.7	612.5	614.7	470.7	612.5		128.9	700	842
Maine		322.5	262.5		157.3	143.7	102.6	95.6	79.7	74.6	69.0	72.6	-139.2	-460	-892
Michigan	375.5	362.6	315.2	269.6		313.9	362.3	371.7					39.6	319	319
Minnesota	112.1	113.5	112.0	122.2	130.6	127.6									
Mississippi	204.0		183.4	146.0	133.9	121.5	128.6	221.4	303.6	386.2	198.6	183.5	79.2	867	1,893
Missouri	277.3	308.4	285.4	281.7	315.6	366.6									
Montana	208.9		218.9	88.1	85.6	76.5	99.0		76.2	98.8	180.0	237.2	2.7	67	444
Nevada	484.7	369.3		278.9	380.4	587.5	436.6	362.1	304.2	381.8	421.5		-38.9	-1,979	-3,094
New Mexico	752.3	819.1	649.7	641.0		576.6	541.9						-145.8	-104	-104

North Carolina	370.7	305.8	298.2		364.2	363.2	384.5	362.3	270.3	289.3	301.8		−18.8	−218	−623
Ohio	180.7	168.9	139.3	145.0	137.4	143.4							−10.9	18	18
Oklahoma	402.7	366.0	383.5	418.1	461.1	476.9	436.9	311.2	414.7	414.0	405.3	268.4	−0.3	−307	−710
Oregon	609.8	588.4	470.6	417.3	371.2	297	311.2	117.7	330.5	316.4		341.8	−217.9	−1,163	−1,450
Pennsylvania	206.9	210.5	219.4	216.7	221.6	223.1	204.8			266.9	288.5		49.3	−46	291
South Carolina	772.9	667.2	777.6	822.1	804.7	756.9	616.2	564.5	628.5				−145.5	−1430	−1958
Tennessee	352	355.3	365.2	406.5	473.6	466.8	490.5	544	542.7	613.5	627.9		160.5	530	1,453
Texas	402.2	431.5	479.6	487.1	420.3	421.4	405.3		395.7	428.4	397.1		−34.6	−116	−161
Utah	279	231.9	216.4	227.0	210.4	218.1	245.6		240.4	247.0			8	218	328
Virginia	269.8	231.3	239.6	233.5	218.4	172.4	177.5		179.1		231.2	194.5	−38.5	−68	74
West Virginia	101.5	110.2	116.7	119.0	82.4	101.5	125.3		104.9	112.4	197.6	187.7	32.3	51	153
Wyoming	305.7	264.6	277.7	243.7	201.0	199.8	217.1		203.0	232.5	205.1		−48.2	51	158
Percentage of states where crime fell													58%	48%	45%
Drop in aggravated assaults per 100,000 people for states where aggravated assault rates fell													−1,228.7	−6,522	−10,452
Increase in aggravated assaults per 100,000 people for states where aggravated assault rates rose													573.7	3,465	6,345

Note: Blanks indicate that not enough information was available to calculate an estimate for those years.

a right-to-carry law is passed merely due to randomness is far less than 0.1 percent—more than 1,000 to 1 odds. The odds that these drops in robbery rates are random are also somewhat long—about 11 to 1. For aggravated assault, while the laws still indicate a small overall reduction in crime, the impact on particular states is essentially random. These odds are similar to testing whether a coin is fair. If you flip a coin twenty times and 70 or 80 percent of your tosses come up heads, you would be very foolish not to bet heads for the next coin flip.

The results are again very similar to those provided in figures 10.1b–10.1e, with murder and rape showing the most dramatic reductions. The average murder rate dropped in 89 percent of the states after the right-to-carry law was passed. Over the first six years after the law, 82 percent of the states experienced a net reduction in murders. Over the first ten years after the law, 85 percent saw a drop. Even in the three states where the average rate went up, the increase was very small, averaging just one percentage point, and statistically insignificant.

There was a similar decline in rape rates. While rape rates didn't compare quite as well in terms of the before-and-after averages (81 percent of the states showed declines, compared to 89 percent for murder). Nevertheless, rape rates showed a slightly more consistent drop across states than murder rates when you compare the crime rates after the law to the rates right before the law went into effect (85 percent for both the six- and ten-year comparisons compared to 82 percent). The average drop for the states whose rape rates fell was over twenty-seven times larger than the average increase for the states that experienced an increase in rape.

While the results for robbery are not anywhere near as overwhelming as for murder and rape, states still experienced a drop in robbery rates by almost a two-to-one ratio. Once again, the drops are much larger than the increases—with the average drops in robbery rates being between 4.4 and 9.9 times larger than the average increases. In fact, as we have pointed out many times in this book, the comparison in this case might underestimate the benefit of right-to-carry laws, because robbery rates were rising before the law and falling afterward. If you concentrate on the changes in robbery rates between the period immediately before the law and up to six or ten years afterward, the average drop experienced by states where robbery rates declined is between 6.4 and 9.9 times bigger than the average increase in the states where robbery rates rose.

Victims face real costs from crime. Although the loss of life and physical and psychological damage are the most important, there are lost earnings, medical care, and the destruction of property that should be included in adding up the costs. Not too surprisingly, murder imposes by far the biggest cost. The estimated total loss from a murder—$3.9 million in 2007 dollars—is far greater than the $115,260 average loss from rape and the $10,758 average loss from robbery. These victimization costs were developed by the National Institute of Justice. If we use these figures, the twenty-nine states that we study save over $30 billion a year, with over half of that coming just from the reduction in murder rates. To put it differently, the average citizen in those states saved $221 each year from other law-abiding citizens carrying concealed handguns. Excluding property crimes, where our results are the least certain, the average citizen still saved $183. Since criminals don't know which people are going to be able to protect themselves from an attack, even those who would never even consider owning a gun, let alone carrying one, benefit from others willing to bear these costs.

The costs are borne by individual gun carriers, who have to pay the price of the gun, licensing fees, and training. These individuals also have to deal with the inconvenience of carrying a gun. It is important to note that higher fees mean that fewer people will carry guns, which reduces the total benefit.[99]

All these tables make another point quite clear. When accounting for the differences in the laws, there is no evidence that states that adopted right-to-carry laws later than others had a different experience. Florida, Maine, and Virginia had the first full year of their laws during the 1980s, but there is little difference in how murder, rape, or robbery rates changed compared with states such as Louisiana, Nevada, and Oklahoma, whose right-to-carry laws started in the 1990s. Even Michigan, whose right-to-carry law was adopted after 2000, experienced substantial benefits.

For example, two-thirds of the states whose right-to-carry laws went into effect during either the 1980s or 1990s saw drops in robbery rates. One of the two states whose laws went into effect after 2000 also showed a drop, while the other, Missouri, showed no change. This pattern casts doubt on the claim that the crack cocaine epidemic during the late 1980s and early 1990s is driving the results, because these results show drops in crime rates whether the right-to-carry laws went into effect before, during, or after the crack epidemic.

Figure 10.2 shows the pattern for murder rates by the decade that the right-to-carry law went into effect. It graphs out what was shown in table 10.5a. Clearly, the murder rates start falling after the law, though

Table 10.6 The impact of right-to-carry laws on victimization costs (millions of 2007 dollars)

	Murder	Rape	Robbery	Aggravated assault	Property crime
Alaska	−$36.91	−$110.29	−$28.61	−$1.26	−$42.19
Arizona	−$67.35	−$19.85	$127.33	−$258.63	$104.84
Arkansas	−$795.17	−$182.53	−$137.97	$38.05	−$264.70
Colorado					
Florida	−$6,652.83	−$1,795.62	−$3,368.81	$40.88	−$2,834.34
Georgia	−$1,490.79	−$118.89	−$208.35	−$53.45	−$0.63
Idaho	$3.50	−$2.61	$3.78	$4.06	$6.84
Kentucky	−$18.56	−$3.15	$28.72	−$6.90	$10.73
Louisiana	−$547.55	−$107.19	−$128.08	$153.92	−$70.19
Maine	−$31.41	$11.93	−$6.57	−$42.26	−$1.13
Michigan	−$289.53		−$149.53	$123.29	−$153.37
Minnesota	−$127.05	−$82.40		$0.00	$0.00
Mississippi	−$122.11	−$68.16	$33.72	$212.79	−$12.96
Missouri			−$0.01		
Montana	−$4.33	$0.24	−$0.08	$16.46	$14.10
Nevada	−$158.07	−$48.00	−$67.20	−$235.82	−$48.57
New Mexico	$70.39	−$11.31		−$8.33	$8.13
North Carolina	−$126.29	−$90.48	$140.17	−$200.92	−$106.80
Ohio	$270.82	−$37.24		$8.73	−$2.81
Oklahoma	−$707.18	−$202.90	−$131.82	−$100.52	−$316.14
Oregon	−$168.72	−$30.24	−$67.03	−$189.06	$38.63
Pennsylvania	−$492.25	−$2.71	$89.37	$147.51	$61.49
South Carolina	$195.55	−$71.77	$43.31	−$332.01	−$42.53
Tennessee	−$282.37	−$209.50	−$50.29	$332.65	−$132.71
Texas	−$3,263.15	−$882.25	−$1,566.65	−$135.67	−$1,619.63
Utah	−$37.02	$27.97	$14.15	$29.44	−$3.00
Virginia	−$421.56	$33.52	$43.51	$19.91	$40.54
West Virginia	−$122.35	−$21.28	−$5.37	$0.00	−$8.16
Wyoming	$2.39	−$5.69	−$0.07	$3.23	$0.17
Total	−$15,419.92	−$4,030.40	−$5,392.38	−$433.91	−$5,374.38
Average per state	−$571.11	−$155.02	−$215.70	−$14.96	−$185.32
Per capita	−$111.38	−$29.11	−$38.95	−$3.13	−$38.82
Excluding Florida:					
Total	−$8,767.10	−$2,234.78	−$2,023.58	−$474.78	−$2,540.04
Average per state	−$337.20	−$89.39	−$84.32	−$16.96	−$90.72
Per capita	−$63.33	−$16.14	−$14.62	−$3.43	−$18.35

Note: Except for the per capita estimates, all dollar amounts are in millions of dollars.
Source: The estimated victimization costs from crime are from Ted R. Miller, Mark Cohen, and Brian Wiersema, "Victim Costs and Consequences: A New Look," Office of Justice Programs, National Institute of Justice, 1996.
Note: Except for the per capita estimates, all amounts are in millions of dollars. All estimates are in 2007 dollars. The victimization costs for the different crime categories are $3,887,200 for murder, $115,260 for rape, $10,758 for robbery, and $12,640 for aggravated assault.

the drop is greater in those states whose laws went into effect in the 1980s than the 1990s. And states that adopted the law after 2000 display a similar pattern—murder rates were rising consistently over the preceding eight years and declined for the first time right after the law went into effect. However, for this last set of states too little time has elapsed to reach any overall conclusion.

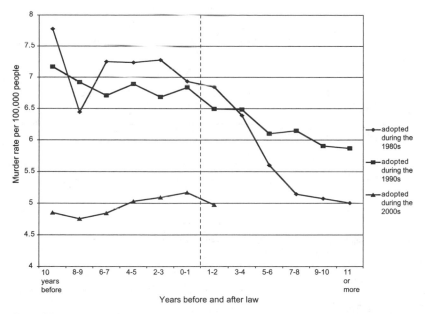

Figure 10.2. Changes in murder rates after adoption of right-to-carry laws by decade of adoption

Obviously, there can be some debate over what factors cause changes in crime rates. Take our graphs for murder. In the nine alternative graphs that follow, I look at many combinations of factors that can explain crime: (a) using the arrest rate in the preceding year; (b) excluding changes in all the other gun-control laws, but keeping everything else; (c) excluding all the measures of demographic change, but keeping everything else; (d) dropping all the measures of income, poverty, unemployment, and population, but keeping everything else; (e) dropping the gun-control laws except the right-to-carry law and dropping all measures of demographics but keeping everything else; (f) dropping the gun-control laws as well as the income, poverty, unemployment, and population variables; (g) dropping the particular demographic variable for the percentage of the population that is neither white nor black males 20–29 years of age; (h) eliminating all control variables but fixed effects; and (i) including crack cocaine use for the 1980–2000 period (see figures 10.3a–10.3i). These different estimates examine how sensitive the results are to the specifications that are used. While I think that most people would accept that the procedures used in the earlier estimates are important in explaining crime rates, all readers might not share that feeling.

The nine figures consistently show that right-to-carry laws reduce murder rates. Given the frequent claims made by critics about cocaine's impact

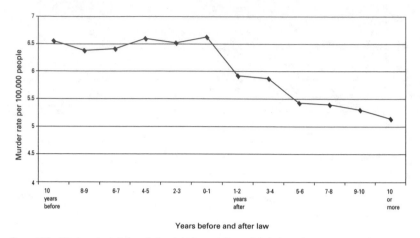

Figure 10.3a. Murder rates before and after right-to-carry law: using the lagged arrest rate

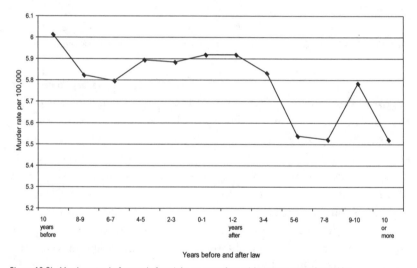

Figure 10.3b. Murder rates before and after right-to-carry law: without gun-control variables

on the measured benefits of right-to-carry laws, it is interesting how large the drop in crime is even when the measure of cocaine use is included. As in the results reported in previous chapters, per capita income and poverty measures have very small and statistically insignificant impacts on crime rates.

Generally, the regulations to obtain permits have effects similar to those

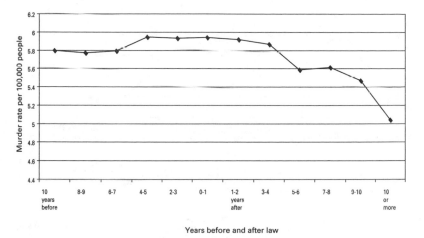

Figure 10.3c. Murder rates before and after right-to-carry law: without demographic control variables

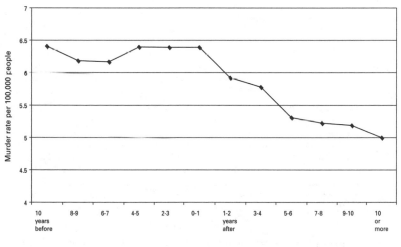

Figure 10.3d. Murder rates before and after right-to-carry law: without the income, poverty, unemployment, and population variables

found in chapter 9. Longer training requirements imply a larger reduction in crime from right-to-carry laws, but the effect drops off at a diminishing rate. There also seems to be an increase in crime when the length of the training requirement is greater than eight hours. Requiring people to train for more than eight hours means that they must attend training for

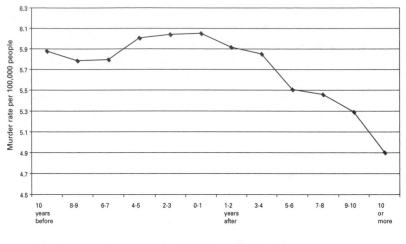

Figure 10.3e. Murder rates before and after right-to-carry law: without the gun-control variables and demographic variables

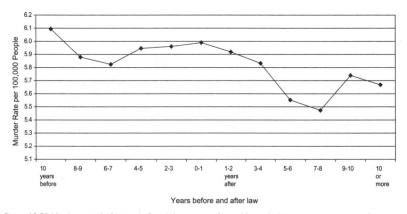

Figure 10.3f. Murder rates before and after right-to-carry law: without the income, poverty, unemployment, population, and gun-control variables

more than one day, and that greatly reduces the number of people who get a permit. The more years a permit lasts, the larger reduction in crime, though the effect is small. Finally, higher age limits before one can obtain a permit appear to be related to more crime, but the effect is only statistically significant for overall violent crime and aggravated assault.

We will discuss these regressions more later in the context of other gun laws.

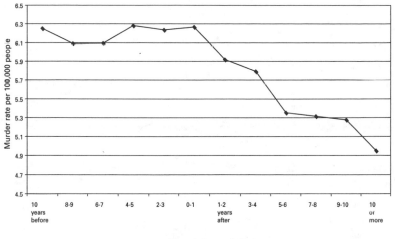

Figure 10.3g: Murder rates before and after right-to-carry law: dropping "percentage of population that is neither white nor black males 20–29 years of age"

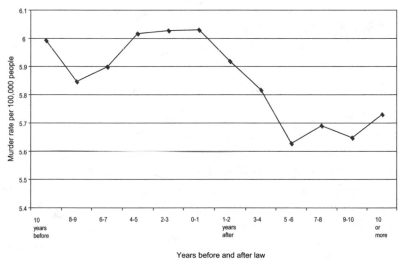

Figure 10.3h. Murder rates before and after right-to-carry law: only accounting for average differences by state and year, no other factors taken into account

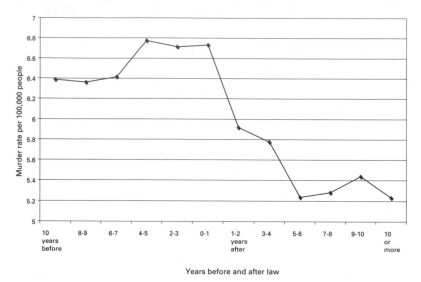

Figure 10.3i. Murder rates before and after right-to-carry law: including crack cocaine, data only available for 1980–2000

Other Research on Guns and Crime

When other scholars have tried to replicate [Lott's] results, they found that the right-to-carry laws simply don't bring down crime.

—Steven Levitt and Stephen Dubner, *Freakonomics* (2005), pp. 133–34

The Numbers

After *More Guns, Less Crime* first appeared in 1998 (with the second edition in 2000), a host of new empirical research was undertaken on the effect of right-to-carry laws.[100] The most recent research continues the earlier pattern of finding reductions in crime, with twelve new refereed studies by economists and criminologists finding reductions in violent crime of various magnitudes. On the other side, one new refereed piece claims that the benefits are small or nonexistent. Weak evidence that concealed handguns may increase crime has been put forward in two nonrefereed publications by Ayres and Donohue.

Here are the results from nine of the twelve studies finding a benefit from right-to-carry laws published since the last edition of this book (see table 10.7; my three articles are excluded from this list):

—Florenz Plassmann and Nicolaus Tideman conclude that "right-to-carry laws do help on average to reduce the number of these crimes."[101]

—Carl Moody states that his findings "confirm and reinforce the basic findings of the original Lott and Mustard study."[102]

—In another paper that Moody coauthored with Thomas Marvell, which studies county crime rates from 1977 to 2000, the authors write that "the evidence, such as it is, seems to support the hypothesis that the shall-issue law is generally beneficial with respect to its overall long run effect on crime."[103]

—Eric Helland and Alex Tabarrok used county crime rates from 1977 to 2000 to find that "shall-issue laws cause a large and significant drop in the murder trend rate" and that "there is considerable support for the hypothesis that shall-issue laws cause criminals to substitute away from crimes against persons and towards crimes against property."[104]

—While calling for more research, David Olsen and Michael Maltz found "a decrease in total homicides," though the different data set they use indicates that the decline was driven entirely by a drop in gun homicides.[105]

—Bruce Benson and Brent Mast argue that their results "are virtually identical to those in [Lott and Mustard]. Therefore, the hypothesis that the [Lott and Mustard estimates] suffer from missing-variable bias owing to the lack of control for the private security industry is rejected."[106]

—David Mustard provides evidence that "after enactment of the right-to-carry laws, states exhibit a reduced likelihood of having felonious police deaths."[107]

—James Q. Wilson, often mentioned as the preeminent criminologist in the United States, reviewed the National Academy of Sciences report on Firearms and Violence and notes that while there might be some debate over some types of violent crime, "I find that the evidence presented by Lott and his supporters suggests that RTC laws do in fact help drive down the murder rate."[108]

—My work with John Whitley concludes that "the longer a right-to-carry law is in effect, the greater the drop in crime."[109]

Different researchers approach the problem from a variety of perspectives by using new statistical techniques, different data sets, or different control variables or by examining a variety of specifications. Despite these differences, the consensus is the same: right-to-carry laws reduce violent crime.[110]

Plassmann and Tideman break down the impact of concealed-handgun laws not only across states but also by each year before and after the law for the years 1977–1992. Their big innovation involves solving what is called

Table 10.7 Modern statistical research on right-to-carry laws and crime by academic economists and criminologists using national panel data

	Studies that found right-to-carry laws reduced violent crime	Studies that claim to find that right-to-carry laws have no discernable effect on violent crime	Studies that found right-to-carry laws increased violent crime
Refereed academic publications	1. Lott and Mustard, *Journal of Legal Studies*, 1997 2. Bartley and Cohen, *Economic Inquiry*, 1998 3. Lott, *Journal of Legal Studies*, 1998 4. Bartley, *Economics Letters*, 1999 5. Benson and Mast, *Journal of Law and Economics*, 2001 6. Moody, *Journal of Law and Economics*, 2001 7. Mustard, *Journal of Law and Economics*, 2001 8. Olsen and Maltz, *Journal of Law and Economics*, 2001 9. Plassmann and Tideman, *Journal of Law and Economics*, 2001 10. Marvell, *Journal of Law and Economics*, 2001 11. Lott and Whitley, *Journal of Law and Economics*, 2001 12. Lott and Whitley, *Journal of Quantitative Criminology*, 2003 13. Helland and Tabarrok, *Advances in Economic Analysis and Policy*, 2004 14. Wilson, *National Academies Press*, 2005 15. Lott and Whitley, *Economic Inquiry*, 2007 16. Moody and Marvell, *Econ Watch*, 2008	1. Black and Nagin, *Journal of Legal Studies*, 1998 2. Ludwig, *International Review of Law and Economics*, 1998 3. Donohue and Levitt, *Quarterly Journal of Economics*, 1999 4. Hood and Neeley, *Social Science Quarterly*, 2000 5. Duggan, *Journal of Political Economy*, 2001 6. Duwe, Kovandzic, and Moody, *Homicide Studies*, 2002 7. Kovandzic and Marvell, *Criminology and Public Policy*, 2003 8. Dezhbakhsh and Rubin, *International Review of Law and Economics*, 2003 9. National Research Council, *National Academies Press*, 2005 10. Kovandzic, Marvell, and Vierauis, *Homicide Studies*, 2005	None
Nonrefereed publications by academics	1. Bronars and Lott, *American Economic Review*, 1998 2. Plassmann and Whitley, *Stanford Law Review*, 2003 3. Lott and Landes, *The Bias Against Guns*, 2003	1. Ayres and Donohue, *American Law and Economics Review*, 1999 (book reviews, unlike papers in this journal, are not refereed)	1. Ayres and Donohue, *Stanford Law Review*, 2003; see also Donohue, "The Impact of Concealed-Carry Laws," 2003 2. Ayres and Donohue, *Econ Watch*, 2009[a]

[a]Just the original paper by Carl Moody and Teb Marvell was refereed by *Econ Watch*. Correspondence with the editor indicates the comment by Ayres and Donohue was published as it was sent into the journal: no refereeing or editing was done for their piece.

the "truncation problem," which occurs in county-level data sets because in some years many counties do not experience certain types of crimes at all—80 percent have no murders, for instance. If the murder rate in a county is zero before the law goes into effect, simple randomness means that sometimes the crime rate will go up, but the reverse cannot happen— crime rates cannot fall below zero. This could bias results for these regressions toward finding an increase in crime from the law. To avoid that, they exclude counties where there were no crimes committed.

Figure 10.4 graphs the regression results that Plassmann and Tideman obtained for murder. Their results are striking. For the ten states that adopted concealed-handgun laws during the period they studied, murder rates were rising or constant prior to the law. After the law was passed, they were all falling. Indeed, with one exception, all Plassmann and Tideman's estimates for murder, rape, and robbery for the ten states that enacted the law from 1977 through 1992 show that crime rates fell during the first full year that the laws were in effect. Even in the one exception (Oregon for robbery), the robbery rates still were much lower in the first three full years after enactment than in any of the five years before the law. Robbery rates (again with the exception of the single year for Oregon) indicate a bigger drop for each additional year that the law is in effect.

David Olsen and Michael Maltz use county-level data from the Supplemental Homicide Report (SHR). At the time of my initial research with David Mustard, the SHR only provided data at the state level, so we could not use it. Fortunately, the SHR data set has since been improved. The SHR is remarkably rich and includes much more detailed characteristics of the victims and murderers than the FBI's *Uniform Crime Reports* (UCR). Further, county-level data are generally preferable to state level data. When you examine changes in crime rates solely at the state level, you likely miss much of what may be happening within a state.[111] There is no reason to expect that changes in law enforcement or other factors are going to have the same impact on crime in all counties within a state.

The overall drop in homicides that Olsen and Maltz find is roughly similar to what I originally reported using county level UCR data. However, the county level SHR data set does produce different results in terms of how murders are committed and who benefits from gun ownership. Olsen and Maltz's results show that after the passage of concealed-handgun laws, murderers rely much less frequently upon guns to kill people. The results are striking and important: murders with guns fall by 21 percent while non-gun murders actually rise by 10 percent, though this rise is not statistically

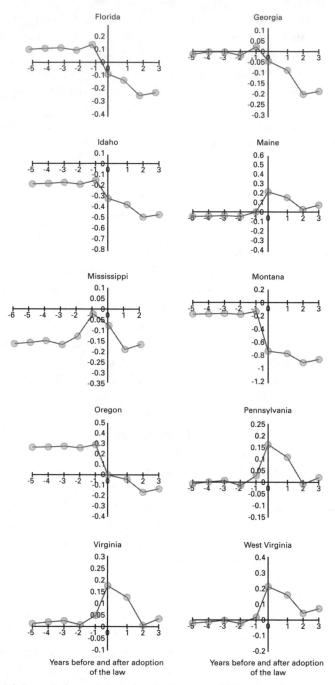

Figure 10.4. Before-and-after trends for murder using Plassmann and Tideman's results

significant. In total, they find that concealed-carry laws lower murder by 7 percent.

Another study presents the effect of right-to-carry laws on police killings. Using data from 1984 to 1996, David Mustard finds that while waiting periods rarely have a significant effect on police deaths, concealed-handgun laws are consistently and significantly related to fewer killings of police. Olsen and Maltz's work dovetails well with Mustard's. If right-to-carry laws result in fewer criminals carrying guns, this might explain why fewer police are murdered.

My paper with John Whitley in 2007 takes into account whether the impact of legalizing abortion on crime altered our results for right-to-carry laws. Using the SHR data from 1980 to 1998, we also find that each additional year that a right-to-carry law was in effect, the murder rate dropped by between 1 and 2.5 percent (with most of the estimates between about 1.9 and 2.5 percent). We also found that legalized abortion led to more single-parent families, which in turn is a well-known cause of delinquent and criminal behavior in children.

The Critics

A number of critics claim that right-to-carry laws have no impact on violent crime. However, there is very little in peer-reviewed professional journals to point to. Even the results that they point to actually hold more evidence that right-to-carry laws reduce crime.

For instance, Mark Duggan claims that my statistically significant results on concealed handguns disappear for several of the violent crime categories when one correctly calculates the statistical significance. However, Duggan has simply misreported his own results and recorded some of his estimated drops in crime as not being statistically significant when in fact they are significant.[112] After those mistakes are corrected, fifteen of his thirty estimates show statistically significant drops in crime, while only one shows a significant increase.

Indeed, all six of his estimates show that right-to-carry laws reduce murder rates, and the results are statistically significant for four of them. These significant reductions occur despite his leaving out all the normal factors that are well known to affect crime rates, such as the arrest rate, the death penalty, prison incarceration rate, poverty, or anything else. These factors are routinely included when economists study crime. In a few estimates, he only accounts for the year-to-year and average county differences in crime rates.

His two estimates that did not yield statistically significant reductions in murder rates are particularly problematic.[113] In one of them, Duggan compares the murder rate the year before the law with the murder rate the year afterward. However, as shown in previous editions of this book, such an approach gives a very misleading result when crime rates are rising before a law and falling afterward. Obviously, this change in trends, from crime going up to going down, would be consistent with the law's being effective in combating crime. But the before-and-after averages would be the same, meaning that Duggan's calculations would falsely imply the law didn't matter. (Recall the earlier discussion and graphs in chapter 9, critique 4, "Do right-to-carry laws significantly reduce the robbery rate?")

Duggan's second estimate without a statistically significant result stems from his ignoring the "truncation problem," noted above by Plassmann and Tideman, and thus treating counties with no reported murders the same as the others. For example, when most counties have zero murders in any given year, no matter how good the law is, murder rates can't fall any further. But simple randomness can mean that sometimes you will see the crime rate rise from zero even though it had no connection with the right-to-carry laws. In his last set of estimates, his analysis of the different violent crime categories included counties with zero crimes. There are a number of ways to statistically adjust for this problem (Tobit, negative binomials, etc.), but Duggan didn't bother to use these techniques—thus biasing his results against finding a drop in crime.

Let's break down the results from five of the more prominent critical papers. Besides Duggan's work, there are papers by Black and Nagin, Ayres and Donohue (1999), Ludwig, and a book chapter by Donohue (2003) that reproduces the regressions shown in Ayres and Donohue (2003), plus a few more. The results are summarized in table 10.8. Out of 177 estimates reported by these critics, only 7 imply a statistically significant increase in crime after the passage of the law. In contrast, 80 imply no statistically significant change, and 90 imply a statistically significant decline in crime. In other words, half the time these critical studies confirm my results. In only 4 percent of the estimates are the results reversed. And those 4 percent contain numerous problems with their regressions, problems that tend to bias their results against finding a beneficial affect.[114]

Take Black and Nagin's state-by-state breakdown. At the 10 percent level, merely three of their estimates imply a statistically significant increase in crime, twenty-two imply no significant change, and fifteen imply a statistically significant decline.[115] And again, as just mentioned, examining only

Table 10.8 Results on violent crime rates from studies critical of my work

Study	Tables in the study	Finding of reduced crime[a]	Finding of no change	Finding of increased crime
Estimates where there is enough information provided to determine statistical significance:				
Black and Nagin	Tables 1 and 2, national effects	12	8	1
Duggan	Table 12	14[b]	15[b]	1
Ludwig	Tables 4 and 5	0	19	0
Ayres and Donohue	Table 1	30 (27)[c]	13 (16)[c]	0
Donohue	Tables 1–4, examining the period from 1977 to 1997, estimates looking at the average drop in crime or the change in trends	34	25	5
Total		90 (87)	80 (83)	7

	Tables in the study	Net benefit from reduced crime	Net cost from increased crime
Estimates where there is not enough information provided to determine statistical significance:[d]			
Donohue[e]	Tables 1–4, net benefit or cost estimated by combining both average drop and trends together	4	0
	Tables 5–8, examining the impacts year by year after the law	4	0
Total		8	0

Sources: D. A. Black and D. S. Nagin, "Do Right-to-Carry Laws Deter Violent Crime?" *Journal of Legal Studies* 27 (1998): 209–19; Ian Ayres and John J. Donohue III, "Nondiscretionary Concealed Weapons Laws: A Case Study of Statistics, Standards of Proof, and Public Policy," *American Law and Economics Review* 1 (1999): 436; Mark Duggan, "More Guns, More Crime," *Journal of Political Economy* 109 (2001): 1086; J. Ludwig, "Concealed-Gun-Carrying Laws and Violent Crime: Evidence from State Panel Data," *International Review of Law and Economics* 18 (1998): 239–54; J. J. Donohue, "The Impact of Concealed Carry Laws," in *Evaluating Gun Policy*, ed. J. Ludwig and P. J. Cook (Washington, DC: Brookings Institution, 2003), 287–325.

Note: Values are the national coefficients from the most critical studies listed in footnote 17 of the report.

[a]Some of these negative significant coefficients are a result of the authors' replicating my earlier work. If these were removed, the numbers for negative significant coefficients would be as follows: Black and Nagin, 8; Duggan, 9; Ayres and Donohue, 25 (22); and totals, 42 (39).

[b]Duggan's study has typos mislabeling the statistical significance of two of his results. See column 2 in table 12 (p. 1110) and the results for rape and aggravated assault. For rape a coefficient of −.052 and a standard error of .0232 produce a t-statistic of 2.24. For aggravated assault a coefficient of −.0699 and a standard error of .0277 produce a t-statistic of 2.52.

[c]Because of downward rounding to 1.6, it is not possible to tell whether the t-statistics reported by Ayres and Donohue are statistically significant at the 10 percent level. The values in parentheses assume that a t-statistic of 1.6 is not significant at the 10 percent level, while the first values assume that a t-statistic rounded off to 1.6 is significant at that level.

[d]Examines the net effect over five years after the right-to-carry law is in effect, for estimates that simultaneously use both a law dummy and trend for the years that the law is in effect.

[e]Calculations taken from Plassmann and Whitley (2003).

Examining the net effect over five years after the right-to-carry law is in effect, for estimates that simultaneously use both a law dummy and trend for the years that the law is in effect.

simple before-and-after averages can be quite misleading, and Black and Nagin, Duggan, Ludwig, and Ayres and Donohue (1999) limit their studies to those averages.

Finally, in a series of papers, none of them peer refereed, Ian Ayres and John Donohue claim that crime rates may possibly rise with the passage of right-to-carry laws. (The book chapter discussed here by Donohue [2003] duplicates the same data and the same regressions.) They provide results for a variety of specifications using data from 1977 to 1997. Their most general results report the relative crime rates by year before and after the adoption of the law and show significant declines in all violent crime categories with patterns that are very similar to those just shown for Plassmann and Tideman.

Nevertheless, Donohue argues that these results provide no evidence that right-to-carry laws reduce violent crime, as the coefficients for crimes like robbery are positive for up to 6 to 7 years after the enactment of the law.[116] But he completely misinterprets his own results. A positive coefficient implies that the crime rates in right-to-carry states are higher than in non-right-to-carry states. But if the coefficient becomes smaller after the passage of the law, as is true here, that means the crime rates in right-to-carry states are falling relative to the crime rates in non-right-to-carry states. The crime rate in right-to-carry states is still higher than in other states, but not by as much as before. Thus, contrary to his own statements, Donohue's study showed that concealed-carry laws actually reduced crime. Figure 10.5 provides fairly dramatic evidence that even Ayres and Donohue's own results show that violent crime rates fall after right-to-carry laws are adopted, and that the drops over the entire period are larger for county- than state-level data. Their results generate similar graphs for the other violent crime categories.

Donohue explains his results this way (pp. 312–13, emphasis added):

> A supporter of the Lott thesis might note that the dummies for the periods more than three years after passage tend to become negative and statistically significant, but in my opinion the coefficient estimates for the dummies lagged beyond three years tend to weaken Lott's case rather than buttress it. . . . The ostensibly growing effect on crime—see the increasingly larger negative numbers after passage in table 8–5—are taken by Lott as evidence that shall-issue laws become more beneficial over time, but something very different is at work. The observed pattern again shows that numerous states *experiencing increases in crime* after passage drop out of the analysis be-

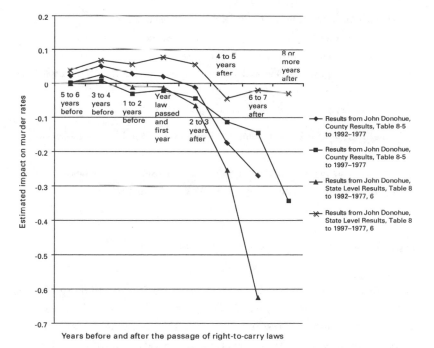

Figure 10.5. Donohue's (2003) estimated impact of right-to-carry laws on murder. From John Donohue, "The Impact of Concealed-Carry Laws," in *Evaluating Gun Policy*, ed. Jens Ludwig (Washington, DC: Brookings Institution Press, 2003), 287–323.

cause these states' laws were adopted too close to 1997 to be included in the estimate for beyond three years. (Indeed, none of the fourteen shall-issue laws that were adopted after the period for inclusion in Lott's original work affect the estimates of these "after three years" dummies).

As mentioned, Donohue makes a significant mistake here when interpreting his own results. True, the coefficients were positive for some of these estimates in the years immediately after passage of right-to-carry laws. As I explained, however, this simply means that the states that passed right-to-carry laws tended to be states with high crime rates. The crucial point here is that the number of crimes still fell—that immediately after the law was passed, crime rates in right-to-carry states were still higher than in other states but by a smaller amount. As the crime rates in right-to-carry states continued to fall, they eventually fell below the crime rates in non-right-to-carry states, and that is when the coefficients become negative. Thus, Donohue's own results clearly show that right-to-carry laws reduce crime.

Is There an Initial Increase in Crime? How Not to Fit a Line to a Curve

While we do not want to overstate the strength of the conclusions that can be drawn from the extremely variable results emerging from the statistical analysis, if anything, there is stronger evidence for the conclusion that these laws increase crime than there is for the conclusion that they decrease it.

—Ian Ayres and John Donohue, *Stanford Law Review*, 2003, p. 1202

Only one article, by Ayres and Donohue who employ a model that combines a dummy variable with a post-law trend, claims to find that shall-issue laws increase crime. However, the only way that they can produce the result that shall-issue laws increase crime is to confine the span of analysis to five years. We show, using their own estimates, that if they had extended their analysis by one more year, they would have concluded that these laws reduce crime.

—Carl Moody and Thomas Marvell, *Econ Journal Watch*, September 2008, p. 291

The above quotes speak for themselves. Donohue's claim that crime rates initially spike up after right-to-carry laws are adopted is made frequently in Ayres and Donohue's research. We have already discussed many issues such as why looking at simple average crime rates before and after the right-to-carry laws go into effect can lead to highly misleading conclusions on how crime rates are changing over time (p. 216). But there is nothing magical about adding simple before-and-after crime rate trends to these before-and-after averages. Indeed, the best way of analyzing the data is to simply look at how the crime rates change year by year. The reason to look at trends is to allow a simple statistical test to see if the before-and-after trends differ from each other.

Ayres and Donohue added a twist to their tests by combining the before-and-after averages with the before-and-after trends, what they call their "hybrid" estimate. There is nothing inherently wrong with this—after all, it is just another way of summarizing the patterns in the data. Nevertheless, one has to be careful that the actual changes in crime rates fit the pattern implied by whatever approach we are using.

Ayres and Donohue argue that when right-to-carry laws are adopted, there is an initial increase in crime and then a gradual decrease. But since none of the year-by-year estimates for violent crime show this initial jump in crime when the law starts, how do Ayres and Donohue reach this conclusion? The answer: It is really just an artifact of how they tried to fit a straight line to a curve.

Take a look at figure 10.6. Ayres and Donohue claim that crime rates are

Figure 10.6. Fitting a line to crime rates that are nonlinear

very slightly declining up until the right-to-carry law is passed and then they start to fall much more dramatically. Suppose that you wanted to fit two lines to the figure (say, the two dashed regression lines in the diagram). One straight line shows how the crime rate changes in the years before the law, and one straight line shows how it changes after the law. The first line is very easy to fit. The second one requires some arbitrary choices. The way Ayres and Donohue choose to position this line is so that it goes right through the middle of the curve for the after-law crime rates. An alternative would have been to have this second line start where the first one had finished (the approach that I had taken in the first and second editions in looking at before-and-after trends). This "predicted" crime rate line for the after-law period thus lies above the true crime rate immediately after the law, falls below the actual crime rate when you get out to year 4 after the law, and then again lies above the actual crime rate when you get out past year 9.

The key is that this "predicted" crime rate does not remotely resemble how the actual crime rate is changing. All this might not have been much of a problem if Ayres and Donohue had tried to reconcile these results with their reported year-by-year estimates (as I discussed at the end of the section "Other Research on Guns and Crime"). But they also made another mistake. Oddly, they used data for states that had these laws in effect for over a decade in order to estimate this after-law regression line, but then they only looked at the net change in crime rates for the first five years that the law was in effect. This only matters because for three of those first five years they are overpredicting the crime rate. Limiting the time that you examine to a period when you are greatly overpredicting the crime rate is what causes the large upward bias in their estimates of how right-to-carry laws alter crime rates.

Steve Levitt has claimed: "When the original Lott and Mustard (1997) data set is extended forward in time to encompass a large number of additional law enactments, the results disappear (Ayres and Donohue, 2003)."[117] That is wrong. It was not because they added additional years of data that these results disappear. The second edition of this book examined crime rates from 1977 to 1996, and the Ayres and Donohue paper added only one year, 1997, to the data set that I had given them. Adding one year of data onto twenty years didn't make a difference in the results. The issue is how they fitted a straight line to crime rate data that weren't straight.

This is where Carl Moody and Ted Marvell enter the debate. Moody and Marvell point out that even using Ayres and Donohue's own estimation over the period of time that they chose, summing the net effects over the first six years shows an overall benefit from the law.

So what is the moral of the story? When you know that the underlying data don't show an initial increase in crime but the simplified method that you are using to test the changes in crime rates implies there is, you had better go back and figure out what you did wrong.

Multiple-Victim Public Shootings

Finally, we should discuss the research by Grant Duwe, Tom Kovandzic, and Carl Moody on multiple-victim public shootings.[118] The three authors claim that the drop in multiple-victim public shootings after right-to-carry laws are adopted is not statistically significant. The problem is that they only looked at a very small subset of attacks, those that left four or more victims killed. Indeed, my earlier work with Bill Landes had also not found a statistically significant result for that one type of attack, but the reason is simple—this way of defining the dependent variable greatly reduces the number of public shootings to just thirty-six incidents over the entire 1977 to 1995 period.[119] Landes and I had examined a range of different types of attacks: two or more murders, three or more murders, two or more injuries or murders, three or more injuries or murders, and four or more injuries or murders. And the results consistently found that right-to-carry laws reduced the number of attacks and the number killed or injured.

Conclusion

In light of all the studies of right-to-carry laws, it is remarkable *that not a single refereed academic study by economists or criminologists* has found a bad effect from these laws. It's also noteworthy that no one has challenged the results that I have gotten for all the other gun-control laws that I have studied in this book.

The Continuing Debate

Clearly, the weight of research in refereed scholarly journals indicates that the basic results have been replicated, which is a central scientific criterion for evaluating an argument. Critics of the more-guns-less-crime thesis have not been content, however, to limit themselves to whether the basic findings stand up against legitimate examinations by others. Instead, they have sought to find chinks in the armor. When even that has not succeeded, they have engaged in misrepresentations and the casting of aspersions. To be blunt, the debate, such as it is, has unfortunately become personalized rather than sticking to the merits of the case—on which my opponents have no case to make. This section will take up some of the issues raised by critics seeking any way they can to call into question the findings both I and others have made.

Can We Trust the Data? Are the County-Level Crime Data Unusable?

Due to problems in the reporting of [county] crime data there are many gaps that need to be filled. The organization that prepared the data filled these gaps using two different estimation (i.e., imputation) procedures; moreover, the change in these procedures was not recognized by and incorporated into the MGLC analysis. Thus, there are so many problems with the county-level crime data sets used in MGLC that its analyses are called into question. We note, however, that the second edition of *More Guns, Less Crime* (Lott, 2000) includes state- and city-level analyses, which are not subject to this particular problem. . . . Not all police agencies provide 12 months of crime data to the FBI . . . And some agencies may not fill out crime reports simply because they rarely have any crime to report. [The

FBI only tries to fill in these gaps for data at the] state, regional, and national level. . . . At this point, county-level crime data cannot be used with any degree of confidence.
—Michael D. Maltz and Joseph Targonski, "A Note on the Use of County-Level UCR Data," *Journal of Quantitative Criminology*, September 2002, pp. 298–99

Maltz and Targonski have a point—there is missing information in the county level-data. But their conclusion "that county-level crime data, as they are currently constituted, should not be used, especially in policy studies" is unjustified. While people who work with data might not want to admit it, all data have errors in them. For example, per capita income in a regression doesn't perfectly measure people's income; people do not report all their income to the government, and there are often typos in the recording of various numbers. These figures are useful, but they are not a perfect measure. Nor does the measure of poverty perfectly evaluate poverty. This is true for every factor that we examine.

Thus, pointing out the mere existence of measurement errors isn't enough. Errors can work to artificially weaken or strengthen results, but normally, if they are random, they simply make it difficult to find any relationship that might exist. But Maltz and Targonski do not ask whether any errors actually affected my results, and that is the key question. The fact that similar results are obtained for city and state data should provide confidence that any problems are minimal. Maltz and Targonski do acknowledge in their article that the "state- and city-level analyses . . . are not subject to [the problem]" for counties.[120] Indeed, one reason why I used city-, county-, and state-level data in the second edition of the book was specifically to double-check that the results are not sensitive to any particular errors in the data.

Fortunately, for each county the FBI provides information on the size of this recording error. Perhaps unsurprisingly, rural counties with few people and small police departments tend to have the most problems reporting their crime numbers accurately. Research that John Whitley and I published found that studying only the counties with the fewest errors produced stronger evidence that right-to-carry laws reduce violent crime.

For example, eliminating those states where at least 20 percent of their counties have unreported crime numbers for cities with at least 30 percent of those county's populations implied that for each additional year after right-to-carry laws were introduced all the violent crime rates fell: murder by 4.8 percent, rape by 1 percent, robbery by 3.5 percent, and aggravated assault by 0.5 percent. The drops for murder, rape, and robbery are statistically significant.[121] Eliminating those states with even smaller levels of error also continued to imply similar drops in violent crime.

Even if county-level data have more errors, there are still trade-offs. For example, Maltz and Targonski acknowledge the point first made in this book, that "aggregating statistics over an entire state can mislead the true nature of a state's population characteristics."

Unfortunately, my other critics have completely ignored the strong results that I obtained from the city-level data that were shown in chapter 9.[122]

Do the Sales of the Fourth-Largest Gun Magazine Accurately Measure Gun Ownership?

My findings demonstrate that changes in gun ownership are significantly positively related to changes in the homicide rate, with this relationship driven almost entirely by an impact of gun ownership on murders in which a gun is used. The effect of gun ownership on all other crime categories is much less marked.

—Mark Duggan, "More Guns, More Crime," October 2001[123]

Other critics have sought other sources of data to test my findings. Mark Duggan's argument would be troubling were it based on gun survey data or actual gun ownership. But Duggan simply relies on sales of the fourth-largest gun magazine, *Guns and Ammo*, as a proxy for ownership— that is, he assumes that sales are connected to gun ownership—and finds that when magazine sales change, murder rates change. The magazine that he used happens to be the only one for which increased sales correspond to increased crime (see table A7.1).

Duggan claimed that he focused on this one magazine for two reasons: "*Guns & Ammo* is focused relatively more on handguns than [*American Rifleman*, *American Hunter*, and *North American Hunters*]," and "sales data for this magazine are available annually at both the state and the county levels." But other magazines better meet those criteria, such as the two largest exclusively handgun-oriented magazines, *Handguns Magazine* and *American Handgunner*. These magazines also have county and state sales figures.

There is a simple reason why *Guns and Ammo* gives such a different result from other gun magazines. It was the only one of the top seven largest gun magazines that experienced a drop in sales during the 1990s.[124] Its drop was smaller than the increase in the other six magazines. During 2001, Skip Johnson, a vice president for *Guns and Ammo's* parent company, Primedia, told me that in the 1990s anywhere from 5 to 20 percent of its national sales in a particular year were purchased by the magazine itself in order to meet its guaranteed sales to advertisers.[125] The copies were then given away for free to dentists' and doctors' offices.

But importantly, Johnson noted that these magazine self-purchases were not distributed in all states or counties, nor were they done randomly. These self-purchased copies were distributed in areas where the magazine thought that gun purchases were going to increase, and this included areas where they thought that crime rates were going up. Thus, it is not very surprising that *Guns and Ammo* is the one magazine whose sales are associated with more homicides. In statistical language this is known as a spurious relationship.

Did Crack Cocaine Confound the Results?

But an alternative explanation is that the crack cocaine problem drove up crime. . . . The regression would identify a relationship between higher crime and the failure to adopt a shall-issue law when the real cause would have been the influence of crack.

—Ian Ayres and John Donohue, *Stanford Law Review*, 2003[126]

One of Ayres and Donohue's greatest concerns is the apparent failure of previous research to account for the differential geographic impact of cocaine on crime. Lott's book (and the Lott and Mustard paper) reported that including price data for cocaine did not alter the results. Using yearly county-level pricing data (as opposed to short-run changes in prices) has the advantage of picking up cost but not demand differences between counties, thus measuring the differences in availability across counties. Research conducted by Steve Bronars and John Lott examined the crime rates for neighboring counties . . . on either side of a state border. When the counties adopting the law experienced a drop in violent crime, neighboring counties directly on the other side of the border without right-to-carry laws experienced an increase. . . . Ayres and Donohue argue that different parts of the country may have experienced differential impacts from the crack epidemic. Yet, if there are two urban counties next to each other, how can the crack cocaine hypothesis explain why one urban county faces a crime increase from drugs, when the neighboring urban county is experiencing a drop? Such isolation would be particularly surprising as criminals can easily move between these counties. . . . Even though Lott gave Ayres and Donohue the cocaine price data from 1977 to 1992, they have never reported using it.

—Florenz Plassmann and John Whitley, *Stanford Law Review*, 2003

The elephant in the room was crack cocaine. The states that did not pass the right-to-carry laws were states that had a big problem with crack-cocaine which had an enormous influence in running up crime.

—John Donohue, "Do Guns Reduce Crime?" debate on National Public Radio, November 5, 2008[127]

One persistent criticism of my work has been that it did not account for an alternative explanation, namely, that crack cocaine explains increases and variation in crime rates, especially murder. Alas, as Plassmann and Whitley note, my critics fail to discuss or even recognize the efforts that David Mustard, others, and I have made to address the drug question. In my own mind, those who have found that right-to-carry laws lower crime rates have shown that the results are not affected by the impact of crack cocaine. The critics have also not done anything themselves to try to show how crack cocaine might explain the results. It is one thing to say that they disagree with how I have dealt with the issue, but to keep asserting that the drug problem has not been accounted for is annoying.

This chapter adds new material to our argument, using new data from Steven Levitt and other academics that purports to measure crack cocaine use.[128] There are some serious questions regarding whether the data actually measure cocaine use. Given how much Levitt's coauthors emphasizes DC's crime problems, it is also surprising that their data ignore DC. (DC's crime problems will be discussed in the next section.) The data are also unexplainably limited to the period from 1980 to 2000. Nevertheless, accounting for their measure of crack cocaine use does not reduce the estimated benefits of right-to-carry laws on crime.

Sensitivity of the Results

The results of the state data regressions were incredibly contingent on an array of factors, such as the inclusion or omission of rather innocuous right-hand side controls. We found a similar fragility with regard to these county data regressions. Indeed, as we were double checking our results, we discovered that we had omitted one of Lott's original controls: Percentage of County Population That Was Not Black or White but Was Male and Aged 20–29; and we were surprised to find that adding this extremely innocuous demographic variable decreased our estimate of the dollar impact that the law's passage had on crime (that we are about to report) by more than twenty percent.
—Ayres and Donohue, *Stanford Law Review*, 2003, p. 1281

"Using a more customary set of demographic controls would have reversed Lott's results."
—John Donohue, "Can You Believe Econometric Evaluations of Law, Policy, and Medicine?" October 16, 2008

How sensitive the results are to the inclusion or exclusion of specific variables or changes in the values of certain variables is important. For were it the case that reasonable changes in the specifications reversed or eliminated the findings presented in this book and elsewhere, it would undermine the argument that more guns lead to less crime. However, the earlier editions of this book have run thousands of estimates to see if the results change with different combinations of control variables. For example, figure 9.11 on page 188 summarizes the results of 20,480 regressions, which took several months to estimate. The results for murder demonstrate that passing right-to-carry laws causes drops in that crime ranging from about 5 to 7.5 percent, a substantial 40 percent range. There should be nothing surprising or troubling about the 20 percent variation that Ayres and Donohue point to, and it is smaller than the range that I show.

The debate really shouldn't be whether right-to-carry laws reduce crime rates by 4 or 5 or 6 or 7 percent. The debate should be over whether the laws reduce or increase crime. Of course, it is better to have larger drops, but as long as crime rates decline, right-to-carry laws protect potential victims.

It makes little sense to study crime rates without trying to account for the many factors already known to affect crime. But as we showed earlier, the empirical results for murder, even those using state-level data, are not sensitive (when properly analyzed) to eliminating even factors that should obviously be included, such as demographics or law enforcement.

Perhaps not too surprisingly, I can't find any work by Ayres, Donohue, or Levitt that subjects their own work to the types of specification searches that they require my work to stand up to. In none of their papers has any of them tried to run all possible combinations of the different factors that might explain crime rates.

But others beside myself have looked at the sensitivity of my results, too. William Bartley and Mark Cohen examine well over sixteen thousand possible combinations of the control variables. Later works by Bruce Benson and Brent Mast, Carl Moody, and Eric Helland and Alex Tabarrok have attempted to test how sensitive the results are in many different ways. Like myself, they have found the results remarkably consistent. As shown earlier in figures 10.3a–10.3i, redoing the possible combinations of the control variables with the data from 1977 through 2005 proved no different.

The National Academy of Sciences Report

So far the debate has focused on technical issues, including the reliability of the data and the sensitivity of the statistical analysis. But there is also a political side. The importance of the right-to-carry debate eventually led the Clinton administration to set up a National Academy of Sciences panel to investigate the relationship between firearms and violence. When the NAS undertakes an examination of a pressing issue, its findings have an authority that is distinctive—based on perceptions of unbiased and fair evaluation of all sides of an issue leading to a consensus among leading experts. Unfortunately, the 2004 National Academy of Sciences (NAS) report on Firearms and Violence[129] has been misrepresented.

Consider the following radio debate:

> John Donohue (Yale University): The National Academy of Sciences convened a panel of talented experts who spent two years looking at John Lott's work, Gary Kleck's work. . . . They concluded the scientific evidence does not support the more guns, less crime proposition. The lone dissenter was someone who was not an econometrician, who admitted in his dissent that he wished he knew more econometrics, and who had previously testified as an expert witness on behalf of the *execrable* NRA. . . . But, again, this is exactly what the National Academy of Sciences looked at. And, they concluded the opposite, that the data did not—
>
> Gary Kleck (Florida State): They did not conclude the opposite.
>
> John Donohue: They concluded that the data does not support the proposition that we're debating today which is that guns reduce crime.
>
> Gary Kleck: No, actually what that report persistently said was, we don't have strong enough evidence to draw firm conclusions about virtually every issue they addressed, so, that was more of a no-decision decision than it was reaching the opposite conclusion, they did not reach the conclusion that making it easy to get a carry permit increases crime. They did not conclude that John Lott was wrong, and basically, you know, you learn nothing from what that particular panel said.
>
> John Donvan (ABC News): I've read the same report and I have to say, Gary, that I read it the same way, actually, it was a bit of a Pontius Pilate moment that didn't know who was right or who was wrong.[130]

Kleck and Donvan were correct that Donohue mischaracterized the 2004 NAS report on firearms and violence.[131] Contrary to Donohue's account, the report actually concluded, "The data available on these questions are too weak to support unambiguous conclusions or strong policy statements." The majority of the panel advocated that more money be available to academics to fund additional research.

James Q. Wilson, the panel's "dissenter," is possibly America's most preeminent criminologist, and he vigorously denies the claim that the NRA ever hired him as an expert witness.[132] Wilson, who had previously served on four similar panels, concluded: "I find that the evidence presented by Lott and his supporters suggests that [right-to-carry] laws do in fact help drive down the murder rate." He argued that the NAS panel simply "show[ed] that different authors have reached different conclusions." Wilson wanted a more critical inquiry, one "to analyze carefully not only the studies by John Lott but those done by both his supporters and his critics. Here, only the work by Lott and his coauthors is subject to close analysis."[133]

Are Those Who Possess a Gun More Likely to Be Shot in an Assault Than Those Not Having a Gun?

People who carry guns are far likelier to get shot—and killed—than those who are unarmed, a study of shooting victims in Philadelphia, Pennsylvania, has found.

—Ewen Callaway, "Carrying a Gun Increases Risk of Getting Shot and Killed," *New Scientist*, October 6, 2009

A study by Charles Branas and coauthors looked at people who had been shot during assaults in Philadelphia between October 15, 2003, and April 16, 2006.[134] The data for this test consists of a "case sample" (677 victims who had been shot in an assault) and a "control" group (684 "matched" individuals who were the same sex, race, and age as those assaulted). The authors conclude that "on average, guns did not protect those who possessed them from being shot in an assault" and that successful defensive gun uses are unlikely. The study, though, suffers from the exact same problems that plagued Arthur Kellermann's work, as we noted early in chapter 2. It is analogous to the hypothetical test we discussed there of whether sick people who have been to a hospital are more likely to die than healthy individuals who never felt the need to go to a hospital to begin with. Presumably that wouldn't be taken as evidence that going to a hospital increases the probability of death. If those who are most likely to be assaulted are more likely to own a gun, it also explains the Branas claim. Guns could make those who own them safer, but not as safe as those who weren't and didn't feel the need to own a gun to begin with.

The "case study" approach makes sense for testing the efficacy of drugs where you are able to randomly determine which patients receive the drug and which receive the placebo. But gun ownership isn't detemined randomly. It is the reason why economists look at changes in people's behavior that occur because of forces beyond their direct control, such as the costs of obtaining a gun. For example, if you institute a ban on handguns, some people who would have owned a gun no longer do so, and researchers can examine the impact that such a change has on crime rates.

As to the claim that successful defensive gun uses are unlikely, the study really provides no evidence on that, because "successful" defensive gun users may completely avoid having to go to police as assault victims. If criminals run away after potential victim brandish their handguns, the events would never be included among their sample of gunshot victims. What one needs to answer this question are surveys on defensive gun use that attempt to identify people who were threatened with crime (not necessarily that they were victims) and that their response protected them. Indeed, the published academic refereed research to make such direct comparisons has found that victims who resisted with guns were less likely to be injured that those who did not.[135]

Data and the Truth

Fundamentally, any academic debate boils down to two issues: how good the data are and whether the tests were done correctly. In capsule form, these issues have been succinctly stated by Steven Levitt and Stephen Dubner in their best-selling *Freakonomics*:

> Then there was the troubling allegation that Lott actually invented some of the survey data that support his more-guns/less-crime theory. Regardless of whether the data were faked, Lott's admittedly intriguing hypothesis doesn't seem to be true. When other scholars have tried to replicate [Lott's] results, they found that the right-to-carry laws simply don't bring down crime. (Pp. 133–34)

As noted above, Levitt's suggestion that my work has not been replicated is totally wrong. Survey data were not even used in my regressions and thus could not have affected the results. In any case, the fact that results have been replicated by those who have put the data together themselves indicates that data could not have been faked. Unfortunately the debate has not stayed on the merits.

Steven Levitt has been one of my most fervent critics for some time, and the above quote from his book was just one of his many attacks on my work. As a result of these allegations, I filed a defamation lawsuit against Levitt and his publishers. The evidence in the lawsuit included a series of e-mail messages exchanged between Levitt and economist John McCall, during which Levitt incorrectly stated that I had "stocked" with only my supporters a conference examining the more-guns-less-crime thesis, that I then had to "buy an issue" of the highly prestigious *Journal of Law and Economics* to publish the results of the conference, and that there was no peer review.[136]

As a result of this litigation, however, Levitt was required to release a letter retracting and clarifying the allegations he made. In what the *Chronicle of Higher Education* called "a doozy of a concession," Levitt conceded that he "knew that scholars with varying opinions had been invited to participate" in the conference because "I received an email from Dr. Lott inviting my own participation." In addition, Levitt acknowledged that I did not engage in "bribery or otherwise exercised improper influence on the editorial process" in the special issue and that "the articles that were published in the Conference Issue were reviewed by referees engaged by the editors of the JLE [*Journal of Law and Economics*]. In fact, I was one of the peer referees."[137]

Nonetheless, charges of faulty data have continued to be made. For example, in his recent book, a coauthor of Levitt's, Ian Ayres, writes that "we found that Lott had made a computer mistake in creating some of his underlying data. For example, in many of his regressions, Lott tried to control for whether the crime took place in a particular region (say, the Northeast) in a particular year (say, 1988). But when we looked at his data, many of these variables were mistakenly set to zero. When we estimated his formula on the corrected data, we again found that these laws were more likely to increase the rate of crime."

One might think from Ayres's comment that there is a mistake in my work with David Mustard or in the earlier editions of this book. However, the research that Ayres is really discussing was not a paper of mine, but a paper published by Florenz Plassmann and John Whitley in the *Stanford Law Review*. Plassmann and Whitley thank me for helping them with their study ("We thank John Lott for his support, comments and discussion"), but this is their own paper, published under their own names.

As to the data mistake, Plassmann and Whitley used the data presented in the second edition of this book, covering the years from 1977 to 1996. There was nothing wrong with those data. The data entry mistakes for their paper arose in the years that were added when they extended the data from 1997 to 2000. Out of over 7 million data entries, about 180 had accidentally been left blank. The significance of some results in one of their tables (table 10.3A) was decreased. Despite the tenor of the critics, this data error was not even crucial for their findings. Further, Plassmann and Whitley had explicitly noted the results in that particular table were biased against finding a decrease in crime, and they had argued that those results should not be given much weight.

Correcting the small data entry errors did not alter the results that Plassmann and Whitley said were the focus of their paper, and their conclusion was still the same: more concealed-handgun permits reduce crime. And Plassmann and Whitley had excellent reasons for the estimates that they thought should be used: "Including all counties with zero crime rates [with the statistical test that Ayres and Donohue use] will bias the estimated benefit of the concealed handgun law towards finding an increase in crime, because no matter how good the law is, it cannot lower the crime rate below zero." Unfortunately, Ian Ayres and John Donohue's responses to Plassmann and Whitely completely ignore these arguments on the proper test as well as the estimates they provide.

This is not the only incorrect claim that Ayres and Donohue make. They have—repeatedly—falsely asserted that I withdrew from coauthorship with Plassmann and Whitley once I saw their criticism.[138] Ayres and Donohue claimed that "we hope that this indicates that the arguments in our Reply have caused the primary proponent of the more guns, less crime hypothesis to at least partially amend his views." It is quite an amazing slur against Plassmann and Whitley to claim that they insisted on publishing research despite a coauthor's withdrawing from the paper over errors.

The inaccuracy of Ayres and Donohue's claim was such that the *Stanford Law Review* felt it necessary to run a very unusual "Clarification," where the editors said that they might not have originally made things sufficiently clear to Ayres and Donohue and noted that "the Editors feel that the impression that some have gotten from Ayres and Donohue's Reply piece is incorrect, unfortunate, and unwarranted."[139]

Being a target of inaccurate accusations has been an unfortunate and unpleasant experience. It certainly would have been preferable if the debate had stuck to the data and their analysis. The hypothesis that more guns connects to less crime has stood up against massive efforts to criticize it.

Fewer Guns, More Crime

If a resident has a handgun in the home that he can use for self defense, then he has a handgun in the home that he can use to commit suicide or engage in acts of domestic violence. If it is indeed the case, as the District believes, that the number of guns contributes to the number of gun-related crimes, accidents, and deaths, then, although there may be less restrictive, less effective substitutes for an outright ban, there is no less restrictive equivalent of an outright ban. . . . In my view, there simply is no untouchable constitutional right guaranteed by the Second Amendment to keep loaded handguns in the house in crime-ridden urban areas.

—Justice Stephen Breyer, dissenting in *District of Columbia v. Heller*, June 26, 2008[140]

The Supreme Court was sharply divided in its recent 5–4 decision striking down DC's handgun ban as unconstitutional. While in the minority, Justice Breyer's strongly worded dissent represented many people's concern about guns. To him, the Second Amendment to the Constitution did not guarantee an individual's right to own a handgun, but even if it did, he believes that such a right could be overridden by the public interest of reducing gun crimes and suicides. The possible harm from guns was central to his dissent, and the words "crime," "criminal," "criminologist," "homicide," "murder," "rape," "robbery," and "victim" were used a total of 109 times in forty-four pages. The term "suicide" was used thirteen times.

Despite the Supreme Court's decision, DC is still fighting to make it extremely difficult for people to own handguns.[141] Nor is the court's decision just one of historical curiosity. As of this writing, the gun ban litigation question has moved on to Chicago and its ban on handguns. A federal district court has upheld Chicago's ban, and an appeals court will next look at the case.[142] When the Chicago case eventually goes before the Supreme Court, it is going to be important whether gun bans are linked to crime and suicides. Studying the effects of recent bans is also useful because it represents the simplest test for the more-guns-less-crime hypothesis.

Gun bans are not imposed just on cities or nations. There are bans for everything from public housing to city parks or schools and universities. Seattle Mayor Greg Nickles announced late in 2008 that he was moving to ban guns on city property, at sporting events, and street fairs.[143] Court cases have recently been filed over gun bans in places from Western Oregon University to public housing in San Francisco.[144] Given all these pushes for gun bans, a systematic discussion across many places that have instituted them seems long overdue.

Comparing DC's Murder Rate to Other Places

So what is the evidence? DC's handgun ban policy has had ample time in the thirty years since it became effective in February 1977 to reveal any beneficial effects. Yet, looking at the data, there is absolutely no evidence that DC's gun ban reduced murder rates.[145] Indeed, there is only one single year after the ban started that the murder rate is below what it was in 1976. The bad crime figures after 1977 cannot be explained away by any general increase that has been occurring in other large cities, the neighboring states of Virginia and Maryland, or the United States generally.

In 1976, DC's murder rate was fifteenth among America's fifty most populous cities. In only one of the years after the ban (1985) did DC rank as low as fifteenth. In fifteen out of the next twenty-nine years after the ban, DC's murder rate had risen to first or second place; in another four years it was fourth. DC's murder rate rose relative to the average city murder rate.

Of course, there are many reasons for crime rates to change. For example, DC's police department underwent many changes, and some were likely detrimental, such as instituting new rules for hiring and promotion.[146] Changes in income and poverty can also matter. It is simple enough to see how DC's crime rates change over time relative to the rest of the country in our regression analysis, with all the factors that we have already talked about accounted for. This is particularly important given the demographic and income changes that were occurring in DC. Running a regression accounting for all these other factors, including demographics, reveals that each additional year that the DC ban was in effect saw DC's relative murder rate rise by 6 percent, and the effect is statistically significant at better than the 1 percent level.

Three simple graphic comparisons show how DC's murder rate rose: DC's murder rate relative to other large cities, as just mentioned, DC's murder rate relative to neighboring Maryland and Virginia, and DC's murder rate relative to the rest of the United States.

Justice Breyer's dissent put a great deal of emphasis on a study published seventeen years earlier in the *New England Journal of Medicine*. This study by Colin Loftin, David McDowall, Brian Wiersema, and Talbert Cottey compared the mean homicide rates before and after the ban.[147] They looked at the period from 1968 through 1987 and claimed that the handgun ban lowered homicide and suicide rates. But there are real questions about how they did their analysis, and we are now fortunate enough to have more and better evidence of what happened after the ban.

Our primary focus will be on murders, not homicides, since homicides include justifiable killings by police and civilians. A drop in civilian justifiable homicides after the handgun ban should actually be viewed as a bad sign because fewer crimes would have been prevented.

THE FIFTY LARGEST CITIES. Figure 10.7 shows how DC's murder rate changed over time relative to the other forty-eight largest cities without a ban on handguns. (Chicago was thus excluded because it was the only other major city among the fifty most populous cities that also banned handguns starting in 1983, and we want to compare cities with a ban to cities without a ban.) City-level data from the FBI are only readily available from 1974 on, so that is the period we start with. During the three years from 1974 to 1976, DC's murder rate averaged 28.5 percent more than the other cities. In 1976, the last year before the ban, its murder rate was not nearly as high, 16 percent greater than the average murder rate for the other large cities. The vertical line in the diagram shows the point at which the ban went into effect, at the beginning of 1977. After the ban, DC's murder rate between 1977 and 1987 averaged 55 percent greater than the average for these other cities, immediately rising to 50 percent above the average and only getting as low as 29.4 percent greater once, in 1985—there is not one single year after the ban when the ratio of DC's murder rate to the average for other cities fell below the preban ratio. Even if we limit ourselves to the period studied by Loftin and his coauthors, it is clear that murder rates rose after the ban.

Extending the data out past 1987 shows how DC's murder rate explodes above the rate in the rest of the cities (figure 10.8). After the ban from 1977 to 2005, the murder rate in DC was on average 91 percent greater than in the other cities. But two criminology professors, James Alan Fox and David McDowall, state:[148]

> [Others have] argued that the rise in violent crimes in the District from 1980 to 1997 establishes that the DC Gun Control Law was ineffective. However, the entire nation experienced an increase in violent crimes during this period because of the emergence of the crack cocaine market and related gang activity.

This is hardly a unique perspective. John Donohue recently claimed:[149]

> John [Lott] mentions what happened in the District of Columbia and it is true that DC did have quite a problem with crime in the late 1980s as did almost all urban areas in the United States because of the crack cocaine problem. Nobody thinks that the crack cocaine problem was a problem caused by a lack of guns, and simply as John does so much in his work where he is a—looking at data in a way that can support a very tendentious conclusion.

Yet DC's murder rate increased relative to other cities even before crack cocaine became an issue in the last half of the 1980s. In addition, crack cocaine affected cities nationwide, and, after 1987, DC's murder rate still increased dramatically relative to the murder rate in other cities. While the crack cocaine epidemic clearly increased DC's murder rate, it is hard to see how cocaine can explain DC's increase in murder rates relative to all other cities either any time from 1977 to 1987 or afterward. DC has continued to

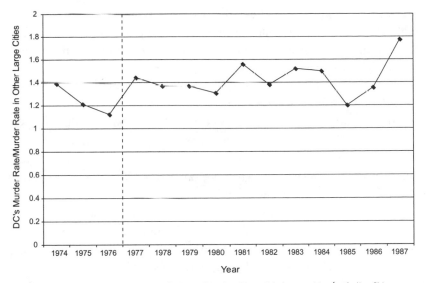

Figure 10.7. Changes in DC's murder rate relative to the other forty-eight largest cities (excluding Chicago from top fifty list, weighted by population)

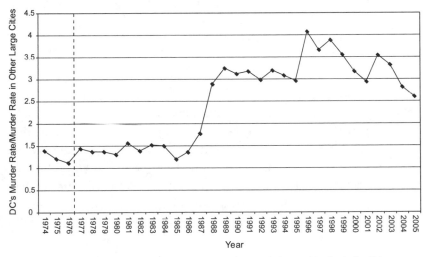

Figure 10.8. Changes in DC's murder rate relative to the other forty-eight largest cities (excluding Chicago from top fifty list, weighted by population)

get worse and worse relative to other cities even since the crack epidemic abated in the early 1990s. DC's murder rate fell much more slowly than other cities. As late as 2007, it was still almost two times that of the average of other large cities.

But to be careful to avoid other possible explanations for DC's rise in murder rates, including crack cocaine, we can re-examine the murder rate regressions and limit the period studied to 1977 to 1987. Would doing so alter our results of the handgun ban's detrimental effects? No, actually the results become even more dramatic—implying that each additional year that the ban was in effect DC's murder rate rose relative to the rest of the United States by 29.9 percent.

If crack was the cause of DC's higher murder rate after 1987, it was a problem that seems to have affected DC dramatically more than other large cities. DC's murder rate not only rose relative to other cities in the late 1980s, but also stayed much higher. How can the crack cocaine problem, which was a national problem affecting many cities, explain DC rising from having the fifteenth highest murder rate in 1976 to place number 1 almost continually from 1988 to 1999 (the exception was only three years from 1993 to 1995, when placed second)? Even if we only concentrated on this later period, their argument would have us believe that crack cocaine dramatically changed DC in a way that it changed no other city.

COMPARISON TO MARYLAND AND VIRGINIA. Perhaps there were regional effects of some nature that influenced crime generally around the DC or mid-Atlantic area. In such a case, the worsening ranking for DC might not be due to gun control, but to the general regional decline. To examine this, we can compare DC and the two states that surround it, Maryland and Virginia. Figure 10.9 examines the period from 1968 through 1987. In the last year before the 1977 ban, DC's murder rate was 197 percent greater than the average murder rate in Maryland and Virginia. Indeed, there was not one single year after the ban was in place when DC's murder rate relative to Maryland and Virginia was as low as it was in 1976.[150] The average murder rate in DC from 1977 to 1987, the period when the ban was in effect, was 257 percent greater than the average for these two states.[151]

Including data past 1987 shows a dramatic additional increase in DC's murder rate relative to Maryland and Virginia (figure 10.10). DC's murder rate averaged 450 percent more than Maryland and Virginia's from 1977 to 2006 (figure 10.10), over twice the ratio of DC to Maryland and Virginia from 1968 to 1976.

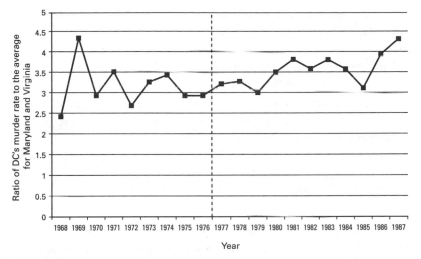

Figure 10.9. Ratio of DC's murder rate to the average for Maryland and Virginia from 1968 to 1987

Figure 10.10. Ratio of DC's murder rate to the average for Maryland and Virginia from 1968 to 2006

Again, comparing DC to Maryland and Virginia provides no evidence that the ban reduced DC's murder rate. If anything, DC's murder rate increased after the ban.

COMPARING DC'S MURDER RATE TO THAT FOR THE UNITED STATES. Examining DC's murder rate relative to the United States' from 1968 to 1987 shows that

DC's murder rate was declining before the ban and rising afterward (figure 10.11). The ban seems to be associated with this adverse change in DC's murder rate relative to the rest of the country. By 1976, DC's murder had fallen to being 3.08 times greater than the United States'. There are only two years after that (1979 and 1985) when the ratio of DC's to the United States' murder rate fell below what it was in 1976. Expanding the data to include the period after 1987 (figure 10.12) continues to show the increase in DC's murder rate relative to the United States' that we observed in figures 10.8 and 10.10. Whether one is looking at the period from 1968 to 1987 or including the later period, there is no evidence that the DC gun ban reduced DC's murder rates.

Comparing Murder Rates to the Number of Murders

The *New England Journal of Medicine* study that Justice Breyer cites didn't look at crime rates; it looked at the number of crimes. That is an important distinction. Imagine a city where the number of murders falls by 10 percent but its population declines by 50 percent. Does that demonstrate that crime conditions are improving? Of course not. The crime rate is usually a much better measure of safety than the number of murders.

Yet, not everyone agrees. John Donohue defended the *New England Journal of Medicine* study's approach:[152]

> If you look at the numbers that John [Lott] had put up, which was interesting, if he had actually showed you the number of murders in DC, they had actually dropped. He showed you the rate. And what was interesting about that was, DC was de-populating tremendously in the seventies, and it was largely the flight of the affluent. So, the group that had the lowest likelihood of engaging in crime. So, crime was going to be, if you used the rates that John showed, it was going to be trending up, because the people remaining in the city had a much, much higher risk of crime. And so, when you make those adjustments, the conclusions are opposite to what John suggested.

There are two responses. One is purely factual. The number of murders didn't "drop" after the handgun ban. You don't get the "opposite" of what I argued. During the first six years after the gun ban went into effect, despite a large drop in population, there was only one year when the absolute number of murders fell below what it was in 1976 (and even then it was drop of only eight murders, a drop of 4 percent). Indeed between 1977 and

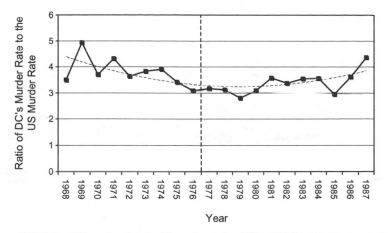

Figure 10.11. Ratio of DC's murder rate to the U.S. murder rate from 1968 to 1987. The dotted line is a simple polynomial curve fitted to these data.

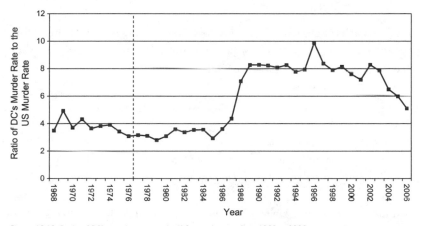

Figure 10.12. Ratio of DC's murder rate to the U.S. murder rate from 1968 to 2006

2005, despite a 20 percent drop in population, there were only four years when the total number of murders was lower than it was in 1976.

The second point concerns demographics. Does the composition of the population matter? Sure it does. And the first and second editions of this book have actually spent a lot of time—more than any previous study—evaluating demographic changes when studying crime. We know that young males commit more crime than other groups. There is more crime in heavily African-American areas. But those concerns are the reason why you look at regressions that account for these changes. As we have already

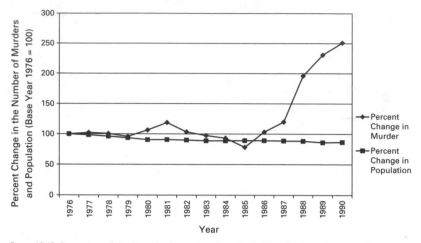

Figure 10.13. Comparison of the change in the number of murders in DC to the change in the number of people living in the city prior to the crack cocaine problem

reported above, DC's murder rates rose relative to the rest of the country even after all the factors—from law enforcement to income and poverty to demographics—have been accounted for.

It Is Not Just DC

The statistics do show a soaring District crime rate. And the District's crime rate went up after the District adopted its handgun ban. But, as students of elementary logic know, after it does not mean because of it. What would the District's crime rate have looked like without the ban? Higher? Lower? The same? Experts differ; and we, as judges, cannot say.

—Justice Stephen Breyer, dissenting in *District of Columbia v. Heller*, June 26, 2008[153]

Justice Breyer is exactly right. DC's crime rates rose after the ban doesn't necessarily mean that the ban caused the increase. Even if the increase wasn't caused by crack cocaine, there could be some other left-out factor that just happened to change at the same time. This is true even though we have run regressions that have attempted to take these different factors into account. One big difference between the earlier work on right-to-carry laws and the current discussion on gun bans is that with thirty-nine states passing right-to-carry laws we have had the same experiment over and over again in many different years in many different places. While it is possible that some left-out factor explains the results in one state or even a few states, the odds that that left-out factor occurred again and again become progressively remote. Of course, there is lots of other evidence for right-to-carry laws: the predicted different effects across different types of crime (multiple-victim shootings should decline more than simple murder), that the size of the drop increases with the percentage of the population with concealed-handgun permits, the comparison of adjacent counties, and so on.

Yet the phenomenon of bans resulting in more crime isn't unique to DC. Every place around the world that has banned guns appears to have experienced an increase in murder and violent crime rates.

Surely DC has had many problems that contribute to crime, but even cities with far better police departments have seen murder and violent crime soar in the wake of handgun bans. Chicago has banned virtually all new handguns since the beginning of 1983 and it now also faces a Supreme Court case challenging its ban.[154] But that handgun ban didn't work at all when it came to reducing violence. Chicago's murder rate fell from 39 to 22 per 100,000 in the eight years before the law and then rose slightly to 23.[155] During the seventeen years from 1983 through 1999, there has been only one year when Chicago's murder rate fell below what it was in 1982, the last year before the ban. Over that same time, the U.S. murder rate fell by 31 percent, from 8.3 to 5.7, and the murder rate for the other nine largest cities dropped by 34 percent, from 17.8 to 11.7 (figure 10.14). Chicago's murder rate doesn't fall below its 1982 murder rate until 2002. It is hard to attribute this eventual drop to the ban, which went into effect twenty years earlier.

Just as it was possible to compare DC's murder rate to other cities, neighboring jurisdictions, and the United States as a whole, one can make the same comparisons for Chicago. Compare Chicago's murder rate to those in other cities among the ten largest or the fifty largest (DC is excluded from this comparison). In both cases, Chicago's murder rate falls relative to the murder rate in other cities up until 1982, when it falls to its lowest value relative to other cities and then rises after that (figure 10.15).

There is a similar relationship when one compares Chicago's murder either to its neighboring counties or to the United States as a whole (figures 10.16, 10.17).[156] If anything, Chicago's murder rate exploded even faster relative to the murder rates in adjacent counties than relative to any of the other comparisons. It is very difficult to see how there is any comparison that can be made that shows that Chicago's murder rate fell after the ban started at the beginning of 1983.

In addition, the experience in other countries is the same, even for island nations that have banned handguns and where borders are easy to moni-

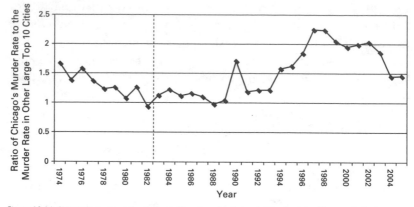

Figure 10.14. Chicago's murder rate relative to the other nine largest cities (weighted by population)

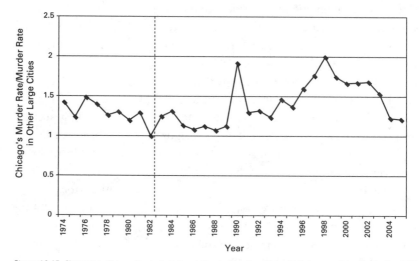

Figure 10.15. Changes in Chicago's murder rate relative to the other forty-eight largest cities (excluding DC from the top fifty list, weighted by population)

tor. These are places that just can't blame the United States or neighboring states for the failure of their gun-control laws. Not only did violent crime and murder not decline as promised; they actually increased.

Great Britain banned handguns in January 1997. But the number of deaths and injuries from gun crime in England and Wales increased an incredible 340 percent in the seven years from 1998 to 2005.[157] The rates of serious violent crime, armed robberies, rapes, and homicide have soared.[158]

The Republic of Ireland and Jamaica also experienced large increases in murder rates after enacting handgun bans in 1972 and 1974, respectively

Figure 10.16. Comparison of Chicago's murder rate to the murder rate in adjacent counties (weighted by population)

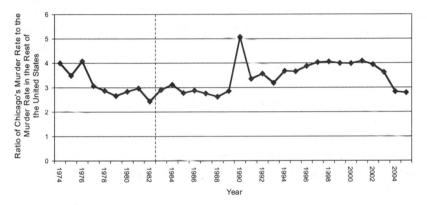

Figure 10.17. Chicago's murder rate relative to the U.S. murder rate

(figures 10.18, 10.19).[159] Since the gun ban, Jamaica's murder rate has soared to become one of the highest in the world, currently at least double that in other Caribbean countries.[160] Jamaica's murder rate hasn't been below 10 murders per 100,000 people since before the gun ban went into effect.[161]

Enforcement efforts have been largely futile. For instance, the weapons the Canadian border guards seize at the U.S. border are overwhelmingly from unwitting U.S. tourists.[162] Few criminals smuggling guns are caught. Jamaica clearly shows that just as drug gangs can bring drugs into a country, they can bring in the guns necessary to protect that valuable property.

The irony is that as drug enforcement increases, the inelastic demand for illegal drugs means that the value gangs attach to protecting their drug turf rises. The same is true in other countries. With recent estimates that up to 80 percent of U.S. crime is gang related—and that, primarily drug gang related—it is likely to be as difficult to remove guns as drugs from these gangs.[163]

Suicides and Guns

One would think that a ban on guns would surely cause a drop in gun suicides. But a graph of the percentage of suicides committed with guns shows no obvious consistent change in the share of suicides committed with guns (figure 10.20).[164] Gun suicides started falling in DC in the early 1970s, a couple of years before the gun ban, but so did nongun suicides (figure 10.21). It is difficult to see any benefit as the drop was virtually identical for both gun and nongun suicides.

What makes these graphs particularly surprising is that a gun ban should, everything else equal, actually cause nongun suicides to rise simply because at least some (if not all) of those who would use guns to commit suicide would use some other way of doing so. After all, the ultimate public policy goal would seem to be to reduce overall suicides and not just one method of committing suicide.

Yet even more perverse results have been obtained. David Cutler, Edward Glaeser, and Karen Norberg have conducted by far the largest study on what factors are related to suicides by juveniles.[165] They find some evidence of a relationship between higher gun ownership and suicide, but that relationship not only disappears but is in fact reversed when they include a variable for the rate at which people go hunting. The higher suicide rate is in fact related to the higher rates at which people in certain counties go hunting, not whether people own a gun. They are unable to discern whether the effect is due to something that arises in areas with a lot of hunters or some other factor, but the evidence clearly indicates that suicide rates are actually lower when gun ownership rates are higher.

Conclusion

Everyone wants to take guns away from criminals. However, the problem with bans is who is most likely to obey them. If the ban primarily disarms law-abiding citizens and not criminals, the ban can have the opposite effect of what was intended.

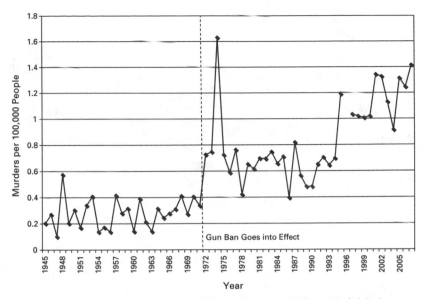

Figure 10.18. Ireland's murder rate. While murder rates in the United States and Jamaica include both murders and manslaughter, Ireland's numbers include only murder. Including manslaughter would probably roughly double the measured murder rate for Ireland for most years. (Murder rate data are not available for 1996.)

Figure 10.19. Jamaica's murder rate. (Murder rate data are not available for 1968 and 1969.)

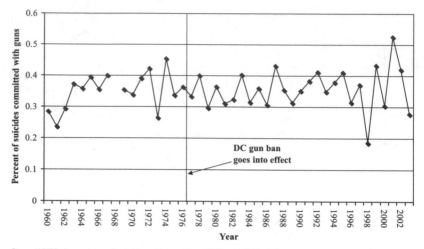

Figure 10.20. Percentage of suicides with guns from 1960 to 2004 for DC

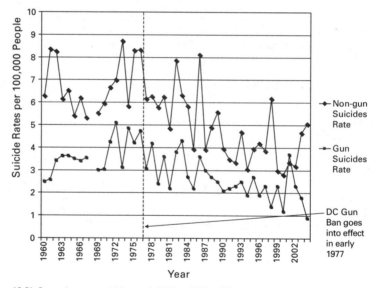

Figure 10.21. Gun and nongun suicide rates in DC from 1960 to 2004

Whether one examines murder rates in DC or Chicago or other countries around the world, there is no evidence that a gun ban reduces murder. Indeed, if anything, the evidence points to the opposite conclusion. DC's rising murder rate cannot be explained as a result of the crack cocaine epidemic during the late 1980s, because this increase started right after the ban was instituted, long before crack cocaine became an issue. Nor can crack cocaine explain why DC's or Chicago's murder rates rose relative to other large cities.

For those interested in evaluating these crime numbers themselves, many of the data can be easily accessed here:

http://www.disastercenter.com/crime/dccrime.htm
http://www.disastercenter.com/crime/mdcrime.htm
http://www.disastercenter.com/crime/vacrime.htm
http://www.disastercenter.com/crime/uscrime.htm
http://johnrlott.tripod.com/Data_for_Graphs.xls

Gun-Free Zones and Permitted Concealed Handguns

In Mumbai, India, on November 26, 2008, cowering armed policemen failed to fire back at terrorists who were attacking the city. A photographer at the scene described his frustration: "There were armed policemen hiding all around the station but none of them did anything. At one point, I ran up to them and told them to use their weapons. I said, 'Shoot them, they're sitting ducks!' but they just didn't shoot back."[166] Unfortunately, only those police who were directly being threatened by the terrorists chose to fire back. At the hotels targeted by the terrorists, security was equally ineffective; while the hotels "had metal detectors . . . none of its security personnel carried weapons because of the difficulties in obtaining gun permits from the Indian government."[167] India has extremely strict gun-control laws, and citizens are effectively banned from being able to carry guns.[168]

Thus, we see that what holds true in America holds true in other countries as well: that law-abiding citizens, not terrorists and criminals, obey gun-control laws.

Israel provides another quite different example. Up until the early 1970s, the Jewish state had to deal with the cold reality of terrorists who would take machine guns into shopping malls, schools, and synagogues and open fire. That type of attack doesn't occur anymore. Why? Israelis realized that armed citizens could stop such attackers before the attackers could shoot many people. Previously, even large numbers of armed soldiers and police had failed to stop the attacks for a simple reason: terrorists have the option of deciding when to attack and whom to attack first. They would either wait for the police and soldiers to leave the area or shoot them first.

Currently, about 10 percent of Jewish Israeli adults are licensed to carry weapons, so determined terrorists have to resort to less effective, secretive routes of attack, such as bombings.[169] Prior to letting citizens carry concealed handguns, terrorist attacks in Israel were committed almost entirely with machine guns. Afterward, bombs were almost always used. The reason for the change was simple. Armed citizens can quickly immobilize a gun-wielding attacker, but no one can respond to a bomber once the bomb explodes. Nevertheless, armed citizens do still stop some bombings before the bombs go off.[170] During waves of terror attacks, Israel's national police chief will call on all permitted citizens to carry their firearms at all times.

Multiple-victim public shooters, like terrorists generally, are kamikaze-like killers who seek to maximize carnage. Even if the killers expect to die anyway (and the vast majority of multiple-victim public shooters do), letting potential victims carry guns can help deter these crimes in the first place simply by reducing the level of carnage the killers believe they can inflict.

Americans have learned this lesson the hard way. Consider the disturbed lone shooter who committed the Northern Illinois University attack in February 2008. One thing was clear: Six minutes proved too long.[171] That's how long it took before police officers were able to enter the classroom. In those short six minutes, five people were murdered, and sixteen wounded. And six minutes is actually record-breaking speed for the police arriving at such an attack. At the Virginia Tech massacre the previous year, hours went by between the first attack and the killer's eventual suicide.[172]

Shortly after the Northern Illinois University attack, five people were killed in the city council chambers in Kirkwood, Missouri. This was despite a police officer being present.[173] In Kirkwood, as often happens in these kinds of attacks, the police officer was the one killed first when the attack started.[174] People cowered or were reduced to futilely throwing chairs at the killer.

Over the last three years there have been shootings at the Westroads Mall in Omaha,[175] the Trolley Square Mall in Salt Lake City,[176] and the Tinley Park Mall in Illinois.[177] These tragedies have one thing in common: they took place in "gun-free zones" where private citizens are not allowed to carry guns.

The malls in Omaha and Salt Lake City were in states that, in principle, let people carry concealed handguns. However, these states let private property owners ban guns provided they post clear signs. These malls were among the very few places in their states that posted such bans.[178] Likewise, the slaughter at Virginia Tech and the other public schools occurred in some of the few areas within their states where people were not allowed to carry concealed handguns. Notably, in the Trolley Square attack, an off-duty police officer fortunately carried a handgun— in violation of the ban- -and shot the attacker before other officers arrived.

Just as we found in chapter 9, extending the results up through 1999 showed that when states passed right-to-carry laws, the rate of multiple-victim public shootings fell by 60 percent. Deaths and injuries from multiple-victim public shootings fell even further, on average by 78 percent, as the remaining incidents tended to involve fewer victims per attack.[179]

That killers often choose gun-free zones for their attacks is not a new phenomenon. Thirteen were killed in the Columbine High School shooting in 1999; twenty-three were shot dead at Luby's Cafeteria in Killeen, Texas, in 1991; and twenty-one were slain at a McDonald's in Southern California in 1984.[180]

Similar horrible incidents occur in other gun-free zones around the world. The Mumbai massacre left 165 victims dead.[181] Since 2001, many European countries—including Finland, France, Germany, and Switzerland—have each suffered at least two major multiple-victim shootings. The worst school shooting in Germany resulted in seventeen killed (four more than were killed at the Columbine High School attack); in Switzerland, one attacker fatally shot fourteen legislators in a regional parliament building; in Finland in 2008, an attack took the lives of ten victims.[182] During a period of just a couple of weeks in April 2009, there were multiple-victim public shootings at a college in Athens, a crowded café in Rotterdam, and a supermarket in Moscow.[183]

Overall, the problem with gun-control laws is not too little regulation, but rather that the regulations disarm law-abiding citizens. Consider a criminal who is intent on massacring people and then planning on taking his own life. He would unlikely be deterred by any penalties for violating gun regulations. For example, expelling students or firing professors for violating campus gun-free zones represent a real life-changing experience for law-abiding citizens—especially since other academic institutions will not admit or hire people who have such gun offenses on their records. But even assuming the killer survives the attack, it is absurd to imagine that after facing multiple life prison sentences or death penalties for killing people, the threat of expulsion from school will be the penalty that ultimately deters the attack.

But citizens and police who pack heat do help, because they can stop a shooting while it is happening. Nevertheless, opposition to guns on campuses is so extreme that some universities even oppose having armed police officers on campus. In the wake of the Virginia Tech shooting, campus police at Brandeis University asked that they be armed to prevent similar tragedies. But the president of the Brandeis Student Union retorted that "the sense of community and the sense of safety would be disturbed very much by having guns on campus."[184] Similarly, Columbus (Ohio) State Community College president Val Moeller worried that "when someone comes on campus and sees armed public safety officers, it indicates that the campus is not safe."[185] Similar objections have been voiced on other campuses.[186]

On or off campus, police with guns are certainly helpful in catching criminals, but there are limits to what we should expect them to accomplish. For example, during the attack at Virginia Tech, each officer on duty had to patrol, on average, well over 250 acres.[187]

Passing right-to-carry laws is only one way to utilize guns to help fight terrorism and other violent crime. President Bush's revival of the Federal Air Marshal Program on airplanes is another. This program for domestic flights started in 1970, but ended in the early 1990s.[188] Evidence indicates that it worked well. There were thirty-eight hijackings in America in 1969, but in 1970—as the marshals were employed—the number of hijackings fell into the twenties for each of the next three years, before finally declining to low single digits. Empirical research by Bill Landes suggests that the marshal program substantially contributed to this drop.[189]

While right-to-carry laws—now operating in thirty-nine states—do reduce violent crime generally, the effect is much larger for multiple-victim shootings. Normally about 2–7 percent of adults in any state have permits, and for most crimes, that means some deterrence. But for a shooting in a public place, where there might be dozens or even hundreds of people present, it will almost ensure that at least someone—someone who is unknown to the attacker—will be able to stop the attacker.

Even when an attack begins, civilians with concealed handguns help limit the carnage. A major factor in how many people are killed or injured is how much time elapses between when the attack starts and when someone—be it citizen or police—arrives on the scene with a gun.[190]

Take the Colorado Springs church shooting in December 2007. A parishioner who had the minister's permission to carry her concealed gun into the church quickly stopped the slaughter before the killer was able to enter the area where thousands of members of the congregation sat.[191] Or take an attack earlier that year on a busy street in downtown Memphis.[192] Or attacks at the Appalachian Law School or high schools in such places as Pearl, Mississippi.[193] In all these incidents, concealed-handgun permit holders stopped what would have clearly escalated into multiple-victim public shootings well before uniformed police could arrive. During 2008, at Israeli schools, armed teachers stopped one terrorist attack and an armed student stopped yet another.[194]

There has been much fear about concealed-handgun permit holders accidentally shooting an innocent bystander when they stop these attacks. This is a legitimate concern. Yet the evidence clearly demonstrates that in practice this is not a problem. Out of all the multiple-victim public shootings that have been stopped by permit holders, no one has indentified a single such incident.[195]

We also have a lot of experience with permitted concealed handguns in schools. Prior to the 1995 Safe School Zone Act, states with right-to-carry laws let teachers and others carry concealed handguns at school. I have not found a single instance when a permitted concealed handgun was improperly used at a school. And neither the National Education Association nor the American Federation of Teachers has been able to point to a problem.

Though in a minority, a number of universities—large public schools such as Colorado State and the University of Utah—let permit holders (both faculty and students) carry concealed handguns on school property.[196] Some other schools, from Dartmouth College to Boise State University, let professors carry concealed handguns.[197] Most of the prohibitions on firearms on college campuses appear to have gone into effect during the early 1990s.[198] Again, no problems have been reported.

Gun-free zones are a magnet for deadly attacks. This applies not only to terrorist attacks, but to crimes generally. Here is one question to think about: If a killer were stalking your family, would you feel safer putting a sign out front announcing, "This home is a gun-free zone"? Probably not, but that is effectively what many places do.

Other Gun-Control Laws

Except for one single study that looks at the Brady Act, researchers following my work have focused exclusively on the impact of concealed handguns. Unfortunately, the work that I did that simultaneously accounted for many gun-control laws—such as state waiting periods and background checks, one-gun-a-month rules, and penalties for using guns in the commission of a crime—has so far been ignored.

But different gun policies all fit together, and it is hardly obvious that one can properly test the impact of right-to-carry laws without attempting to account for these other laws. Since different gun-control laws sometimes get passed at the same time as right-to-carry laws, inclusion of these other laws is the only way to separate out which law is causing the change in crime rates. The singular focus on right-to-carry laws in so many of these studies suggests that these authors don't believe that these other gun-control laws matter. I have made available the data that David Mustard and I put together as well as the later data in this book on the subject so others could without much effort examine the impact of these other laws.

The other major gun-control laws that we will turn our attention to are gun show regulations, bans on so-called Saturday night specials (inexpensive guns), the assault weapons ban, and the Castle Doctrine. In each section below, I will report the results that were obtained from accounting for these laws in the regressions used to produce figures 10.1a–10.1i. Those figures factored in the impact of all these other gun control laws on the crime rate.

Assault Weapons Ban

Despite many studies of bans on so-called assault weapons, economists and criminologists have yet to find any benefit from either state or federal bans. Analyzing the impact of the 1994 federal ban during its first seven years, Christopher Koper, Daniel Woods, and Jeffrey Roth wrote:

> We cannot clearly credit the ban with any of the nation's recent drop in gun violence. And, indeed, there has been no discernible reduction in the lethality and injuriousness of gun violence, based on indicators like the percentage of gun crimes resulting in death or the share of gunfire incidents resulting in injury, as we might have expected had the ban reduced crimes with both [assault weapons] and [large capacity clips].[199]

Banning some semiautomatic guns when there exist other semiautomatic guns that fire the same bullets at the same rapidity and do the same damage cannot be expected to have much of an impact.

During the 2004 presidential campaign, Senator John Kerry would remark: "I never contemplated hunting deer or anything else with an AK-47."[200] Governor Howard Dean explained his support for extending the assault weapons ban the same way: "Deer hunters don't need to have assault weapons."[201] The assault weapons ban unfortunately conjures up images of machine guns used by the military. Such weapons are surely not very useful in hunting deer. Yet the 1994 federal assault weapons ban had nothing to do with machine guns, only semiautomatics, which fire one bullet per pull of the trigger. The AK-47s banned by the assaults weapons ban were civilian, semiautomatic versions of the gun. The firing mechanisms in semiautomatics and machine guns are completely different. The entire firing mechanism of a semi-automatic gun has to be gutted and replaced to turn it into a military AK-47.

Does the assault weapons ban have any impact on crime after all? I used two different ways to estimate the impact of both the state and federal assault weapons bans on crime rates (tables 10.9, 10.10). One measures the simple before-and-after average crime rate and the other measures the before-and-after crime rate trends. The simple averages were used in the results shown in figures 10.1a–10.1i. Only using trends shows a significant impact of the law on crime rates, and the longer the ban has been in effect, the greater the increase in murder and robbery. The effects are actually quite large, indicating that each additional year the ban remains in effect raises both murder and robbery rates by around 3 percent. Rape also rises, but only slightly.

Presumably if assault weapons are to be used in committing any particular crime, they will be used for murder and robbery, but the data appear more supportive of an adverse effect of assault weapons bans on murder and robbery rates.

Gun Show Regulations

Despite the impression created by the term gun show "loophole," there are no different rules for buying a gun at a gun show than anywhere else.[202] Gun-control groups, such as Third Way (formerly Americans for Gun Safety) identify eighteen states that have closed the loophole, but interestingly, prior to 2000, only three of these states had laws that even mentioned gun shows.

So how can a state close a gun show loophole if the laws didn't even mention the term "gun show"? The issue is really private handgun transfers. What usually constitutes "closing the loophole" is mandating background checks for private transfers of handguns. Since 1994, federal law has required background checks for all handguns purchased through dealers. The checks were extended to long guns in 1998. But regulating transfers

Table 10.9 Enactment dates of state assault weapons bans

State	Date law went into effect	Penalty for violation
California	Jan. 1, 1990	Felony: 4–8 years in prison
California	Mar. 4, 1998—state appellate court ruled that the 1990 ban was unconstitutional	
California	Jan. 1, 2000—a new assault weapons bill went into effect	Felony: 4–8 years in prison
Hawaii	July 1, 1992	Class C felony: 5 years in prison
Maryland	June 1, 1994	Fine of $1,000–10,000 and/or 1–10 years imprisonment
Massachusetts	Oct. 21, 1998	Felony: not more that 3 years or $5,000 or both
New Jersey	May 30, 1990	Crime of the 3rd degree, knowingly violating regulatory provisions is a crime of the 4th degree
New York	Nov. 1, 2000	Class D violent felony: criminal possession of a weapon in the 3rd degree
Federal assault weapon ban	Sept. 13, 1994, through Sept. 13, 2004	

Table 10.10 Two simple ways of looking at the impact of the assault weapons bans

	Murder	Rape	Robbery	Aggravated assault
Change in the average crime rate when the ban goes into effect	0.4%	−3.0%	3.0%	−2.1%
Change in the crime rate calculated from the difference in the annual change in crime rates in the years before and after adoption of an assault weapon ban	3.2%*	1%**	2.7%*	0.1%

Note: The specifications reported earlier for figures 10.1a–10.1i use the simple dummy variable approach reported here, but using the before-and-after trends does not alter the earlier results.
* Statistically significant at least at the 1 percent level for an F-test.
** Statistically significant at least at the 5 percent level for an F-test.

by private individuals—such as those occurring at gun shows—has been left to the states (see table 10.11).

The theory linking "gun show loopholes" and crime is fairly straightforward. To the extent that background checks on private transfers prevent criminals from getting guns, crime rates will be reduced. But its impact depends upon two factors: how many criminals actually get guns from gun shows and the ability of criminals to get guns from substitute sources. There is also a trade-off: Increased regulations on private transfers can reduce the number of gun shows and make it more difficult for law-abiding citizens to get guns—guns that could have been used to protect against crime.

To help determine where criminals obtained their firearms, the Bureau

Table 10.11 Enactment dates of state laws requiring background checks on the private transfer of handguns

State	Date enacted	Type of penalty for not conducting check	Type of penalty for providing false information
California	Jan. 1, 1991	Misdemeanor	Misdemeanor
Colorado	Mar. 31, 2001	Class 1 misdemeanor	Class 1 misdemeanor
Connecticut	Oct. 1, 1994	Class D felony	Fine of not more than $500 and/or imprisonment for not more than 3 years
Hawaii	Before 1977	Misdemeanor	Class C felony
Illinois	Before 1977	Class A misdemeanor	Perjury
Indiana	Until Nov. 11, 1998	Class B misdemeanor	Class C felony
Iowa	July 1, 1991	Simple misdemeanor	Class D felony
Maryland	Oct. 1, 1996	Misdemeanor	Misdemeanor
Massachusetts	Before 1977	Felony	Fine of $500–$1,000 and/or 6 months to 2 years imprisonment
Michigan	Before 1977	Felony	Felony
Missouri	Sept. 28, 1981	Class A misdemeanor	Class A misdemeanor
Nebraska	Sept. 6, 1991	Class 1 misdemeanor	Class 4 felony
New Jersey	Before 1977	Crime of the 4th degree	Crime of the 3rd degree
New York	Before 1977	Class A misdemeanor	Class A misdemeanor
North Carolina	Dec. 1, 1995	Class 2 misdemeanor	Class H felony
Oregon	Dec. 7, 2000	Class A misdemeanor	Class A misdemeanor
Pennsylvania	Oct. 11, 1995	Misdemeanor of the 2nd degree	Felony of the 3rd degree
Rhode Island	Before 1977	Fine of not more than $1,000 and/or imprisonment of up to 5 years	Imprisonment of up to 5 years
Tennessee	Until Nov. 11, 1998	Class A misdemeanor	Class A misdemeanor

of Justice Statistics conducted a survey of eighteen thousand state prison inmates in 1997, the largest survey of inmates ever conducted.[203] Fewer than 1 percent of inmates (0.7 percent) who possessed a gun indicated that they obtained it at a gun show. When combined with guns obtained from flea markets, the total rises to 1.7 percent. These numbers are dwarfed by the 40 percent who obtained their guns from friends or family and the 39 percent who obtained them on the street or from illegal sources. These numbers are also very similar to a 1991 survey, a survey that indicated that only 0.6 percent of inmates had obtained their guns from guns shows and 1.3 percent from flea markets. Other surveys of criminals report a similar range of estimates.[204] A detailed discussion of the research on gun show regulations as well as the costs that background checks impose on gun sales is provided in chapter 8 of my book *The Bias Against Guns*.

Despite all the emphasis on gun shows, there is no empirical research linking gun show regulations to decreased crime rates. If anything, the evidence points in the other direction. Earlier work that I have done using state-level data from 1977 to 2000 implies that gun show regulations not only significantly reduce the number of gun shows by up to 24 percent, but also increase murder and robbery rates. I found no statistically significant impact of background checks for handguns purchased through dealers, a result also found consistently in research by others. Enacting the assault weapons ban and instituting waiting periods did have one effect in my research: it significantly reduced the number of gun shows.[205]

The number of gun shows in the United States peaked in 1996 at 2,907 and has continually fallen since then under both the rest of the Clinton administration and the Bush administration.[206] By 2005, there were 1,792 gun shows, a drop of 38 percent from the peak and just slightly below the 1,800 gun shows that took place in 1990.

Mark Duggan, Randi Hjalmarsson, and Brian Jacob have conducted more recent work. They find that gun shows modestly reduce homicides and have no impact on suicides within twenty-five miles of the gun show.[207] If their result is correct, the reduction in gun shows that I find from closing the gun show loophole may explain why closing the loophole could increase murder and robbery rates. Closing down gun shows is more likely to deprive law-abiding citizens of a relatively inexpensive source of guns than to prevent criminals from getting guns.

The results in table 10.12 imply little impact from closing the gun show loophole. While murder and robbery rates appear to rise, neither increase is statistically significant. Nor is the change in aggravated assaults significant. Although rape is reduced and the reduction is significant, it is unclear how to interpret this lone result, since guns are very rarely used in the commission of rape. In fact, unlike the other violent crime categories, the FBI *Uniform Crime Reports* don't even list how many rapes are committed with guns. What is probably most clear from this result is that closing the gun show loophole does not reduce defensive gun uses that stop rapes.

Castle Laws

Fourteen states adopted Castle Laws in just 2006 alone. It is hard to think of any gun-control law that has been adopted in so many states in just a single year. Yet, this book represents the first research on the impact that the so-called Castle Doctrine, or Castle Law, has on crime rates. These Castle Laws eliminate the requirement that people in their own homes retreat as far

Table 10.12 The impact of "closing" the gun show loophole on violent crime rates

	Murder	Rape	Robbery	Aggravated assault
Change in the average crime rate after the gun show loophole is closed (%)	2%	−3.0%***	3.0%	−2.1%

Note: Examining the before-and-after average crime rates from closing this loophole was accounted for in figures 10.1a–10.1i.
***Statistically significant at least at the 10 percent level for two-tailed *t*-test.

as possible before defending themselves. By removing this requirement, victims do not risk misjudging how far they should retreat. As a result, committing crimes in a home becomes more risky for the criminal. Castle Laws take away worries for a law-abiding citizen about breaking the law by not retreating as far as possible, a delay that might be potentially harmful. Indeed, three of the cases discussed earlier in the section on prosecutions of concealed-handgun permit holders ("Concealed-Carry Permit Holders: Villains or Saints?") noted judgment calls where prosecutors apparently didn't believe that the victims had done enough to avert the attack prior to firing their guns.

On the other hand, there could be some unintended consequences where gun owners might shoot too quickly—leading to the shooting being classified as either murder or manslaughter and thus potentially increasing crime rates. One recent case in Colorado Springs during the end of December 2008 has been pointed to as the type of tragedy that might arise from the Castle Doctrine, and it received widespread international attention.[208] As initially reported, 22-year-old Sean Kennedy had been drinking heavily; he had gotten lost and knocked on the back door of the wrong house and got shot.

But later reports indicated that the residents might have had some justification for their shooting, noting that Kennedy "had broken a window and was trying to get inside a back door when he was shot and killed by the homeowner Sunday night" while those inside were screaming at him to leave.[209] The residents had also reportedly called 911 and "reported that someone was trying to break into the house" before they fired their gun.[210] There is also a mention that Kennedy had "broken" the door. In any case, it appears that the improper actions with guns that many feared would happen after the law are quite rare.

While thirty states have now passed Castle Laws, there are not yet many changes in the law to study. Only seven states enacted such laws during our sample period, between 1977 and the end of 2005, and three of the seven adopted the laws between 2003 and 2005 (table 10.13). While the results (table

Table 10.13 Enactment dates of Castle Doctrine laws

State	Date law went into effect
Alabama	June 1, 2006
Alaska	June 20, 2006
Arizona	Apr. 24, 2006
California	Before 1977
Colorado	June 6, 1995
Connecticut	1973
Delaware	Before 1977
Florida	Oct. 1, 2005
Georgia	July 1, 2006
Hawaii	Before 1977
Idaho	Oct. 1, 2006
Illinois	July 28, 2004
Indiana	July 1, 2006
Kansas	May 26, 2006
Kentucky	July 12, 2006
Louisiana	Aug. 15, 2006
Massachusetts	Before 1977
Michigan	July 26, 2006
Minnesota	Before 1977
Mississippi	July 1, 2006
Montana	Before 1977
New Mexico	1978
North Carolina	1993
Oklahoma	Oct. 1, 2006
Rhode Island	Before 1977
South Carolina	June 9, 2006
South Dakota	July 1, 2006
Utah	2003
Virginia	Before 1977
Washington	1999[a]

Source: Information from "Summary Of 'Duty to Retreat' Law in All 50 States" (NRA/ILA Office of Legislative Counsel, Fairfax, VA, 2008) and factiva searches.
[a]No law; legal precedent only: "The law is well settled that there is no duty to retreat when a person is assaulted in a place where he or she has a right to be"(Washington State Supreme Court, citing a 1999 ruling; http://www.washapp.org/Opinion.aspx?id=16).

10.14) suggest an overall reduction in violent and property crimes, too few years with the law in place are available to examine the before-and-after trends in crime rates.

Conclusion

Only rarely does a man of ideas witness in his own lifetime, the opportunity to actually see one of his ideas change history. For a scholar who wrote a controversial book in

Table 10.14 The impact of the Castle Doctrine on violent crime rates

	Murder	Rape	Robbery	Aggravated assault	Property crime	Burglary	Larceny	Auto theft
Change in the average crime rate after adoption of Castle Doctrine	−9%*	−18%*	6.7%***	−14.1%*	−6%*	−3.5%	−8.8%*	13%*

Note: The before-and-after average crime rates from enacting this law were accounted for in figures 10.1a–10.1i.

* Statistically significant at least at the 1 percent level for two-tailed *t*-test.

*** Statistically significant at least at the 10 percent level for two-tailed *t*-test.

the 1990s, arguing that, where there is more gun ownership there is actually less crime, that history-making experience took place. Legislatures across the country took hold of the ideas in that book, and passed laws allowing for the carrying of concealed weapons, that indeed was history-making. The author of that idea and of the book that contained those ideas, is our first debater tonight, speaking for the motion, "Guns reduce crime," John Lott.

—John Donvan of *ABC News Nightline* giving the introduction to the Intelligence Squared U.S. debate on October 28, 2008[211]

John Donvan's judgment in the above quote is extremely generous—indeed, probably too generous. There are lots of factors that went into this debate, and it is hard to evaluate how important each one was. The most crucial thing, though, is clear: if permit holders weren't extremely law abiding and if there were problems with right-to-carry laws, most states would not have adopted them. It would also have sparked calls for repealing concealed-handgun laws that had already been adopted, but no state has even held a legislative hearing on doing that. The lack of serious political debate on these points reflects that the evidence has been so clear. David Mustard and I may have noticed the facts before others, but the evidence has also spoken for itself.

It is easy to see why some people think that banning guns will make others safer, but gun-free zones, whether on college campuses or at the city or country level, have not disarmed criminals. Everyone wants to disarm criminals, but the problem we face is one faced with all types of gun-control laws: who is most likely to obey the law? Time after time, it is the most law-abiding citizens, the people who we don't have anything to worry about, who are disarmed and made vulnerable, not the criminals. However well meaning, banning guns only makes the lives of criminals easier.

During the past year, gun control has become a heated issue again. Calls for rebanning so-called assault weapons and regulating gun shows are again all the rage. The media have also gotten desperate trying to promote gun control. Take an ABC show from April, 2009. The network aired a heavily promoted, hour-long *20/20* special called "If I Only Had a Gun." It is ABC's equivalent of NBC's infamous exploding gas tanks in General Motors pickups, where NBC rigged the truck to explode. With states debating whether to eliminate gun-free zones at universities, there are few sacred cows in the gun-control debate that are not being questioned.

The show started and ended by claiming that allowing potential victims to carry guns would not help keep them safe—not even with hundreds of hours of practice firing guns. No mention was made of the actual multiple-victim public shootings stopped by people with concealed handguns, nor did the reporters describe who actually carried out such shootings. Instead, ABC presented a rigged experiment where one student in a classroom had a gun.

But sometimes even the best editors can't hide everything the camera sees. The experiment was set up to make the student fail. It did not resemble a real-world shooting. The same scenario is shown three times, but in each case the student with the gun is seated in the same seat—the center seat in the front row. The attacker not only is a top-notch shooter—a firearms expert who teaches firearms tactics and strategy to police—but also obviously knows precisely where the student with the gun is sitting.

Each time the experiment is run, the attacker first fires two shots at the teacher in the front of the class and then turns his gun directly on the very student with the gun. The attacker wastes no time trying to gun down any of the unarmed students. Thus, very unrealistically, between the very first shot setting the armed student on notice and the shots at the armed student, there is at most two seconds. The armed student is allowed virtually no time to react and, unsurprisingly, fails under the same circumstances that would have led even experienced police officers to fare poorly.

But in the real world, a typical shooter is not a top-notch firearms expert and has no clue about whether or not anyone might be armed and, if so, where that person is seated. If you have fifty people—a pretty typical college classroom—and the armed student is unknown to the attacker, he or she is given a tremendous advantage. Actually, if the experiment run by *20/20* seriously demonstrated anything, it was the problem of relying on uniformed police or security guards for safety: the killer instantly knows whom to shoot first.

Yet, in the ABC experiment, the purposefully disadvantaged students are not just identified and facing (within less than two seconds) an attacker whose gun is already drawn. They are also forced to wear unfamiliar gloves, a helmet, and a holster. This only adds to the difficulties the students face in handling their guns.

Given this odd setup, the second student, Danielle, performed admirably well. She shot the firearms expert in his left leg near the groin. If real bullets had been used, that might well have disabled the attacker and cut short his shooting spree.

What this book has tried to do is describe real-world cases where people have used guns to defend themselves and others. We have tried to use hard data to answer questions about what rules and regulations will save lives. Ten years have passed since this book was first written. While the previous editions involved the largest studies of crime at that time, even more data are now available, and many more states have adopted right-to-carry laws. A lot more work by many academics has been done on gun-control regulations. There are certain points that are beyond dispute.

1. By any measure, concealed-handgun permit holders are extremely law abiding.

2. Even the number of anecdotal news stories of defensive gun uses completely dwarfs any possible bad actions by permit holders with their concealed handguns.

3. No refereed academic articles by economists or criminologists claim that right-to-carry laws have a significant bad effect on crime rates.

Regarding the academic debate, it is obvious that a nerve has been struck. The language and accusations used by some can be distracting and disturbing, but the strongest opponents of allowing people to defend themselves have made what are at best simple mistakes that, when corrected, show the opposite of what they claim.

Refereed academic journal articles by economists and criminologists continue to show estimates that range from indicating large benefits from right-to-carry laws to claiming to show no change in crime rates. Yet, even those studies that claim that there is no benefit provide more evidence of benefits than no effect and much more evidence of benefits than costs.

At some point the risk of gun-free zones is going to have to be seriously discussed. Whether one looks at city or country gun bans or even smaller gun bans involving malls or schools, bans increase violence and murder.

The gun-control debate has changed dramatically over the last decade. In the past the question was how much guns caused crime. The debate now is over whether there are benefits from gun ownership and how large those benefits are.

APPENDIX ONE   How to Account for the Different Factors
                 That Affect Crime and How to Evaluate
                 the Importance of the Results

The research in this book relies on what is known as *regression analysis,* a statistical technique that essentially lets us "fit a line" to a data set. Take a two-variable case involving arrest rates and crime rates. One could simply plot the data and draw the line somewhere in the middle, so that the deviations from the line would be small, but each person would probably draw the line a little differently. Regression analysis is largely a set of conventions for determining exactly how the line should be drawn. In the simplest and most common approach—ordinary least squares (OLS)—the line chosen minimizes the sum of the squared differences between the observations and the regression line. Where the relationship between only two variables is being examined, regression analysis is not much more sophisticated than determining the correlation.

The regression *coefficients* tell us the relationship between the two variables. The diagram in figure A1.1 indicates that increasing arrest rates decreases crime rates, and the slope of the line tells us how much crime rates will fall if we increase arrest rates by a certain amount. For example, in terms of figure Al, if the regression coefficient were equal to −1, lowering the arrest rate by one percentage point would produce a similar percentage-point increase in the crime rate. Obviously, many factors account for how

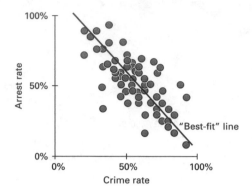

Figure A1.1. Fitting a regression into a scatter diagram

crime changes over time. To deal with these, we use what is called *multiple regression analysis*. In such an analysis, as the name suggests, many explanatory (or exogenous) variables are used to explain how the endogenous (or dependent) variable moves. This allows us to determine whether a relationship exits between different variables after other effects have already been taken into consideration. Instead of merely drawing a line that best fits a two-dimensional plot of data points, as shown in figure A1.1, multiple regression analysis fits the best line through an *n*-dimensional data plot, where *n* is the number of variables being examined.

A more complicated regression technique is called *two-stage least squares*. We use this technique when two variables are both dependent on each other and we want to try to separate the influence of one variable from the influence of the other. In our case, this arises because crime rates influence whether the nondiscretionary concealed-handgun laws are adopted at the same time as the laws affect crime rates. Similar issues arise with arrest rates. Not only are crime rates influenced by arrest rates, but since an arrest rate is the number of arrests divided by the number of crimes, the reverse also holds true. As is evident from its name, the method of two-stage least squares is similar to the method of ordinary least squares in how it determines the line of best fit—by minimizing the sum of the squared differences from that line. Mathematically, however, the calculations are more complicated, and the computer has to go through the estimation in two stages.

The following is an awkward phrase used for presenting regression results: "a one-standard-deviation change in an explanatory variable explains a certain percentage of a one-standard-deviation change in the various crime rates." This is a typical way of evaluating the importance of statistical results. In the text I have adopted a less stilted, though less precise formulation: for example, "variations in the probability of arrest account for 3 to 11 percent of the variation in the various crime rates." As I will explain below, standard deviations are a measure of how much variation a given variable displays. While it is possible to say that a one-percentage-point change in an explanatory variable will affect the crime rate by a certain amount (and, for simplicity, many tables use such phrasing whenever possible), this approach has its limitations. The reason is that a 1 percent change in the explanatory variable may sometimes be very unlikely: some variables may typically change by only a fraction of a percent, so assuming a one-percentage-point change would imply a much larger impact than could possibly be accounted for by that factor. Likewise, if the typical change in an explanatory variable is much greater than 1 percent, assuming a one-percentage-point change would make its impact appear too small.

The convention described above—that is, measuring the percent of a one-standard-deviation change in the endogenous variable explained by a one-standard-deviation change in the explanatory variable—solves the problem by essentially normalizing both variables so that they are in the same units. Standard deviations are a way of measuring the typical change that occurs in a variable. For example, for symmetric distributions, 68 percent of the data is within one standard deviation of either side of the mean, and 95 percent of the data is within two standard deviations of the mean. Thus, by comparing a one-standard-deviation change in both variables, we are comparing equal percentages of the typical changes in both variables.[1]

The regressions in this book are also "weighted by the population" in the counties or states being studied. This is necessitated by the very high level of "noise" in a particular year's measure of crime rates for low-population areas. A county with only one thousand people may go through many years with no murders, but when even one murder occurs, the murder rate (the number of murders divided by the county's population) is extremely high. Presumably, no one would believe that this small county has suddenly become as dangerous as New York City. More populous areas experience much more stable crime rates over time. Because of this difficulty in consistently measuring the risk of murder in low-population counties, we do not want to put as much emphasis on any one year's observed murder rate, and this is exactly what weighting the regressions by county population does.

Several other general concerns may be anticipated in setting up the regression specification. What happens if concealed-handgun laws just happen to be adopted at the same time that there is a downward national trend in crime rates? The solution is to use separate variables for the different years in the sample: one variable equals 1 for all observations during 1978 and zero for all other times, another equals 1 for all observations during 1979 and zero otherwise, and so on. These "year-dummy" variables thus capture the change in crime from one year to another that can only be attributed to time itself. Thus if the murder rate declines nationally from 1991 to 1992, the year-dummy variables will measure the average decline in murder rates between those two years and allow us to ask if there was an additional drop, even after accounting for this national decline, in states that adopted nondiscretionary concealed-handgun laws.

A similar set of "dummy" variables is used for each county in the United States, and they measure deviations in the average crime rate across counties. Thus we avoid the possibility that our findings may show that nondiscretionary concealed-handgun laws appear to reduce crime rates simply because the counties with these laws happened to have low crime rates to begin with. Instead, our findings should show whether there is an additional drop in crime rates after the adoption of these laws.

The only way to properly account for these year and county effects, as well as the influences on crime from factors like arrest rates, poverty, and demographic changes, is to use a multiple-regression framework that allows us to directly control for these influences.

Unless we specifically state otherwise, the regressions reported in the tables attempt to explain the natural logarithms of the crime rates for the different categories of crime. Converting into "logs" is a conventional method of rescaling a variable so that a given absolute numerical change represents a given percentage change. (The familiar Richter scale for measuring earthquakes is an example of a base-10 logarithmic scale, where a tremor that registers 8 on the scale is ten times as powerful as one that registers 7, and one that registers 7 is ten times as powerful as one that registers 6.) The reason for using logarithms of the endogenous variable rather than their simple values is twofold. First, using logs avoids giving undue importance to a few, very large, "outlying" observations. Second, the regression coefficient can easily be interpreted as the percent change in the endogenous variable for every one-point change in the particular explanatory variable examined.

Finally, there is the issue of *statistical significance.* When we estimate coefficients in a regression, they take on some value, positive or negative. Even if we were to take two completely unrelated variables—say, sunspot activity and the number of gun permits—a regression would almost certainly yield a coefficient estimate other than zero. However, we cannot conclude that any positive or negative regression coefficient really implies a true relationship between the variables. We must have some measure of how certain the coefficient estimate is. The size of the coefficient does not really help here—even a large coefficient could have been generated by chance.

This is where statistical significance enters in. The measure of statistical significance is the conventional way of reporting how certain we can be that the impact is different from zero. If we say that the reported number is "positive and statistically significant at the 5 percent level," we mean that there is only a 5 percent chance that the coefficient happened to take on a positive value when the true relationship in fact was zero or negative.[2] To say that a number is statistically significant at the 1 percent level represents even greater certainty. The convention among many social scientists is usually not to affirm conclusions unless the level of significance reaches 10 percent or lower; thus, someone who says that a result is "not significant" most likely means that the level of significance failed to be as low as 10 percent.

These simple conventions are, however, fairly arbitrary, and it would be wrong to think that we learn nothing from a value that is significant at "only" the 11 percent level, while attaching a great deal of weight to one that is significant at the 10 percent level. The true connection between the significance level and what we learn involves a much more continuous relationship. We are more certain of a result when it is significant at the 10 percent level rather than at the 15 percent level, and we are more certain of a result at the 1 percent level than at the 5 percent level.

ARREST RATE: The number of arrests per crime.

CRIME RATE: The number of crimes per 100,000 people.

CROSS-SECTIONAL DATA: Data that provide information across geographic areas (cities, counties, or states) within a single period of time.

DISCRETIONARY CONCEALED-HANDGUN LAW: Also known as a "may-issue" law; the term *discretionary* means that whether a person is ultimately allowed to obtain a concealed-handgun permit is up to the discretion of either the sheriff or judge who has the authority to grant the permit. The person applying for the permit must frequently show a "need" to carry the gun, though many rural jurisdictions automatically grant these requests.

ENDOGENOUS: A variable is endogenous when changes in the variable are assumed to caused by changes in other variables.

EXOGENOUS: A variable is exogenous when its values are as given, and no attempt is made to explain how that variable's values change over time.

EXTERNALITY: The costs of or benefits from one's actions may accrue to other people. External benefits occur when people cannot capture the beneficial effects that their actions produce. External costs arise when people are not made to bear the costs that their actions impose on others.

NONDISCRETIONARY CONCEALED-HANDGUN LAW: Also

known as a "shall-issue" or "do-issue" law; the term *nondiscretionary* means that once a person meets certain well-specified criteria for obtaining a concealed-handgun permit, no discretion is involved in granting the permit—it must be issued.

POOLED, CROSS-SECTIONAL, TIME-SERIES DATA: Data that allow the researcher not only to compare differences across geographic areas, but also to see how these differences change across geographic areas over time.

REGRESSION: A statistical technique that essentially lets us fit a line to a data set to determine the relationship between variables.

STATISTICAL SIGNIFICANCE: A measure used to indicate how certain we can be that the impact of a variable is different from some value (usually whether it is different from zero).

TIME-SERIES DATA: Data that provide information about a particular place over time. For example, time-series data might examine the change in the crime rate for a city over many years.

Description of the Data

This appendix provides a detailed discussion of the variables used in this study and their sources. The number of arrests and offenses for each crime in every county from 1977 to 1992 were provided by the FBI's *Uniform Crime Reports* (UCR). The UCR program is a nationwide, cooperative statistical effort by over 16,000 city, county, and state law-enforcement agencies to compile data on crimes that are reported to them. During 1993, law-enforcement agencies active in the UCR program represented over 245 million U.S. inhabitants, or 95 percent of the total population. The coverage amounted to 97 percent of the U.S. population living in Metropolitan Statistical Areas (MSAs) and 86 percent of the population in non-MSA cities and in rural counties.[1] The *Supplementary Homicide Reports* of the UCR supplied the data on the sex and race of victims and on whatever relationship might have existed between victim and offender.[2]

The regressions report results from a subset of the UCR data set, though we also ran the regressions with the entire data set. The main differences were that the effect of concealed-handgun laws on murder was greater than what is reported in this study, and the effects on rape and aggravated assault were smaller. Observations were eliminated because of changes in reporting practices or definitions of crimes; see *Crime in the United States* for the years 1977 to 1992. For example, from 1985 to 1994, Illinois operated under a unique, "gender-neutral" definition of sex offenses. Another example involves Cook County, Illinois, from 1981 to 1984, which experienced a large jump in reported crime because of a change in the way officers were trained to report crime.

The additional observations that were either never provided or were dropped from the data set include those from Arizona (1980), Florida (1988), Georgia (1980), Kentucky (1988), and Iowa (1991). Data for counties containing the following cities were also eliminated for the crime rates listed: violent crime and aggravated assault for Steubenville, Ohio (1977–89); violent crime and aggravated assault for Youngstown, Ohio (1977–87); violent crime, aggravated assault, and burglary for Mobile, Alabama (1977–85); violent crime and aggravated assault for Oakland, California (1977–90); violent crime and aggravated assault for Milwaukee, Wisconsin (1977–85); all crime categories for Glendale, Arizona (1977–84); violent crime and aggravated assault for Jackson, Mississippi (1977 and 1982); violent crime and aggravated assault for Aurora, Colorado (1977 and 1982); violent crime and aggravated assault for Beaumont, Texas (1977 and 1982); violent crime and aggravated assault for Corpus Christi, Texas (1977 and 1982); violent crime and rape for Macon, Georgia (1977–81); violent crime, property crime, robbery, and larceny for Cleveland, Ohio (1977–81); violent crime and aggravated assault for Omaha, Nebraska (1977–81); all crime categories for Eau Claire, Wisconsin (1977–78); all crime categories for Green Bay, Wisconsin (1977); and all crime categories for Little Rock, Arkansas (1977–79).

The original *Uniform Crime Report* data set did not have arrest data for Hawaii in 1982. These missing observations were supplied to us by the Hawaii UCR program. In the original data set several observations included two observations for the same county and year identifiers. The incorrect observations were deleted from the data.

For all of the different crime rates, if the true rate was zero, we added 0.1 before we took the natural log of those values. It is not possible to take the natural log of zero, because any change from zero is an infinite percentage change. For the accident rates and the supplementary homicide data, if the true rate was zero, we added 0.01 before we took the natural logs of those values.[3]

The number of police in a state, the number of officers who have the power to make arrests, and police payrolls for each state by type of officer are available for 1982 to 1992 from the U.S. Department of Justice's *Expenditure and Employment Data for the Criminal Justice System*.

The data on age, sex, and racial distributions estimate the population in each county on July 1 of the respective years. The population is divided into five-year age segments, and race is categorized as white, black, and neither white nor black. The population data, with the exception of 1990 and 1992, were obtained from the U.S. Bureau of the Census.[4] The estimates use modified census data as anchor points and then employ an iterative proportional-fitting technique to estimate intercensal populations. The process ensures that the county-level estimates are consistent with estimates of July 1 national and state populations by age, sex, and race. The age distributions of large military installations, colleges, and institutions were estimated by a separate procedure. The counties for which special adjustments were made are listed in the report.[5] The 1990 and 1992 estimates have not yet been completed by the Bureau of the Census and made available for distribution. We estimated the 1990 data by taking an average of the 1989 and 1991 data. We estimated the 1992 data by multiplying the 1991 populations by the 1990–91 growth rate of each county's population.

Data on income, unemployment, income maintenance, and retirement were obtained by the Regional Economic Information System (REIS). Income maintenance includes Supplemental Security Insurance (SSI), Aid to Families with Dependent Children (AFDC), and food stamps. Unemployment benefits include state unemployment insurance compensation, Unemployment for federal employees, unemployment for railroad employees, and unemployment for veterans. Retirement payments include old-age survivor and disability payments, federal civil employee retirement payments, military retirement payments, state and local government employee retirement payments, and workers compensation payments (both federal and state). Nominal values were converted to real values by using the consumer price index.[6] The index uses the average consumer price index for July 1983 as the base period. County codes for twenty-five observations did not match any of the county codes listed in the ICPSR codebook. Those observations were deleted from the sample.

Data concerning the number of concealed-weapons permits for each county were obtained from a variety of sources. Mike Woodward, of the Oregon Law Enforcement and Data System, provided the Oregon data for 1991 and after. The number of permits available for Oregon by county in 1989 was provided by the sheriff's departments of the individual counties. Cari Gerchick, Deputy County Attorney for Maricopa County in Arizona, provided us with the Arizona county-level conviction rates, prison-sentence lengths, and concealed-handgun permits from 1990 to 1995. The Pennsylvania data were obtained from Alan Krug. The National Rifle Association provided data on NRA membership by state from 1977 to 1992. The dates on which states enacted enhanced-sentencing provisions for crimes committed with deadly weapons were obtained from a study by Marvell and Moody.[7] The first year for which the enhanced-sentencing variable equals 1 is weighted by the portion of that first year during which the law was in effect.

For the Arizona regressions, the Brady-law variable is weighted for 1994 by the percentage of the year for which it was in effect (83 percent).

The Bureau of the Census provided data on the area in square miles of each county. Both the total number of unintentional-injury deaths and the number of those involving firearms were obtained from annual issues of *Accident Facts* and *The Vital Statistics of the United States*. The classification of types of weapons is from *International Statistical Classification of Diseases and Related Health Problems*, vol. 1, 10th ed. The handgun category includes guns for single-hand use, pistols, and revolvers. The total includes all other types of firearms.

The means and standard deviations of the variables are reported in appendix 4.

APPENDIX FOUR   National Sample Means and Standard Deviations

Table A4.1 National Sample Means and Standard Deviations

Variable	Observations	Mean	Standard deviation
Gun ownership information:			
Nondiscretionary law dummy	50,056	0.16	0.368
Arrests rates (ratio of arrests to offenses)			
Index crimes[a]	45,108	27.43	126.73
Violent crimes	43,479	71.31	327.25
Property crimes	45,978	24.03	120.87
Murder	26,472	98.05	109.78
Rape	33,887	57.83	132.80
Aggravated assault	43,472	71.37	187.35
Robbery	34,966	61.62	189.50
Burglary	45,801	21.51	47.299
Larceny	45,776	25.57	263.71
Auto theft	43,616	44.82	307.54
Crime rates (per 100,000 people)			
Index crimes	46,999	2,984.99	3,368.85
Violent crimes	47,001	249.08	388.72
Property crimes	46,999	2,736.59	3,178.41
Murder	47,001	5.65	10.63
Murder rate with guns (from 1982 to 1991 in counties with more than 100,000 people)	12,759	3.92	6.48
Rape	47,001	18.78	32.39
Robbery	47,001	44.69	149.21
Aggravated assault	47,001	180.05	243.26
Burglary	47,001	811.8642	1,190.23
Larceny	47,000	1,764.37	2,036.03
Auto theft	47,000	160.42	284.60
Causes of accidental deaths and murders (per 100,000 people)			
Rate of accidental deaths from guns	23,278	0.151	1.216175
Rate of accidental deaths from causes other than guns	23,278	1.165152	4.342401
Rate of total accidental deaths	23,278	51.95	32.13482
Rate of murders (handguns)	23,278	0.44	1.930975
Rate of murders (other guns)	23,278	3.478	6.115275

Table A4.1 (*continued*)

Variable	Observations	Mean	Standard deviation
Income data (all values in real 1983 dollars)			
Real per-capita personal income	50,011	10,554.21	2,498.07
Real per-capita unemployment insurance	50,011	67.58	53.10
Real per-capita income maintenance	50,011	157.23	97.61
Real per-capita retirement (over age 65)	49,998	12,328.5	4,397.49
Population characteristics			
County population	50,023	75,772.78	250,350.4
County population per square mile	50,023	214.33	1421.25
State population	50,056	6,199,949	5,342,068
State NRA membership (per 100,000 people)	50,056	1098.11	516.0701
Percent voting Republican in presidential election	50,056	52.89	8.41

ªIndex crimes represent the total of all violent and property crimes.

Table A4.2 Average percent of the total population in U.S. counties in each age, sex, and race cohort from 1977 to 1992 (50,023 observations)

	10–19 years of age	20–29 years of age	30–39 years of age	40–49 years of age	50–64 years of age	Over 65 years of age
Black male	0.9%	0.8%	0.5%	0.4%	0.4%	0.4%
Black female	0.9%	0.8%	0.6%	0.4%	0.5%	0.6%
White male	7.3%	6.8%	6.4%	4.9%	6.5%	5.4%
White female	6.8%	6.6%	6.3%	5.0%	6.9%	7.5%
Other male	0.2%	0.2%	0.2%	0.1%	0.1%	0.1%
Other female	0.2%	0.2%	0.2%	0.1%	0.1%	0.1%

APPENDIX FIVE

Continuation of the Results from Table 4.2:
The Effect of Demographic Characteristics
on Crime

Table A5.1 The effect of demographic characteristics on crime

The following assume a 1 percent change in the portion of the population in each category	Violent-crime rate	Murder rate	Rape rate	Aggravated assault rate	Robbery rate	Property-crime rate	Burglary rate	Larceny rate	Auto-theft rate
Percent of population that is black, male, and in the following age ranges:									
10–19	6%	11%	4%	9%***	11%***	13%*	7%**	17%*	5%
	(5%)	(8%)	(3%)	(7%)	(6%)	(22%)	(7%)	(25%)	(6%)
20–29	0%	7%	8%**	-5%*	-1%	-1%	-2%	-1%	1%
	(0%)	(4%)	(4%)	(3%)	(0%)	(2%)	(2%)	(1%)	(1%)
30–39	4%	11%**	-8%*	20%*	1%	4%	-1%	0%	15%*
	(2%)	(4%)	(3%)	(9%)	(0%)	(4%)	(0%)	(0%)	(11%)
40–49	-2%	-34%*	90%*	-37%*	-1%	-2%	-3%	19%*	-68%*
	(1%)	(9%)	(22%)	(11%)	(0%)	(1%)	(1%)	(10%)	(32%)
50–64	18%**	-35%*	-15%	29%*	-1%	-5%	9%	-13%***	6%
	(7%)	(11%)	(4%)	(10%)	(0%)	(4%)	(4%)	(9%)	(3%)
65 and over	12%	-14%	44%*	11%	17%	-4%	6%	-10%	-34%*
	(5%)	(4%)	(12%)	(4%)	(4%)	(3%)	(3%)	(6%)	(18%)
Percent of population that is black, female, and in the following age ranges:									
10–19	0%	4%	4%	-7%	-18%	8%*	2%	16%*	-18%*
	(0%)	(3%)	(2%)	(6%)	(11%)	(14%)	(2%)	(23%)	(22%)
20–29	-10%*	-22%*	18%*	-19%*	-22%*	-10%*	-17%*	-1%	-25%*
	(7%)	(13%)	(9%)	(13%)	(11%)	(14%)	(13%)	(1%)	(26%)
30–39	12%*	-8%	15%*	9%*	38%*	13%*	27%*	9%*	17%*
	(7%)	(4%)	(6%)	(5%)	(14%)	(14%)	(16%)	(9%)	(14%)

Table A5.1 (*continued*)

The following assume a 1 percent change in the portion of the population in each category	Violent-crime rate	Murder rate	Rape rate	Aggravated assault rate	Robbery rate	Property-crime rate	Burglary rate	Larceny rate	Auto-theft rate
40–49	1% (0%)	59%* (19%)	−74%* (21%)	27%* (10%)	−7% (2%)	6% (4%)	−5% (2%)	−3% (2%)	48%* (27%)
50–64	−21%* (11%)	20%*** (9%)	10% (4%)	−5% (3%)	7% (2%)	−2% (2%)	−22%* (12%)	1% (1%)	12% (9%)
65 and older	−20%* (11%)	31%* (14%)	−52%* (21%)	−16%** (8%)	−37%* (14%)	−20%* (22%)	−39%* (23%)	−12%** (12%)	24%* (19%)
Percent of population that is white, male, and in the following age ranges:									
10–19	−1% (1%)	−3% (2%)	1% (0%)	4%** (4%)	0% (0%)	−1% (1%)	1% (1%)	0% (0%)	−6%* (8%)
20–29	1% (1%)	6%* (5%)	4%* (3%)	2% (2%)	4%* (3%)	0% (1%)	2%** (2%)	0% (1%)	−2% (3%)
30–39	−1% (0%)	−1% (1%)	−4% (2%)	7%* (6%)	−7%* (4%)	−5%* (8%)	−3%*** (2%)	−6%* (8%)	−6%* (7%)
40–49	−1% (1%)	−2% (1%)	9%* (4%)	−4% (2%)	−11%* (5%)	−15%* (17%)	−10%* (7%)	−13%* (13%)	−10%* (8%)
50–64	−1% (0%)	−5% (3%)	4% (2%)	−9%* (7%)	−14%* (8%)	−13%* (20%)	7%* (6%)	−11%* (14%)	−27%* (31%)
65 and over	−13%* (15%)	2% (2%)	4% (4%)	−17%* (18%)	4% (3%)	−14%* (33%)	−12%* (15%)	−14%* (28%)	−11%* (19%)

Percent of population that is white, female, and in the following age ranges:

10–19	2% (2%)	5% (3%)	7%* (5%)	−1% (1%)	6%** (4%)	8%* (15%)	8%* (8%)	9%* (14%)	9%* (12%)
20–29	1% (1%)	−4%*** (3%)	6%* (4%)	4%** (4%)	1% (1%)	−1% (2%)	−4%* (5%)	3%** (5%)	−3%*** (4%)
30–39	2% (2%)	4% (3%)	14%* (8%)	3% (2%)	−1% (0%)	4%* (6%)	2% (1%)	7%* (5%)	−10%* (12%)
40–49	−9%* (5%)	0% (0%)	−7%** (3%)	0% (0%)	−2% (1%)	6%* (7%)	−4%* (2%)	7%* (7%)	−2% (1%)
50–64	0% (0%)	1% (1%)	2% (1%)	8%* (6%)	3% (2%)	10%* (17%)	6%* (6%)	11%* (16%)	11% (13%)
65 and over	6%* (9%)	−7%* (8%)	6%* (7%)	8%* (12%)	−9%* (9%)	2%** (6%)	5%* (8%)	4%* (9%)	−5%* (10%)

Percent of population that is other males in the following age ranges:

10–19	25%** (11%)	66%* (23%)	56%* (18%)	19% (7%)	54%* (16%)	16%*** (13%)	27% (13%)	15% (11%)	60% (38%)
20–29	−12%** (4%)	14% (4%)	−17%** (4%)	−6% (2%)	1% (0%)	8%* (5%)	0% (0%)	20%* (11%)	−41% (18%)
30–39	23%* (6%)	−30% (6%)	−19% (4%)	40%* (9%)	−10% (2%)	−18%** (9%)	−43% (12%)	−4% (2%)	65% (24%)
40–49	13% (2%)	−36% (5%)	−24% (3%)	−19% (3%)	78%* (9%)	3% (1%)	24%** (4%)	−23%*** (7%)	46%* (11%)
50–64	−9% (2%)	−16% (3%)	24% (4%)	−28% (5%)	−40%** (6%)	−2% (1%)	27%** (6%)	−20% (7%)	−42%** (13%)
65 and over	35%** (6%)	−26% (3%)	87%* (10%)	102%* (15%)	−27% (3%)	−8% (2%)	19% (3%)	−23%*** (6%)	−18% (4%)

Table A5.1 (*continued*)

The following assume a 1 percent change in the portion of the population in each category	Violent-crime rate	Murder rate	Rape rate	Aggravated assault rate	Robbery rate	Property-crime rate	Burglary rate	Larceny rate	Auto-theft rate
Percent of population that is other females in the following age ranges:									
10–19	−3%	−73%*	−11%	12%	−35%**	−18%**	−29%*	−23%**	−27%**
	(1%)	(25%)	(3%)	(5%)	(10%)	(14%)	(13%)	(16%)	(17%)
20–29	−13%	−33%**	21%*	9%	−30%	−15%**	−32%**	−33%**	−56%*
	(4%)	(8%)	(5%)	(3%)	(6%)	(9%)	(11%)	(18%)	(26%)
30–39	−22%*	−11%	16%	−17%	−22%	−9%	27%*	−28%*	−75%*
	(6%)	(2%)	(3%)	(4%)	(4%)	(4%)	(8%)	(12%)	(28%)
40–49	−14%	57%**	8%	18%	−48%**	25%**	28%*	70%*	−15%
	(2%)	(8%)	(1%)	(3%)	(6%)	(8%)	(5%)	(20%)	(4%)
50–64	−10%	44%	−66%*	−27%	37%	−5%	−49%*	16%	31%***
	(2%)	(7%)	(10%)	(5%)	(5%)	(2%)	(11%)	(6%)	(9%)
65 and over	44%*	6%	−37%**	−44%*	−36%**	−11%	−14%	−5%	−59%*
	(7%)	(1%)	(4%)	(6%)	(4%)	(3%)	(2%)	(1%)	(13%)

*The result is statistically significant at the 1 percent level for a two-tailed *t*-test.
**The result is statistically significant at the 5 percent level for a two-tailed *t*-test.
***The result is statistically significant at the 10 percent level for a two-tailed *t*-test.

APPENDIX SIX   Data and Additional Results for Chapter 10

Table A6.1 Means and standard deviations for variables for state-level data set from 1977 to 2005

Variable	Observations	Mean	Standard deviation	Minimum	Maximum
Natural log of murder rate	1,477	1.663805	0.7535024	−2.302585	4.394449
Natural log of rape rate	1,470	3.436527	0.4527471	0	4.897914
Natural log of robbery rate	1,477	4.606105	0.9641285	1.166271	7.398854
Natural log of aggravated assault rate	1,477	5.465097	0.6679146	1.997418	7.350902
Arrest rate for murder	1,443	82.51287	49.81053	0	1363.16
Arrest rate for rape	1,422	28.34408	15.90256	0	368.171
Arrest rate for robbery	1,439	34.38413	17.31153	0	310.63
Arrest rate for aggravated assault	1,446	42.64555	18.83171	0	343.5685
Execution rate	1,476	0.0018315	0.0069163	0	0.0997791
Prisoners as a percentage of the population	1,478	0.0031395	0.0029579	0.0000262	0.0561262
Greater than or equal to 10 years before law	1,479	0.1670047	0.3731063	0	1
8–9 years before law	1,479	0.0385396	0.1925599	0	1
6–7 years before law	1,479	0.0392157	0.194734	0	1
4–5 years before law	1,479	0.0392157	0.194734	0	1
2–3 years before law	1,479	0.0392157	0.194734	0	1
0–1 years before law	1,479	0.0392157	0.194734	0	1
1–2 years after law	1,479	0.0378634	0.1909304	0	1
3–4 years after law	1,479	0.032454	0.1772634	0	1
5–6 years after law	1,479	0.0311021	0.1736524	0	1
7–8 years after law	1,479	0.0311021	0.1736524	0	1
9–10 years after law	1,479	0.0290737	0.16807	0	1
11–12 years after law	1,479	0.0162272	0.1263909	0	1

13–14 years after law	1,479	0.0135227	0.1155371	0	1
15 or more years after the law	1,479	0.0148749	0.1210932	0	1
Training hours required	1,479	1.252874	2.821413	0	16
Training hours required squared	1,479	9.524679	29.10097	0	256
Training hours required >8	1,479	0.1156187	0.3198752	0	1
Permit duration in years	1,479	1.323867	1.955158	0	8
Age required for permit	1,479	6.853955	9.533732	0	23
Permit fees	1,479	22.67433	42.28191	0	219.0849
Permit fees squared	1,479	2300.677	6100.163	0	47,998.21
One-gun-a-month rule	1,479	0.0365112	0.186718	0	1
Neighboring state has one-gun-a-month rule	1,479	0.0993915	0.2975878	0	1
Assault weapons ban	1,479	0.354977	0.4666294	0	1
Castle Doctrine	1,479	0.2151761	0.4105261	0	1
Saturday night special	1,479	0.0892495	0.2852	0	1
Regulations on private transfers	1,479	0.2734909	0.4446851	0	1
State population	1,479	4,988,618	5,505,221	0	3.62E+07
Unemployment rate	1,479	5.945571	2.022835	2.2	18
Poverty rate	1,479	13.2191	5.488303	2.9	129
Real per capita income	1,479	14,367.35	2,863.493	8,587.184	27,041.21
Real per capita unemployment payments	1,479	68.08383	41.86245	10.48574	403.6979
Real per capita income maintenance payments	1,479	185.6606	70.61742	45.84409	552.4575

Table A6.1 (*continued*)

Variable	Observations	Mean	Standard deviation	Minimum	Maximum
Percentage of the population by sex, race, and age:					
Black male 10–19 years of age	1,479	0.8328599	0.8871636	0.01642	5.45238
White male 10–19 years of age	1,479	6.257005	1.431695	1.21827	9.55684
Neither male 10–19 years of age	1,479	0.4455137	0.7688774	0.02724	5.72339
Black female 10–19 years of age	1,479	0.8740414	0.9543196	0.02013	6.31461
White female 10–19 years of age	1,479	6.370946	1.497998	1.38595	9.92206
Neither female 10–19 years of age	1,479	0.4427511	0.7457205	0.02888	5.39289
Black male 20–29 years of age	1,479	0.8814284	1.017257	0.01565	7.25909
White male 20–29 years of age	1,479	6.428597	1.493398	1.85564	10.59611
Neither male 20–29 years of age	1,479	0.4574014	0.8148456	0.02696	6.57483
Black female 20–29 years of age	1,479	0.9458942	1.147497	0.01144	8.40541
White female 20–29 years of age	1,479	6.561392	1.588738	1.8211	10.00352
Neither female 20–29 years of age	1,479	0.4594413	0.791113	0.02851	6.24559

Black male 30–39 years of age	1,479	0.801526	0.8907323	0.00809	5.69006
White male 30–39 years of age	1,479	6.255831	1.217634	1.67978	9.51396
Neither male 30–39 years of age	1,479	0.4593404	0.8215571	0.01779	5.90577
Black female 30–39 years of age	1,479	0.8726103	1.010259	0.00463	6.53929
White female 30–39 years of age	1,479	6.415199	1.258567	1.67469	9.44145
Neither female 30–39 years of age	1,479	0.4669651	0.8115325	0.01889	5.72763
Black male 40–49 years of age	1,479	0.6467276	0.7169999	0.00586	4.44523
White male 40–49 years of age	1,479	5.288351	1.298221	1.28408	8.65968
Neither male 40–49 years of age	1,479	0.3649927	0.6834877	0.01525	5.41537
Black female 40–49 years of age	1,479	0.7102121	0.8227117	0.00204	5.44682
White female 40–49 years of age	1,479	5.439538	1.286688	1.49004	8.52743
Neither female 40–49 years of age	1,479	0.381±887	0.6850796	0.01623	5.3861
Black male 50–64 year of age	1,479	0.6855771	0.7729429	0.00236	4.95675
White male 50–64 year of age	1,479	5.867447	1.255093	1.6931	9.81465

Table A6.1 *(continued)*

Variable	Observations	Mean	Standard deviation	Minimum	Maximum
Percentage of the population by sex, race, and age:					
Neither male 50–64 year of age	1,479	0.3626394	0.6681734	0.02167	5.28878
Black female 50–64 year of age	1,479	0.763614	0.8955906	0.00168	5.75757
White female 50–64 year of age	1,479	6.101135	1.308835	1.8069	10.00725
Neither female 50–64 year of age	1,479	0.3780827	0.6964578	0.02227	5.79369
Black male over 64 years of age	1,479	0.5470208	0.6538146	0.000713	4.11721
White male over 64 years of age	1,479	4.851585	1.274724	0.9776	7.63618
Neither male over 64 years of age	1,479	0.2767989	0.5631171	0.01591	4.54086
Black female over 64 years of age	1,479	0.643306	0.792862	0.000996	6.03449
White female over 64 years of age	1,479	5.451655	1.553272	0.8869	9.49874
Neither female over 64 years of age	1,479	0.2982582	0.6113198	0.01638	5.73696

Table A6.2 The probability that any year's crime rate is different from the crime rate during years 0–1 before the law was enacted, as shown in figures 10.1a–10.1i

	Murder	Probability that year's murder rate is different from years 0–1 before the law	Rape	Probability that year's rape rate is different from years 0–1 before the law	Robbery	Probability that year's robbery rate is different from years 0–1 before the law	Aggravated assault	Probability that year's aggravated assault rate is different from years 0–1 before the law
Greater than or equal to 10 years before law	0.797		1.417		0.888		0.711	
8–9 years before law	0.770		1.473		0.931		0.695	
6–7 years before law	0.770		1.460		0.948		0.702	
4–5 years before law	0.799		1.486		0.920		0.679	
2–3 years before law	0.792		1.463		0.921		0.672	
0–1 years before law	0.795		1.476		0.945		0.646	
1–2 years after law	0.735	56.9%	1.404	43.8%	0.946	96.0%	0.528	21.6%
3–4 years after law	0.716	45.4%	1.306	6.9%	0.931	94.8%	0.510	15.9%
5–6 years after law	0.637	13.5%	1.300	5.8%	0.903	77.4%	0.459	5.0%
7–8 years after law	0.623	10.0%	1.320	9.4%	0.947	95.6%	0.547	29.9%
9–10 years after law	0.614	9.6%	1.356	21.3%	0.927	92.3%	0.542	29.2%
11–12 years after law	0.597	7.3%	1.287	5.7%	0.896	74.4%	0.558	38.1%
13–14 years after law	0.537	2.2%	1.341	19.0%	0.842	47.9%	0.525	23.6%
15 or more years after the law	0.482	0.6%	1.358	25.5%	0.835	44.8%	0.521	22.4%

Table A6.3 Regression for murder that corresponds to the estimates shown in figure 10.1b

Variable	Coefficient	Absolute t-statistic	Probability
Arrest rate for murder	−0.00047	2.86	0.004
Execution rate	−3.020	2.71	0.007
Prisoners as a percentage of the population	−7.312	1.92	0.055
Greater than or equal to 10 years before law	0.797	4.16	0
8–9 years before law	0.770	4	0
6–7 years before law	0.770	3.98	0
4–5 years before law	0.799	4.1	0
2–3 years before law	0.792	4.04	0
0–1 years before law	0.795	4.07	0
1–2 years after law	0.735	4.13	0
3–4 years after law	0.716	4.02	0
5–6 years after law	0.637	3.55	0
7–8 years after law	0.623	3.47	0.001
9–10 years after law	0.614	3.35	0.001
11–12 years after law	0.597	3.15	0.002
13–14 years after law	0.537	2.81	0.005
15 or more years after the law	0.482	2.53	0.011
Training hours required	−0.022	1.74	0.082
Training hours required squared	0.001	1.02	0.309
Training hours required >8	−0.014	0.47	0.636
Permit duration in years	−0.015	1.07	0.284
Age required for permit	0.018	3.22	0.001
Permit fees	0.002	1.83	0.067
Permit fees squared	0.000001	0.2	0.839
One-gun-a-month rule	0.001	0.03	0.976
Neighboring state has one-gun-a-month rule	0.167	5.13	0
Assault weapons ban	0.004	0.11	0.91
Castle Doctrine	−0.088	2.73	0.006
Saturday night special	0.303	3.67	0
Regulations on private transfers	0.020	0.88	0.378
State population	0.000	1.2	0.23
Unemployment rate	−0.032	5.23	0
Poverty rate	−0.002	1.36	0.174
Real per capita income	0.000	0.59	0.555
Real per capita unemployment insurance payments	0.001	2.42	0.016
Real per capita income maintenance payments	0.000	1.95	0.051

Table A6.3 (*continued*)

Variable	Coefficient	Absolute t-statistic	Probability
Percentage of the population by sex, race, and age:			
Black male 10–19 years of age	0.685	1.29	0.199
White male 10–19 years of age	−0.405	2.78	0.006
Neither male 10–19 years of age	2.362	3.1	0.002
Black female 10–19 years of age	−0.836	1.64	0.1
White female 10–19 years of age	0.383	2.69	0.007
Neither female 10–19 years of age	−1.880	2.52	0.012
Black male 20–29 years of age	0.462	1.07	0.284
White male 20–29 years of age	0.446	3.66	0
Neither male 20–29 years of age	0.879	1.06	0.291
Black female 20–29 years of age	−0.345	0.83	0.405
White female 20–29 years of age	−0.491	4.05	0
Neither female 20–29 years of age	−0.821	0.98	0.328
Black male 30–39 years of age	−1.199	2.28	0.023
White male 30–39 years of age	−0.511	3.01	0.003
Neither male 30–39 years of age	2.767	3.09	0.002
Black female 30–39 years of age	0.935	1.91	0.057
White female 30–39 years of age	0.597	3.54	0
Neither female 30–39 years of age	−3.145	3.48	0.001
Black male 40–49 years of age	0.847	1.45	0.148
White male 40–49 years of age	0.402	2.44	0.015
Neither male 40–49 years of age	−3.866	4.24	0
Black female 40–49 years of age	−0.561	1.11	0.269
White female 40–49 years of age	−0.412	2.49	0.013
Neither female 40–49 years of age	3.962	4.32	0
Black male 50–64 year of age	2.055	4.91	0
White male 50–64 year of age	−0.020	0.16	0.87
Neither male 50–64 year of age	−0.697	0.94	0.348
Black female 50–64 year of age	−1.617	4.64	0
White female 50–64 year of age	0.080	0.67	0.503
Neither female 50–64 year of age	−0.196	0.26	0.792
Black male over 64 years of age	−0.589	2.14	0.033
White male over 64 years of age	−0.172	3.25	0.001
Neither male over 64 years of age	1.118	2.86	0.004
Black female over 64 years of age	0.756	3.54	0
White female over 64 years of age	−0.008	0.17	0.864
Neither female over 64 years of age	−0.406	1.2	0.231

Using Gun Magazine Sales as a Proxy
for Gun Ownership

Table A7.1 examines whether changes in gun
magazine sales are related to changes in gun
ownership rates. Changes in the sales of the six
gun magazines are related to the gun ownership
rate in a state.[1] Information on gun ownership
rates is from the National Opinion Research Corporation's General Social Survey. Survey data
was readily available from 1977 to 1998, though
they are not available for every year and the
sample size is relatively small.[2] While I have used
the larger CBS News General Election Exit Poll
or the Voter News Survey in the past,[3] I will use
the General Social Survey here because Duggan
refers to it.[4] Two different measures of gun ownership were derived from General Social Survey:
a simple rate at which people own guns and the
rate at which households owned guns.[5]

The regressions in table A7.1 attempt to account for the average differences in gun ownership across states and any national changes
in gun ownership rates across years. What the
table shows is that the gun magazines that most
closely proxy the survey data are the two NRA
publications, *American Hunter* and *American Rifleman*, and *Handguns* magazine. For these three magazines, increasing magazine sales by 1 percent is
associated with an increased gun ownership rate
of anywhere from 0.34 to 0.52 percent.

Guns and Ammo is positively related to the survey data, but the relationship is not statistically

significant and is only about a third to a half as large as for the three most closely related magazines. Duggan provides a similar analysis using only *Guns and Ammo* and claims to provide a significant positive relationship between survey data and magazine sales, but while he uses the data at the state level, he weights the polling data by regional and not state-level demographic characteristics. Of the six magazines, *Guns and Ammo* ranked fourth in its ability to explain changes in the survey data, and its effect was never statistically different from zero.

So do increases in either gun magazine sales or survey data precede changes in murder? To answer this I added the sales of the different gun magazines into the crime regressions reported earlier in this book. This allows us to account for the impact that other factors have on murder rates. These include the arrest rate for murder, the death penalty execution rate, the population density, the unemployment rate, the poverty rate, per capita income, per capita welfare payments, and detailed demographic information on the share of the population by age, sex, and race.[6]

The results are reported in table A7.1. If more sales of a gun magazine lead in a year or two to higher murder rates, it appears to occur only for the fourth largest magazine, *Guns and Ammo*, where a 1 percent increase in magazine sales increases murder rates by 0.24 percent the following year and by 0.17 percent two years later. What is puzzling with these results is that handguns are used to commit most murders (indeed, that is the reason that Duggan claims to focus on *Guns and Ammo*). Yet, the relationship between the two purely handgun magazines and murder rates is essentially zero, with coefficients that are less than 18 percent of the size of the *Guns and Ammo* coefficients in three of the four cases. Almost the same results are obtained when homicide or firearm homicide data are used. *Guns and Ammo* magazine is the only magazine that ever implies a statistically significant relationship for both previous years of sales.

Table A7.1 Effect of gun magazine sales on murder rate

Name	Average annual national sales from 1990 to 1999	Percent change in the rate that guns are owned in households from increasing magazine sales one year earlier by 1 percent	Percent change in murder rate from increasing magazine sales one year earlier by 1 percent	Percent change in murder rate from increasing magazine sales two years earlier by 1 percent
Guns and Ammo	147,110	0.28%	0.25%*	0.17%**
American Handgunner	1,027,854	0.19%	0.04%	0.03%
Handguns	1,328,805	0.50%***	0.10%	0.002%
American Hunter	569,108	0.58%*	0.19%	−0.31%***
American Rifleman	148,308	0.79%*	0.32%	−0.12%
North American Hunter	766,326	0.10%	−0.11%	−0.08%

* The result is significant at the 1 percent level for a two-tailed *t*-test
** The result is significant at the 5 percent level for a two-tailed *t*-test
*** The result is significant at the 10 percent level for a two-tailed *t*-test

NOTES

CHAPTER ONE

1. ABC News/Washington Post Poll, April 21–24, 2009; Graduate Institute of International Studies, *Small Arms Survey* (London: Cambridge University Press, 2007); and U.S. Department of Commerce, Bureau of the Census, *Statistical Abstract of the United States* (Washington, DC: U.S. Government Printing Office, 2009). And discussions of older data are available in Gary Kleck, *Targeting Guns* (Hawthorne, NY: Aldine de Gruyter Publishers, 1997); and David B. Kopel, *Guns: Who Should Have Them?* (Amherst, NY: Prometheus Books, 1995), pp. 260–61, 300–301. The estimates on the number of guns are very sensitive to the rate at which guns are assumed to wear out. Higher depreciation rates produce a lower estimated current stock. About a third of all guns are handguns.

A recent poll by the *Dallas Morning News* indicated that "52 percent of the respondents said they or a member of their household own a gun. That response is consistent with Texas Polls dating to 1985 that found more than half of Texans surveyed own guns.

"In the latest poll, of those who said they owned a gun, 43 percent said they had two to five guns; 28 percent said they had one; and 19 percent said they had more than five guns. And of the gun owners polled, 65 percent said they had some type of shooting instruction." See Sylvia Moreno, "Concealed-Gun Law Alters Habits of Some Texans, Poll Finds Supporters, Foes Disagree About What That Means," *Dallas Morning News*, Nov. 3, 1996, p. 45A. The number of people owning guns is examined in more detail in chapter 3.

2. For example, in Chicago 59 percent of police officers report never having had to fire their guns. See Andrew Martin, "73% of Chicago Cops Have Been Attacked While Doing Their Job," *Chicago Tribune*, June 17, 1997, p. A3.

3. Dawn Lewis of Texans Against Gun Violence provided a typical reaction from gun-control advocates to the grand jury decision not to charge Gordon Hale. She said, "We are appalled. This law is doing what we expected, causing senseless death." Mark Potok, a Texan, said that the concealed-gun law saved his life. "I did what I thought I had to do," (*USA Today*, Mar. 22, 1996, p. 3A). For a more recent

evaluation of the Texas experience, see "Few Problems Reported After Allowing Concealed Handguns, Officers Say," *Fort Worth Star-Telegram,* July 16, 1996. By the end of December 1996, more than 120,000 permits had been issued in Texas.

4. Japan Economic Newswire, "U.S. Jury Clears Man Who Shot Japanese Student," *Kyodo News Service,* May 24, 1993; and Lori Sharn, "Violence Shoots Holes in USA's Tourist Image," *USA Today,* Sept. 9, 1993, p. 2A.

5. Gary Kleck, *Point Blank: Guns and Violence in America* (Hawthorne, NY: Aldine de Gruyter Publishers, 1991).

6. John R. Lott, Jr., "Now That the Brady Law Is Law, You Are Not Any Safer Than Before," *Philadelphia Inquirer,* Feb. 1, 1994, p. A9. For a more detailed breakdown of police shootings in the larger U.S. cities, see William A. Geller and Michael S. Scott, *Deadly Force: What We Know* (Washington, DC: Police Executive Research Forum, 1992).

7. "Mexican Woman Who Killed Would-Be Rapist to Turn to Activism," *Associated Press Newswire,* Feb. 12, 1997, dateline Mexico City.

8. For many examples of how guns have prevented rapes from occurring, see Paxton Quigley, *Armed and Female* (New York: St. Martin's, 1989).

9. Newspaper stories abound. Examples of pizza deliverymen defending themselves can be found in the *Chicago Tribune,* May 22, 1997, p. 1; *Baltimore Sun,* Aug. 9, 1996, p. B1; *Tampa Tribune,* Dec. 27, 1996, p. A1; and *Los Angeles Times,* Jan. 28, 1997, p. B1. Another recent example involved a pizza deliveryman in New Paltz, NY (*Middletown (New York) Times Herald Record,* Jan. 25, 1997). Examples of thwarted carjackings (*Little Rock Democrat-Gazette,* Aug. 3, 1996) and robberies at automatic teller machines (*York (Pennsylvania) Daily Record,* April 25, 1996) are also common.

For a case in which a gun was merely brandished to stop an armed street robbery, see the *Annapolis Capitol,* Aug. 7, 1996. Other examples of street robberies that were foiled by law-abiding citizens using concealed handguns include the case of Francisco Castellano, who was shot in the chest during an attempted street robbery by two perpetrators but was able to draw his own handgun and fire back. Castellano's actions caused the robbers to flee the scene (Corey Dada and Ivonne Perez, "Armed Robbery Botched as Restaurateur Shoots Back," *Miami Herald,* Aug. 3, 1996, p. B6.) The following story gives another example: "Curtis Smalls was standing outside the USF&G building when he was attacked by two thugs. They knocked him down, robbed, and stabbed him. Mr. Smalls pulled a .38-caliber revolver and shot both attackers, who were later charged with this attack and two other robberies and are suspects in at least 15 more robberies." This story was described in "Gun Laws Render Us Self-Defenseless," *Baltimore Sun,* Sept. 27, 1996. See also Charles Strouse, "Attacker Killed by His Victim," *Fort Lauderdale (Florida) Sun-Sentinel,* Sept. 16, 1997, p. 4B; Henry Pierson Curtis, "Bicyclist Kills Man Who Tried to Rob Him," *Orlando Sentinel,* Sept. 19, 1997, p. D3; and *Florence (Alabama) Times Daily,* Dec. 27, 1996, for other examples. Examples of foiled carjackings can be found in "Guns and Carjacking: This Is My Car," *Economist,* Sept. 20, 1997. Many other types of robberies have been foiled by people carrying concealed handguns. In at least one case, citizens carrying concealed handguns in Jacksonville, Florida may have saved a restaurant waitress from being shot ("Pistol-Packing Seniors in Florida Wound Robber," Reuter Information Service, Sept. 24, 1997, 6:15 P.M. EDT). For another example, see Clea Benson, "Wounded Barmaid Kills Gunman in Holdup," *Philadelphia Inquirer,* Jan. 23, 1997, p. R1.

10. Stories involving defensive uses of guns in the home are featured even more prominently. For example, four intruders forced their way into the home of two elderly women, struggled with them, and demanded their car keys. The attack stopped only after one of the women brandished her handgun ("Pistol-Packing Grandmas Honored by Sheriff," *Associated Press Newswire,* Feb. 16, 1997 2:30 P.M. EST, dateline Moses Lake, WA). In another case a twenty-three-year-old burglar "pummeled" a 92-year-old man and "ransack[ed]" his house. The burglar left only after the elderly man reached his gun ("Burglar Puts 92-Year-Old in the Gun Closet and Is Shot," *New York Times,* Sept. 7, 1995, p. A16). Although the defensive

use of guns in the home is interesting, my focus in this book is on the effects of allowing citizens to carry concealed handguns.

11. Not all news stories of defensive uses involve shots being fired. For example, the *Arizona Republic* reported the following: "In January 1995, a permit-holder who lives in Scottsdale pulled a handgun from a shoulder holster and scared off two men armed with aluminum baseball bats who attempted to rob him near 77th Street and East McDowell Road. No shots were fired." ("In Arizona, High Numbers of Concealed-Weapon Permit Holders Are Found in the Suburbs," *Arizona Republic,* Mar. 17, 1996.)

12. "Mom Saves Self and Child with Handgun," *Atlanta Constitution,* Nov. 12, 1996, p. E2.

13. See *Los Angeles Times,* Jan. 28, 1997, p. B1. Similarly, Pete Shields, Handgun Control, Inc.'s founder, wrote that "the best defense against injury is to put up no defense—give them what they want or run. This may not be macho, but it can keep you alive." See Pete Shields, *Guns Don't Die, People Do* (New York: Arbor, 1981).

14. Problems exist with the National Crime Victimization Survey both because of its nonrepresentative sample (for example, it weights urban and minority populations too heavily) and because it fails to adjust for the fact that many people do not admit to a law-enforcement agency that they used a gun, even defensively; such problems make it difficult to rely too heavily on these estimates. Unfortunately, this survey is the only source of evidence on the way the probability of significant injury varies with the level and type of resistance.

15. Lawrence Southwick, Jr., "Self-Defense with Guns: The Consequences," *Journal of Criminal Justice,* vol. 8 (2000), tables 5 and 6; see also Kleck, *Point Blank.*

16. For example, see David B. Kopel, *The Samurai, the Mountie, and the Cowboy* (Amherst, NY: Prometheus, 1992), p. 155; and John R. Lott, Jr., "Now That the Brady Law Is Law, You Are Not Any Safer Than Before," *Philadelphia Inquirer,* Feb. 1, 1994, p. A9.

17. James D. Wright and Peter Rossi, *Armed and Considered Dangerous: A Survey of Felons and Their Firearms* (Hawthorne, NY: Aldine de Gruyter Publishers, 1986).

Examples of anecdotes in which people successfully defend themselves from burglaries with guns are quite common. For example, see "Burglar Puts 92-Year-Old in the Gun Closet and Is Shot," *New York Times,* Sept. 7, 1995, p. A16. George F. Will, in "Are We 'a Nation of Cowards'?" *Newsweek,* Nov. 15, 1993, discusses more generally the benefits produced from an armed citizenry.

18. See Wright and Rossi, *Armed and Considered Dangerous,* p. 150.

19. Ibid., p. 151.

20. *Baltimore Sun,* Oct. 26, 1991; referred to in Don Kates and Dan Polsby, "Of Genocide and Disarmament," *Journal of Criminal Law and Criminology* 86 (Fall 1995): 252.

21. Rebecca Trounson, "Anxiety, Anger Surround Return of Young Survivors," *Los Angeles Times,* Mar. 14, 1997, p. A1.

22. It is possible that both terrorists and citizens are worse off because of the switch to bombings if shootings would have involved targeted attacks against fewer citizens.

23. David Firestone, "Political Memo: Gun Issue Gives Mayor Self-Defense on Crime," *New York Times,* Mar. 7, 1997, p. B1.

24. Using an on-line retrieval search, it is easy to find many news articles and letters to the editor that repeat this common claim. For example, one letter to the editor of the *Newark Star-Ledger* (Oct. 12, 1996) stated that "over half the firearm homicides are committed not by criminals but by friends, family members, and lovers—people with no criminal record."

25. The sum of these percentages does not equal precisely 100 percent because fractions of a percent were rounded to the nearest whole percent.

26. Captain James Mulvihill recently testified before the U.S. Senate that "the greater L.A. area suffers under the weight of more than 1,250 known street gangs, whose membership numbers approximately 150,000. These gangs are responsible for nearly 7,000 homicides over the last 10 years, and injury to thousands of other people." (Prepared testimony of Captain

James Mulvihill, commander of the Safe Streets Bureau for Sheriff Block of Los Angeles County before the Senate Judiciary Committee, Apr. 23, 1997.)

27. I would like to thank Kathy O'Connell of the Illinois Criminal Justice Information Authority for taking the time to provide me with such a detailed breakdown of these data.

28. Many such murders also end up in the "undetermined relationship" category.

Probably the best known study of who kills whom is by Daly and Wilson. They examined nonaccidental homicide data for Detroit in 1972. In contrast to my emphasis here, however, they focused exclusively on trying to explain the composition of murders when relatives killed relatives. Of the total of 690 murders committed in Detroit in 1972, 243 (47.8 percent) involved unrelated acquaintances, 138 (27.2 percent) involved strangers, and 127 (25 percent) involved relatives. Of this last category, 32 (4.6 percent) involved blood relatives, and 80 (11.6 percent) victims were spouses (36 women killed by their husbands, and 44 men killed by their wives). The percentage of Chicago's murders involving relatives in 1972 was very similar (25.2 percent), though by the 1990–95 period the percentage of murders involving relatives had fallen to 12.6 percent (7.2 percent involving spouses). For the information about Detroit, see Martin Daly and Margo Wilson, *Homicide* (Hawthorne, NY: Aldine de Gruyter Publishers, 1988).

29. Kathy O'Connell of the Illinois Criminal Justice Information Authority provided these data.

30. See also Daniel D. Polsby, "From the Hip: The Intellectual Argument in Favor of Restrictive Gun Control Is Collapsing. So How Come the Political Strength of Its Advocates Is Increasing?" *National Review* (Mar. 24, 1997): 35–36.

31. In these seventy-five largest counties in 1988, 77 percent of murder arrestees and 78 percent of defendants in murder prosecutions had criminal histories, with over 13 percent of murders being committed by minors, who by definition cannot have criminal records. This implies that 89 percent of those arrested for murders must be adults with criminal records, with 90 percent of those being prosecuted. See Bureau of Justice Statistics Special Reports, "Murder in Large Urban Counties, 1988," (Washington, DC: U.S. Department of Justice, 1993), and "Murder in Families" (Washington, DC: U.S. Department of Justice, 1994); see also Don B. Kates and Dan Polsby, "The Background of Murders," Northwestern University Law School working paper (1997).

32. The average victim had 9.5 prior arraignments, while the average offender had 9.7. David M. Kennedy, Anne M. Piehl, and Anthony A. Braga, "Youth Violence in Boston: Gun Markets, Serious Youth Offenders, and a Use-Reduction Strategy," *Law and Contemporary Problems* 59 (Winter 1996): 147–96.

33. The relationship between age and sex and who commits murders holds across other countries such as Canada; see Daly and Wilson, *Homicide,* pp. 168–70.

34. James Q. Wilson and Richard J. Herrnstein, *Crime and Human Nature,* (New York: Simon and Schuster, 1985), p. 177. Wilson and Herrnstein also discuss in chapter 3 evidence linking criminality to physical characteristics. The surveys that they summarize find evidence that criminality is more likely among those who are shorter and more muscular.

35. Ibid., pp. 204–7; see also Michael K. Block and Vernon E. Gerety, "Some Experimental Evidence on the Differences between Student and Prisoner Reactions to Monetary Penalties," *Journal of Legal Studies* 24 (Jan. 1995): 123–138.

36. John J. Dilulio, Jr., "The Question of Black Crime," *The Public Interest* 117 (Fall 1994): 3–24; and "White Lies About Black Crime," *The Public Interest* 118 (Winter 1995): 30–44.

37. While there are many sources of misinformation on the deaths that arise from handguns, some stories attempt to clarify claims. For example, a *Nando Times* (www.nando.com) news story (Oct. 26, 1996) reported that "during a campaign visit here this week, President Clinton met with the widow of a police officer killed in the line of duty and later during a political rally cited his death as a reason to outlaw armor-piercing bullets. What he did

not tell his audience, however, was that the officer died in an auto accident, not from gun-fire. . . . Neither a bulletproof vest nor a ban on 'cop-killer bullets,' however, would have saved Officer Jerome Harrison Seaberry Sr., 35. He was responding to a radio call for backup on Christmas night last year when 'he lost control of his vehicle, going too fast . . . hit a tree head-on, and the vehicle burst into flames,' said Lake Charles Police Chief Sam Ivey. Armor-piercing bullets, Ivey said, 'had nothing to do with it.'"

38. National Center for Injury Prevention, *Injury Mortality Statistics* (Atlanta: Centers for Disease Control, 1999).

39. Editorial, "The Story of a Gun and a Kid," *Washington Times,* May 22, 1997, p. A18.

40. Joyce Price, "Heston Attacks Trigger-Lock Proposal: Actor Begins Role as NRA Executive," *Washington Times,* May 19, 1997, p. A4.

41. Currently, the impact of gun locks is difficult to test simply because no state requires them. Seven states (California, Connecticut, Florida, Hawaii, Minnesota, New Jersey, and North Carolina) and the District of Columbia have laws regarding proper storage, but these laws do not mandate a particular method of storage.

42. W. Kip Viscusi, "The Lulling Effect: The Impact of Child-Resistant Packaging on Aspirin and Analgesic Ingestions," *American Economic Review* (May, 1984): 324–27.

43. The Department of Justice's National Institute of Justice recently released a government-funded study entitled "Guns in America: National Survey on Private Ownership and Use of Firearms," by Philip Cook and Jens Ludwig. The study used poll evidence from 2,568 adults in 1994 to claim that "20 percent of all gun-owning households had an unlocked, loaded gun at the time of the survey. The report cited the accidental deaths of 185 children under the age of 14, and many times that number of accidental shootings. For each death, there are several accidental shootings that cause serious injuries." Fifty percent of respondents were said to have stored an unloaded gun that was unlocked. The Justice Department's press release quoted Attorney General Janet Reno as claiming that "these results show how dangerous unlocked guns are to children. That's why we must pass the child-safety-lock provision in the President's Anti-Gang and Youth Violence Act of 1997, now before Congress. A locked gun can avoid a family tragedy." Ignoring problems with the survey itself, several problems exist with these conclusions. First, the report does not show that those 20 percent of gun-owning households with "unlocked, loaded" guns were responsible for the 185 firearm deaths of children. We would be interested to know if the 20 percent of households included children. Second, the report only concentrates on the costs, while ignoring any possible benefits. One question that might be useful in considering benefits is this: Where did those with unlocked, loaded guns tend to live? For example, were they more likely to live in urban, high-crime areas? (See Department of Justice, *PR Newswire,* May 5, 1997.)

Unfortunately, despite issuing press releases and talking to the press about their findings, neither the Department of Justice, nor professors Cook or Ludwig, nor the Police Foundation, which oversaw the government grant, have made any attempt to release their data at least by August 1997.

44. U.S. Department of Commerce, Bureau of the Census, *Statistical Abstract of the United States* (Washington, DC: U.S. Government Printing Office, 1995). A common claim I will discuss later is that "more than half of all firearm deaths occur in the home where the firearm is kept." As noted in the text, since one-half of all firearm deaths are suicides, this should come as no surprise.

45. Editorial, *Cincinnati Enquirer,* Jan. 23, 1996, p. A8. Others share this belief. "It's common sense," says Doug Weil, research director at the Center to Prevent Handgun Violence, in Washington. "The more guns people are carrying, the more likely it is that ordinary confrontations will escalate into violent confrontations" (William Tucker, "Maybe You Should Carry a Handgun," the *Weekly Standard,* Dec. 16, 1996, p. 30).

46. For these arguments, see P. J. Cook, "The Role of Firearms in Violent Crime," in M. E.

Wolfgang and N. A. Werner, eds., *Criminal Violence* (Newbury, NJ: Sage Publishers, 1982); and Franklin Zimring, "The Medium Is the Message: Firearm Caliber as a Determinant of Death from Assault," *Journal of Legal Studies* 1 (1972): 97–124.

47. P. J. Cook, "The Technology of Personal Violence," *Crime and Justice: Annual Review of Research* 14 (1991): 57, 56 n. 4. Cook reported 82,000 defensive uses for an earlier period. The irony of Cook's position here is that his earlier work argued that the National Crime Victimization Survey radically underreports other violence-related events, including domestic violence, rapes, and gunshot woundings linked to criminal acts; see Gary Kleck, *Targeting Guns* (Hawthorne, NY: Aldine de Gruyter Publishers, 1997).

It is easy to find people who argue that concealed handguns will have no deterrent effect. H. Richard Uviller writes that "more handguns lawfully in civilian hands will not reduce deaths from bullets and cannot stop the predators from enforcing their criminal demands and expressing their lethal purposes with the most effective tool they can get their hands on." See H. Richard Uviller, *Virtual Justice: The Flawed Prosecution of Crime in America* (New Haven: Yale University Press, 1996), p. 95.

48. For instance, the University of Chicago's National Opinion Research Center states that reported gun ownership rates are much lower in urban areas. In the nation's twelve largest cities, just 18 percent of all households report owning a gun. Women in rural areas appear to own guns at about three times the rate that women in the twelve largest cities do. For a discussion about how these numbers vary between urban and rural areas generally or for women across areas, see James A. Davis and Tom W. Smith, *General Social Surveys, 1972–1993: Cumulative Codebook* (Chicago: National Opinion Research Center, 1993); and Tom W. Smith and Robert J. Smith, "Changes in Firearm Ownership Among Women, 1980–1994," *Journal of Criminal Law and Criminology* 86 (Fall 1995): 133–49. This issue is discussed further in chapter 3.

49. Gary Kleck provides an excellent discussion of the methodological weaknesses in the National Crime Victimization Survey. As an example, he writes, "Unfortunately, 88 percent of the violent crimes reported to the [National Crime Victimization Survey] in 1992 were committed away from the victim's home. Thus, by the time the self-protection question is asked, almost all the [respondents] who in fact had used a gun for self-protection know that they had already admitted that the incident occurred in a place where it would be a crime for them to have possessed a gun" (see Kleck, *Targeting Guns*).

50. Still another survey deals more directly with the number of lives potentially saved by defensive gun uses. It reports that potential victims believe that each year, 400,000 people "almost certainly" saved a life by using a gun, though even the researchers providing this estimate believe that the number is too high. See Gary Kleck and Marc Gertz, "Armed Resistance to Crime: The Prevalence and Nature of Self-Defense with a Gun," *Journal of Criminal Law and Criminology* 86 (Fall 1995): 150, 153, 180, 180–2; see also Gary Kleck, "Critique of Cook/Ludwig Paper," undated manuscript, Dept. of Criminology, Florida State University). Recent evidence confirms other numbers from Kleck's and Gertz's study. For example, Annest et al. estimate that 99,025 people sought medical treatment for nonfatal firearm woundings. When one considers that many criminals will not seek treatment for wounds and that not all wounds require medical treatment, Kleck's and Gertz's estimate of 200,000 woundings seems somewhat plausible, though even Kleck and Gertz believe that this is undoubtedly too high, given the very high level of marksmanship that this implies for those firing the guns. Even if the true number of times that criminals are wounded is much smaller, however, this still implies that criminals face a very real expected cost when they attack armed civilians. For discussions of the defensive use of guns, see J. L. Annest et al., "National Estimates of Nonfatal, Firearm-Related Injuries: Beyond the Tip of the Iceberg," *Journal of the American Medical Association* (June 14, 1995): 1749–54; and Lawrence Southwick, Jr., "Self-Defense with Guns: The Consequences," *Managerial and Decision Economics* (forthcoming).

51. Information from telephone call to Susan Harrell, Administrator, Bureau of License

Issuance for the state of Florida in Tallahassee. David Kopel writes that "in Florida as a whole, 315,000 permits had been issued by December 31, 1995. Only five had been revoked because the permit holder committed a violent crime with a gun." See David Kopel, "The Untold Triumph of Concealed-Carry Permits," *Policy Review* 78 (July–Aug. 1996), see also Stan Schellpeper, "Case for a Handgun-Carry Law," *Omaha World-Herald*, Feb. 6, 1997, p. 27; and Clayton E. Cramer and David B. Kopel, "'Shall Issue': The New Wave of Concealed-Handgun Permit Laws," *Tennessee Law Review* 62 (Spring 1995): 679, 691. An expanded version of this last article is available from the Independence Institute, 14142 Denver West Parkway, Suite 185, Golden, Colorado, 80401–3134.

52. Cramer and Kopel, "New Wave of Concealed-Handgun Permit Laws," pp. 691–92.

53. Bob Barnhart, "Concealed-Handgun Licensing in Multnomah County," mimeo (Intelligence/Concealed Handgun Unit: Multnomah County, Oct. 1994).

54. See *Richmond Times Dispatch*, Jan. 16, 1997.

55. Schellpeper, "Case for a Handgun-Carry Law," p. 27.

56. "Packin' and More Peaceful," *Las Vegas Review-Journal*, Aug. 5, 1996, p. 6B.

57. Kentucky State Police Trooper Jan Wuchner is also quoted as saying that he has "heard nothing around the state related to crime with a gun committed by permit holders. There has been nothing like that that I've been informed of." See Terry Flynn, "Gun-Toting Kentuckians Hold Their Fire," *Cincinnati Enquirer*, June 16, 1997, p. A1.

58. Lee Anderson, "North Carolina's Guns," *Chattanooga Free Press*, May 31, 1997, p. A4.

59. Lawrence Messina, "Gun-Permit Seekers Not the Criminal Type," *Charleston Gazette*, July 28, 1997, p. C1.

60. This is the incident discussed in note 3 that occurred during the beginning of 1996 in Texas. As for citizens with concealed handgun permits coming to the aid of police officers see the end of note 68.

61. Peter Hermann, "Unarmed Resident Slain by Intruder; Victim's Rifle Taken by Authorities," *Baltimore Sun*, Sept. 19, 1996, p. B1.

62. Christi Parsons and Andrew Martin, "Bead Drawn on Gun Law," *Chicago Tribune*, May 22, 1997, p. 1; the article includes a long list of such cases, not all of which ended with the charges being dropped. For example,

In Chicago, two motorists, both U.S. Marine Recruiters, were charged with felonies for allegedly having guns in their car when stopped by police for a minor traffic violation. State Rep. Joel Brunsvold (D-Milan) said a downstate woman who kept an assembled rifle in her car to shoot rodents on her farm was pulled over and charged with a felony, as if she had been planning a drive-by shooting. And in March, Chicago Bears defensive end Alonzo Spellman was charged with a felony after volunteering to a police officer during a traffic stop that he had a handgun inside his car.

63. Stephen Singular, *Talked to Death* (New York: Beech Tree Books, 1987), p. 142. In several other tragic cases people have carried concealed handguns because of death threats, only to be arrested by the police for carrying them; see, for example, Kristi Wright, "Executive Decision," *Omaha World-Herald*, June 8, 1997, p. 1E.

64. A recent case in Oklahoma illustrates how a gun allowed an elderly woman to defend herself:

An 83-year-old woman proved her aim was good Tuesday morning as she shot a burglar trying to get inside her home. Delia Mae Wiggins's home has been burglarized four times. She was beaten by a burglar in November. And she wasn't going to let it happen again. When she heard someone trying to break into her home at about 5 A.M., Wiggins said she grabbed a gun that had been loaded for nine years but never fired. She told police an intruder removed her window-unit air conditioner to enter her home. She said she warned the intruder she was armed. Then she pulled the trigger, hitting the intruder in the thigh. The man backed out the window and fled. (Robert Medley, "83-Year-Old Woman Shoots Fifth Burglar to Try to Victimize Her," *Oklahoma City Daily Oklahoman*, May 21, 1997.

This case also illustrates another point, because it involves a crime where the perpetrator would have been classified as knowing the intended victim. The attacker had just a few days earlier "mowed a lawn at a rental property for her."

65. Kristi O'Brien, "Concealed-Gun Legislation Bottled Up Again," *Copley News Service* (Apr. 15, 1997).

66. As Lon Cripps, the police chief in Langsberg, Montcalm County, Michigan, said in discussing concealed handguns, "There comes a time when you have to take responsibility for your own life. Police officers just aren't always going to be there" (*Detroit News*, June 14, 1996).

67. States where less than 10 percent of the members responded to the poll were excluded from the polling numbers reported by the National Association of Chiefs of Police.

68. Recent legislative testimony during 1997 provides similar evidence. In testifying before the Kansas House of Representatives on behalf of the Kansas State Lodge of the Fraternal Order of Police, Joseph T. Gimar said, "We . . . continue our support of the [right-to-carry] legislation with the belief that the citizens of Kansas will use it responsibly. . . . I have gone to great lengths to speak to as many national [Fraternal Order of Police] members as possible, many in jurisdictions that have concealed-carry statutes, but [I] have been unable to find any that were in opposition to their statutes." (For this and other quotations by law-enforcement officers, see Gary K. Hayzlett, "Kansans Should Get to Carry and Conceal Arms," *Kansas City Star*, Mar. 21, 1997.)

Many stories involve armed citizens, some with licensed concealed handguns, who have come to the aid of police officers who are being attacked. For example,

> Shapiro was arrested April 9 after punching and kicking Howey police Officer David Kiss in the face and mouth during a State Road 48 traffic stop, which also involved his wife, Susan Jane Shapiro.
>
> The melee didn't break up until a Mission Inn employee who was passing by shot Mark Shapiro in the back of his left knee.
>
> The passer-by, Vincent McCarthy, 46, of Eustis, had a permit to carry his .25-caliber automatic pistol and will not be charged, Lake sheriff's authorities said.
>
> The Howey Town Council earlier this week commended McCarthy for coming to the aid of Kiss. (Linda Chong, "Man Gets House Arrest in Law Officer's Beating," *Orlando Sentinel Tribune*, May 16, 1992, p. 8)

69. Related stories can be found in the *Alva (Oklahoma) Review Courier*, Jan. 8, 1995; the *Tuscaloosa News*, Jan. 12, 1995; and the *Houston Post*, Jan. 22, 1994; see "Gun-Control Survey" *Law Enforcement Technology* (July–Aug. 1991), pp. 14–15.

Police officers are well aware that off-duty officers have often been able to thwart crimes because they were armed. News stories on such cases are easy to find; see, for example, Deborah Hastings, "Girl Killed in California During Stop for Ice Cream on Parents' Anniversary," *Associated Press*, June 18, 1997, dateline Los Angeles, 02:50 A.M. EDT).

70. See Richard Connelly, "Handgun Law's First Year Belies Fears of 'Blood in the Streets,'" *Texas Lawyer*, Dec. 9, 1996, p. 2.

71. See the *Florida Times-Union*, May 9, 1988, and *Palm Beach Post*, July 26, 1988.

72. Flynn, "Gun-Toting Kentuckians Hold Their Fire," p. A1.

73. However, other polls, such as one done by the Johns Hopkins Center for Gun Policy and Research, a group that I will discuss again in chapter 7, argue that people favor more restrictions on gun ownership and claim that 82 percent favored mandatory registration of all handguns (Larry Bivens, "Most Want Child-Proof Handguns, Poll Shows," *Detroit News*, Mar. 14, 1997, p. A5).

74. Zogby International, "Strong Majority of Independents, Democrats, and Obama Voters Support Right to Carry a Firearm," PR Web, Aug. 4, 2009. Tom Smith, "1996 National Gun-Policy Survey of the National Opinion Research Center: Research Findings," (Chicago: National Opinion Research Center, Mar. 1997), p. 21.

75. Lydia Saad, "Before Recent Shootings, Gun-Control Support Was Fading," Gallup poll, Apr. 8, 2009. Smith, "1996 National Gun Policy Survey," pp. 8–9. The survey did include overwhelmingly positive responses to many questions on additional safety regulations for guns. I believe that many of these responses would have been significantly altered if the questions had been posed in terms of the trade-off between safety benefits and estimates of their costs, or if terms describing dangers to children had been eliminated (especially, as already noted in the text, since the number of children harmed by gun accidents is probably much smaller than most people believe).

76. Ibid., p. 13. The other major deciding factor for people's views on gun control appears to be whether they trust government. Those who do trust government are much more in favor of gun control.

77. Erika Schwarz (the first runner-up in the 1997 Miss America Pageant) decided to obtain a gun after a gunman stole her car when she pulled into her driveway. "It's about time they allow citizens to protect themselves. I don't advocate taking the law in your own hand. But in a situation where you're cooped up in a car or house and somebody wants to harm you, this is a good law." Erika Schwarz said that after a carjacking she had been afraid to drive at night. (Guy Coates, "Beauty Gets Ready to Shoot Carjackers " *Chattanooga Free Press*, Aug. 14, 1997, p. B7). Similar stories are told by others who were motivated to obtain firearms training. A recent *Wall Street Journal* story discussed the reasons given by fourteen people who enrolled in a self-defense class run by Smith & Wesson: "The budget analyst had a knife held to her throat in a crowded Manhattan bar. Ms. Denman awoke 18 months ago in her rural home to find a masked, armed burglar at the foot of her bed. He'd kicked in her deadbolted door, and shot at her several times before fleeing. She dialed 911, and then waited 45 minutes for help to arrive." See Caitlin Kelly, "Gun Control," *Wall Street Journal,* Sept. 12, 1997, p. A20.

78. "Georgia Lawmakers Quietly Vote Themselves the Right to Carry Weapons," *Associated Press,* dateline Atlanta, Mar. 19, 1996, 11:09 P.M. EST.

79. According to Larry Mason of the Association of California Deputy District Attorneys, "The association is . . . glad prosecutors have been permitted to protect themselves and that they can continue to do so for their own peace of mind and well-being" (quoted in Greg Krikorian, "Lungren Rules Prosecutors Can Carry Guns to Offices," *Los Angeles Times,* July 25, 1997, p. B1).

The Fraternal Order of Police has also strongly supported legislation that would allow current or retired police officers to carry concealed handguns with them wherever they travel within the United States. (Prepared testimony of Bernard H. Teodorski, National Vice President, Fraternal Order of Police, before the House Committee on the Judiciary, Subcommittee on Crime *(Federal News Service,* July 22, 1997.)

80. *Los Angeles Times,* Jan. 4, 1996, p. E1; Louis Graham, "Officials, Celebs Become Gun-Toting Sheriff's Deputies in Long Tradition," *Memphis Commercial Appeal,* Oct. 3, 1994, pp. 1A, B7; and Clayton B. Cramer and David B. Kopel, "'Shall Issue': New Wave of Concealed-Handgun Permit Laws" (Independence Institute: Golden Colorado, Oct. 17, 1994).

81. See note 77 above.

82. See Adriel Bettelheim, "Campbell Gunning for Concealed-Weapon Proposal," *Denver Post,* June 8, 1997, p. A31.

83. Gary Marx and Janan Hanna, "Boy Called Unfit for Murder Trial," *Chicago Tribune,* Jan. 18, 1995, p. 3; and Joan Beck, "The Murder of Children," *St. Louis Post-Dispatch,* Oct. 24, 1994, p. B19.

84. Maggi Martin, "Symphony of Life Ended Too Quickly for Musician: Grieving

Friends Say Man Stabbed in Lakewood Had Much to Give," *Cleveland Plain Dealer,* July 12, 1995, p. 1A.

85. John Stevenson, "Jurors Begin Deliberating Stroud's Fate," *Durham (North Carolina) Herald-Sun,* Feb. 9, 1995, p. C1.

86. In 1992, only three states did not allow insanity as a defense (Idaho, Montana, and Utah), but even in these states, insanity can be used in determining whether a person had intent.

87. See Dan Kahan and Martha Nussbaum, "Two Conceptions of Emotion in Criminal Law," *Columbia Law Review* 96 (Mar. 1996): 269–374.

88. *Model Penal Code* § 2100.3(1)(b) (1980).

89. See Kahan and Nussbaum, "Emotion in Criminal Law," *Columbia Law Review:* 315–17.

90. *Bullock v United States,* 122 F2d 214 (DC Cir 1941).

91. Kahan and Nussbaum, "Emotion in Criminal Law," *Columbia Law Review:* 325.

92. Anne Lamoy, "Murder Rate in KCK Lowest Since 1991," *Kansas City Star,* Jan. 1, 1997, p. C1.

93. John H. Kagel, Raymond C. Battalio, Howard Rachlin, and Leonard Green, "Demand Curves for Animal Consumers," *Quarterly Journal of Economics* 96 (Feb. 1981): 1–16; John H. Kagel, Raymond C. Battalio, Howard Rachlin, and Leonard Green, "Experimental Studies of Consumer Demand Behavior Using Laboratory Animals," *Economic Inquiry* 13 (Jan. 1975): 22–38; Raymond C. Battalio, John H. Kagel, and Owen R. Phillips, "Optimal Prices and Animal Consumers in Congested Markets," *Economic Inquiry* 24 (Apr. 1986): 181–93; Todd Sandler, "Optimal Prices and Animal Consumers in Congested Markets: A Comment," *Economic Inquiry* 25 (Oct. 1987): 715–20; Raymond C. Battalio, John H. Kagel, and Owen R. Phillips, "Optimal Prices and Animal Consumers in Congested Markets: A Reply," *Economic Inquiry* 25 (Oct. 1987): 721–22; and Raymond C. Battalio, John H. Kagel, Howard Rachlin, and Leonard Green, "Commodity Choice Behavior with Pigeons as Subjects ," *Journal of Political Economy* 84 (Feb. 1981): 116–51.

94. William M. Landes, "An Economic Study of U.S. Aircraft Hijacking, 1961–1976," *Journal of Law and Economics* 21 (Apr. 1978): 1–29.

95. Alfred Blumstein and Daniel Nagin, "The Deterrent Effect of Legal Sanctions on Draft Evasion," *Stanford University Law Review* 28 (1977): 241–76.

96. For a particularly well-done piece that uses data from another country, see Kenneth Wolpin, "An Economic Analysis of Crime and Punishment in England and Wales, 1894–1967," *Journal of Political Economy* 86 (1978): 815–40. For a recent survey of papers in this area, see Isaac Ehrlich, "Crime, Punishment, and the Market for Offenses," *Journal of Economic Perspectives* 10 (Winter 1996): 43–67.

97. Alfred Blumstein, Jacqueline Cohen, and Daniel Nagin, eds., *Deterrence and Incapacitation: Estimating the Effects of Criminal Sanctions on Crime Rates* (Washington, DC: National Academy of Sciences, 1978), pp. 4, 7. Economists have responded to this report; see Isaac Ehrlich and Randall Mark, "Fear of Deterrence: A Critical Evaluation of the 'Report of the Panel on Research on Deterrent and Incapacitation Effects,'" *Journal of Legal Studies* 6 (June 1977): 293–316.

98. Wallace P. Mullin, "Will Gun Buyback Programs Increase the Quantity of Guns?" Michigan State University working paper (Mar. 1997), and Martha R. Plotkin, ed., *Under Fire: Gun Buy-Backs, Exchanges, and Amnesty Programs* (Washington, DC: Police Executive Research Forum, 1996).

CHAPTER TWO

1. The Supreme Court Justices would not uphold broad protections for gun ownership "if they thought blood would flow in the streets." This point was made by Professor Daniel Polsby in a talk given at the University of Chicago, February 20, 1997. As he points out, the Supreme Court would not have allowed the publication of the Pentagon Papers, despite the

NOTES TO PAGES 23-27 | 377

arguments about the freedom of the press, if it had posed a severe military risk to the United States. It is not the role of this book to debate the purpose of the Second Amendment. However, the argument that the Second Amendment implies broad protection of gun ownership seems quite strong. William Van Alstyne argues that the reference to a "well-regulated Militia" refers to the "ordinary citizen" and that it was emphatically not an allusion to "regular armed soldiers." It was ordinary citizens who were to bring their own arms to form an army when the Republic was in danger. The amendment was viewed as the ultimate limit on a government's turning against the will of the people. See William Van Alstyne, "The Second Amendment Right to Arms," *Duke Law Review* 43 (Apr. 1994): 1236–55.

2. The opposite of endogenous is exogenous. An exogenous change in something is an independent change, not a response to something else. In reality, almost everything is to some extent related to something else, so the distinction between exogenous and endogenous is a matter of degree. Since models and statistical methods must put a limit on how much to include, some variables will always be treated as "exogenously given" rather than dependent on other variables. For the social sciences, this is a constant headache. Virtually any study is open to the criticism that "if variable X depends upon variable Y, your results are not necessarily valid." In general, larger studies that rely on more data have better chances of reliably incorporating more relationships. Part of the process of doing research is determining which relationships may raise important concerns for readers and then attempting to test for those concerns.

3. With purely cross-sectional data, if one recognizes that differences may exist in crime rates even after all the demographic and criminal-punishment variables are accounted for, there are simply not enough observations to take these regional differences into account. One cannot control for more variables than one has observations to explain.

The problem with time-series data is the same. Time-series studies typically assume that crime follows a particular type of time trend (for example, they may simply assume that crime rises at a constant rate over time, or they may assume more complicated growth rates involving squared or cubic relationships). Yet almost any crime pattern over time is possible, and, as with cross-sectional data, unexplained differences over time will persist even after all the demographic and criminal-punishment variables are accounted for. Ideally, one could allow each year to have a different effect, but with time-series data we would again find that we had more variables with which to explain changes than we had observations to explain.

4. Gary Kleck and E. Britt Patterson, "The Impact of Gun Control and Gun-Ownership Levels on Violence Rates," *Journal of Quantitative Criminology* 9 (1993): 249–87.

5. David McDowall, Colin Loftin, and Brian Wiersema, "Easing Concealed Firearm Laws: Effects on Homicide in Three States," *Journal of Criminal Law and Criminology* 86 (Fall 1995): 193–206.

6. Arthur L. Kellermann, et al., "Gun Ownership as a Risk Factor for Homicide in the Home," *New England Journal of Medicine* (Oct. 7, 1993): 1084–91.

7. Ibid., p. 1084.

8. The interesting letter that provoked this response from Kellermann et al. was written by students in a graduate statistics class at St. Louis University. See the *New England Journal of Medicine* (Feb. 3, 1994): 366, 368. The estimated rate at which defensive gun uses result in the death of the criminal is derived by comparing the estimated number of defensive gun uses with the number of justifiable homicides. The justifiable-homicide number is obviously an underestimate, and it implies that the actual rate of criminal deaths from defensive gun uses is somewhat higher than reported in the text, but it could be several times higher and not affect the overall statement.

9. Recent attempts to relate the crime rate to the prison population concern me. Besides difficulties in relating the total prison population to any particular type of crime, I think it is problematic to compare a stock (the prison population) with a flow (the crime rate). See,

for example, Steven Levitt, "The Effect of Prison Population Size on Crime Rates: Evidence from Prison Overcrowding Litigation," *Quarterly Journal of Economics* 111 (1996): 144–67.

10. Gary S. Becker, "Crime and Punishment: An Economic Approach," *Journal of Political Economy* 76 (Mar./Apr. 1968): 169–217. See also, for example, Isaac Ehrlich, "Participation in Illegitimate Activities: A Theoretical and Empirical Investigation," *Journal of Political Economy* 81 (1973): 521–65; Michael K. Block and John Heineke, "A Labor Theoretical Analysis of Criminal Choice," *American Economic Review* 65 (June 1975): 314–25; William M. Landes, "An Economic Study of U.S. Aircraft Hijacking, 1961–1976," *Journal of Law and Economics* 21 (Apr. 1978): 1–29.; John R. Lott, Jr., "Juvenile Delinquency and Education: A Comparison of Public and Private Provision," *International Review of Law and Economics* 7 (Dec. 1987): 163–75; James Andreoni, "Criminal Deterrence in the Reduce Form: A New Perspective on Ehrlich's Seminal Study" *Economic Inquiry* 33 (July 1995): 476–83; Morgan O. Reynolds, "Crime and Punishment in America," (Dallas: National Center for Policy Analysis, June 1995); and Levitt, "Effect of Prison Population Size on Crime Rates."

11. John R. Lott, Jr., "Do We Punish High-Income Criminals Too Heavily?" *Economic Inquiry* 30 (Oct. 1992): 583–608.

12. John R. Lott, Jr., "The Effect of Conviction on the Legitimate Income of Criminals," *Economics Letters* 34 (Dec. 1990): 381–85; John R. Lott, Jr., "An Attempt at Measuring the Total Monetary Penalty from Drug Convictions: The Importance of an Individual's Reputation," *Journal of Legal Studies* 21 (Jan. 1992): 159–87.

13. This approach is also known as controlling for "fixed effects," where a separate dummy variable is used to account for each county.

14. James Q. Wilson and George L. Kelling, "Making Neighborhoods Safe," *Atlantic Monthly,* Feb. 1989, and "Broken Windows," *Atlantic Monthly,* Mar. 1982.

15. Arson was excluded because of a large number of inconsistencies in the data and the small number of counties reporting this measure.

16. Robbery includes street robbery, commercial robbery, service station robbery, convenience store robbery, residence robbery, and bank robbery. (See also the discussion of burglary regarding why the inclusion of residence robbery creates difficulty with this broad measure.) After I wrote the original paper, two different commentators attempted to argue that "If 'shall-issue' [a synonym for "nondiscretionary"] concealed-carrying laws really deter criminals from undertaking street crimes, then it is only reasonable to expect the laws to have an impact on robberies. Robbery takes place between strangers on the street. A high percentage of homicide and rape, on the other hand, occurs inside a home— where concealed-weapons laws should have no impact. These findings strongly suggest that something else—not new concealed-carry laws—is responsible for the reduction in crime observed by the authors." See, for example, Doug Weil, "Response to John Lott's Study on the Impact of 'Carry-Concealed' Laws on Crime Rates," *U.S. Newswire,* Aug. 8,1996. The curious aspect of the emphasis on robbery over other crimes like murder and rape is that if robbery is the most obvious crime to be affected by gun-control laws, why have virtually no gun-control studies examined robberies? In fact, Kleck's literature survey only notes one previous gun-control study that examined the issue of robberies ("Guns and Violence: An Interpretive Review of the Field," Social Pathology 1 [Jan. 1995]: 12–47). More important, given that the FBI includes many categories of robberies besides those that "take place between strangers on the street," it is not obvious why this category should exhibit the greatest sensitivity to concealed-handgun laws.

17. "NRA poll: Salespeople No. 1 for Permit Applications," *Dallas Morning News,* Apr. 19, 1996, p. 32A.

18. For example, see Arnold S. Linsky, Murray A. Strauss, and Ronet Bachman-Prehn, "Social Stress, Legitimate Violence, and Gun Availability," Paper presented at the annual meetings of the Society for the Study of Social Problems, 1988; and Clayton E. Cramer and

David B. Kopel, "'Shall Issue': The New Wave of Concealed-Handgun Permit Laws," *Tennessee Law Review* 62 (Spring 1995): 680–91.

19. Among those who made this comment to David Mustard and me were Bob Barnhart, Manager of the Intelligence/Concealed Handgun United of Multnomah County, Oregon; Mike Woodward, of the Oregon Law Enforcement Data System; Joe Vincent of the Washington Department of Licensing Firearms Unit; Alan Krug, who provided us with the Pennsylvania Permit data; and Susan Harrell of the Florida Department of State Concealed Weapons Division. Evidence for this point with respect to Virginia was obtained from Eric Lipton, "Virginians Get Ready to Conceal Arms: State's New Weapon Law Brings a Flood of Inquiries," *Washington Post,* June 28, 1995, p. A1, who notes that "analysts say the new law, which drops the requirement that prospective gun carriers show a 'demonstrated need' to be armed, likely won't make much of a difference in rural areas, where judges have long issued permits to most people who applied for them. But in urban areas such as Northern Virginia—where judges granted few permits because few residents could justify a need for them—the number of concealed weapon permits issued is expected to soar. In Fairfax, for example, a county of more than 850,000 people, only 10 now have permits." See also Cramer and Kopel, "New Wave of Concealed-Handgun Permit Laws," pp. 679–758.

20. For example, see Kleck and Patterson, "Impact of Gun Control and Gun-Ownership Levels on Violence Rates."

21. The sex ratios in Alaska are quite large. For example, white males outnumber white females in the 20–29 age range by 19 percent, while the difference for the United States as a whole is 3 percent. The same ratio for the 30–39 age range is 12 percent in Alaska and 1 percent nationally. Yet the greatest differences occur for blacks. In Alaska black males outnumber black females in the 20–29 age range by 40 percent, while in the rest of the United States the reverse is true, with black females outnumbering (nonincarcerated) black males by 7 percent.

22. While no reliable data are available on this question, a couple of polls indicate that the number of otherwise law-abiding citizens who carry concealed handguns may be substantial. The results of a recent Oklahoma poll showed that up to 6 percent of Oklahoma residents already carry concealed handguns either on their persons or in their cars; see Michael Smith, "Many Permits to Go to Lawbreakers," *Tulsa World,* May 5, 1996, p. A15. The margin of error in the poll was 3.5 percent, which is substantial, given the small value with which this error is compared.

23. Sam Peltzman, "The Effects of Automobile Safety Regulation," *Journal of Political Economy* 83 (Aug. 1975): 677–725.

24. Steven Peterson, George Hoffer, and Edward Millner, "Are Drivers of Air-Bag-Equipped Cars More Aggressive? A Test of the Offsetting-Behavior Hypothesis," *Journal of Law and Economics* 38 (Oct. 1995): 251–64.

25. Kieran Murray, "NRA Taps into Anger of Mid-American Gunlovers," *Reuters Newswire,* dateline Dallas, Apr. 21, 1996.

26. At least since the work of Isaac Ehrlich, economists have also realized that potential biases exist from using the offense rate as both the variable that one is seeking to explain and as the denominator in determining the arrest rate. To see this, suppose that mistakes are made in measuring the crime rate (and mistakes are certainly made) because of recording inaccuracies or simply because citizens may change the rates at which they report crime over time. Accidentally recording a crime rate that is too high will result in our recording an arrest rate that is too low, since the arrest rate is the total number of arrests divided by the total number of crimes. The converse is also true: When too low a crime rate is recorded, the arrest rate that we observe will be too high. Obviously, this problem will make it appear that a negative relationship exists between arrest rates and crime even if no relationship exists. There is also the concern that increasing crime rates may lower arrest

rates if the same resources are being asked to do more work. See Isaac Ehrlich, "Participation in Illegitimate Activities: A Theoretical and Empirical Investigation," *Journal of Political Economy* 81 (1973): 548–53.

CHAPTER THREE

1. The 1988 poll's margin of error was 1.1 percent, while that of the 1996 poll was 2.2 percent.

2. In order to obtain the rate at which people in the general population owned guns, I weighted the respondents' answers to give less weight to groups that were overrepresented among voters compared to their share in the overall population, and to give greater weight to those groups that were underrepresented. Twenty-four categories of personal characteristics were used to compute these weightings: white males and females, and black males and females, aged 18–29; neither black nor white males and females 18–29; white males and females, and black males and females 30–44; neither black nor white males and females 30–44; white males and females, and black males and females 45–59; neither black nor white males and females 45–59; white males and females, and black males and females over 59; neither black nor white males and females over 59.

3. This argument has been made explicitly in the press many times. See, for example, Scott Baldauf, "As Crime Shrinks, Security Is Still Growth Industry," *Christian Science Monitor,* Oct. 2, 1996, p. 1.

4. Alix M. Freedman, "Tinier, Deadlier Pocket Pistols Are in Vogue," *Wall Street Journal,* Sept. 12, 1996, P. B1.

5. The primary concern here is that letting people check those parts of a list that apply will result in fewer positive responses than asking people to answer individual questions about each item. As one way of checking the importance of this concern, I examined whether other questions that changed in a similar way between the two polls experienced a change in the same direction as that shown for gun ownership. The two questions that I looked at—regarding marriage and whether children less than 18 lived with the respondent—moved in the opposite direction. Relatively more people indicated these responses in the 1988 poll when the questions were presented in a list than did so when they were presented with separate questions about these characteristics. I have also done extensive research using other questions involving marriage and children under 18 living with the respondent that were part of a "check as many as apply" question. That research provides extremely strong evidence that these questions were answered consistently between 1988 and 1996. See John R. Lott, Jr. and Larry W. Kenny, "How Dramatically Did Women's Suffrage Change the Size and Scope of Government?" University of Chicago School of Law working paper (1997). The relative differences in gun ownership across groups is also consistent with recent work using other polls by Edward Glaeser and Spencer Glendon, "Who Owns Guns?" *American Economic Review* 88 (May 1998).

The empirical work that will be done later will allow us to adjust for the changes in the reported level of gun ownership that might result from the change in this question.

6. I appreciate Tom Smith's taking the time to talk to me about these issues on May 30, 1997.

7. Gun owners within each of the twenty-four categories listed in note 2 above may have particular characteristics that cause them to vote at rates that differ from the rates at which other people vote. One would hope that some of that difference would be accounted for in the detailed demographic characteristics, but there is a good chance that this may not occur. Several attempts were made to see how large this effect might be by asking, for example, whether gun owners were more or less likely not to have voted in previous elections. This question has also been broken down to account for those who are old enough to have voted previously. For 1988, the difference in gun ownership between those who were voting for the first time and those who had voted previously was 3 percent (23.2 percent of those vot-

ing for the first time and 26.2 percent of those who were not owned guns). Limiting this question to people who were 30 years of age or older produced an even smaller difference: 28.9 percent of first-time voters owned guns versus 27.5 percent of those who had voted previously. Similarly, for the question of whether voters in 1988 had also voted in 1984, the difference was also 3 percent (23 percent of those who did not vote in 1984 and 26.4 percent of those who did owned guns).

Because most people voted, a 13 percent increase in the proportion of the general population owning guns would require an even greater drop in gun ownership among those who didn't vote in order for gun ownership to have remained constant. For some groups, such as women, for whom gun ownership among voters increased by over 70 percent, the increase is so large and the percent of women voting so high that an 80 percent drop in gun ownership among nonvoting women would have been required for gun ownership among women to have remained constant.

8. Indeed, making this adjustment produces a number that is much closer to that found in other polls of the general population, such as the National Opinion Research Center's 1996 National Gun-Policy Survey, which finds that 42 percent of the general adult population owns guns.

9. The data are available from the ICPSR at the University of Michigan as ICPSR 4181. The National Election Pool General Election Exit Polls, 2004, National Data National Election Pool, Edison Media Research Mitofsky International, March 2005.

10. Richard Morin, "Surveying the Damage," *Washington Post*, November 21, 2004, p. B1. Evidence that the underlying vote data did not involve fraud is provided by Kevin Hassett and John R. Lott, Jr., "Voting Technology and Voter Fraud: A Test Using Exit Poll Data," American Enterprise Institute working paper, February 2005.

11. Evaluation of Edison/Mitofsky Election System 2004 prepared by Edison Media Research and Mitofsky International for the National Election Pool, January 19, 2005 (http:// abcnews.go.com/images/Politics/EvaluationofEdisonMitofskyElectionSystem.pdf).

12. The initial exit poll survey results that were reported on election day used a weighting that "for the national exit poll overstated the proportion of women in the electorate." That problem was fixed in the weightings that were released after that date. Weightings for the share of voters who were Republican or conservative could also have been introduced to rectify the skewness in the survey, but this was not done.

13. The previous peak in murder rates occurred at the end of Prohibition in the early 1930s, with the peak of 9.7 murders per 100,000 people being reached in 1933. The 1996 murder rate of 7.3 murders per 100,000 people seems tame by comparison. Indeed many people, such as Milton Friedman, have argued that much of the change in murder rates over time has been driven by the country's war on drugs and its earlier war on alcohol. Even the gradual increase in murder rates leading up to the Nineteenth Amendment's adoption in 1991 corresponds with passage of individual state laws. Kansas, Maine, and North Dakota enacted prohibition laws between 1880 and 1890. Five states enacted prohibition in 1907–1909, followed by twelve more between 1912 and 1915 and another twelve between 1916 and 1918. Obviously, all this points to the importance of other factors in the murder rate, and that is part of the reason why I include a measure of drug prices in my estimates to explain why crime rates change over time. See Ernest H. Cherrington, *The Evolution of Prohibition in the United States of America* (Westerville, OH: Tem-Press, 1920); Edward B. Dunford, *The History of the Temperance Movement* (Washington, DC: Tem-Press, 1943); D. Leigh Colvin, *Prohibition in the United States,* (New York: George H. Doran, 1926); as well as state statutes (as a check).

14. While I will follow Cramer and Kopel's definition of what constitutes a "shall-issue" or a "do-issue" state (see "'Shall Issue': The New Wave of Concealed-Handgun Permit Laws," *Tennessee Law Review* 62 [Spring 1995]), one commentator has suggested that it is not appropriate to include Maine in these categories (Stephen P. Teret, "Critical Comments on a Paper by Lott and Mustard," School of Hygiene and Public Health, Johns Hopkins University,

mimeo, Aug. 7, 1996). Neither defining Maine so that the "shall-issue" dummy equals zero nor removing Maine from the data set alters the findings shown in this book.

15. While the intent of the 1988 legislation in Virginia was clearly to institute a "shall-issue" law, the law was not equally implemented in all counties in the state. To deal with this problem, I reran the regressions reported in this paper with the "shall-issue" dummy equal to both 1 and 0 for Virginia.

16. I rely on Cramer and Kopel for this list of states. Some states, known as "do-issue" states, are also included in Cramer and Kopel's list of "shall-issue" states, though these authors argue that for all practical purposes these two groups of states are identical. See Cramer and Kopel, "New Wave of Concealed-Handgun Permit Laws," pp. 679–91.

17. The Oregon counties providing permit data were Benton, Clackamas, Columbia, Coos, Curry, Deschutes, Douglas, Gilliam, Hood River, Jackson, Jefferson, Josephine, Klamath, Lane, Lincoln, Linn, Malheur, Marion, Morrow, Multnomah, Polk, Tillamook, Umatilla, Washington and Yamhill.

18. In economics jargon I would say that I am interacting the sentence length with year-dummy variables.

19. These variables are referred to as county fixed-effects, where a separate dummy variable is set equal to 1 for each individual county.

20. See appendix 4 for the list and summary statistics.

21. For example, see James Q. Wilson and Richard J. Herrnstein, *Crime and Human Nature* (New York: Simon and Schuster, 1985), pp. 126–47.

22. However, the effect of an unusually large percentage of young males in the population may be mitigated because those most vulnerable to crime may be more likely to take actions to protect themselves. Depending upon how responsive victims are to these threats, the coefficient for a variable like the percent of young males in the population could be zero even when the group in question poses a large criminal threat.

23. Edward L. Glaeser and Bruce Sacerdote, "Why Is There More Crime in Cities?" Harvard University working paper, Nov. 14, 1995.

24. For a discussion of the relationship between income and crime, see John R. Lott, Jr., "A Transaction-Costs Explanation for Why the Poor Are More Likely to Commit Crime" *Journal of Legal Studies* 19 (Jan. 1990): 243–45.

25. A brief survey of the laws, excluding the changes in the rules regarding permits, reveals the following: Alabama made no significant changes in these laws during the period. Connecticut law gradually changed its wording from "criminal use" to "criminal possession" from 1986 to 1994. Florida has the most extensive description of penalties; the same basic law (790.161) persists throughout the years. An additional law (790.07) appeared only in 1986. In Georgia, a law (16-11-106) that does not appear in the 1986 edition appears in the 1989 and 1994 editions. The law involves possession of a firearm during commission of a crime and specifies the associated penalties. Because this legal change might have occurred at the same time as the 1989 changes in the rules regarding permits, I used a Lexis search to check the legislative history of 16-11-106 and found that the laws were last changed in 1987, two years before the permit rules were changed (*Official Code of Georgia, Annotated,* at 16-11-106 [1996]). Idaho has made no significant changes over time. In Indiana and Maine no significant changes occurred in these laws during the period. In Mississippi, Law 97-37-1 talks explicitly about penalties. It appears in the 1986 version but not in the 1989 or the 1994 versions. Montana enacted some changes in punishments related to unauthorized carrying of concealed weapons, but no changes in the punishment for using a weapon in a crime. New Hampshire, North Dakota, Oregon, Pennsylvania, and Washington made no significant changes in these laws during period. In South Dakota, Law 22-14-13, which specifies penalties for commission of a felony while armed, appears in 1986 but not 1989. In Vermont, Section 4005, which outlines the penalties for carrying a gun when committing a felony, appears in

1986 but not in 1989 or 1994. Virginia and Washington made no significant changes in these laws during the period. West Virginia had Law 67-7-12 on the books in 1994, but not in the earlier versions. It involves punishment for endangerment with firearms. Removing Georgia from the sample, which was the only state that enacted changes in its gun laws near the year that the "shall-issue" law went into affect, eliminates the chance that the other changes in gun laws might affect my results and does not appreciably alter those results.

26. Thomas B. Marvell and Carlisle E. Moody, "The Impact of Enhanced Prison Terms for Felonies Committed with Guns," *Criminology* 33 (May 1995): 247, 258–61.

27. Marvell and Moody's findings (see note 22 above) show that the shortest time period between these sentencing enhancements and changes in concealed-weapon laws is seven years (Pennsylvania). Twenty-six states passed their enhancement laws prior to the beginning of my sample period, and only four states passed such laws after 1981. Maine, which implemented its concealed-handgun law in 1985, passed its sentencing-enhancement laws in 1971.

28. The states that had waiting periods prior to the beginning of the sample are Alabama, California, Connecticut, Illinois, Maryland, Minnesota, New Jersey, North Carolina, Pennsylvania, Rhode Island, South Dakota, Washington, and Wisconsin. The District of Columbia also had a waiting period prior to the beginning of my sample. The states that adopted this rule during the sample period are Hawaii, Indiana, Iowa, Missouri, Oregon, and Virginia.

CHAPTER FOUR

1. More precisely, it is the percentage of a one-standard-deviation change in the crime rate that can be explained by a one-standard-deviation change in the endogenous variable.

2. All the results are reported for the higher threshold required with a two-tailed t-test.

3. One possible concern with these initial results arises from my use of an aggregate public-policy variable (state right-to-carry laws) on county-level data. See Bruce C. Greenwald, "A General Analysis of the Bias in the Estimated Standard Errors of Least Squares Coefficients," *Journal of Econometrics* 22 (Aug. 1983): 323–38; and Brent R. Moulton, "An Illustration of a Pitfall in Estimating the Effects of Aggregate Variables on Micro Units," *Review of Economics and Statistics* 72 (1990): 334. Moulton writes, "If disturbances are correlated within the groupings that are used to merge aggregate with micro data, however, then even small levels of correlation can cause the standard errors from the ordinary least squares (OLS) to be seriously biased downward." Yet this should not really be a concern here because of my use of dummy variables for all the counties, which is equivalent to using state dummies as well as county dummies for all but one of the counties within each state. Using these dummy variables thus allows us to control for any disturbances that are correlated within any individual state. The regressions discussed in table 4.2 reestimate the specifications shown in table 4.1 but also include state dummies that are interacted with a time trend. This should thus not only control for any disturbances that are correlated with the states, but also for any disturbances that are correlated within a state over time. Finally, while right-to-carry laws are almost always statewide laws, there is one exception. Pennsylvania partially exempted its largest county (Philadelphia) from the law when it was passed in 1989, and it remained exempt from the law during the rest of the sample period. However, permits granted in the counties surrounding Philadelphia were valid for use in the city.

4. However, the increase in the number of property crimes is larger than the decrease in the number of robberies.

5. While I adopt the classifications used by Cramer and Kopel in "'Shall Issue': The New Wave of Concealed-Handgun Permit Laws," Tennessee Law Review 62 (Spring 1995), some are more convinced by other classifications of states (for example, see Doug Weil, "Response to John Lott's Study on the Impact of 'Carry-Concealed' Laws on Crime Rates," *U.S. Newswire*, Aug. 8, 1996; and Stephen P. Teret, "Critical Comments on a Paper by Lott and Mustard," School

of Hygiene and Public Health, Johns Hopkins University, mimeo, Aug. 7, 1996). Setting the "shall-issue" dummy for Maine to zero and rerunning the regressions shown in table 4.1 results in the "shall-issue" coefficient equaling –3% for violent crimes, –8% for murder, –6% for rape, –4.5% for aggravated assault, –1% for robbery, 3% for property crimes, 8.1% for automobile theft, 0.4% for burglary, and 3% for larceny. Similarly, setting the "shall-issue" dummy for Virginia to zero results in the "shall-issue" coefficient equaling –4% for violent crimes, –9% for murder, –5% for rape, –5% for aggravated assault, –0.11% for robbery, 3% for property crimes, 9% for automobile theft, 2% for burglary, and 3% for larceny. As a final test, dropping both Maine and Virginia from the data set results in the "shall-issue" coefficient equaling –2% for violent crimes, –10% for murder, –6% for rape, –3% for aggravated assault, 0.6% for robbery, 3.6% for property crimes, 10% for automobile theft, 2% for burglary, and 4% for larceny.

6. This information is obtained from Mortality Detail Records provided by the U.S. Department of Health and Human Services.

7. This assumption is implausible for many reasons. One reason is that accidental handgun deaths occur in states without concealed-handgun laws.

8. Given the possible relationship between drug prices and crime, I reran the regressions in table 4.1 and included an additional variable for cocaine prices. One argument linking drug prices and crime is that if the demand for drugs is inelastic and if people commit crimes in order to finance their habits, higher drug prices might lead to increased levels of crime. Using the Drug Enforcement Administration's STRIDE data set from 1977 to 1992 (with the exceptions of 1988 and 1989), Michael Grossman, Frank J. Chaloupka, and Charles C. Brown, ("The Demand for Cocaine by Young Adults: A Rational Addiction Approach," NBER working paper, July 1996), estimate the price of cocaine as a function of its purity, weight, year dummies, year dummies interacted with eight regional dummies, and individual city dummies. There are two problems with this measure of predicted prices: (1) it removes observations during a couple of important years during which changes were occurring in concealed-handgun laws, and (2) the predicted values that I obtained ignored the city-level observations. The reduced number of observations provides an important reason why I do not include this variable in the regressions shown in table 4. 1. However, the primary impact of including this new variable is to make the "shall-issue" coefficients in the violent-crime regressions even more negative and more significant (for example, the coefficient for the violent-crime regression becomes –7.5%, –10% for the murder regression, –7.7% for rape, and –11% for aggravated assault, with all of them significant at more than the 0.01 level). Only for the burglary regression does the "shall-issue" coefficient change appreciably: it becomes negative and insignificant. The variable for drug prices itself is negatively related to murders and rapes and positively and significantly related, at least at the 0.01 level for a one-tailed t-test, to all the other categories of crime. I would like to thank Michael Grossman for providing me with the original regressions on drug prices from his paper.

9. In contrast, if we had instead inquired what difference it would make in crime rates if either all states or no states adopted right-to-carry concealed-handgun laws, the case of all states adopting concealed-handgun laws would have produced 2,000 fewer murders; 5,700 fewer rapes; 79,000 fewer aggravated assaults; and 14,900 fewer robberies. In contrast, property crimes would have risen by 336,410.

10. Ted R. Miller, Mark A. Cohen, and Brian Wiersema, *Victim Costs and Consequences: A New Look* (Washington, DC: National Institute of Justice, Feb. 1996).

11. See Sam Peltzman, "The Effects of Automobile Safety Regulation," *Journal of Political Economy* 83 (Aug. 1975): 677–725.

12. To be more precise, a one-standard-deviation change in the probability of arrest accounts for 3 to 11 percent of a one-standard-deviation change in the various crime rates.

13. Translating this into statistical terms, a one-standard-deviation change in the percentage of the population that is black, male, and between 10 and 19 years of age explains 22 percent of the ups and downs in the crime rate.

14. This is particularly observed when there are more black females between the ages of 20 and 39, more white females between the ages of 10 and 39 and over 65, and females of other races between 20 and 29.

15. In other words, the second number shows how a one standard-deviation change in an explanatory variable explains a certain percent of a one-standard-deviation change in the various crime rates.

16. While I believe that such variables as the arrest rate should be included in any regressions on crime, one concern with the results reported in the various tables is over whether the relationship between the "shall-issue" variable and the crime rates occurs even when all the other variables are not controlled for. Using weighted least squares and reporting only the "shall-issue" coefficients, I estimated the following regression coefficients.

How do average crime rates differ among states with and without nondiscretionary laws?

Crime rates	Crime rates in states with nondiscretionary concealed-handgun laws compared to those without the law (regressing the crime rate only on the variable for the law)	Crime rates in states with nondiscretionary concealed-handgun laws compared to those without the law after adjusting for national trends (regressing the crime rate on the variable for the law and year-dummy variables)
Violent crimes	−40%	−57%
Murder	−48	−52
Rape	−16	−28
Aggravated assault	−38	−57
Robbery	−62	−75
Property crime	−17	−20
Auto theft	−31	−43
Burglary	−28	−24
Larceny	−11	−15

Note: The only factors included are the presence of the law and/or year-specific effects. All these differences are statistically significant at least at the 1 percent level for a two-tailed *t*-test. To calculate these percentages, I used the approximation 100 [exp(coefficient) − 1].

17. The time-trend variable ranges from 1 to 16: for the first year in the sample, it equals 1; for the last year, it is 16.

18. Other differences arise in the other control variables, such as those relating to the portion of the population of a certain race, sex, and age. For example, the percent of black males in the population between 10 and 19 is no longer statistically significant.

19. If the task instead had been to determine the difference in crime rates when either all states or no states adopt the right-to-carry handgun laws, the case of all states adopting concealed-handgun laws would have produced 2,048 fewer murders, 6,618 fewer rapes, 129,114 fewer aggravated assaults, and 86,459 fewer robberies. Non-arson property crimes also would have fallen by 511,940.

20. Generally, aggregation is frowned on in statistics anyway, as it reduces the amount of information yielded by the data set. Lumping data together into a group cannot yield any new information that did not exist before; it only reduces the richness of the data.

21. Eric Rasmusen, "Stigma and Self-Fulfilling Expectations of Criminality," *Journal of Law and Economics* 39 (Oct. 1996): 519–44.

22. In January 1996, women held 118,728 permits in Washington and 17,930 permits in Oregon. The time-series data available for Oregon during the sample period even indicate that 17.6 percent of all permit holders were women in 1991. The Washington state data were obtained from Joe Vincent of the Department of Licensing Firearms Unit in Olympia,

Washington. The Oregon state data were obtained from Mike Woodward of the Law Enforcement Data System, Department of State Police, Salem, Oregon. Recent evidence from Texas indicates that about 28 percent of applicants were women ("NRA poll: Sales people No. 1 for Permit Applications," *Dallas Morning News,* Apr. 19, 1996, p. 32A).

23. For an interesting discussion of the benefits to women of owning guns, see Paxton Quigley, *Armed and Female* (New York: E. P. Dutton, 1989).

24. Unpublished information obtained by Kleck and Gertz in their 1995 National Self-Defense Survey implies that women were as likely as men to use handguns in self-defense in or near their homes (defined as in the yard, carport, apartment hall, street adjacent to home, detached garage, etc.), but that women were less than half as likely to use a gun in self-defense away from home. See Gary Kleck and Marc Gertz, "Armed Resistance to Crime: The Prevalence and Nature of Self-Defense with a Gun," *Journal of Criminal Law and Criminology* 86 (Fall 1995): 249–87.

25. Counties with real personal income of about $15,000 in real 1983 dollars experienced 8 percent drops in murder, while mean-income counties experienced a 5.5 percent drop.

26. Lori Montgomery, "More Blacks Say Guns Are Answer to Urban Violence," *Houston Chronicle,* July 9, 1995, p. A1. This article argues that while the opposition to guns in the black community is strong, more people are coming to understand the benefits of self-protection.

27. For an excellent overview of the role of race in gun control, see Robert J. Cottrol and Raymond T. Diamond, "The Second Amendment: Toward an Afro-Americanist Reconsideration," *Georgetown Law Review* 80 (Dec. 1991): 309.

28. See William Van Alstyne, "The Second Amendment Right to Arms," *Duke Law Review* 43 (Apr. 1994): 1236–55. In slave states prior to the Civil War, the freedoms guaranteed under the Bill of Rights were regularly restricted by states because of the fear that free reign might lead to an insurrection. As Akhil Reed Amar writes, "In a society that saw itself under siege after Nat Turner's rebellion, access to firearms had to be strictly restricted, especially to free blacks." See Akhil Reed Amar, "The Bill of Rights and the Fourteenth Amendment," *Yale Law Journal* 101 (Apr. 1992): 1193.

29. *Associated Press Newswire,* May 9, 1997, 4:37 P.M. EDT. As the *Washington Times* recently noted, this story "comes at an awkward time for the administration, since President Clinton has spent the last week or two berating Republicans for failing to include in anti-crime legislation a provision requiring that child safety locks be sold with guns to keep children from hurting themselves" (Editorial, "The Story of a Gun and a Kid," *Washington Times,* May 22, 1997, p. A18).

30. The conversation took place on March 18, 1997, though regrettably I have misplaced the note containing the representative's name.

31. John Carpenter, "Six Other States Have Same Law," *Chicago Sun-Times,* Mar. 11, 1997, p. 8.

32. John J. Dilulio, Jr., "The Question of Black Crime," *The Public Interest* 117 (Fall 1994): 3–24. Similar concerns about the inability of minorities to rely on the police was also expressed to me by Assemblyman Rod Wright (D-Los Angeles) during testimony before the California Assembly's Public Safety Committee on November 18, 1997.

33. One additional minor change is made in two of the earlier specifications. In order to avoid any artificial collinearity either between violent crime and robbery or between property crimes and burglary, violent crimes net of robbery and property crimes net of burglary are used as the endogenous variables when robbery or burglary are controlled for.

34. The Pearson correlation coefficient between robbery and the other crime categories ranges between .49 and .80, and all are so statistically significant that a negative correlation would only appear randomly once out of every ten thousand times. For burglary, the correlations range from 0.45 to 0.68, and they are also equally statistically significant.

35. All the results in tables 4.1 and 4.4 as well as the regressions related to both parts of figure 4.1 were reestimated to deal with the concerns raised in chapter 3 over the "noise" in arrest rates arising from the timing of offenses and arrests and the possibility of multiple

offenders. I reran all the regressions in this section by limiting the sample to those counties with populations over 10,000, over 100,000, and then over 200,000 people. The more the sample was restricted to larger-population counties, the stronger and more statistically significant was the relationship between concealed-handgun laws and the previously reported effects on crime. This is consistent with the evidence reported in figure 4. 1. The arrest-rate results also tended to be stronger and more significant. I further reestimated all the regressions by redefining the arrest rate as the number of arrests over the last three years divided by the total number of offenses over the last three years. Despite the reduced sample size, the results remained similar to those already reported.

36. More formally, by using restricted least squares, we can test whether constraining the coefficients for the period before the law produces results that yield the same pattern after the passage of the law. Using both the time-trend and the time-trend-squared relationships, the F-tests reject the hypothesis that the before and after relationships are the same, at least at the 10 percent level, for all the crime categories except aggravated assault and larceny, for which the F-tests are only significant at the 20 percent level. Using only the time-trend relationship, the F-tests reject the hypothesis in all the cases.

37. The main exception was West Virginia, which showed large drops in murder but not in other crime categories.

38. See Thomas B. Marvell and Carlisle E. Moody, "The Impact of Enhanced Prison Terms for Felonies Committed with Guns," *Criminology* 33 (May 1995): 259–60.

39. I should note, however, that the "nondiscretionary" coefficients for robbery in the county-level regressions and for property crimes using the state levels are no longer statistically significant.

40. Toni Heinzl, "Police Groups Oppose Concealed-Weapons Bill," *Omaha World-Herald,* Mar. 18, 1997, p. 9SF.

41. A simple dummy variable is used for whether the limit was 18 or 21 years of age.

42. Here is one example: "Mrs. Elmasri, a Wisconsin woman whose estranged husband had threatened her and her children, called a firearms instructor for advice on how to buy a gun for self-defense. She was advised that, under Wisconsin's progressive handgun law, she would have to wait 48 hours so that the police could perform the required background check.

"Twenty-four hours later, . . . Mrs. Elmasri's husband murdered the defenseless woman and her two children" (William P. Cheshire, "Gun Laws No Answer for Crime," *Arizona Republic,* Jan. 10, 1993, p. C1.) Other examples can be found in David B. Kopel, "Background Checks and Waiting Periods," in *Guns: Who Should Have Them,* ed. David B. Kopel (Amherst, NY: Prometheus Books, 1995.) Other examples tell of women who successfully evaded these restrictions to obtain guns.

In September 1990, mail carrier Catherine Latta of Charlotte, N. C, went to the police to obtain permission to buy a handgun. Her ex-boyfriend had previously robbed her, assaulted her several times, and raped her. The clerk at the sheriff's office informed her that processing a gun permit would take two to four weeks. "I told her I'd be dead by then," Latta recalled.

That afternoon, Latta bought an illegal $20 semiautomatic pistol on the street. Five hours later, her ex-boyfriend attacked her outside her house. She shot him dead. The county prosecutor decided not to prosecute Latta for either the self-defense homicide or the illegal gun. (Quoted from David B. Kopel, "Guns and Crime: Does Restricting Firearms Really Reduce Violence?" *San Diego Union-Tribune,* May 9, 1993, p. G4.)

For another example where a woman's ability to defend herself would have been impaired by a waiting period, see "Waiting Period Law Might Have Cost Mother's Life," *USA Today,* May 27, 1994, p. 10A.

43. Quoted in David Armstrong, "Cities' Crime Moves to Suburbs," *Boston Globe,* May 19, 1997, pp. 1 and B6.

CHAPTER FIVE

1. While county-level data were provided in the *Supplementary Homicide Reports,* matching these county observations with those used in the *Uniform Crime Reports* proved unusually difficult. A unique county identifier was used in the *Supplementary Homicide Reports* that was not consistent across years. In addition, some caution is necessary in using both the Mortality Detail Records and the *Supplementary Homicide Reports,* since the murder rates reported in both sources have relatively low correlations of less than .7 with the murder rates reported in the *Uniform Crime Reports.* This is especially surprising for the supplementary reports, which are derived from the *Uniform Crime Reports.* See U.S. Department of Justice, FBI staff, *Uniform Crime Reports* (Washington, DC: U.S. Govt. Printing Office) for the years 1977 to 1992.

2. Indeed, the average age of permit holders is frequently in the mid- to late forties (see, for example, "NRA poll: Salespeople No. 1 for Permit Applications," *Dallas Morning News,* Apr. 19, 1996, p. 32A.) In Kentucky the average age of permit holders is about fifty (see Terry Flynn, "Gun-Toting Kentuckians Hold Their Fire," *Cincinnati Enquirer,* June 16, 1997, p. Al).

3. This is the significance for a two-tailed t-test.

4. Similar breakdowns for deaths and injuries are explored in much more depth in a paper that I have written with William Landes; see William Landes and John R. Lott, Jr., "Mass Public Shootings, Bombings, and Right-to-Carry Concealed-Handgun Laws," University of Chicago working paper, 1997.

5. A second change was also made. Because of the large number of observations noting no deaths or injuries from mass public shootings in a given year, I used a statistical technique known as Tobit that is particularly well suited to this situation.

6. The results shown below provide the estimates for the simple linear time trends before and after the adoption of the law. They demonstrate that for each year leading up to the passage of the law, total deaths or injuries from mass public shootings rose by 1.5 more per 10 million people and that after the passage of the law, total deaths or injuries fell by 4 more per 10 million people. The difference in these two trends is statistically significant at the 1 percent level for a two-tailed t-test. It is interesting to note that higher murder arrest rates, although they deter murderers, do not seem to deter perpetrators of mass public shootings.

Linear time trends for deaths and injuries from mass public shootings before and after adoption of concealed-handgun law

	Total deaths and injuries per 100,000 population
Average annual change for years after adoption of the law	−0.04***
Average annual change for years before adoption of the law	0.015***
Arrest rate for murder	−0.0003

***Statistically significant at least at the 10 percent level for a two-tailed *t*-test
Note: numbers are negative; years furthest beyond adoption are the largest

7. See appendix 4 for the means and standard deviations of the variables used in these regressions.

8. Again, this is stating that a one-standard-deviation change in arrest rates explains more than 15 percent of a one-standard-deviation change in crime rates.

9. Running the regressions for all Pennsylvania counties (not just those with more than 200,000 people) produced similar signs for the coefficient for the change in concealed-

handgun permits, though the coefficients were no longer statistically significant for violent crimes, rape, and aggravated assault. Alan Krug, who provided us with the Pennsylvania handgun-permit data, told us that one reason for the large increase in concealed-handgun permits in some rural counties was that people used the guns for hunting. He told us that the number of permits issued in these low-population, rural counties tended to increase most sharply in the fall around hunting season. If people were in fact getting large numbers of permits in low-population counties (which already have extremely low crime rates) for some reason other than crime, it would be more difficult to pick up the deterrent effect of concealed handguns on crime that was occurring in the larger counties.

10. A one-standard-deviation change in conviction rates explains 4 to 20 percent of a one-standard-deviation change in the corresponding crime rates.

11. I reran these regressions using the natural logs of the arrest and conviction rates, and I consistently found statistically larger and even economically more important effects for the arrest rates than for the conviction rates.

12. For example, see Dan M. Kahan, "What Do Alternative Sanctions Mean?" *University of Chicago Law Review* 63 (1996): 591–653.

13. See John R. Lott, Jr., "The Effect of Conviction on the Legitimate Income of Criminals," *Economics Letters* 34 (Dec. 1990): 381–85; John R. Lott, Jr., "An Attempt at Measuring the Total Monetary Penalty from Drug Convictions: The Importance of an Individual's Reputation," *Journal of Legal Studies* 21 (Jan. 1992): 159–87; John R. Lott, Jr., "Do We Punish High-Income Criminals Too Heavily?" *Economic Inquiry* 30 (Oct. 1992): 583–608.

14. Put differently, six of the specifications imply that a one-standard-deviation change in the number of concealed-handgun permits explains at least 8 percent of a one-standard-deviation change in the corresponding crime rates.

15. Philip Heymann, a former deputy attorney general in the Clinton administration and currently a law professor at Harvard University, wrote, "None of this [the drop in crime rates] is the result of . . . the Brady Act (for most guns were never bought by youth from licensed gun dealers)." See "The Limits of Federal Crime-Fighting," *Washington Post,* Jan. 5, 1997, p. C7.

16. For a discussion of externalities (both benefits and costs) from crime, see Kermit Daniel and John R. Lott, Jr., "Should Criminal Penalties Include Third-Party Avoidance Costs?" *Journal of Legal Studies* 24 (June 1995): 523–34.

17. Alix M. Freedman, "Tinier, Deadlier Pocket Pistols Are in Vogue," *Wall Street Journal,* Sept. 12, 1996, pp. B1, B16.

18. One hundred and eighty-two million people lived in states without these laws in 1991, so the regressions would have also implied nine more accidental deaths from handguns in that year.

19. Given the very small number of accidental deaths from handguns in the United States, the rate of such deaths in the vast majority of counties is zero, and the last two columns of table 5.6 again use Tobit regressions to deal with this problem. Limitations in statistical packages, however, prevented me from being able to control for all the county dummies, and I opted to rerun these regressions with only state dummy variables.

20. For example, see Nicholas D. Kristof, "Guns: One Nation Bars, the Other Requires," *New York Times,* Mar. 10, 1996, sec. 4, p. 3. For some evidence on international gun ownership rates see Munday and Stevenson, *Guns and Violence* (1996): 30.

21. See Ian Ayres and Steven Levitt, "Measuring Positive Externalities from Unobservable Victim Precaution: An Empirical Analysis of Lojack" NBER working paper 5928 (1997); and John Donohue and Peter Siegelman, "Is the United States at the Optimal Rate of Crime?" *Journal of Legal Studies* 27 (Jan. 1998).

22. See notes 12 and 13 above.

CHAPTER SIX

1. Isaac Ehrlich, "Participation in Illegitimate Activities: A Theoretical and Empirical Investigation," *Journal of Political Economy* 81 (1973): 548–51. Except for the political variables, my specification accords fairly closely with at least the spirit of Ehrlich's specification, though some of my variables, like the demographic breakdowns, are much more detailed, and I have a few other measures that were not available to him.

2. See also Robert E. McCormick and Robert Tollison, "Crime on the Court," *Journal of Political Economy* 92 (Apr. 1984): 223–35, for a novel article testing the endogeneity of the "arrest rate" in the context of basketball penalties.

3. These last two variables are measured at the state level.

4. Phil Cook suggested this addition to me. In a sense, this is similar to Ehrlich's specification, except that the current crime rate is broken down into its lagged value and the change between the current and previous periods. See Ehrlich, "Participation in Illegitimate Activities," p. 557.

5. The natural logs of the rates for violent crime and property crime were used.

6. These estimates are known as two-stage least squares.

7. Ehrlich raises the concern that the types of two-stage, least-squares estimates discussed above might still be affected by spurious correlation if the measurement errors for the crime rate were serially correlated over time. To account for this, I reestimated the first-stage regressions predicting the arrest rate without the lagged crime rate, which made the estimated results for the nondiscretionary law dummy even more negative and more statistically significant than those already shown. See Ehrlich, "Participation in Illegitimate Activities" p. 552 n. 46.

8. Still another approach would be to estimate what are known as Tobit regressions, but unfortunately no statistical package is available that allows me both to control for all the different county dummy variables and to use the Tobit procedure.

CHAPTER SEVEN

1. The Violence Policy Center grew out of the National Coalition to Ban Handguns.

2. Douglas Weil, the research director for Handgun Control, Inc., has publicly disagreed with the claim that most gun-control advocates initially refused to comment on my study. In a letter to the *Washington Times*, Weil wrote,

> The *Washington Times* editorial ("Armed and Safer," Aug. 14) is misinformed and misguided. The *Times* falsely claims that gun-control proponents "initially refused to read" John Lott's and David Mustard's study of the impact of laws regarding the right to carry concealed guns, and that I attacked the researchers' motivations rather than challenge the study "on the merits." This charge is untrue.
>
> One look at the study would prove the *Times* wrong. On the title page of the study, several pro-gun-control researchers are credited for their comments "on the merits" of the study. Included in this list are David McDowall, a criminologist at the University of Maryland; Philip Cook, an economist at Duke University; and myself, research director for the Center to Prevent Handgun Violence.
>
> Upon reviewing the study, I found Mr. Lott's methodology to be seriously flawed. I told Mr. Lott that his study did not adequately control for the whole range of ways that state and local governments attempt to lower the crime rate. In Oregon, for example, the same legislation that made it easier to carry a concealed handgun included one of the toughest new handgun-purchase laws in the country—a 15-day waiting period and fingerprint-background check on all purchases. . . .
>
> I gladly shared my critique of this study with Mr. Lott and will now reiterate it here; as someone fully credentialed to evaluate Mr. Lott's and Mr. Mustard's work,

I would have recommended that the paper be rejected. (See Douglas Weil, "A Few Thoughts on the Study of Handgun Violence and Gun Control," *Washington Times,* Aug. 22, 1996, p. A16.)

While it is true that I thanked Mr. Weil in my paper for a comment that he made, his single comment was nothing like what his letter to the *Times* claimed. Before he explained his concerns to the press, he and I had no discussions about whether I had controlled for "ways that state and local governments attempt to lower the crime rate," possibly because my study not only controls for arrest and conviction rates, prison sentences, the number of police officers and police payroll, but also waiting periods and criminal penalties for using a gun in the commission of a crime.

Mr. Weil's sole comment to me came after two previous telephone calls over a month and a half in which Mr. Weil had said that he was too busy to give me any comments. His sole comment on August 1 was that he was upset that I had cited a study by a professor, Gary Kleck, with whom Weil disagreed. I attempted to meet this unusual but minor criticism by rewriting the relevant sentence on the first page in a further attempt to dispassionately state the alternative hypotheses.

Mr. Weil's claims are particularly difficult to understand in light of a conversation that I had with him on August 5. After hearing him discuss my paper on the news, I called him to say how surprised I was to hear about his telling the press that the paper was "fundamentally flawed" when the only comment that he had given me was on the reference to Kleck. Mr. Weil then immediately demanded to know whether it was true that I had thanked him for giving comments on the paper. He had heard from people in the news media who had seen a draft with his name listed among those thanked. (On August 1, I had added his name to the list of people who had given comments, and when the news of the paper suddenly broke on August 2 with the story in *USA Today,* it was this new version that had been faxed to the news media.) He wanted to know if I was trying to "embarrass" him with others in the gun-control community, and he insisted that he had not given me any comments. I said that I had only done it to be nice, and I mentioned the concern that he raised about the reference to Kleck. Weil then demanded that I "immediately remove [his] name" from the paper.

3. This was not my only experience with Ms. Glick. On August 8, 1996, six days after the events of August 2 described above, I appeared with her on MSNBC. After I tried to make an introductory statement setting out my findings, Ms. Glick attacked me for having my study funded by "gun manufacturers." She claimed that I was a "shill" for the gun manufactures and that it was important that I be properly identified as not being an objective academic. She also claimed that there were many serious problems with the paper. Referring to the study, she asserted that it was a fraud.

I responded by saying that these were very serious charges and that if she had some evidence, she should say what it was. I told her that I didn't think she had any such evidence, and that if she didn't, we should talk about the issues involved in the study.

At this point the moderator broke in and said to Ms. Glick that he agreed that these were very serious charges, and he asked her what evidence she had for her statements. Glick responded by saying that she had lots of evidence and that it was quite obvious to her that this study had been done to benefit gun manufacturers.

The moderator then asked her to comment further on her claim that there were serious problems with the study, and she stated that one only had to go to page 2 before finding a problem. Her concern was that I had used data for Florida that was a year and a half old. The moderator then asked her why this was a problem, since I couldn't be expected to use data that was, say, as recent as last week. Ms. Glick responded by saying that a lot of things could have changed since the most recent data were available. I then mentioned that I had obtained more recent data since the study had been written and that the pattern of people not using permitted guns improperly had held true from October 1987 to December 31, 1995.

A more recent exchange that I had with the Violence Policy Center's President, Josh Sugarmann, on MSNBC on February 24, 1997, involved the same accusations.

4. Douglas Weil, from the Center to Prevent Handgun Violence, a division of Handgun Control, wrote the following to the *Washington Times:* "Given that Mr. Lott has published 70 papers in peer-reviewed journals, it is curious that he has chosen a law review for his research on concealed-gun-carrying laws" (*Washington Times,* Aug. 22, 1996, p. A16).

5. Scott Harris, "To Build a Better America, Pack Heat," *Los Angeles Times,* Jan. 9, 1997, p. B1. In many ways, my study was indeed fortunate for the coverage that it received. It appears that no other study documenting the ability of guns to deter crime has received the same level of coverage. MediaWatch, a conservative organization tracking the content of television news programs, reviewed every gun-control story on four evening shows (ABC's *World News Tonight,* CBS's *Evening News,* CNN's *The World Today,* and NBC's *Nightly News*) and three morning broadcasts (ABC's *Good Morning America,* CBS's *This Morning,* and NBC's *Today*) from July 1, 1995 through June 30, 1997. MediaWatch categorized news stories in the following way: "Analysts counted the number of pro- and anti-gun-control statements by reporters in each story. Pieces with a disparity of greater than 1.5 to 1 were categorized as either for or against gun control. Stories closer than the ratio were deemed neutral. Among statements recorded as pro-gun control: violent crime occurs because of guns, not criminals, and gun control prevents crime. Categorized as arguments against gun control: gun control would not reduce crime; that criminals, not guns are the problem; Americans have a constitutional right to keep and bear arms; right-to-carry concealed weapons laws caused a drop in crime." MediaWatch concluded that "in 244 gun policy stories, those favoring gun control outnumbered stories opposing gun control by 157 to 10, or a ratio of almost 16 to 1 (77 were neutral). Talking heads were slightly more balanced: gun-control advocates outnumbered gun-rights spokesmen 165 to 110 (40 were neutral)." The news coverage of my study apparently accounted for 4 of the 10 "anti-gun control" news reports. (*Networks Use First Amendment Rights to Promote Opponents of Second Amendment Rights: Gun Rights Forces Outgunned on TV,* MediaWatch, July 1997.)

6. One of the unfortunate consequences of such attacks is the anger that they generate among the audience. For example, after Congressman Schumer's letter to the *Wall Street Journal,* I received dozens of angry telephone calls denouncing me for publishing my *Wall Street Journal* op-ed piece on concealed-handgun laws without first publicly stating that the research had been paid for by gun manufacturers. Other letters from the Violence Policy Center making these funding claims produced similar results.

Understandably, given the seriousness of the charges, this matter has been brought up by legislators in every state in which I have testified before the state legislature. Other politicians have also taken up these charges. Minnesota State Rep. Wes Skoglund (DFL-Minneapolis) provided one of the milder statements of these charges in the *Minneapolis Star Tribune* (Mar. 29, 1997, p. A13): "Betterman [a Minnesota state representative] uses a much-publicized study by John Lott Jr., of the University of Chicago, to back up her claims about the benefits of her radical gun-carry law. . . . But what no one has told you about Lott's study is that it has been found to be inaccurate and flawed. And Betterman didn't tell you that the study was funded by the Olin Foundation, which was created by the founder of Winchester Arms."

7. I telephoned Ms. Rand to ask her what evidence she had for her claim that the study was "the product of gun-industry funding" and reminded her that the public relations office at the University of Chicago had already explained the funding issue to her boss, Josh Sugarmann, but Ms. Rand hung up on me within about a minute.

8. Alex Rodriquez, "Gun Debate Flares; Study: Concealed Weapons Deter Crime," *Chicago Sun-Times,* Aug. 9, 1996, p. 2. Kotowski made his remark at a press conference organized by the Violence Policy Center, whose president, Josh Sugarmann, had been clearly told by the

press office at the University of Chicago on August 6 that these charges were not true (as the letter by William E. Simon shown later will explain). Catherine Behan in the press office spent an hour trying to explain to him how funding works at universities.

9. *Chicago Tribune,* Aug. 15, 1996.

10. "Study: Concealed Guns Deterring Violent Crime," *Austin American Statesman,* Aug. 9, 1996, p. A12.

11. The brief correction ran in the *Austin American Statesman,* Aug. 10, 1996.

12. As Mr. Simon mentions, one journalist who looked into these charges was Stephen Chapman of the *Chicago Tribune.* One part of his article that is particularly relevant follows:

> Another problem is that the [Olin] foundation didn't (1) choose Lott as a fellow, (2) give him money, or (3) approve his topic. It made a grant to the law school's law and economics program (one of many grants it makes to top universities around the country). A committee at the law school then awarded the fellowship to Lott, one of many applicants in a highly competitive process.
>
> Even the committee had nothing to do with his choice of topics. The fellowship was to allow Lott—a prolific scholar who has published some 75 academic articles— to do research on whatever subject he chose. . . .
>
> To accept their conspiracy theory, you have to believe the following: A company that derives a small share of its earnings from sporting ammunition somehow prevailed on an independent family foundation to funnel money to a scholar who was willing to risk his academic reputation (and, since he does not yet have tenure, his future employment) by fudging data to serve the interests of the firearms lobby— and one of the premier research universities in the world cooperated in the fraud. (See Stephen Chapman, "A Gun Study and a Conspiracy Theory," *Chicago Tribune,* Aug. 15, 1996, p. 31.)

13. A Gannett Newswire story quoted a spokeswoman for the Coalition to Stop Gun Violence who made similar statements: "But Katcher said the study . . . was funded by the Olin Foundation, which has strong ties to the gun industry. The study has 'been proven by a series of well-known, well-respected researchers to be inaccurate, false, junk science,' she said." (Dennis Camire, "Legislation before Congress Would Allow Concealed Weapons Nationwide," Gannett News Service, June 6, 1997.)

14. John R. Lott, Jr., "Should the Wealthy Be Able to 'Buy Justice'?" *Journal of Political Economy* 95 (Dec. 1987): 1307.

15. "Notebook," *The New Republic,* Apr. 14, 1997, p. 10.

16. After much effort, Randy was eventually able to get Cynthia Henry Thielen, a Hawaiian State Representative, to participate in the radio program.

17. Richard Morin, "Unconventional Wisdom: New Facts and Hot Stats from the Social Sciences," *Washington Post,* Mar. 23, 1997, p. C5.

18. It is surely not uncommon for academics to write letters to their local newspapers or to national or international publications, and indeed such letters were also written (see, for example, *The Economist,* Dec. 7, 1996, p. 8). But to track down the letters of everyday citizens to local newspapers and send replies is unusual.

19. The *Springfield State Journal-Register,* Nov. 26, 1996. Steven Teret, director of the Center for Gun Policy and Research wrote dozens of letters to newspapers across the country. They usually began with statements like the following: "Recently in a letter to the editor dated October 19, Kurt Amebury cited the work of two University of Chicago professors" (*Orlando Sentinel,* Nov. 16, 1996, p. A18); "Recently the *Dispatch* published a letter to the editor citing the work of two researchers" (*Columbus Dispatch,* Nov. 16, 1996, p. A11); "The *State Journal-Register* Oct. 28 published two letters citing research by the University of Chicago's John Lott" (*Springfield State Journal-Register,* Nov. 13, 1996, p. 6); or "A recent letter to the editor . . ." (*Buffalo News,* Nov. 17, 1996, p. H3). In late November, I asked Stephen Teret how many newspapers he had

sent letters to. He would not give me an exact count, but he said "dozens" and then listed the names of some major newspapers to which they had written. It is curious that none of the effort put into responding to my paper by the Center has gone into writing a comment for submission to the *Journal of Legal Studies*, where my original paper was published. Nor has the Center prepared a response for any other scholarly journal.

20. My opinion piece appeared in the *Omaha World-Herald*, Mar. 9, 1997, p. B9.

21. *Virginia Code Annotated*, § 18.2–3088 (1988).

22. This discussion relies on conversations with Clayton Cramer.

23. This point is similar to the "broken-window" argument made by Wilson and Kelling; see James Q. Wilson and George L. Kelling, "Making Neighborhoods Safe," *Atlantic Monthly*, Feb. 1989.

24. Some robberies also involve rape. While I am not taking a stand on whether rape or robbery is the primary motivation for the attack, there might be cases where robbery was the primary motive.

25. Information obtained from Kathy O'Connell at the Illinois Criminal Justice Information Authority.

26. For example, see Douglas Weil, "A Few Thoughts on the Study of Handgun Violence and Gun Control," *Washington Times*, Aug. 22, 1996, p. A16.

27. The durability of these initial false claims about Florida's crime rates can be seen in more recent popular publications. For example, William Tucker, writing in the *Weekly Standard*, claims that "Florida crime rates remained level from 1988 to 1990, then took a big dive. As with all social phenomena, though, it is difficult to isolate cause and effect." See William Tucker, "Maybe You Should Carry a Handgun," *Weekly Standard*, Dec. 16, 1996, p. 30.

28. In an attempt to facilitate Black's and Nagin's research, I provided them not only with all the data that they used but also computer files containing the regressions, in order to facilitate the replication of each of my regressions. It was thus very easy for them to try all possible permutations of my regressions, doing such things as excluding one state at a time or excluding data based on other criteria.

29. Dan Black and Dan Nagin, "Do 'Right-to-Carry' Laws Deter Violent Crime?" Carnegie-Mellon University working paper, Dec. 18, 1996, p. 5.

30. In addition, because the regressions use individual county dummy variables, so that they are really measuring changes in crime rates relative to each county's mean, one need not be concerned with the possibility that the average crime rates for the years that are farthest beyond the adoption of the concealed-handgun laws are being pulled down by relatively low crime rates in some states.

31. Ian Ayres and Steven Levitt, "Measuring Positive Externalities from Unobservable Victim Precaution: An Empirical Analysis of Lojack," NBER working paper 5928 (1997). The main issue with their empirical estimates, however, is whether they might be overestimating the impact from Lojack because they do not control for any other responses to higher auto-theft rates. For example, while higher auto-theft rates might trigger implementation of Lojack, they might also increase purchases of other antitheft devices like The Club. In addition, the political support for altering the distribution of police resources among different types of crimes might also change. Unfortunately, neither Ayres and Levitt nor Lojack has made the information on the number of Lojacks installed available to other researchers. My attempts to replicate their results with dummy variables have found insignificant effects.

32. Ultimately, however, the levels of significance that I have tested for are the final arbiters in deciding whether one has enough data, and the results presented here are quite statistically significant.

33. Daniel W. Webster, "The Claims That Right-to-Carry Laws Reduce Violent Crime Are Unsubstantiated," The Johns Hopkins Center for Gun Policy and Research, copy obtained March 6, 1997, p. 5.

34. Jens Ludwig, "Do Permissive Concealed-Carry Laws Reduce Violent Crime?" George-town University working paper (Oct. 8, 1996), p. 12.

35. "Battered Woman Found Not Guilty for Shooting Her Husband Five Times," *San Francisco Examiner,* Apr. 9, 1997.

36. In Chicago from 1990 to 1995, 383 murders (or 7.2 percent of all murders) were com-mitted by a spouse.

37. For a detailed discussion of how Black's and Nagin's arguments have changed over time, see my paper entitled "'If at First You Don't Succeed . . .': The Perils of Data Mining When There Is a Paper (and Video) Trail: The Concealed-Handgun Debate," *Journal of Legal Studies* 27 (January 1998), forthcoming.

38. Black and Nagin, "Do 'Right-to-Carry' Laws Deter Violent Crime?" Carnegie-Mellon working paper, version of December 18, p. 5, n. 4.

39. The December 18, 1996, version of their paper included a footnote admitting this point:

> Lott and Mustard weight their regression by the county's population, and smaller counties are much more likely to have missing data than larger counties. When we weight the data by population, the frequencies of missing data are 11.7% for homi-cides, 5.6% for rapes, 2.8% for assaults, and 5% for robberies.

In discussing the sample comprising only counties with more than 100,000 people, they write in the same paper that "the (weighted) frequencies of missing arrest ratios are 1.9% for homicides, 0.9% for rapes, 1.5% for assaults, and 0.9% for robberies."

40. For rape, 82 percent of the counties are deleted to reduce the weighted frequencies of missing data from 5.6 to 0.9 percent. Finally, for robbery (the only other category that they examine), 82 percent of the observations are removed to reduce the weighted missing data from 5 to 0.9 percent.

41. The reluctance of gun-control advocates to share their data is quite widespread. In May 1997 I tried to obtain data from the Police Foundation about a study that they had recently released by Philip Cook and Jens Ludwig, but after many telephone calls I was told by Earl Hamilton on May 27, "Well, lots of other researchers like Arthur Kellermann do not release their data." I responded by saying that was true, but that it was not something other researchers approved of, nor did it give people much confidence in his results.

42. See William Alan Bartley, Mark Cohen, and Luke Froeb, "The Effect of Concealed-Weapon Laws: Estimating Misspecification Uncertainty," Vanderbilt University working paper (1997).

CHAPTER EIGHT

1. Allison Thompson, "Robber Gets Outgunned on Westside," *Jacksonville (Florida) Times-Union,* Sept. 24, 1997, p. B1.

2. Craig Jarvis, "Pizza Worker's Husband Shoots Masked Bandit," *Raleigh News and Observer,* Dec. 11, 1996, p. B3.

3. Other work that I have done indicates that while hiring certain types of police officers can be quite effective in reducing crime rates, the net benefit from hiring an additional police officer is about a quarter of the benefit from spending an equivalent amount on concealed handguns. See John R. Lott, Jr., "Does a Helping Hand Put Others At Risk? Affirmative Ac-tion, Police Departments, and Crime," University of Chicago working paper (July 1997).

4. The cost of public prisons runs about twice this rate; see Mike Flaherty, "Prisons for Profit; Can Texas System Work for Wisconsin's Overflowing System," *Wisconsin State Journal,* Feb. 16, 1997, p. Al.

5. Fox Butterfield, "Serious Crime Decreased for Fifth Year in a Row," *New York Times,* Jan. 5, 1997, p. 10.

6. Michael Fumento, "Are We Winning the Fight Against Crime?" *Investor's Business Daily*, Feb. 5, 1997, p. A34.

7. Yet there never was much controversy over this issue: when Congress debated the law, no one, not even the National Rifle Association, opposed background checks. The dispute was over a five-day waiting period versus an "instant check."

8. Fumento, "Fight Against Crime," p. A34.

9. After the Supreme Court decision, Arkansas completely stopped the background checks, while Ohio has essentially gutted the rules by making background checks voluntary. In addition, as "Ohio Deputy Attorney General Mark Weaver said, the responsibility for conducting background checks rests with counties and cities in most states—rather than with statewide agencies—and . . . 'hundreds of counties' stopped doing checks after the Supreme Court ruling." (Joe Stumpe, "Arkansas Won't Touch Gun Checks 'Unwarranted,' Chief Cop Says," *Arkansas Democrat-Gazette*, July 29, 1997, p. 1A.

10. Bureau of Alcohol, Tobacco, and Firearms, *A Progress Report: Gun-Dealer Licensing and Illegal Gun Trafficking*, Washington, DC: Department of the Treasury, Bureau of Alcohol, Tobacco, and Firearms (Jan. 1997). John Lott, "A Fair Shot: New Legislation Claims to Ease the Unfair Burden on Gun-Stores," *National Review Online*, July 26, 2006; and Michael Doyle, "Number of U.S. Gun Dealers Has Plunged," *Roanoke Times*, Sept. 20, 2009.

11. Many other restrictions on gun use have prevailed during the last couple of years, even some that appear fairly trivial. For example, in 1996 alone thirteen states voted on initiatives to restrict hunting. The initiatives were successful in eleven of the states. Congressman Steve Largent from Tulsa, Oklahoma, claims that the new rules are "part of a national effort to erode our ability to hunt. . . . It wasn't a local effort. It was a national effort." Not only were the initiatives strongly supported by animal rights activists, but they also received strong support from gun-control advocates. It is probably not lost on gun-control advocates that support for gun control seems to be strongest among those who grew up in households without guns and that making hunting less attractive is one long-term way to alter support for these initiatives. See Janet Pearson, "A 'Fair Chase': Keep the Sport in Hunting" *Tulsa World*, Nov. 17, 1996, p. G1.

12. For most government agencies that try to obtain higher funding, exaggerating the problems helps justify such higher funding. Michael Fitzgerald, a spokesman for the BATF in Chicago, is quoted as saying that 1 percent of federal license holders are estimated to be illegally running guns. "If that figure is accurate, the reduction of . . . dealers should eliminate a substantial number of traffickers." See Jim Adams, "Number of Licenses Falls Dramatically: Crime Law Puts Squeeze on Gun Dealers; Zoning Can Be Used to Keep Gun Sales Out of Private Homes," *Louisville Courier-Journal*, Mar. 20, 1997, p. A1.

13. During the last few years, the BATF has been much more aggressive in harassing law-abiding gun owners and retailers. A recent study using 1995 data, by Jim Couch and William Shughart, claims not only that the BATF refers dramatically more criminal fire arm violations to prosecutors in states that have more National Rifle Association members, but that Clinton's own U.S. attorneys have declined to prosecute a much greater percentage of the cases referred to them in these states. They estimate that 54 percent of the variation across states in the BATF's criminal referrals is explained simply by the number of NRA members in a state, and that about a quarter of these higher requests for prosecutions are declined by U.S. attorneys. See Jim F. Couch and William F. Shughart I, "Crime, Gun Control, and the BATF: The Political Economy of Law Enforcement," University of Mississippi working paper presented at the March, 1997, Public Choice Meetings in San Francisco.

14. I cannot end, however, without at least mentioning several excellent law-review articles on the issue of what was intended in the Second Amendment: see Nelson Lund, "The Second Amendment, Political Liberty, and the Right to Self-Preservation," *Alabama Law Review* 33 (1988): 103–47; Robert J. Cottrol and Raymond T. Diamond, "The Fifth Auxiliary Right," *Yale Law Journal* 104 (1995): 309–42; Don B. Kates, "Handgun Prohibition and

the Original Meaning of the Second Amendment," *University of Michigan Law Review* 82 (1983): 204 68; William Van Alstyne, "The Second Amendment Right to Arms," *Duke Law Review* 43 (Apr. 1994): 1236–55; and Sanford Levinson, "The Embarrassing Second Amendment," *Yale Law Journal* 99 (Dec. 1989): 637–89. Legal scholars seem to be in general agreement on the way the Second Amendment's use of the word *militia* is so completely misinterpreted in current discussions of what the amendment means. The only twentieth-century case in which the Supreme Court directly interpreted the Second Amendment was *United States v. Miller*, 307 US 174 (1939). The court was quite clear that historical sources "showed plainly enough that the Militia comprised all males physically capable of acting in concert for the common defense." The court accepted "the common view . . . that adequate defense of the country and laws could be secured through the Militia—citizens primarily, soldiers on occasion."

The framers of the Constitution were also very clear on this issue. James Madison wrote in the Federalist papers that if a standing army threatened citizens' liberties, it would be opposed by "a militia amounting to near a half-million citizens with arms in their hands"; see Clinton Rossiter, ed., *The Federalist* no. 46 (1961): 299. An excellent discussion of this and related issues is presented by David L. Franklin and Heather L. O'Farrell in their University of Chicago Moot Court brief on *Printz and Mack v United States*, Apr. 18, 1997.

CHAPTER NINE

1. Dates were established by doing a Nexis search. During 1996, Kentucky, Louisiana, and South Carolina enacted "shall-issue" laws. However, these did not go into effect until extremely late in the year. Louisiana did not even start issuing applications until the end of September (Lisa Roland, "Applications for Concealed Handgun Permits to Be Issued This Week," *Gannett News Service*, Sept. 20, 1999). In Kentucky, permits were also not issued until the very end of the year (Michael Quinlan, "Concealed Guns: Permits Will Take Time, Law Will Go into Effect Tomorrow," *Louisville Courier-Journal*, Sept. 30, 1996, p. A1). South Carolina's law went into effect August 22, 1996, but its permitting process also took a couple of months to start actually issuing permits (Kathy Steele, "Women with Guns on Rise," *Augusta (GA) Chronicle*, Apr. 11, 1997, p. B2).

2. While I believe the much more interesting question is how crime rates change before and after the adoption of right-to-carry laws, the states with right-to-carry laws in effect for at least one year in 1996 had an average violent crime rate of 446.6 per 100,000 people, while the states with more restrictive "may-issue" rules had a violent crime rate of 592.6, and states banning concealed handguns a rate of 789.7. The main reason for not focusing on these numbers is simply that it ignores whether these states tended to be the lowest-crime-rate states even before they adopted right-to-carry laws. One method that partially accounts for this concern is to examine the cross-sectional data using the demographic, poverty, income, and other variables that have been employed throughout the book. After controlling for these other factors, the presence of a right-to-carry law implies a violent crime rate 15 percent lower than the absence of a law implies, and the effect is quite statistically significant, with a t-statistic that is significant at better than the .01 percent level for a two-tailed t-test.

3. David Hemenway, "Book Review of *More Guns, Less Crime*," *New England Journal of Medicine*, Dec. 31, 1998, pp. 2029–30.

4. Jens Ludwig, "Concealed-Gun-Carrying Law and Violent Crime: Evidence from State Panel Data," *International Review of Law and Economics* 18 (Sept. 1998): 239–54.

5. The Northeast includes Connecticut, Delaware, the District of Columbia, Maine, Maryland, Massachusetts, New Hampshire, New Jersey, New York, Pennsylvania, Rhode Island, and Vermont; the South includes Alabama, Arkansas, Florida, Georgia, Louisiana, Mississippi, Missouri, North Carolina, Oklahoma, South Carolina, Tennessee, Texas, and Virginia; the Midwest includes Illinois, Indiana, Iowa, Kansas, Kentucky, Michigan, Minnesota, Nebraska, North Dakota, Ohio, South Dakota, West Virginia, and Wisconsin; the

Rocky Mountains include Arizona, Colorado, Idaho, Montana, Nevada, New Mexico, Utah, and Wyoming; and the Pacific states include Alaska, California, Hawaii, Oregon, and Washington.

6. Because of the criticism that it is unrealistic to use a simple dummy variable, I have decided to focus from the beginning on the more realistic approach that examines the before- and after-law trends in crime rates.

7. The results using the old specifications also continue to be very similar.

8. As another test of the sensitivity of the results, I also reestimated the before-and-after trends by limiting them to ten years before and after the adoption of the right-to-carry laws. The results equivalent to table 9.1 are −3.1 percent for violent crime, −0.8 percent for murder, −2.0 percent for rape, −2.6 percent for robbery, −3.3 percent for aggravated assault, and −0.4 percent for property crime. All the violent-crime category results are significant at least at the .01 percent level except for murder, which is significant at the 4 percent level.

9. See also figures 7.7–7.9.

10. Glenn Puit, "Survey: Gun Sales Increasing since Grocery Store Shooting," *Las Vegas Review-Journal,* June 24, 1999, p. 4A; and "Gun Sales up 30 Percent This Year," *Associated Press Newswire,* dateline San Francisco, Aug. 28, 1999. The *Las Vegas Review-Journal* article mentions that "Firearms instructors also said they have seen a jump in the number of people wanting to know the requirements to carry a concealed weapon. And, Las Vegas police have seen an increase in requests for concealed weapons permits in recent weeks." The Associated Press story mentions that "Others say recent crime stories in the news, from the shooting rampage at a Los Angeles Jewish day camp to the tourist killings in Yosemite National Park, have motivated gun buyers."

11. The average murder rate for states over this period is 7.57 per 100,000; for rapes, 33.8; for aggravated assaults, 282.4; and for robberies, 161.8. A 4 percent change in murders is 0.3 per 100,000, a 7 percent change in rape is 2.4 per 100,000, a 5 percent change in aggravated assaults is 14.1 per 100,000, and a 13 percent change in robberies is 21 per 100,000. By contrast, a one-percentage-point increase in the population with permits is 1,000 per 100,000.

12. While small, lightweight guns are available and new materials have also made it possible to make lighter guns, most handguns weigh about the same as a laptop computer. Carrying them around requires some significant inconvenience.

13. More precisely, I replaced the predicted percentage of the population with permits with the predicted percentage of the population with permits divided by the permit fee. This is the same as the interactions done earlier looking at the percentage with permits multiplied by county demographics.

14. Ideally, one would also want to use the expected variation in permit rates across counties (though those data were not available at the time that I put these results together), but since I am examining all counties in the state, the state permitting rates at least allow us to rank the relative impact of right-to-carry laws across states.

15. The different drafts of their paper also went through different specifications.

16. Edward E. Leamer, "Let's Take the Con Out of Econometrics," *American Economic Review* 173 (Mar. 1983): 31–43; and Walter S. McManus, "Estimates of the Deterrent Effect of Capital Punishment: The Importance of the Researcher's Prior Beliefs," *Journal of Political Economy* 93 (Feb. 1985): 417–25.

17. I also included a tenth variable that examined the percentage of the adult population that was in prison, but there were sufficient theoretical objections to including this that I have decided not to report these results in the text. The major theoretical problem is that this variable is a "stock" while the crime rate is a "flow." In other words, the prison population is created by the number of people who are convicted and sentenced over many years and not just how harsh the current sentences are. In fact, if tough sentencing in the past makes it more likely that current criminals will not be sentenced to prison terms as long as those of past criminals (e.g., because of a takeover of the prison system by the courts),

it is possible that there might even be a negative relationship between the prison population and the current toughness of the system. The bottom line is that past punishment is
only roughly related to current punishment, particularly when average state differences
are already being taken into account through fixed effects and when regional yearly fixed
effects have also been added.

18. In a powerful piece, Isaac Ehrlich and Zhiqiang Liu show that classic economics papers concerning the law of demand, production theory, and investment theory would fail
this test (Isaac Ehrlich and Zhiqiang Liu, "Sensitivity Analyses of the Deterrence Hypothesis: Let's Keep the Econ in Econometrics," *Journal of Law and Economics* 42 [Apr. 1999]: 455–88).
Because of this strong bias toward not finding "true" relationships, Leamer and McManus
have dropped off the 10 percent most extreme values on both ends of their estimates when
they have reported their results. Yet even this does not protect most studies from having
their results determined to be "fragile" by this test.

19. One problem from excluding the arrest rate was never clearly made in the first edition of this book. The reason using the arrest rate forces some county observations to be
dropped is that when the number of crimes is zero, the arrest rate is "undefined." Including
counties with zero crime rates biases the results toward not finding an effect because crime
rates cannot fall below zero. Since these counties already have a zero crime rate, the passage
of the right-to-carry law can produce no benefit. The more counties with zero crime rates
that are included, the more the estimated benefit from the law will move toward zero.

My work with Steve Bronars also examined whether replacing the crime-specific arrest
rates with the overall violent-crime or property-crime arrest rates altered the results, and
we found that it had no impact on the results. There are few counties which have no violent
crimes of any type, so there are few missing observations for the violent-crime arrest rate
(Stephen G. Bronars and John R. Lott, Jr., "Criminal Deterrence, Geographic Spillovers, and
Right-to-Carry Laws," *American Economic Review* 88 (May 1998): 475–79).

20. While I find it difficult to believe that anyone would argue that demographic factors are not important in explaining crime rates, I did try a couple of specification tests.
Paring the demographic variables down to the percentage of the population that is black,
the percentage of the population that is white, the percentage of the population that is
male, and the percentage of the population in the six different age classifications leaves the
results essentially unchanged. Eliminating the demographic variables entirely reduces the
estimated drop in violent-crime rates from right-to-carry laws by at most one percentage
point.

21. The way that the county-level data were compiled was changed in 1994. Prior to that
time those jurisdictions within a county which provided data for fewer than six months
were estimated to have the same offense rates as the rest of the county. From 1994 onward,
the imputation method was applied only to counties with less than three months of data.
For jurisdictions with at least six months of data prior to 1994 and at least three months of
data after that time, the jurisdiction was calculated to have $12/N$ offenses, where N is the
number of months reported.

Because of concerns that this might affect estimates using data after 1993, I reran the
regressions reported in table 9.1 by including a variable for the change in a county's crime
rate between 1993 and 1994. This change variable was included for the 1994–1996 observations to account for the relative differences that this change in measurement might have
had across different counties. The results are similar to those already reported. The annual
difference in the trends in violent-crime rates before and after the passage of a right-to-carry
law are −1.4 percent for murder, −2.94 percent for rape, −2.8 percent for robbery, and −3.12
percent for aggravated assault. All the results are significant at better than the .01 percent
level with F-tests of 17.36, 83.33, 87.38, and 87.31, respectively.

22. These data draw on research that I am currently conducting with Kevin Cremin.
Kevin collected all the data used here on policing policies.

23. "[The] problem-solving effort began essentially as directed patrol operations designed to identify patterns of offending or known offenders and to deploy police to catch the offenders. All gradually evolved into quite different efforts that involved activities other than arrest and agencies other than the police. The attack on burglaries in the housing projects involved surveying tenants, cleaning the projects, creating a multiagency task force to deal with particular problems in the housing projects, and organizing the tenants not only to undertake block watches but also to make demands on city agencies. The attack on thefts from cars eventually involved the inclusion of police officers in the design of new parking lots to make them less vulnerable to theft. The attack on prostitution and robbery involved enhanced code enforcement against hotels and bars that provided the meeting places for prostitutes and their customers as well as decoy operations" (Christopher Slobogin, "Why Liberals Should Chuck the Exclusionary Rule," *University of Illinois Law Review* 99 (1999): 363.

24. The data on community-oriented policing, problem-oriented policing, and the broken-windows strategy were primarily obtained by using the Westlaw "News" database. For community policing, the search took the form [name of city] & "community policing" & DA(BEF 1/1/1997) & DA(AFT 1/1/1975). For problem-oriented policing, the search took the form ("Problem Solving Policing" or "Problem-Solving Policing" or "Problem Oriented Policing" or "Problem-Oriented Policing") & DA(AFT 1/1/1975) & DA(BEF 1/1/1997). Finally, for the broken-windows strategy, the search consisted of "Broken Window" & Crime & DA(AFT 1/1/1975) & DA(BEF 1/1/1997) AND NOT "Broken Windows." Other sources were also investigated. For community policing, the sources included Robert C. Trojanowicz and Hazel A. Harden, "The Status of Contemporary Community Policing Programs," National Center for Community Policing, 1985; Washington State University, Division of Governmental Studies and Services (DGSS), surveys of police administrators conducted at three-year intervals between 1978 and 1994; Anna Sampson, "National Survey of Community Policing Strategies, 1992–93"; and Robert C. Trojanowicz et al., "Community Policing: A Survey of Police Departments in the United States," 1994. However, the only one of these studies which identifies the cities is the 1985 Trojanowicz and Harden study. The authors of the other studies were unwilling to identify the cities in their samples. For the broken-windows strategy, George Kelling's book was also used to identify additional cities (George L. Kelling, *Fixing Broken Windows: Restoring Order and Reducing Crime in Our Communities* [New York: Free Press, 1998]).

25. John R. Lott, Jr., "Does a Helping Hand Put Others at Risk? Affirmative Action, Police Departments, and Crime," *Economic Inquiry* (forthcoming).

26. For example, policing policies may have changed because of concerns about future crime rates. Not adopting the change might have resulted in even more crime.

27. Bartholomew Sullivan, "Students Recall 'Unreal' Rampage," *Commercial Appeal*, June 11, 1998, p. A1.

28. Lance Gay, "New Gun Measure Wouldn't Have Halted School Tragedies," *Cleveland Plain Dealer*, May 30, 1999, p. 19A.

29. Pam Belluck and Jodi Wilgoren, "Shattered Lives—a Special Report: Caring Parents, No Answers, in Columbine Killers' Pasts," *New York Times*, June 29, 1999, p. A1; and Virginia Culver, "Pastor Comforts Gunman's Family," *Arizona Republic*, May 1, 1999, p. D7.

30. Evelyn Larrubia, Ted Rohrlich, and Andrew Blankstein, "Suspect Scouted 3 Prominent L.A. Jewish Sites as Targets," *Los Angeles Times*, Aug. 13, 1999, p. 1.

31. An earlier attempt by Congress to pass this law was never really enforced and was struck down by the Supreme Court in 1995. The 1995 law put in simple "boiler plate" language requiring that prosecutors make a finding that the gun or parts of the gun had been involved in interstate commerce.

32. These results are available at http://ssrn.com/abstract=272929. If the variance doesn't equal the mean, the appropriate test is to use a negative binomial, which no longer requires this assumption. Redoing the results presented in this chapter with a negative binomial

produces results extremely similar to those that will be reported. For example, redoing the right-to-carry estimates for table 6.6 with a negative binomial produces

Murders in multiple-victim public shootings: 71%, z = 2.496, significant at the 1.3% level

Injuries in multiple-victim public shootings: 83%, z = 3.414, significant at the 0.1% level

Attempted or actual bombings: 67%, z = 3.821, significant at the 0.1% level

33. To illustrate, let the probability that a single individual is carrying a concealed handgun equal .10. Assume further that there are 10 individuals in a public place. Then the probability that at least one of them is armed is $1 - .9^{10}$, or about .65.

34. *Baltimore Sun*, Apr. 30, 1999.

35. Greg Pierce, "Professional Viewpoint," *Washington Times*, Sept. 3, 1999, p. A5.

36. Even so-called smart locks, which are activated by one's fingerprint or by a special ring with a computer, pose several types of risks. With locks activated by fingerprints, a spouse would be unable to use the gun to come to the other person's rescue if the gun were coded for the other person. The person must also correctly position the finger on the fingerprint reader. Small differences in the angle of the finger may leave the gun inoperable even for the designated user.

37. This discussion is based upon research that I am currently doing with John Whitley.

38. Peter Cummings, David C. Grossman, Frederick P. Rivara, and Thomas D. Koepsell, "State Gun Safe Storage Laws and Child Mortality Due to Firearms," *Journal of the American Medical Association* 278 (Oct. 1, 1997): 1084–86.

39. U.S. General Accounting Office, "Accidental Shootings: Many Deaths and Injuries Caused by Firearms Could Be Prevented" (Washington, DC: U.S. General Accounting Office, Mar. 1991).

40. An article in the *Journal of the American Medical Association* does not control for any other factors but claims that 23 percent of the accidental gun deaths for children under fifteen would have been prevented by these storage rules. In 1996, this would have amounted to thirty-two lives if the laws had been in effect for the entire country. One obvious mistake that this article made was that it made no attempt to account for the normal downward trend in accidental gun deaths that would have continued to at least some extent even without these safe-storage laws. Since no other variables were being controlled for, all of the drop was being attributed to the new law (Cummings et al., "State Gun Safe Storage Laws").

41. As of this writing, the Violence Policy Center still has a section of its Web site entitled "Funder of the Lott CCW Study Has Links to the Gun Industry" at http://www.vpc.org/fact_sht/lottlink.htm.

42. M. W. Guzy, "Soft Logic on Hard Facts on Guns," *St. Louis Post-Dispatch*, July 22, 1998, p. B7.

43. Shelley Kiel [state senator in Nebraska], "Some Gun Restrictions Needed," *Omaha World-Herald*, July 11, 1998, p. 11.

44. Kevin Beck, "Conceal Carry," *St. Louis Post-Dispatch*, Aug. 12, 1998.

45. Minnesota Representative Wesley Skoglund on PBS's *Almanac*, Sept. 26, 1998.

46. Take for example a June 21, 1999, discussion between two people on alt.fan .cecil-adams:

"Dutch Courage": hey, did you know Lott's study was funded by a gun manufacturer? I did. That's a little suspicious, don't you think?

"Shawn Wilson": Actually, it wasn't.

"Dutch Courage": You're right, it was a foundation founded by the owner of a gun company, which is now an ammunition company, and further the foundation

has large holdings in this company, and several of the directors of this foundation are men with standing within the company which shares the name. So much for his reputation as an honest scholar and academic reputation, eh?

47. Linnet Myers, "Go Ahead . . . Make Her Day," *Chicago Tribune*, May 2, 1999, p. C12. See also Diane Carman, "Gun-Bill Premise Is Bogus," *Denver Post*, Mar. 23, 1999, p. B1: "While gun-control activists have criticized Lott's work because it is funded in part through a grant from the Olin Foundation, which was founded by the largest manufacturer of ammunition in the U.S., [Jens] Ludwig argues that the debate about the grant money 'only distracts people. The study fails on its merits.'"

48. This quote is from the Web site of Handgun Control, Inc. (http://www.handgun-control.org/lott.htm). The Violence Policy Center's claim that I believe that "increases in the percent of minority police officers increase crime rates" can be found at http://www.vpc.org/fact_sht/wholott.htm. Of course, the Violence Policy Center fails to mention the rest of the abstract in question, which points out that the paper (Lott, "Does a Helping Hand Put Others at Risk?") will investigate "whether these increases in crime are due to changes in the quality of all new police officers or just minority officers."

49. The previous footnote provides references for this claim on gun-control Web sites. Similar statements were made by Luis Tolley, the western regional director for Handgun Control, Inc., at a debate that I participated in at Claremont College, and Tom Diaz, an analyst for the Violence Policy Center, has made this claim a couple of times when we appeared on radio shows together.

50. Lott, "Does a Helping Hand Put Others at Risk?"

51. The selective quoting was obviously a well-orchestrated campaign, with newspaper editorials also getting involved in repeating the statements by Handgun Control. Consider the following editorial attack on me: "In May 1998, for instance, he published the following in a police research journal: 'Increasing black officers' share of the police force by one percentage point increases murders by four percent, the violent crimes by seven percent, and property crimes by eight percent. . . . More black and female officers are also associated with declines in both the arrest and conviction rates'" (Editorial, "A Lott More Guns," *St. Louis Post-Dispatch*, Mar. 23, 1999, p. B6). They failed to quote some other sentences in this same piece, such as "Not all black officers nor all white officers nor all officers of any other race are of the same quality. Some black officers are undoubtedly better at reducing crime than most potential white officers, and some white officers are probably better than most potential black officers. The question is how to select those officers who will do the best job. There is the possibility that choosing applicants by race or sex could work against hiring the best officers available. . . . One must be very clear about what is happening, however. The large impact of more black officers indicates that more than just the quality of new minority recruits or new minority promotions are affected. Indeed, changing tests to employ a greater percentage of blacks appears to make it more difficult to screen out lower-quality candidates generally, including whites and other racial groups" (John R. Lott, Jr., "Who Is Really Hurt by Affirmative Action?" *Subject to Debate*, May 1998, pp. 1, 3).

52. William F. Shughart II, "More Guns, Less Crime: Understanding Crime and Gun Control Laws: Review," *Southern Economic Journal* 65, no. 4 (Apr. 1, 1999): 978.

53. Bruce L. Benson, "Review of *More Guns, Less Crime*," *Public Choice* 100 (Sept. 1999), nos. 3–4: 309.

54. Stan Liebowitz, "Handgun Argument Is Loaded," *Dallas Morning News*, June 21, 1998.

55. Nelson Lund, "Gunning Down Crime: The Statistics of Concealed Weapons," *Weekly Standard*, June 1, 1998.

56. Joanne Eisen and Paul Gallant, "Scientific Proof That Gun Control Increases the Cost of Crime," *Shield*, Summer 1998, p. 42.

57. I really don't take most threats very seriously, and I believe that it is just people blowing off steam. The worst threats usually come over the telephone, though I did have some regular writers from Canada who would express the hope that someone would get a gun and kill either me or my family members. The one e-mail threat that was forwarded to me by one of the editors at the University of Chicago Press gives some idea of the types of comments I received:

> Pass along the word, to that soulless weasel and absolutely irresponsible chicken-shit John M. Lott that he better change his name and get some plastic surgery because his days of [obscenities deleted] of the NRA's [obscenities deleted] will be quickly coming to a crashing close if he keeps trying to pass off unethical, and second rate statistics with his pseudoscience rhetorical sylogisms.
>
> My point—someone is going to become very angered by the view of this imbecile, and is going to get a concealed hand-gun permit and find where he lives and make a point. I won't lose sleep knowing that one more moron is dead, but I feel that he should be warned none-the-less. Also, if John Lott had any integrity he'd make it possible to reach him. Since the little scatmuncher is playing hide and seek by having no-available e-mail adress, whoever reads this please forward this too him. This is not a threat, just a warning.
>
> Sometimes when views of cretins like this are expressed I think "love it or leave it," and man, if our scholars get any stupider and any more immoral than Mr. Lott I'm out of this shit house. I nearly packed my bags.

58. Matt Bai, "Is He the Smoking Gun?" *Newsweek*, Jan. 25, 1999, Business section.

59. "According to the Federal Bureau of Investigation's *Uniform Crime Report*, from 1992 to 1997, states which made it easier for citizens to carry concealed handguns had a significantly smaller drop in their crime rates than states which chose not to loosen their concealed weapons laws" (Brian Morton [associate director of communications for Handgun Control and the Center to Prevent Handgun Violence], "John Lott's Gun Research Doesn't Hold Up to Review," *Fort Wayne Journal Gazette*, Aug. 15, 1999, p. 3C).

Even when others would state that the FBI indeed did not produce these claims, Handgun Control's press release was put on the same footing as my research. Consider the following: "The Center to Prevent Handgun Violence did a 1999 analysis of crime statistics that came to a conclusion opposite of Mr. Lott's, and their study (like his) is open to review by experts in many fields" (Molly Ivins, "More Guns, Less Crime? Are You Sure?" *Fort Worth Star-Telegram*, Aug. 15, 1999). For clarification, the Center to Prevent Handgun Violence is part of Handgun Control, and Sarah Brady serves as the head of both organizations. Many similar statements were made by the media in Missouri during the debate over the concealed-handgun law.

60. For example, a December 1998 press release on children and gun violence had South Carolina and Colorado ranking similarly in terms of how liberal their right-to-carry laws were, but by January 1999, in a press release examining the change between 1992 and 1997, Colorado was listed as having a more restrictive law than South Carolina. The only motivation that I can conjecture for the change was that it helped get them the different results that they wanted.

61. "In stark contrast, a review of the national Uniformed Crime Reporting data, which is compiled by the FBI each year from state and local law enforcement agencies, indicates that the violent crime rate has fallen in all states by an average of 19 percent from 1992–97" (Richard Cook, "Don't Buy the Pro-Gun Arguments," *Kansas City Star*, Mar. 11, 1999, p. B7).

62. Peter Squires, "Review of More Guns, Less Crime," *British Journal of Criminology* 39, no. 2 (Spring 1999): 318–20.

63. My book does not even cite this quotation, though I mentioned it in an earlier re-

search paper because it was "quite relevant" to the debate over concealed handguns: it illustrates both the possibility of deterrence and the fears about the possible disasters that such laws could lead to.

Still other recent discussions in medical journals continue claiming that the nondiscretionary concealed-handgun laws for "several counties . . . were misclassified" and that the National Academy of Sciences deemed it inappropriate to account for arrest rates when researchers tried to explain changes in crime (see Arthur Kellermann and Sheryl Heron, "Firearms and Family Violence," *Emergency Medicine Clinics of North America,* Aug. 1999, pp. 699–708). Of course, responses 4 and 9 on pages 132–33 and 142 in this book addressed the first concern and page 18 discussed the second one.

64. http://www.handguncontrol.org/gunowner/statflaw.htm.

65. Doug Weil, Handgun Control's research director, provided the only response that I know of to my research on the Brady law by claiming that "Since John's data does not cover the years following implementation of the Brady Act, it's hard to know how he can claim to have studied the impact of the Brady law on crime rates or criminal access to guns" ("More Guns, Less Crime?: A Debate between John Lott, Author of *More Guns, Less Crime,* and Douglas Weil, Research Director of Handgun Control, Inc.," an online debate sponsored by *Time* magazine, transcript from July 1, 1998.) In fact, my book examined data up through 1994, the first year that the Brady law was in effect.

66. Romesh Ratnesar, "Should You Carry A Gun? A New Study Argues for Concealed Weapons," *Time,* July 6, 1998, p. 48.

67. I responded by saying that he was doing more than simply reporting these statements as claims when he used phrases like "Lott dropped" or "the book does not account." More importantly, readers were likely to believe that he had looked at the material and that he would not print something, even if the critics claimed it was true, unless it was true. Again, he emphasized that his role was that of a reporter and not to take sides in the debate.

I had called Romesh in part to tell him that I planned to send in a letter clarifying these points, and *Time* magazine did print a letter. Undoubtedly he played some role in guaranteeing that the letter was published, but it seems doubtful that the letter carried the same weight as a statement by the reporter about whether he could verify if the claims made against me were true. The letter in *Time* magazine was printed in the Aug. 3, 1998, issue under the heading "More about Concealed Weapons." It read:

> While your piece "Should You Carry a Gun?" [July 6] was generally favorable toward my new book, *More Guns, Less Crime,* it contained seriously misleading statements. Despite accusations by some critics, my study on the effect that carrying concealed weapons has on crime absolutely did not ignore "counties that had no reported murders or assaults for a given year." In contrast to the tiny samples in previous work by others, I used data on all the counties in the U.S. that were available when I did the study on the years from 1977 to 1994. It is likewise false that I did "not account for fluctuating factors like poverty levels and police techniques." Among the factors I included in the analysis were poverty, income, unemployment, arrest and conviction rates, the number of police officers and police expenditures per capita, as well as the impact that the prevention of less serious crimes has on more serious ones.

68. Ivins, "More Guns, Less Crime? Are You Sure?"

69. Tom Teepen, "A Modest Proposal: Let's Arm the Teachers," *Atlanta Journal and Constitution,* Sunday, May 17, 1998, p. 2G.

70. The following letter of mine appeared in the *Atlanta Journal and Constitution,* May 24, 1998, p. 6B:

> Tom Teepen's column "A modest proposal: Let's arm the teachers," Perspective, May 17), an attack on my new book "More Guns, Less Crime" (University of Chicago

Press), contained misleading information. He claimed that "Lott can't fairly compare 1988 and 1996 exit polls on gun ownership, as he does, because the questions were asked differently." Yet on pages 36–37 in my book, I point out this fact and discuss in detail what impact this has on estimates of changing gun ownership.

Citing a paper in the *Journal of Legal Studies*, Teepen claimed that I make a "fundamental gaffe" by failing to consider other anti-crime variables. My book provides the first systematic national evidence and examines the crime, accidental gun death, and suicide rates for all 3,054 counties in the United States by year from 1977 to 1994. No other study on crime has attempted to account for anywhere near as many different factors that could have affected crime rates over time. Unlike the Centers for Disease Control and Prevention's claim that homes with guns were "more likely to experience suicide," or have "a member of the family killed by another member or by an acquaintance," I did not focus on data from only one or a few cities for only one year. There is no evidence that these claims are correct.

Obviously, bad things can happen with guns, but guns also prevent bad things from happening to people. The evidence in my book indicates that many more lives are saved than lost from gun ownership.

71. An editor at the *Fort Worth Star-Telegram*, Bob Davis, was very helpful, and he took the time to read my book to evaluate whether a mistake had been made. He printed a response by me in his newspaper, and he asked Creators Syndicate, which distributes Ms. Ivins's commentary, to make the response available to other newspapers around the country that carried Ms. Ivins's column. Unfortunately, despite repeated promises by Creators to do so, they never followed through on this.

72. Let me just give a couple of other examples.

Even John Lott admits that 58 percent of homicides are committed either by family members or friends and acquaintances, not criminals. (Richard Scribner, [director of the Injury Control Research Center], "More Guns Don't Mean a Safer Society," *New Orleans Times-Picayune*, Apr. 28, 1999, p. B6)

Dr. Lott's own analysis accounts for only about 10 percent of why some crime rates have fallen. We need to explain the other 90 percent before concluding that the "best" social policy is to carry more handguns. (Shela Van Ness, "More Guns, Less Crime? This Isn't Just a 'Good Guy' vs. 'Bad Guy' Issue," *Chattanooga Times / Chattanooga Free Press*, May 9, 1999, p. H1)

For the first point, not only do I not "admit" this, but my book points out that this claim is extremely misleading because the term "acquaintances" primarily includes rival gang members killing each other or drug buyers and drug sellers killing each other. As to the second point, the estimates shown in this book explain about 80–95 percent of the variation in crime rates.

73. The *Chronicle of Higher Education* noted that the opposition to my book also showed up in the University of Chicago Press, this book's publisher. The *Chronicle* reported that "The book also caused a mini-revolt at Chicago, where salespeople initially blanched at the prospect of pitching it to bookstores. Some cited personal views about guns; others thought that the book would alienate booksellers" (Christopher Shea, "'More Guns, Less Crime': A Scholar's Thesis Inflames Debate over Weapons Control," *Chronicle of Higher Education*, June 5, 1998, p. A14).

74. In this case, the dummy must be interpreted as whether the law raised or lowered the crime rate as quickly as the quadratic time trend would predict.

75. This example is taken from David D. Friedman's Web site, www.best.com/~ddfr/Lott_v_Teret/Lott_Mustard_Controversy.html.

76. Virtually identical complaints have been posted on the Handgun Control, Inc., Web

site, where Handgun Control writes: "To this day, John Lott has failed to provide any statistical evidence of his own that counters Black and Nagin's finding that Lott's conclusions are inappropriately attributed to changes in concealed-carry laws. Until Lott can do this, it is inappropriate for him to continue to claim that allowing more people to carry concealed handguns causes a drop in crime."

77. Dan A. Black and Daniel S. Nagin, "Do Right-to-Carry Laws Deter Violent Crime?" *Journal of Legal Studies* 27 (Jan. 1998): p. 213.

78. What is mystifying to me is how others have also continued to make this claim. Hashem Dezhbakhsh and Paul H. Rubin claim that "We believe that Lott and Mustard's findings are suspect, mainly because of the way they parameterize and measure the effect of permissive handgun laws on crime. They model the effect as a shift in the intercept of the linear crime equation they estimate at the county level. This approach is predicated on two assumptions: (i) all behavioral (response) parameters of this equation (slope coefficients) are fixed (unaffected by the law), and (ii) the effect of the law on crime is identical across counties" (Hashem Dezbakhsh and Paul H. Rubin, "Lives Saved or Lives Lost? The Effects of Concealed-Handgun Laws on Crime," *American Economic Review Papers and Proceedings*, May 1998, p. 468).

79. http://www.best.com/-ddfr/Lott_v_Teret/Friedman_on_B_and_N.html. A great deal of debate about my research and other gun-related research takes place on the Internet in discussion groups such as talk.politics.guns or on Web sites such as David Friedman's, which allows for a very detailed discussion of the issues. The give and take also allows people to ferret out the weaknesses and strengths of different arguments.

80. Benson, "Review of *More Guns, Less Crime*" p. 312.

81. An example of one of the other criticisms is by Ayres and Donohue where they write that "the ultimate criticism of Lott will be that the model is too flawed to provide any information on the effect of the law. . . . One of the strongest results to emerge from Lott's book is that shall issue laws, as he models them, lead to higher property crime. If you don't believe this, then you cannot endorse any of Lott's findings. But, to believe that property crime rose you must believe that the rate of robbery fell, because the only reason that more concealed handguns would cause property crime to go up is that some other money-generating activity became less available or less attractive. One would hardly expect that someone desiring to beat up an individul would instead decide to steal a car if the assaultive option were foreclosed. But since the robbery results are arguably weak, it is hard to tell a convincing story that would explain the alleged shift from violent crime to property crime that the Lott model attributes to shall issue laws" (Ian Ayres and John J. Donohue III, "Nondiscretionary Concealed Weapons Laws: A Case Study of Statistics, Standards of Proof, and Public Policy," *American Law and Economics Review* 1, nos. 1–2 (Fall 1999): 436–70).

82. The "recidivism" referred to by Ayres and Donohue is actually not a good measure for what they are discussing, since recidivism refers to whether criminals keep on committing a crime after they have been punished by the legal system.

83. Ayres and Donohue raise another issue that should be discussed at least briefly, and that is the use of the percentage of a state's population that is in prison as an enforcement variable. They find that including this variable strengthens the results, but while the variable provides some information, there are some important theoretical problems with it. One problem is that the prison population and the crime rate are simply in different units. The prison population measures a "stock," while the crime rate represents a "flow." The simplest comparison is between the amount of water in a bathtub (a stock) and the rate at which water is flowing into the bathtub (a flow). The amount of water in the bathtub is only loosely related to the current flow into it because it depends upon not only flows in previous periods but also the rate at which water is flowing out of it. A second problem is that I have focused on county-level data because of the heterogeneity in law enforcement across counties within a state, and this variable is available only at the state level.

84. For example, Sarah Brady, "Q: Would New Requirements for Gun Buyers Save lives? Yes: Stop Deadly, Unregulated Sales to Minors, at Gun Shows and on the Internet," *Insight*, June 21, 1999, p. 24; or "More Guns, Less Crime? A Debate between John Lott and Douglas Weil."

85. Gary Kleck, *Targeting Guns: Firearms and Their Control* (Hawthorne, NY: Aldine de Gruyter Publishers, 1997), p. 371.

86. This is true whether one uses the 430,000 instances in 1997 in which crimes with guns were reported to police in the *Uniform Crime Report* or the number that is about twice as large from the National Crime Victimization Survey.

87. Frank Main, "Taxpayers Pay Big Part of Gunshot Victims' Bills," *Chicago Sun-Times*, Aug. 4, 1999, p. 30.

88. Another survey by gun-control advocates claims that "four million legal handgun owners sometimes carried guns for protection 'in connection with work.' Two-thirds of those who carried handguns said they kept them in their vehicles, while the others said they sometimes carried them. . . . The researchers said about 56 percent of those who carried handguns outside of work did so fewer than 30 days per year, while 22 percent said they rarely left home without a gun" (Will Hacker, "Majority of Owners Cite Security Concerns," *South Bend Tribune*, June 29, 1997, p. A6).

89. Janelle Hartman, "Assailant Gets Shot by Victim," *Eugene (OR) Register Guard*, Mar. 11, 1998, p. 1.

90. Nicole Marshall, "Concealed Gun Carrier Subdues Suspect: Man Reportedly Had Snatched Toddler," *Tulsa World*, Jan. 31, 1998.

91. Frank J. Murray, "Arizona Gun Owner's Courage Led to Scary Arrests," *Washington Times*, May 2, 1999, p. C8.

92. Laurie Mason, "Customer Stops Would-Be Robber," *Bucks County Courier Times*, Dec. 13, 1998, p. 7C.

93. Edward W. Lempinen, "Robber Shot Dead," *Newsday*, Aug. 3, 1999, p. A3; "Concealed Carry Permit Pays Off," *Local Cincinnati-Northern Kentucky TV 9 Evening News*, Aug. 19, 1999; Tom Jackman and Maria Glod, "A Glimmer of Hope, Then Violent Death," *Washington Post*, June 21, 1999, p. B1; "Carjacking Suspect Critically Wounded," *Arizona Republic*, June 5, 1999, p. B2; and Joe Brogan, "Rent Collector Shoots, Kills Riviera Robber," *Palm Beach Post*, Jan. 14, 1999, p. B1.

A case from the end of 1998 that deserves some mention involved an eighty-one-year-old Chicago native who defended himself by illegally carrying a concealed handgun—a gun that he wasn't even allowed to own legally in Chicago, let alone carry with him.

In the pre-dawn hours Tuesday, 81-year-old Bruno Kosinski looked like an easy mark for a robbery. Kosinski, a frail man with thinning white hair who shuffles his feet as he walks slightly hunched over, was getting into his car in Ukrainian Village when he felt something wet on his head. In a few brief moments, two teenagers allegedly squirted pepper spray in his face, pushed him to the ground, took his wallet and, still unsatisfied, threatened to kill him, police said. Kosinski did something authorities said was rare: The 5-foot-5 elderly man used a concealed handgun he carries in his pants. Without saying a word, he got to his feet and fired once. . . . Kosinski, admitting he illegally carried a concealed handgun, was unapologetic. "I don't feel at all sorry that it happened," said Kosinski. . . ."The least that I could do was defend myself." (Bechetta Jackson and Todd Lightly, "Aged Hold-Up Victim Shoots Teen Suspect," *Chicago Tribune*, Dec. 8, 1998, sec. 2, p. 8)

94. Mene Tekel Upharsin, "Homeowner Grabs Gun for Self-Defense, Assists Police in Capture of Escaped Murderer," *Associated Press Newswire*, Aug. 21, 1999, 8:37 EDT. What would have become a multiple-victim public shooting at a business in July 1999 was stopped by a person with a concealed handgun ("Gunman Turns Weapon on Gun Store Employees,

Is Wounded in Shootout," *St. Louis Post-Dispatch* (from Reuters), July 7, 1999, p. A11; and see also Thomas Sowell, "Why Does Media Hide Benefits of Arming Citizens?" *Bergen County (NJ) Record*, July 19, 1999, p. L3). Typical is the story of a Greenville, North Carolina, restaurant owner who prevented a robbery with a gun that he carried with him all the time "in the small of his back" (Travis Fain, "Man Shot, Killed in Attempted Robbery," *Daily Reflector*, June 2, 1999, p. B1). Other articles on prevented robberies from June 1999 can be found in the *Providence Journal*, June 18, 1999; the *Prescott (AZ) Daily Courier*, June 13, 1999; the *Augusta (GA) Chronicle*, June 16, 1999; and the *Aiken (SC) Standard*, June 2, 1999.

95. "Man Charged in Robbery Hurt in Intimidation Bid," *Buffalo News*, Jan. 16, 1999; "Cops: Woman Shot by Man She Tried to Rob," *Orlando Sentinel* (from Associated Press), Jan. 10, 1999, p. B4; Seth Muller, "Homeowner Fires .357 at Night Burglar," *Martinsburg (WV) Journal*, Mar. 2, 1999; Valerie Bauertein, "Woman Kills an Intruder in Her Home," *Winston-Salem Journal*, Mar. 2, 1999, p. A1; "Woman Shoots Golf Stalker to Death during Attack," *Palm Beach Post* (from Associated Press), May 12, 1999, p. A11; Kirk Swauger, "Shooter's Brother: Break-in Not First," *Johnstown (PA) Tribune-Democrat*, Apr. 10, 1999, p. A1; Bill Blair, "West End Man Slays Intruder," *Johnstown (PA) Tribune-Democrat*, Apr. 9, 1999, p. A1; Bill Hanna, "Robbery Victim Shoots Suspect," *Fort Worth Star-Telegram*, June 15, 1999; Mark Duncan, "Hall of Fame Cowboy Stems Tragedy at Ranch: Family Survives Knife Attack," *Yavapai County (AZ) Daily Courier*, June 13, 1999, p. A1; Dan Richardson, "Armed Homeowner Drives Off Intruder," *Valley News (VT)*, July 2, 1999; Heather Romero, "Intruder Is Wounded As Shots Fly 'All Over,'" *Arizona Daily Star*, July 3, 1999, p 1B; Beena A. Hyatt, "Intruder Is Killed in Home," *Chattanooga Times*, July 22, 1999, p. B1; Kate Folmar and Luise Roug, "Late-Night Intruder Gets More Than He Bargained For," *Los Angeles Times*, Aug. 2, 1999, Orange County edition, p. B1; and "Home-owner Shoots Man Climbing into Window," *Knoxville (TN) Knox-News Sentinel*, Aug. 1, 1999.

96. While I find the claims greatly exaggerated, another recent study has come out claiming that sixty-four children under the age of two die every year from sleeping with their parents (Shari Roan, "Baby's First Year: Dangerous to Doze with Baby Alongside?" *Los Angeles Times*, Oct. 4, 1999, p. S1).

97. Brenda Rodriguez, "Notes Begin to Tell Story of Rampage in Atlanta: Killer Wanted to Exact Revenge," *Dallas Morning News*, July 31, 1999, p. 1A.

98. Rhonda Cook, "To the Rescue: Salesman Grabs Gun, Prevents Tragedy," *Atlanta Journal and Constitution*, Aug. 3, 1999, 1B; Lyda Longa and David Pendered, "Armed Patient Shot in Grady," *Atlanta Journal and Constitution*, Aug. 4, 1999, p. 1B; Hannity and Colmes, Fox News Network, Aug. 11, 1999 (21:30 EST); and "Armed Georgia Defenders Thwart Two Gunmen," *Washington Times* (from Reuters), Aug. 4, 1999, p. A9.

99. Carol Robinson, "Gunman Opens Fire at Alabama Business," *New Orleans Times-Picayune*, Aug. 6, 1999 p. A17.

100. Editorial, "Lethal Weapon," *Daily News of Los Angeles*, May 6, 1999, p. N20.

101. Elaine Gale, "Grieving Mother Haunted by Crash Scene," *Los Angeles Times*, May 6, 1999, p. A1.

102. A Nexis search of news stories for the one week after both incidents indicates that Buford Furrow was mentioned in the news about five times as often as Steve Abrams, and that while news accounts of Furrow tended to be full-feature news stories, virtually all of the mentions of Mr. Abrams were fairly minor recounts of the Associated Press story that ran on him. Later in the day it was discovered that Furrow had killed a U.S. Post Office worker, but the initial news coverage was based upon the attack at the community center.

Other writers have done an excellent job of pointing out these biases (Sowell, "Why Does Media Hide Benefits of Arming Citizens?" p. L3; Jeff Jacoby, "Media Bias Revealed by Crimes That Go Unnoticed," *San Jose Mercury News*, Aug. 24, 1999).

103. This total includes 427 incendiary bombings. Eleven deaths and 29 injuries were classified as "noncriminal" (Bureau of Alcohol, Tobacco, and Firearms, "Arson and Explosives: Incidents Report, 1997" [Department of the Treasury, 1999]). For an example of a recent

knife attack that injured several people on an Amtrak train see Editorial, "Speak Up," *Dayton Daily News,* Sept. 2, 1999.

104. For example, CNN's *Late Edition with Wolf Blitzer,* May 2, 1999, 12:00 A.M. EST.

105. Tom Diaz, *Making a Killing: The Business of Guns in America* (New York: New Press, 1999).

106. Ruth Teichroeb, "Hearing Today for Boy Expelled over Squirt Gun," *Seattle Post-Intelligencer,* Sept. 22, 1998, p. B1; Mike Martindale, "OU Acts after Police Take Youth into Custody after Call," *Detroit News,* Aug. 13, 1999; Pete Falcone, "Student Expelled for Toting BB Gun," *Bloomington (IL) Pantagraph,* May 27, 1999, p. A2; Cathy Cummins, "Expulsion Law's Author Says Schools Have Gone Too Far," *Rocky Mountain News,* Feb. 23, 1998, p. A4; and "Howitzer Picture Cut From Yearbook," *Associated Press Newswire,* Oct. 28, 1999, 3:16 EDT. These different incidents were said to violate schools' "zero tolerance" policy.

107. This information on the number of words in different gun-control laws was compiled by Alan Korwin (Alan Korwin, *The California Gun Owner's Guide* [Phoenix: Bloomfield Press, 1999], *The Texas Gun Owner's Guide* [Phoenix: Bloomfield Press, 1998]; and *Gun Laws of America* [Phoenix: Bloomfield Press, 1997]).

108. Terry L. Anderson, Charles W. Baird, Randy E. Barnett, et al. [letter signed by 290 academics], "Disarming Good People," *Washington Times,* June 16, 1999, p. A17. The correct number of 294 signatories was noted in John R. Lott, Jr., "More Gun Controls? They Haven't Worked in the Past," *Wall Street Journal,* June 17, 1999, p. A26.

109. Dale Anema, "A Father at Columbine High," *American Enterprise,* Sept./Oct. 1999, pp. 48–50.

CHAPTER TEN

1. Matt Bai, "The Gun Crowd's Guru," *Newsweek,* Mar. 12, 2001.

2. John Donohue, "The Final Bullet in the Body of the More Guns, Less Crime Hypothesis," *Criminology and Public Policy* 2, no. 3 (2003): 397–410. In an interview for the *Wichita Eagle* (Kansas), Donohue would claim in 2003, "It borders on fraud for anyone to try to make the case that there is a drop in crime," and "Lott's earlier work failed to account for the peak and subsequent decline in violent crime related to the advent of crack cocaine in the 1980s." *Wichita Eagle,* Oct. 12, 2003.

3. John J. Donohue, "Can You Believe Econometric Evaluations of Law, Policy, and Medicine," address given at the University of Virginia Law School, Oct. 24, 2008. The paper was said to contain a discussion that Donohue has in a forthcoming book.

4. See the section "Fewer Guns, More Crime" for a detailed discussion of claims by Steven Levitt regarding these claims.

5. Jordy Yager, "New Rule Prompts Fears of Guns at Inauguration," *Hill,* Dec. 27, 2008 (http://thehill.com/leading-the-news/new-rule-prompts-fears-of-guns-at-inauguration-2008-12-27.html).

6. Rep. Rob Bishop, "Telling the Second Amendment to Take a Hike," *Human Events,* Jan. 15, 2009 (http://www.humanevents.com/article.php?id=30284&page=1).

7. There is some debate about whether Iowa should be classified as a right-to-carry state or as a may-issue state, but for the empirical work in this book it isn't relevant, because it did not change its law during the period that I have examined since 1977. For convenience, I will classify Iowa as being more restrictive than some do and classify it as a may-issue state.

8. Still, even if Alabama's concealed-permit rate for the entire state is as low as the lowest urban county for which numbers are readily available (and urban counties tend to have lower rates of permits than rural areas), it would mean that more than 300,000 people in Alabama have permits—possibly the highest rate of any state in the country.

9. Information obtained from State and Local Affairs Department for the National Rifle Association's Institute for Legislative Action (July 28, 2008) and confirmed again on March 3, 2009.

10. "Well-Armed Lawmakers," *State* (Columbia, SC), Mar. 8, 2008 (http://www.feedzilla .com/news-archive/usa/2008-03-08-columbia.html).

11. Andy Sher, "1 in 4 State Legislators Holds Gun Permit," *Chattanooga Times Free Press*, Mar. 1, 2009 (http://timesfreepress.com/news/2009/mar/01/1-4-state-legislators-holds-gun -permit/).

12. Joanne Kimberlin, "Tech Massacre Only Heated Up the Gun Debate in Virginia," *Virginian-Pilot*, Mar. 2, 2008 (http://hamptonroads.com/2008/03/tech-massacre-only-heated -gun-debate-virginia).

13. Phillip Morris, "Run-In Changes Lawmaker's Stance," *Cleveland Plain Dealer*, May 15, 2007, p. B1.

14. Richard Stenger, "Armed Pilots Offer Added Protection, New Danger," CNN.com, Sept. 26, 2001.

15. John R. Lott, Jr., "P.C. Air Security: When Will Our Pilots Be Armed?" *National Review Online*, Sept. 2, 2003.

16. I worked with several of the pilots' unions over helping let pilots again carry guns. I did not accept any payments from them for the work that I did.

17. Serena Parker, "Arming Airline Pilots," *Voice of America News*, Sept. 4, 2003. See also John R. Lott, Jr., "Marshals Are Good, but Armed Pilots Are Better," *Wall Street Journal Europe*, Jan. 2, 2004 (http://online.wsj.com/article/SB107299581523057500.html?mod=opinion %255Feurope%255Fcommentaries).

18. Based on conversations with Tracy Price and Bob Lambert with the Airline Pilots Security Alliance and union representatives from Southwest and American Airlines.

19. Based on conversations both with pilots' union officials and with officials from the Transportation Security Administration during 2002 and 2003.

20. John R. Lott, Jr., "Arming of Pilots Is Way Overdue," *Los Angeles Times*, Apr. 14, 2003.

21. Ben Dubose, "Pilot's Gun Goes Off on US Airways Flight," *Los Angeles Times*, Tuesday, Mar. 25, 2008.

22. See a press release from the Airline Pilots Security Alliance, "Blame Shifts to TSA in Pilot's Gun Mishap," Mar. 27, 2008 (http://secure-skies.org/doc/PRESS%20RELEASE%20-%20 BLAME%20SHIFTS%20TO%20TSA%20IN%20PILOTS%20GUN%20MISHAP.pdf).

23. For example, John Donohue debating at the Contemporary Club in Charlottesville, Virginia, on October 22, 2008. After I described the gun going off in the cockpit, Donohue said: "John made the exact point that I made, I said that the gun went off in the cockpit and basically John [Lott]'s attitude, the NRA attitude, is sort of like NASA's view when they are bringing down the spaceships. They crash them into the earth and most of the time they don't hit anybody because there is a lot of ocean there." Quote from recording of the debate.

24. John R. Lott, Jr., "Letting Teachers Pack Guns Will Make America's Schools Safer," *Los Angeles Times*, July 13, 2003.

25. While I will discuss some of the problems with the Brady Campaign listing of incidents with permit holders, it is still interesting to note that their list does not contain a single example involving a school. See "CCW License Holders: 'Law-Abiding Citizens?'" on the Brady Campaign Web site, accessed Jan. 10, 2009 (http://www.bradycampaign.org/facts/ research/?page=incident&menu=gvr). My own extensive research as well as calls to the NEA and the AFT confirm this.

26. "Do Guns Reduce Crime?" debate on National Public Radio, Nov. 5, 2008 (broadcast available at http://www.npr.org/templates/story/story.php?storyId=96409853).

27. Ibid.

28. I also talked with Philip Ward, the assistant managing editor at the *Sun-Sentinel*. When I noted that none of the stories by O'Matz and Maines had any examples of permit holders committing crimes in their stories he said: "Well, I would say that answers your question." See also Megan O'Matz and John Maines, "Investigation Reveals Criminal Pasts of

Those Toting Guns," *South Florida Sun-Sentinel*, Jan. 28, 2007. Megan O'Matz can be reached at momatz@sun-sentinel.com and John Maines at jmaines@sun-sentinel.com.

29. This is based on a series of e-mail exchanges during December 2008 and January 2009 and telephone conversations with Sally Kestin and Philip Ward on February 17, 2009.

30. "Texas Concealed Handgun Law and Selected Statutes, 2007–2008," Texas Department of Public Safety, Austin, Oct. 2007 (http://www.txdps.state.tx.us/ftp/forms/LS-16.pdf).

31. Katie Brown, "Permit Changes Opposed: Blind Man Who Passed Defends Tests," *Bismarck Tribune*, Nov. 25, 2005.

32. Information obtained from Donna J. Street, administrative supervisor, Arizona Department of Public Safety, Concealed Weapons Permit Unit, P.O. Box 6488, Phoenix, AZ 85005; phone: 602-223-2704.

33. Jaime Holguin, "Arizona Gunman Had Threatened School," CBSNews.com, Oct. 29, 2002 (http://www.cbsnews.com/stories/2002/10/30/national/main527553.shtml).

34. Division of Licensing, Florida Department of Agriculture and Consumer Services, "Concealed Weapon/Firearm Summary Report, October 1, 1987–November 30, 2008" (http://licgweb.doacs.state.fl.us/stats/cw_monthly.html).

35. When asked about the July 1997 murder case involving Joseph Corcoran, Berkey said that case had been improperly reported as his having a permitted concealed handgun.

36. Jim Hannah, "Shooting Stirs Vigilante Justice Fears," *Cincinnati Enquirer*, Jan. 7, 2002, p. B1.

37. Information on the number of active permits is available from Dawson Bell, "Michigan Sees Fewer Gun Deaths—with More Permits," *Detroit Free Press*, Jan. 6, 2008, p. A1. Michigan State Police, "Concealed Pistol Licensure Annual Report, July 1, 2006 to June 30, 2007" (http://www.michigan.gov/documents/msp/CCW_Annual_Report_2006-2007_228850_7.pdf).

38. See the various issues of the Concealed Pistol Licensure Annual Report for Michigan that are available at http://www.michigan.gov/msp/0,1607,7-123-1591_3503_4654-77621-,00.html.

39. This information was supplied by Matt Connor with the Missouri Department of Revenue, and it covers the year up until December 11, 2008. Seventeen permits were revoked due to a protection order issued by a court, 78 were revoked due to disqualifying convictions, and one is just listed as being revoked by a court. In addition, two permits were suspended.

40. Ted Richardson, Montana Department of Justice, 406-444-2800. I talked to him during December 2008.

41. All quotes here are from a telephone conversation that I had with Rosemary Ruby during January 2009.

42. "North Carolina Concealed Handgun Permit Statistics by County, 12/01/1995 thru 12/31/2008" (http://sbi2.jus.state.nc.us/crp/public/other/conceal/Dec%2031_2008%20Data.pdf).

43. All quotes here are from a telephone conversation that I had with Tamara Road during January 2009.

44. For example, in Johnston County, the information was provided to me by Angie Butts, an administrative assistant.

45. John Futty, "Few Concealed-Carry Permits Revoked, Records Show," *Columbus Dispatch*, Aug. 13, 2006 (http://www.dispatch.com/live/contentbe/dispatch/2006/08/13/20060813-C6-00.html).

46. Attorney General of the State of Ohio, "Ohio's Concealed Handgun Law: 2008 Report to the Governor and General Assembly," Mar. 1, 2008 (http://www.ag.state.oh.us/le/prevention/concealcarry/docs/07_cc_annual_rpt.pdf).

47. "Gun Law Marks Its First Year," *Cincinnati Post*, Apr. 9, 2005, p. A1.

48. Pennsylvania State Police. "Firearm Record Information by County for 2007."

49. Pennsylvania State Police, "Firearm Record Information by County" for 2003 to 2006.

50. Conversations with Pennsylvania State Police Public Information Office press secretary Jack Lewis and Lt. Annette Quinn, Jan. 16, 2009.

51. Pennsylvania State Polic, "Firearm Record Information by County for 2007."

52. Conversations with Kim Stolfer, chairman of Firearm Owners Against Crime, Jan. 19, 2009.

53. Telephone conversation with Stolfer, Jan. 19, 2009.

54. In 2006, there were 61,539 convictions for misdemeanors and felonies among those without a concealed-handgun permit ("Conviction Rates for Concealed Handgun License Holders, Reporting Period: 01/01/2006–12/31/2006," Texas Department of Public Safety, http:// www.txdps.state.tx.us/administration/crime_records/chl/ConvictionRatesReport2006 .pdf). The adult population was 16,925,604.

55. This information is available in "Conviction Rates for Concealed Handgun License Holders, Reporting Period: 01/01/2006–12/31/2006," Texas Department of Public Safety, http:// www.txdps.state.tx.us/administration/crime_records/chl/ConvictionRatesReport2006 .pdf; "Conviction Rates for Concealed Handgun License Holders, Reporting Period: 01/ 01/2005–12/31/2005," Texas Department of Public Safety, http://www.txdps.state.tx.us/ administration/crime_records/chl/ConvictionRatesReport2005.pdf; "Conviction Rates for Concealed Handgun License Holders, Reporting Period: 01/01/2004–12/31/2004," Texas Department of Public Safety, http://www.txdps.state.tx.us/administration/crime_records/chl/ ConvictionRatesReport2004.pdf; "Conviction Rates for Concealed Handgun License Holders, Reporting Period: 01/01/2003–12/31/2003," Texas Department of Public Safety, http://www .txdps.state.tx.us/administration/crime_records/chl/ConvictionRatesReport2003.pdf; and "Conviction Rates for Concealed Handgun License Holders, Reporting Period: 01/01/2002– 12/31/2002," Texas Department of Public Safety, http://www.txdps.state.tx.us/administration/ crime_records/chl/ConvictionRatesReport2002.pdf.

56. Over the four years from 2005 to 2008, the rate at which new permits were denied was 1.3 percent. The reasons given for not issuing a permit include an alcohol violation, a protective order, that the person was wanted, a firearm offense, being a threat to oneself or another, domestic violence, moral turpitude, abuse of a controlled substance, conviction of a felony, and other. Thirty-eight percent of the denials were due to alcohol violations. Fourteen percent were due to moral turpitude. Thirteen percent were due to felonies.

One quote on the issuance of concealed-handgun permits in Utah has gotten some attention. A March 22, 2002, article in the *Salt Lake Tribune* quotes Joyce Carter, the then supervisor of the Bureau of Criminal Identification firearms section, "It's an extremely small percentage that have been revoked. But they're not all straight, law-abiding citizens. . . . I would hazard a fairly educated guess that better than 50 percent of the applicants have a criminal history of some kind." But there seems to be some debate whether the reporter accurately quoted Carter. Regarding the 50 percent claim, Carter told me on January 6, 2009, that "I am going to say that is wrong. I don't remember making that statement or even where or when I would have made it, but I have heard others quote it back to me." Nicole Starks, who replaced Carter as supervisor, said that "I don't think that it is 50 percent." There is at least one other mistake in the story. Clark Aposhian said that the reporter also confused arrests for murder with convictions. The article claimed that four permit holders had committed murder, and the actual number was two. See Dan Harrie, "Crimes Trigger Revocation of 584 Concealed-Weapon Permits," *Salt Lake Tribune*, Mar. 25, 2002, p. A1.

57. The officer had gotten a concealed-handgun permit so that he didn't have to go through the background checks when he bought a gun. Information provided by Clark Aposhian.

58. Chris Lynch, records analyst, Wyoming Division of Criminal Investigations, clynch@ dci.wyo.gov.

59. I did talk to some county offices in Colorado. In 2006, 95 revocations occurred for arrest, but there is no available information on how many of those revocations resulted in conviction. Revocations for arrest account for about 0.35 percent of active permits. The counties that I contacted were very helpful but were unable to provide me with information on convictions. Laurie Thomas, the concealed-handgun permit coordinator for El Paso County, told me that they didn't follow up to see if the arrests resulted in conviction, though she did say that none of the 24 revocations in 2006 resulted in those permit holders applying for their permits to be reinstated. Two of the 24 revocations involved prohibited use of a firearm, but Ms. Thomas told me that those types of cases usually "simply involve, I say simply because it doesn't involve the use of the gun, being drunk or intoxicated . . . while in possession of a firearm." However, she was not sure of the actual facts of those two cases. Ms. Thomas was available at 719-520-7249. See also http://www.rmgo.org/faq/CCW %20Permits%20by%20county.pdf.

60. Interestingly, Texas has the most murders by permit holders, and it also has one of the strictest concealed handgun laws—having the longest training and retraining requirements, among the highest fees for permits, and strictest restrictions on who can get permits. The Texas number is obtained by comparing Texas Department of Public Safety numbers with news reports to get more detail on each case, though this might overestimate the total because cases in the DPS conviction numbers which could not be confirmed as involving guns were assumed to involve guns. The numbers were based on calls to those state agencies that collect permit records as well as their annual reports on permit holders discussed earlier, reports from the Brady Campaign and the Violence Policy Center, and news reports. "Signature Grand Shooting an Apparent Murder-Suicide," NBC 6, Miami, FL, Apr. 29, 2003 (http://www.nbc6.net/news/2166227/detail.html); "South Florida Couple, Dog Dead in Apparent Murder-Suicide," *Orlando News*, Jan. 12, 2004 (http://www.clickorlando.com/news/ 2758332/detail.html); Louis Mockewich in Philadelphia (Associated Press, "Man Convicted of Shooting Neighbor over Snow Shoveling," Jan. 27, 2000); Jamie Cokes in Pittsburgh ("Local News, Homicide Conviction," *Pittsburgh Post-Gazette*, Nov. 8, 2002, p. B4); William Manies in Knoxville, Tennessee (Don Jacobs, "Judge Retains Gun Permit despite State Law; Statute Relies on Applicants' Honesty," *Knoxville News-Sentinel*, Oct. 1, 2000, p. B1; the crime occurred in December 1999); Shirley Henson in Alabama (Jay Reeves, "Woman Sentenced to 13 Years for 'Road Rage' Killing," Associated Press, Dec. 4, 2000; the crime occurred in November 1999); Scott Stone in North Carolina (Betsy Blaney, "Custody Loss Prompts Separation Violence," *Chicago Tribune*, Nov. 7, 1999, p. N8; the murder actually took place in Texas); John Corcoran in Indiana (Niki Kelly, "Corcoran Execution Is July 21; Killed 4 Men inside City House in '97; Federal Appeal Planned," *Fort Wayne (IN) Journal Gazette*, June 16, 2005, p. 1C); Geraldine Beasley in Ohio was convicted of voluntary manslaughter (Associated Press, "Woman Accused of Shooting Beggar Had Her Concealed Weapon Permit," *Bryan Times*, Aug. 13, 2007); Terrance Hough, Jr., in Ohio was convicted of murder (Associated Press, "Firefighter Charged in 3 Killings at Party," *Columbus Dispatch*, July 7, 2007); David Ragsdale in Utah (Janice Peterson, "David Ragsdale Gets 20 Years to Life in Prison in Wife's Murder," *Daily Herald*, Jan. 30, 2009); Jason K. Hamilton in Maine was involved in a murder-suicide (Taryn Brodwater, Bill Morlin, and Amy Cannata, "Shooter Linked to Ayrans," *Spokesman-Review*, May 23, 2007); Aaron P. Jackson in Virginia was involved in a murder-suicide (Nick Miroff, "Four Dead in Murder, Suicide in Va.," *Washington Post*, May 7, 2008); Ashford Thompson killed Joshua Miktarian in Twinsburg Township, Ohio, in July (Macollvie Jean-Francois, Brian Haas, Andrew Tran, and Rachel Hatzipangos, "Police Report: Federal Agent's Death Due to Road Rage," *South Florida Sun-Sentinel*, Aug. 7, 2008; and Karen Farkas, "Man Indicted in Killing," *Cleveland Plain Dealer*, July 22, 2008, p. B2).

As this book was going to press, the Violence Policy Center released a report entitled "CCW Total Killed," claiming that from May 2007 through December 2009, permit holders had killed 107 people. Thirty-six of the sixty-two cases involved instances where someone was charged and not convicted of murder. Take Reginald Royal's case, where the media report, "Royals saw the victim had a gun in his pocket. He saw it because he displayed it" and that he was confronted by four men who threatened him (Michelle Washington, "Waterside Shooting Was Self-Defense, Accused Man Says," *Virginian-Pilot,* March 29, 2009). Other cases included instances where there was no evidence that a permit holder had committed the crime (indeed, the police did not know who had committed it), cases that never made it to court because they obviously involved self-defense (e.g., the case of Charles Podany, who obviously used his gun to protect himself from a man who was beating him; Jessica Vander Velde, "Man Shot after Speeding Confrontation," *St. Petersburg Times,* March 2, 2008), and cases where no prison time was imposed even when there was a conviction (e.g., Willie Donaldson's case, which involved self-defense). Even a quick examination indicates that many of these cases are exactly the self-defense type of cases that legislators wanted to let occur. Instead of being counted as a cost of right-to-carry laws, they should be counted as a benefit.

61. Associated Press, "Jury Sent Home, to Return and Continue Deliberations," Associated Press Newswire, Sept. 28, 1999.

62. Associated Press, "Man Killed After Argument," Associated Press Newswire, Feb. 26, 1999.

63. Associated Press, "Wallace Found Guilty of Negligent Homicide," Associated Press Newswire, Sept. 29, 1999.

64. Associated Press, "Man Killed After Argument."

65. Associated Press, "Jury Sent Home, to Return and Continue Deliberations"; Associated Press, "Wallace Found Guilty of Negligent Homicide."

66. Deon Hampton, "Charge Filed in Road-Rage Homicide: A Former Security Guard Who Said He Feared for His Life Was Not Justified in Shooting Another Man, the D.A. Says," *Tulsa World,* Sept. 27, 2007.

67. Bill Braun, "Plea Deal Reached in Fatal Shooting," *Tulsa World,* May 30, 2008, A1.

68. Mike Glenn, "Longshoreman Charged in Fatal Eastside Shooting," *Houston Chronicle,* Apr. 25, 2006, p. B3.

69. Identity of person engaging in the attack based on discussion with Brian Rogers of the *Houston Chronicle.*

70. Brian Rogers, "Convicted Killer Ordered to Serve 10 Years' Probation; Attorney Says Man Was Defending Himself at the Time of Fatal Shooting," *Houston Chronicle,* July 22, 2008.

71. See "Comments Opposing Proposed Rule to Allow the Carrying of Loaded, Hidden Firearms in National Park Areas and National Wildlife Refuges" from the Brady Campaign Web site, accessed Jan. 10, 2009 (http://www.bradycampaign.org/xshare/pdf/fedleg/national-park-comments.pdf).

72. Associated Press, "Public-Safety Department Lists 23 Concealed-Gun Incidents; House Panel Tracking Law's Effects, Enforcement," *Dallas Morning News,* July 17, 1996.

73. Ralph Winingham, "Although Cleared of Murder Charge, Memories Remain," *San Antonio Express-News,* Sept. 7, 1997, p. 29A.

74. "CCW License Holders: 'Law-Abiding Citizens?'" on the Brady Campaign Web site, accessed Jan. 10, 2009 (http://www.bradycampaign.org/facts/research/?page=incident&menu=gvr).

75. Bill Braun, "Man Cleared in Fatal Shooting: Slaying Case Is First Involving a Legally Concealed Weapon," *Tulsa World,* Feb. 12, 1999, p. 17.

76. William C. Rempel and Lianne Hart, "Murder Case Puts New Focus on Texas' Concealed Gun Law," *Los Angeles Times,* Nov. 2, 2000, p. A5.

77. Both the Brady Campaign and the Violence Policy Center have tracked cases—the Brady Campaign up through the beginning of 2007 and the Violence Policy Center up through the end of 1998. Their Web sites were last checked on January 10, 2009. The Brady Campaign's list of crimes by permit holder is at http://www.bradycampaign.org/xshare/

pdf/reports/no-gun-left-behind.pdf and http://www.bradycampaign.org/facts/research/
?page=incident&menu=gvr. The list for the Violence Policy Center is available at http://
www.vpc.org/Studies/ltk2cont.htm.

78. In 2007, that equals 0.017 murders per 100,000 permit holders. By contrast, for the
United States has a whole, 4.47 adults were arrested for committing murder out of every
100,000 adults. "Expanded Homicide Data Table 3," in "Crime in the United States 2007,"
FBI *Uniform Crime Reports* (http://www.fbi.gov/ucr/cius2007/offenses/expanded_information/
data/shrtable_03.html). These calculations assume an adult population in the United States
of 227 million in 2007.

79. The other cases are these:

Thibodaux, Louisiana (Jan. 1, 2009)—"Police said a city man was shot and wounded
Thursday night while trying to rob another at gunpoint near a Canal Boulevard convenience store. . . . No charges have been filed against [the armed victim]" (John DeSantis,
"Police Say Victim Shot Robbery Suspect," *Thibodaux Daily Comment*, Jan. 2, 2009; http://www
.dailycomet.com/article/20090102/ARTICLES/901029977/1212?Title=Police_say_victim_
shot_robbery_suspect).

Anniston, Alabama (Dec. 24, 2008)—"A would-be robber was shot dead overnight
Wednesday and his alleged accomplice was wounded after they attempted to commit a
robbery at a gas station near Anniston. Calhoun County Sheriff Larry Amerson said . . . he
acted in self-defense" (Associated Press, "Robbery Suspect Shot Dead, Alleged Accomplice
Wounded," *Huntsville Times*, Dec. 25, 2008; http://blog.al.com/breaking/2008/12/robbery_
suspect_shot_dead_alle.html).

Orlando, Florida (Dec. 23, 2008)—Three men attempted to rob a woman in a mall
parking lot. Two of the men were wrestling with the woman. A permit holder shot one of
the suspects in the leg ("Police: Bystander Shoots Robber in Mall Parking Lot," WESH.com,
Thursday, Dec. 23, 2008; http://www.msnbc.msn.com/id/28380721/).

80. "Police: Man Shoots, Kills Suspect in Hammond Robbery Attempt," *Northwest Indiana Times*, Jan. 12, 2009; http://nwitimes.com/articles/2009/01/12/news/top_news/
docce29b62cf028c9ef8625753c00081c82.txt).

81. In this second follow-up story they mention that the individual who fired his gun defensively had a concealed-handgun permit. "Police: Statements Support Self Defense Claim
in Fatal Shooting," *Northwest Indiana Times*, Jan. 12, 2009; http://www.thetimesonline.com/
articles/2009/01/12/updates/breaking_news/doc496ba228600bb151954649.txt).

82. "Victim Kills Robbery Suspect at Car Wash," WFTV.com, Jan. 9, 2009 (http://www
.wftv.com/news/18451573/detail.html).

83. "Police: Man Shoots, Kills Armed Robber at Car Wash," WESH.com (Orlando),
Jan. 10, 2009 (http://www.wesh.com/news/18451432/detail.html).

84. "2 Men Sought After Customer Saves Clerk from Robber," WESH.com (Orlando),
Jan. 7, 2009 (http://www.msnbc.msn.com/id/28518530/).

85. "West Park Homeowner Kills Robber," *Florida Today*, Dec. 26, 2008 (http://www
.floridatoday.com/article/20081226/BREAKINGNEWS/81226044/1006/NEWS01).

86. "Dog Walker Kills Armed Teen Robber, Police Say," MyFoxDFW, Dec. 18, 2008 (http://
www.myfoxdfw.com/myfox/pages/News/Detail?contentId=8100189&version=5&locale
=EN-US&layoutCode=TSTY&pageId=3.2.1).

87. Jared Broyles, "Concealed Carry Permit Comes in Handy for Woman in Fort
Smith," KFSM.com, Channel 5 News, Dec. 18, 2008 (http://www.kfsm.com/Global/story
.asp?S=9541680).

88. Minnesota's permit system was prevented from issuing more permits from July 2004
to June 2005.

89. The means and standard deviations for the state-level data are shown in appendix
table 10A.1.

90. Change.gov, the Office of the President-Elect, under Agenda, under Urban Policy,

under the headline "The Obama-Biden Plan" (http://change.gov/agenda/urbanpolicy_agenda/).

91. One could add up the list of places where permitted concealed handguns are prohibited, and I have done that in some of my research, but it is also somewhat arbitrary, because it assumes that all prohibited places are equally important to permit holders. Grambsch is a public health researcher who estimates that later adoption of right-to-carry laws gives states reduced benefits, but despite my suggestion to her, there is no attempt to account for later states having more restrictive laws. Patricia Grambsch, "Regression to the Mean, Murder Rates, and Shall-Issue Laws," *American Statistician* 62, no. 4 (2008): 289–95.

92. "Bill Would Allow Prosecutors Guns in Court," KCTV Channel 5 News, Jan. 23, 2009 (http://www.kctv5.com/news/18546809/detail.html). Gorman isn't alone. Reno County prosecutor Thomas Stanton says, "We act to insure those who violate the laws of Kansas receive consequences for their actions. This can lead to prosecutors being targets of violent acts perpetrated by defendants, their families and their friends." Stanton said that he would carry a concealed firearm, but the prohibitions on where he can carry a gun makes it impracticable. Tim Carpenter, "Concealed-Carry Bill Would Let Prosecutors Be Armed in Court," *Topeka Capital-Journal*, Jan. 21, 2009 (http://cjonline.com/stories/012109/sta_379727801.shtml).

93. Nancy Badertscher, "Georgia Law: Guns Allowed in More Places: 79% More Apply for Firearms Permit," *Atlanta Journal-Constitution*, Feb. 1, 2009 (http://www.ajc.com/services/content/printedition/2009/02/01/gunpermits02011.html).

94. For Florida's information see http://licgweb.doacs.state.fl.us/stats/cw_active.html. The explosion in Utah's issuing of permits in 2008 was due to out-of-state residents (http://www.des.utah.gov/bci/documents/2008Q4.pdf).

95. Following Donohue, "The Final Bullet in the Body of the More Guns, Less Crime Hypothesis," and F. Plassmann and John Whitley, "Confirming 'More Guns, Less Crime,'" *Stanford Law Review*, 2003, pp. 1313–69, I will do the year-by-year affects by two-year intervals.

96. The drops are statistically significant at better than the 10 percent level by years 5 and 6 after the law was put in place. These levels of significance are calculated using robust standard errors. By years 11 and 12, the drop is statistically significant at the 5 percent level, and by years 15 or more later, the drop is significant at better than the 1 percent level. A breakdown of the year-by-year levels of significance is shown in appendix 10.2.

97. The drop in violent crime is statistically significant at 7 percent level by years 3 and 4 after the law.

98. The drop is statistically significant at the 2 percent level by years 3 and 4 after the law.

99. The estimated benefits from reduced property crimes shown in table 10.6 depend a lot upon what set of estimates are used. For example, if the change in average crime rates before and after the law had been used, property crimes would have been associated with an equally large increase in victimization costs, reducing the total gain to the states by about one-third.

100. Ian Ayres and John Donohue, "Nondiscretionary Concealed Weapons Laws: A Case Study of Statistics, Standards of Proof, and Public Policy," *American Law and Economics Review* 1 (1999): 436; William Bartley and Mark Cohen, "The Effect of Concealed Weapons Laws: An Extreme Bound Analysis," *Economic Inquiry* 36 (Apr. 1998): 259; Daniel Black and Daniel Nagin, "Do Right-to-Carry Laws Deter Violent Crime?" *Journal of Legal Studies* 27 (1998): 209; Stephen Bronars and John R. Lott, "Criminal Deterrence, Geographic Spillovers, and Right-to-Carry Laws," *American Economic Review* 88 (1998): 475.

101. F. Plassmann and T. N. Tideman, "Does the Right to Carry Concealed Handguns Deter Countable Crimes? Only a Count Analysis Can Say," *Journal of Law and Economics* 44 (2001): 771–98.

102. C. E. Moody, "Testing for the Effects of Concealed Weapons Laws: Specification Errors and Robustness," *Journal of Law and Economics* 44, no. 2, pt. 2 (2001): 799–813.

103. Carlisle Moody and Thomas Marvell, "The Debate on Shall-Issue Laws," *Econ Journal Watch*, Sept. 2008, pp. 269–93.

104. E. Helland and A. Tabarrok, "Using Placebo Laws to Test 'More Guns, Less Crime,'" *Advances in Economic Analysis and Policy* 4, no. 1 (2004).

105. D. E. Olsen and M. D. Maltz, "Right-to-Carry Concealed Weapons Laws and Homicide in Large U.S. Counties: The Effect on Weapons Types, Victim Characteristics, and Victim-Offender Relationships," *Journal of Law and Economics* 44 (2001): 747–70.

106. B. L. Benson and B. D. Mast, "Privately Produced General Deterrence," *Journal of Law and Economics* 44 (2001): 725–46.

107. D. B. Mustard, "The Impact of Gun Laws on Police Deaths," *Journal of Law and Economics* 44 (2001): 635–57.

108. James Q. Wilson, "Dissent," in *Firearms and Violence: A Critical Review*, ed. Charles F. Wellford, John V. Pepper, and Carol V. Petrie (Washington, DC: National Academies Press, 2005), appendix A.

109. John R. Lott, Jr., and John Whitley, "Safe Storage Gun Laws: Accidental Deaths, Suicides, and Crime," *Journal of Law and Economics* 44, no. 2, pt. 2 (Oct. 2001): 659–89.

110. The only study that tried to retest my results for the Brady Act was by Jens Ludwig and Philip Cook, and they also found that the law had no statistical impact on murder rates or overall accidental gun deaths or suicides. Their study did not examine the one crime category for which I found an increase in crime, rapes. Even though they concede that the Brady Act had no effect on total suicides, they claim that it reduced suicides for those over age 55. A closer look at narrower age groupings contradicts the pattern that they predict. The reduced incidence of firearm suicides for persons over 54 is overwhelmingly driven by the change for just those from ages 55 to 64, but this subcategory has the lowest suicide rate for those over age 54 and has the highest gun ownership rate. The different age groups experienced apparently random increases and decreases in firearm suicides after enactment of the law: the groups aged 35–44 years, 45–54 years, and older than age 85 all show increases in firearm suicides after the Brady Act. (See Jens Ludwig and Philip Cook, "Homicide and Suicide Rates Associated with Implementation of the Brady Handgun Violence Prevention Act," *Journal of the American Medical Association*, Aug. 2, 2000, pp. 585–91; and John R. Lott, Jr., "Impact of the Brady Act on Homicide and Suicide Rates," *Journal of the American Medical Association*, Dec. 6, 2000, p. 2718.)

111. In fact, there is frequently much more variation in crime rates or other individual characteristics across counties within a state than there is across states. For example, 80 percent of the counties in the United States have zero murders in any given year, and even the states with the highest murder rates contain many counties without any murders.

112. To obtain the level of statistical significance for his table 12, column 2, one must divide the coefficients by the reported standard errors. When that is done, four of the five violent crime rates indeed show a statistically significant reduction after the passage of the right-to-carry law. The *t*-statistics for these coefficients when they are corrected are at least 2.3 for a two-tailed *t*-test. See Mark Duggan, "More Guns, More Crime," *Journal of Political Economy* 109 (2001): 1110, table 12.

113. Two other points need to be made. First, Duggan provides no evidence that the adjustments that he makes are appropriate (indeed, my original paper with Mustard discussed these adjustments). Second, examining the before-and-after trends produce extremely statistically significant results. Duggan chose only to report the results for the before-and-after averages.

114. Of the two significant positive coefficients, one by Black and Nagin includes separate nonlinear time trends for each state (see chapter 9, critique 2, "Does it make sense for

nonlinear time trends for each state?" for a discussion of this). The one significant result from Duggan uses differences even though he doesn't do any tests for whether this is the appropriate specification. (In fact, Moody, "Testing for the Effects of Concealed Weapons Laws," p. 805, tests for unit roots and finds that county crime rates are stationary.)

There is one paper by Dezhbakhsh and Rubin that is critical of my work, but I have not included it in table 10.7, because it is a shorter version of the exact same empirical work that is already included in the list. They also do not investigate the differences in crime rates before and after right-to-carry laws are adopted (Hashem Dezhbakhsh and Paul H. Rubin, "Lives Saved or Lives Lost? The Effects of Concealed-Handgun Laws on Crime," *American Economic Review Papers and Proceedings* 88 (May 1998): 468–74). This has been discussed in other parts of this book.

115. Black and Nagin mark only the levels of statistical significance at the 5 percent level. There are a number of negative coefficients with statistical significance between the 5 and 10 percent levels.

116. For example, Ian Ayres and John J. Donohue III, "Shooting Down the More Guns, Less Crime Hypothesis" (draft version available from author), p. 20, write: "Note that for a number of the violent crime categories, very large negative estimated coefficients are found on some of the dummies for more than 6 years after passage. As noted, only a small portion of the entire array of shall issue states contribute to these estimates, thereby allowing a substantial drop in crime in an early passing state (whether caused by the shall issue law or not) to have a disproportionate effect in estimating a post-passage dummy or linear trend."

117. Steven Levitt, "Understanding Why Crime Fell in the 1990s: Four Factors That Explain the Decline and Six That Do Not," *Journal of Economic Perspectives* 18 (Winter 2004): 175.

118. Grant Duwe, Tom Kovandzic, and Carl Moody, "The Impact of Right-to-Carry Concealed Firearm Laws on Mass Public Shootings," *Homicide Studies*, Nov. 1, 2002.

119. John R. Lott, Jr., and William M. Landes, "Acts of Terror with Guns: Multiple Victim Shootings," in *The Bias Against Guns* (Washington, DC: Regnery, 2003), chapter 6.

120. It was also nice of Maltz and Targonski to state: "We should note that the authors of these studies were not aware of the extent of the problems with the data they used. In fact, they went to great lengths to secure the best possible data and conferred with many people (including an author of this paper) prior to performing their analysis" (Michael D. Maltz and Joseph Targonski, "A Note on the Use of County-Level UCR Data," *Journal of Quantitative Criminology*, Sept. 2002, p. 298.)

121. John R. Lott, Jr., and John Whitley, "Measurement Error in County-Level UCR Data," *Journal of Quantitative Criminology* 19, no. 2 (June 2003): 185–98.

122. The city-level data also answer another related objection. A referee for this book argued that right-to-carry laws "required local police agencies to perform fingerprinting of carry permit (CP) applicants, as well as other administrative tasks in processing applications, it placed a strain on agencies with less manpower relative to the demand for their services. This caused the agencies to withdraw personnel who compiled the (voluntary) UCR statistics and reassign them to the CP-related tasks mandated by the state legislature." While such a bias might affect county-level data, there is no bias that this creates in either city- or state-level data. Since all three types of data imply the same change in violent crime rates, it provides evidence against the claim that the results are driven by a bias in the county data. If this is a problem, eliminating the counties with the most missing data should cause the results to become less negative, but that is not the case.

123. See Duggan, "More Guns, More Crime," p. 1086.

124. There is also work that finds that magazine sales did not precede increases in murder rates. Carlisle E. Moody and Thomas B. Marvell, "Guns and Crime," *Southern Economic Journal* 71 (2005): 720–36.

125. Based on a telephone call with Mr. Johnson on December 5, 2001.

126. Ayres and Donohue, "Shooting Down the More Guns, Less Crime Hypothesis," p. 1296.

127. http://www.npr.org/templates/story/story.php?storyId=96409853.

128. See Roland Fryer, Paul Heaton, Steven Levitt, and Kevin Murphy, "Measuring the Impact of Crack Cocaine," *Social Science Research Network*, May 2005 (http://ssrn.com/abstract=720405).

129. Charles F. Wellford, John V. Pepper, and Carol V. Petrie, eds., *Firearms and Violence: A Critical Review* (Washington, DC: National Research Council of the National Academies and National Academies Press, 2004), p. 2.

130. "Do Guns Reduce Crime?"

131. Wellford, Pepper, and Petrie, *Firearms and Violence*, p. 2.

132. E-mail correspondence from James Q. Wilson to me, November 25, 2008. In e-mail correspondence with me on January 6, 2009, John Donohue did not accept this response from Wilson.

133. Wilson, "Dissent," p. 269.

134. Charles C. Branas, Therese S. Richmond, Dennis P. Culhane, Thomas R. Ten Have, and Douglas J. Wiebe, "Investigating the Link between Gun Possession and Gun Assault," *American Journal of Public Health* 99, no. 11 (Nov. 2009): 1–7.

135. Gary Kleck and Miriam A. Delone, "Victim Resistance and Offender Weapon Effects in Robbery," *Journal of Quantitative Criminology* 9 (1993): 55–81; Lawrence Southwick, "Self-Defense with Guns," *Journal of Criminal Justice* 28 (2000): 351–370; and Jongyeon Tark and Gary Kleck, "Resisting Crime," *Criminology* 42 (2004): 861–909.

136. The complete text of Levitt's letter is available at http://johnrlott.blogspot.com/2007/08/steve-levitts-correction-letter.html.

137. David Glenn, "Unusual Agreement Means Settlement May Be Near in 'Lott v. Levitt,'" *Chronicle of Higher Education*, July 27, 2007.

138. Unfortunately, the *Stanford Law Review*'s correction piece hasn't stopped Ayres and Donohue from continuing to make this claim even six years later. In a new paper that they released in 2009 just two days before I finished writing this book, Ayres and Donohue made the claim again, writing: "After we pointed out that our corrections of Lott's errors had rendered statistically insignificant all of the Lott, Plassmann, and Whitley results, Lott removed his name from the reply to Ayres and Donohue (2003a), which then was published—with the errors uncorrected—as Plassmann and Whitley (2003)."

Or take this example from another piece by Donohue that was published after the *Stanford Law Review* correction: "Lott acted somewhat incongruously in dropping his name from his reply to my work with Ian Ayres on the eve of publication. Ayres and I showed that virtually every regression in Lott's reply to our paper in the *Stanford Law Review* was incorrect due to Lott's coding errors." Donohue, "The Final Bullet in the Body of the More Guns, Less Crime Hypothesis," pp. 397–410.

139. A copy of the *Stanford Law Review* "Clarification" can be found at http://johnrlott.tripod.com/clarification.pdf.

140. See http://www.law.cornell.edu/supct/pdf/07-290P.ZD1.

141. Vivian S. Chu, "District of Columbia v. Heller: The Supreme Court and the Second Amendment," Congressional Research Service report for Congress, Jan. 15, 2009.

142. *National Rifle Association, et al. v. City of Chicago* and *National Rifle Association, et al. v. Village of Oak Park*, filed December 4, 2008, in the United States District Court for the Northern District of Illinois, Eastern Division, *Case 1:08-cv-03697* 4, 2008 (http://www.chicagoguncase.com/wp-content/uploads/2008/12/dist_ct_nra_opinion.pdf).

143. Kim Murphy, "Proposed Seattle Gun Ban May Draw New Fire," *Los Angeles Times*, Nov. 25, 2008.

144. Suzanne Pardington, "Oregon Universities' Gun Ban Faces Legal Test," *Oregonian*, Feb. 20, 2009 (http://www.oregonlive.com/news/index.ssf/2009/02/oregon_universities_

gun_ban_fa.html); Windsor Genova, "Rifle Association Suit Seeks End to Chicago, San Francisco Gun Bans," *Gant Daily*, June 27, 2008 (http://www.gantdaily.com/news/35/ARTICLE/24122/2008-06-27.html).

145. DC's brief and various amici point to murder as the violent crime category that was reduced after the DC handgun ban went into effect during February 1977. No other violent crime rate is pointed to.

146. John R. Lott, Jr., "Does a Helping Hand Put Others at Risk? Affirmative Action, Police Departments, and Crime," *Economic Inquiry* 38, no. 2 (Apr. 2000): 239–77.

147. Colin Loftin, David McDowall, Brian Wiersema, and Talbert J. Cottey, "Effects of Restrictive Licensing of Handguns on Homicide and Suicide in the District of Columbia," *New England Journal of Medicine* 325 (1991): 1615.

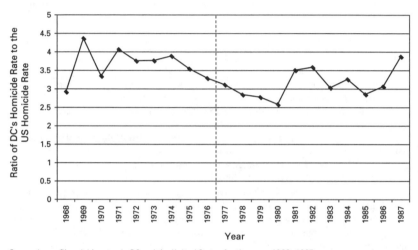

Comparison of homicide rates in DC and the United States for the years 1968–1987

148. James Alan Fox and David McDowall, "Brief of Professors of Criminal Justice as Amici Curiae in Support of the Petitioners," submitted to the Supreme Court of the United States in *District of Columbia v. Heller*, no. 07-290, Jan. 11, 2008 (http://www.gurapossessky.com/news/parker/documents/07-290tsacprof.ofcrim.just.pdf).

149. The debate between John Donohue and myself took place at the Contemporary Club in Charlottesville, Virginia, on October 22, 2008.

150. The average ratio from 1968 to 1976 was 219 percent compared to the average rate of 257 percent from 1977 to 1987.

151. Gary Kleck compares the changes in DC's murder rate to the changes in Baltimore's.

152. "Do Guns Reduce Crime?"

153. See http://www.law.cornell.edu/supct/pdf/07-290P.ZD1.

154. The Chicago Handgun Freeze of 1982 stopped the registration of handguns after April 10, 1982, but a lawsuit was immediately filed by Jerome Sklar, an individual who had moved to Chicago from Skokie, Illinois, on April 15. The case *Sklar v. Byrne* (*Federal Supplement*, vol. 556, p. 736 [Northern District of Illinois, 1983]) did not have a judgment entered until February 1983, and enforcement of Chicago's ordinances did not begin until that date. The Seventh Circuit didn't reach its decision in *Quilici v. Village of Morton Grove* upholding Morton Grove's ban on handguns until December 6, 1982. Richard Pearson, the executive director of the Illinois State Rifle Association, said that Chicago didn't really enforce the ban until the be-

ginning of 1983, when these legal cases had run their course. Chicago's registration rules had been in effect since 1968. I interviewed Victor Quilici, the plaintiff in *Quilici v. Village of Morton Grove*, on January 9, 2009. I also interviewed Kenneth Denberg, the lawyer who had filed Sklar's case in District Court, on January 14, 2009, but he was unable to add anything to this discussion (312-704-3000). See Illinois Citizens for Handgun Control, "Sample Firearms Regulations in Illinois Municipalities—Four Types of Local Ordinances in Effect in Illinois in 1983 and the Judicial Opinions Regarding Their Constitutionality," National Institute of Justice, 1983 (http://www.ncjrs.gov/App/Publications/abstract.aspx?ID=96896). I also talked to Richard Pearson, the head of the Illinois State Rifle Association, by telephone on January 9, 2009.

155. The FBI's UCR had data on cities with more than 10,000 people between 1974 and 2005.

156. The adjacent counties in Illinois are Lake, Will, DuPage, Kane, and McHenry. In Indiana, there is also Lake County.

157. David Leppard, "Ministers 'Covered Up' Gun Crime," *London Times*, Aug. 26, 2007.

158. David Kopel, *The Samurai, the Mountie, and the Cowboy* (Amherst, NY: Prometheus Books, 1992), pp. 73–78.

159. Don B. Kates and Gary A. Mauser, "Would Banning Firearms Reduce Murder and Suicide: A Review of International Evidence," *Harvard Journal of Law and Public Policy* 30 (Spring 2007): 651–94.

160. For Anguilla, Antigua and Barbuda, Dominica, Grenada, Montserrat, Saint Kitts and Nevis, Saint Lucia, and Saint Vincent and the Grenadines, the average murder rate rose to 19.9 per 100,000 people in 2007. The murder rate in Trinidad and Tobago rose to a historical high of 30.6. That same year, Jamaica's murder rate was at 58. "A Caribbean Crime Wave," *Economist*, Mar. 20, 2008 (http://www.economist.com/displayStory.cfm?story_id=10903343&fsrc=RSS).

161. Jamaica's crime data were obtained from a variety of sources. Its murder data from 1960 to 1967 were obtained from Terry Lacey, *Violence and Politics in Jamaica, 1960–70* (Manchester: Manchester University Press, 1977). Professor Gary Mauser obtained the data from 1970 to 2000 from a Professor A. Francis in Jamaica and the data from 2001 to 20006 from the Statistical Institute of Jamaica (http://www.statinja.com/stats.html). Jamaica's population estimates were obtained from NationMaster.com (http://www.nationmaster.com/graph/peo_pop-people-population&date=1975).

162. "While Firearms Seized at Border on Rise, Majority of Guns Caught from Vacationers, not Smugglers," *Global Travel Industry News*, May 18, 2008 (http://www.eturbonews.com/2554/while-firearms-seized-border-rise-majority-gu). The article originally appeared in the *Toronto Sun*.

163. National Gang Intelligence Center, U.S. Department of Justice, "National Gang Threat Assessment 2009," Jan. 2009 (http://www.usdoj.gov/ndic/pubs32/32146/index.htm). See also Kevin Johnson, "FBI: Burgeoning Gangs Behind up to 80% of U.S. Crime," *USA Today*, Jan. 29, 2009, p. A1 (http://www.usatoday.com/news/nation/2009-01-29-ms13_N.htm).

164. Loftin et al.'s suicide analysis (like his homicide analysis) looked only at raw numbers, not rates, and therefore failed to account for DC's decline in population. By ignoring rates, Loftin implied a somewhat larger drop in suicides than actually occurred. A graph showing the number of suicides instead of the suicide rate can be found in Loftin et al., "Effects of Restrictive Licensing in Handguns," p. 1620.

165. D. M. Cutler, E. L. Glaeser, and K. E. Norberg, "Explaining the Rise in Youth Suicide," in Risky Behavior Among Youths: An Economic Analysis, ed. J. Gruber (Chicago: University of Chicago Press, 2001), pp. 219–69.

166. Jerome Taylor, "Mumbai Photographer: I Wish I'd Had a Gun, Not a Camera; Armed Police Would Not Fire Back," *Belfast Telegraph* (Northern Ireland), Nov. 29, 2008 (http://www.belfasttelegraph.co.uk/news/world-news/article14086308.ece).

167. Yaroslav Trofimov, Geeta Anad, Peter Wonacott, and Matthew Rosenberg, "India Security Faulted as Survivors Tell of Terror," *Wall Street Journal*, Dec. 1, 2008, p. A1 (http://online.wsj.com/article/SB122809281744967855.html).

168. Abhijeet Singh, "Gun Ownership in India" (http://www.abhijeetsingh.com/arms/india/).

169. In 2002, there were about 6.5 million people living in Israel. Of those, 81 percent were Jews and 63 percent were over 20 years of age (http://www.jafi.org.il/agenda/2001/english/wk3–1/14.asp and http://www.un.org/Depts/unsd/social/youth.htm). Arabs were restricted from obtaining concealed-handgun permits. At the time of this writing Israel had 340,000 handgun permit holders, though they were planning on issuing 40,000 more permits ("Army Issuing 40,000 Handgun Permits," IsraelNN.com, Mar. 6, 2002 [http://www.israelnationalnews.com/news.php3?id=19628]). Related information can be found at http://www.jpost.com/Editions/2002/03/06/LatestNews/LatestNews.44715.html, though this second story appears to include only a portion of all the permit holders.

170. See Lott and Landes's discussion in "Acts of Terror with Guns" for examples.

171. Steven Gray, "How the NIU Massacre Happened," *Time*, Feb. 16, 2008 (http://www.time.com/time/nation/article/0,8599,1714069,00.html?cnn=yes).

172. "Worst U.S. Shooting Ever Kills 33 on Va. Campus: 15 Others Wounded as Panic Grips Virginia Tech for 2½ Hours," MSNBC.com, Apr. 17, 2007 (http://www.msnbc.msn.com/id/18134671/).

173. Associated Press, "Gunman Who Killed 5 at Missouri Council Meeting Left Suicide Note 'Truth Will Come Out,'" FoxNews.com, Feb. 8, 2008 (http://www.foxnews.com/story/0,2933,329767,00.html).

174. http://www.foxnews.com/video2/player06.html?020808/020808_studiob_thornton&Studio_B&%26%2392%3B%26%2339%3BNot%20Right%20or%20Wrong%26%2392%3B%26%2339%3B&%26%2392%3B%26%2339%3BNot%20Right%20or%20Wrong%26%2392%3B%26%2339%3B&US&-1&News&335&&&new.

175. John Keenan, "Few Merchants See Need to Post No-Weapons Signs," *Omaha World-Herald*, Mar. 28, 2007 (http://4.bp.blogspot.com/_2SW2_lbrxgY/R1gZwy1WaWI/AAAAAAAAAE8/a6HSha-Arys/s1600-h/Picture+5.png).

176. A picture of the warning signs at the mall can be seen in John R. Lott, Jr., "Evidence that Trolley Square Mall in Utah Occurred in a 'Gun Free Zone,'" Johnrlott.blogspot.com, Feb. 15, 2007 (http://johnrlott.blogspot.com/2007/02/proof-that-trolley-square-mall-in-utah.html).

177. Associated Press, "5 Dead in Illinois Mall Shooting; Suspect Still on the Loose," FoxNews.com, Feb. 3, 2008 (http://www.foxnews.com/story/0,2933,327908,00.html).

178. An article in the *Omaha World-Herald* noted: "Signs banning guns from privately owned businesses haven't exactly popped up all over the Omaha area." Keenan, "Few Merchants See Need to Post No-Weapons Signs."

179. See Lott and Landes, "Acts of Terror with Guns."

180. Ibid.

181. Trofimov et al., "India Security Faulted as Survivors Tell of Terror."

182. "18 Dead in German School Shooting," BBC News, Apr. 26, 2002 (http://news.bbc.co.uk/2/hi/europe/1952869.stm); Nick Allen, "Finland School Shooting: Gunman Planned Massacre for Six Years," *London Telegraph*, Sept. 24, 2008 (http://www.telegraph.co.uk/news/worldnews/europe/finland/3071235/Finland-school-shooting-Gunman-planned-massacre-for-six-years.html); "'Grudge' Behind Swiss Gun Massacre," CNN, Sept. 27, 2001 (http://archives.cnn.com/2001/WORLD/europe/09/27/switzerland.shooting/index.html); and John Lichfield, "Gunman with a Grudge Kills Four in French Shooting Spree," *Independent*, Oct. 30, 2001 (http://www.independent.co.uk/news/world/europe/gunman-with-a-grudge-kills-four-in-french-shooting-spree-633112.html). Another attack at a German school in

2006 wounded eleven people ("I Loathe People: Ex-pupil Wounds 11 in German School Shooting," *Spiegel Online International*, Nov. 20, 2006 (http://www.spiegel.de/international/ 0,1518,449492,00.html)).

183. "Greek Gunman Dies After Shooting," BBC, Apr. 10, 2009 (http://news.bbc.co.uk/ 2/hi/europe/7993401.stm); "One Killed in Dutch Café Shooting," BBC, Apr. 11, 2009 (http:// news.bbc.co.uk/2/hi/europe/7994731.stm); and David Nowak, "Moscow Policeman Opens Fire in Public, Kills 3," Associated Press, Apr. 27, 2009.

184. Marcella Bombardieri, "Campus Police Renew Call to Carry Arms," *Boston Globe*, Apr. 28, 2007 (http://www.boston.com/news/local/articles/2007/04/28/campus_police_ renew_call_to_carry_arms/).

185. Scott Buhrmaster, "Should Campus Cops Carry Guns? One College President Says No," Policeone.com, Nov. 19, 2003.

186. Fred Abraham, "No One Benefits from Arming of UNI Safety Officers," *Cedar Falls Courier*, May 6, 2007 (http://www.wcfcourier.com/articles/2007/05/06/columnists/guest_ column/c904ad59385a60bd862572d1006016b0.txt).

187. "Safety and Security on the Virginia Tech Campus," Division of Student Affairs, Virginia Tech University, as posted on May 30, 2007 (http://www.dsa.vt.edu/family/Safetylisting .php). Since that time the campus police force has expanded by a third.

188. William M. Landes, "An Economic Study of U.S. Airline Hijacking, 1961–1976," *Journal of Law and Economics* 21 (Apr. 1978): 1–32.

189. Ibid.

190. "Ohio Trainer Makes the Case for Single-Officer Entry Against Active Killers," Policeone.com, May 14, 2008 (http://www.policeone.com/active-shooter/articles/1695125 -Ohio-trainer-makes-the-case-for-single-officer-entry-against-active-killers/). The article says: "'Time is our worst adversary in dealing with active killers,' Borsch told *Force Science News*. 'We're racing what I call "the Stopwatch of Death." Victims are often added to the toll every several seconds.'" Brendan Keefe, "When Seconds Count: Stopping Active Killers," WCPO.com, Nov. 21, 2008 (http://www.wcpo.com/news/local/story/When-Seconds-Count -Stopping-Active-Killers/_yls0jTxAkK8QJR1NKbePA.cspx). Keefe's news article notes: "Based on the Virginia Tech data, top tactics training facilities determined the first officer on scene should make entry immediately with an aggressive attack on the shooter. Every minute the officer waits for back-up, another three or more people could die. In other words, while it was once considered suicide for a lone officer to take on an active killer, it is now considered statistical homicide for him not to do so."

191. P. Solomon Banda, "Year After Attack, Colorado Church Guard Reflects," Policeone .com, Dec. 8, 2008 (http://www.policeone.com/patrol-issues/articles/1763667-Year -after-attack-Colo-church-guard-reflects/). Jeanne Assam had prior experience as a police officer.

192. "Armed Citizens Stop Memphis Street Shooter," WBIR.com, Mar. 8, 2007 (http:// www.wbir.com/news/local/story.aspx?storyid=43109). A copy of the article can also be found at http://johnrlott.blogspot.com/2007/03/two-concealed-handgun-permit-holders .html.

193. Josh White, "Law School Shooter Pleads Guilty, Former Student Avoids Death Penalty in Deal on Va. Slayings," *Washington Post*, Feb. 28, 2004, p. B3. "Mississippi v. Luke Woodham," Court TV archives (http://www.courttv.com/archive/trials/woodham/).

194. "Counselors' Heroism Foils Terror Attack in Gush Etzion Seminary High School," Jan. 25, 2008 (http://web.israelinsider.com/Articles/Security/12596.htm). Tzippe Barrow, "Terrorists Target Israeli Students," CBNNews.com, Jan. 25, 2008 (http://www.cbn.com/ CBNnews/310078.aspx). News Agencies, "Jerusalem Yeshiva Student: I Shot the Terrorist Twice in the Head," Haaretz.com, July 7, 2008 (http://www.haaretz.com/hasen/spages/ 961703.html).

195. A recent segment on ABC's *20/20* mentioned this as a possibility, but the reporters were not able to identify a single example of this either ("If I Only Had a Gun," http://abcnews.go.com/2020/story?id=7298996&page=1).

196. Joshua Molina, "Utah Students Hide Guns, Head to Class," CNN.com, Feb. 21, 2008 (http://www.cnn.com/2008/US/02/20/cnnu.guns/index.html). See also the chart "Guns on Campus" (http://www.cnn.com/2008/US/02/20/cnnu.guns/index.html#cnnSTCOther1).

197. Discussions with faculty members at a number of schools indicate that the rules are somewhat more flexible for them (e.g., Robert G. Hansen at the Tuck Business School and Charlotte Twight in the economics department at Boise State University, who consulted their faculty handbooks).

198. For example, the University of Colorado Board of Regents enacted a weapons control policy in 1994 (*Students for Concealed Carry on Campus v. The Regents of the University of Colorado*, District Court, El Paso County, State of Colorado, Case Number 2008CV6492, Motion to Dismiss,).

199. See the conclusion in Christopher Koper, Daniel Woods, and Jeffrey Roth, "An Updated Assessment of the Federal Assault Weapons Ban: Impacts on Gun Markets and Gun Violence, 1994–2003," report to the National Institute of Justice, United States Department of Justice, June 2004.

200. John R. Lott, Jr., "Candidates Confused on Gun Ban," Fox News, Wednesday, Nov. 19, 2003.

201. Ibid.

202. For a very useful reference see David B. Kopel, "Should Gun Shows Be Outlawed? McCain Bill Does Much More than Impose Background Checks" (issue paper no. 1-2002, Independence Institute, Golden, CO, Jan. 23, 2002) (http://www.davekopel.com/2A/IP/gunshows2.htm).

203. Caroline Wolf Harlow, "Firearm Use by Offenders," Bureau of Justice Statistics, U.S. Department of Justice, Nov. 2001. An earlier study using the same survey data found slightly higher rates of criminal guns acquired from gun shows (1.7 percent) or flea markets (1.7 percent), but a discussion with Ms. Harlow indicated that the later study had used a "cleaned up" version of the survey data. Apparently there had been several coding and other errors in the original version of the data. The earlier study was John Scalia, "Federal Firearm Offenders, 1992–98," Bureau of Justice Statistics, U.S. Department of Justice, June 2000.

204. James D. Wright and Peter Rossi, *Armed and Considered Dangerous: A Survey of Felons and Their Firearms* (Hawthorne, NY: Aldine de Gruyter Publishers, 1986).

205. Lott and Landes, *The Bias Against Guns*, chapter 8.

206. Surprisingly, the Bureau of Alcohol, Tobacco, and Firearms used the same source when examining 1998 and claimed that there were 4,442 such shows, when the total given to me by Bruce Wolberg, advertising manager for the Gun Show Calendar, was 2,630. The differences across some states was substantial and affected the rankings. For example, Texas is 213 instead of the BATF's 472. Pennsylvania is now 138 instead of 250, Florida 178 instead of 224, and Illinois 103 instead of 203.

Back in 2002 after repeated attempts, James Knowles, my research assistant at the time, finally got John D'Angelo at the BATF to answer questions about these discrepancies. James told me that, according to D'Angelo, "it would be better to use our own numbers than the numbers from the report, unless I hear otherwise from him. He asks what we expect from him in response to our question. He explained that he could not find the exact documentation for the manual counts and said that he will look into it a little further but that he is not optimistic that he will find it. He said that he would call back," but he never did. D'Angelo's telephone number is 202-927-8500.

207. Mark Duggan, Randi Hjalmarsson, and Brian Jacob, "The Effect of Gun Shows on Gun-Related Deaths: Evidence from California and Texas" (National Bureau of Economic Research working paper, Oct. 2008).

208. "Colorado's 'Make My Day' Law Eyed in Home Shooting," *Taiwan News*, Jan. 1, 2009; and Catherine Ellsworth, "Colorado Home Owner Could Avoid Murder Charges Under 'Make My Day' Law," *London Telegraph*, Jan. 3, 2009.

209. "New Details in Springs Shooting," KRDO.com, Jan. 4, 2009 (http://www.krdo.com/Global/story.asp?S=9604233).

210. Sue McMillin and Bill Vogrin, "Mistaken for Thief, Man Gunned Down," *Colorado Springs Gazette*, Dec. 29, 2008 (http://www.gazette.com/articles/police_45478_article.html/kennedy_house.html).

211. "Do Guns Reduce Crime?" Rosenkranz Foundation/Intelligence Squared US, Oct. 28, 2008.

APPENDIX ONE

1. Although this jargon may appear overwhelming, it is actually fairly simple. Consider the following example. Suppose we wish to present findings that height and SAT scores are correlated among college-bound students. Instead of reporting that an additional inch is related to an increase in test scores of so many points, we can compare standard-deviation changes, which would be equivalent to reporting the results as comparisons of changes in percentile height with percentile changes in the SAT scores.

2. To phrase this in terms of the earlier discussion of standard deviations, with a symmetric distribution, there is a 32 percent probability that a variable will take on a value that is more than one standard deviation different from its mean, and only a five percent probability that it will be more than two standard deviations away from the mean.

APPENDIX THREE

1. U.S. Department of Justice, *Crime in the United States, 1994* (Washington, DC: U.S. Department of Justice, 1994.) I also wish to thank Tom Bailey of the FBI and Jeff Maurer of the Department of Health and Human Services for answering questions concerning the data used in this paper.

2. The Inter-University Consortium for Political and Social Research number for this data set was 6387, and the principle investigator was James Alan Fox of Northeastern University College of Criminal Justice.

3. Dropping the zero crime values from the sample made the "shall-issue" coefficients larger and more significant, but doing the same thing for the accident-rate regressions did not alter "shall-issue" coefficients. (See also the discussion at the end of the section headed "Using County and State Data for the United States" in chapter 4).

4. For further descriptions of the procedures for calculating intercensus estimates of population, see ICPSR (8384): U.S. Department of Commerce, Bureau of the Census, *Intercensal Estimates of the Population of Counties by Age, Sex, and Race (United States), 1970–1980* (Ann Arbor, MI: ICPSR, Winter 1985). See also Bureau of the Census, *Methodology for Experimental Estimates of the Population of Counties by Age and Sex: July 1, 1975,* Current Population Reports, series P-23, no. 103, and *Census of Population, 1980: County Population by Age, Sex, Race, and Spanish Origin (Preliminary OMB-Consistent Modified Race)*.

5. U.S. Department of Commerce, Bureau of the Census, *Methodology for Experimental Estimates of the Population of Counties by Age and Sex: July 1, 1975,* Current Population Reports, series P-23, no. 103; see also Bureau of the Census, *Census of Population, 1980: County Population by Age, Sex, Race, and Spanish Origin (Preliminary OMB-Consistent Modified Race)*, pp. 19–23.

6. U.S. Department of Commerce, *Statistical Abstract of the United States,* 114th ed., table 746, p. 487.

7. Thomas B. Marvell and Carlisle E. Moody, "The Impact of Enhanced Prison Terms for Felonies Committed with Guns," *Criminology* 33 (May 1995): 259–60.

APPENDIX SEVEN

1. The regression is natural log of gun ownership given by General Social Survey on the natural log of per capita magazine sales and state and year fixed effects

2. The survey was not conducted every year. Initial years when the gun questions were not asked are 1972, 1975, 1978, 1983, and 1986. Beginning in 1988, the gun questions were asked every year but of only two-thirds of the total survey sample. There was no funding for surveys in 1979 and 1981, and beginning in 1994 the survey was switched to biennial (even years). The survey data are also weighted by the demographics in each individual state. Over the entire period, "owngun" was "refuse to answer" for 156 out of the total 24,855 observations with a response to that variable.

3. See chapter 3.

4. Compared to other surveys such as the CBS General Election Exit Poll, with over 36,000 observations in 1988, and the Voter News Service Poll, with over 3,400 people surveyed in 1996, the General Social Survey only surveys 899–1,973 in any given year. While the General Social Survey will not provide a very accurate picture of gun ownership in any given state in a year, the much larger number of years over which the survey is provided allows us to investigate trends.

5. The household rate was calculated by assuming that married women owned guns at the same rate as married men of the same race and age grouping.

6. Using weighted least squares where the weight was the state population, I estimated

$\ln(\text{murder rate}) = a_0 + b_1 \ln(\text{magazine sales for the preceding year}) + b_2 \ln(\text{magazine sales two years previously}) + b_3$ arrest rate for murder $+ b_4$ death penalty execution rate $+ b_5$ state population $+ b_6$ state population squared $+ b_7$ unemployment rate $+ b_8$ poverty rate $+ b_9$ real per capita income $+ b_{10}$ real per capita unemployment insurance payments $+ b_{11}$ real per capita welfare payments $+ b_{12}$ real per capita retirement payments $+ b_{13}$ 36 different demographic variables that measure the percentage of the state population in different age, sex, and race divisions $+$ state fixed effects $+$ year fixed effects

To deal with the endogeneity issues involved in using the arrest rate for murder in explaining the murder rate, I also tried using the arrest rate for violent crime, and the results were virtually identical. Removing the arrest rate entirely also produced similar results.

BIBLIOGRAPHY

Akhil Reed Amar. "The Bill of Rights and the Fourteenth Amendment." *Yale Law Journal* 101 (Apr. 1992).

Andreoni, James. "Criminal Deterrence in the Reduce Form: A New Perspective on Ehrlich's Seminal Study." *Economic Inquiry* 33 (July 1995).

Annest, J. L; J. A. Mercy; D. R. Gibson; and G. W. Ryan. "National Estimates of Nonfatal, Firearm-Related Injuries: Beyond the Tip of the Iceberg." *Journal of the American Medical Association* (June 14, 1995).

Ayres, Ian, and Steven Levitt. "Measuring Positive Externalities from Unobservable Victim Precaution: An Empirical Analysis of Lojack." NBER working paper 5928 (1997).

Bartley, William Alan; Mark A. Cohen; and Luke Froeb. "The Effect of Concealed-Weapon Laws: Estimating Misspecification Uncertainty." *Economic Inquiry* 36 (1997).

Battalio, Raymond C; John H. Kagel; and Owen R. Phillips. "Optimal Prices and Animal Consumers in Congested Markets." *Economic Inquiry* 24 (Apr. 1986).

———. "Optimal Prices and Animal Consumers in Congested Markets: A Reply." *Economic Inquiry* 25 (Oct. 1987).

Battalio, Raymond C; John H. Kagel; Howard Rachlin; and Leonard Green. "Commodity Choice Behavior with Pigeons as Subjects." *Journal of Political Economy* 84 (Feb. 1981).

Becker, Gary S. "Crime and Punishment: An Economic Approach." *Journal of Political Economy* 76 (Mar./Apr. 1968).

Block, Michael K., and Vernon E. Gerety. "Some Experimental Evidence on the Differences between Student and Prisoner Reactions to Monetary Penalties." *Journal of Legal Studies* 24 (Jan. 1995).

Block, Michael K., and John Heineke. "A Labor Theoretical Analysis of Criminal Choice." *American Economic Review* 65 (June 1975).

Blumstein, Alfred, and Daniel Nagin. "The Deterrent Effect of Legal Sanctions on Draft Evasion." *Stanford University Law Review* 28 (1977).

Blumstein, Alfred; Jacqueline Cohen; and Daniel Nagin,

eds. *Deterrence and Incapacitation: Estimating the Effects of Criminal Sanctions on Crime Rates.* Washington, DC: National Academy of Sciences, 1978.

Bureau of Alcohol, Tobacco, and Firearms. *A Progress Report: Gun-Dealer Licensing and Illegal Gun Trafficking.* Washington, DC: Department of the Treasury, Bureau of Alcohol, Tobacco, and Firearms, Jan. 1997.

Bureau of Justice Statistics Special Reports. "Murder in Large Urban Counties, 1988." Washington, DC: US. Department of Justice, 1993.

———. "Murder in Families." Washington, DC: U.S. Department of Justice, 1994.

Cherrington, Ernest H. *The Evolution of Prohibition in the United States of America.* Westerville, OH: Tem-Press, 1920.

Colvin, D. Leigh. *Prohibition in the United States.* New York: George H. Doran Co., 1926.

Cook, P. J. "The Role of Firearms in Violent Crime," in M. E. Wolfgang and N. A. Werner, eds., *Criminal Violence.* Newbury, NJ: Sage Publishers, 1982.

———. "The Technology of Personal Violence." *Crime and Justice: Annual Review of Research* 14 (1991).

Cottrol, Robert J., and Raymond T. Diamond. "The Second Amendment: Toward an Afro-Americanist Reconsideration." *Georgetown Law Review* 80 (Dec. 1991).

Cramer, Clayton E., and David B. Kopel. "'Shall Issue': The New Wave of Concealed-Handgun Permit Laws." *Tennessee Law Review* 62 (Spring 1995). A longer version of this study is available from the Independence Institute, 14142 Denver West Parkway, Suite 185, Golden, Colorado, 80401–3134.

Daly, Martin, and Margo Wilson. *Homicide.* Hawthorne, NY: Aldine de Gruyter Publishers, 1988.

Davis, James A., and Tom W. Smith. *General Social Surveys, 1972–1993: Cumulative Codebook.* Chicago: National Opinion Research Center, 1993.

Donohue, John, and Peter Siegelman. "Is the United States at the Optimal Rate of Crime?" *Journal of Legal Studies* 27 (Jan. 1998).

Dilulio, John J., Jr. "The Question of Black Crime." *The Public Interest* 117 (Fall 1994).

———. "White Lies About Black Crime." *The Public Interest* 118 (Winter 1995).

Dunford, Edward B. *The History of the Temperance Movement.* Washington, DC: Tem-Press, 1943.

Ehrlich, Isaac. "Participation in Illegitimate Activities: A Theoretical and Empirical Investigation." *Journal of Political Economy* 81 (1973).

———. "Crime, Punishment, and the Market for Offenses." *Journal of Economic Perspectives* 10 (Winter 1996).

Ehrlich, Isaac, and Randall Mark. "Fear of Deterrence: A Critical Evaluation of the Report of the Panel on Research on Deterrent and Incapacitation Effects." *Journal of Legal Studies* 6 (June 1977).

Geller, William A., and Michael S. Scott. *Deadly Force: What We Know.* Washington, DC: Police Executive Research Forum, 1992.

Glaeser, Edward L., and Bruce Sacerdote. "Why Is There More Crime in Cities?" Harvard University working paper, Nov. 14, 1995).

Glaeser, Edward, and Spencer Glendon. "Who Owns Guns?" *American Economic Review* 88 (May 1998).

Greenwald, Bruce C. "A General Analysis of the Bias in the Estimated Standard Errors of Least Squares Coefficients." *Journal of Econometrics* 22 (Aug. 1983).

Grossman, Michael; Frank J. Chaloupka; and Charles C. Brown. "The Demand for Cocaine by Young Adults: A Rational Addiction Approach." NBER working paper, July 1996.

Kagel, John H.; Raymond C. Battalio; Howard Rachlin; and Leonard Green. "Experimental Studies of Consumer Demand Behavior Using Laboratory Animals." *Economic Inquiry* 13 (Jan. 1975).

———. "Demand Curves for Animal Consumers." *Quarterly Journal of Economics* 96 (Feb. 1981).

Kahan, Dan M. "What Do Alternative Sanctions Mean?" *University of Chicago Law Review* 63 (1996).

Kahan, Dan, and Martha Nussbaum. "Two Conceptions of Emotion in Criminal Law." *Columbia Law Review* 96 (Mar. 1996).

Kates, Don B., and Dan Polsby. "The Background of Murders." Northwestern University Law School working paper (1997).

Kates, Don, and Dan Polsby. "Of Genocide and Disarmament." *Journal of Criminal Law and Criminology* 86 (Fall 1995).

Kellermann, Arthur L., et al. "Gun Ownership as a Risk Factor for Homicide in the Home." *New England Journal of Medicine* (Oct. 7, 1993).

Kennedy, David M.; Anne M. Piehl; and Anthony A. Braga. "Youth Violence in Boston: Gun Markets, Serious Youth Offenders, and A Use-Reduction Strategy." *Law and Contemporary Problems* 59 (Winter 1996).

Kermit, Daniel, and John R. Lott, Jr. "Should Criminal Penalties Include Third-Party Avoidance Costs?" *Journal of Legal Studies* 24 (June 1995).

Kleck, Gary. *Point Blank: Guns and Violence in America.* Hawthorne, NY: Aldine de Gruyter Publishers, 1991.

——. *Targeting Guns.* Hawthorne, NY: Aldine de Gruyter Publishers, 1997.

——. "Guns and Violence: An Interpretive Review of the Field." *Social Pathology* 1 (Jan. 1995).

Kleck, Gary, and Marc Gertz. "Armed Resistance to Crime: The Prevalence and Nature of Self-Defense with a Gun." *Journal of Criminal Law and Criminology* 86 (Fall 1995).

Kleck, Gary, and E. Britt Patterson. "The Impact of Gun Control and Gun-Ownership Levels on Violence Rates." *Journal of Quantitative Criminology* 9 (1993).

Kopel, David B. *The Samurai, the Mountie, and the Cowboy.* Amherst, NY: Prometheus Books, 1992.

——. *Guns: Who Should Have Them?* Amherst, NY: Prometheus Books, 1995.

Landes, William M. "An Economic Study of U.S. Aircraft Hijacking, 1961–1976." *Journal of Law and Economics* 21 (Apr. 1978).

Law Enforcement Technology magazine. "Gun-Control Survey." *Law Enforcement Technology* (July–Aug. 1991).

Levinson, Sanford. "The Embarrassing Second Amendment." *Yale Law Journal* 99 (Dec. 1989).

Levitt, Steven. "The Effect of Prison Population Size on Crime Rates: Evidence from Prison Overcrowding Litigation." *Quarterly Journal of Economics* 111 (1996).

Lott, John R., Jr. "Juvenile Delinquency and Education: A Comparison of Public and Private Provision." *International Review of Law and Economics* 7 (Dec. 1987).

——. "Should the Wealthy Be Able to 'Buy Justice'?" *Journal of Political Economy* 95 (Dec.1987).

——. "The Effect of Conviction on the Legitimate Income of Criminals." *Economics Letters* 34 (Dec. 1990).

——. "A Transaction-Costs Explanation for Why the Poor Are More Likely to Commit Crime." *Journal of Legal Studies* 19 (Jan. 1990).

——. "An Attempt at Measuring the Total Monetary Penalty from Drug Convictions: The Importance of an Individual's Reputation." *Journal of Legal Studies* 21 (Jan. 1992).

——. "Do We Punish High-Income Criminals Too Heavily?" *Economic Inquiry* 30 (Oct. 1992).

——. "The Concealed-Handgun Debate." *Journal of Legal Studies* 27 (Jan. 1998): forthcoming.

Lott, John R., Jr., and Larry W. Kenny. "How Dramatically Did Women's Suffrage Change the Size and Scope of Government?" University of Chicago Law School working paper (1997).

Lott, John R., Jr., and William M. Landes. "Multiple Victim Public Shootings, Bombings, and

Right-to-Carry Concealed Handgun Laws." University of Chicago Law School working paper (1997).

Lott, John R., Jr., and Stephen G. Bronars. "Criminal Deterrence, Geographic Spillovers, and Right-to-Carry concealed Handgun Laws." *American Economic Review* 88 (May 1998).

Lund, Nelson. "The Second Amendment, Political Liberty, and the Right to Self-Preservation." *Alabama Law Review* 33 (1988).

Marvell, Thomas B., and Carlisle E. Moody. "The Impact of Enhanced Prison Terms for Felonies Committed with Guns." *Criminology* 33 (May 1995).

McCormick, Robert E., and Robert Tollison. "Crime on the Court." *Journal of Political Economy* 92 (Apr. 1984).

McDowall, David; Colin Loftin; and Brian Wiersema. "Easing Concealed-Firearm Laws: Effects on Homicide in Three States." *Journal of Criminal Law and Criminology* 86 (Fall 1995).

Miller, Ted R.; Mark A. Cohen; and Brian Wiersema. *Victim Costs and Consequences: A New Look.* Washington, DC: National Institute of Justice, Feb. 1996.

Moulton, Brent R. "An Illustration of a Pitfall in Estimating the Effects of Aggregate Variables on Micro Units." *Review Economics and Statistics* 72 (1990).

Mullin, Wallace P. "Will Gun Buyback Programs Increase the Quantity of Guns?" Michigan State University working paper (Mar. 1997).

Munday, R. A. L, and J. A. Stevenson. *Guns and Violence: The Debate Before Lord Cullen.* Essex, England: Piedmont Publishers, 1996.

Peltzman, Sam. "The Effects of Automobile Safety Regulation." *Journal of Political Economy* 83 (Aug. 1975).

Peterson, Steven; George Hoffer; and Edward Millner. "Are Drivers of Air-Bag-Equipped Cars More Aggressive? A Test of the Offsetting-Behavior Hypothesis." *Journal of Law and Economics* 38 (Oct. 1995).

Plotkin, Martha R., ed. *Under Fire: Gun Buy-Backs, Exchanges, and Amnesty Programs.* Washington, DC: Police Executive Research Forum, 1996.

Polsby, Daniel D. "From the Hip: The Intellectual Argument in Favor of Restrictive Gun Control Is Collapsing. So How Come the Political Strength of Its Advocates Is Increasing?" *National Review,* Mar. 24, 1997.

Quigley, Paxton. *Armed and Female.* New York: St. Martin's, 1989.

Rasmusen, Eric. "Stigma and Self-Fulfilling Expectations of Criminality." *Journal of Law and Economics* 39 (Oct. 1996).

Reynolds, Morgan O. "Crime and Punishment in America." Dallas: National Center for Policy Analysis, June 1995.

Sandler, Todd. "Optimal Prices and Animal Consumers in Congested Markets: A Comment." *Economic Inquiry* 25 (Oct. 1987).

Shields, Pete. *Guns Don t Die, People Do.* New York: Arbor, 1981.

Singular, Stephen. *Talked to Death.* New York: Beech Tree Books, 1987.

Smith, Tom W. "1996 National Gun-Policy Survey of the National Opinion Research Center: Research Findings." Chicago: National Opinion Research Center, Mar. 1997.

Smith, Tom W, and Robert J. Smith. "Changes in Firearm Ownership Among Women, 1980–1994." *Journal of Criminal Law and Criminology* 86 (Fall 1995).

Southwick, Lawrence, Jr. "Self-Defense with Guns: The Consequences." *Journal of Criminal Justice* 28 (2000): 351–70.

Teret, Stephen P. "Critical Comments on a Paper by Lott and Mustard." School of Hygiene and Public Health, Johns Hopkins University, mimeo, Aug. 7, 1996.

U.S. Department of Commerce, Bureau of the Census. *Statistical Abstract of the United States.* Washington, DC: U.S. Government Printing Office, 1995.

Uviller, H. Richard. *Virtual Justice: The Flawed Prosecution of Crime in America.* New Haven, CT: Yale University Press, 1996.

Van Alstyne, William. "The Second Amendment Right to Arms." *Duke Law Review* 43 (Apr. 1994).

Viscusi, W. Kip. "The Lulling Effect: The Impact of Child-Resistant Packaging on Aspirin and Analgesic Ingestions." *American Economic Review* (May, 1984).

Wilson, James Q., and Richard J. Herrnstein. *Crime and Human Nature.* Simon and Schuster, New York, N.Y. 1985.

Wilson, James Q., and George L. Kelling. "Making Neighborhoods Safe." *Atlantic Monthly,* Feb. 1989.

Wolpin, Kenneth. "An Economic Analysis of Crime and Punishment in England and Wales, 1894–1967." *Journal of Political Economy* 86 (1978).

Wright, James D., and Peter Rossi. *Armed and Considered Dangerous: A Survey of Felons and Their Firearms.* New York: Aldine de Gruyter Publishers, 1986.

Zimring, Franklin. "The Medium Is the Message: Firearm Caliber as a Determinant of Death from Assault." *Journal of Legal Studies* 1 (1972).

SUPPLEMENTARY ENTRIES FOR SECOND EDITION

Ayres, Ian, and John J. Donohue III. "Nondiscretionary Concealed Weapons Laws: A Case Study of Statistics, Standards of Proof, and Public Policy." *American Law and Economics Review* 1, nos. 1–2 (Fall 1999): 436–70.

Bartley, William Alan. "Will Rationing Guns Reduce Crime?" *Economics Letters* 62 (1999): 241–43.

Bartley, William, and Mark Cohen. "The Effect of Concealed Weapons Laws: An Extreme Bound Analysis." *Economic Inquiry* 36 (Apr. 1998): 258–65.

Benson, Bruce L. "Review of More Guns, Less Crime." *Public Choice* 100, nos. 3–4 (Sept. 1999): 309–13.

Black, Dan A., and Daniel S. Nagin. "Do Right-to-Carry Laws Deter Violent Crime?" *Journal of Legal Studies* 27 (Jan. 1998): 209–19.

Bronars, Stephen G., and John R. Lott, Jr. " Criminal Deterrence, Geographic Spillovers, and Right-to-Carry Laws." *American Economic Review* 88 (May 1998): 475–79.

Cummings, Peter, David C. Grossman, Frederick P. Rivara, and Thomas D. Koepsell. "State Gun Safe Storage Laws and Child Mortality Due to Firearms." *Journal of the American Medical Association* 278 (Oct. 1, 1997): 1084–86.

Dezbakhsh, Hashem, and Paul H. Rubin. "Lives Saved or Lives Lost? The Effects of Concealed-Handgun Laws on Crime." *American Economic Review Papers and Proceedings* 88 (May 1998): 468–74.

Diaz, Tom. *Making a Killing: The Business of Guns in America.* New York: New Press, 1999.

Ehrlich, Isaac, and Zhiqiang Liu. "Sensitivity Analyses of the Deterrence Hypothesis: Let's Keep the Econ in Econometrics." *Journal of Law and Economics* 42 (Apr. 1999): 455–88.

Eisen, Joanne, and Paul Gallant. "Scientific Proof That Gun Control Increases the Cost of Crime." *Shield,* Summer 1998, p. 42.

Harrison, Glenn W., David Kennison, and Katherine M. Macedon. "Legal Guarantee of the Right to Bear Arms: Can It Be Justified Empirically?" University of South Carolina working paper, December 1999.

Hemenway, David. "Book Review of More Guns, Less Crime." *New England Journal of Medicine,* Dec. 31, 1998, pp. 2029–30.

Kellermann, Arthur, and Sheryl Heron. "Firearms and Family Violence." *Emergency Medicine Clinics of North America* 17 (Aug. 1999): 699–708.

Kelling, George L. *Fixing Broken Windows: Restoring Order and Reducing Crime in Our Communities.* New York: Free Press, 1998.

Korwin, Alan. *The California Gun Owner's Guide.* Phoenix: Bloomfield Press, 1999.

———. *Gun Laws of America.* Phoenix: Bloomfield Press, 1997.

————. *The Texas Gun Owner's Guide*. Phoenix: Bloomfield Press, 1998.

Leamer, Edward E. "Let's Take the Con Out of Econometrics." *American Economic Review* 73 (Mar. 1983): 31–43.

Lott, John R., Jr. "Does a Helping Hand Put Others at Risk? Affirmative Action, Police Departments, and Crime." *Economic Inquiry,* vol. 38 (April 2000), forthcoming.

————. "Who Is Really Hurt by Affirmative Action?" *Subject to Debate,* May 1998, pp. 1, 3.

Lott, John R., Jr., and John E. Whitley. "Safe Storage Gun Laws: Accidental Deaths, Suicides, and Crime." Yale Law School working paper, October 1, 1999.

Ludwig, Jens. "Concealed-Gun-Carrying Law and Violent Crime: Evidence from State Panel Data." *International Review of Law and Economics* 18 (Sept. 1998): 239–54.

McManus, Walter S. "Estimates of the Deterrent Effect of Capital Punishment: The Importance of the Researcher's Prior Beliefs." *Journal of Political Economy* 93 (Feb. 1985): 417–25.

Miron, Jeffrey A. "Violence, Guns, and Drugs: A Cross-Country Analysis." Boston University working paper, December 9, 1999.

Moody, Carlisle E. "Testing for the Effects of Concealed Weapons Laws: Specification Errors and Robustness." College of William and Mary, Department of Economics, working paper, December 19, 1999.

Mustard, David B. "The Impact of Gun Laws on Police Deaths." University of Georgia working paper, November 1999.

Olson, David, and Michael Maltz. "Magic Bullets, Deterrence, and Gun Laws." Loyola University Chicago working paper, December 1999.

Plassman, Florenz, and T. Nicolaus Tideman. "Does the Right to Carry Concealed Handguns Deter Countable Crimes? Only a Count Analysis Can Say." State University of New York at Binghamton working paper, May 19, 1999.

————. "Geographical and Temporal Variation in the Effects of Right-to-Carry Laws on Crime." Virginia Polytechnic Institute and State University working paper, November 19, 1999.

Shughart, William F., II. "More Guns, Less Crime: Understanding Crime and Gun Control Laws: Review." *Southern Economic Journal* 65, no. 4 (Apr. 1, 1999): 978–81.

Slobogin, Christopher. "Why Liberals Should Chuck the Exclusionary Rule." *University of Illinois Law Review* 99 (1999): 363–446.

Squires, Peter. "Review of More Guns, Less Crime." *British Journal of Criminology* 39, no. 2 (Spring 1999): 318–20.

U.S. General Accounting Office. "Accidental Shootings: Many Deaths and Injuries Caused by Firearms Could Be Prevented." Washington, DC: U.S. General Accounting Office, Mar. 1991.

SUPPLEMENTARY ENTRIES FOR THIRD EDITION

Ayres, Ian, and John Donohue. "Shooting Down the 'More Guns, Less Crime' Hypothesis." *Stanford Law Review* 55, no. 4 (2003): 1202–1309.

Benson, B. L., and B. D. Mast. "Privately Produced General Deterrence." *Journal of Law and Economics* 44 (2001): 725–46.

Chu, Vivian S. "District of Columbia v. Heller: The Supreme Court and the Second Amendment." CRS report for Congress, Jan. 15, 2009.

Cutler, D. M., E. L. Glaeser, and K. E. Norberg. "Explaining the Rise in Youth Suicide." In "Risky Behavior Among Youths: An Economic Analysis," ed. J. Gruber, pp. 219–69. Chicago: University of Chicago Press, 2001.

Donohue, John. "The Final Bullet in the Body of the More Guns, Less Crime Hypothesis." *Criminology and Public Policy* 2, no. 3 (2003): 397–410.

Duggan, Mark. "More Guns, More Crime." *Journal of Political Economy* 109, no. 5 (Oct. 2001): 1086–1114.

Duggan, Mark, Randi Hjalmarsson, and Brian Jacob. "The Effect of Gun Shows on Gun-Related Deaths: Evidence from California and Texas." National Bureau of Economic Research working paper, Oct. 2008.

Duwe, Grant, Tom Kovandzic, and Carl Moody. "The Impact of Right-to-Carry Concealed Firearm Laws on Mass Public Shootings." *Homicide Studies*, Nov. 1, 2002.

Fox, James Alan, and David McDowall. "Brief of Professors of Criminal Justice as Amici Curiae in Support of the Petitioners." Submitted to the Supreme Court of the United States in *District of Columbia v. Heller*, no. 07-290, Jan. 11, 2008.

Harlow, Caroline Wolf. "Firearm Use by Offenders." Bureau of Justice Statistics, U.S. Department of Justice, Nov. 2001.

Helland, E., and A. Tabarrok. "Using Placebo Laws to Test 'More Guns, Less Crime.'" *Advances in Economic Analysis and Policy* 4, no. 1, article 1 (2004).

Intelligence Squared. "Do Guns Reduce Crime?" Debate on National Public Radio, Nov. 5, 2008.

Kopel, David B. "Should Gun Shows Be Outlawed? McCain Bill Does Much More than Impose Background Checks." Issue paper no. 1-2002. Independence Institute, Golden, CO, Jan. 23, 2002.

Koper, Christopher, Daniel Woods, and Jeffrey Roth. "An Updated Assessment of the Federal Assault Weapons Ban: Impacts on Gun Markets and Gun Violence, 1994–2003." Report to the National Institute of Justice, United States Department of Justice, June 2004.

Levitt, Steven. "Understanding Why Crime Fell in the 1990s: Four Factors That Explain the Decline and Six that Do Not." *Journal of Economic Perspectives* 18 (Winter 2004): 163–90.

Loftin, Colin, David McDowall, Brian Wiersema, and Talbert J. Cottey. "Effects of Restrictive Licensing of Handguns on Homicide and Suicide in the District of Columbia." *New England Journal of Medicine* 325 (1991): 1615–20.

Lott, John R., Jr. *The Bias Against Guns*. Washington, DC: Regnery Press, 2003.

Lott, John R., Jr., and John Whitley. "Safe Storage Gun Laws: Accidental Deaths, Suicides, and Crime." *Journal of Law and Economics* 44, no. 2, pt. 2 (Oct. 2001): 659–89.

———. "Measurement Error in County-Level UCR Data." *Journal of Quantitative Criminology* 19, no. 2 (June 2003): 185–98.

Maltz, Michael D., and Joseph Targonski. "A Note on the Use of County-Level UCR Data." *Journal of Quantitative Criminology*, Sept. 2002.

Moody, C. E. "Testing for the Effects of Concealed Weapons Laws: Specification Errors and Robustness." *Journal of Law and Economics* 44, no. 2, pt. 2 (2001): 799–813.

Moody, C. E., and Thomas Marvell. "The Debate on Shall-Issue Laws." *Econ Journal Watch*, Sept. 2008, pp. 269–93.

Mustard, D. B. "The Impact of Gun Laws on Police Deaths." *Journal of Law and Economics* 44 (2001): 635–57.

National Gang Intelligence Center, U.S. Department of Justice. "National Gang Threat Assessment 2009." Jan. 2009.

Olsen, D. E., and M. D. Maltz. "Right-to-Carry Concealed Weapons Laws and Homicide in Large U.S. Counties: The Effect on Weapons Types, Victim Characteristics, and Victim-Offender Relationships." *Journal of Law and Economics* 44 (2001): 747–70.

Plassmann, F., and T. N. Tideman. "Does the Right to Carry Concealed Handguns Deter Countable Crimes? Only a Count Analysis Can Say." *Journal of Law and Economics*, 44 (2001): 771–98.

Plassmann, F., and John Whitley. "Confirming 'More Guns, Less Crime,'" *Stanford Law Review*, 2003, p. 1313–69.

Scalia, John. "Federal Firearm Offenders, 1992–98." Bureau of Justice Statistics, U.S. Department of Justice, June 2000.

Wilson, James Q. "Dissent." Appendix A in *Firearms and Violence: A Critical Review*, ed. Charles F. Wellford, John V. Pepper, and Carol V. Petrie. Washington, DC: National Academies Press, 2005.

Wellford, Charles F., John V. Pepper, and Carol V. Petrie, eds. *Firearms and Violence: A Critical Review*. Washington, DC: National Research Council of the National Academies and National Academies Press, 2004.

INDEX

Brady law (Brady Act), 15, 38, 92–93, 93t, 112, 166–67, 198–99, 202, 233, 325, 347, 404n65, 417n110
Branas, Charles, 302
Breyer, Stephen, 306–7, 312, 314
"broken window" effect, 28, 394n23
broken-windows strategy (policing policy), 171, 191, 207
Bronars, Steve, 298, 399n19
Brown, David M., 241
Bunker, Archie, 206
Bureau of Alcohol, Tobacco, and Firearms (BATF), 167, 396n13, 424n206
burglary, 28–30, 62, 178, 187, 191, 201; hot, 5–6, 201
burglary rates, 75–77, 81; and arrest rate, 60; and concealed-handgun laws, 66, 71, 107, 112; potential reduction, 63; and right-to-carry laws, 263f, 264
Bush, George W. (former U.S. president), 324

California, 148, 153, 233
Callaway, Ewen, 302
campaign to impugn the findings of the study, 204
Campbell, Ben Nighthorse, 16
carjackings, foiled, 368n9
Carroll, Thomas, 17
Carter, Joyce, 412n56
Castle Doctrine, 236–37, 254, 326, 331–32, 332t, 333t
Cato Institute, 125, 127
causality, 27, 30, 157, 210
Centers for Disease Control and Prevention, 405n70
Center to Prevent Handgun Violence, 390n2, 392n4, 403n59
Chapman, Stephen, 128, 393n12
children: and gun violence, 403n60; as victims, 9–10 (see also murder rates: juvenile)
child safety locks. See gun locks
Clinton, Hillary, 204
Clinton, William (former U.S. president), 10, 166–67, 232, 300, 370n37, 386n29, 396n13
Coalition to Stop Gun Violence, 202, 393n13
Cohen, Mark, 300
Colorado, 413n59
Colorado Springs church shooting (2007), 324–25
Columbine High School (Littleton, Colorado, 1999), 195, 230, 233, 323
concealed-handgun laws, 7, 12–15, 20–21, 27, 30, 35, 56–57, 63–64, 97–98, 197, 237, 342; and arrest rates, 62, 64, 65t, 107, 117, 124; benefit to blacks, 56, 71, 98, 183, 165–66, 181, 184; benefit to women, 56, 68, 98, 165; and the elderly, 182f, 182–84; and income data, 71, 72f, 98, 182, 183f, 184; and percentage of

population that is black, 182–84, 183f; and percentage of population that is female, 182–84; and population density, 68–71, 70f, 81, 86, 87t, 98, 182f, 183–84; by state, 48, 52f, 81, 84; variation across states, 89, 90–91t
concealed-handgun law studies. See gun control studies
concealed-handgun permits, 26 (see also permits); held by state legislators, 240
concealed handguns, 11, 16, 21; case for allowing, 6; restrictions on where they can be carried, 255–58
consent decrees, 191–92
control variables, 77, 101, 157, 171, 186, 300. See also specific variables
conviction rates, 106–7, 112, 119, 135, 158, 160, 164, 170, 191, 195
Cook, Philip J., 11, 371n43, 372n47, 390n4, 390n2 (chap. 7), 395n41, 417n110
cost of crime, 59–60, 61t, 64, 113, 118–19, 181, 202, 219, 274–75, 276t
Cottey, Talbert, 307
Couch, Jim, 396n13
court cases, 240; Supreme, 166–67
crack cocaine epidemic (late 1980s), 221, 277, 298–99, 308–10, 314, 321, 409n2
Cramer, Clayton E., 136, 381n14
Cremin, Kevin, 399n22
crime: by blacks, 9; effect on number of permits issued, 178; "irrational," 17; statistics, 23; violent versus property, 28, 29t, 138
crime cycles (crime waves), 79–81, 134–35, 147, 167, 171, 208–10
crime patterns, 213f; variability, 377n3
crime rates, 57, 63, 120–21, 135–36, 147, 161, 254, 292, 300, 342; in adjacent counties, 94, 95t; changes in, 28, 259, 261, 265, 361t; demographic characteristics, 54, 148, 155, 351t (see also demographic variables); District of Columbia, 314; and gun ownership, 117–18, 117t; and gun ownership, worldwide, 116; and income data, 54–55, 57, 62–63, 155, 186, 254, 277, 296; and individual safety, 35; and maintenance payments, 186; mean, 135, 137, 149; and population density, 54, 57, 60–62, 155, 186; and poverty, 57, 155, 170–71, 186, 207, 254, 277, 287, 296; predicted, 293–94; by region, 171–72; related to concealed-handgun laws, 49, 58t; related to handgun use, 27; relative to arrest rates, 32, 36, 57, 60, 75, 86, 95, 97, 99, 107, 110, 112, 119, 120, 122–23, 190–91, 379n26; relative to number of permits granted, 171–72, 179, 180t, 187, 188f, 189f, 226; relative to prison populations, 287, 377n9, 398n17, 406n83; relative to unemployment, 55, 57, 120, 155, 171, 186, 277; and retirement payments, 186; by state, 53t, 155; among states with and without